THESE UNITED STATES

CONCISE EDITION
THESE
UNITED STATES

The Questions of Our Past

Volume I to 1877

Irwin Unger

New York University

PRENTICE HALL, *Upper Saddle River, New Jersey 07458*

Library of Congress Cataloging-in-Publication Data

The Library of Congress has catalogued the one volume edition as follows:

UNGER, IRWIN.
    These United States : the questions of our past / Irwin Unger. —
Concise ed./Combined ed.
      p. cm.
    Includes index.
    ISBN 0-13-081551-9
    1. United States—History. I. Title.
E178.1.U54 1999
973—dc21   98-40954
                                  CIP

Interior design and production manager: Judy Winthrop
Acquisitions editor: Todd Armstrong
Editorial director: Charlyce Jones Owen
Editorial assistant: Holly Jo Brown
Manufacturing buyer: Lynn Pearlman
Marketing manager: Sheryl Adams
Photo researcher: Diana Gongora
Photo director: Lorinda Morris-Nantz
Cover designer: Joe Sengotta
Cover art: Jasper Johns, (b. 1930) "Three Flags" 1958,
              encaustic on canvas. Whitney Museum
              of American Art. Photograph by Geoffrey
              Clements. © Jasper Johns/Licensed
              by VAGA, New York, NY.

> *To Rita and Mickey, Libby and Arnie,*
> *Phyllis and Jerry, and Norma and David—once more*

© 1999 by Prentice-Hall, Inc.
Simon & Schuster/A Viacom Company
Upper Saddle River, New Jersey 07458

Printed in the United States of America
10 9 8 7 6 5 4 3

Photo credits appear on page A-69. They are a
continuation of the copyright page.

ISBN 0-13-081549-7

Prentice-Hall International (UK) Limited, *London*
Prentice-Hall of Australia Pty. Limited, *Sydney*
Prentice-Hall Canada Inc., *Toronto*
Prentice-Hall Hispanoamericana, S.A., *Mexico*
Prentice-Hall of India Private Limited, *New Delhi*
Prentice-Hall of Japan, Inc., *Tokyo*
Simon & Schuster Asia Pte. Ltd., *Singapore*
Editora Prentice-Hall do Brasil, Ltda., *Rio de Janeiro*

BRIEF TABLE OF CONTENTS

CONTENTS

MAPS

ABOUT THE AUTHOR

Pulitzer Prize winning historian Irwin Unger has been teaching American history for over twenty-five years on both coasts. Born and largely educated in New York, he has lived in California, Virginia, and Washington State. He is married to Debi Unger and they have five children, now all safely past their college years. Professor Unger formerly taught at California State University at Long Beach and the University of California at Davis. He now teaches at New York University, where he has been since 1966.

Professor Unger's professional interests have ranged widely within American history. He has written on Reconstruction, the Progressive Era, and on the 1960s. His first book, *The Greenback Era,* won a Pulitzer Prize in 1965. Since then he has written *The Movement: The New Left* and (with Debi Unger) *The Vulnerable Years, Turning Point: 1968* and *The Best of Intentions* about the Great Society. He also teaches a wide range of courses, including the introductory U.S. history survey, the Civil War and Reconstruction Era, the Gilded Age, U.S. economic history, and the United States during the 1960s.

PREFACE

These United States, Concise Edition, represents a major change from the previous versions of the work. Most important it is a "concise" edition, about one-fourth shorter than its predecessor. Our goal here has been to survey American history for a college audience in a briefer format to facilitate readability and reduce the price of the work to students. The condensing process has not, I believe, sacrificed essential material. Rather, redundant examples, overextended treatment, and marginal topics have been eliminated, a process that drew on reviewers' and adopters' evaluations. We have also reduced the number of illustrations and maps to contain costs and removed the "Portraits" from the main body of the text and placed them in a separate booklet. One final change is chronological updating to include events since the last edition.

In most significant ways the book's plan remains the same, however. First, unlike virtually every other introductory text, it still has a single author and speaks in a single voice. I hope readers will agree that a book by an individual has inherent advantages over one composed by a committee. Second, each chapter is still organized around significant questions, each designed to challenge students with the complexity of the past and to compel them to critically evaluate different viewpoints. This plan, I believe, makes the learning of history a quest, an exploration, rather than the mere absorption of a mass of facts. Yet, at the same time, "the facts" are made available. *These United States* provides the ample "coverage" of standard texts.

The word "standard" here does not mean old-fashioned. Though *These United States* discusses political, diplomatic, and military events, it also deals extensively with social, cultural, and economic matters. It concerns itself not only with "events," moreover, but also with people, currents, and themes. It is not old-fashioned in another way: it expands the "canon" to include those who traditionally have been excluded from the American past and seeks to embrace the enormous diversity of the American people. The reader will find in *These United*

States women as well as men; people of color as well as those of European extraction; youths as well as adults; the poor as well as the rich; artists, writers and musicians as well as politicians and diplomats.

Here, then, is the Concise Edition of *These United States.* I hope that, like its precursors, it meets with favor among faculty and students and serves both as a successful teaching instrument and an absorbing introduction to the American past.

IRWIN UNGER
Department of History
New York University

ACKNOWLEDGMENTS

Every author incurs debts in writing or revising a book such as this. I have been the beneficiary of particularly generous help and advice and I would like to acknowledge it here.

My thanks to my editor Todd Armstrong who came to Prentice Hall late in the revision process but helped greatly in expediting it. Susan Alkana's editorial advice and services were invaluable during the early and mid-phase of the revisions. I should also like to thank Charlyce Jones Owen for her valuable supervisory help, Darcy Betts for her marketing skills and Judy Winthrop for her expertise as production editor. A number of my fellow academics were generous enough to read and evaluate the manuscript for this Concise Edition. They include: William M. Leary, University of Georgia; Michael Haridopolos, Brevard Community College; Stephen L. Hardin, The Victoria College; David G. Hogan, Heidelberg College. My thanks also to the scholars and teachers who evaluated earlier editions: James F. Hilgenburg, Jr., of Glenville State College; Johanna Hume of Alvin Community College; Robert G. Fricke of West Valley College; Steve Schuster of Brookhaven College; Kenny Brown of the University of Central Oklahoma; Paul Lucas of Indiana University; and last, but assuredly not least, Irving Katz, also of Indiana University. Though I did not invariably follow their advice, I always took it seriously.

* ANCILLARY INSTRUCTIONAL MATERIALS *

These United States Concise Edition comes with an extensive package of ancillary materials.

For the Instructor

Test Item File prepared by James Sargent of Virginia Western Community College contains multiple choice questions, essay questions, identification questions, and matching questions.

Instructor's Manual prepared by John Soares includes chapter summaries, learning objectives, suggestions for lecture topics, essay or classroom discussion topics, and suggestions for projects or term papers.

Prentice Hall Custom Test, available in Windows, DOS, and Macintosh formats, provides questions from the printed test item file for generating multiple versions of tests.

For the Students

Study Guides, Volumes I and II, include commentary, definitions, identifications, map exercises, short-answer exercises, and essay questions.

Historical Documents and Portraits have been extracted from the unabridged version of the text and compiled as a separate supplement for students, available at no charge when shrinkwrapped (at the instructor's request) to the text. The Historical Portraits consist of biographical information about a representative figure from each chapter, while the Historical Documents are excerpts from primary source readings.

1

THE NEW WORLD ENCOUNTERS THE OLD

Why 1492?

Every schoolchild knows that Columbus "discovered" America in 1492. It is a "fact" firmly established in our national consciousness. Yet Columbus did not discover America, if by that statement we mean he was the first person to encounter the two great continents that lie between Europe and Asia. At least two other groups stumbled on the Americas before Columbus. Sometime between 40,000 BCE and 12,000 BCE people from northeast Asia reached the "New World" from across the Pacific and gradually spread across the vast new lands. We call their descendants Indians, though many prefer to call them Native Americans. Then about 1000 CE, Scandinavians called Norsemen touched North America coming from northern Europe.

Given these earlier encounters, is there any special significance to that famous year 1492? Should we drop it from our list of crucial dates and substitute 40,000 BCE or 1000 CE? If we keep 1492, how do we justify it? Did Columbus's landing in the Caribbean have a greater impact on the world than the two earlier events, or does our traditional emphasis simply mark our Europe-centered biases? What did Columbus's discovery mean, both to those in the Old World of Europe, Asia, and Africa and to those already living in the Americas? To answer these questions let us look at the first discovery and its significance.

* THE NATIVE AMERICANS *

The first Americans were migrants from eastern Siberia on the northern portion of the Asian mainland. Physically, they belonged to the same human stock as the modern Chinese, Japanese, and Koreans. The migrants were people who depended on roots, berries, seeds, fish, and game for food. Decreasing rainfall in their Asian homeland, perhaps, forced them eastward to stay alive. Today their journey would be stopped by the Bering Sea, but in that distant era a land bridge joined Alaska to Siberia. Once in North America the migrants gradually moved southward, and within a thousand years had spread from just below the Arctic Ocean to the stormy southern tip of South America. They had also increased enormously in numbers. From perhaps a few hundred or a few thousand original immigrants, by 1492 the Indian population of the Americas had swelled to over 50 million, a figure about equal to that of contemporary Europe.

As their numbers grew over the centuries the descendants of these Asian people diversified into many groups with distinct languages, cultures, and political and economic systems. By about 3000 BCE some had begun to practice agriculture, with "maize" (corn) as their chief crop and the staple of their diet. They also grew tomatoes, squash, various kinds of beans, and, in South America, potatoes. Surpluses from agriculture transformed Indian life. Abundant food led to larger populations and also to more diverse societies. Classes of priests, warriors, artisans, and chiefs appeared. In the most fertile agricultural regions great civilizations arose with a technological prowess, artistic sophistication, and political complexity comparable to the civilizations of Asia and Europe.

THE GREAT INDIAN CIVILIZATIONS.   One of these Indian civilizations, that of the Mayas, built great ceremonial and administrative cities in the dense rain forests of Yucatan and Central America. Mayan society was composed of many separate urban centers, each independent and governed by a group of priests. It also developed a culture of great sophistication: The Mayas alone among the American Indian peoples had a written language and books, and their mathematicians developed the idea of zero as a number place long before Europeans did.

The Aztecs to the north, in central Mexico, were a more warlike people than the Mayans. Around 1300 CE they settled on the site of what is now Mexico City. Led by powerful rulers, the Aztecs conquered virtually all their neighbors, creating a great empire of 5 million inhabitants in central Mexico. In the course of their many wars the Aztec rulers took thousands of prisoners and enormous quantities of feathered headdresses, jade jewelry, and beautiful gold and silver ornaments. The treasure went into the coffers of the rulers and their nobles; the prisoners, by the thousands, had their hearts cut out in public ceremonies to appease the Aztec war god.

In the coastal mountains of South America, the Incas created an empire that paralleled the Aztec domain to the north. At its height, 7 million people lived within its borders. Strong rulers like the Aztec chiefs, the Inca emperors built fortresses on the Andes mountainsides and a network of roads that held their farflung state together. The Inca people were among the most skilled metallurgists of the time, making weapons, tools, and ornaments of gold, silver, copper, and bronze. The Inca privileged classes lived comfortably, but the sick and handicapped were also provided for by the government. Inca society has sometimes been compared to a modern social welfare state.

This is a reconstruction of what Cortés and his men saw when they arrived at "the great city of Mexico." The structure at the center of the plaza is the altar where prisoners were sacrificed to the Aztec gods.

THE INDIANS OF NORTH AMERICA.   North of these great Indian civilizations were less complex, smaller-scale cultures and societies. By 1492 there was a substantial population perhaps as many as 9 million people, in what is now the United States and Canada. This population was diverse in culture, economy, and social organization. There were twelve distinct language groups in present-day United States, each embracing numerous individual tribes. The various tribes also had differing economies. Some were composed of hunters and food gatherers, others of cultivators of maize, beans, squash, melons, and tobacco.

Indian dwellings ranged from tepees of skin-covered poles, the typical homes of the western Plains Indians, to the impressive lodges made of wooden beams covered with bark built by the Iroquois and other eastern peoples. Among the Hurons and many southeastern groups these structures were often grouped into towns surrounded by stockades. Although some Indian tribes were isolated and self-sufficient, others relied on traders who traveled long distances by canoe on the lakes and rivers to exchange goods with other tribes.

Many tribes were skilled in handicrafts, making beautiful pottery, light and swift birchbark canoes, and implements of copper. Some wove a kind of cloth

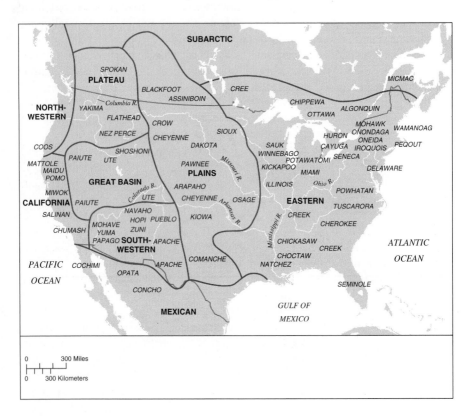

Indian Tribes of North America

from the inner bark of trees. Others, however, lived very simply, with few artifacts. The numerous peoples of California, for example, blessed with a mild climate and abundant food, made do with minimal clothing and crude houses. Only their beautiful basketwork revealed their skills with materials.

Politically, these peoples varied greatly. The Indians of the Iroquois Confederacy, or Six Nations, were a powerful and warlike league, the terror of its Indian neighbors and the scourge of later European settlers. On the other hand, the Delaware were peaceful and the Chippewas of present-day Ohio lived in many small bands that had little in common besides language. Tribal government varied widely. The Natchez of the lower Mississippi River Valley were ruled by an absolute despot called the Great Sun, who was chosen by the female Suns when his predecessor died. The Iroquois had a kind of representative political system. Female clan heads elected both the male delegates to the Confederacy council and the sachems, or chiefs, who governed the Six Nations.

Religion was important among virtually all Native Americans. Most believed in an ultimate being, the creator of nature, humankind, and all the good things of life. Indians held that spiritual forces resided in all living things. Like other religious peoples, they expressed their feelings about the change of seasons, hunting, death, love, and war in elaborate ceremonies that included dances, songs, feasts, and the wearing of vivid costumes and masks.

The Europeans, who would soon be arriving in North America, held very different views of nature. In the Judeo-Christian cosmology, the Bible said humans should "have dominion over the fish of the sea and over the birds of the air and over every living thing that moves upon the earth." The Judeo-Christian view of "man the master" was reinforced by the contemporary European cultural theme of raw nature as dangerous, a "wilderness" of threatening animals, insects, poisonous plants, and "savages," a place to be avoided or tamed to man's use. An even more powerful force guiding Europeans in their relations to nature was avarice. Nature represented latent wealth and opportunity for personal riches. To stand in the way of exploiting nature's bounty not only hobbled the enterprising individual but violated the laws of human progress. Associated with these attitudes were European views of property. The white settlers of America believed in exclusive individual possession of land, timber, minerals, and other natural resources and measured status by how much of these a person owned.

While Indians were not incapable of altering nature to meet their needs—their pursuit of big game in the earliest years following migration from Asia may have exterminated the mammoths and wild horses that occupied the Americas—they were not driven by a lust for limitless resource-consuming possessions and so were not generally willing to sacrifice present satisfactions for remote future ones. Nor did they accept the European concept of private land ownership. Land, they believed, belonged to the whole tribe, not the individual. In many ways the Indian view of human relations with the natural world was the reverse of the European. Taken together, these differing attitudes toward nature and property would have significant consequences for future Indian–European relations.

* THE FIRST EUROPEAN "DISCOVERY" *

Europeans first touched the Americas long before Columbus. According to early Scandinavian sagas, in 986 CE a ship on the way to European-settled Greenland commanded by a Norwegian merchant, Bjarni Herjulfsson, was driven off course by a storm and narrowly escaped being dashed to pieces on an unfamiliar coast. The land Herjulfsson and his crew encountered—probably Newfoundland or Labrador—was covered with "forests and low hills." The Europeans were not interested in this new land and did not disembark. When they finally reached Greenland, however, they reported their discovery.

Ever on the lookout for new lands to settle, other Scandinavians soon followed up on Herjulfsson's lead. In the year 1000, Leif Ericsson, a founder of the Greenland colony, sailed westward to investigate reports of the new country. He and his party found it relatively warm, densely forested, with streams that overflowed with salmon. Finding what they later described as grapes, and hoping perhaps to encourage settlement, they dubbed the new country Vinland (Wineland) the Good.

Would-be Norse settlers followed Leif Ericsson to Vinland. In 1010 or thereabouts, three boatloads of Greenlanders set out to establish permanent communities in North America. Indian attacks drove them away, but the Norse apparently made other efforts to colonize the new country. In 1960, archaeologists discovered the remains of a small Norse village at L'Anse aux Meadows in northern Newfoundland. The find confirmed for the first time the sagas of medieval Scandinavian exploration. But the simple structures and the primitive tools uncovered also suggest how feeble the Norse colonizing effort was.

Some garbled knowledge of the Norse discoveries spread to other parts of Europe. Yet nothing happened. The first European contact with the Americas did not "take." Europe quickly forgot the eleventh-century Norse voyages to North America. It was as if they had never taken place.

* THE RISE OF MODERN EUROPE *

The isolation of the Americas of course did not last. The Old World eventually intruded into the New, and within a few generations the collision of these two different worlds completely transformed both societies. To the people of Europe this contact with the Americas seemed a "discovery"; actually, it was a meeting. As one scholar has written: "Columbus did not discover a new world; he established contact between two worlds already old."

MEDIEVAL EUROPE. Why did Europe fail to follow up on the Norse voyages of the eleventh century? Why did it respond differently in 1492? What had happened during the centuries separating Leif Ericsson from Columbus to change the way Europeans reacted to the momentous meeting of the two worlds?

Eight hundred years before the Norse voyages, the Roman Empire had joined all parts of the Western European world into a peaceful, prosperous, civilized whole. Then, during the period 500–700 CE, came the Germanic invasions, the Muslim conquest of the southern and eastern Mediterranean, and the devastating attacks on Europe by the Scandinavian Vikings. To protect life and property, barons' castles sheltered the common folk against raiders and brigands. Before long, however, the barons themselves became the source of disorder as they battled one another for land and power. By the eighth or ninth century all long-range travel and trade within Europe and between Europe and other parts of the world had become unsafe. Goods, except for a few high-profit luxury items, ceased to move over the decaying Roman roads or along pirate-infested sea routes.

Not surprisingly, Europe ceased to be an economic unit. Italy retained its cities and trade, but elsewhere each small region of the continent was forced to become self-sufficient. By the year 1000, particularly north of the Alps, a fragmented, localized economic system had replaced the unified, complex organization of the Roman Empire. Europe was poor, politically divided, beset by local wars and civil disorder, its people largely illiterate and unfree. Each nobleman's estate or manor—with its manor house, peasants' village, and surrounding fields—had to provide all the food, implements, and other commodities it needed. With each manor supplying its own needs, there was little reason to produce a surplus or find new ways to increase the output of crops or other goods. Cities that had once been great centers of commerce and industry declined, with many disappearing entirely.

Most Europeans during this era were unfree peasants or serfs. Like farm animals, they went with the land when it was passed on from one nobleman to another through inheritance or conquest. In return for the right to till the soil, the peasant family gave the lord part of its crop plus various other payments in the form of work. Money seldom changed hands. Instead, exchanges and obligations were discharged through crops, animals, or services. Illiterate, superstitious, and often malnourished, as well as exploited, the serfs of Europe were a severe brake on economic change.

Even during the darkest of the "Dark Ages" Europe had a small merchant class. But in the centuries from 700 to 1000 traders wielded little economic power and suffered from low social status. Neither serfs nor priests nor feudal lords, they did not fit into the medieval social order, which presupposed a rural society composed of tilling peasants, praying clergymen, and fighting noblemen. Nor did Roman Catholicism, the religion of virtually all Western Europeans, find commerce congenial. The Church held that all economic relations must be subject to moral guidelines and was suspicious of merchants who looked only to profits. These attitudes undoubtedly reinforced the economic backwardness of Europe.

By the year 1000, Europe had disintegrated politically as well as economically. Kings reigned in France, England, Portugal, and other realms, but they were not like later monarchs. They did not have armies, navies, or corps of civil servants. Instead, they relied on their vassals—the feudal nobility—to supply them with men and arms in emergencies and to administer the customary law in their districts. Nor did the monarchs of this era have large financial resources. No European kingdom imposed uniform national taxes. Although theoretically supreme, kings were often inferior in wealth and power to one or more of the feudal lords who supposedly owed them allegiance.

The one institution that held Western Europe together during the early Middle Ages was the Roman Catholic Church. Retaining many features of the Roman imperial government—the Latin language, a corps of literate officials, and a supreme head, the pope, residing in Rome—the Church preserved many of the values and much of the culture and organizational skill of the ancient world. Possessing a virtual monopoly of literacy, priests and church officials provided essential services to kings and nobles as scribes and administrators. But the medieval church was no substitute for powerful secular rulers.

Nor was the Church's learning as useful for practical affairs as it might have been. Indeed, its attention to the salvation of the individual's soul focused Europeans' minds on the afterlife rather than on worldly matters. This emphasis discouraged the creative curiosity about nature and the physical world felt by men and women of ancient times.

In the year 1000, in short, Europe could not rise to the challenge of the newfound world to the west. It did not have the economic or technical resources, the political and social cohesion, or even the interest to do so. The disorganized, politically feeble, largely illiterate Europe of Leif Ericsson's time was incapable of responding to the Norse encounter with America.

THE LURE OF THE EAST.   Five hundred years later, when Columbus returned from the Caribbean to report the discovery of a new route to "the Indies," Europe reacted powerfully and decisively. Europe's response reflected the remarkable revival of trade and commerce in the half millennium between Leif Ericsson and Columbus. This revival would eventually undermine feudalism and the self-sufficient manor-based economy on which it rested.

In part the change followed contact with the Islamic civilization that rimmed the eastern, southern, and western shores of the Mediterranean Sea. For centuries Western Christians were content with what they had. But then, at the very end of Leif Ericsson's eleventh century, thousands of Europeans set out as Crusaders for Palestine to recover the Holy Sepulcher, Jesus' tomb, from the Muslim "infidels" who occupied the Holy Land. After the Crusaders captured Jerusalem in 1099, Europeans settled in the newly conquered Levant on the eastern edge of the Mediterranean. Compared with the rude commodities of France, England, and Germany, the silks, cotton, spices, cabinetwork, pottery, and weapons of the Muslims were marvels of delicacy and sophistication. Many Europeans appreciated the skills and artistry of Muslim craftsmen, developed a taste for sugar, silks, fine leatherwork, and other luxury goods of the Islamic world, and came to respect Muslim science and philosophy. This was the beginning of a change in European attitudes and awakening to the opportunities of commercial relations with distant lands and cultures.

Even more intriguing were the riches of the distant Orient. By the eleventh century a lucrative trade had sprung up between Europe and remote China and

India. Italian textiles, arms, and armor, along with north European copper, lead, and tin, moved eastward; silk, jewels, and spices westward. The eastern end of the trade was in the hands of Asian traders—Chinese, East Indians, and Arabs. The western end was carried on largely by Italians from Venice and Genoa. Their immense profits soon made the Venetians and Genoese the envy of other European traders.

The most important part of this East–West exchange was the spice trade. In the Middle Ages spices seemed indispensable to civilized living. They retarded decay, relieved the blandness of daily fare, and disguised the poor quality of unrefrigerated meat. Europeans used many locally grown herbs to flavor their food, but none of these could compare to pepper, cloves, nutmeg, and cinnamon, which came only from India, Ceylon, and the "Spice Islands" of present-day Indonesia.

Contact with Islam and the revival of long-distance trade were accompanied by a change in attitude toward money and the making of money. Monarchs and nobles could no longer afford to revile and oppress traders, for they were now becoming rich capitalists whose wealth might be needed to pay royal debts or procure arms. New rules granted merchants privileges and provided them with protection. Before long the Church relaxed its ban against charging interest for lending money. Banking soon became both a respectable and a highly profitable enterprise.

The contact with the East also helped break down the self-sufficient manorial system. Before long the nobility had acquired a passion for the wondrous luxuries of Islam and the Orient. But to buy them they needed cash, and cash, in an era when almost all economic relations were based on payment in locally produced commodities or in services, was scarce. The need for cash soon changed these economic relations. Now serfs might be allowed to rent the land for money. They might be permitted to buy their freedom or to purchase some land and become freeholders. Meanwhile, up-to-date nobles tried to improve their own cultivation methods to guarantee a surplus that they could sell for money in the growing towns. By the thirteenth or fourteenth century the revival of trade had led to the breakdown of the manorial system in many parts of Western Europe and the appearance of a small-landowner class.

The revival of trade also encouraged the growth of cities and the flowering of urban life. As trade returned, new cities sprang up and old ones expanded. Former serfs flocked to the towns with their markets, warehouses, docks, and shops to work for wages, as laborers, artisans, and craftsmen, and to enjoy the greater freedom and variety of city life. Besides the older centers of Italy, newer towns arose along the Baltic and North seas to distribute the goods of the East and to serve the growing commerce of northern Europe.

THE NATION-STATE. The urban merchant class was a powerful force for change in early modern Europe. The burghers, or *bourgeoisie* (from burgh or bourg, meaning "town"), were natural foes of the unruly barons whose constant wars made travel unsafe and who levied expensive tolls on trade. What they wanted was peace, order, and economic unity to permit goods and people to move safely and freely over long distances. Only a friendly and powerful central authority could assure such conditions.

The interests of the merchants made them the natural allies of feudal kings. And the kings quickly found uses for the merchants. They were the source of borrowed money to finance armies that could impose internal order and put down disobedient vassals. Their literacy could free monarchs from reliance on priests and bishops as administrators. The revival of trade and subsequent creation of a money economy made it possible to impose national taxes. Before long, the modern nation-state, with its dedicated civil servants, its armies and navies, and its capacity to mobilize capital and resources to achieve national goals, had emerged in place of the disjointed, hidebound, feeble feudal kingdoms in Western Europe.

These political changes had immense implications for European relations with the rest of the world. The new nation-states were powerful instruments of European policy and ambition. The new rulers could marshal, organize, and focus vast forces to serve European ends and project these forces thousands of miles across the seas. In quest of wealth, the new centralized national states would finance exploration and conquest. Their early successes would reinforce the expansion process until it came to feed on itself.

REVOLUTIONS IN THOUGHT AND COMMUNICATION. Intellectual and cultural shifts also made 1492 different from a.d. 1000. People in the Middle Ages had little sense of historical change. To medieval Christians all that had preceded the birth of Jesus was a prelude to that great event; all that followed was a long epilogue that would culminate in Christ's Second Coming and the "end of days." Early medieval people gave the ancients little credit for their contributions to civilization and, in fact, knew little about them.

Then, in fourteenth-century Italy, scholars began to discover that the Greeks and Romans knew many things that they did not. This new realization was probably sparked by the interchange with Greek-speaking Constantinople and the Muslim Mediterranean world, which had preserved and translated many ancient Greek and Latin authors and thinkers. It was reinforced by the discovery of hundreds of ancient manuscripts hidden in monasteries, churches, and libraries for almost a thousand years.

The new contact with classical antiquity was a wonderfully stimulating experience. Encountering a new civilization, even one long dead, made European culture richer and more complex. At the same time it gave Europeans a new confidence in their own society and in themselves. The ancients were great and creative people, surely, but their achievements were not beyond reach of the moderns.

The interest in history and literature inspired by contact with the Greek and Roman world, (the new "humanism") secularized the way many people thought; that is, it deflected their attention from religion and salvation toward the things of this world. The humanism of the era we call the Renaissance was not the irreligious, materialistic, and pleasure-obsessed set of attitudes people used to believe it was. But it did create new concern with the laws of physical nature and new appreciation of the beauties of form, color, and line.

The new attitudes were immeasurably helped by the invention of printing. In ancient and medieval times books had to be copied laboriously by hand and so were rare and expensive. By the end of the Middle Ages the revival of trade had created a new class of literate men and women, but the high cost of recording people's thoughts inevitably slowed the spread of ideas and knowledge. A way to print pages from movable type, developed by German craftsmen and perfected by Johann Gutenberg of Mainz, spread throughout Europe in the fifteenth century. By 1500, about 1,000 printers were working in the trade, and they had published 30,000 separate book titles in some 6 million copies.

Many of these books were religious, but there were also scientific works, works on navigation, and numerous accounts of discoveries in the Far East and West. Columbus's description of his first voyage to the "Indies" was quickly printed and widely circulated and read. The new inexpensive printed book created a large audience for new information and guaranteed that Europeans would not forget America a second time.

NEW TECHNOLOGY.   Advances in navigation and naval architecture also helped Europe exploit its encounter with the Americas after 1492. In the year 1000 the Norse captains had located their position on the open sea by sighting the sun with the naked eye and guessing their speed. By 1492, Europeans had adopted the compass, consisting of a magnetized needle attracted to the north magnetic pole attached to a card marked with directions. Now a ship captain could calculate his direction even when the pole star was obscured by clouds and more accurately than sighting the sun. By the fifteenth century, European navigators were also beginning to calculate latitude with the quadrant and astrolabe.

Improvements in navigation were accompanied by advances in ship design. The merchant ship of medieval Europe was a tubby vessel with a rudder at the side and a single large square sail useful only when the wind blew directly from behind. Gradually these ships were modified to carry adjustable sails and mount their rudders at the stern. Now, by "tacking"—following a zigzag course toward one's destination—vessels could sail without the wind directly astern. Faster, more maneuverable, and more stable ships such as caravels, carracks, galleons expanded Europe's reach. These nautical changes gave Europeans the equipment needed to undertake long ocean voyages with relative confidence.

One more innovation was needed before Europeans were equipped to subdue the world: gunpowder. It was first used to propel missiles from cannons early in the fourteenth century, and used in siege operations against walled cities. Cannon were soon installed aboard ships as well. With time, guns were miniaturized so that by 1360 some soldiers carried primitive hand-held small arms. When combined with the horse, pike, metal armor, and steel sword, these weapons would prove devastating against the native peoples of the Americas.

A Portuguese galleon, of the sort that enabled Europeans to conquer the oceans and helped create the Portuguese empire in the sixteenth century. The gun ports on the sides and stern are realistic in this contemporary engraving, but the men on deck—and the fish—are exaggerated in size.

∗ EUROPEAN EXPANSION ∗

By the 1400s, fueled by advances in navigation, trade, and the rise of the bourgeoisie and nation-state, Europeans were launched on a campaign to explore the world and make contact with other lands and peoples. The quest began with the effort of Prince Henry of Portugal, later known as Henry the Navigator, to seek out new lands to the south and west. Henry was not a fully modern man impelled by curiosity or hope of profits. Rather, his chief concern was to find the legendary Christian kingdom of Prester John and reunite him and his people with the main body of Christendom.

To advance these goals Henry organized and financed a program of exploration along the west coast of Africa. Each year ships left Portugal to venture ever farther south, their captains spurred on by Henry's financial rewards for progress. By 1445, Dinis Dias had rounded Cape Verde and reached the humid, fertile part of the African coast below the Sahara. Ten years later Alvise da Cadamosto sighted the Senegal and Gambia rivers and discovered the Cape Verde Islands.

After Henry's death his work was taken over by the kings of Portugal who sought an all-sea route to India, Cathay (China) and Xipangu (Japan) around the southern end of the African continent and across the Indian Ocean. If the Portuguese could bypass the Italian and Muslim middlemen and go to the source itself, all the profits of trade with the farthest East would be theirs.

In 1488, Bartolomeu Dias finally rounded the tip of Africa. Encouraged by Dias's report, Vasco da Gama set out from Portugal for India in July 1497. The following May his four ships arrived at Calicut, where he collected a valuable cargo of pepper, ginger, cloves, and cinnamon. He returned home safely in 1499, the first European to sail directly from Europe to India and back.

Once opened, the route around Africa became a busy thoroughfare. To expedite the trade in spices, silks, drugs, and other precious goods, the Portuguese established trading posts in Africa, along the Malabar coast of India, in Ceylon, and on the islands of Indonesia. The Portuguese commercial empire soon expanded to the western Pacific. By 1550 the small Atlantic nation had established a virtual monopoly of the European spice trade.

COLUMBUS AND THE SPANISH EXPLORATIONS.   The success of the Portuguese aroused the envy of the rulers of Europe's other new nation-states. Eventually the Dutch, the French, and the English would challenge Portugal's stranglehold on the Eastern spice trade around Africa. But meanwhile, a Genoese adventurer and visionary named Cristoforo Colombo (Christopher Columbus) had arrived at an alternative that not only promised a shorter route to the East but also seemed likely to avoid a direct confrontation with the Portuguese.

Columbus's scheme was simple, though based on false premises. Columbus thought that only a narrow body of water lay between Europe and the Indies. So a ship sailing west, after only a few weeks, should reach Asia and its riches.

After unsuccessfully peddling his idea to every prince of Western Europe, Columbus finally interested the rulers of Spain. These joint monarchs, Ferdinand of Aragon and Isabella of Castile, had just concluded a centuries-long crusade against the infidel "Moors," and were looking for new worlds to conquer. Pledging her jewels as security, Isabella borrowed from a Spanish religious order some of the money Columbus needed. The rest came from the small city of Palos, whose burghers, as punishment for an infraction of Spanish law, she ordered to supply "the Admiral" with three small vessels. The total cost of the expedition was about 2 million maravedis (today about $14,000), a great fortune that could not have been gathered for such a purpose 500 years earlier, in Norse times. With this sum Columbus fitted out his three small ships and on August 3, 1492, he and his crew of ninety left Palos. They arrived at the Caribbean island of San Salvador ten weeks later, almost exactly five centuries after the first European had sighted North America (though they believed they had reached the Indies).

Columbus's first voyage was followed by three others, each better equipped than the first. The "Admiral of the Ocean Sea" explored the Caribbean, surveyed its major islands, and touched the mainland of the Americas at several points. He also established the first permanent European communities in the

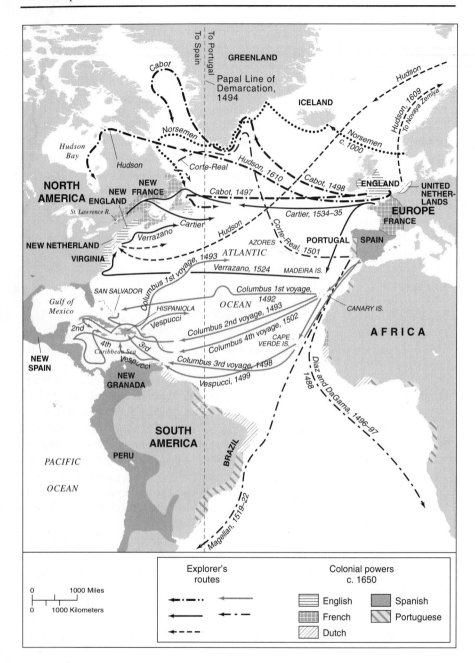

Voyages of Exploration

New World. Columbus's expeditions were followed by many more whose leaders established European settlements on the Caribbean islands. From these settlements in turn Spanish commanders launched expeditions to the mainland. One of these, under Vasco Nuñez de Balboa, crossed the Isthmus of Panama in 1513, its members becoming the first Europeans to see the eastern shore of the Pacific Ocean.

But Spain's ambitions went beyond "the Indies." In 1519 the Spanish crown sent the Portuguese navigator Ferdinand Magellan to find an ocean route to the Far East by sailing west. In November 1520, Magellan discovered the stormy strait at the southern tip of South America that bears his name, sailed through it, and launched his small fleet onto the vast Pacific. Months later, after harrowing experiences with hunger, scurvy, and thirst, he arrived in the Philippines, off the Asian mainland. There he was killed in a skirmish with the natives. Eventually one of his vessels reached Spain by sailing westward around Africa. Though the route was far too long to be practical for the Europe–Asia trade, Magellan's voyage proved that the Americas were not part of the Indies. It was also the first circumnavigation of the globe, a milestone for humankind.

SPAIN ENCOUNTERS THE INDIAN CIVILIZATIONS. Spain's conquests soon made it master of two continents. In 1519 the Spaniard Hernando Cortés set out from Cuba with 600 men, 17 horses, and 10 cannons, landed at Veracruz, and marched to the Aztec capital of Tenochtitlán (Mexico City). The Aztec ruler, Moctezuma II, believed that the invaders were gods returned to the world of men. His warriors, moreover, were startled and demoralized by the Spaniards' strange horses and firearms. Taking advantage of this combination of trust and fear, the Spaniards seized Moctezuma and plundered the overflowing Aztec treasury. After Moctezuma's death, his successors sought to rally the people of Mexico against the invaders, but few Indian nations would cooperate. The final blow to Aztec hopes was a devastating epidemic of smallpox caught from the Europeans. By 1521 all resistance was over. The mighty Aztec empire had fallen to a few hundred Europeans.

The conquest of Mexico was soon followed by the fall of the Inca empire in Peru. The *conquistador* this time was Francisco Pizarro, a young man of lowly birth, who, while in Panama, had heard of a great native empire full of wealth along the Pacific coast of South America. In 1532, after a 45-day climb up the high wall of the Andes from the coast, Pizarro and his 102 men and 62 horses reached the frontier of Peru. The Inca ruler, Atahualpa, confident of his own strength, allowed them to advance unchecked. When he finally encountered the Europeans, they attacked, cut down 5,000 Indian warriors, and took the Inca emperor prisoner. The royal captive offered the Spaniards a roomful of silver and gold to buy his freedom. Pizarro accepted. Then, with the treasure safely in his hands, he had Atahualpa bound to a stake and strangled. Inca resistance continued for some time after this, but over the next few years the Europeans extended their control over the whole of the vast Inca domain, from modern Colombia to what is now central Chile.

The conquest of the Mayas was slower and less dramatic because there was no single Mayan state to confront the invaders. Not until about 1550 were the Mayan communities of middle America subjugated and placed firmly under the control of the Spanish king. The last great native civilization of the Americas was now gone.

Meanwhile Spanish explorers, friars, soldiers, and settlers—moved by greed, curiosity, ambition, and zeal to save souls—pushed their reconnaissance of the Americas into what is now the United States. In 1565 they established the first European settlement on the North American mainland at St. Augustine, in present-day Florida. Thirty years later Don Juan de Oñate, moving north from Mexico, brought settlers to present-day New Mexico. In 1609 these European colonists founded the city of Santa Fe.

SPAIN'S RIVALS. By 1600 Spain had conquered virtually all of Central and South America except for Brazil. This eastward extension of South America had been awarded to Portugal by the Treaty of Tordesillas in 1494 which, with the sanction of the Pope, divided the non-European world between the two Iberian nations.

At first Spain's claims in America were unchallenged, and wealth from the New World poured in. Gold and silver confiscated from the Indians was soon joined by additional streams of precious metals flowing from new mines in Peru and Mexico. From 1500 to 1650 Spain extracted almost 20,000 tons of silver and 200 tons of gold from its American colonies. In addition, cocoa, tobacco, dyes, and other American products found ready markets throughout Europe, providing another source of Spanish income. All this New World bounty helped make Spain the richest and most powerful nation in Europe.

But the Spanish monopoly could not last indefinitely. Other European rulers questioned the Pope's decision to divide the non-European world between Spain and Portugal. As the French king Francis I remarked to the Spanish ambassador in 1540, "The sun shone for him as for others," and where, he wondered, in "Adam's will" had the Americas been divided between Spain and its Iberian neighbor.

England was the first northern European country to join the scramble for a share in the New World. In 1496 King Henry VII authorized a Venetian captain, John Cabot, to sail west "to seeke out, discouer, and finde whatsoeuer isles, countryes, regions or prouinces of the heathens and infidels whatsoeuer they be. . . ." Cabot made two voyages to North America, sighting either Nova Scotia or Newfoundland, and sailing down the Atlantic coast as far as the Delaware or Chesapeake Bays. The English government did not follow up on these voyages, but Cabot's report of codfish in Newfoundland waters attracted many fishermen from France and England to the area. More important, his voyages became the basis for English claims to North American territory.

France joined the quest for overseas wealth in 1524, when Francis I dispatched the Florentine mariner Giovanni da Verrazano to seek out the Far East by the still-elusive western sea route. Verrazano touched land probably somewhere along the Carolina coast, and sailed north as far as Nova Scotia. Later Francis sent mariner Jacques Cartier to explore the coasts of Newfoundland, Prince Edward Island, and the Gaspé Peninsula. On a second voyage Cartier sailed up the St. Lawrence River to the site of present-day Montreal. Cartier's voyages did not lead immediately to successful settlements, but they gave France a claim to part of North America.

The Dutch began exploring relatively late. By the beginning of the seventeenth century most of modern Holland had achieved autonomy from Spain and was developing into a prosperous country dominated by aggressive merchants and bankers. In 1609 a group of these capitalists, joined as partners in the Dutch East India Company, hired Henry Hudson, an English sea captain, to find a water route to the Far East through North America. Hudson failed to find this "Northwest Passage," but he added to Europe's geographical knowledge and Holland's claim to part of North America by sailing down the Atlantic coast from Newfoundland to Virginia. During this trip Hudson explored Cape Cod and Delaware Bay and sailed partway up the broad river that now bears his name.

These expeditions were only a small part of the sixteenth- and early seventeenth-century exploration of the Americas. There were scores of other expeditions along every coast and into every accessible bay, inlet, and navigable river of the two western continents. Meanwhile, Spanish captains like Hernando de Soto and Francisco Vásquez de Coronado, and the Frenchman Samuel de Champlain, pushed deep into the heartland of North America. By about 1650 Europeans knew the essential outlines of the two New World continents and had even learned much of their remote interiors.

✳ THE COLUMBIAN EXCHANGE ✳

In 1552 the Spanish historian Francisco López de Gómara declared "the greatest event since the creation of the world (excluding the incarnation and the death of Him who created it) is the discovery of the Indies." If we discount the word discovery and allow for some exaggeration, López was correct: Few if any events have so changed the history of the world as the encounter of Europeans and Native Americans at the end of the fifteenth century. The resulting interaction of culture, products, ideas, and diseases—the "Columbian Exchange—altered human destiny.

In Central and South America, Europeans quickly swept away all traces of Indian self-rule, save for a few remote interior regions. North of Mexico the process of conquest was slower but no less thorough. Vicious warfare against the Indians was part of the history of every European colonial power.

At times, the kings of Spain, France, and England sought to protect their new Indian subjects. Friars, priests, and ministers sometimes denounced the cruel treatment of the native Americans. Yet even when Europeans refrained from outright murder, they treated the native peoples harshly. In the Spanish colonies Indians were enslaved and sometimes worked to death. Well into the nineteenth century Indians in Spanish-held lands remained "peons" whose lot resembled that of medieval serfs. In the English colonies the more nomadic North American tribes generally escaped forced labor only by slipping away into the forest.

Contact with Europeans injured the native peoples even when whites intended no harm. Because of their long geographic separation, humans of the Old and the New Worlds had developed immunities to different diseases. As a result, neither people could fend off the infections of the other. Europeans encountered a virulent form of syphilis in America, and it quickly spread over all of Europe. Thousands broke out in horrible sores and died before anyone knew how to deal with the malady. The Indians suffered far more. Even European childhood diseases such as measles became killing scourges among populations without protective antibodies. Smallpox, too, along with tuberculosis and cholera, hit the native populations hard. In Mexico the 25 million Indians of 1519 were reduced, primarily by disease, to 2.5 million by 1600. Along the Atlantic coast of North America a similar grim process took place. In 1656 Adriaen Van der Donck reported that the Indians of New Netherlands claimed "that before the arrival of the Christians, and before the small pox broke out amongst them, they were ten times as numerous as they now are. . . . " Indeed, the English and Dutch occupations of the eastern coast were greatly facilitated by the European plagues that had spread to North America from the south and decimated the native population even before the Europeans themselves appeared on the scene.

Syphilis fell like a scourge on Europe shortly after Columbus returned from the New World. It was the real "Montezuma's Revenge." The picture of a victim was drawn by the German artist Albrecht Dürer in 1496.

Disease was only part of the damage that Europeans inflicted on Indian societies. In many areas native agriculture was destroyed by the great herds of sheep and cattle introduced by the conquerors. European manufactures swamped native crafts and undermined native skills. European "fire water"—brandy, wine, whisky—created serious alcoholic dependence. Even efforts to implant the Christian faith often did harm. The European missionaries hoped to benefit the Indians by bringing them the blessings of Christianity. Some friars and priests won converts by their example of humility, kindness, and courage; others, however, fiercely attacked every aspect of the Indians' religion. Bishop Diego de Landa of Yucatán destroyed thousands of Mayan books in his effort to root out idolatry, impoverishing both the Mayas themselves and our knowledge of their civilization and history.

EUROPE BENEFITS. The transatlantic encounter after 1492 was no less momentous for Europeans than for Native Americans. But the effects were almost diametrically opposite. With few exceptions (such as the scourge of syphilis), the contact between the Americas and Europe benefited Europe dramatically. Its fabulous American treasure catapulted Spain into the first rank of European powers. Simultaneously, the deluge of American gold and silver stimulated European trade, commerce, and industry. Rising prices produced by the influx of precious metals further weakened the feudal system by accelerating the conversion of labor services into cash payments. The treasure also provided national rulers with enormous new incomes, giving them an additional edge over their unruly and disobedient vassals. Finally, the events following 1492 accelerated the rise to wealth and influence of the merchant-capitalists who entered the American trade. In short, the "discovery" of America speeded the modernization of Europe that was already well under way when Columbus sailed from Palos.

The transatlantic contact also provided Europeans with an enormously expanded and improved diet. Potatoes and Indian corn would eventually become staples consumed by millions of Europeans. Tomatoes, pumpkins, a wide assortment of beans, and many new fruits were also brought eastward to be widely grown in Europe. Rubber and chicle (the raw material for chewing gum) were other useful American borrowings. Not all the plant imports were seen as blessings: Some would consider tobacco almost as serious a scourge as syphilis, and there are those who have their doubts about chicle. Yet it is clear that America was a botanical, as well as a mineral, treasure trove.

The relative ease with which Europeans conquered the New World peoples encouraged European arrogance—on the theory, apparently, that strength and ferocity equaled virtue. After observing the Aztecs' mass sacrifices of war captives, the Spanish were certain that the native religions were bloodthirsty superstitions. But not all Europeans found their prejudices reinforced. Some felt wonder at the variety of the world's cultures. Some saw native Americans as "noble savages" living in the same state of simplicity and grace that Adam and Eve had enjoyed in the Garden of Eden. It is not surprising that the first modern utopia was conceived by Sir Thomas More in 1516, soon after the Spanish discoveries. This contact with new cultures widened Europe's horizons and produced new fields of knowledge and new intellectual disciplines, including the predecessors of anthropology and sociology.

✳ **CONCLUSIONS** ✳

We focus on 1492 as the date of America's discovery for several good reasons then. One of these, no doubt, is that we tend to accept a Europe-centered view of the world. But from any cultural perspective, Columbus's landing at San Salvador in 1492 was a transforming event. For the millions living in the Americas, the change was a social disaster marked by disease, misery, bondage, and cultural disintegration. For Europe as a whole, 1492 marked the beginning of a new era of geographic, intellectual, and economic expansion.

By 1500 Europeans were also about to embark on the greatest mass migration of all time, one that would eventually pull 100 million human beings westward across the Atlantic. We have seen something of the "forces" that led to this momentous occurrence. Let us now consider the personal motives that impelled countless ordinary, and not-so-ordinary, individuals to risk their lives and their fortunes to create new communities in the strange lands across the ocean.

2

THE OLD WORLD COMES TO AMERICA

What Brought Europeans and Africans to the New World?

1517–21	Martin Luther launches the Protestant Reformation
1527–39	Henry VIII of England defies the pope and declares himself head of a new Church of England
1577	Elizabeth I of England privately begins to promote exploration and colonization in America
1587–88	Sir Walter Raleigh founds England's first American settlement on Roanoke Island
1607	The London Company establishes the first permanent English settlement at Jamestown
1619	The first Africans in British North America arrive at Jamestown; The House of Burgesses is established as Virginia's legislature
1620	The Pilgrims settle at Plymouth on Cape Cod Bay
1624	The Dutch establish New Netherland in the Hudson Valley
1629	Puritans receive a charter for Massachusetts Bay Colony
1632	Lord Baltimore is granted a charter to found Maryland
1635	Roger Williams establishes Rhode Island at Providence
1636	Bostonian Thomas Hooker founds colony at Hartford, Connecticut; Dissenter Anne Hutchinson is banished from Massachusetts
1664	New Netherland becomes the English colony of New York
1681	William Penn receives a charter to found the Quaker colony of Pennsylvania
1701	East Jersey and West Jersey are united as a single province
1701–03	Delaware is separated from Pennsylvania and becomes a separate colony
1732	James Oglethorpe founds Georgia as refuge for English debtors

As we have seen, North America was not an empty continent when Columbus first stumbled on San Salvador in October 1492. Yet today the Indian population of the United States represents only about 1 percent of the total. The rest are descendants of men and women who crossed the oceans from some part of the Old World after 1492.

Immigration to America is one of the great sagas of world history and a central part of our national experience, lasting for hundreds of years, and continuing today. Here, we will consider the first wave of Old World settlement, the one that began in the early seventeenth century and continued to United States independence in the 1770s.

Early explorers by sea claimed they had found an earthly paradise, a "fruitful and delightsome" land with "most sweet savours" wafting from its shores. But most Europeans took these descriptions with a large grain of salt. Europeans of the day were often repelled by raw, untamed nature. America, with its vast gloomy forests, its wild beasts, and its painted "savages," seemed beset by "thorns and thistles." Besides, there was the ordeal of getting there. During the two to four months the average transatlantic passage took in the seventeenth and eighteenth centuries, crews and passengers were packed into tiny ships, confined below deck in bad weather, and fed on salt meat, worm-infested ship's biscuit, and foul water. "Ship fever," a form of typhus, frequently raged through these vessels, carrying off old and young alike. During the age of sail, thousands went to watery graves without ever seeing their new homeland. Finding and developing America's great potential resources was risky and time-consuming.

Yet despite the fears, the discomforts, and the risks, both promoters and settlers staked their money and their lives on the gamble of America. Promoters conceived, organized, financed, and led expeditions to the coast of North America and then guided them through their formative years. Settlers, both men and women, actually risked themselves personally, contributing to new colonies with their own lives. What moved these people? Was their goal wealth? Did they crave adventure? Were they seeking prestige? Were they primarily in quest of religious or political freedom?

* THE ARISTOCRATIC IMPULSE *

Many early colony promoters were driven by the desire for glory, adventure, status, and power. England about the year 1600 was full of young gentlemen and aristocrats who found life at home uninteresting and confining. Under the English laws of primogeniture ("the first born"), the eldest son of a "gentle" family alone inherited his father's estate and, if a nobleman, the family title. Younger sons turned to the army or the professions; others, swallowing the typical disdain of "gentlemen" for mere trade, entered business. Still others sought out rich wives. None of these alternatives fully compensated for the accident of being born in the wrong birth order, and by the early years of the seventeenth century many younger sons had begun to look expectantly at America. They often envisioned a

New World version of England as it was, where they might live as feudal noblemen amidst the trappings of chivalry and hereditary privilege.

The English gentleman of this period did not enjoy soiling his hands with physical labor. He also typically disdained the bourgeois virtues of prudence, patience, and frugality, and valued and cultivated boldness, passion, and open-handed hospitality. Such men saw exploration and colonization of the New World as a bold adventure.

THE ROANOKE ATTEMPT.   The noble promoters of English colonization in America did not learn easily that settlement in North America required more substantial virtues than aristocratic gallantry and courage. In 1587 Sir Walter Raleigh sent an expedition to present-day North Carolina under the immediate command of John White. Women and children went along, but the enterprise included a large group of gentlemen with coats of arms to identify them and their descendants as members of the new feudal aristocracy to be established in America.

The colonists arrived on Roanoke Island off North Carolina too late to plant a crop and had to rely on the Indians for food. In less than a year the settlement had disappeared, apparently destroyed by the local Indians, who probably had lost patience with the Europeans' dependence on them.

ARISTOCRATIC ENTREPRENEURS.   The aristocratic yearning for adventure and disdain for work continued to handicap English colonists long after Raleigh's failure. The first permanent English settlement in North America, established at Jamestown in 1607, for instance, would also suffer from the idleness of gentlemen more interested in finding gold, carving out personal estates, or despoiling the Indians than in clearing the land, raising crops, and founding self-sustaining communities. Still, we must not dismiss the contribution of aristocratic impulses to settlement of the New World.

In the "proprietary" colonies most royal charters conferred on a "proprietor" the powers of a great feudal lord. The 1632 royal charter for Maryland, for example, gave George Calvert (Lord Baltimore) the right to create special titles of nobility and confer them on his friends and associates. These vassals in turn would rule over a population of tenants, the American equivalent of serfs, who would pay "quit rents" that resembled medieval labor services. The Carolina colony, established in the 1660s, was slated to have "landgraves," a new kind of titled nobleman, ruling over rent-paying commoners. Even the Dutch tried a feudal plan in their colony along the Hudson River. Any Dutch gentleman who brought fifty settlers to New Netherland could claim a sixteen-mile stretch of land along any navigable river. Here he might reign as "patroon," or lord of the manor.

All these attempts to establish a feudal system in America eventually failed. There were simply too many applicants for the position of manor lord and too few for the entry level job of serf. The proprietors and would-be landgraves quickly found that they could not compete with colonies where land was cheap and distinctions of rank not so sharp. In the end the schemes to re-create a feudal world in America had to be abandoned.

* THE PROFIT MOTIVE *

A more effective motive for colony promotion was the simple yen for wealth. Whether we consider the role of national governments or of private promoters, the desire for riches overshadowed the desire for rank and titles in summoning forth colony-founding energies.

MERCANTILISM AND THE NATION-STATE. Few Europeans were more eager to exploit the wealth of the New World than kings and princes. Rulers were obviously inspired by Spain's successful example. But they were also influenced by a group of thinkers called *mercantilists,* whose goal was to strengthen their own nation and elevate it above all others. The key to international supremacy, these publicists held, was treasure, gold and silver. These "sinews of war" enabled rulers to hire soldiers, buy weapons, build navies, and conduct an ambitious foreign policy.

The English mercantilists hoped, of course, that their own nation, like Spain, would discover fabulous deposits of silver and gold in its overseas possessions. But even if England were not so lucky, an overseas empire would provide vital products—sugar, tobacco, dyewoods, citrus fruit, furs, and timber—that it would otherwise have to buy from foreign countries and export gold and silver to pay for. England, moreover, would be able to sell surpluses of colonial goods for hard cash and so draw coin from other nations.

The colonies might also become ready markets for English goods. Mercantilist Richard Hakluyt the Younger, in his *Discourse Concerning Westerne Planting* (1584), pictured the North American Indians clothed in English woolens, sleeping in English beds, and using English tools. Eventually hundreds of ships would criss-cross the ocean, carrying American products to Britain and British products to America. Employment in Britain would leap, turning the thousands of dangerous jobless "sturdy beggars" who roamed the English countryside into busy artisans and seamen.

Hakluyt addressed his book directly to Elizabeth, England's shrewd and ambitious queen. But at first the queen avoided directly challenging Spain's claim to sole possession of North America. She encouraged Raleigh's attempts at settlement, but preferred to work behind the scenes. In 1577 she financed the half-exploratory, half-piratical around-the-world expedition of "sea dog" Sir Francis Drake, which established England's claim to present-day California and British Columbia and made Drake and the queen rich from the proceeds of a captured Spanish treasure galleon.

After Elizabeth's death in 1603, the English crown proved more willing to defy Spain openly. Yet none of the Stuart monarchs who followed used public funds to finance a colonization project directly. Rather, under James I and his successors, the crown provided exclusive charters and grants to proprietors and commercial companies, thereby encouraging them to risk their own capital. It suspended laws that restricted emigration from England to help colony promoters people their grants. As we shall see, it conferred various economic privileges on producers of colonial products needed in Britain. Finally, it provided military and naval protection to new settlements. All told, it is hard to see how British North America could have been created and successfully nurtured without the aid of the English nation-state.

MERCHANTS AND PROFITS.   English merchants too were directly moved by the profit motive, hoping to get rich by trading in the furs, timber, metals, and tropical products that the colonies could supply, by transporting passengers to the new settlements, and by speculating in land.

Unfortunately, few individual merchants could afford the large sums needed in the early stages of exploration and settlement. Few foresaw just how difficult it would be to make a colony a profitable enterprise, but commercial investors recognized the wisdom of reducing the risk by pooling their capital with others. Accordingly, merchants sold shares in "joint stock" companies that resembled modern corporations. These shares entitled investors to profits in proportion to their investment and spread the risk if the company's ventures failed. Shareholders often had other privileges as well, such as a personal claim to a certain amount of land in the New World, or the right to trade with the Indians on their individual accounts.

JAMESTOWN: A COMMERCIAL ENTERPRISE.   The first of the commercially inspired colonies—and the first permanent English "plantation" in the New World—was Jamestown in Virginia. Backed by two groups of merchants, one from London and the other from Plymouth and Bristol, in 1606 the promoters of the enterprise secured a charter from the crown that established two Virginia companies.[1] One of these, the Plymouth Company, had the right to plant settlements anywhere between the Potomac and what is now Bangor, Maine. The second, the London Company, was given the right to settle between Cape Fear in present-day North Carolina and the site of what is now New York City. The overlapping strip was open to both.

Both groups got off to a shaky start. In the summer of 1607 the Plymouth Company deposited forty-four men at Fort St. George, on a rocky projection of the Maine coast as the preliminary to a larger effort the following year. After one cruel winter the Maine settlers had had enough; when spring came, the survivors returned home. Discouraged, the Plymouth group abandoned colonization.

In early 1607 the better-financed Londoners dispatched three vessels and 105 passengers to the Virginia coast. The promoters hoped that the new settlement—called Jamestown after James I—would be self-sustaining. When the vessels departed for home with a cargo of clapboards soon after landing settlers and supplies, it seemed that all would be well.

It was not. Not a single one of the first settlers was a woman, a fatal flaw obviously in what was meant to be a self-sustaining colony. Thirty-six, moreover,

---

[1] "Virginia" was the name Raleigh had given to the entire eastern seaboard of the present-day United States in honor of his patron Elizabeth, the "virgin queen."

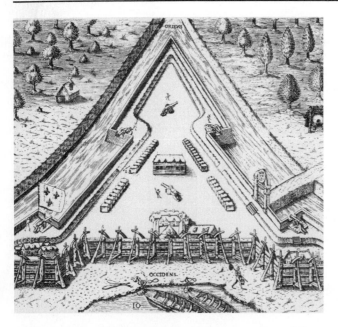

A very early view of the fort at Jamestown by an artist rather indifferent to rules of perspective. Still, it captures the primitive nature of this first successful European settlement in British America.

were gentlemen who could not be expected to soil their hands with manual labor. Besides, the site of the town near the James River was swampy and malarial.

During the first summer the colonists, considered employees of the company, planted orange trees, cotton, and exotic melons rather than the grain they needed for food. Meanwhile, despite the efforts of John Smith, head of the seven-man governing council, to get them to cooperate, they squabbled and fought. The winter was still worse. In January a company ship arrived from England, bringing 120 new settlers to reinforce the surviving 38. This further strained the settlement's limited resources. Soon after, a fire destroyed all the houses and storehouses. The colonists were now virtually without food, but instead of foraging for supplies, they threw themselves into a frantic search for gold.

Fortunately, Smith was able to keep the settlers alive. He stopped the gold hunt and put men to work building, planting crops, and producing pitch, tar, and wood ashes. To tide the settlers over until harvest time, he negotiated with Powhatan, the local Indian chief, for food. The game, corn, fish, and other supplies Powhatan gave them cut the death toll to fewer than a dozen during the winter of 1608–1609.

Smith's successors failed to maintain good relations with the Indians. Powhatan's warriors soon attacked settlers on the colony's outskirts and drove them back to Jamestown proper, where overcrowding and bad sanitation killed many. The winter of 1609–1610 was Jamestown's tragic "starving time." Food was so scarce that some colonists resorted to cannibalism. In the spring, when another contingent of settlers arrived, the supply situation became even more critical; at one point the colony's leaders decided to abandon the settlement altogether.

The following year, 1611, was the turning point. Under Sir Thomas Dale strong leadership was restored. When, in 1612, colonist John Rolfe learned that the native tobacco could be made palatable to Europeans, the colonists discovered their true vocation: tobacco growing. In a few years English smokers were paying premium prices for "Virginia leaf."

The new tobacco crop quickly made Jamestown into a boom town. Small fortunes were quickly made and quickly lost; gambling, drunkenness, and crime became rampant. Yet tobacco provided a solid base for growth even when tobacco prices came down after 1630. For the remainder of the colonial period Virginia and its neighbor, Maryland, provided most of the better tobacco Europeans consumed.

The London Company's policies contributed to the colony's continued growth and stability after 1612. In 1616 the company began to give land to settlers, previously merely company employees. Effort would now confer benefits on the worker himself. A year later the company started to grant large tracts of land called "Hundreds" to enterprising people willing to buy stock in the company for the sake of establishing their own "particular plantations." In 1619 the company created a legislative assembly consisting of a governor-appointed council and an elected House of Burgesses, the first representative political body in the New World. To cap the campaign to build a self-sustaining colony, the company also began to pay the ship passage of young women from England to become wives of the settlers.

In the midst of these gains, Virginia was plunged into a devastating Indian war. Until 1622 Powhatan had used the Europeans to offset his tribal enemies; they in turn had counted on him for food during lean times. Neither side much liked the other. A few company officials believed in the possibility of an integrated community, but most settlers despised the Indians. As a Jamestown official noted, "There is scarce a man amongst us that doth soe much as afforde them [the Indians] a good thought in his hart and most men with their mouthes give them nothinge but maledictions and bitter execrations."

For a while Powhatan's successor, Opechancanough, ignored the insults. But when the expanding white population threatened Indian claims, he decided to strike. In March 1622, Opechancanough's warriors attacked the unsuspecting Virginia settlers, killing 357 men, women, and children. The English struck back with a war of extermination, wiping out whole communities and resorting to such tactics as setting out casks of poisoned wine for unsuspecting Indians to drink. When the smoke of their campaign had cleared, the English had virtually destroyed the tribes of coastal Virginia and ended the "Indian menace."

Still, profits eluded the London Company. Between 1607 and 1624 it declared not a single dividend, and indeed kept calling for additional funds from its shareholders to stave off bankruptcy. In 1624 the crown intervened, annulled the company's charter, and made Virginia a royal colony under a governor appointed by the king.

The Virginia experience was not unique. Few joint-stock colonizing ventures made money for their investors. The Plymouth Company effort along the Maine coast failed dismally. Dutch investors in the joint-stock Dutch West India Company established several settlements along the Hudson River from 1624 on, but the Dutch never considered their colony much of a commercial success. When the English captured New Netherland in 1664 (and renamed it New York), the Dutch did little to get it back. Few people made money, from these merchant-promoted settlements. Nevertheless, the joint-stock company proved to be an invaluable way of pooling economic resources and harnessing the profit motive to the task of founding colonies in America.

∗ "THE BEST POOR MAN'S COUNTRY" ∗

Aristocrats and rich merchants, though useful as promoters and leaders, could scarcely populate the new English settlements by themselves. Few chose to leave the wealth and comfort of Britain, and in any case, there were not many of them to begin with. Immigrants in large numbers had to be drawn from the "common" people; America had to be made attractive to laborers, artisans, servants, shopkeepers, and farmers—both men and women—if the new settlements were to take root and prosper.

And attractive it became. In the seventeenth century about 155,000 came from England alone. In the eighteenth century the number of European arrivals increased. During the fifteen years preceding the American Revolution (1760–1775) alone, 125,000 emigrants left the British Isles (England, Scotland, Wales, and Ireland) for mainland North America, while another 12,000 immigrants arrived from Germany and Switzerland. The majority of immigrants were young. Youth, with its physical strength, adaptability, and sense of adventure, was required by the new land, and the infant settlements received them gladly.

MIXED MOTIVES.   Most immigrants to America during the seventeenth and eighteenth centuries came willingly, though not always wisely. Some were propelled by boredom, some fled from the law or from unpleasant jobs or difficult family circumstances. In 1732, philanthropists led by James Oglethorpe founded Georgia as a haven for English debtors, who were then often jailed when they could not pay their creditors. (Georgia was the last British colony to be established in North America, and would still be a sparsely settled community at the time of the Revolution.)

Only a small number of immigrants were feckless runaways, lawbreakers, or debtors, however. According to the surviving lists of seventeenth-century immigrants from London and Bristol, some were orphan boys sent to the colonies by the church authorities to relieve British taxpayers of the burden of supporting them. The adult males emigrating through Bristol were mostly farmers; those departing through London mostly artisans and tradesmen—carpenters, weavers, shipbuilders, wheelwrights, barrelmakers, and cobblers. All in all, scholars believe, a disproportionate number of departing English were craftspeople and artisans from the cities and towns. Propelling these people from their homeland were low wages, increasingly high rents, bad harvests, and severe depression in the woolen industry.

About a quarter of the immigrants on the London and Bristol lists are women. Most were in their early twenties, the usual age of marriage in Britain. They were probably fleeing an environment where husbands were scarce as were economic opportunities for unmarried women. Going beyond the London and Bristol lists, the proportion of women immigrants to colonial America varied according to the development stage of the particular colony, with more women immigrants when a community had passed beyond the pioneer phase. At the same time, some colonies—Massachusetts, Connecticut, and Pennsylvania, for example—were the destination of whole families, even in the early years, including wives, mothers, daughters, and sisters.

HIGH WAGES AND CHEAP LAND.   In addition to the forces pushing people from Europe, other forces were pulling them to America. During the seventeenth and early eighteenth centuries colony promoters hired agents to travel through Britain and the European continent recruiting colonists. These "Newlanders," wearing jewels and fancy clothes, circulated among the peasants, telling the ignorant that America's mountains were full of precious metals and that its springs gushed milk and honey.

It was not all humbug. The New World was no paradise, but ordinary people could expect to make real gains by moving to America. Success required hard work, but hard work paid richer dividends than in Europe. The reason was simple. North America was a vast continent bursting with resources that could be turned into wealth. The missing ingredient was labor, and those who could supply it were certain to receive a higher economic reward than at home.

For Europeans, then, colonial America promised high wages. Still better, it promised cheap land. This fact was well understood by seventeenth-century colony promoters, who soon began to offer a free "headright" of fifty or a hundred acres to settlers who paid their own way to the New World, and even more to those who subsidized additional settlers. Where land was not actually given away, it was sold cheaply. Proprietor William Penn, for example, sold 15,000 acres in Pennsylvania to a group of Germans for £300, less than 5 cents an acre.

INDENTURED SERVANTS.   Though America exerted a strong pull on the peasants and laborers of Europe, the Atlantic passage for a single person in the seventeenth century—about $100 in today's money—was far more than any laborer or landless husbandman could afford. The solution for most would-be settlers was a labor contract (an indenture) whereby, in exchange for passage, immigrants agreed to work for an employer in America for a specified time at a certain wage or a specified amount of food, clothing, and shelter.

There were several kinds of indentured servants. The most fortunate possessed a needed or uncommon skill and therefore could get favorable terms before leaving home. These "servants" normally agreed to work for four years, with their labor contract describing the trade they would work at and defining acceptable working conditions. The indenture frequently also promised "freedom dues"—clothes, tools, and even land—when the contract expired. "Redemptioners" were less fortunate. Most of these were German and Swiss refugees from war and hard times during the eighteenth century. Redemptioners usually moved as whole families. They arranged for merchants to pay their fare and agreed to reimburse them when they arrived in America. If they could not somehow find the passage money immediately upon arrival, the merchant or his agent could sell their services for a time sufficient to recover the debt. This arrangement sometimes led to the break-up of families.

The life of an indentured servant was often hard. They usually worked from ten to fourteen hours a day, six days a week. Masters had the right to whip them for disobedience or laziness. Normally, they could not marry, vote, or engage in trade. Their indenture and their persons could be transferred from one master to another without their permission. If they ran away, their terms of service could be extended. Many failed to survive the difficult indenture period and were buried in unmarked graves.

Yet many did attain success in America, working off their contracts and establishing themselves as free farmers or craftspeople. News of their achievements drifted back to Europe and inspired others to follow, thus ensuring the indenture system's survival despite its risks and uncertainties. While most of New England was peopled by free families who either paid their own way or were sponsored by the community, by 1750 a large part of the white population from Pennsylvania southward was composed of indentured servants or their descendants.

* INVOLUNTARY IMMIGRANTS *

Many thousands of men and women were brought across the Atlantic against their will. Involuntary immigration was an unadorned product of greed. The inducements colonial promoters offered to would-be settlers were often not enough to attract the laborers needed to do the heavy work of the colonies. Especially in the southern colonies, planters without abundant labor could not take advantage of cheap land and a ready market for their crops of tobacco, rice, and indigo in Europe. Rather than forgo profits, they were willing to pay good prices for forced labor from whatever source they could find.

INVOLUNTARY EUROPEAN IMMIGRANTS. Some of the involuntary immigrants were Europeans. During the seventeenth and eighteenth centuries kidnappers operated in every English port, enticing the young, naive, or intemperate aboard ship to carry them to America to sell as indentured servants. More numerous were "His Majesty's Seven Year Guests"—convicts given the choice of going to America as seven-year indentured servants or facing a hangman's noose at home. Those who accepted "transportation" were pardoned and turned over to merchants, who bore the expense of the transatlantic trip in exchange for the right to sell the convicts' labor to the colonists.

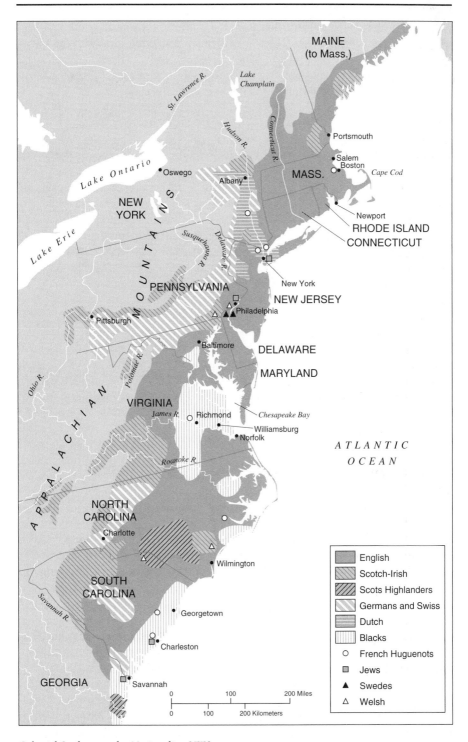

Colonial Settlements by Nationality, 1770

Every colonial legislature protested this dumping of England's "fellons and other desperate villaines" on America. Parliament remained unmoved, however, and the planters of Maryland and Virginia, where most felons were sent, were generally happy to have their labor. Historians estimate that some 20,000 convicts were sent to America during the eighteenth century alone.

BLACK SLAVES. Indentured servants, convicted felons, and kidnapped youths notwithstanding, labor remained in short supply in America, especially in the regions south of Pennsylvania. Europe, it seemed, simply could not send enough workers to satisfy the needs of the New World's profit-making enterprises.

But Africa could in the form of captive slaves. Though slavery no longer existed in Christian Europe, it survived in Islamic lands and existed in Africa itself among the indigenous peoples. The Portuguese, the Spanish, and later the French, Dutch, and English responded to the lure of profits and readily adopted the system for their labor-short American colonies. Many Europeans rationalized slavery by arguing that the African peoples were "heathens" who worshiped idols, or "naked savages" who might benefit from contact with Christian, "civilized" people.

The Africans brought to the Americas were plucked primarily from peoples and nations along Africa's Atlantic coast, largely between present-day Guinea and Angola. These West Africans practiced agriculture and had brought to high levels the arts of weaving, metalworking, pottery making, and wood and ivory carving. The bronze sculptures of Benin, the silver and gold jewelry of the Yoruba, and the rugs and carpets of the Asante were beautiful artifacts. West Africans were also talented in the arts of government. Powerful states such as Benin, Congo, Dahomey, and Ghana brought order and prosperity to large areas of Africa, conducting foreign affairs in much the same way as contemporary European kingdoms.

The slave trade that ripped these people from their homes was a well-organized system by the end of the seventeenth century. At first Europeans themselves captured slaves along the Guinea coast. But whites could not withstand West Africa's tropical diseases and by 1700 the white slavers had come to rely on African merchants and chiefs as middlemen to supply them with prisoners of war or with victims snatched by raiders from the interior of the African continent. Chained together, these unfortunate people were brought overland to the coast by the merchants or by war parties. There they were sold to the European traders for guns, powder, cloth, beads, and rum.

Once aboard ship, the next step in the African slave trade was the infamous "middle passage" to America. "Slavers" as small as ninety tons—ships scarcely bigger than a modern fishing boat—were sometimes packed with 400 slaves besides the crew and supplies. The captives were chained together to prevent rebellion. Wise captains attempted to keep them healthy, but slaves lived in filth below deck where temperatures rose into the nineties, and inevitably the death rate was appalling. Some slave vessels arrived in the Americas with well over half their passengers dead from dysentery, smallpox, or some European disease to which Africans had little natural resistance.

The first slaves reached the English mainland colonies in 1619 when a Dutch vessel unexpectedly put in at Jamestown with a cargo of twenty Africans. Over the next thirty or forty years a small trickle of blacks were brought to the Chesapeake region and most, it seems, were kept as bondservants for a few years and then freed much like indentured servants.

At first the market for slaves in the plantation colonies was limited despite the labor shortage. The mortality rates of all immigrants to the southern plantation colonies were extremely high during the early years of settlement, and so the lifetime service of a black slave offered little advantage over short-term white servitude. By the 1660s or 1670s, however, life expectancies in the southern colonies rose as settlers learned how to deal with American diseases and as food supplies improved. At this point high-priced slaves for life began to promise an economic advantage over cheaper four-year indentured servants.

Racial attitudes as well as economics played a part in establishing slavery in North America. White indentured servants were protected by law from the worst physical abuse; women servants could not be exploited sexually. If the master of an indentured servant violated the custom of the country or the terms of the contract, he or she could be sued by the servant. Except briefly in the earliest period, Africans enjoyed no such rights. The English were prejudiced against the physical characteristics of Africans and viewed them as lesser beings. Brutally torn away from all that was familiar, brought among strangers, surrounded by other captives who did not speak their language, and confronted with an alien landscape and an unfamiliar climate, blacks were in no position to protect themselves.

As the slave system fully matured, its victims were subject to ever more elaborate "slave codes" that defined their legal position in detailed ways and placed severe restrictions on their movements and conduct. Under these codes they became "chattel property," to be bought, sold, inherited, and bequeathed like houses, horses, or plows. As slaves became more valuable as property, the planters sought to increase their number. Prices rose and each year more and more were imported from Africa or from the Caribbean islands which served as way stations for African laborers. Some 300,000 Africans were landed at the docks of the mainland colonies during the seventeenth and eighteenth centuries. More than ten times as many slaves were brought to the Caribbean and Latin America during this period. There, the high profits on the sugar plantations permitted the owners to bring in few women, work the males to death, and then replace them by importing new male slaves. The Chesapeake planters, who made smaller profits on tobacco, could not afford such an extravagant system, and from the beginning they imported female slaves as well. The relatively high proportion of women, plus the healthier conditions of the North American mainland than the New World tropics, resulted in a rapid increase in the slave population through an excess of births over deaths. By 1759 more than a fifth of the inhabitants of mainland British America were black slaves, and many of these were native-born Americans.

* AMERICA AS A RELIGIOUS HAVEN *

Americans like to think of their country as a haven for the oppressed. And while the yearning for land and a better living standard pulled more people from the Old World to the New than any other force, America did serve as a refuge for thousands of transatlantic migrants fleeing Old World oppression. In the seventeenth century most of these were refugees from religious intolerance and they came primarily to the settlements north of the Chesapeake, especially to New England and Pennsylvania, imprinting on these communities many of their values and characteristics.

Religious refugees came from every class of European society. At the top were rich merchants and landed gentlemen who sought to aid their poorer co-religionists. In the case of Massachusetts, many of the gentry actually joined the migration to America. Most of those who came to escape persecution at home, however, were ordinary laborers, artisans, farmers, housewives, servants, and shopkeepers, much like those who came to escape poverty. Most of those fleeing religious oppression had no interest in freedom of worship for its own sake. They were often as intolerant toward others as their persecutors were toward them. Their complaint was merely that the wrong people were dictating the religious rules. It is not surprising, then, that such refugees would often become persecutors in turn when they found themselves in a position to dictate religious beliefs and practices.

THE REFORMATION. To understand the flight from persecution we must look at the religious scene in sixteenth- and seventeenth-century Europe. Until the 1520s virtually all Western Europeans were Roman Catholic Christians who believed that men and women achieved salvation and avoided eternal damnation through accepting Jesus, participating in the sacraments, and embracing the Catholic creed. Through its rituals, ceremonies, ministries, and confessionals, the all-embracing Catholic Church provided solace and hope for the multitude and cloistered refuge for those with a contemplative bent. Its spiritual authority was reinforced by its stewardship of the Bible, which was available only in Latin, the language of the ordained clergy and a small lay elite. The supreme head of the Catholic Church, the pope, the Vicar of Christ, seated in Rome, was the final authority in matters of faith and morals. He also sought at times to assert temporal power over the rulers of the European states.

By 1500 many Europeans had become critical of the Catholic Church. Some objected to church governance through a hierarchy of priests, bishops, and cardinals as unwarranted by the original Gospels. Some believed Church doctrines had drifted far from the views of Jesus and the early Church Fathers. Many found the Church too worldly or even immoral. Popes, bishops, and even ordinary priests seemed obsessed with wealth and secular power. Monasteries and convents were no longer centers for the contemplative life, but havens for the idle and the dissolute. To the growing number of skeptics it seemed that the Church had become hypocritical, venal, and corrupt and in need of fundamental reform.

In 1517 Martin Luther, an Augustinian friar, attacked the Church's sale of papal letters remitting punishment for sin to raise money for building the magnificent new St. Peter's basilica in Rome. He soon moved on to deny the Church's claim to be the guardian of the gates of heaven and asserted in its place that salvation was a transaction between God and the individual, needing no priest as intermediary. Luther also denounced the self-imposed isolation of monks and nuns and insisted that all Christians participate in the world's affairs. In theology he denied the Catholic emphasis on "good works" as the road to salvation and substituted the idea of faith: only God could confer salvation; it could not be earned by deeds, however pious or numerous.

Luther's demands for change quickly spread through Europe. Before long the reform movement expanded into a thorough assault on Church ceremony, worldliness, papal power, and the belief that the sacraments of the Church were essential to salvation. The attack begun by Luther against the established religious order eventually touched many other aspects of life, producing the continent-wide upheaval known as the Protestant Reformation.

For a while the Reformation scarcely affected England. King Henry VIII accepted the Catholic Church's doctrines and forms of worship. But when the pope refused to annul Henry's marriage to Catherine of Aragon and excommunicated him in 1533 for marrying Anne Boleyn, the king declared himself supreme head of the Church of England. He also authorized an English translation of the Bible so that it might be read by all literate people, and dissolved the monasteries, confiscating their vast property.

For the next century England became a battleground between the forces of Catholicism and Protestantism. Under Elizabeth I, a Protestant Church of England (the Anglican Church) emerged, controlled by the English crown but retaining many of the old religion's ceremonies and beliefs. This outcome did not please everyone. Some English people refused to accept Anglicanism and remained loyal Catholics. Others sought to go beyond Anglicanism to embrace the tenets of John Calvin, a French Protestant reformer, who had established his headquarters at Geneva.

Calvinists insisted that all humans were sinful and wicked. As one English Calvinist expressed it, "every natural man and woman is born as full of sin as a toad of poison, as full as ever his skin can hold. . . . " Such beings obviously deserved damnation and could not ransom themselves through good works. But God, in his infinite mercy and out of regard for Jesus's sacrifice of His earthly life, would save a few. These few "elect" were predestined to be saved from hell, since God, who determined all, had selected them at the beginning of time.

English Calvinists demanded that the Church of England "purify" itself entirely of Catholic belief and ceremonies and abandon the bishop-run church-governing structure that it still retained from the old religion. At first these "Puritans" were content to remain within the official Anglican Church as "dissenters" or "nonconformists," working to change it from the inside. Eventually, after being harassed and persecuted, many became "separatists" who renounced the Church of England entirely.

In the half century following Elizabeth's death in 1603, England experienced a religious churning that threatened to tear the country apart. New sects rose to prominence, each, it seemed, more extreme and unusual than the preceding one. Some of these "sectaries" were intensely hostile to the existing social system, despising and denouncing political absolutism, class deference, intellectual authority, and even private property. But even the more moderate Nonconformists and the remaining Catholics seemed to deny the authority of the crown and the unity of the nation, besides endangering their own souls and infecting with error all who came in contact with them.

THE PILGRIMS OF PLYMOUTH.   By the early 1600s several religious minorities had abandoned hope of change in England and begun to consider emigration. The first to depart was a small body of radical Puritan Separatists, the Pilgrims. In 1608 this group moved to Leiden in the Netherlands, a refuge for religious minorities from all over Europe. For a while they prospered, but as time passed the little congregation began to fear for its survival and its purity of belief in the face of the easygoing religious ways of the Dutch. In 1617 the Pilgrim leaders decided to move the congregation to "Virginia," where they could maintain their preferred mode of life and form of worship without distraction. After selling their possessions in Holland and securing loans from the London Company and from Thomas Weston, a London merchant, about thirty of the Pilgrims departed for England. At Southampton they joined a larger group of nonseparatists hired to work in the colony by the profit-seeking Weston. On September 16, 1620, after many difficulties and much delay, the 180-ton Mayflower, with 149 passengers and crew, sailed from Plymouth harbor for America.

The Pilgrims' original destination was the region near the mouth of the Hudson River but severe storms drove them to the north and they decided to stay at Cape Cod Bay where they had touched land. Fearful that the nonseparatists ("strangers") among them might dominate the community, and worried that their charter might not have legal force because the region was outside the London Company's grant, the Pilgrims adopted the Mayflower Compact before leaving ship. This short document established a civil government with powers "to enact, constitute, and frame such just and equal Laws, Ordinances, Acts, Constitutions, and Offices, from time to time, as shall be thought most meet and convenient for the general Good of the Colony."

During the first winter the colonists, who called their settlement Plymouth after their port of departure, suffered grievously from disease. Fortunately, the weather was relatively mild and the Indians proved helpful. One, Squanto, had been seized by a European trader years before and taken to England, where he had learned the English language. He and Massasoit, the grand sachem of the local Wampanoags, befriended the colonists, teaching them how to plant maize and other native plants and showing them the best fishing streams. In spite of this aid, the Pilgrim community, like almost all early English settlements, went through a "starving time" that first winter. By spring nearly half the colonists were dead. During the summer, however, the survivors put the Indians' teachings to good use; by fall their storehouses were well stocked. In November 1621 they celebrated their success with a harvest festival that has come down to us, after many twists and bypaths, as Thanksgiving.

The Plymouth colony expanded slowly, reaching a population of about 1,000 in 1640 and 3,000 in 1660. Although life was hard, William Bradford and the other Pilgrim leaders never forgot that their mission was to found a godly colony. Yet Plymouth's religious orthodoxy was never intolerant or harsh. For seventy years the "Old Colony" modestly prospered. Then, in 1691, it was absorbed into the Massachusetts Bay community.

THE MASSACHUSETTS BAY PURITANS. Until the 1620s the Puritan dissenters had hoped to reform the established Church of England. By the middle of that decade, however, they feared for the future of the godly in a nation ruled by Charles I and Anglican Archbishop William Laud. Laud considered Puritan doctrines wicked and erroneous and, in cooperation with the king, he suppressed Puritan books, forbade Puritans to preach, and attempted to impose Anglican practices and beliefs on all dissenters. In 1629 when Charles dissolved the Puritan-friendly Parliament and assumed personal rule of England, it was clearly time to leave.

A few Puritans had already departed. In 1625 forty had emigrated to the fishing colony of Salem, north of present-day Boston. Now a number of prominent Puritan gentlemen procured a royal charter for a new colony, establishing the Massachusetts Bay Company, a corporation authorized to own and govern all land between the Merrimack and Charles rivers, from the Atlantic to the Pacific. The charter also prescribed a structure for the new Massachusetts Bay Company that omitted the provision, common to such grants, that the governor, assistants, and freemen of the company had to remain in England to do business.

In the summer of 1629 the promoters of emigration persuaded John Winthrop, a Cambridge University-educated gentleman and attorney, to accept the governorship of the company. Winthrop agreed on condition that the settlers bring the company's charter to New England where it would be out of reach of the English authorities, enabling the colonists to enjoy virtual autonomy in their political and religious affairs. Reflecting on the hard fate of the Virginia colonists, Winthrop noted the differences between the two ventures. The Virginia settlers, he wrote, had fallen into "great and fundamental errors" because, among other things, "their mayne end was Carnall and not religious." The new community would avoid that mistake.

In fact there were "carnall" reasons for the Puritan migration as well. In addition to Winthrop's appeals and the desire to escape Laud's harassment, a depression in the English wool industry in the late 1620s helped push the Puritans to the New World. Men and women facing both persecution and hunger sold their property, paid their debts, and signed up for Massachusetts. In the early spring of 1630 four well-equipped, crowded vessels left for New England. They were soon followed by seven more. The Puritan settlers were generally more prosperous and more socially prominent than the Pilgrims and other separatists.

John Winthrop expected the Massachusetts Bay Colony to be an example of order, morality, and conformity for wayward humanity. "We shall be as a City upon a Hill, the eies of all people are uppon us." (Courtesy of American Antiquarian Society)

In a few months 1,000 settlers were building cabins, clearing fields, and planting crops in the Shawmut (Boston) area. Despite some sickness and a few untimely deaths the first year, settlers continued to arrive and the population grew quickly. By 1640 Massachusetts had about 9,000 inhabitants, almost as many as Jamestown, founded thirty-three years earlier.

OFFSHOOTS OF THE MASSACHUSETTS BAY COLONY. Religious oppression in America itself would soon become a colonizing force. Under John Winthrop and the other learned Puritan "magistrates," Massachusetts Bay was dominated by religion. All adult male family heads who were full-fledged members of the church were considered "freemen" and allowed to participate in political decisions. Women were denied all political rights, as were many men who were not church members or who owned no property. The leaders of the colony did not welcome those who did not accept Puritan religious views. As John Cotton, a prominent Puritan minister later noted, "the design of our first planters was not toleration, but [they] were professed enemies of it. . . . Their business was to settle, and (as much as in them lay) secure Religion to Posterity according to that way which they believed was of God." Before long, political and religious intolerance had begun to drive independent-minded people out of the Bay Colony itself.

One of the first to go was the Reverend Thomas Hooker. Though himself a minister, Hooker demanded that church membership not be a requirement for voting. When the Massachusetts authorities refused to yield, Hooker joined with others who were leaving the Bay Colony to find better land. Hooker's group established a colony at Hartford and adopted the Fundamental Orders, a form of government that, though scarcely democratic, gave the magistrates less power than they had in the Bay Colony and imposed a more lenient religious test for full citizenship. Soon after, other former residents of Massachusetts established New Haven on the north shore of Long Island Sound. Still other communities, peopled from Plymouth, Massachusetts Bay, and the Connecticut River settlements themselves, sprang up nearby. In 1662 the river communities and those on the sound were merged as the self-governing colony of Connecticut.

Roger Williams, another Puritan minister who came to Massachusetts in 1631, promptly quarrelled with the Bay Colony's religious leaders over whether the community had fully separated from the Church of England and whether its charter was legal. He also denounced the practice of requiring church attendance and the payment of taxes to support the Puritan clergy. In 1635 the Massachusetts authorities ordered his arrest and Williams fled to Narragansett Bay, just east of Connecticut. There he bought land from the Indians and established the community of Providence Plantation, becoming the father of the Rhode Island colony. The new colony's key principles were the complete separation of religion and government (separation of church and state), toleration of all religious beliefs, and the sovereignty of the people.

Other dissenters soon flocked to the Narragansett area. One of the most remarkable was Anne Hutchinson, "a woman of ready wit and bold spirit," who, like Williams, had tangled with the leading clergymen of the Bay Colony over religious doctrine. Hutchinson espoused the idea that only those infused with the Holy Spirit could preach the word of God and that only a few, herself included, could determine to whom the Holy Spirit had been revealed. Besides threatening the leadership of the Bay Colony ministers, Hutchinson's outspokenness also defied the principle of female subordination. The church leaders summoned her to a hearing and demanded that she retract her views and cease to preach. She refused and threatened that if they continued to persecute her, God would ruin them, their posterity, and "this whole State." Shocked by her boldness and presumption, the leaders expelled Hutchinson from the church and declared her a heretic. She and some of her followers soon moved to Aquidneck near Providence.

Other exiles and dissenters also came to the Narragansett region, enlarging the population of the little cluster of towns. In 1663 King Charles II granted Rhode Island and Providence Plantation a royal charter as a separate colony.

PENN'S WOODS.   Pennsylvania, too, was the offshoot of religious persecution—in this case of the Quakers, as outsiders called those belonging to the Society of Friends. Quakers believed that to understand God's will people needed only to consult their "inner light"; there was no need for an elaborate credo and a trained clergy. In the 1640s and 1650s, Quaker "enthusiasts" traveled through

England passionately preaching their message of the inner light, and advising their listeners to throw off the vanities of the world and renounce war and excessive respect for authorities.

The Anglican clergy, and many orthodox English people, considered Quaker behavior and teachings even more offensive than those of the Puritans. One contemporary called them "a new fanatic sect, of dangerous principles, who show no respect to any man, magistrate, or other, and seem a melancholy, proud sort of people. . . . " The English government feared the Quakers' contempt for a "hireling ministry" and their refusal to take oaths or pay church tithes. In 1655 the government ordered the Quakers to desist from their disorderly practices and enforced the command by a flock of legal prosecutions.

During the 1650s Quaker missionaries fanned out from England, many going to the British colonies. Here, too, they were persecuted. Except in Rhode Island, their emotional preaching and breaches of religious decorum resulted in savage punishment. For refusing to desist from preaching, several Quakers were whipped and imprisoned in Massachusetts. Between 1659 and 1661, four were hanged.

In the 1670s a few Quaker families from England settled along the Delaware River in an area that in 1701 would join with Puritan-settled East Jersey to form the royal province of New Jersey. In 1681, William Penn, who had become a "Friend" against his influential father's strong wishes, secured a charter from Charles II for a giant block of land along the Delaware River to repay a debt the crown owed Admiral Penn. In addition, the king's brother gave Penn three counties along the lower Delaware River, which would become the separate colony of Delaware in 1701.

Even before this grant Penn had prepared the way for a mass migration of Quakers to Pennsylvania (Penn's Woods) by constructing a "frame of government" for the colony and a set of laws. The result was one of the most enlightened political systems in the contemporary world. In Pennsylvania any male who owned or rented a small amount of land or who paid any taxes would be allowed to vote. No taxes would be imposed on anyone without the approval of the elected colonial legislature. All trials were to be before juries. In place of the long list of crimes punishable by death in England, in Pennsylvania there would be only two capital crimes: treason and murder. No atheists were to be admitted to the colony, but all who believed in God, regardless of their denomination, were welcome and would be allowed to worship in peace.

In 1682 Penn visited his new colony to observe the laying out of Philadelphia, one of the first modern planned cities. During this visit he also cemented cordial relations with the local Indians by paying generously for their land. Settlers soon began arriving in large numbers, drawn by Penn's policies of selling land at low prices and extending religious liberty to all Christians. Pennsylvania attracted not only thousands of British Quakers, but also French Protestants (Huguenots), who were in disfavor in Catholic France, and many German Pietists (radical Protestants), victims of persecution by German Catholics and Lutherans alike. By 1689, with 12,000 inhabitants, the colony was already a going concern.

THE LIMITS OF RELIGIOUS TOLERATION. Seventeenth-century religious dissidents from Europe also settled in Maryland, the Carolinas, and New Netherland. Maryland was a particular refuge for George Calvert's Catholic co-religionists, though it also attracted Puritan and Anglican Protestants. In New Netherland the tolerant Dutch attracted religious minorities from almost every part of the Western world—Huguenots from France, Jews from the Portuguese colony of Brazil, and assorted religious refugees from Germany, England, Massachusetts, and elsewhere. By the end of Dutch rule in 1664, the small colony—and especially its chief town, New Amsterdam on Manhattan Island—had become a cosmopolitan community inhabited by a score of nationalities and a wide assortment of religious groups.

America, then, served as a refuge for religious dissenters from Europe. Pennsylvania, New Netherland, Rhode Island, and, for a while, Maryland, accorded the right to worship to a wide array of faiths. But religious toleration was far from universal even in the mainland British colonies. In few places were Catholics or Jews allowed to practice their religion openly. Toleration, if accorded at all, generally meant toleration only for Protestants of various kinds.

In many colonies, as we have seen, even Protestants who differed from the founding denomination suffered disabilities. In most of New England only Puritans were welcome. In southern New York and most of the colonies south of Pennsylvania only Anglicans enjoyed full civil and religious rights. In both Calvinist and Anglican colonies ministers of the favored ("established") churches received support from the provincial treasury through tithes—religious taxes—imposed on all residents of the colony regardless of their religious preferences. All other clergy had to rely on their parishioners to support their churches and pay their salaries, if allowed to preach at all. Yet taken as a whole, religious toleration was more complete and general in the British mainland colonies than elsewhere in the Western world.

✳ CONCLUSIONS ✳

The motives, then, of those who promoted and those who settled the American colonies present a mixed picture. Americans may prefer to see their country as founded primarily on freedom, a refuge for those fleeing oppression and bigotry, but at best this view is only partly true. New England, Pennsylvania, and, to a lesser extent, Maryland, New Jersey, and Delaware assuredly served as havens for religious dissenters. But they themselves exhibited religious tolerance only for select groups. Nowhere, except perhaps in Rhode Island and New Netherland, were those of every religious persuasion welcome. Nor should we forget that for many men and women who crossed the Atlantic America was the opposite of a haven: It was a prison. For thousands of transported European felons and for an even larger number of Africans, America was a place of bondage.

For those who came voluntarily, moreover, the strongest lure was not freedom; it was economic and social opportunity. Capitalists could make profits from trade, land speculation, and commercial agriculture; gentlemen could raise their status and restore their diminished fortunes; rulers could enrich their realms and make themselves more powerful. The expectations of Europeans who had only their lives to invest were more modest, perhaps, but they, too, were primarily economic. Most ordinary men and women crossed the Atlantic to acquire the economic independence and decent comfort that the social and economic systems of England and continental Europe denied them. Opportunity was America's basic premise in the beginning and would remain so throughout its history.

3

COLONIAL SOCIETY

How Did Old World Life and Culture Change in the Wilderness?

1636	Harvard, in Massachusetts, is the first college to be founded in the colonies
1642, 1647	Massachusetts Bay Colony enacts compulsory school laws
1662	The "Half-Way Covenant" allows the children of Massachusetts Bay church members to join the congregation without a conversion experience
1675–78	Indian–white tensions erupt into King Philip's War in New England
1675	Bacon's Rebellion in Virginia
1692	Twenty-one men and one woman are executed in the Salem, Massachusetts, witch trials
1705	Virginia's legislature establishes a Propositions and Grievances Committee to receive public petitions proposing new laws
1732	Publication of the first issue of Benjamin Franklin's *Poor Richard's Almanack*
1734–37	Congregationalist minister Jonathan Edwards sparks a religious revival in New England
1739	Stono Rebellion of South Carolina slaves
1740	George Whitefield's "Methodism" leads to a "Great Awakening" throughout the colonies
1746–52	Benjamin Franklin's experiments with electricity earn him international fame

In 1782, shortly before the Revolutionary War ended, J. Hector St. John de Crèvecoeur, a French gentleman who had settled in the American colonies, asked a question that would be posed in various forms again and again: "What, then, is the American, this new man?" Crèvecoeur's answer was that the American was a mixture of the old and the new. He was an individual who leaving behind all his ancient prejudices and manners, receives new ones from the mode of life he has embraced, the new government he obeys, and the new rank he holds. . . . Americans are the western pilgrims, who are carrying along with them that great mass of arts, sciences, vigour, and industry which began long since in the east; they will finish the great circle. . . .

Americans, then, were not simply transplanted Europeans, according to Crèvecoeur. They had brought with them to the new land many of the habits and much of the cultural heritage of the Old World. But they had also left behind a good deal, and much of what they had taken with them had been transformed in their new circumstances.

Were Crèvecoeur's conclusions correct? Had the human mixture of the colonies blended into a new type? Was there a distinctive American culture by the eve of the Revolution? Or were Americans merely transplanted Europeans with attitudes, values, and institutions directly traceable to the European continent? In what sense and in what ways were Americans "new," and if they were new, how had they become so?

✻ A NEW MIXTURE IN A NEW LAND ✻

Two powerful factors clearly worked to transform immigrants to colonial America: a different physical environment, and a different mixture of human beings.

A NEW PHYSICAL ENVIRONMENT. Unlike Europe, America, as late as the Revolution, was still almost entirely a forested wilderness. Most of the population of the British colonies was confined to a narrow strip of coast between the Appalachian Mountains and the sea. Beyond the coastal tidewater region tongues of settlement extended along the rivers that rose in the mountains, but much of the "West" was a vast expanse of forest dotted by a few clearings and threaded by Indian trails. Even in the 1770s only five American towns had more than 10,000 inhabitants—Boston, Newport, New York, Philadelphia, and Charleston. Nor did the settled countryside much resemble its European counterpart with its trim fields, neat fences and hedgerows, stone barns, and well-built farmhouses. Everywhere in colonial America there were more woods than cleared land and even established farms with their timber dwellings and scraggly wood fences seemed impermanent and ill-tended by European standards.

Travel in this great wilderness was slow and uncomfortable. Roads were dirt tracks through the forest; bridges were logs laid across stones. The mounted riders of the continental postal service took three weeks to cover the 310 miles from Boston to Philadelphia. Inns were scarce and generally squalid.

DIVERSITY AMONG THE EUROPEANS. The population mix of the colonies was far more hetereogeneous than Europe's. Even in its European ingredients the colonial population was diverse. In the seventeenth century, streams of French, Dutch, Swedes, and Germans joined the largely English population. Between 1700 and 1775 about 100,000 Germans crossed the Atlantic to the mainland British colonies. Many went to Pennsylvania; others settled in western Maryland and western Virginia. Presbyterians from Scotland had displaced the conquered Catholics in northern Ireland in the early seventeenth century, prospering in their new homes by raising cattle and weaving linen until the British government imposed duties on imports from Ulster, severely damaging the Scotch-Irish economy. Masses of Ulster Protestants soon flocked to America. Many went to the Pennsylvania backcountry to the west of the older settled regions. Others moved into western Virginia and then down through the Great Valley (the Shenandoah) and the frontier counties of the Carolinas as far as northern Georgia.

Crèvecoeur claimed that in America "individuals of all nations are melted into a new race of men." But even white Europeans often refused to mingle, much less melt. The result was a lumpy demographic stew rather than a smooth puree. Most groups retained their characteristics generation after generation, practicing their own religion, speaking their own language, pursuing their own customs, and marrying within their own fold.

The Germans, because they were numerous and slow to assimilate, aroused the suspicion of English-speaking Pennsylvanians. In the 1750s Benjamin Franklin penned an exasperated outburst against the "Palatine boors" that expressed a widely held view among British Pennsylvanians of the dangers they posed:

> Advertisements intended to be general are now printed in Dutch [German] and English. The signs in our streets have inscriptions in both languages, in some places only German. They begin of late to make all their . . . legal instruments in their own language . . . which . . . are allowed in our courts, where the German business so increases that there is continued need of interpreters; and I suppose within a few years they will also be necessary in the Assembly, to tell one half of our legislators what the other half say. In short, unless the stream of importation can be turned from this to other colonies . . . they will so outnumber us that . . . we . . . will . . . not be able to preserve our language, and even our government will become precarious.

The Scotch-Irish were not always warmly welcomed either. In Pennsylvania the authorities feared that they would violate the rights of the Indians and set off a major Indian war. These fears were not unfounded. The newcomers were the very image of the frontiersmen of legend: tall, red-haired, quick to anger, hospitable, fiercely independent. Such hot-blooded people did not get along well with their neighbors and were constantly embroiled in disputes and quarrels with the Indians. Yet they made valuable additions to the American population. Herdsmen and hunters rather than farmers, they filled in the colonial backcountry, where their qualities made them useful, if sometimes troublesome, pioneers.

NATIVE AMERICANS. From the beginning, European–Indian contacts affected both sides in profound ways. Generally the two societies remained distinct although they interacted where they touched.

Some of the interactions were clearly benign. The early settlers of New England had learned Indian farming techniques and borrowed from the Native Americans many food plants and recipes whose Indian names—squash, hominy, and succotash, for example—entered the English language. For their part, the Indians acquired the colonists' muskets, cloth, iron implements, and other goods through trade in beaver pelts and deerskins.

More commonly, however, the transfer from European to Indian proved damaging to the latter. The Indians were quickly entangled in the transplanted economy of the Europeans, especially the fur trade. Though not the perfect ecological heroes posited by sentimentalists, Indians usually did not place too heavy a burden on the animal life of the forest. But when whites appeared, ready to trade metal tools, guns, cloth, and "firewater" for animal pelts, many succumbed to temptation. Wherever the fur trade flourished it decimated the beaver and other animal populations. Increasingly, moreover, the Indians became dependent on trade with whites and less able to do without the white man's goods. The fire water proved particularly harmful. Drunkenness and alcoholism became a corrosive part of Indian life, damaging the health of individuals and tearing at the very fabric of Indian society.

From a strict cultural perspective, however, the exchange between Indian and European was relatively superficial in the British colonies. Colonists of English and Scottish extraction did not mix as readily with the Indians as did the Spanish in Mexico and Florida and the French in Canada. In addition, people of northern European origins intermarried less often with the Indians than did whites of southern European extraction.

Protestants also lacked the zeal for saving heathen souls that their Catholic rivals in Canada, Brazil, and New Spain displayed. In the 1660s the Reverend John Eliot, a Bay Colony Puritan minister, translated the Bible "into the Indian tongue." In all, Eliot established fourteen towns of "praying Indians" with over 1,000 Indian converts. By the mid-1670s there were perhaps 4,000 Christian Indians in New England. In the 1740s, the Moravians, German Protestant Pietists, set out to convert the Indians in Pennsylvania without destroying their culture. Still, the total conversion effort in Protestant America was relatively feeble.

Indeed, rather than Christian love, Indian–white relations in British-America were generally marked by hostility and violence. The competing view of land ownership often led to troubles. Outside Pennsylvania, where the white Quaker officials respected Indian rights, Indian–white contacts produced constant warfare. We have already seen how, in 1622, tensions between the Jamestown settlers and the Virginia coastal tribes tripped off a massacre of white colonists and a war that destroyed the power of the Indians in the region. In the 1630s the Pequot War decimated the Indian population of eastern Connecticut. Most serious of all, during the first century of settlement, was King Philip's War, which erupted in New England in the mid-1670s. In this conflict the tribes of southern New England, under the leadership of Philip (Metacomet), son of the Plymouth colony's benefactor, Massasoit, attacked the settlers of Massachusetts for encroaching on their lands and hunting grounds. The Narragansetts of Rhode Island and the Nipmucks of Connecticut soon joined Philip's Wampanoag warriors in the struggle.

Armed for the first time with guns, the Indians devastated the white settlements with their hit-and-run tactics. Before long the colonists adopted Indian

*This is a contemporary drawing
of Metacomet, usually called King Philip.
He looks rather gentle here,
but he proved a formidable enemy
of the New England settlers.*

methods of warfare: surprise raids, ambushes, and even scalping. Eventually the war against the "savages" made the colonists savage. Soon they were torturing prisoners and using large dogs to tear the Indians apart. In the end the Europeans' superior numbers and organization prevailed. By 1676 the southern New England tribes were defeated and subdued.

King Philip's War exacted an enormous toll of both sides. According to one estimate, one-sixteenth of the white male population of New England died in the fighting. One casualty of the war was Eliot's praying Indians. Although they had remained loyal to the whites, they were interned for three years on Deer Island, where they were forced to live on shellfish. Many died. Philip himself was captured and shot, and many of his followers were sold into slavery in the Caribbean or indentured as servants to whites. Indian lands were awarded to the victorious white soldiers. After 1676 the New England Indians ceased to be a challenge to the white population except on the remote frontiers.

COLONIAL BLACKS.   In 1760 about 325,000 of the approximately 1.6 million people in British North America were black. Of these, 12,000 lived in New England, another 25,000 in the middle colonies (New York, New Jersey, and Pennsylvania), and the remainder in the southern colonies, with Virginia and South Carolina far in the lead. Almost all of these people were slaves; only a few hundred were "free people of color."

Black workers were a vital part of the laboring class in colonial America. In New England and the middle colonies black slaves were employed as day laborers, seamen, house servants, or craftsmen's assistants in the ports and towns. In the Chesapeake region and the Carolinas, on the other hand, slaves formed the backbone of the labor force on the plantations and farms, producing tobacco, rice, indigo, and grain. Even in the southern plantation colonies, however, many blacks worked as house servants and artisans.

This forced labor on colonial farms, plantations, and in towns transformed the culture of enslaved Africans. Slaves had to learn occupations that were not part of their African culture. In South Carolina, Virginia, and elsewhere they quickly acquired trades such as bricklaying, "plaistering," wig making, silversmithing, and gunsmithing. The cultural exchange was not all one way, however. Slaves brought skills and knowledge from Africa and used them in America. West Africans were familiar with boats and the sea; in South Carolina many of them worked as fishermen. They introduced the West African perriauger—a kind of canoe—for transportation along the Sea Islands and through the many rivers and streams of the Carolina coastal lowlands. Slaves also introduced West African agricultural products to South Carolina, including melons, gourds, and probably even rice. Black cooks learned the techniques of European cuisine but they contributed their own ingredients such as sesame seeds and red pepper. In fact, much of the South's distinctive cooking is derived from the merger of African and European elements.

The African family and kinship systems also survived the transplant to America. In most of the slaves' original homelands each individual was tied to the community through elaborate kinship networks. In their new homes, husbands and wives, parents and children, were often separated against their will. But the inherited networks made it possible for slaves to remain in touch with distant relatives for many years, despite infrequent chances for face-to-face contact.

Little is known about the religion of the first generation or two of American slaves. Most West Africans worshiped the spirits of the dead, who were believed to remain close by, protecting their descendants. It seems likely that the first slaves tried to practice their religion much as they had at home, though far from the graves of their venerated ancestors. But there is evidence that transfer to America was destructive to the African religious system as a whole. It is also clear that many discrete practices—belief in amulets, conjurers, faith healing—survived the Atlantic leap and flourished on the new soil.

In most of the colonies few efforts were made at first to convert the Africans to Christianity, in part because Christians were not supposed to enslave their fellow Christians. Nonetheless, there is evidence that slaves absorbed the Europeans' faith to some degree in this early period, merely through contact. In the middle of the eighteenth century formal conversion of slaves became more common. By this time a new emotionalism had developed in Protestantism, and it made Christianity more attractive to many slaves.

The lot of the colonial slave varied from place to place, from time to time, and from master to master. In New England slaves were relatively well treated because they often lived in close contact with whites in a family setting. In the South the system was harsher. Some masters abused their slaves cruelly. The Virginian Robert Carter underfed his slaves and expected them to make up the deficiency by raising their own food in their spare time. The slaves' housing was often minimal. One eighteenth-century white Virginian, forced to take shelter one evening in a "Negro cabin" with six blacks, reported that the shack "was not lathed or plaistered, neither ceiled nor lofted above . . . one window, but no glass in it, not even a brick chimney, and as it stood on blocks about a foot above the ground, the hogs lay constantly under the floor, which made it swarm with flies."

Colonial slaves were harshly disciplined and tightly controlled. In seventeenth-century South Carolina, slaves judged guilty of offenses such as murder, striking a white person, or plotting an insurrection could be castrated, branded, and burned alive. In the eighteenth century whipping replaced most of the earlier sentences, but whipping too was a brutal and terrifying experience. Slaves who left their plantations were required to carry "tickets" indicating their owners' permission to be away from home. Mounted patrols stopped blacks on the roads, entered black homes for inspection, and confiscated black-owned firearms.

Despite these efforts to impose discipline, colonial blacks found ways to express their hatred of the slave system. They deliberately destroyed their master's tools, injured cattle and horses, damaged crops, and ran away. South Carolina slaves often escaped to the Spanish settlements in Florida. Some slaves fled to the Indian frontier. To discourage flight, Virginia allowed anyone who encountered a runaway to kill him on sight without penalty.

The most serious slave protest was group rebellion. Nowhere in the mainland English colonies did slaves mount a large-scale uprising or set up independent black communities, as they did in Brazil, Surinam, and places in the Caribbean. But there were several organized rebellions during the colonial period. In New York City in 1712 twenty-five slaves armed with knives, axes, and guns set fire to a white man's outhouse. When whites rushed to save the burning structure, the slaves attacked them, killing nine. The authorities called out the militia, who quickly rounded up the insurrectionists. Twenty-one were executed.

The Stono Rebellion in South Carolina—a far more serious threat to white rule—began near Charleston in September 1739 when a group of slaves broke into a storehouse and seized arms and supplies. Fleeing south toward Spanish Florida, the rebels gathered recruits, and attacked any white who got in their way. The militia soon caught up with the fugitives and killed them all. Thirty whites and forty-four blacks lost their lives. The Stono Rebellion sent a shock wave through South Carolina. White South Carolinians would never feel entirely safe again.

* REGIONS *

NEW ENGLAND, MIDDLE COLONIES, THE SOUTH. Diversity in colonial America also extended to patterns of settlement. Much of New England was divided into "towns," small communities of about 500 with a central village and adjacent fields and woods. The New England town was a relatively homogeneous community. All of its members belonged to the same Puritan faith;

most came from the same part of east-central England. Most town residents were members of farm families, but each community also had a minister, a schoolmaster, artisans, and craftspeople of various kinds. The dwellings within the village center were distributed around the perimeter of the "common," an open space where sheep and cattle grazed and where the community held its militia "musters" and conducted other collective activities. The village church, with its austere white exterior and tall steeple, usually bordered the common. Each family normally had a garden parcel close to its dwelling and larger fields, distant from the town center, where it grew its chief crops.

Life in the typical New England town was placid and orderly. Community decisions were made through the monthly town meeting. Though women, minors, servants, and nonchurchgoers were disfranchised, a sizable proportion of the adult males voted. These towns, one scholar has said, were "peaceable kingdoms," where disputes were readily resolved and a wide consensus achieved by discussion. They were also ideal settings for community activities, whether educational or religious. Some of the edge that New England has enjoyed in science, the arts, and business enterprise has been ascribed to the compact settlement of the New England town, which made schools more practical than where settlement was more scattered.

In the middle colonies (New York, New Jersey, and Pennsylvania), on the western border, and in the South, such tight-knit communities were rare, except in a few places, like Long Island, where New Englanders had settled. Instead, settlement patterns were open and scattered. Families lived on detached farms, often separated from their neighbors, especially on the western frontier, by large stretches of forest. In the middle colonies commerce helped create a sprinkling of small cities, but in the Chesapeake region (Maryland and Virginia) and the Carolinas, these were uncommon. Aside from a few provincial capitals such as Williamsburg, Virginia, Annapolis, Maryland, and the port of Charleston, little approaching a true city could be found in the region south of Pennsylvania until almost the very end of the colonial era.

Given these patterns of land occupation, it is not surprising that historians have supposed that the life of the typical Pennsylvanian or Virginian, say, entailed far less intense community involvement than that of the contemporary New Englander. But did it? A study by Darrett and Anita Rutman of Middlesex County, Virginia, in the period 1659–1750 demonstrates that communities in the Chesapeake region were not the chaotic, impersonal places often assumed. Though the people of Middlesex County did not come together each month in a formal legislative town meeting as in New England, they had their equivalent social, if not political occasion, in the monthly county court day. On court days, not only were criminal and civil cases heard by the magistrates, but people without court business came for the horse racing, the liquid refreshment, the gossip, and the chance to renew acquaintanceships and do business.

Studies such as the one by the Rutmans have narrowed the gap between New England and the colonial South. Moreover, there is reason to think that we have exaggerated the communal solidarity of many towns in New England. A recent study of Marblehead and Gloucester, both in Massachusetts, shows, for example, that community solidarity and homogeneity were often lacking even in the Bay Colony, especially in the ports and the fishing communities.

Though we can no longer draw such sharp contrasts between the social texture of New England and that of the South, it remains true that differences did affect the course of regional development.

EAST–WEST DIFFERENCES. Among the regional divisions that marked colonial society, East–West differences were especially troublesome. Much of the sectional tension involved the Indians.

It was on the frontier that the white population brushed against Indian groups unwilling to surrender additional lands or permit Europeans to settle among them. In the clashes that ensued, the authorities in the older coastal areas, preferring to preserve order at all costs, sometimes sided with the Indians against the western frontiersmen. This response created resentment between East and West.

These East–West tensions first appeared in Virginia, where by the 1670s settlers had pushed beyond the Tidewater into the Piedmont, the hilly plateau region immediately to the west. Piedmont settlers soon came to feel that the Tidewater planters who controlled the provincial government were unconcerned with the problems. They especially resented the indifference to Indian attacks on the frontier.

In 1675 and 1676, when Indian warfare broke out on the frontier, Virginia governor Sir William Berkeley called for restraint. The frontiersmen, under the leadership of Nathaniel Bacon, ignored him and attacked local Indian villages, almost wiping them out. Berkeley marched to the scene with 300 armed men determined to "call Mr. Bacon to accompt." By the time he arrived, Bacon and his followers had disappeared into the forest, where they mounted further attacks on the local tribes, friendly and hostile alike. Now a hero in the Piedmont, Bacon was elected to the House of Burgesses and took his seat in Jamestown, accompanied by armed partisans to see that he was not arrested.

The rebellious delegates passed measures to liberalize voting, open offices to small property holders, make taxes less burdensome for poorer colonists, and improve defenses against the Indians. Bacon soon demanded to be made commander of all the colony's armed forces. Berkeley refused, but the assembly, afraid of Bacon's armed supporters, yielded. Bacon soon departed with his men for the frontier, intent on killing more Indians. A series of maneuvers between militia loyal to the governor and Bacon's partisans ended with the burning of Jamestown in September 1676. In this moment of triumph Bacon suddenly died of a "Bloody Flux," ending his cause. Berkeley was not forgiving and hanged thirty-seven of Bacon's followers. Bacon's Rebellion was over.

Pennsylvania too began to experience Indian–white and East–West tensions as the frontier was settled. The Scotch-Irish settlers had complained for years that the Quaker-dominated government in Philadelphia did not support them adequately against the Indians. In December 1763, a mob of frontiersmen from the towns of Paxton and Donegal took the law into their own hands and attacked a group of peaceful Conestoga Indians, killing six. When the horrified Pennsylvania assembly ordered the "Paxton Boys" arrested, the enraged westerners marched on Philadelphia, prepared to get "justice" at the point of a gun. For a while it looked as if the colony would be thrown into civil war. Fortunately, Benjamin Franklin intercepted the rebels and negotiated a solution. Though further violence was avoided, this near-rebellion left a legacy of sectional antagonisms within Pennsylvania that lasted to the end of the century.

* FAMILIES *

The diverse ethnic and cultural ingredients in British North America continued to be separate, and new regional differences developed. But this does not mean that the New World environment did not broadly affect transplanted Old World institutions, attitudes, and practices. On the contrary, the new setting profoundly modified many Old World forms, helping to produce a society identifiably American.

BIRTH RATES, DEATH RATES, AND FAMILY SIZE. Even the most fundamental institution of all, the family, was altered by the new American environment. Exposed to New World conditions, the European family became both larger and more egalitarian than it had been in the mother country.

Famines, plagues, and wars ravaged seventeenth-century Europe and cut down thousands of men, women, and children before their time. By itself this situation would have limited family size. It was also typical of early modern Britain that, except for the aristocracy, the nuclear family consisted of parents and young children. Once grown, children were expected to establish their own households. This custom, coupled with the high death rates in this period, made for relatively small families, not more than four or five people.

The new American environment created a different family pattern. In New England from the beginning, people lived longer. During the seventeenth century the average life expectancy for men in Plymouth Colony came close to that of our own day. In Dedham, in the Bay Colony, death rates were half those of contemporary Europe. At the same time, in most of the New England towns birth rates were high, usually higher than in Europe. The net effect of these low death rates and high birth rates was to create larger families in New England than on the other side of the Atlantic.

At first the family history of the southern colonies was quite different. Most early immigrants to Maryland and Virginia were single men who came either as planters or servants. The authorities tried to attract women by paying their passage, but their success was limited. In 1704, for example, only about 7,200 of the 30,000 Europeans in Maryland were women. Most male Virginians and Marylanders were forced to remain bachelors.

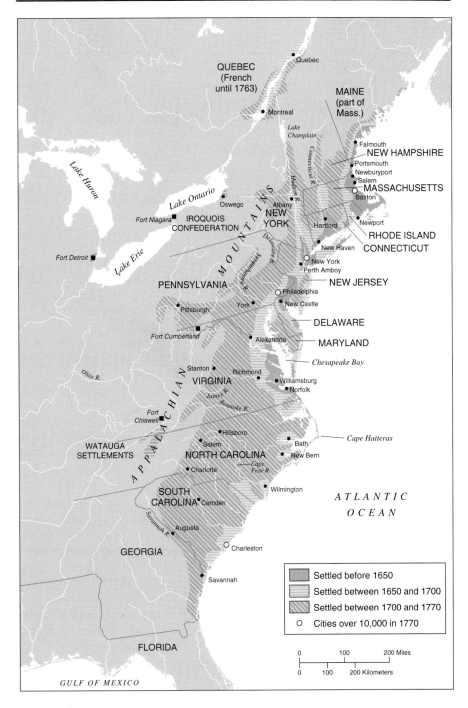

QUEBEC
(French
until 1763)

Quebec

MAINE
(part of
Mass.)

Montreal

Lake
Champlain

Falmouth
NEW HAMPSHIRE
Portsmouth
Newburyport
Salem
MASSACHUSETTS
Boston

Lake Huron

Lake Ontario

Oswego
Fort Niagara   IROQUOIS
CONFEDERATION

Albany
NEW
YORK

Hartford

Newport

RHODE ISLAND
CONNECTICUT

New Haven

Fort Detroit

Lake Erie

New York
Perth Amboy

NEW JERSEY

PENNSYLVANIA

Philadelphia

New Castle

DELAWARE

Pittsburgh   York

Fort Cumberland

MARYLAND

Alexandria

Ohio R.

Stanton

Richmond

VIRGINIA

Williamsburg
Norfolk

Chesapeake Bay

James R.

Roanoke R.

Fort
Chiswell

Hillsboro

Cape Hatteras

WATAUGA
SETTLEMENTS

Salem

NORTH CAROLINA

Bath

New Bern

Charlotte

Cape
Fear R.

SOUTH
CAROLINA Camden

Wilmington

ATLANTIC
OCEAN

Savannah R.

Augusta

GEORGIA

Charleston

Savannah

	Settled before 1650
	Settled between 1650 and 1700
	Settled between 1700 and 1770
O	Cities over 10,000 in 1770

0   100   200 Miles

0   100   200 Kilometers

FLORIDA

GULF OF MEXICO

Colonial Settlement, 1650–1770

The generally unhealthy state of the Chesapeake region also held down family formation. Malaria and dysentery killed many people in early colonial Virginia and Maryland and hit pregnant women particularly hard. In addition, European diseases were carried to the Chesapeake region by the tobacco-collecting vessels that came directly to each planter's dock. In South Carolina the rice-growing lowlands with their "agues" continued to be unhealthy well into the 1800s.

Still, as time passed, an ever-larger proportion of the Chesapeake and Carolina population consisted of the native-born, a development that equalized the numbers of males and females. This return to a normal sex ratio made more marriages possible, so that by the eighteenth century the family became the normal household unit even in the South. Meanwhile, because of closer commercial contact with other parts of the world, smallpox, malaria, and other illnesses invaded New England, increasing mortality rates. By the later years of the colonial period the disparity in size between the southern and northern colonial family had virtually disappeared.

The difference between European and American demographic characteristics, however, never entirely vanished during the colonial period. As late as 1790 American families were larger than their European counterparts. Population grew faster, too. Because land was cheaper and more abundant in America than in Europe, young people could afford to marry early. In the absence of birth control they usually had many children. Even without heavy immigration this would have made for a rapid population increase. But the flood of European immigrants magnified the effects.

FAMILY ROLES.   In colonial America the family served many functions. It was, for one thing, the center of education and training. Parents taught young children their first "letters" and their earliest religious precepts. A father taught his sons how to farm, repair tools, hunt, and fish. If he was a craftsman, he taught his son his trade. Girls learned from their mothers how to cook, bake, sew, weave, and spin.

The family was also a "little commonwealth" within which people's lives were prescribed and regulated and acceptable social behavior taught and enforced. Fathers were the rulers in these small political units; the law in the Puritan colonies even allowed them the power of life and death over their children. This patriarchal system was reinforced by the father's control over the family land and property. In the southern colonies, with their looser settlement patterns and their more abundant fertile land, this arrangement was probably not a serious problem for children. In early New England, however, where towns were limited in size and where fathers usually lived to ripe old age, grown sons were often forced to live in their parents' household, subject to continued patriarchal control, or to become tenants on their father's land. Fortunately, New England sons had an escape route. By the beginning of the eighteenth century an ever-larger number were leaving the crowded Massachusetts and Connecticut towns to move to cheap land in the Berkshire Hills, the Green Mountains, New Hampshire, and Maine.

Within the colonial family the roles of fathers and mothers differed distinctly. Fathers typically carried on the family's public functions—such as casting its vote, serving in the militia, filling governmental positions—and its work outside the home. Mothers were responsible for private domestic matters and for acting as "helpmeets" to their husbands. Within this limited domain women had considerable power. Mothers were expected to supervise the children, particularly the youngest ones. But in addition to their household duties, many married women helped in the family business, supplemented family income by running their own small businesses or by selling surplus produce or handmade goods, and helped organize church functions.

However inferior their status to American men, American women had greater privileges than women in Europe. Colonial men often recognized the value of women's work. In one Plymouth community a man was denied a license to run a tavern because he had no wife to help him in the business. Laws of the times granted American women higher legal status than their English sisters. Divorce was easier for wronged wives. Husbands who abused their spouses, especially in New England, were often reprimanded by the authorities. And colonial widows were entitled to a larger fixed amount of their husbands' estates than was common in the mother country.

Yet it remains true that the colonial woman's role and status were inferior to the man's. Even their services as wives and mothers conferred little freedom or prestige on colonial women, and many felt keenly their subordination. Their response was more often resignation than rebellion, however. As one South Carolina woman noted, her "self-denying duties" were "a part of the curse pronounced upon Eve" and nothing could be done about it.

Servants, who usually lived with their employers or masters, were often treated as part of the family. Masters had the authority to discipline them and sometimes were obliged to provide them with an education. In the South, slaves were in some ways members of the master's family, too. In law, slaves were treated as the children of their masters or mistresses, who, like parents, were expected to provide food, clothing, and shelter, and to mete out rewards and punishments.

The structure and power relations of colonial families were not static. They evolved over time, and by the eighteenth century a new pattern, according to historian Philip Greven, had begun to emerge, though the older, patriarchal one remained very much alive. This new "genteel" type flourished among richer, better-educated, and less pious Americans. It appeared late because wealth, comfort, and a secular outlook were relatively late developments in America.

Genteel families were bound together by affection rather than by authority and fear; they were more child-centered. Fathers were less insistent on their despotic rights and were more likely to accept the autonomy of their wives and children. One effect was the greater freedom of adult children to choose their spouses rather than have them selected by their parents. Scholars have theorized that the soaring rate of premarital pregnancy in the late eighteenth century may have reflected the desire of grown daughters and sons to force the consent of fathers to marriages they would otherwise have forbidden.

* EVERYDAY LIFE *

To describe coherently how colonial Americans lived presents many problems. The colonial era lasted 170 years by conventional measure (from 1607 to 1776). During that interval habits, customs, styles, and values changed. Daily life in the colonial era also differed among classes, races, nationalities, and regions. Yet some common qualities of daily life can be extracted from the immense diversity.

Housing among the earliest settlers was generally primitive. The first Europeans to touch shore dug caves in the hillsides, or put up lean-tos and canvas tents. But as soon as possible the settlers built in styles familiar at home. Until well into the eighteenth century, farmhouses in the northern colonies were made by driving posts into the ground, siding the structures with clapboard, and capping them with a wood-shingled roof. Many of these were no larger than twenty-by-twenty feet and rose a story-and-a-half, the "half" being a loft reached by an inside ladder. Each of these structures had a fireplace, often of logs partially protected from fire by clay plastering. They were usually unpainted, as paint was imported and expensive. To exclude cold weather, in the absence of glass, householders used wooden shutters. These kept out the rain and wind but they also excluded the daylight, and such dwellings were often dark, dank places.

Even in the eighteenth century, rooms in colonial homes were seldom differentiated by function. People slept, washed, dined, sat, and entertained in whatever room was handy, though there were sleeping lofts in houses with more than one story and most homes had kitchens with a table and fireplace for cooking. Sanitary facilities were primitive. People often bathed—when they did bathe—outdoors. They used privies set some distance from the house to keep the flies away. There were no window screens in those days, and mosquitoes and flies often made life in summer an ordeal. Rooms lacked closets. Clothes were folded away in chests or hung on pegs on the wall. Furniture was sparse and crude. Meals were consumed on tables made of boards set on trestles. Benches and stools were more common than chairs. Beds were hard mattresses stuffed with grass or feathers laid over a web of rope attached to a wood frame. Tableware—bowls, plates, trenchers—consisted of hollowed-out wood at first and then later of pewter, a silver-gray alloy of copper and lead. Spoons were common but forks were rare until late in the colonial period.

Housing in the towns was generally better than in the countryside. Town structures were more often of brick or stone than farm houses. As dwelling places for the colonies' prosperous merchants, shopkeepers, and skilled artisans, the towns also had many of America's largest and most luxurious private houses, buildings with two or three stories, many bedrooms, parlors, and multiple fireplaces. Some of these were designed by professional architects. In the South a few show plantation homes matched the luxury of the best town houses in Salem, Newport, Boston, and Philadelphia.

Food was abundant but plain. The forests and waters provided game, fish, fowl, berries, fruits, and nuts in abundance. The settlers planted European parsnips, turnips, carrots, cabbage, and onions in their kitchen gardens. They also sowed wheat where it would grow and raised hogs, sheep, cattle, and chickens. They borrowed maize and beans from the Indians. These ingredients they consumed roasted, stewed, or in the form of breads and various sorts of mushes or porridges. Frying with lard was a common way to prepare meats, especially in the South. Breakfast often consisted of a porridge of grain mixed with milk and flavored with molasses. The main meal was dinner served in the afternoon and often featuring a stew with meat and vegetables. Supper often repeated breakfast or was leftovers from dinner. In the towns, especially of New England, fish such as cod and herring was a common article of diet. Cuisine, generally, was not very flavorful, at least by our standards. Most cooks used few spices and did little to preserve natural flavors. None of this was especially healthy. The fat content of colonial food was high; the vitamin content undoubtedly low. Still, its variety and abundance made it superior to the diet of contemporary Europeans. Americans were on average taller and heavier than were Western Europeans as early as the 1770s, a fact attesting to their superior nutrition.

Colonial Americans scorned water as a thirst quencher. At the outset milk was one of the few alternatives, but as soon as possible the colonists turned to beer, wine, hard cider, and distilled liquors, the latter mostly rum made from West Indies molasses. By the eighteenth century tea had become common, but through most of the colonial era beverages containing alcohol were the drink of choice. This practice cannot have contributed to longevity, and drunkenness was a common colonial problem.

American dress was tied to class and occupation. The male farmer wore, on workdays, a linen shirt under a tight jacket called a "doublet." Below the waist he wore knee breeches, usually of wool but often of leather, ending in long cotton or linen stockings. His feet were shod either in moccasins or boots, depending on the season. The city artisan often supplemented this dress with a leather apron. Women of the farm or artisan class typically wore a three-piece outfit: a long skirt, a bodice, and sleeves that were attached to the bodice by ties at the armholes. Headgear for men consisted of woolen caps; for women, hoods or scarves.

Needless to say, dress was fancier among the richer colonists. Breeches and bodices were often velvet or satin; leather shoes had silver buckles. Men wore three-cornered hats of beaver felt, at least by the eighteenth century. Wigs became the almost universal head covering among "gentlemen" during the early eighteenth century, though at times, in the towns, even slaves wore them. Heavy, hot, and expensive, wigs eventually were replaced by longish hair whitened with chalk and tied in a queue behind. Rich women wore slippers of satin or morocco leather, and donned long skirts over several layers of petticoats. In the eighteenth century they adopted the hoop-petticoat, an outside skirt stiffened with whalebone. Women often wore their bodices low-cut. Slim waists were prized and the middles of prosperous young women and matrons were confined by tight-laced corsets.

The workweek was a six-day affair for most colonial people. Only on Sunday did work cease, and for the pious that did not mean leisure but church-going that took up long hours followed by sedate occupations such as visiting, reading, and conversation.

Life revolved around the seasons more than today. Most men were farmers and their year was governed by the crop-growing cycle of spring plowing and planting, summer weeding and hoeing, and fall harvesting. Winter on the farm was devoted to fence and house repair, handicrafts, and the like. Women's tasks were less affected by the season. Each week, whether summer or winter, brought the same routine of washing, cooking, nursing, house cleaning.

The colonists, except for the most devout, craved amusement for their leisure hours. In the South people enjoyed horse racing and indulged in "blood sports," such as cockfighting and bull baiting. Colonial boys played games with a ball and a bat that resembled modern baseball. In the winter, northern children ice-skated and sledded. Males in general hunted and fished.

∗ GOVERNMENT ∗

COLONIAL POLITICAL STRUCTURE. British immigrants to America brought with them the political ideas, customs, and practices of the mother country. On the local level, for example, both the town in New England and the church vestry in the South were political units transplanted from Britain. Beginning with Virginia in 1619, settlers were empowered one by one to set up legislatures resembling Parliament in each of the British mainland colonies. These were given different names in different colonies (General Court, House of Burgesses, General Assembly), and like Parliament usually had a lower and an upper house.

Each colony also had a chief executive, the equivalent of the English monarch. In royal colonies (in 1776, New Hampshire, Massachusetts, New York, New Jersey, Maryland, Virginia, North Carolina, South Carolina, and Georgia) the governor was appointed by the British sovereign. In proprietary colonies (Pennsylvania and Delaware, and New York, Maryland, and the Carolinas before they became royal colonies) the governor represented the proprietor, the man who held the original charter. Only in Connecticut and Rhode Island was the governor elected by the local enfranchised citizens. No matter how he was chosen, the governor usually could veto acts by the colonial legislature, much as, in theory at least, the English sovereign could veto acts of Parliament.

As time passed, the governors were forced to give up some of their power to the assemblies. At first British authorities refused to consider these bodies true legislatures. One British official described them as only "so many Corporations at a distance, invested with an Ability to make Temporary By Laws for themselves." But the distance from England, official British policy of ignoring restrictions on the colonies to allow them to prosper and thus enrich England, and inefficiency in administering colonial affairs, encouraged the colonial legislatures to expand their powers. Early in the eighteenth century the colonial lower houses forced the governors to allow them to debate freely without executive interference, to judge the qualifications of their own members, to exclude crown officials from their deliberations, and to meet when and for as long as they wished. Most important, they forced the governors to surrender to them "the power of the purse." By the middle of the eighteenth century the assemblies had moved from granting an annual lump-sum appropriation to the governor to spend as he saw fit to earmarking appropriations for specific periods. They also began to pay the governors' salaries for a single year—and only at the end of it—to guarantee their good behavior. In several colonies these efforts to control the governors touched off furious battles. By the 1750s most of these struggles had been decided in favor of the legislatures.

By the end of the colonial era the provincial assemblies were miniature parliaments exercising almost all the hard-won rights of their English model, including control over taxation, expenditures, the salaries of officials, military and Indian affairs, and everything that affected religion, education, and what we today would call welfare. The legislatures' power was not unlimited, however. Governors continued to veto laws they opposed. And even if the governor approved a measure, it could be "disallowed" by the Privy Council in England. Especially during the early years of the eighteenth century, however, the English government did little to restrain the colonial assemblies, and during this period of "salutary neglect" much real political power slipped into the hands of the colonists.

VOTERS AND THEIR REPRESENTATIVES. Although the framework of the colonial governments was similar to that of Great Britain, political power was more widely diffused in the colonies than in Britain. The upper houses of the colonial legislatures, the councils, were appointed and were composed typically of landed gentlemen, prosperous lawyers, and rich merchants. But membership was not hereditary, as it was in the English House of Lords.

More significant was the relatively broad electorate that chose the colonial lower houses. By modern standards the colonial franchise was severely limited. Slaves, of course, could not vote, nor could indentured servants. Though at times some women exercised considerable public authority, no colonial female had the right to vote. Even free white adult males had to own land or houses, or lease them for a long period, to qualify as voters. This was only one side of the picture, however. Property was so easily acquired and so widely held in America that the election laws disqualified relatively few free adult males from voting. Furthermore, traditional requirements linking church membership to voting privileges were undermined by the growing diversity of religions in America. The end result was a relatively broad franchise. In various Rhode Island towns in the mid-eighteenth century, for example, 60 percent or more of the total adult male population was eligible to vote. In some New York districts up to 80 percent of all adult males had the vote. In Massachusetts, according to conservative Governor Thomas Hutchinson, "anything with the appearance of a man" was allowed to exercise the franchise.

Though many ordinary people could vote, colonial officials were not carbon copies of the colonial population. Colonial voters generally preferred to send the local squire, a prosperous merchant, or a rising young lawyer to the House of Burgesses or House of Assembly rather than a farmer, craftsman, or small shopkeeper. Local officials were also members of the elite. Southern vestries appointed their own successors and were dominated by the "squirearchy" of rich planters, who resembled the county gentry of England. Nor was the town, the basic governmental unit in New England, entirely democratic. Virtually all adult males participated in the town meeting, but town leaders were generally men of high status. In a word, the political system of colonial America was not democratic.

On the other hand, political deference—submission to social superiors—was decidedly weaker in America than in England. When the local squire ran for office, he had to campaign hard and promise to abide by the wishes of the voters. Candidates were expected to act democratically and avoid aloofness. During election campaigns they made it a point to mingle with the electors and offer them "refreshment," liquid or otherwise.

We must conclude that colonial government was neither predominantly democratic nor predominantly aristocratic; it displayed both tendencies. Democracy as we know it did not exist anywhere in the seventeenth- and eighteenth-century world. But as political institutions were transferred from England to America, they were changed in ways that allowed greater popular freedom and self-determination.

* RELIGION *

Organized religion was another institution that changed in the New World. White settlers brought with them a great variety of faiths—Presbyterian, Quaker, Baptist, Anglican, Lutheran, Mennonite, Catholic, Jewish, and others. Before long, under the special conditions in America, the practices of many of these groups began to diverge from their European norms.

GUARDING THE FLAME IN NEW ENGLAND. The Puritans who immigrated to Massachusetts did not come to found a separate church. Rather, they came to escape the harsh repression of a powerful state and the Anglican bishops. But once free of these restraints, they created the New England Way, a distinctive pattern that differed from both the Puritanism and the Anglicanism of Old England.

One of the differences involved church structure. In the Old World, bishops or a council of church elders (presbyters) ruled the church. But in America the sparseness of the white population and the relative isolation of settlements encouraged church government by individual self-governing congregations. Each group of Christians, led by their ministers, developed, in the words of the Reverend John Cotton, "complete liberty to stand alone." This system was called Congregationalism.

The New England Way also changed Puritan doctrine. At the heart of the Puritan faith as it evolved in Britain was the Calvinist notion that since Adam's fall only the "elect" (the "saints"), solely through God's mercy, would be saved from hell. But in New England the alternate idea of the "covenant" appeared: People could effect their salvation by entering into a kind of contract with God by which the Lord would agree to guarantee them the faith needed for salvation. Thus saints were not predestined, but "reborn," or converted.

These saints, the Puritans believed, would not only behave virtuously, but would also avoid wicked thoughts. Their faith thus placed a tremendous moral and emotional burden on the New England Puritans. Some became tortured souls obsessed with a sense of their own sinfulness. Michael Wigglesworth, a Congregational minister at Malden, kept a diary between 1653 and 1670 in which he constantly lamented his depravity. A typical entry noted:

> Peevishness, vain thoughts, and especially pride still prevail in me. I cannot think one good thought; I cannot do anything for God but presently pride gets hold of me. . . . I fear there is much sensuality and doting upon the creature in my pursuit of the good of others.

New England Puritans closely linked religion and government. The law required everyone to attend church services and pay taxes to support the Congregational ministry, regardless of their religious preference. But not all church attenders were church members: Only those who had experienced conversion could belong to the church. And only converted males could vote or hold office, although all were expected to obey the laws. Massachusetts was a community where God was considered the ruler and his will was expressed through the church leaders. Though clergymen did not hold office, they advised the secular rulers, and were consulted in all matters that pertained to public life and community policy. Questions that we today would consider matters of personal preference were treated as public issues subject to law. Sexual behavior in all its aspects fell under close public control; so did family concerns, such as children's disobedience. Blasphemy was a serious crime punishable by the authorities, as was breaking the Sabbath by game playing, drinking, or levity. Public education was intended not only to transmit skills and secular culture but also to imbue religious principles.

For a time it seemed possible to establish in Massachusetts a truly godly community—"a City upon a Hill"—where holiness might guide every aspect of life and people might avoid the corruptions of England. But as time passed, New Englanders increasingly turned to worldly affairs and shifted their attention from God to gain. By the middle of the seventeenth century the pious Puritan was already giving way to the get-ahead, enterprising Yankee. Before long many church members failed to experience conversion and so their children could not be admitted to church membership. This shrinking of the elect left many people without civil rights and threatened the churches with much-diminished membership. The answer was the Half-Way Covenant, which provided that persons who had been baptized and who led virtuous lives could become "half-way" church members. No conversion experience was necessary. These people could not participate in the Lord's Supper, one of the few sacraments remaining in Calvinism, but they were no longer disqualified from normal civil rights.

The new policy eased the crisis, but it did not check the erosion of orthodoxy in the Puritan colony. Some historians have connected the notorious Salem witchcraft trials of 1692, during which more than twenty persons were put to death for consorting with the Devil, with this Puritan decline. The panic may have been fanned by the earnest efforts of the Puritan clergy, including the Reverend Cotton Mather, to raise a new fear of sin and thus revive the orthodox church.

THE HIGH CHURCH IN THE WILDERNESS.   The American environment affected other Protestant denominations as well. In the Anglican communities on the Chesapeake local circumstances wore down traditional religion even more than in New England. With its elaborate ceremonies and complex organization, the Anglican Church was less suited to early America than Puritanism, a condition made more trying by the distance between settlements and plantations in the Chesapeake area and the absence of cities and towns.

It was especially difficult to maintain the traditional governance of the church. In England bishops ruled the Anglican Church, but no bishop came to America during the colonial period. Low salaries, isolation from the amenities of civilization, and the absence of substantial towns made English Anglican ministers reluctant to accept duties in America. And with no bishop in the colonies, young Americans who desired to become clergymen had to travel to England for ordination. Because few were willing to make the voyage, many parishes were forced to do without an ordained spiritual leader or to accept an inferior one. The net effect was that in Virginia, Maryland, and elsewhere the Church of England moved toward a congregational system, placing control of religious matters in the hands of the vestry, the ruling lay group of the parish.

Nor were the Congregationalists and the Anglicans the only troubled religious bodies. By the beginning of the eighteenth century most of the transplanted European denominations were losing ground. On the frontiers of New York, New Jersey, and Pennsylvania the German Lutherans and Pietists and the Scotch-Irish Presbyterians were slow to form congregations. In eastern Pennsylvania, as the Quaker community grew richer, its members replaced piety with worldliness.

THE GREAT AWAKENING.   The general decline of orthodoxy created a vacuum in the lives of many people. Among farmers, craftspeople, and other ordinary men and women, religion came increasingly to seem remote and unsatisfying. This attitude eventually triggered a religious resurgence that we call the Great Awakening.

The movement began in the 1720s as a series of revivals among the Presbyterians and Dutch Reformed groups in the middle colonies. During the next decade it was infused with new power by the Congregational minister Jonathan Edwards of Northampton, Massachusetts. In 1729 Edwards began to preach the old Calvinist doctrine of predestination, calling people back to God and threatening them with eternal damnation for their sins. Edwards's theology was old-fashioned, but his emotional preaching style was new, and his sermons shocked the traditionalists, who considered them unseemly. Ordinary people, however, flocked to hear him preach at his Northampton church. Before long clergymen throughout New England were emulating Edwards's hellfire-and-damnation sermons.

In 1738 the English preacher George Whitefield visited America and turned the Great Awakening into a religious event of continental proportions. Whitefield was a spellbinder who preached the traditional old-time Calvinism of predestination and damnation for all but an elect. Benjamin Franklin, skeptical of organized religion in general and of Whitefield's appeals for money to found an American orphanage in particular, went to hear the preacher, but was resolved not to contribute to his cause. "I had in my pocket, a handful of copper money, three or four silver dollars, and five pistoles in gold," Franklin later wrote. "As he proceeded I began to soften, and concluded to give the copper, another stroke of his oratory determined me to give the silver; and he finished so admirably that I emptied my pocket wholly into the collector's dish, gold and all."

The doctrines of the revivalists varied. Some were Calvinists who believed most souls damned. Others were Arminians who rejected predestination and assumed a forgiving God. But most of their followers embraced their passionate appeal for surrender to Jesus and a commitment to live an exemplary Christian life rather than their theology. Whitefield, Edwards, and the other revivalists presented these views so simply and with such emotional effect that thousands were brought back to religion. Attacked by educated people as "shouters," "enthusiasts," and disturbers of the peace, the revivalists of the Great Awakening were immensely successful among common people. Many joined, or rejoined, the older denominations. Within these churches congregations and clergy soon divided between those who followed the decorous old way—the Old Lights—and those who followed the emotional new way—the New Lights. Many more people flocked to newer denominations such as the Baptists and later the Methodists. Thus, by producing new sects and dividing congregations and ministers, the Great Awakening further diversified religious expression in America.

THE ENLIGHTENMENT. The Great Awakening lured many ordinary people back into the traditional religious fold. But by the middle of the eighteenth century many educated men and women in America were turning not to traditional religion but to a new set of secular beliefs we call the Enlightenment.

This major alteration in the way Western thinkers perceived the world was rooted in the scientific revolutions of the day, especially in the ideas of Sir Isaac Newton. In the new view the world appeared a rational, orderly place, operating not according to the immediate will of God but by changeless natural laws. Several important concepts followed from this view: First, that as members of this rational universe, human beings were good, not sinful; second, that by use of their reason, human beings could discover the natural laws of the universe; third, that knowledge of these laws would enable people to control their environment and society; and finally, that the inevitable result of this control would be "progress" toward a happier, more virtuous and prosperous society. Science played a significant role in this world picture because it was by means of scientific method—observation and experiment—that natural laws could be discovered.

A few members of the "enlightened" elite rejected all religion and became agnostics or atheists. Most, however, chose deism. Deists continued to believe in God, but theirs was a god who operated through natural laws, not miracles. He showed himself through nature, not Christian revelation. God's role in the world was much like that of a clockmaker—a being who makes a clock, winds it up, and then leaves it to work by its own mechanical laws.

Deism developed late in the colonial period and affected only a small group of Americans. The deists, however, were an influential group—including Benjamin Franklin, Thomas Jefferson, Ethan Allen, and Thomas Paine—who would have influence in the world of ideas disproportionate to their numbers.

* INTELLECTUAL AMERICA *

The conditions that changed the social, political, and religious institutions transplanted from Europe also molded colonial science, education, and the professions. For better or worse, intellectual development in America lagged behind or diverged from the Old World experience.

SCIENCE.　The seventeenth century was an era of immense progress in the natural sciences. It was the time when Galileo first used the telescope to observe the solar system, William Harvey detected the circulation of the blood, Johannes Kepler formulated the laws governing the orbits of the planets, and Isaac Newton discovered the basic laws of motion and the role of gravity. These scientists were all Europeans, however; Americans made few contributions to basic scientific theory.

Neither the social nor physical environment of colonial America encouraged theoretical science. Engaged in a day-to-day struggle to earn a living, the colonists tended to be interested in practical, not theoretical, matters. Moreover, even at the very end of the colonial era the scaffolding necessary for a flourishing scientific enterprise was absent. Theoretical science requires laboratories, patronage, centers of learning, and stimulating contact among thinkers. Colonial America—lacking large accumulations of wealth, inhabited by a sparse and scattered population, and far from the intellectual centers of the Western world—was not a likely birthplace for a Harvey, a Galileo, a Kepler, or a Newton. Twenty-five Americans were elected before 1776 to the prestigious British scientific body, the Royal Society of London, but they were honored for their acute observations of natural phenomena, not for grand theories or major intellectual breakthroughs.

Only one colonial scientist deserves comparison with the best of Europe: Benjamin Franklin. Franklin's experiments in the 1740s and 1750s contributed to an early understanding of electricity and won him an honorary doctorate from a European university. Yet among the practical Americans "Doctor" Franklin was largely famous for his invention of the lightning rod to protect buildings from electrical storms and for the efficient parlor stove that bears his name.

EDUCATION.   In America, education also took on a distinctive cast. At the lower levels American education was advanced for its day. Primary schools, staffed by both men and women, existed in every colony by the mid-eighteenth century, but educational opportunities varied greatly. More boys than girls attended schools, a fact reflected in the higher literacy rate of colonial men than women. Slaves received no formal education, though a few learned to read and write. There were also strong regional inequalities in access to education. Because of the scattered settlement pattern in the southern colonies, it was hard to bring together a concentration of pupils sufficient to support a local school. Rich planters hired private tutors for their sons and daughters, and occasionally these tutors also instructed the sons and daughters of the planter's poorer neighbors. But educational opportunities in the southern colonies were generally limited, especially for the children of common farmers.

The more densely settled northern colonies, particularly New England, did better by their young people. The Dutch in New Netherland were quick to establish schools supported by the colonial treasury. Still more conscientious were the Massachusetts Puritans, who believed that it was essential to salvation for individuals to be able to read and understand the Scriptures for themselves. In 1647 the Massachusetts General Court required each town in the province with fifty families to establish a "petty" school to teach children to read and write. Any town with at least a hundred households was also required to establish a "grammar" school (high school) to prepare students for college and the learned professions. The purpose of the law, the legislators noted, was to defeat "ye ould deluder, Satan"; but its most important effect was to create in New England a body of literate people probably unique among contemporary Western communities.

Educated Americans tried to nurture higher education even in the crude early settlements. In 1636, just six years after the Puritans settled Massachusetts, Bay Colony authorities established Harvard College in Cambridge, to create the literate, educated ministry the Puritans considered vital to religion. Massachusetts's example was soon followed by other colonies. By the time of the Revolution eight other institutions of higher learning had been established: the College of William and Mary (1693); Yale (1701); the College of New Jersey, later called Princeton (1746); Queen's College, later called Rutgers (1766); King's College, later called Columbia (1754); the College of Philadelphia, later called the University of Pennsylvania (1754); Rhode Island College, later called Brown University (1764); and Dartmouth (1769). Like Harvard, most of these colleges were sponsored by religious denominations. They turned out men with "liberal" educations who either became clergymen or, after further training, entered one of the other traditional learned professions—law or medicine.

LAW AND MEDICINE.   Colonial conditions molded professional education, too. In England members of the legal profession endured a long and elaborate training process at the old and respected Inns of Court. English lawyers included

Harvard College in the mid-1700s, a century after its founding.

attorneys to start the legal machinery going, solicitors to offer legal advice, notaries to prepare legal documents, and barristers to plead cases. The structure resembled England's class system: an elite at top with lesser folk beneath.

The struggling colonists could not support this elaborate and expensive system. In America there was only one all-purpose attorney, who drew up documents and briefs, advised clients, and pleaded cases in courtrooms. Instead of attending law schools, lawyers learned by working in law offices, reading standard law books, attending court, and performing minor legal chores for senior attorneys. Toward the end of the colonial period, however, the legal profession drew closer to its English model. Some Americans began to go to London for legal training. But despite America's growing exposure to English forms, the English legal structure remained too cumbersome for America, with its weaker system of higher education and its more open class structure.

A similar simplification took place in the colonial medical profession. Despite scientific advances in medicine in seventeenth-century Europe, medical men still embraced theories of disease expounded by ancient or medieval authorities. These theories usually ascribed disease to some imbalance in the four "humors"—choler, blood, bile, and phlegm. The physician's task was to determine the nature of the imbalance and restore equilibrium—often, as it happened, with harsh and ineffective remedies. Fortunately for Americans, the European physicians' learned ignorance could not be transplanted easily to North America. In Europe doctors trained at the universities. Few cared to surrender the high fees and status they enjoyed in Europe to come to the American wilderness, nor did American colleges teach medicine until the eve of the Revolution. Moreover, the exotic drugs and preparations used by European doctors were hard to duplicate in America.

The dilution of European practices in the colonies probably improved medical care. Colonial medical practitioners, like colonial legal practitioners, learned by apprenticeship and from day-to-day contact with patients. Without mistaken theories to lead them astray, doctors relied on experience, observation, and common sense. Instead of purges, poultices, bleeding, and the foul potions prescribed in Europe, they turned to local herbs, often ones recommended by the Indians, for cures. Even when these did no good, they generally did little serious harm.

The American medical profession was also structured more democratically than the European. The shortage of trained personnel created opportunities for people who could not have practiced in England. Many medical practitioners in the colonies were women, and a number of slaves and free blacks were respected for their medical knowledge. Cotton Mather, who became a crusader for smallpox vaccination over the objections of European-trained physicians, first learned about the procedure from his black slave, a man named Onesimus.

* THE ARTS *

In the fine arts colonial American accomplishments generally fell well below the best of Europe. Early American writing was predominantly nonfiction with an emphasis on biography, travel descriptions, religious exposition, and history. Much of it is today of interest only to academic students. At times, however, these works achieved some distinction. William Bradford's *Of Plimmoth Plantation,* an account of the founding and early days of the Pilgrim colony, was a heartfelt and effective narrative, though it was not published until many years after its author's death. The *Magnalia Christi Americana* (1702), by New Englander Cotton Mather, the scion of a distinguished Bay Colony ministerial family, is a rich encyclopedic review of New England's early history, replete with biographies, descriptions of wondrous happenings, and defenses of the New England way. In the South, Robert Beverley, an American-born planter, wrote the epically proportioned *The History and Present State of Virginia* (1705), a work that reveals the author's compassion for the Indians and his hope that Virginia would become a pastoral paradise.

Fiction was sparser. The first American novel did not appear until after independence, but there were several talented colonial poets. The best perhaps was Edward Taylor, an English-born minister educated at Harvard College. Taylor wrote more than 200 devotional poems full of rich imagery and subtle nuances. Unfortunately, almost none of his poetry was published until the 1930s. Anne Bradstreet of Andover, Massachusetts—a "Tenth Muse lately sprung up in America," her publisher called her—was more fortunate. Bradstreet had come to Massachusetts as a bride with the first Puritan wave in 1630 at the age of eighteen. Like many pioneer women, she had been dismayed by the crude frontier environment. But, as was expected of colonial women, she accepted her fate. "I changed my condition and was marryed," she later wrote, "and came into this country, where I found a new world and new manners, at which my heart rose [that is, was stirred against it]. But after I was convinced it was the way of God, I submitted to it. . . . " During the next forty years, amid the cares and labors of raising eight children and attending to her busy husband, she wrote reams of verse. Her later work, with its unaffected language and faithful images of the American landscape, is the first authentic American poetry.

Although imaginative literature did not flourish in colonial America, newspapers, broadsides, pamphlets, instructional books, and almanacs were produced in abundance. The colonists read widely because they needed practical information. Newspapers were read by proportionately more Americans than Europeans; they contained vital information about colonial affairs. Almanacs were useful to farmers and merchants, who had to know about prices and the weather. In the hands of Benjamin Franklin, the famous *Poor Richard's Almanack* came close to being a form of creative literature. Besides the usual data on planting times, seasonal changes, tides, eclipses, and the like, *Poor Richard's* contained entertaining little word sketches by "Richard Saunders" (Franklin's pseudonym) and pithy maxims that have become part of America's folk heritage.

Though Americans lagged badly behind Europeans in the fine arts, they excelled in the production of functional objects. This bent helps to explain the relatively high level of painting in the colonies. Colonial artists did not, like their European counterparts, paint dramatic landscapes, cavorting gods and goddesses, or heroic battle scenes. Instead, they focused on portraits, the most practical genre of painting. Here they could count on a ready market for their efforts. In the absence of photography, wealthy merchants and planters, who had little interest in art for art's sake, turned to painters to glorify their affluence and preserve their likenesses and those of their family for posterity.

The earliest American artists were amateurish daubers who often paid the rent by painting signs for merchants or inn keepers. Then, toward the end of the colonial era, John Singleton Copley and Benjamin West, of Boston and Philadelphia, respectively, began to attract wealthy patrons. But even in the second century of settlement, America could not hold onto its most talented artists. In 1760 West left for Rome and soon after settled in England. In 1775 Copley too left for Britain, in part to escape attack as a Loyalist, but also to expand his artistic horizons.

American architecture was also primitive and limited at first. As we saw, the earliest settlers lived in lean-tos, dugouts, and tents. Later in the first century of settlement, they began to imitate European models. Upper class seventeenth-century houses in Massachusetts and Virginia resembled Tudor English buildings, replete with gables and small-paned leaded windows. Even the log cabin was a European borrowing, brought to the Delaware Bay region in the seventeenth century by Swedes and Finns.

In time, American architecture became more original. The new elite style of the eighteenth century took its name—Queen Anne or Georgian—from the English monarchs of the day. With its regularly spaced rows of windows, white-trimmed brick, and fine detailing at doors and openings, Georgian architecture was not strictly speaking a native genre at all. But it was adapted to American needs and circumstances in ways that frequently transcended mere imitation. The best of eighteenth-century colonial architecture blended admirably with the American environment; to this day Independence Hall in Philadelphia and domestic buildings like William Byrd's Virginia mansion, Westover, convey a sense of a vigorous provincial society evolving a distinctive cultural tradition.

A similar progression from imitation to innovation can be observed in the minor arts and the crafts. In the seventeenth century there were few skilled craftsmen in the colonies, and the settlers either used English artifacts or made their own crude ones. But by the eighteenth century many talented workers in brass, pewter, glass, silver, clay, and wood had immigrated to America from England and the Continent. Meanwhile, the skills of both white and black Americans had matured to a high level. Paul Revere of Boston combined native inspiration with imported forms and designs to create exquisite bowls, trays, and tea services in silver. At his glassworks at Mannheim, Pennsylvania, the German entrepreneur Henry William Stiegel produced glassware that is still eagerly collected. Skill and creativity marked the approach of colonial women to functional crafts, such as recycling bits of material into boldly designed quilts. Their work is now being recognized and appreciated as the expression of artistic sensitivities that transcended the drudgeries of primitive life in the New World.

* CONCLUSIONS *

Crèvecoeur was right. By the eve of the Revolution America was no longer a carbon copy of Europe, and Americans were not simply transplanted Europeans.

Several factors had contributed to the change. British North America included a mixture of racial and ethnic components unknown in Europe; even the European ingredients of this mix were present in different proportions and existed in different relationships to one another than in the Old World. The Indian and African elements in the New World mixture were completely unknown to Europeans; yet they affected the military practice, technology, language, and customs of the new society.

In addition to the changes that accompanied the mingling of diverse cultures, there were those produced by the special physical and social environment of the New World. The abundance of land relative to the population made for better health, larger families, and ultimately a larger electorate and a more democratic political system. The relative scarcity of women allowed them some freedom to take on nontraditional roles and helped improve their legal status. A more scattered population and a less elitist social structure made it difficult to implant complex European institutions intact; as a result, the legal and medical professions were simplified and transformed. Meanwhile, the absence of a substantial leisure class, of great universities, and of private and government patronage altered the character of the arts and learning, pushing them toward greater practicality.

Nevertheless, we must qualify Crèvecoeur's announcement of a "new man" in America. Many of the distinctive national and cultural groups existed side by side without blending. In the case of blacks and Indians, their contributions were deliberately inhibited by the European majority. It would take generations before the blending process could produce a uniform new cultural mix, and the process is not complete today, nor will it ever be.

And there is another qualification to the Crèvecoeur formula. At the end of the colonial period, as wealth increased and transatlantic communication improved, the culture of the colonial elite began to move closer to Britain's. In many ways, by the eve of the Revolution, religion, the professions, the arts, and political life had begun to take on the characteristics of the mother country. In 1775 American society was becoming a provincial offshoot of Europe.

Yet the differences remained and the convergence would soon slow. By the mid-eighteenth century the actual interests of Americans and English people had begun to draw apart. British–American differences would soon produce a crisis that would sever the imperial connection and create a separate American nation and with it a still more distinctive culture.

4

MOVING TOWARD INDEPENDENCE

Why Did the Colonists Revolt?

1651	England passes the first "navigation act" to prevent Dutch intrusion into the colonial trade
1688	The overthrow of James II begins the "Glorious Revolution" in England
1699	The Wool Act; France establishes the settlement of "Louisiana" on the Gulf of Mexico
1721–48	The period of "salutary neglect"
1732	The Hat Act
1733	The Molasses Act
1750	The Iron Act
1754	Benjamin Franklin proposes the Albany Plan of Union to the colonies, but it is never adopted
1754–63	The French and Indian War: Colonists disobey England's ban on all trade with France and its colonies; War with France ends with the Treaty of Paris; Colonial settlement west of Appalachians prohibited by the Proclamation of 1763
1764	The Sugar Act; The Currency Act
1765, 1766	The Quartering Acts
1765	The Stamp Act; The Intercolonial Stamp Act; Congress resolves that colonists should be taxed only by a representative legislature
1765–66	New York and other cities respond to the Stamp Act by adopting nonimportation agreements
1766	Parliament repeals the Stamp Act, but reaffirms with the Declaratory Act its right to legislate for the colonies
1767	The Townshend (or Revenue) Acts provoke another boycott of British goods
1770	Parliament repeals Townshend duties, except those on tea; The Boston Massacre

1773	The Tea Act threatens to undercut the colonial smuggling trade; East India Company tea is destroyed in the Boston Tea Party
1774	Boston harbor is closed by the Coercive (or Intolerable) Acts; The First Continental Congress attacks Britain's restrictions on colonial trade
1775	Armed confrontation at Lexington and Concord

Few events in American history are as momentous as the great struggle that ended with independence in 1783. Yet the causes of this crucial upheaval have long been controversial. Thomas Jefferson believed that Britain's "deliberate, systematical plan of reducing us to slavery" had spurred Americans to take the drastic step of declaring their freedom. John Adams recalled many years later that the British threat to establish Anglican bishops in America had "spread a universal alarm against the authority of Parliament." A third group of contemporaries stressed economic strains in the imperial relationship. In 1766 British customs officials in Rhode Island complained bitterly that the interests of "the Mother Country & this Colony" were "deemed by the People almost altogether incompatible, in a commercial View. . . . " Any official who attempted to defend British trade policies had been "threatened as an Enemy to this Country. . . . "

Which of these explanations is correct? Is each partly correct? Is one fundamental and the others secondary? Let us consider the economic one first.

✳ THE COLONIAL ECONOMY ✳

What was the colonial economy like; what were its strengths and weaknesses? Did British policy foster prosperity or hinder it? Did Americans have valid economic grievances against the mother country?

AGRICULTURE. On the eve of the Revolution agriculture employed 80 percent of the colonial working population and created most of the wealth produced. A majority of American cultivators were small farm owners, "yeomen," engaged in mixed agriculture—growing corn, rye, wheat; raising cattle, sheep, horses, hogs; and planting fruit trees, potatoes, and vegetables. The farmer's own family consumed most of these products, but except on the distant frontier, farmers sold a part of their output to townspeople or even to customers overseas. In most places the farmer's labor force consisted almost entirely of himself and his family.

American farmers were not especially efficient or innovative by the best European standards. Except for the German settlers of Pennsylvania, the colonists impressed foreign visitors as slovenly cultivators who neglected the fertility of the soil and the care and improvement of their livestock. The critics were right, but there was a simple reason for their behavior: American farmers could rely on the sheer abundance of fresh, fertile land to carry them through. As Thomas Jefferson remarked, "We can buy an acre of new land cheaper than we can manure an old one." In later years Americans would learn to regret this wasteful attitude, but in colonial America it suited the circumstances of the time and place.

Colonial agriculture varied by region. In New England the soil was so rocky almost everywhere except in the Connecticut Valley and a few other favored spots, that local farmers, it was said, had to shoot the seed into the unyielding ground with a gun. Connecticut produced some surplus livestock, grain, and dairy products for export, and Rhode Island raised horses for the Caribbean trade. But with these exceptions New England agriculture had mostly local importance.

In contrast, New York, New Jersey, and Pennsylvania were the "bread colonies," harvesting large surpluses of wheat from their fertile fields. They converted this grain to flour in the region's many gristmills and exported much of it to the Caribbean or southern Europe. In addition, the bread colonies exported potatoes, beef, pork, and other farm products.

The Chesapeake region, including the colonies of Virginia and Maryland, was British America's great tobacco-growing area. By the mid-eighteenth century tobacco cultivation had moved from the Tidewater region to the Piedmont plateau where the soils were fresher and more productive, leaving the remaining coastal farmers to switch to grain. The Piedmont planters faced more difficult transportation problems than their Tidewater predecessors. Located above the "fall line," where the eastward-flowing streams dropped sharply to the coastal plain, they could not put their crops directly aboard ships tied to their own dock. Instead, they sold their tobacco to local merchants who packed the leaf into huge hogsheads. These they rolled to towns like Richmond or Petersburg, which lay along the fall line, and loaded them aboard ships for shipment to foreign buyers.

By the 1770s Maryland and Virginia were shipping about 100 million pounds of tobacco annually—worth £1 million, or about $50 million in modern money—to the pipesmokers and snuff taker of Europe. The Chesapeake region also became a major grain exporter, with most going to the south of Europe and the West Indies.

Rice was the major crop of the South Carolina lowlands, although some was also grown in North Carolina and Georgia. Requiring vast amounts of water, as well as a long growing season, rice was suited to the swampy coastal regions of the most southerly colonies and proved highly profitable there. In 1710 South Carolina exported 1.5 million pounds. By 1770 the rice-growing colonies, with South Carolina far in the lead, exported almost 84 million pounds. Most of it went to England, the sugar plantations of the Caribbean, and southern Europe.

The lowland areas of South Carolina and Georgia also produced indigo, a blue dye widely used for coloring woolen cloth. The crop was introduced in the 1740s by Eliza Lucas Pinckney, an enterprising young woman newly arrived from the Caribbean island of Antigua. Helped by a British government bounty of six pence a pound, the production and export of indigo quickly leaped. By 1770 almost 600,000 pounds of indigo were being shipped from the port of Charleston each year.

Tar, pitch, resin, and turpentine, extracted from pine trees and widely employed in the shipping and paint industries, were other extractive products of the southern colonies. The British encouraged naval-store production within its overseas empire by offering a bounty and by 1770 North Carolina was exporting naval stores worth about £35,000 each year, almost all of it to Great Britain.

FISHING AND WHALING.   The sea was one of the earliest sources of food and wealth for New England. The first Massachusetts settlers caught hake, haddock, halibut, and mackerel in local waters for their own tables. By the mid-1630s they were beginning to sell the preserved catch to distant customers. By the eighteenth century the cod fish had become the major haul.

Each season hundreds of vessels sailed from the towns of Gloucester, Marblehead, Salem, and other ports to fish for cod at the Grand Banks off Newfoundland. These small craft were manned by crews who received between a sixth and a tenth of the season's catch as their share, with the rest going to the boat owners. The cod was an important item in the Massachusetts economy. Salted and dried, the best grades were sent to Catholic southern Europe and to the "Wine Islands" of Madeira and the Canaries off Africa, while the worst went to the West Indies to feed the sugar planters' slaves. The trade in dried fish represented a large part of the Bay Colony's total exports.

Whaling was another profitable enterprise of the northern colonies. At first whaling was confined to small New England and Long Island ports. In the eighteenth century, as the local whale supply declined, capitalists fitted out larger vessels for trips well out into the Atlantic. The whalers from Nantucket, New Bedford, and Sag Harbor were not interested in the flesh of the great mammals. Their goal was whale oil, the liquid rendered from whale blubber, which supplied much of the lighting fuel for colonial lamps, and spermaceti, a waxy substance from the heads of sperm whales, used to make fine candles.

COLONIAL INDUSTRY.   Besides the 80 percent who tilled the soil, perhaps 5 percent of the colonial work force were full-time craftsmen, "mechanicks," or artisans, in the cities, towns, and villages. In addition, thousands of rural colonists produced finished or semi-finished goods at home for sale on a part-time basis.

Almost all colonial manufactured goods were produced by hand. Colonial farm women spun wool and flax fiber into yarn and then wove it on hand looms into cloth. Farm women also molded candles from wax extracted from bayberries. They churned butter and made cheese from milk supplied by the family cow, and pressed cider from apples, and perry from pears. Rural men also used the home as a workshop. Farmers often devoted the long winter evenings to carving ax handles, gunstocks, and other wooden articles.

In the towns, full-time craftsmen, using hand tools, manufactured items for customers in their workshops. Coopers made barrels as containers for flour, tobacco, sugar, rum, and other bulk goods. Wheelwrights crafted wheels for carts,

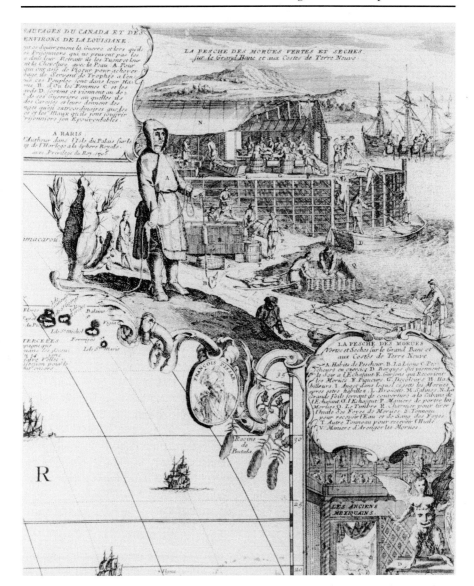

A French illustration of the colonial Grand Banks cod fishery.
The racks in the background were used for drying the fish.

wagons, and coaches. Cordwainers produced shoes; blacksmiths made nails, horseshoes, shovels, and edged tools; tanners produced the leather that others made into shoes, aprons, saddles, and other items. Every growing colonial village needed housing and the demand was met by carpenters, masons, bricklayers, and various laborers. As communities became richer and more populous, colonial craftspeople became ever more skilled. By the eve of the Revolution they were producing beautiful silverware and fine furniture. In addition, the small cities were full of barbers, tailors, milliners, and other skilled providers of services for the prosperous consumer.

Even in the cities the typical manufacturing establishment was a small workshop run by the owner with the help, perhaps, of a young apprentice and an older journeyman who had not yet set up shop for himself. The urban master craftsman generally lived above his shop, which was both a little manufacturing establishment and a retail store. Much of his work was done on direct order from a customer, but he usually made additional wares in slack times to have ready for buyers coming to the door. Sometimes he sold his surplus to traveling peddlers. Often the craftsman's wife handled the selling in the front while he and his helpers turned out the product in the back.

Only a very few colonial enterprises resembled the modern factory with hired labor, expensive machinery, and the separation of workplace from home. With water power widely available, mills with waterwheels and machinery, often made of wood, sprang up in every colony to do especially heavy work. There were few settled localities without sawmills to cut boards and gristmills to grind grain into flour. A few of the most successful grain millers—merchant millers—established large-scale operations and overseas markets for their flour.

Shipbuilding was one of the largest-scale industries in colonial America. By 1670 Massachusetts had turned out 730 vessels, and between 1696 and 1713 the colony built more than 1,000 ships of almost 70,000 tons total displacement. Besides the shipyards along the Charles River, there were large ship-building establishments in Salem; Portsmouth, New Hampshire; Newport, Rhode Island; and Philadelphia, each employing scores of workers. In addition to the shipyards themselves, the major ports acquired scores of sail-making establishments and ropewalks to provide rigging for the vessels.

Another relatively large-scale, factorylike colonial manufacturing enterprise was iron making. By the middle of the eighteenth century its center was Pennsylvania, though New Jersey, Maryland, and Virginia also had large furnaces producing pig iron from ore. By 1700 the American colonies were producing about 2 percent of the world's total pig iron; by the 1770s they accounted for 15 percent.

COMMERCE.   Commerce or trade was the final and, next to agriculture, the most important, leg of the colonial economy. Ultimately, it was foreign markets that drove the colonial economy. Foreign buyers provided the means for raising the colonial economy above the subsistence level. Commerce sustained the bread colonies, which relied on the Caribbean market to absorb their surplus grain and provisions. Without markets in Britain and Europe the southern tobacco, rice, indigo, and naval-stores colonies would have been far poorer. Both overseas and intercolony trade supported the shipbuilding, sail-making, and rope-making industries and encouraged flour milling, lumbering, barrel-making, and iron manufacture.

Exports helped Americans pay for the paper, hardware, pottery, and cloth, as well as wines, the latest books, fine furniture, and scientific instruments that came only from Britain, the Continent, or the Wine Islands. To pay for these goods,

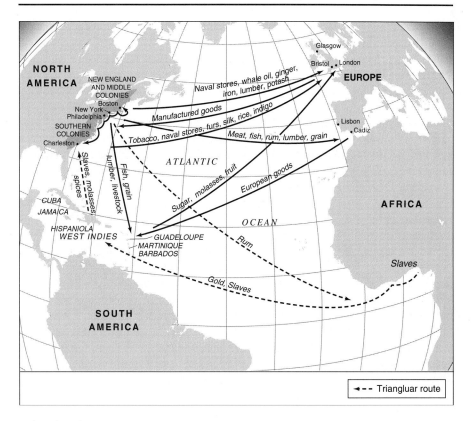

Colonial Trade Routes

Americans needed coin or commercial credits from sales of their own goods abroad. Unfortunately, colonial trade relations were out of balance geographically. England needed the tobacco, rice, indigo, and naval stores of the Chesapeake region and the Carolinas; these colonies, accordingly, easily earned the credits needed to pay for what they imported from the mother country. But the major northern products—fish, grain, and cattle—were not wanted in Great Britain since it produced its own. Because each year the northern colonies bought more from Britain than they sold to it, they were forced to find other customers whose purchases would offset the British deficit.

The Caribbean served this role. In the West Indies the planters concentrated all their energies on growing sugar cane for the European market. Their neglect of everything but sugar made them excellent customers for cheap food, horses, lumber, and barrels from the northern mainland colonies. By 1700, hundreds of vessels from northern ports sailed to the islands each year, laden with provisions, flour, and dried fish to feed the slaves and their masters, and with lumber, wooden hoops, and staves to build structures and to package sugar, rum, and molasses.

Once he had found buyers for his miscellaneous cargo, the New England or middle-colony merchant accepted payment in several forms. The colonies acquired a wide assortment of shillings, doubloons, guilders, and pieces of eight in the West Indies. But molasses and sugar were also acceptable. These could be consumed directly at home, or the molasses could be converted into rum and traded with the Indians for furs or exported overseas. The trader could also accept bills of exchange on England—receipts that the planters received when they sold their sugar in England. These represented credits that could be used like cash to pay for English goods or clear debts owed to English creditors. With their holds full of molasses and some West Indies cotton or citrus fruit, and the captain's strongbox stuffed with coin or bills of exchange, the ship sailed home to Boston, Providence, New York, or Philadelphia.

The transatlantic slave trade also helped cancel the commercial deficit with the mother country. Most of the slaves carried from Africa to America in the eighteenth century were transported by the French, the British, or the Dutch. But some were carried by slavers out of Boston and Newport. The typical New England slave trader sent a small vessel with a cargo of rum distilled from West Indies molasses to the west coast of Africa. There the Yankee captain exchanged some rum for British goods, such as iron, cloth, gunpowder, cheap jewelry, and glass with a trader from London or Bristol. With this mixed stock of goods he bought slaves from an African middleman and loaded the human cargo aboard his vessel. He then returned to the Caribbean where he sold the captives for the same coin, molasses, or bills of exchange that other cargo brought. Only a small proportion of the slaves stolen from Africa were transported directly to the Carolinas or the Chesapeake on the mainland. Many came first to the Caribbean.

WEALTH AND INEQUALITY.   How did Americans fare, overall, under this evolving economic system? And did its benefits fall on each person equally?

By one measure—population growth—the American community prospered mightily during the colonial era. Benjamin Franklin was right when he claimed that Americans doubled in numbers every twenty-five years. In 1680 there were fewer than 80,000 settlers along the Atlantic coast of British North America. By 1700 there were about a quarter of a million. Fifty years later population had passed the million mark and by 1770 had soared above 2 million. This surge in part marked the heavy immigration from the Old World to America, itself a sign of prosperity. But it also marked the abundance of land and food that encouraged early marriage and large families and prevented the malnutrition and famine that cruelly pruned population elsewhere in the contemporary world. It is in some ways the most convincing measure of sustained colonial prosperity.

And despite the explosion of people, during each decade average per capita income grew. Output, that is, expanded even faster than population. The best estimate that we have suggests that overall per person growth of output in colonial America ran about 0.6 percent a year. This was unusually high for a preindustrial society and was fast enough to double the average colonial's income over the course of 120 years. By the eve of the Revolution, Alice Hanson Jones has said, the standard of living in British North America, was "probably the highest achieved for the great bulk of the population in any country up to that time."

Surinam was a Dutch sugar-growing colony on South America's Atlantic coast. It was an important trading partner for British North America, and especially for Rhode Island. In this 1758 John Greenwood painting we see a group of Rhode Island sea captains —including a future governor of Rhode Island and a future commander in chief of the Continental Navy—rowdily enjoying their layover in Surinam before returning home with sugar, molasses, and rum. Note the black servants at lower right and upper left.

But of course not everyone benefited equally from the high and growing prosperity. The group most obviously excluded from the benefits of a growing economy was the slaves. By 1770 there were about 460,000 black slaves in the mainland colonies out of a total population of some 2.1 million. Obviously they did not receive very much of the wealth that their labor produced.

For free rural Americans, the location of land and how it was held and the size of landholdings determined individual levels of prosperity. Yeoman farmers who grew crops only to supply their own family needs seldom were rich. Commercial agriculture made for prosperity, but it also encouraged inequality. In towns close to the Boston market, for example, where farmers sold to urban consumers, there was a sharp division between rich and poor. In 1771 about a quarter of the taxpayers in Milton and Roxbury were landless, while the wealthiest 10 percent owned 46 percent of the real estate. In general, both less wealth and greater equality were to be found in the frontier regions of each colony, where land per person was abundant and major markets too distant to support commercial agriculture. In the South the picture was similar: Regions of subsistence farming had many landowners and a high degree of equality. By contrast, the commercial rice- and indigo-growing Carolina coast and the tobacco-growing Chesapeake tidewater were the realms of the great slaveholding gentry.

In the towns, marketable skills counted as much as real estate in determining an individual's prosperity. Apprentices, journeymen, laborers, and seamen made up the urban lower class. Fully trained craftsmen and shopkeepers did better; at the top of the pyramid were the merchants and professionals. Those merchants who sold goods door to door in nearby rural areas were poor by comparison with the great overseas traders who sent their ships to Europe, Africa, or the West Indies. It was difficult to break into the ranks of the overseas traders, but the class was not completely closed to the energetic, ambitious, or lucky.

Obviously, economic inequalities existed in the American colonies. But were these inequalities growing or diminishing in the years before the Revolution? Were the rich getting richer and the poor getting poorer?

The most recent studies seem to show that inequality was increasing in the larger cities and in rural parts of the older settled regions. The opening of new settlements, however, offset this trend to some extent, for the colonial frontier remained a region where there were few rich and few poor. And even in the older sections, we must not forget that the overall income trend was upward. Almost all free Americans were getting richer. The growing gap was not because the poor were getting poorer in absolute terms. It resulted from the fact that those at the top were increasing their wealth and incomes faster than those at the bottom. All in all, as Robert Beverley had written of Virginia early in the eighteenth century, America was "the best poor Man's Country in the World."

* COSTS AND BENEFITS OF EMPIRE
BEFORE 1763 *

How did America's place in the British Empire affect its economic circumstances? And did its economic place within the empire, in turn—or the colonists' perception of that place—influence how they felt about their political ties to Great Britain.

THE ECONOMIC BALANCE SHEET. As we look at the colonial economy it is clear that there were both benefits and losses from the imperial relationship. From the 1650s on the colonists were forced to accept a multitude of restrictions on their trade with other parts of the world. Though frequently violated or circumvented, these restrictions limited their ability to work out their own economic destiny.

As we saw in Chapter 2, colonies were supposed to enrich the mother country by supplying it with exotic commodities and hard-to-get raw materials, by consuming its surplus manufactures, and by providing jobs to a host of people engaged in the colonial trade. With these potential benefits in mind, beginning in 1650, Parliament enacted measures called the Navigation Acts. To keep the enterprising Dutch from profiting from the carrying trade within the empire and between the empire and other nations, they decreed that all ships engaged in such trade must be owned by either Britons or Americans, built in either Britain or America, captained by a subject of the British crown, and manned, predominantly, by such subjects. Other Navigation Acts established lists of "enumerated articles" that had to be shipped to England first whatever their ultimate destination. The lists included the most valuable colonial exports such as sugar, tobacco, rice, naval stores, and indigo. Another law provided that, except for salt for the New England fisheries, wine from Madeira and the Azores, and servants and horses from Scotland and Ireland, all European commodities sent to the colonies had to be shipped from England, rather than from their place of origin, and in English-built ships.

Besides excluding foreigners from the imperial trade and encouraging shipping and shipbuilding, these measures were intended to make England the distribution center for goods entering or leaving the colonies. They would guarantee British merchants a key role in the colonial overseas trade and allow the British government to levy a tax on all goods passing through Great Britain. To enforce the Navigation Acts and collect duties imposed on overseas trade, the British government stationed a host of customs commissioners in the colonial ports.

The British also sought to limit the manufactures of the mainland colonies to preserve them as markets for British producers and prevent colonial competition with home producers. The Wool Act of 1699 forbade the export of wool yarn or cloth from any American colony either to Europe or any other American colony. The Hat Act of 1732 prohibited the export of American hats from one colony to another and imposed strict limits on the number of workers in any hat-making shop. Finally, two Iron Acts, of 1750 and 1757, sought to encourage the production of American bar and pig iron—raw materials for the British iron and steel industry—but to restrict the colonial iron-finishing industry that the British wanted to keep for themselves. This measure forbade the construction in the colonies of rolling and slitting mills, of forges, and of steel furnaces.

Americans undoubtedly were penalized by these trade regulations. The enumerated tobacco sent to Europe, mostly from Maryland and Virginia, had to be unloaded and then reloaded in England first. The charges for this roundabout method of export to Europe were high, and the planters lost money because of it. American consumers in turn were penalized by the rule that European goods must first be sent to England before crossing the Atlantic.

Were the impediments imposed on the colonies by these regulations severe? To answer this question fairly, we should consider not just costs such as these, but the overall economic benefits of the empire as well. The foremost benefit was that Britain assumed the expense of the empire's defense. During the seventeenth and eighteenth centuries, as we shall see, four great European wars placed the colonies in danger. The British army and navy often proved indispensable to colonial safety. Recognizing their stake in the outcome, the colonists contributed money and men themselves; but most of the cost by far was borne by the British. Without the mother country's contribution, the colonies would have been forced to lay out millions of pounds in extra taxes, a financial burden that would have lowered their incomes and retarded their economic growth.

It is also important to recognize that in restricting the imperial trade to subjects of the king, Parliament meant Americans as well as Britons. American-built ships, owned by American merchants, with American crews, were as much entitled under the Navigation Acts to protection against Dutch competition and the privileges of the imperial trade as their counterparts in England, Scotland, or Ireland. Under this arrangement American shipbuilding flourished so that by the 1763–1775 period the thirteen continental colonies produced vessels worth £300,000 each year. About half this output was sold to British merchants. During these same years American ship owners earned an estimated £600,000 annually by carrying cargo and passengers to and from various points within the empire.

And America received other economic benefits as part of the empire. The British paid bounties to encourage production of items that did not compete with English-made goods and for raw materials that were needed by English manufacturers; these brought thousands of pounds a year to American indigo growers, pig-iron manufacturers, and naval-stores producers.

The measures to restrict colonial manufacturers do not fall either in the debit or credit columns. The Iron Act, aimed at finished iron products, did little to restrain the colonial iron industry because it was not rigorously enforced. As for the Wool and Hat acts, they did not, as we might suppose, kill off promising industries. The intention of these measures was clear: They were designed to limit future growth that might injure British producers. Still, in their day they probably had little effect.

On the whole, the American experience within the mercantile system was positive. And Americans recognized, generally, how much they gained economically from the imperial relationship. Before 1763 only one economic measure, the Molasses Act of 1733, caused serious friction. This imposed a high tax on molasses, sugar, and rum brought into the colonies from the Dutch, French, and Spanish West Indies. Intended to protect the British Caribbean sugar planters from the competition of lower-cost foreign producers, the act threatened the profitable trade between New England and the foreign West Indies. Yankee merchants responded by turning the smuggling of foreign sugar and molasses into a fine art. The law, never strictly enforced, became a virtual dead letter.

THE POLITICAL LEDGER.   When we measure the political debits and credits of the British–American relationship, we encounter a similar even balance through the 1760s. There were indeed periods of rather strict imperial governance. During the reigns of Charles II (1660–1685) and James II (1685–1688), the British authorities tried to tighten imperial control. In 1684 they revoked the Massachusetts Bay charter and soon after merged New England, New York, and New Jersey into the Dominion of New England. Under the stern rule of Governor Sir Edmund Andros, residents of the northern colonies were denied the right to tax themselves or to make laws regulating their day-to-day concerns. In the proprietary colonies farther south, the crown sought to impose direct royal control.

This effort at tight imperial regulation, while stirring deep fears among the colonists, proved short-lived. In 1689 a British coalition of Whig leaders, champions of Protestantism, and partisans of Parliament, inspired by the liberal political ideas of John Locke and other Whig thinkers, deposed the Catholic ruler James II. They then invited Mary, James's Protestant daughter, and her husband,

William of Orange, to rule England in his place. Accompanying the offer was the Declaration of Rights, establishing Parliamentary supremacy in England and bolstering the rights of individuals as against the crown.

This so-called Glorious Revolution echoed loudly in America. Led by the Puritan clergy, Massachusetts rebels arrested Governor Andros and his subordinates and shipped them all back to England. The Dominion of New England was dissolved and the individual colonies separated once more, though Massachusetts absorbed Plymouth colony and the sparsely settled region of Maine. Efforts to restore the former Bay Colony charter, allowing virtual self-rule, failed, however. Despite loud protest, in 1691 Massachusetts had to accept a new charter with a royal governor at the top, royal review of all legislation, and a property qualification for voting to replace the old religious test. Notwithstanding the Massachusetts experience, the thrust of the Glorious Revolution was to guarantee to the crown's subjects on both sides of the Atlantic a large measure of self-government through powerful representative legislatures and assemblies.

By the early eighteenth century, then, the colonists had achieved a large measure of political autonomy. The English Privy Council was still permitted to "disallow" measures passed by the colonial legislatures and approved by the colonial governors; but of some 8,500 colonial laws submitted to the council, only 469 were declared null. Nor was the Board of Trade, which shared colonial administration with the governors and the Privy Council, any more coercive. From 1721 to 1748, when Sir Robert Walpole and the Duke of Newcastle were the crown's chief advisers, the English government gave higher priority to colonial economic growth than to tight and tidy English rule. This era of "salutary neglect" helped encourage an even greater sense than before that the colonists were self-governing in all internal matters.

THE ISSUE OF RELIGION.   Before 1763, then, Americans had little reason to complain of British political or economic oppression. But what about the religious oppression John Adams spoke of?

A majority of colonists were Protestant nonconformists of some kind. Some of these charged that the Anglicans intended to establish "a tyranny over the bodies and souls of men," destroy the religious liberties of Americans, and restrict public office to members of the Anglican Church. Most of all they feared the British would create Anglican bishops for the colonies, who would rule over American religious affairs as they did those of England.

In fact, British officials recognized that American religious dissenters were often firm supporters of the crown. Such people, in the words of one, "should not be provoked or alienated" by imposing bishops on them. The British government did occasionally interfere in colonial religious matters, but it was usually to insist that toleration be extended to some unpopular denomination, rather than to restrict religious expression. Though intolerant Americans sometimes were offended by such intrusion, few ever felt seriously threatened. In religion, as in politics and economics, the conflicts between mother country and colonies remained muted before 1763.

* THE CRISIS OF EMPIRE *

Whatever was true during the first century and a half of British settlement, after 1763, many of the most influential and articulate people in the colonies would begin to find the system of imperial administration galling and the actions of the British government intolerable. Before long they would demand that they be changed. The dramatic change of heart would be linked to the end of the French threat to English America.

THE ENGLISH–FRENCH CONFRONTATION. French Canada (New France) and English America had been planted at approximately the same time. Thereafter the two communities had evolved in different ways. By the mid-eighteenth century Canada was a sparsely settled region with some 55,000 farmers cultivating the lands of the gentry, ruled autocratically by a royal governor. Pious and conservative, the French Canadians accepted the dominance of the seigneurs, the church, and the appointed royal officials without serious question.

Friction between English America and New France was almost preordained. Both communities were political extensions of their respective mother countries and inevitably became enmeshed in the quarrels of the two European arch-rivals. Both were also religious antagonists. Before long Catholic New France and Protestant English America took up the fierce political and religious conflicts that had beset the European world for two centuries.

Just as important as these transplanted European quarrels were the tensions native to America itself. New France and "new England" vied over control of the fishing trade in Newfoundland and over competing claims in the Caribbean. Even closer to home was rivalry over the fur trade with the Indians. The British had the advantage of cheaper and better trade goods; the French, on the other hand, were more effective in winning the personal allegiance of the Indians. Canadian traders went to the Indians for furs rather than waiting for the Indians to deliver them to the European settlements. They lived with the Indians and often married Indian women. Their half-European, half-Indian children in turn forged bonds that the English seldom could match. French religious institutions also gave them an advantage with the Indians. Unlike the Protestants to the south, French Catholics were effective in converting Indians to Christianity.

In the late 1680s Britain and France confronted one another in the first of four major wars that would extend over several continents simultaneously. In King William's War (1689–1697), Massachusetts colonial troops captured the French stronghold of Port Royal in modern Nova Scotia. The post was returned to France, however, by the Treaty of Ryswick (1697), which ended the conflict. The French soon moved to occupy the vast Mississippi Valley, a region also claimed by the American colonists under their provincial charters. In 1699 the French established an outpost at Cahokia, near present-day St. Louis; in 1703 they placed a fort at Kaskaskia in southern Illinois. They also planted settlements on the Gulf Coast and along the shores of the Great Lakes. When war broke out again in 1702 (Queen Anne's War, 1702–1713), French troops and their Indian allies clashed with the Anglo-Americans in a vast arc from Maine to the outskirts of Louisiana, as the French called their new colony in the North American interior. By the Treaty of Utrecht (1713), ending this conflict, England acquired Newfoundland, Acadia (renamed Nova Scotia), and the Hudson Bay region.

Following the Treaty of Utrecht, the French sought to consolidate their hold on Louisiana by establishing new posts and settlements in the disputed region. In 1718 they estblished New Orleans near the mouth of the Mississippi. The British countered by constructing Fort Oswego on Lake Ontario and fortifying the northern frontier against the pro-French Abenakis. When war between Britain and France broke out again (King George's War, 1740–1748), both sides once more clashed in North America. New England troops captured the French strong point of Louisbourg in Nova Scotia, while in New York William Johnson, the province's commissary of Indian affairs, induced the Iroquois to attack the French. In retaliation the French and their Indian allies raided Albany and burned Saratoga.

THE FRENCH AND INDIAN WAR. These three wars were extensions of disputes that originated in Europe. The most destructive and momentous of all the colonial wars, however, started over an issue of more immediate concern to many Americans.

French expansion into the Mississippi Valley seemed to threaten the very existence of the British colonies as self-governing Protestant communities. Besides, a string of interior French colonies promised to block westward expansion. Colonial farmers looking for fresh, fertile lands for themselves and their children would be walled off and confined to the dwindling acres east of the mountains. Would-be speculators in western lands, who were especially prominent and vocal in Pennsylvania and Virginia, would be denied their expected windfall profits from land sales.

The crisis came in what is now western Pennsylvania and Ohio. Here, Pennsylvania fur traders had established a string of trading posts to collect pelts from the Indians. Hoping to head off further English encroachment, the French, under the Marquis Duquesne, determined to build a chain of forts from Lake Erie to the Forks of the Ohio at what is now Pittsburgh. In 1753 a construction party of several hundred Frenchmen and Indians established three stockades along Lake Erie and on French Creek. Still left to construct when winter came was the projected post at the strategic Forks, where the Allegheny and Monongahela join to form the Ohio River.

News of the French project alarmed Governor Robert Dinwiddie of Virginia. Dinwiddie responded by dispatching a tall, young Virginia squire, George Washington, with a force of armed men to warn the French to leave. Washington failed in his mission. The following year, after the French had completed Fort Duquesne at the Forks, Washington returned to oust them by force. The young Virginian foolishly allowed himself to engage the French though outnumbered ten to one. At Fort Necessity, a hurriedly constructed American stockade, the French took the intruders prisoner. When released from captivity, Washington and his little force returned to the Virginia capital, Williamsburg, carrying news that the French were on the verge of making good their claim to the great interior valley.

The confrontation of a few hundred men in western Pennsylvania triggered the French and Indian War, a struggle lasting from 1754 to 1763. In 1756 the conflict spread to Europe itself when Britain and Prussia concluded an alliance against France, which in turn allied itself with Austria and then, in 1762, with Spain. Because Britain, France, and Spain were all great imperial nations, the struggle quickly turned into a "world war." Before it was over, armies and fleets had grappled in the Mediterranean, the Caribbean, the Far East, India, and on the European continent, as well as in the dense forests of North America. At first the war went badly for the English. But then, in 1757, William Pitt the Elder took over its management and brought Britain a series of brilliant victories that changed the course of history.

In America, as elsewhere, the war started badly for the Anglo-Americans when, during the summer of 1755, the British general, Edward Braddock, suffered a serious defeat at the hands of the French and their Indian allies in an attempt to capture Fort Duquesne. On July 9 Braddock's small force of 1,400 British redcoats, 450 Virginia militiamen under Washington, and 50 Indian scouts, after hacking their way through the dense Pennsylvania forest, encountered 600 French and 200 Indians seven miles from the French post. With flags flying and bagpipes playing, the British advanced in a line in the approved European fashion. But the battle quickly degenerated into a wild melee with the French and Indians pouring deadly fire into the advancing redcoats and Americans from concealed positions on either side. Wounded mortally, Braddock ordered a retreat. As the combined Anglo-American force limped back to their base, they were attacked by the enemy from behind every tree and rock. Of the 1,900 men who had set out, only 500 arrived home safely.

Other British commanders were more successful. In the fall of 1758 General John Forbes resumed the effort to oust the French from the Forks of the Ohio. Seeing Forbes' powerful Anglo-American army approaching, the Indians of the Ohio country deserted the French. On November 24 the handful of French soldiers remaining at Fort Duquesne blew it up and fled, leaving it to the British, who reconstructed it as Fort Pitt. Impressed by this British victory, the Indians turned on their former French allies and virtually drove them out of the upper Mississippi Valley.

A still more brilliant British triumph came in the summer of 1759 when General James Wolfe and an army of 4,500 redcoats scaled the heights above the St. Lawrence River and deployed on the Plains of Abraham outside the walls of Quebec, the political and religious capital of French Canada. The French commander was the able Marquis de Montcalm, but his force consisted only of ill-trained provincial troops. They bravely attacked but in the face of the redcoats' deadly musket volleys, quickly fell back to the town and soon after surrendered. Both commanders died in the battle. With the fall of Quebec, followed later by the capture of Montreal, French power in Canada collapsed.

The war dragged on for many months following the fall of New France. In 1761 prime minister Pitt, despite his successes, resigned. The new king, George

III, replaced him with Lord Bute and other "Tory" advisers who were more friendly to the idea of royal power than Pitt and his fellow Whigs. By this time the British people were weary of the war, which had cost them well over £100 million and had pushed taxes to record levels. In February 1763 the British, French, and Spanish signed the Treaty of Paris ending the war.

The treaty made sweeping changes in the political map of North America. By its terms France ceded Cape Breton Island and all of Canada to Great Britain and recognized the region from the Appalachians to the Mississippi and from the Great Lakes to Florida as British territory. Spain, France's ally, gave Florida, including much of the eastern Gulf Coast, to England. In return for this loss, Spain gained from the French what they had retained of Louisiana; that is, the portion west of the Mississippi. Other territory changed hands in India, Africa, and the Caribbean. To the Americans the crucial matter was that powerful France was now virtually eliminated from the entire North American continent.

The end of the French presence abruptly altered American attitudes toward the British Empire. As long as the French were nearby, the Americans clung to the protection of England. Now that the French menace was gone, the colonists could afford to consider the disadvantages of their subordinate relationship with the Empire. Moreover, the French and Indian War had created serious tensions between the British government and its American subjects that now clamored to be resolved.

BRITISH–AMERICAN RELATIONS DURING THE WAR. From the British point of view, the Americans had not been the best of subjects during the war. Defying the Rule of 1756 forbidding wartime trade between the colonies and France, American vessels had sailed to the French Caribbean islands, carrying, in exchange for sugar, needed supplies excluded by the British naval blockade. American merchants had also exchanged American flour and fish for French wines and gold at Hispaniola, initially a neutral Spanish port, despite Pitt's complaint that this trade enabled the enemy "to sustain and protect" the "long and expensive War."

The British government sought to stop the illegal wartime commerce with France by issuing writs of assistance, general search warrants allowing customs officials to inspect private property to determine whether smuggled goods were present. Though such writs had been issued before, they now angered colonial merchants, who saw them as a dangerous violation of the rights of private citizens. In 1760 several Boston traders hired attorney James Otis to argue against the legality of the writs. In a fiery address that John Adams later called the "first scene of the first act of opposition" to British authority in America, Otis denounced the writs as "against the fundamental principles of law" and the British constitution, and hence void. In the end the writs were upheld by the Massachusetts court and confirmed by the later Townshend Acts, but they were never effectively used in the Bay Colony.

Besides flouting wartime trade regulations, the colonists had also resisted paying their share. To help meet war costs, Pitt had imposed a "requisition" system whereby each colonial assembly would share with the British treasury the expense of recruiting and supplying troops. In addition, the British would re-imburse the colonial legislatures for part of their initial outlays in the following year. This was an extremely generous scheme, British officials said, since the Americans were fighting the French as much for themselves as for the mother country. Yet time and again, it seemed to British officials, the Americans had failed to do their part. They had delayed voting money for defense or even refused out-right to do so. According to Lord Loudon, British commander in chief in Amer-ica, it had been "the constant study of every province . . . to throw every expense on the Crown and bear no part of the expense of this war themselves."

The Americans had also been unable to cooperate in a common policy to-ward the Indians. In 1754 the British Board of Trade had issued a call for a colo-nial congress to consider Indian–white relations generally and find a way to induce the tribes south of the Great Lakes to support the Anglo-American cause against the French. Only New England, New York, Pennsylvania, and Maryland sent delegates to the meeting at Albany. The results were not impressive. The con-gress recommended a number of measures to meet Indians complaints against American fur traders and land speculators and charges that the British govern-ment had failed to protect them against the French. It also adopted a proposal made by Benjamin Franklin for a political union of all the continental colonies to exercise jurisdiction over Indian affairs and deal with the overall problem of west-ern development. Yet none of the separate colonies wished to surrender control over western policy. The congress's recommendations were not adopted, and Indian–white relations remained chaotic.

Indian problems soon worsened. In the wake of the British conquest of the West, hundreds of American traders crossed the Appalachian Mountains. They cheated the Indians and plied them with drink. At the same time scores of Ameri-can, Scottish, and English speculators besieged Parliament, demanding land grants in the West that could be sold to eager would-be settlers. A flood of small farmers was already pouring into the Pittsburgh region, displacing the local In-dians. British officials in the West were no more sensitive to Indian feelings than the Americans. Lord Jeffrey Amherst despised the "savages" and advised spread-ing smallpox among them. In 1762 Amherst abruptly cut off the food and am-munition traditionally supplied to the Indians during the winter.

To the northern tribes Amherst's act seemed the last straw. By this time a ma-jor Indian renewal movement was under way, inspired by a religious leader called the "Prophet," who urged his people to abandon white ways and reassert their in-dependence. In May 1763, led by Pontiac, one of the Prophet's disciples, the In-dians attacked Fort Detroit, triggering a fierce Indian uprising throughout the West that in two months drove virtually all the whites back over the mountains. The British struck back and by the summer of 1764 had put down Pontiac's re-bellion. But the affair highlighted the chaos in Indian affairs and, more generally, Britain's problems in controlling its empire.

THE PROCLAMATION OF 1763.   With the French and Indian war over, British as well as American attitudes toward the empire changed. In general, the

Whig leaders who had governed England had accepted the validity of colonial claims to autonomy in managing local affairs. Philosophically, they had opposed the assertion of royal power at home, and this attitude had carried over to their view of how to govern America. But the Tory government of Lord Bute and Chancellor of the Exchequer George Grenville supported the crown against Parliament and had little use for colonial "pretensions" to self-rule. Given the experience of the war and the Indian problem, tighter administration of the empire, they felt, was clearly needed.

The first move to tighten colonial control was the Proclamation of 1763. This measure prohibited colonists from settling west of the Appalachians and required all those already there "forthwith to remove themselves." East of the mountains, colonists were forbidden to purchase land directly from the Indians. The entire trans-Appalachian region was to be placed under the control of the British commander in chief and to remain an exclusive Indian preserve until further notice. Through the proclamation the British hoped to pacify the Indians and to give themselves time to contrive a rational permanent policy for disposing of the crown's lands, especially in the West. Eventually colonists would be allowed to move across the mountains, but not before Indian claims had been dealt with and an orderly system of land transfer and settlement worked out.

However rational its goals, the proclamation dismayed many Americans. Those who had anticipated profits from land speculation, fur trading, and farming saw their hopes for gain go up in smoke. Among the influential land promoters of Virginia, the check on western settlement seemed designed to permit Englishmen to grab an unfair share of speculative profits in the American West. For small farmers, the new western policy, by closing the frontier escape hatch, seemed likely to widen the gap between rich and poor.

CHANGES IN BRITISH TAX POLICY.   Even more disturbing to most Americans, however, was Parliament's effort to raise revenue in America. The British government had long imposed duties on certain imports through laws like the Molasses Act, but their primary purpose had been to regulate commerce, not to extract money from the Americans. Now there were other considerations. Britain after 1763 labored under an immense debt that was costing it £4.5 million a year in interest alone. Military costs, too, were certain to continue. Britain would have to maintain an expensive army to protect the colonists against the Indians and prevent the return of the French. The conclusion was obvious: Make the Americans help pay the bill.

The first revenue measure of the Grenville ministry was the Sugar Act (1764). This law imposed import duties on non-English cloth, indigo, coffee, wine, sugar, and molasses. The tax on molasses was especially offensive. Even though the new duty was actually lower than the earlier Molasses Act rates, the money was now really to be collected. Smuggling had made the old law a sham; the new law forced American merchants to pass through a thicket of certificates, affidavits, oaths, and inspections and added a new vice-admiralty court to try suspected smugglers under rules that put more of the burden of proof than previously on the accused.

North America, 1763

Most American merchants balked at this renewed effort to exclude them from the profitable foreign West Indies market. The Navigation Acts had pressed only lightly on the colonies thus far, largely because the Americans had offset their disadvantages through trade with the Caribbean. By cutting off trade with the foreign West Indies, the Sugar Act not only threatened profits but also endangered the northern colonists' elaborate adjustments to the requirements of the imperial economy.

THE STAMP ACT.   The Proclamation of 1763 injured Virginians primarily; the Sugar Act promised to hurt New England and the middle colonies. The Grenville ministry next proposed a measure that angered powerful groups in every one of the colonies and threatened the political autonomy that Americans as a whole had gained over a century of effort.

During the summer of 1763 Grenville decided to impose on America a tax on legal documents and other items, to be paid with stamps purchased from the British treasury. Under the new law a revenue stamp had to be affixed to all professional licenses, court documents, papers concerning land transfers or exports or imports, all private contracts, newspapers, and even college diplomas. These stamps were to be paid for in gold or silver, and the money collected was to be set aside for exclusive use in the colonies. Violations of the law would be tried in both the ordinary and the admiralty courts.

Before proceeding with the measure, Grenville had the foresight to consult with agents who represented colonial interests at the seat of empire. The Americans were dubious about such a tax, but the colonial legislatures, Grenville learned, would not accept the alternative of taxing themselves. Under the circumstances, he refused to abandon his scheme. In early 1765, after a brief debate, Parliament passed the momentous Stamp Act.

Two other measures supplemented Grenville's program of tightening imperial control. The Quartering Act (actually two separate measures of 1765 and 1766) required colonial authorities to provide barracks and supplies for British troops or, in lieu of barracks, to make provision for billeting troops in inns or unoccupied dwellings. The Currency Act (1764) forbade colonial legislatures to issue legal tender paper money. Previously applied only to New England, the prohibition was now extended to all the colonies.

The Quartering Act seemed a dangerous extension of British military power in America; the Currency Act hampered the colonial legislatures' efforts to provide a circulating medium in place of scarce coin. Neither law, however, produced the wave of outrage that greeted the Stamp Act.

The Stamp Act touched almost every aspect of colonial social and economic life—the professions, commerce, the press, and education. It penalized two of the most articulate and influential groups in the colonies—lawyers and newspaper publishers. It also threatened the hard-won authority of colonial assemblies, which had previously exercised the power to levy taxes. Furthermore, the Stamp Act raised profound and disturbing constitutional issues. First, were the colonies subordinate to Great Britain, or equal partners in the empire? Second, must American colonists pay taxes imposed by Parliament, where they were not formally represented? Few colonists expected their representatives to be seated in the English Parliament; rather, they wanted Parliament to recognize the authority of colonial assemblies, including their exclusive authority to tax Americans. Unlike most of the post-1763 British measures, by jeopardizing all the colonies equally, the Stamp Act created a common bond of opposition to British policies. It was probably one of the most foolish and inexpedient bills passed by the British Parliament in its long history.

News of the Stamp Act reached the colonies in mid-April 1765. In May the Virginia House of Burgesses, goaded by the young firebrand lawyer Patrick Henry, boldly resolved that Americans had all the rights of Englishmen and that only their own legislatures could tax them. Virginia's action electrified Americans everywhere. Newspapers all over the colonies praised the resolutions and denounced British policy. Other colonial assemblies quickly joined the House of Burgesses in attacking the act, and the Massachusetts General Court called for a colonial congress to meet in October to consider united action in the crisis.

But outraged citizens did not wait until the congress met. In almost every colony the new law stirred up violence. Mobs of artisans, shopkeepers, sailors, and merchants, some organized as "Sons of Liberty," burned effigies of Grenville and royal officials in America and physically attacked tax collectors and supporters of the new tax. In Boston the protesters set fire to the house of Lieutenant Governor Thomas Hutchinson. So effective was this intimidation that almost all the official stamp distributors resigned their royal commissions.

By the time the Stamp Act Congress convened in New York (October 7–25, 1765), the act was a dead letter in every colony except Georgia, where an unusually firm governor succeeded in making the citizens comply with it. The congress adopted petitions addressed to the king, the House of Lords, and the House of Commons. Although mild in tone, they insisted once again that Americans could be taxed only by bodies that represented them directly.

The petitions did little to move the British government, and mob violence only angered Grenville and other English conservatives. A few English Whig leaders, such as Edmund Burke, supported the Americans on the grounds of justice, but in the end it was economic pressure that killed the tax. The merchants of England, skeptical of the Stamp Act from the outset, grew increasingly hostile to the measure when it became clear that the law was disastrous for trade with America. In some places in the colonies legal processes for enforcing commercial contracts stalled. Still more dismaying were the Nonimportation Agreements initiated by New Yorkers and widely adopted in the other colonies by which citizens pledged not to buy British goods, and merchants agreed not to import them. The resulting drop in transatlantic trade soon brought many British manufacturers and exporters to the brink of bankruptcy.

Parliament yielded to the complaints of the English merchants. On March 18, 1766, it repealed the detested measure but simultaneously adopted the Declaratory Act, affirming its right to legislate for the colonies "in all cases whatsoever." In effect, the English government was telling the Americans that it acknowledged the stamp tax as a mistake, but that it would not accept the principle of "no taxation without representation" that had been marshaled to oppose it.

THE TOWNSHEND ACTS.   The rejoicing that followed news of the repeal of the Stamp Act was short-lived. In January 1766 the New York assembly refused to contribute support for British troops as required by the Quartering Act. Over the summer hostile feelings arose between New York citizens and British soldiers, and several Americans were injured in violent clashes between redcoats and Sons of Liberty, the secret organization formed to protest the Stamp Act. At the urging of Charles Townshend, Grenville's successor, Parliament suspended the New York legislature's powers in mid-1767.

During the debate over taxation, Townshend had noticed that Americans made a distinction between a tax for raising revenue and one intended to regulate commerce. The first, they said, was a dangerous novelty; the second was traditional and acceptable. "Champagne Charlie"—a witty, charming, but shallow man—now seized on this distinction as a way around American resistance to revenue taxes. In May 1767 he proposed legislation that proved almost as foolish and inept as the Stamp Act: the Revenue Act of 1767.

Commonly referred to as the Townshend Acts, the law imposed new import duties on glass, red and white lead, painters' colors, paper, and tea. The imposts (taxes) were to be paid in coin and the money used to pay royal officials in the colonies, thereby ending their dependence on colonial legislatures for their salaries. The Townshend Acts also authorized the colonial higher courts to issue writs of assistance to help customs officers search private property for violations of the new law. A companion measure established a board of customs commissioners with headquarters in Boston and new vice-admiralty courts in Halifax, Philadelphia, and Charleston to enforce both old and new trade regulations.

"Patriots," as the opponents of Britain's policies were called, once more demanded a boycott of British goods through Nonimportation Agreements. This time the colonial merchants were determined to keep the violence under control, and for a while they succeeded. Before long, however, the public began to defy the customs commissioners openly. In a number of places mobs rescued ships and cargoes held for suspected smuggling. In Rhode Island the courts were intimidated into acquitting accused smugglers.

The disorder never became as widespread as it had during the Stamp Act crisis, but it seemed sufficiently alarming to the royal governor of Massachusetts, Sir Francis Bernard, to require drastic action. Responding to Bernard's reports, the British government ordered the military commander in chief, Thomas Gage, to move troops from New York to Boston. At the same time the British ministry sent the governor two more regiments of redcoats from Britain. The troops were greeted with hostility and deep suspicion by Bostonians, who were convinced that the soldiers were there to intimidate the colony and arrest Patriot leaders.

Meanwhile in Britain, pressure mounted to repeal the Townshend duties. They had brought relatively little revenue and by encouraging a second boycott had led to another drastic drop in Anglo-American trade. Once more adopting an expedient course, Parliament canceled the duties in 1770, except for a three-penny tax on each pound of tea. By now, even such firm friends of America as William Pitt were beginning to fear that the colonists were determined to overturn the basic laws governing commercial relations between Britain and the colonies.

FEARS FOR COLONIAL RELIGIOUS AUTONOMY. The tightening of imperial bonds was not confined to the political and economic spheres. In religion, too, the advent of the crown's Tory advisers tripped off efforts to limit colonial autonomy. In March 1763 the archbishop of Canterbury, head of the Church of England, wrote that he and his fellow bishops finally intended to "try our utmost for bishops" at the next session of Parliament. The colonies did not have an episcopal structure; this void, the archbishop said, would have to be remedied.

The archbishop's scheme to attach the colonies more securely to Anglicanism eventually failed. Yet controversy over the religious issue continued to rage, constantly fed by rumors that the effort to establish Anglican bishops in America had not ended. Especially in New England where hostility to Anglicanism had always been intense, many colonists came to believe that there was a plot to impose upon them bishops, tithes for the Church of England, and even laws restricting public office to Anglicans. Inevitably the religious and political issues merged. The link between these issues seemed confirmed by the role of the Anglican clergy in America. Unlike the dissenting ministers, who were often the most vehement enemies of the Grenville and Townshend programs, clergy of the Church of England generally opposed active resistance to the stamp tax and Townshend duties, urging their flocks to obey the law and show respect for royal officials.

PATRIOT INSECURITY. Before 1763 most Americans had been proud of their British heritage, and even those whose ancestors came from other lands had acknowledged their allegiance to Britain. Thereafter, they drifted away from this loyalty and eventually developed a rationale for autonomy that would carry them all the way to independence.

In part the process reflected American social insecurity. Yes, Americans were affluent and relatively free, but this condition, unusual among societies of the day, seemed precarious. As historian Gordon S. Wood has noted, "the people were acutely nervous about their prosperity and the liberty that made it possible." He also describes the resentment that many of them felt against those who, owing to their connections with the British royal government, had special advantages in the scramble for wealth and "preferment," favors in the form of office or lucrative business arrangements. The patriot leaders were not modern democrats, but neither did they favor a system that conferred permanent privilege on a few. Above all they despised the hereditary principle entrenched in the British monarchy— that birth to the right parents conferred, by right, permanent and unchallengeable advantages regardless of merit.

PATRIOT IDEOLOGY. During the imperial crisis of 1763–1776 some of the best minds of America were devoted to the task of justifying colonial "rights." At various stages of the British–American conflict such men as John Dickinson, Thomas Jefferson, John Adams, and Benjamin Franklin published letters, pamphlets, and editorials that indicted British policies in the name of fundamental political principles. At times their writing was important largely for its immediate political utility. Dickinson's *Letters from a Farmer in Pennsylvania to the Inhabitants of the British Colonies* (1767–1768) for example, was an attack on the Townshend duties that emphasized the illegality of collecting internal taxes in America as opposed to merely regulating commerce. But there were also searching and thorough defenses of American freedom and the right to resist authority that, taken together, announced a new philosophy of government and a new perspective on the individual's relations to it.

Few of the pamphleteers and writers were entirely original thinkers. They borrowed widely from European, especially English, sources, especially from the radical Whig publicists of the late 1680s and 1690s, who had sought to justify the Glorious Revolution against James II and later had worked out arguments to limit the power of the crown. John Locke's *Treatise Of Civil Government* was a particuularly important source of ideas. Society, said Locke, was based on an agreement between ruler and ruled to preserve the natural rights of man inherent in the order of the universe. Although obedience to a just ruler was required by this "social contract," defiance of tyranny was also an obligation.

Patriots almost always maintained that they were defending traditional rights guaranteed under the unwritten British constitution and endangered by either the king or his chief ministers. Far from demanding what was legitimate obedience from their subjects, they argued, the tyrants in Britain were attempting to subvert rights sanctioned both by history and by the laws of nature. Such arguments became vital weapons in the Patriot arsenal; as incorporated in the Declaration of Independence, they would be handed down to later Americans as part of their political heritage.

The Whig thinkers also provided Americans with a moral rationale for independence. In England, political dissenters during the early eighteenth century had come to regard English society as corrupt. Compared with the past, royal officials were mere "placemen" who served royal power with no other aim but to grow rich. England itself had grown grossly wealthy, its people a prey to luxury and vice.

Americans seized on this bleak picture enthusiastically, using it to support the Patriot position. In contrast to corrupt Britain, American society was pure and unspoiled. The colonists still lived honestly and simply. But would all this not end if Bute, Grenville, and the rest had their way? If Americans did not resist, surely a horde of locusts in the shape of royal officials would descend on America and consume its substance, meanwhile exposing the colonists to the dissipations and moral laxity that the young society till now had been spared. If for no other reason than to preserve American virtue, British policies must be resisted at all costs.

MASSACRE IN BOSTON.   As the journalists, pamphleteers, and lawyers learnedly or passionately argued the extent of natural rights, ordinary men and women grew ever more hostile to British policy and restless at the visible symbols of British authority. Some outburst of violence was probably inevitable in Boston. The city in 1770 was a hotbed of anti-British feeling, and townspeople and redcoats had been trading insults ever since the soldiers had arrived from New York. To make matters worse, many Boston artisans deeply resented the fact that British soldiers were taking part-time jobs and so depriving them of scarce work. Then, one evening in March, a mob attacked a British sentry at his post. The soldier called for help, and when the squad dispatched to rescue him arrived, they encountered a rapidly growing, angry crowd. At some point someone gave the command for the redcoats to fire. When the smoke of the muskets cleared, three Americans lay dead and several were wounded, two of whom later died.

The incident threatened to touch off a major uprising. The townspeople, Governor Hutchinson reported, were in a perfect frenzy and might attempt to drive out all 600 redcoats stationed in Boston. If they attacked, it would plunge the colony into full-scale rebellion against the crown, the consequences of which would be too horrible to contemplate. Although unsure of his authority, Hutchinson quickly ordered the arrest of the soldiers involved in the "massacre" and directed that the British troops be removed from their barracks in town to Castle William in Boston harbor. From there they could continue to guard the city but would no longer be in direct contact with the irate citizens. Eventually seven of the redcoats were tried for the massacre. Ably defended by John Adams and Josiah Quincy, five were acquitted and two received light sentences.

THE GASPÉE INCIDENT.   Repeal of the Townshend duties in April 1770 cooled the argument between Britain and America. Yet the next two or three years were not without jarring incidents of American defiance and British reprisal.

The most serious of these was the Gaspée incident, involving a British revenue cutter operating out of Narragansett Bay. On June 9, 1772, while pursuing a suspected smuggler, the vessel ran aground on the Rhode Island coast near Providence, a hotbed of Patriot sentiment. That evening a group of the town's prominent citizens boarded the vessel, wounded its commander, disarmed the crew, and burned the ship to the keel. This was not only a crime against the king's property, but also a blatant attack on a royal officer. Royal officials immediately posted a large reward for information leading to the conviction of the guilty parties and convened a commission of leading American Loyalists to investigate the affair. But no one chose, or dared, to come forward with information, and royal officials could only fume with frustration.

THE TEA ACT.   The Gaspée affair notwithstanding, the period between 1771 and 1773 was one of relative calm. During these years the Patriot cause, with few new outrages to feed on, went into eclipse. The militant Sons of Liberty pledged to compel the British government to rescind the remaining duty on tea and tried to force merchants to continue the Nonimportation Agreements. They failed. Instead, British–American trade revived—to the joy of the merchants, who no longer saw any purpose in boycotting English wares now that the other Townshend duties were dead. Meanwhile, Americans evaded the tea duty by smuggling in their favorite beverage from Dutch sources.

Now the government in England blundered once more and set in motion the final phase of the British–American confrontation. After decades of growing profit in trade with India and the Far East, the British East India Company had been brought to the edge of ruin by mismanagement and fraud. Its last remaining asset, 18 million pounds of tea, could not be sold because taxes in Britain and America made smuggled Dutch tea cheaper. To help the company, the British government, under the Tea Act of 1773, eliminated an export duty on British tea. Though the new law retained the existing three-pence-a-pound import duty on tea brought to America, this new arrangement would allow the East India Company to undersell American merchants who sold smuggled tea. By allowing the company to forgo the auction of its product in Britain and sell directly to various favored American consignees, the new law meant it could bypass or undersell even the "fair traders," those American merchants who obeyed the law and bought only English tea. The scheme, it seemed, might be the beginning of a new policy to favor those merchants in the colonies who supported British policies and penalize those who did not.

In each major port artisans, shopkeepers, and merchants gathered to condemn this latest threat to American liberty. Information was passed from cities to villages and from colony to colony through the Committees of Correspondence, building a broad and organized resistance. The radicals urged all Americans to abstain from drinking tea. Patriot women responded by turning to native concoctions that Patriot drinkers loyally pronounced "vastly more agreeable" than anything out of India.

In Boston during the winter of 1773 the Tea Act ignited an explosion that initiated the final steps to military confrontation. Leading the Boston radicals were the fiery Samuel Adams, organizer of the Massachusetts Sons of Liberty, and a prominent merchant, John Hancock. In late November the first tea-carrying vessels had arrived in Boston. On the evening of December 16 a group of Patriots dressed as Mohawk Indians boarded the ships and dumped the contents of 342 chests of tea—worth £10,000—into the harbor. Hundreds of people watched from the wharf as a thick layer of tea leaves spread over the water. They did not know it, but they were watching part of the British Empire sink beneath the waves.

THE "INTOLERABLE ACTS".   Between March and May 1774, following other attacks on tea-carrying vessels, an angry Parliament passed the so-called Intolerable or Coercive Acts. The first of these punished Boston by closing the port to all commerce until the East India Company had been paid for its tea. The second, intended to prevent local juries from frustrating enforcement of imperial trade regulations, allowed royal officials accused of crimes while stopping a riot or collecting revenue to be sent to Britain for trial. The third modified the charter of Massachusetts by giving the royal governor enlarged appointive powers and limiting the authority of the town meetings, which had served as forums for anti-British radicals.

Patriots considered two other measures passed at this time, though not reprisals for the Boston Tea Party, equally "intolerable." The first extended the provisions of the Quartering Acts so that troops might be lodged in private dwellings. The second, the Quebec Act, established a highly centralized administration for the province of Quebec, Canada, won during the French and Indian War, and granted toleration for the Catholic religion that most of the French population embraced. The law also extended the boundaries of Quebec south to the Ohio River. Protestant Americans, revealing their age-old prejudices, objected to this acceptance of Catholicism. Citizens of Virginia, Connecticut, and Massachusetts denounced the extension of Canada into the area south of the Great Lakes as violating provincial claims to the region under founding charters.

THE FIRST CONTINENTAL CONGRESS.   In response to widespread demand for a united colonial front against the Intolerable Acts, fifty-five delegates representing all the colonies except distant Georgia, met at Philadelphia in early September 1774. This First Continental Congress was composed of men with widely differing views. There were radicals, who claimed that American rights were founded on natural law and that, accordingly, Parliament could not abridge them in any way. There were also moderates who argued that American liberties came ultimately from the British constitution and that Parliament had the right to legislate at least on matters of imperial trade. Conservatives, led by Joseph Galloway of Pennsylvania, proposed a plan to establish a political union between Britain and America under a crown-appointed "president-general" and a kind of super Parliament. It was narrowly defeated.

During the debate a copy of the Suffolk Resolves, recently drafted in Massachusetts, arrived in Philadelphia. These condemned the Intolerable Acts and urged the people of Massachusetts to establish an armed militia, boycott British goods, and withhold taxes from the royal government. Presented to the delegates, the Suffolk Resolves were endorsed as the congress's own resolutions. In its own Declaration of Rights and Grievances the congress sharply attacked virtually all British trade legislation since 1763 and established a Continental Association, which forbade the importation or consumption of British goods and urged an embargo on colonial exports as well. The congress resolved to meet the following May if American grievances had not been redressed by then.

The First Continental Congress was a milestone on the road to American solidarity. Until this time provincial legislatures had acted independently to protest British actions; there had been no body that could claim to speak for Americans as a whole. Now, in 1774, another and greater crisis had finally broken through the selfish localism that had so often governed colonial relations. Americans would continue to resist surrendering local political autonomy to a collective government. But they had taken the first step toward political union.

LEXINGTON AND CONCORD.   In the next months the Patriot leaders prepared for the worst. In every colony men joined militia units, collected arms, ammunition, and gunpowder, and began to engage in military drill. In Massachusetts these groups were called Minute Men because they were expected to "Stand at a minute's warning in Case of alarm." In other provinces the assemblies voted to send money and supplies to the people of Massachusetts, who were suffering economically under the Intolerable Acts. Meanwhile, General Gage, now installed as governor of Massachusetts, prepared his forces for a Patriot attack. Gage particularly feared the Boston Committee of Safety, headed by John Hancock, which had been formed to coordinate Patriot military actions and to call out the Minute Men at the sign of further British provocation.

In mid-April Gage received orders to enforce the Intolerable Acts, by military action if necessary, and to stop Patriot preparations for armed defense. He immediately dispatched a force of 700 men to Concord to destroy Patriot arms caches. Learning of the redcoat destination, the Boston Committee of Safety sent Paul Revere and William Dawes to alert the countryside and warn Hancock and Sam Adams, staying at nearby Lexington, to escape. When the redcoats arrived at Lexington at dawn on April 19, 1775, they found seventy Minute Men waiting for them. After repeated British commands to disperse, the outnumbered Americans complied. At this point someone fired a shot. The British then let off several volleys, killing eight Americans. The Americans replied but got the worst of the exchange. At the end of the skirmish the British occupied Lexington Common.

The redcoats now marched to Concord, where they destroyed some Patriot supplies. By this time the countryside had been thoroughly aroused, and as the British troops straggled back to Boston, they were attacked on every side by colonial militia. The twenty-one miles to Boston became a murderous gauntlet as Minute Men fired at the redcoats from behind walls, barns, and trees. By the time the British reached the safety of Charlestown, 250 had been killed or wounded. Also dead were almost 100 Americans.

* CONCLUSIONS *

Lexington and Concord turned a disagreement into a war. For the next eight years North America would be the arena for struggling armies. At the end there would be an independent United States.

In one sense this momentous result was the climax of the long process we observed in Chapter 3 that had helped to create a distinctive society and culture in America and a feeling among the colonists that they were not simply transplanted Europeans. It was also related to the growing economic and political maturity of British North America. Here, ironically, British policy was itself largely responsible. Unlike the other European colonial powers, Britain had done much to foster colonial political autonomy and economic prosperity. By 1763 British North America had the population, the material resources, and the political self-confidence to defy one of Europe's most powerful nations.

But cultural, political, and economic maturity by themselves were not enough for revolution. The ties to Britain remained too strong. The actual imperial crisis was precipitated by the special circumstances after 1763. One crucial matter was the French and Indian War. By relieving the colonists of a long-standing danger, it weakened American dependence on Britain. At the same time it loaded the British taxpayer with debt and demonstrated to Pitt's Tory successors that the Americans could not be counted on to bear the burdens of empire in an acceptable way.

However justified from the British perspective, the policies adopted after 1763 were foolishly conceived and executed. A few in Britain saw that the American colonies had become a mature society fast approaching England in wealth and numbers; but most Englishmen and, most crucially, King George's Tory ministers could see them only as disobedient children. Charging ahead blindly, Britain imposed measures that threatened many occupational and economic groups, deeply disturbed the elite merchants, lawyers, and planters, and aroused fears among many thousands of ordinary people that they were about to be enslaved and exploited by harpies in the shape of bishops and royal officials.

In short, we cannot separate the economic, religious, and political strands of causation. All these factors motivated the colonists, who eventually sought independence; and in each of these areas we find a common anxiety: fear of oppression. It was a fierce colonial attachment to self-determination in all spheres that was the ultimate source of the American Revolution.

5

THE REVOLUTION

How Did It Change America?

1775	The Second Continental Congress meets in Philadelphia; it declares war on Britain, organizes the Continental Army under George Washington, authorizes a navy, and appoints a Committee of Secret Correspondence; Ethan Allen captures Fort Ticonderoga; The Battle of Breed's (Bunker) Hill in Boston
1776–79	Main theater of war is in middle colonies; Philadelphia and Yorktown occupied by the British
1776	Paper money "continentals" printed; Thomas Paine's *Common Sense*; in Congress Richard Lee of Virginia introduces a resolution of independence from Britain; Congress approves the Declaration of Independence; Congress appoints a committee to plan for a permanent constitution
1777	Congress recommends that states sell Loyalist property; Horatio Gates defeats General Burgoyne at Saratoga, the turning point of the war; Congress approves a draft of the Articles of Confederation
1778	France and the American colonies establish a military alliance
1779	Spain declares war on Great Britain
1779–81	Main theater of war shifts to the southern colonies
1781	Final victory at Yorktown; Articles of Confederation ratified; The colonial monetary system collapses; Congress appoints Robert Morris to organize Bank of North America to strengthen public credit
1782	Americans and British agree on a preliminary peace treaty dealing with the states' western boundaries, fishing rights off Newfoundland, British garrisons in the West, colonial debts, and payment for Loyalist property

1783	The Treaty of Paris brings full independence; Massachusetts court interpretation of the state constitution prohibits slavery; thereafter slavery is illegal in the Bay State
1786	Virginia legislature adopts the principle of separation of church and state in an act drafted by Jefferson

Writing in the summer of 1775, shortly after Lexington and Concord, John Adams described an encounter with a person he had defended in court as an attorney. The man—"a common Horse Jockey," Adams called him—greeted the Founding Father on the road. "Oh! Mr. Adams," he exclaimed, "what great Things have you and your Colleagues done for us! We can never be grateful enough to you. There are no Courts of Justice now in this Province, and I hope there will never be another!" Adams was appalled. Would the future of America be as the "common Horse Jockey" hoped? Would the colonies, in the course of changing governments, jettison all law to protect lives and property and turn their entire social structure upside down? "If the Power of the Country should ever get into such hands," remarked Adams, "and there is great danger that it will, to what purpose have we sacrificed our Time, Health, and every Thing?"

Adams and other moderate Americans worried throughout the war about a takeover of power by the less respectable people of the colonies. Their concern was understandable. Eight years of bitter fighting followed the skirmishes at Lexington and Concord. During that time the American community expended vast amounts of energy and wealth and sacrificed thousands of lives. Surely a struggle of this magnitude—one, moreover, fought in the name of freedom from tyranny—could be expected to undermine conventional values, transform traditional relationships, and weaken long-standing institutions. Did it? The obvious and fundamental result of the American Revolution was independence. But how profoundly did the Revolution change American society? Did Adams's fears prove justified?

∗ AMERICAN PROSPECTS ∗

Americans found it hard to predict what lay ahead in the days following Concord and Lexington. Ties of memory, habit, interest, and affection, and fears of the unknown, all acted as deterrents to a complete break with England. Few as yet wanted independence. Even among the most ardent Patriots the common hope was that Britain would see the light, abandon its punitive policies, and reconsider its fundamental relations with America. This hope was reflected in John Dickinson's Olive Branch Petition adopted by the Second Continental Congress in July 1775, declaring that the colonists remained loyal to King George and asking him to intervene to protect his American subjects against Parliament's tyranny.

Loyalists, needless to say, were even less willing to break with the past. Whether Loyalist or Patriot, virtually all Americans in the spring of 1775 recoiled at the thought of complete independence.

Whatever their ultimate goals, Americans recognized that armed resistance to the mighty British Empire was a risky policy. Britain was probably the strongest nation on earth in 1775. On the face of it, the British had an enormous advantage over the Americans in numbers, military experience, and political cohesion. But they also labored under great difficulties. British military and naval power had declined since the end of the French and Indian War in 1763. Meanwhile, France had rebuilt its military forces and was in a position to challenge Britain again. More serious, Britain's victories in the recent war had left it isolated. France, Spain, Holland, and Russia all feared British power and had grievances that they hoped to redress. These nations, especially France, were potential American allies in 1775. Their hostility to Great Britain would prove indispensable to the American cause.

Britain also faced enormous strategic problems in fighting a war in America. The British Isles were three thousand miles from the military scene, and troops and supplies sent to the battlefields would take two or three months to arrive. When they finally did, the troops would have to fight on unfamiliar terrain, often surrounded by a hostile populace. Americans were on their home ground, close to supplies and manpower, and able to apply the strength they had to the battle at hand.

Yet the "rebels," too, faced colossal difficulties. Several hundred thousand Americans were not only opposed to the Patriot cause but were willing to risk their lives and property to defeat it. The Loyalists would be a great source of strength to the British. Several regiments of Loyalists would fight ferociously against their countrymen. Loyalist troops would be widely feared and detested by the Patriots for their zeal in the crown's cause.

MILITARY FORCES. Few Americans had military experience, let alone the knowledge required for raising, equipping, and leading a large army. A few colonials had served as officers during the French and Indian War, but none, not even George Washington, had held a rank higher than colonel. And the professional foreign soldiers who flocked to America seeking military appointments were often incompetent. The French nobleman, the Marquis de Lafayette, the Germans Johann Kalb (known as Baron de Kalb) and Baron Friedrich Wilhelm von Steuben, and the Pole Thaddeus Kosciusko were skilled soldiers. But there was no officer on the American side who had the experience of commanding large bodies of troops in the field or of planning military strategy for a whole continent.

The colonists were better off in ordinary military manpower. Americans believed then, and would continue to believe for most of their history, that a volunteer soldier was better than a hired mercenary. British redcoats, and still more the Hessians— German soldiers hired by the British king to help put down the rebellion—supposedly lacked the spirit of those fighting for their homeland with freedom in their hearts.

The variety of uniforms in Baron Von Closen's watercolors of colonial troops suggests the fragmentation of Patriot forces during the Revolution. Note the black soldier at the far left.

In reality, American soldiers lacked the rigorous training of the redcoats and this difference often strongly favored the British. On the other hand, most Americans knew how to use a rifle or musket, and in fact, their lack of traditional European military experience helped as much as it hurt. At the outset of a battle, British soldiers were trained to fire unaimed volleys at their opponents and trust to the sheer volume of lead to shock and disrupt the enemy. The ranks would then charge the foe with drawn bayonets. These tactics worked well enough on the open fields of Europe, where opposing armies faced each other in full view. But in the forests that covered so much of the colonies, where men could hide behind every tree and bush, they were unsuitable. Troops equipped with accurate Kentucky rifles, deployed from behind cover were often far more effective. The British tried to modify their tactics to suit American conditions. Loyalist troops, moreover, were familiar with guerrilla fighting and were valuable auxiliaries to the British army. But on the whole, American commanders and enlisted men remained better adapted to war in the colonies than the British.

The Patriot leaders could not count on a consistent and stable supply of manpower. It was one thing for a young man to turn out with his gun for a local skirmish or a few weeks of soldiering. It was another, however, to enlist as a regular in the Continental Army, fight battles against professional soldiers, subject himself to military discipline, and spend months or possibly years away from home and family. It proved hard for the Continental Congress and the individual states to raise troops. At first patriotism was enough to bring in recruits; later, cash bounties and promises of land were necessary to induce men to enlist. Once in the army, the new recruits were hard to keep. Many served just a few months and then, with or without official leave, returned to civilian life. Almost 400,000 men passed through the Continental armies during the war, but George Washington never had more than 20,000 troops under his command at one time.

Supplying the army was also a problem for the Americans. There were many fine gunsmiths in the colonies, but they produced so many types and sizes of weapons that securing the proper ammunition was difficult. There was also a shortage of gunpowder and shot, and the dearth at times threatened to put the entire American army out of action. Artillery was in especially short supply, for the country was not yet capable of manufacturing cannon.

American shipyards could not build ships of the line, the battleships of the day, and the Continental navy could scarcely challenge the British fleet in direct battle. But Americans could produce excellent small craft that served effectively as privateers—armed private ships commissioned to attack the enemy. Privateers provided most of the American naval punch. Licensed by Congress with "letters of marque" to prey on British commerce, they attacked enemy merchant ships even within sight of the British coast. During the war privateers captured 3,200 British ships, at immense cost to Great Britain and its citizens. Privateering helped to balance the great losses suffered by northern shippers from the British blockade of American harbors and seizure of hundreds of American merchant vessels on the high seas.

CREATING A GOVERNMENT. At the beginning, the Second Continental Congress was the country's only central political authority. Although it regularly passed resolutions and proposed emergency measures, the Congress was not an effective government. Sovereignty continued to reside in the individual state governments; in fact, the assemblage in Philadelphia was more like a diplomatic conference of sovereign states than a government. In the end, implementation of every proposal Congress made depended on the support of the thirteen state legislatures, and these as often ignored its wishes as obeyed them.

Despite its limitations, for many months the Second Continental Congress acted as the government for the American people. It created the Continental Army with George Washington as commander in chief. On May 29, 1775, it adopted an address to the people of Canada asking them to join in resisting British tyranny. In July it approved the Olive Branch Petition; and after that was rejected by the king, it disavowed American allegiance to Parliament. That same month Congress established a post office department and appointed commissioners to negotiate peace treaties with the Indians. In the fall of 1775 it authorized a navy for the "United Colonies," and soon after appointed a five-man Committee of Secret Correspondence to approach Britain's European enemies for aid.

WARTIME FINANCE. Still the Americans lacked a strong, effective central government. One of Congress's chief weaknesses was that it had no power to tax. Americans were unused to heavy taxation and during the various colonial wars of the past the individual colonies had met the problem by issuing paper money. Now, once more, Congress and the states resorted to the printing press to pay military contractors, the army, and public officials. The paper money issued by Congress was called "continentals," and by 1780 notes with a face value of $200 million had been circulated. The states issued almost as much during the same period.

The American folk expression "not worth a continental" suggests the fate of this paper money. At first the continentals and state notes kept their face value surprisingly well. But as the volume of issues grew, their purchasing power fell. By 1780, $40 in continentals was worth less than $1 in gold and silver coin. Paper money prices soared so high that a bushel of corn that had sold for $1 in Massachusetts in the spring of 1777 sold for $80 by the summer of 1779.

In a modern nation such hyperinflation is likely to produce social and economic disaster. And the inflation during the struggle for independence did harm some Americans. Patriots who bought Congress's bonds ("loan office certificates") or who accepted "commissary" or "quartermaster certificates"—government IOUs—in payment for supplies and services lost money when prices soared. Inflation also hurt officers and men of the Continental Army and the state forces, whose pay plummeted in value. Still, the effects were limited. No one in those days had bank accounts or life insurance, and in this predominantly rural, agricultural economy relatively few worked for money wages or paid cash for the food they ate or the clothes they wore. Inflation, then, had far milder effects than it would today. And in any event, neither Congress nor the state governments had any real alternative given the tax-avoidance traditions of America and Congress's inability to tax.

∗ THE ROAD TO INDEPENDENCE ∗

EARLY BATTLES. Following the skirmishes at Lexington and Concord, General Gage found himself besieged in Boston by several thousand New England troops. In early June 1775 he prepared to dislodge the rebels from Dorchester Heights. The Americans countered by fortifying Breed's Hill (not Bunker Hill, as legend has it) in Charlestown, across the harbor from Boston. On June 17 British naval vessels began firing on the Americans, and at noon 2,400 redcoats landed on the Charlestown peninsula. Twice the heavily laden "lobster-backs" trudged up Breed's Hill into the murderous fire of the Americans entrenched on top; twice they retreated. The third time General William Howe ordered them to drop their packs and charge with fixed bayonets. This time the redcoats swept the Americans off their perch and off nearby Bunker Hill as well. At the end of the day the British held the field, but at the cost of over 200 dead. Though technically an American defeat, the Battle of Bunker Hill was a moral victory that helped convince Americans they could stand up to British regulars.

Bunker Hill had been preceded by Ethan Allen's daring capture of the small British garrison at Fort Ticonderoga on Lake Champlain. It was followed by a double American thrust northward, led by Benedict Arnold and Richard Montgomery, against Montreal and Quebec, designed to deprive Britain of its Canadian base of operations against the Americans. The expedition was dogged by bad luck and nearly led to disaster for the Americans. Montgomery took Montreal, but

Quebec, defended by British regulars and Canadians who had rejected Congress's invitation to join the struggle against England, held out. In the battle to capture Quebec, Montgomery was killed, Arnold wounded, and several hundred Americans killed or captured.

In the South the early fighting went better for the Americans. There a force of Virginians and North Carolinians encountered the royal governor of Virginia, Lord Dunmore, and his army of white Loyalists and black slaves. The blacks had been promised their freedom if they supported the king. Lord Dunmore's small force fought enthusiastically but was overwhelmed by the Patriots.

The year 1776 began well for the Patriot cause. In a series of actions in the Carolinas between February and June, the Americans beat off the attacks of generals Sir Henry Clinton and Charles Cornwallis. In March, after Continental troops had dragged the artillery captured at Ticonderoga down to within range of Boston, General Howe evacuated the city. The British never seriously threatened New England again.

TURNING POINTS.   As the months of fighting passed, many of the remaining emotional ties to Britain snapped. The use of Hessian mercenaries, the king's contemptuous rejection of the Olive Branch Petition, the December 1775 British proclamation declaring the colonies in open rebellion, and the closing off of all formal commerce with the rebellious Americans—these acts made it increasingly clear to Patriots that reconciliation was impossible. A critical event in the South was Lord Dunmore's arming of the slaves, a move that violated one of the South's strongest racial taboos. Chesapeake planters who had previously held back now rushed to support the Patriot cause.

With each passing day, then, Patriots found it easier to consider independence from Britain as their goal. Their need for allies provided an additional push toward independence. The French leaders viewed the British troubles in America with glee. Resentful of their defeat in the French and Indian War, they hoped to see proud Britain humbled and France restored to an important place in North America. Both France and Spain considered Britain a threat to their Caribbean possessions and expected a weak, independent America to be easier to deal with than the mighty British Empire. Early in 1776 the French foreign minister, the Count de Vergennes, sounded out Spain on aid to the Americans. Soon both countries began to funnel secret money and supplies to the colonists. Americans welcomed the aid but realized that all-out French and Spanish support depended on their own willingness to fight for independence, for only independence would accomplish what the two continental powers wanted: a crippled Britain.

Yet something more was needed to convince most Patriots that they should take the final step. Though disillusioned with Parliament and the king's ministers, Americans retained a touching faith in the king himself and hoped he would see the light. A forty-seven page pamphlet called *Common Sense,* published in early 1776 by a recent immigrant from England, Thomas Paine, destroyed their last illusions. In bold and ringing phrases Paine denounced King George and the British government and insisted that the time had come to sever completely the ties with Britain. Calling George the "royal brute," Paine helped to destroy the colonists' awe of the crown and respect for the king. Far from being a benevolent father to his people, George had unleashed the wrath of redcoats, Hessians, Indians, and desperate slaves on them. He was not worthy of their esteem. Furthermore, monarchy was a form of government condemned by God; kings were "crowned ruffians." Concluded Paine: "The blood of the slain, the weeping voice of nature cries, 'tis time to depart'."

INDEPENDENCE DECLARED. Paine's stirring polemic sold 120,000 copies in three months and was read throughout the colonies. Tories denounced it as treasonous and certain to encourage "republican" views—that is, ideas of popular government. *Common Sense* had an immense impact on Patriots. Washington found it "working a powerful change in the minds of many men." In April a convention of North Carolinians authorized the colony's delegates in Congress to support independence. Virginia, the most populous colony, did the same the following month. Then, on June 7, 1776, Virginia delegate Richard Henry Lee introduced a resolution in the Continental Congress that the United Colonies "are, and of right ought to be, free and independent States." In response to this motion, Congress appointed Thomas Jefferson, Benjamin Franklin, John Adams, Roger Sherman, and Robert Livingston to prepare a document declaring and justifying American independence. At the end of June a draft of the proposed statement, composed largely by Jefferson, was sent to Congress. On July 2, Congress voted unanimously for the principle of independence, and on July 4 it formally approved the revised Declaration of Independence.

The Declaration contained a detailed indictment of King George for cruelties, crimes, and illegal political acts against humanity and America. George was made into a villain who personified British wrongdoing. It was also a statement of the principles governing the drastic action proposed. The signers adopted Paine's radical antimonarchism and the views of the 1689 Whig publicists to justify independence. The people's consent, not the divine right of kings, was the ultimate source of political authority, they declared. Governments were established to assure citizens of "certain unalienable rights," including the rights to "Life, Liberty and the pursuit of Happiness." These words were borrowed from Locke, but significantly changed. Locke had written "life, liberty, and property." Jefferson and his colleagues, though deeply respectful of property, shifted the emphasis to the dignity of individuals and their right to personal fulfillment. The declaration also asserted boldly and bluntly that "all men" were "created equal."

The words that followed these expressed the view, borrowed from the English Whigs, that the people had the right to overthrow a government not based on the "consent of the governed." Revolution should not be resorted to "for light and transient causes." But when, as in this case, "a long train of abuses and usurpations" had been committed, with the goal of an "absolute Despotism," then it was the people's right "to throw off such Government, and to provide new Guards for their future security." Though written in the heat of military and political crisis, the declaration was a moving defense of human freedom, and it would inspire millions around the globe for generations to come.

* THE FIGHT FOR INDEPENDENCE *

The Declaration of Independence was greeted throughout the nation with bonfires, toasts, fireworks, and pealing bells. But there was still a long way to go before the reality of independence could be established. The British, certainly, did not take the declaration at face value. In September 1776 General Howe and his brother, Admiral Richard Howe, met on Staten Island with Benjamin Franklin, John Adams, and Edmund Rutledge, representing Congress, and offered the Americans reconciliation. But first they would have to rescind the Declaration of Independence. The three Americans listened and then firmly rejected the terms. The fighting went on.

THE WAR IN THE EAST, 1776–1777. The war was not going well for the Americans. Howe, in fact, had opened the September negotiations only after trouncing the Americans soundly. Foreseeing Howe's move to make New York the base for British operations in America, Washington had moved his victorious troops south from Boston soon after the British evacuated that city. In July of 1776 Howe landed his forces on Staten Island opposite New York City. At the end of August, with 20,000 men under his command, he attacked Washington's troops on Long Island (Brooklyn Heights) and forced them to flee first to Manhattan, then to White Plains, and then across the Hudson to New Jersey. Howe occupied New York City, and the British kept it until the end of the war. At the very end of the year Washington partly redeemed his defeat in New York by attacking a force of Hessians at Trenton. The German troops, their vigilance impaired by too much Christmas cheer, were taken by surprise, and almost a thousand surrendered to the Americans.

The year 1777 held mixed fortunes for the rebels. Washington won an important victory at Princeton in January and cleared the British out of much of New Jersey. But in the summer Howe and Cornwallis routed the American general Anthony Wayne and occupied Philadelphia, forcing Congress to flee to avoid capture.

Still, 1777 brought the turning point of the war. During the summer, while Howe was moving on Philadelphia, British troops under General John Burgoyne were advancing south from Canada. The British plan was to split the colonies along the line of Lake Champlain and the Hudson River. As Burgoyne moved south, General Clinton in New York was to advance up the Hudson. Clinton did move north but failed to link up with the force coming south. In late June Burgoyne's army of 8,000 British, Canadians, Indians, and Germans left Quebec and advanced on Fort Ticonderoga. They captured the fort but were soon struggling through the dense forests of northern New York, using up their supplies and getting farther and farther from their Canadian base. Near Lake George, Burgoyne's

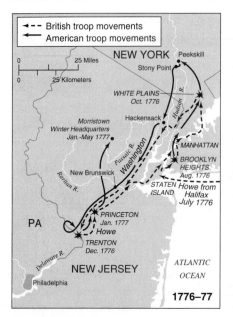

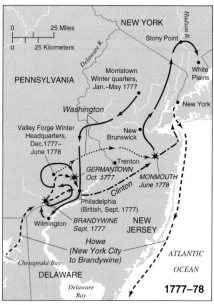

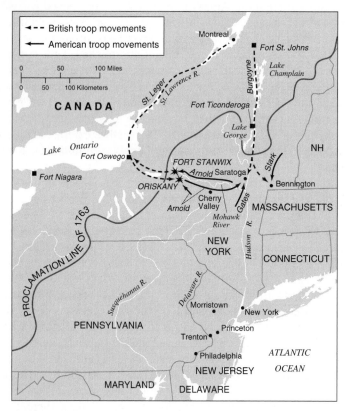

Central Campaigns, 1776–1778

troops encountered stiff resistance from the troops of Horatio Gates. Gates's army consisted of Continental regulars and New England militia who had flocked to his ranks to avenge the brutal killings of civilians by Burgoyne's Indian allies. Burgoyne sought to retreat northward, but the move to escape was futile. At Saratoga he was surrounded, and on October 17, 1777, "Gentleman Johnnie" surrendered his remaining 6,000 men.

THE FRENCH ALLIANCE. The victory at Saratoga convinced the French that the Americans might well make good their claim to independence. In September 1776 Congress had dispatched Silas Deane, Benjamin Franklin, and Arthur Lee to Europe to negotiate treaties with Britain's enemies. Progress at first was slow. Not until January 1778 did Vergennes, the French minister of foreign affairs, tell the American envoys that France was prepared to ally itself with the United States. Soon after that he and the American representatives negotiated two important treaties. The first guaranteed each nation free trading rights with the other. The second was an alliance for joint military effort against Britain, to last until the United States had won its freedom. Each party promised not to conclude a peace with England without the other's consent.

In early May Congress ratified the French treaties. France was now in the war as America's ally. Spain declared war on Britain the following year. The Dutch, too, having clashed with the British over their smuggling of munitions to the rebels through their Caribbean possessions, broke relations with Britain in early 1781, though they never formally declared war. Soon French, Spanish, and later Dutch money—both gifts and loans—began to pour into America, enabling Congress to pay for much-needed arms, food, and equipment. Several other northern European nations, including Russia, Sweden, Prussia, and Denmark, organized the League of Armed Neutrality to keep their vessels supplying the Americans from being stopped by Britain. In all, by the end of the Revolution, Britain had been isolated and placed on the diplomatic defensive. European aid proved indispensable to America.

WAR IN THE WEST. The war that engulfed the older communities of the East also cast its lurid light across the West. On almost every colonial frontier Americans competed with the British for the friendship and aid of the Indians. In this struggle the British often had the advantage: They possessed the trade goods that the Indians wanted and, unlike the American settlers, posed no threat to the Indians' possession of ancestral lands.

The Cherokees proclaimed their allegiance to George III but were fought off by the settlers of western North Carolina in 1775. The infant settlements in eastern Kentucky, established by Richard Henderson and Daniel Boone only months before Lexington and Concord, were more exposed to British-inspired Indian attack. In the summer of 1776 bands of Shawnee and Delaware drove the Kentuckians into refuge in the settlement's three main villages. These remained havens for many whites throughout the war, but away from the log walls of the village stockades, hostile Indians pounced on isolated travelers, stole livestock, and prevented farmers from planting crops.

On the New York frontier the plight of the Americans was even worse. There the British had the support of the powerful Iroquois, under their chief Joseph Brant, and many Loyalists, organized as the Tory Rangers. In the first clash in the region in August 1777, American militia at Fort Stanwix stopped a British advance designed to reinforce Burgoyne, but soon afterward a supporting party of Americans under General Nicholas Herkimer was caught in an ambush at Oriskany, losing 200 men to a force of Indians, Loyalists, and Hessians under Colonel Barry St. Leger. During 1778, the Loyalists attacked the inhabitants of the Wyoming Valley in Pennsylvania and massacred hundreds while the Iroquois spread panic throughout upper New York.

By this time it was clear that defensive policies in the West had not worked. In the summer of 1778 the Kentuckians, led by George Rogers Clark, determined on their own to go on the attack. Clark and his men soon seized most of the northwestern settlements established by the French a generation before. In 1779 Congress itself finally sent several expeditions to nail down the West for the United States. Forays led by Clark himself and by Colonel Daniel Brodhead and General John Sullivan succeeded, but others failed and threatened to undo much of their work. By the time the war ended, the Americans were in firm possession of the frontier in the South, but the British controlled the Northwest. The war in the West ended in a draw.

EASTERN BATTLES, 1778–1780.   It was in the older settlements that the war was won. At news of the British defeat at Saratoga in 1777, Lord North, now prime minister, expressed his heartfelt desire to get out of the "damned war." By now British taxpayers were complaining of the war's high costs, and British merchants, badly hurt by the loss of American trade, were in desperate straits. Hoping to avert the impending alliance between France and America, North dispatched a commission under the Earl of Carlisle to offer the Americans new terms for reconciliation, including ending all efforts to impose revenue taxes on America and suspending all parliamentary acts for America passed since 1763. When this effort failed, North offered to resign; but the king, who remained stubbornly and bitterly opposed to American independence, insisted that he remain.

The Americans, too, had their problems after Saratoga. In fact, the winter of 1777–1778 is generally considered the low point for Washington's army. Worn down by sickness and losses, the Continental Army withdrew to winter quarters at Valley Forge, just twenty miles from Philadelphia, where the British were living in comfort. Valley Forge was a wretched place. Recent fighting had left the area denuded of supplies. Food and clothing might have been brought in, but a breakdown of supply services left the men cold, hungry, and ill-clothed. To make matters worse, discontent was rife among the officers, whose salaries were small and often unpaid. Eventually Congress improved the pay situation, and a new quartermaster general, Nathanael Greene, established a more efficient supply service. Even so, the Continental Army barely survived the awful winter.

For the next three years the fighting went on intermittently and inconclusively. In the winter of 1778–1779 the British won control of Georgia by taking Savannah and Augusta. In 1780 General Sir Henry Clinton captured Charleston, South Carolina, along with 5,000 American troops and 300 guns. Heartened by Clinton's victory, suppressed South Carolina Loyalists now rushed to take up arms against their countrymen. Horatio Gates, the hero of Saratoga, attempted to retake the state for Congress, but was badly beaten by Cornwallis at Camden.

Fighting continued in the north as well. In August 1778 a joint Franco-American operation to capture Newport failed when a storm drove off the French fleet under Admiral d'Estaing. In New Jersey, New York, and the West the Americans were more successful. In July 1779 Anthony Wayne's troops captured a British garrison of 700 at Stony Point on the Hudson at the cost of only 15 American lives. In August "Lighthorse Harry" Lee drove the last British troops out of New Jersey.

VICTORY AT YORKTOWN.   The years 1780 and 1781 were full of confused advances and retreats, and American morale sank almost as low as during the Valley Forge winter. In May 1780 Washington's troops near Morristown, New Jersey, nearly mutinied. Restlessness among front-line regiments continued through the following year. In January 1781 troops on the Pennsylvania and New Jersey lines did rebel.

The lowest ranks of the army were not the only ones disaffected. In the fall of 1780, papers carried by captured British Major John André revealed that General Benedict Arnold, now commanding the American troops at West Point, planned to surrender his vital post to the British. When Arnold learned of André's capture, he fled to the British lines and eventually became an officer in the king's forces.

Although initially discouraging, the year 1781 brought final military victory at Yorktown. The Yorktown campaign opened in April 1781, when General Cornwallis marched north from his base in North Carolina, hoping to crush the American forces in Virginia. He soon collided with troops under Lafayette. For four months Cornwallis and Lafayette danced around one another without reaching a showdown. When Wayne came to Lafayette's aid, the British commander retreated to the coast, hoping to establish a base where the Royal Navy could protect and supply him.

Washington heard of Cornwallis's move while he was besieging the British at New York. He quickly abandoned his effort to recapture the city and moved south. The moment was especially favorable because the French fleet under Count de Grasse could now join the attack. De Grasse soon stationed his ships off the Virginia coast, where Lafayette had pushed Cornwallis onto the narrow Yorktown peninsula. On September 14 Washington's troops and 5,000 French soldiers led by the Count de Rochambeau arrived at Yorktown. Bit by bit, remorseless French and American pressure reduced the area under British control. Cornwallis had counted on help from the sea, but the French fleet was too strong for the British navy. Under relentless attack, Cornwallis notified Henry Clinton, his superior in New York: "If you cannot relieve me very soon, you must prepare to hear the worst."

General Clinton set out on his rescue mission on October 19. But he was too late. Three days earlier Cornwallis had made a desperate attempt to escape across the York River and had been frustrated by a storm. Seeing all hope for his army gone, the British general resolved to surrender. On October 19, 1781, 7,000 British and Hessian troops laid down their arms. Legend has it that as the defeated army marched out of its camp, the British military bands played a tune called "The World Turned Upside Down." The musicians' choice was prophetic. Yorktown was not only the last important battle of the war; it was also the end of the old British Empire.

∗ THE ARTICLES OF CONFEDERATION ∗

Victory had come not a moment too soon. By the fall of 1781 the United States was in serious financial trouble, its monetary system collapsing and prices and wages soaring out of sight. In the last months of the war Congress appointed Robert Morris, a shrewd Philadelphia businessman, as superintendent of finance. He proceeded to reorganize the government's financial affairs, strengthen the public credit, and eliminate waste in the budget. Soon after taking office he also organized the Bank of North America, the first commercial bank in the United States.

The closing months of the war also saw the beginning of a new American government. It had taken the states almost five years to agree on a new political structure. In the meantime, as we have seen, the Continental Congress had acted as the American government. Little more than a convention of sovereign powers, it had not been effective, and since the beginning of the war it had been clear to most American leaders that the country needed a more formal and permanent central authority. In June 1776 Congress had appointed a committee led by John Dickinson of Delaware to establish a constitution for the United States that would end all doubt about congressional authority to conduct war and would provide the structure for a permanent union. The committee's proposal called for a legislature in which each state would have one vote. The new congress would have fairly broad powers, but not the power to tax—Americans remained tax-shy. Instead, it might ask the states for contributions proportional to their population.

The Dickinson scheme immediately came under attack. Delegates from large states complained that small states would be overrepresented since each, regardless of population, would have one vote in the proposed congress. At the same time, states with large slave populations thought that basing financial contributions on total population was unfair. Slaves, they pointed out, were only property, not citizens, and so should not be counted.

The major stumbling block, however, was that the plan gave the proposed congress the power to set westward limits to the states, to grant lands to private parties in regions beyond those limits, and to create new states in the West. This scheme stepped on many toes. Seven states claimed that their boundaries extended well into the trans-Appalachian region. Six states, on the other hand— New Hampshire, New Jersey, Rhode Island, Pennsylvania, Delaware, and Maryland—had no claims to western lands and favored Congressional control.

Why, they asked, should the common struggle to win independence lead to a few states grabbing the western domain that all had fought for? Maryland and Pennsylvania investors had added worries: they had bought lands in the northwest from the Indians and feared that Virginia's claims would nullify their purchases.

The opponents of the initial plan delayed its consideration until the fall of 1777. This time, with the provision that each state would have one vote, it passed Congress. To go into effect the plan now needed acceptance by all the states. It won the support of twelve by the end of 1778, but Maryland refused to go along with it because her big neighbor, Virginia, still retained title to the lion's share of the upper Mississippi Valley. Months of jockeying followed until the Virginia delegates agreed to accept congressional control of the western region. Finally, in March 1781, with Maryland's objections withdrawn, Congress announced the formal adoption of the Articles of Confederation.

The Articles were a clear improvement over the old arrangements. Most important, they formalized the union of the American states. In specific terms, they gave legal standing to several powers that the Continental Congress had exercised earlier. The Confederation Congress could conduct war and foreign affairs, make commercial treaties, and negotiate with the Indians. It could borrow and coin money and issue bills of credit. The Articles also gave Congress the new power to manage public lands in the West.

Yet many imperfections remained. The new government consisted of only a legislature; it had no separate executive or judicial branches. And not all of the new Congress's powers were exclusive. The states could continue to deal directly with foreign governments and engage in war with Congress's consent. They could borrow, maintain mints, and issue bills of credit even without Congressional approval. The states also had the sole right to legislate in matters concerning debts, contracts, and private affairs. Most important of all, they alone could levy taxes. And if experience showed that changes in the Articles were desirable, they would be hard to make; amendments required the consent of every state.

Still, the Articles of Confederation were a substantial move toward American national unity. The Continental Congress had been a makeshift, purely voluntary association entered into to deal with the imperial crisis. Now, with the Articles of Confederation, for the first time there was a permanent American government, one that would speak for the citizens of all the states.

∗ SOCIAL CHANGE ∗

The growing sense of a common nationality was only one of many changes that the war initiated. As Americans looked around them between 1775 and 1783, many were certain that they were also witnessing a social revolution. American Loyalists, particularly, believed the rebels were more intent on overthrowing the social order than in righting the wrongs of imperial government. The Reverend Samuel Peters of Connecticut called the Patriots "ungovernable, righteous and high-handed moberenes." Another Yankee Loyalist saw Patriot control of Massachusetts after 1775 as the triumph of the rabble:

Everything I see is laughable, cursable, and damnable; my pew in the church is converted into a pork tub; my house into a den of rebels, thieves and lice, my farm in possession of the very worst of all God's creatures; my few debts all gone to the devil with my debtors.

The suffering these Tories had endured at the hands of their rebel fellow Americans doubtless colored their attitudes. But even Patriots felt uneasy about the class resentment and the "levelling spirit" that disorder and change had brought to the surface. Langdon Carter of Virginia worriedly reported to Washington that some Patriots in his neighborhood wanted "a form of government that, by being independent of rich men, every man would then be able to do as he pleased." John Adams, after recounting his meeting with the disrespectful "Horse Jockey," described earlier, exclaimed: "Surely we must guard against this Spirit and these Principles or We shall repent of all our Conduct. . . . "

Carter, Adams, and other moderates feared that what had begun as a dispute over the governing of the empire was turning into a social revolution. A number of modern historians, too, have seen the War of Independence as an internal revolution. As one, Carl Becker, expressed it, the war with Britain was as much over "who shall rule at home" as over "home-rule."

A REVOLUTIONARY EXPERIENCE? The French Revolution of 1789 and the Russian Revolution of 1917 are prototypes of what most of us consider social revolutions. These events are abrupt and often violent overthrows of an elite that has monopolized power and enjoyed much of a society's wealth and privileges, by new rulers, claiming to speak for the poor and the powerless. The victors then expel or exterminate the old "oppressors," seize their property, and distribute it among "the people." Let us consider whether this model resembles the course of events in America between 1775 and 1783. Was the American struggle for independence a social revolution?

The term revolution *does* fit some of the change during these years. The fate of the American Loyalists, about 20 percent of the population, resembles the fate of the French elite at the end of the eighteenth century and the Russian at the beginning of the twentieth. During and immediately after the Revolutionary War, some 80,000 Loyalists fled the United States to settle in Upper Canada (present-day Ontario), the Canadian Maritime Provinces, England, and the West Indies. Often they left hurriedly, just before the Patriot mob intent on hanging or tar-and-feathering arrived. Many abandoned their property—which the Patriot state governments usually confiscated—or sold it in a panic at knockdown prices. This exile and confiscation or forced sale of property looks very much like social revolution. By removing an elite of rich landowners, prosperous attorneys, and successful merchants and dividing their property among those, presumably poorer Americans who remained, surely America became more democratic and more equal.

The facts only partially support such a conclusion, however. Loyalists were not all from the upper crust. They came from every sector of colonial society. Many of the leading Tories certainly were "high-toned" folk. Rich merchants and landlords, successful lawyers, royal officials, and many of the Anglican clergy supported the British cause. On the other hand, many poor people, especially in rural areas, also chose to fight for the king. In New York, the tenants of the Hudson Valley landlords were promised the lands of Patriot patroons if they remained loyal, and many did. In the back country of the Carolinas, where small farmers bitterly resented the political domination by the rich Patriot leaders on the seaboard, there were yeoman Loyalists. There were even black Tories. Lured by promises of freedom if they deserted their masters and fought the rebels, thousands of blacks joined the crown's forces. So alarming was this defection that, to counter it, Congress reversed Washington's policy of rejecting black enlistees in the Continental Army. Thereafter, black soldiers, both slaves and free men, fought in the American army. Nevertheless, many blacks continued to prefer the king. When the war ended, hundreds of them refused to remain in the land where they had been enslaved and departed for Canada or the Caribbean with other Loyalists.

Patriots, too, came from both the highest and lowest ends of colonial society. Slaves, as we noted, fought for the Patriot cause, as did seamen, apprentices, artisans, and journeymen of the port towns. But so did a large portion of the colonial elite, from the planters of the South to the great merchants of New England and the middle colonies. As for the middle class of small farmers and shopkeepers, it was they, or at least their sons, who formed the backbone of the Continental Army. In short, the Patriots were anything but "a rabble," as some Tories claimed. They were a cross section of the American people.

So there were only marginal differences between the social standing of those who supported independence and stayed in America and those who fought it and left. The Tory exodus did not deprive the country of a ruling class as did the departure of emigrés from France in the 1790's and "white Russians" from the land of the czars in 1917–1918. The exodus, accordingly, lends little support to the idea of an American social revolution between 1775 and 1783.

And what of the redistribution of wealth, the second standard by which we may identify a social revolution? The property of many Loyalist grandees, especially those who fled to the British lines during the war, was indeed taken by state governments. Did these seizures revolutionize existing property-holding patterns? Probably not. Late eighteenth-century America was not, after all, a society of a few great landlords and a vast landless peasantry, like France in 1789 and Russia in 1917. Many people already owned land, and the amount confiscated from the Tories could not have affected the balance very much. Even if every acre seized had been handed over to the landless, it would not have done much to equalize land-holding. Besides, when the states sold the confiscated farm acres and town lots, they did not generally go to the "common folk." Much of it, it seems, was snapped up by Patriot landholders or speculators. Existing inequalities, if anything, were probably magnified by the resale of confiscated Tory real estate.

It seems clear, then, that the expulsion and expropriation of the Loyalists did little to change the social profile of the community or the nature of property-holding in America. But this is not to say that the Revolution did not liberalize American life. Indeed, there is good evidence that it helped in many ways to make America a more democratic community.

DEMOCRATIZATION. Even if the Tory exiles included members of the "lower orders" and the middle class, historian Gordon Wood believes that a large proportion of the families at the very apex of colonial life departed en masse. Though not numerous, they were particularly powerful and their departure, he believes, broke the crust, allowing new families to rise. This new upper class depended more on merit and achievement and less on "connections" for its wealth and power.

More significant, perhaps, was the growing concern for equity and social justice that accompanied the Revolution. Slavery, the most blatant social inequity in America, was weakened by the Revolution.

Although white Americans were mostly concerned with their own rights and freedoms, the dispute with Britain following 1763 forced them to ponder the issue of human liberty. Not all Patriots were able to protest colonial servitude to Britain and at the same time ignore the slaves' bondage. How can we "reconcile the exercise of slavery with our professions of freedom," Richard Wells, a Philadelphia Patriot, asked pointedly. John Allen, a Baptist minister in Massachusetts, accused his fellow Americans of hypocrisy in refusing to admit the evil of slavery. "Blush . . . ye trifling patriots! who are making a vain parade of being advocates for the liberties of mankind, [and] . . . are . . . thus making a mockery of your profession by trampling on the sacred and natural rights and privileges of Africans."

Happily, the attack on slavery went beyond words. In 1775, the Quakers in Philadelphia established the first antislavery society. Five years later Pennsylvania passed the first law providing for the gradual freeing of slaves. In 1783 the Massachusetts courts interpreted the state constitution as prohibiting slavery, and thereafter slavery was illegal in the Bay State. Other northern states soon followed these leaders, ending slavery either by judicial act or by adopting gradual emancipation laws for slaves who reached a stipulated age. Even in the South slavery was affected by the Revolutionary ferment of egalitarianism. Prominent Patriots such as Jefferson and Henry Laurens, imbued with the ideals of the Enlightenment, attacked the system. Several southern legislatures passed laws making it easier for masters to free (manumit) their own slaves and restricting the slave trade in various ways. By the end of the century, in every state from Pennsylvania northward, slavery was on the way to extinction, and it seemed to some Americans that even in the South it was in decline.

Another sign of the revolutionary zeal for freedom was the decline of indentured servitude, the system of unfree labor that had met the work needs of the colonies and helped facilitate the transfer of people across the Atlantic from Europe. In the new atmosphere of challenge to authority many Americans began to think that keeping people in near bondage, even if only for a period of years, was anachronistic. Believing that indenture was "contrary to . . . the idea of liberty" America had "so happily established," in 1784 a group in New York raised a public subscription for a shipload of servants so they would not have to accept the condition of indentured servitude.

Lawbreakers too benefited from the changes in attitudes awakened by the struggle for independence. Before the Revolution, and for years after, men and women convicted of felonies were often subject to brutal penalties. Criminals were placed in stocks, branded, whipped, and mutilated. The list of crimes with death as the penalty was appallingly long. After 1776, however, several states reduced the number of crimes punishable by hanging and replaced torture and the lash with imprisonment. In Pennsylvania, soon after independence, some effort was even made to replace harsh punishments with reformation of offenders. The purpose of sentencing, said the state legislature, should be "to reclaim rather than destroy. . . . " Years would pass before other states would imitate Pennsylvania, but clearly in this area too the Revolution was a minor watershed.

Finally, there was improvement in the status of women. During the war American women had contributed to the Patriot cause in age-old ways. They made blankets and shirts for Washington's army and spun woolen cloth to offset restricted British imports. They took over jobs and businesses in the absence of male family heads. "I find it necessary to be directress of our husbandry," Abigail Adams wrote John in 1776, and "I hope in time to have the reputation of being as good a farmer as my partner has of being a good statesman." They also expanded their horizons. Some became active in fund-raising for the Continental Army or participated in other Patriot causes. Others developed interests in public issues they had neglected before and joined political discussion groups. A very few women actually engaged in combat. Mary Ludwig Hays McCauley, better known as Molly Pitcher, took her husband's place behind a cannon at the Battle of Monmouth when he was overcome by the heat.

Some women expected their sex to benefit as a group from the war. The spirited Abigail Adams wrote her husband in 1776 that "in the new code of laws" then being considered by Congress—that is, the Articles of Confederation—it was important for the legislators to "remember the ladies and be more generous and favorable to them" than their predecessors had been. "Do not," she urged, "put such unlimited powers in the hands of the husbands."

Abigail Adams and those who thought like her would not fully realize their hopes. And yet the war and the forces it released did have some effect on women's circumstances. In New England the rhetoric of freedom led to liberalized divorce laws that placed women on virtually the same plane as men in seeking legal separation from a brutal or unfaithful spouse. In many states, the laws for the first time recognized the equal right of sons and daughters in inheritance and gave women greater control over their property. The years of debate over American rights also stimulated the first feminist questioning of existing female education. Most of the great battles for female "emancipation" lay in the future. Yet we must not dismiss the revolutionary impulse entirely as a force for female liberation.

NEW POLITICS.   The political system also felt the liberalizing effects of the great upheaval. As they transformed themselves from provinces to "states," the former colonies changed royal charters to constitutions. In some the structural changes were relatively modest. In others, however, there were more sweeping changes. Virginia, Pennsylvania, North Carolina, and Massachusetts ended or reduced the gross underrepresentation of their frontier counties. Pennsylvania, Delaware, North Carolina, Georgia, and Virginia liberalized their franchises so that almost any white male taxpayer, no matter how poor, could vote. Most states reduced the power of the executive branch, considered aristocratic, by taking away the governor's veto over laws passed by the assemblies. Pennsylvania entirely eliminated the legislature's upper house, thereby concentrating all power in the lower one, and fragmented the executive branch by replacing the governor with an executive council of thirteen members. Virginia and several other states pioneered an important democratic advance by adopting formal written bills of rights guaranteeing freedom of speech, conscience, assembly, petition, and privacy, as well as the right to trial by jury and other legal safeguards for the individual.

A final democratic innovation of these years was the constitutional convention, a meeting called for the specific purpose of altering the fundamental frame of government. Only such a convention, it was believed, could validly express the wishes of the people. Its decisions, especially when confirmed by a direct vote of the electors (referendum), took precedence over actions of a mere legislature. First put in practice by Massachusetts during the Revolutionary era, the concept that a convention best expressed the will of the people governed the call for the federal Constitutional Convention in 1787. It was a major contribution to democratic theory and practice.

The use of conventions to frame instruments of fundamental law reflected the new idea that in some ultimate sense "the people" alone were the source of power. Republicanism was a related concept. Republicans wished to reduce the role of birth, breeding, rank, and family influence in political life. These seemed relics of colonial days and royal government when, despite the widespread franchise, Americans had acknowledged hereditary authority and shown deference to officials. Now, said republicans, only talent, virtue, and devotion to the common good should qualify a person for political advancement and high office.

We must qualify the view that the Revolution liberalized political ideology, however. The leaders of the Revolution were carried by the logic of their opposition to royal government to condemn hereditary privileges, but few of them ever got over their fear of pure democracy, in which numbers alone counted and everyone was politically equal. Though they acknowledged that "the people" were the source of power, they did not include women, blacks, Indians, and men without some property in the term. Moreover, except for a few "violent men"—or, as we would say, radicals—republicans did not believe that elected representatives should submit totally to the wishes of the voters. Instead, they favored a "mixed" government in which the popular voice representing "numbers" would be tempered by "talent" of superior leaders.

PRIVILEGE.   Colonial law had upheld the privileged position of several specific institutions and individuals; here, too, the Revolution had a liberalizing effect. In those states with an established Anglican Church there was progress toward the complete religious toleration and separation of church and state that we have come to consider peculiarly American. It was inevitable that Anglicanism, the denomination most closely associated with the English crown, should lose standing after the Declaration of Independence. But the whole idea of an established church had become increasingly distasteful to Patriots. During the war, Jefferson, allied with Virginia's Baptists, Methodists, and other dissenters, fought to disestablish Anglicanism in the state. Afterwards, he and his allies secured passage of the Bill for Establishing Religious Freedom (1786). Other states also disestablished the Anglican church, and several of them removed the remaining restrictions on non-Protestant voting and office-holding.

The Congregationalists' privileged position was a tougher nut to crack. Though many New Englanders had become Baptists, the religious outsiders at first made little progress toward ending the special status of the region's Congregational churches. Unlike the Anglicans, Congregationalism was not identified with the mother country. In fact, the Congregational clergy had been among the most ardent defenders of the Patriot cause. This close association with the fight against Britain gave the Congregational establishment an extended lease on life. Connecticut did not disestablish the Congregational church until 1818. In Massachusetts its privileged position lasted until 1838. It took more than half a century, then, before New England finally achieved the separation of church and state that came elsewhere during the 1780s and 1790s. Yet on the whole, in religious matters too, the Revolution was a major liberalizing force in American life.

The Revolution also ended entail and primogeniture, two practices that reinforced economic inequality and privilege. *Entailing* was a legal procedure that allowed a property holder to forbid his heirs to sell their inheritances. *Primogeniture* was the practice of favoring the firstborn son in inheritances in the absence of a will providing for a more equal property distribution. Together these two practices were designed to preserve large landholdings and buttress the power and wealth of aristocratic families. In 1776, Jefferson drafted a law that abolished entail in Virginia. Similar laws were soon adopted in other states. In 1777, the Georgia legislature prohibited primogeniture, and by 1800 the practice was dead everywhere in America.

* MAKING THE PEACE *

Much of this liberating change took place against the background of war. But the terms of peace had to be settled before their effects could be felt.

France and the United States had agreed not to negotiate a separate peace with Great Britain, but both countries found it hard to resist working out their own arrangements. By 1781 the French were tired of the war and beset by financial problems so serious that they would soon threaten the French monarchy's survival. Having achieved their prime goal of humbling the arrogant British, they saw little reason to continue the fighting. The Americans, too, if conceded their independence, had little reason to fight on. However, there was stubborn Spain. The 1778 treaty with France that brought Spain into the war promised that it be given Gibraltar—the great British fortress guarding the Atlantic entrance of the Mediterranean—if Spanish troops could capture it. But month after month the British defenders held out against the Spanish siege, depriving the Madrid government of its goal. If France stuck by its European ally, it looked as if peace—and American independence—depended on the transfer of a pile of rock.

Fortunately, the American peace negotiators proved adept. In early 1782 Lord North, discredited by the defeat at Yorktown, finally resigned and his successor, the Marquis of Rockingham, prepared to concede independence to America. When Rockingham died, negotiations with the Americans were taken over by Lord Shelburne, a man willing to accept American independence only as a last resort. But Shelburne miscalculated. He sent to Paris as British negotiator, Richard Oswald, a philosophical Scottish gentleman, an old friend of Benjamin Franklin from the Philadelphian's London days. Oswald proved to be exceptionally accommodating. When Franklin proposed a settlement that included as "necessary" terms independence "full and complete in every sense," the total evacuation of all British troops from American soil, boundaries for the new nation that extended to the Mississippi in the west and the Great Lakes to the north, and free access for American fishermen to the Grand Banks off Newfoundland, Oswald saw no objections. Nor did he even balk at one of Franklin's secondary, but "desirable," terms: the concession of Canada to the new American nation!

At Versailles a lady offers Benjamin Franklin a laurel wreath, perhaps to replace the fur cap he often wore to charm the French court. Franklin, a marvelous diplomat, secured formal recognition of the United States and a military and commercial alliance with France; later he helped negotiate the Treaty of Paris, which brought the war to a close.

But difficulties with France soon intervened. Franklin trusted Vergennes, the French foreign minister, but Franklin's colleague, John Jay, who had joined in the Paris negotiations, did not. Jay correctly believed that the French did not intend to make peace until Spain, France's other ally, got what it wanted from the war. But beyond its obligations to its ally, France wanted different things from the peace than the United States. Seeking to protect their own rights on the Grand Banks, the French were unwilling to stand behind American claims to fishing rights off Newfoundland. Vergennes even seemed ready to accept boundaries for the United States that surrendered much of the lower Mississippi Valley to Spain and conceded the northwest to Great Britain.

Hoping to divide its enemies and save Gibraltar, Britain pushed its separate negotiations with the United States. On October 5, 1782, Jay and Oswald, without France, agreed on a draft for preliminary articles of peace, not to go into effect, however, until France and Britain had entered into a similar preliminary agreement. The terms at their core included all of Franklin's earlier primary demands. In London the British ministry insisted that compensation for Loyalist property confiscated during the war and repayment in British money for all debts owed by Americans to British creditors be added to these terms. John Adams, now in Paris to join the negotiations, urged acceptance of these features, and they were included in the final draft.

As finalized, the peace articles acknowledged American independence. The new nation's boundaries would be generous: in the west the Mississippi; to the south to Spanish Florida; to the northwest the Great Lakes; and in the northeast an ill-defined line roughly corresponding to the present Canadian-American boundary. The British agreed to allow Americans to fish off Canadian territorial waters and promised to evacuate American territory still under British occupation "with all convenient speed." In return, the United States promised to place "no lawful impediment" in the way of repayment by Americans of debts owed British creditors and agreed to recommend that the states restore to the Loyalists their civil rights and their confiscated property.

Before signing, the American negotiators considered whether to first inform the French of the peace terms and ask their permission to proceed. Besides the moral obligation enjoined by the 1778 Franco-American treaty, Congress had so instructed them. They decided against it for fear that France, with its own agenda, would scuttle the agreement. Yet they could not cut France out entirely. After the treaty was initialled, Franklin went to tell Vergennes of their action. Sheepishly admitting some "impropriety" to the French Foreign Minister, he urged him strongly to accept the agreement. The French by now were thoroughly tired of the war, and Vergennes chose not to be offended. Instead, he approached the Spanish ambassador in Paris and told him that American perfidy had left France unable to support Spain's claims to Gibraltar any longer. The Count de Aranda saw the light. With this hurdle pushed aside, Spain and France concluded a peace with Great Britain. On September 3, 1783, all these preliminary negotiations, including the Anglo-American articles of agreement, were incorporated into the Treaty of Paris. The great struggle for independence was over.

* CONCLUSIONS *

At news of the peace, a wave of elation and thanksgiving surged through the country. So intense was the joy in Philadelphia that prudent citizens urged the city fathers to restrain the celebration to keep it from getting out of hand.

The jubilant mood could not last. Americans now confronted the problems of repairing the damage of seven long years of war and learning how to function as an independent state. The difficulties would be formidable. The war had caused extensive physical destruction to both the cities and the countryside. In the South the British had carried off thousands of slaves and destroyed dikes and dams. New Jersey, "cockpit of the Revolution," where so many battles had been fought, had been ravaged by advancing and retreating armies. All this damage would have to be repaired.

There would be social mending to do as well. Loyalists—those who had not fled for good—would have to be reconciled to the new regime. Several thousand free blacks in the North would have to be absorbed into the larger society. But on the whole, these adjustments would be minor. American society had not undergone a true social revolution. The war had accelerated processes that had long been moving the American community toward greater democracy, legal equality, and religious toleration. Between 1776 and 1783, religious establishments had been severely undercut, slavery had been eroded, the treatment of women and prisoners had improved, and the few surviving vestiges of feudalism had been swept away. Yet compared with the fundamental upheaval that marked the great French Revolution of 1789 and the Russian and Chinese revolutions of our own century, these were relatively small changes.

But if America had not experienced a major social revolution, it did undergo a political one. From a colony it became an independent nation. The Revolutionary War was primarily a colonial war of independence. If it resembles any upheaval of recent times, it is the decolonization struggles of African and Asian peoples after World War II. And the problems that the new nation would face belonged largely in the same realm: the political. Though the war had advanced the unity of English-speaking America and helped create a sense of shared nationality, it had not forged a cohesive nation. Previous republics had always been small, homogeneous city-states. Never had one been so huge in extent. Could this unusual creation called the United States, with its 900,000 square miles and 3 million people, survive and prosper as an independent republic? In the next few years the issue would be put to the test.

6

THE ORIGINS OF
THE CONSTITUTION

By Popular Demand?

1781	Articles of Confederation ratified; Congress proposes a duty on imports to raise revenue, but it is defeated by Rhode Island
1783	Congress proposes another import duty, it is defeated by New York; Fearing attack by unpaid American troops, Congress flees Philadelphia; Robert Morris sends Empress of China to open trade with China
1784	Spain refuses to allow Americans to transship their goods from New Orleans
1785	Congress adopts the Land Ordinance of 1785, a model for future federal land policy; Maryland and Virginia sign an agreement about navigation rights on the Potomac and in the Chesapeake Bay
1785–87	Shays's Rebellion in Massachusetts
1787	The Ordinance of 1787 prohibits slavery in the Northwest Territory and establishes that new states carved from it will be fully equal to the original states; Constitutional Convention meets at Philadelphia, state delegations approve the completed draft of the Constitution
1788	Delaware, Pennsylvania, New Jersey, Georgia, and Connecticut ratify the Constitution; Massachusetts ratifies with a request for a Bill of Rights; Rhode Island rejects; Maryland, South Carolina, and New Hampshire ratify; Congress certifies adoption of the Constitution; Virginia ratifies with a request for a Bill of Rights; New York ratifies; Congress adopts the first ten amendments to the Constitution (the Bill of Rights); Rhode Island and North Carolina ratify
1789	George Washington becomes president; John Adams, vice president

The great nineteenth-century English statesman William Gladstone once described the American federal Constitution as "the most remarkable work—in modern times—to have been produced by the human intellect at a single stroke in its application to political affairs." Clearly the Constitution is not a perfect document, for we have amended it twenty-six times. But few citizens today would deny that our frame of government has served the nation extraordinarily well over more than two centuries.

It required a prodigious act of faith and will to abandon the Articles of Confederation and replace them with a new political framework for the federal union. The states had ratified the Articles only six years earlier, and although by no means perfect, they had established the sort of political union most Americans wanted. Indeed, to the end of the Confederation period, the Articles would have many loyal supporters. Obviously the influential Americans who assembled in Philadelphia in the summer of 1787 to create a new constitution for the United States must have had a change of heart. Who were these people and what caused them to alter their views?

The origins of the federal Constitution have interested historians for many years. In the nineteenth century it was usually held that the failings and inadequacies of the Articles were so obvious that all could see them. John Fiske called the Confederation period—the time between the British surrender at Yorktown in 1781 and the establishment in 1788 of the new federal government under the Constitution—the "Critical Period." He believed that during these years the nation was "rapidly drifting toward anarchy." Because the Articles were unable to provide the political and social glue to hold the country together, the calling of the Constitutional Convention and the adoption of the document it produced were merely the logical and valid results of broad public concern. The Constitution, in effect, carried to its natural conclusion the nationalistic trend of the Revolution itself.

Fiske's view reflected the patriotic self-congratulation that was common among nineteenth-century Americans. In our own century this has given way to greater skepticism. Just before World War I, Charles A. Beard attacked Fiske's interpretation. The Critical Period, he said, was not very critical. The United States was "in many respects steadily recovering order and prosperity," and "the economic condition of the country seemed to be improving." Ultimately, Beard wrote, the only important group suffering under the Articles had been those who held the wartime securities of the Continental and state governments. These few but powerful individuals wanted the public debts fully repaid, and feared that the state governments and the Confederation Congress would yield to pressure from taxpayers to scale down or repudiate the debts. A democratic system would favor the taxpayers. To protect their interests, creditors had to establish a strong central government that could check the power of majorities and also had sufficient taxing power to pay the public debts. The American federal Constitution of 1787, Beard and his disciples insisted, was a reactionary document intended to restore the power an elite had lost during the Revolution. It was not justified by broad national need or demanded by popular majority; instead, it was intended to protect the economic interests of the powerful.

Let us examine the state of the nation in the 1780s to see which of these interpretations is more convincing, to see how and why the Constitution replaced the Articles of Confederation and became the fundamental law under which Americans have lived for more than two centuries.

* AMERICA IN THE 1780s *

AGRICULTURE. Peace with Britain brought economic troubles to American farmers. During the war years armies had swept across the countryside, destroying fences and barns, burning crops and farmhouses. On the frontier Indian raids had pushed back the line of settled farming. In the Carolinas the dikes that controlled the tidal streams in the rice country had been damaged by hostile troops and by neglect. In Virginia the flight of Loyalist slaves and the removal of others by the British had seriously depleted the labor force on the plantations. In 1783 America faced a major repair job.

In time the physical damage and the labor disruption were mended, but political changes continued to cause difficulties for American agriculture. The severing of imperial ties had unforeseen consequences for farmers. Once the war ended, the British government rescinded the bounty that it had paid indigo planters, and indigo virtually disappeared as a crop from the Carolina coast. The bounty on naval stores also ceased. At the same time Britain imposed a high tax on imported American tobacco. Before independence, when Americans had been subjects of King George, American agricultural commodities had found a ready market in the British West Indies. Now, as foreigners, Americans could no longer expect special rights in British-controlled markets. Shortly before the war ended, the English government clamped down on the export of many mainland commodities to their Caribbean possessions. Farmers of Massachusetts, the Connecticut and Hudson valleys, eastern Pennsylvania, and the grain-growing areas of the Chesapeake were thus deprived of markets for their surpluses. Unsold crops piled up; farm prices fell.

Frontier farmers beyond the Appalachians also faced difficult times after 1783. By the war's end thousands of settlers lived across the mountains in what is now Kentucky and Tennessee. These people raised the food they consumed but relied on the eastern states or Europe for salt, guns, powder, shot, plows, cloth, notions, and small luxuries. They could pay for these imports with surplus grain or meat or with furs, skins, and lumber gathered from the surrounding forests. But how could they get these goods to market? As the crow flies, the farmers of eastern Kentucky and Tennessee were not very far from the seaboard. Unfortunately, the trip by pack animals across the Allegheny and Blue Ridge mountains was hard, slow, and expensive.

The Mississippi and its tributaries were the natural links between the western farmers and the outside world. The westerners could load their products on rafts or flatboats, float them south with the current, and land them at New Orleans to be shipped to the east coast or the Caribbean by oceangoing vessels. But under the 1763 treaty ending the French and Indian War, Spain controlled the mouth of the Mississippi, and Spain demanded payment of a stiff tax to allow Americans to land their wares at New Orleans. Although the Spanish had supported the Americans during the Revolution, they both considered the revolt a dangerous example to their own discontented colonies and feared the Americans would one day seize the weakly held Spanish lands in the West. Why help them prosper? The potentially busy Mississippi waterway accordingly remained closed, while surplus crops went unsold and western farmers did without coveted manufactured goods.

COMMERCE. The imperial Navigation Acts had restricted direct American trade with many parts of the world, with Americans forbidden to export directly to northern Europe, and most European imports coming by way of Britain. Enumerated articles had to go to Britain on the way to their ultimate destination. Though there had been no legal impediments to colonial voyages to the distant East, English merchants had been so dominant in the trade with China, India, and the East Indies that Americans had, in effect, been excluded. With the Navigation Acts gone and newly independent Americans more confident of their prowess, enterprising men jumped at the chance to develop trade with new customers and to open new trading routes. For the first time American ships visited places such as Copenhagen, Rotterdam, Stockholm, Bremen, and even the Russian west coast of North America. In 1783 Robert Morris opened direct trade with China when he and his associates sent the "Empress of China" on a voyage to Canton that brought extraordinary returns to the promoters. Thereafter, American vessels from Boston, Salem, New York, Philadelphia, and other east coast ports regularly rounded "the Horn" or "the Cape" on the way to the East Indies and China. Trade with France, much restricted before 1776, swelled under the Franco-American treaty of 1778, which gave Americans special privileges in French dominions. American commerce with the French, Dutch, and Danish West Indies also grew.

Yet the new trade routes did not compensate for the loss of British imperial customers. Americans were excluded from commerce with the British West Indies, and could no longer trade with the Newfoundland and Nova Scotia fisheries. Nor could New England and middle states shipbuilders count on a protected market for their vessels in the empire. American-built ships were now "foreign" and no longer given a privileged position in the imperial trade. Britain also placed a high duty on American whale oil. The results of all these changes were damaging. By the end of the 1780s, American foreign commerce had partly recovered from wartime and immediate postwar disruption. By 1790 Americans exported more than they had in 1772. But measured on a per capita basis, American exports were 30 percent lower in 1790 than in the average year just before the war for independence.

Other problems beset the country's commercial interests. After 1783 the agents of British firms set up offices and warehouses in every American port and began to push Americans out of the large transatlantic trade in British goods. Before long British vessels were even carrying British products from port to port along the Atlantic coast at the expense of American coastal traders. American merchants demanded that the United States favor imports carried by American ships and exclude foreigners from the coastal trade. Such laws would be American navigation acts, no different from the British restrictions against which colonial Americans had rebeled. But few Americans saw the irony; self-interest was enough to overcome consistency.

INDUSTRY. The livelihoods of city artisans, mechanics, and craftspeople—the "manufacturers" of the day—were also uncertain in the immediate postwar era. During the war consumers in many areas had been forced to turn to domestic artisans for goods formerly imported from Great Britain. American manufacturers had flourished until, with the return of peace, consumers went on a spending spree for British wares. Suddenly the American cabinetmakers, weavers, hat makers, tailors, silversmiths, and cobblers found their shops empty of customers.

The "manufacturers" appealed to the state legislatures for help. One Massachusetts petition sought relief for "persons out of employ who have wives and

A 1790 view of Mississippi commerce in New Orleans. In the center of the picture is a keelboat; to the right a flatboat. The river's width is greatly reduced.

children asking for bread." Several states came to the rescue. They exempted some industries from taxes, lent money to others, and offered premiums to investors and inventors. What the artisans really wanted, however, was tariff protection—high duties that would make foreign imports expensive and thus force American consumers to buy the home product. Massachusetts, Rhode Island, New Hampshire, Connecticut, Pennsylvania, New York, and several southern states did impose taxes on imports.

Unfortunately for the new nation's industries and their workers, the piece-meal system of state duties was ineffective. The states tried to avoid conflicts with one another by exempting goods imported from other states. This practice simply nullified the duties. Importers in states without tariffs sent foreign goods into neighboring states disguised as American-made commodities. New York engaged in a preposterous trade war against New Jersey and Connecticut over this evasion. In 1787 the New York legislature decreed that foreign goods coming through the two neighboring states must pay four times the duties of American goods. New Jersey retaliated by making New York pay £30 a month for the privilege of maintaining the Sandy Hook lighthouse on New Jersey property. Connecticut imposed duties on goods coming from New York.

The economic warfare among the states never went very far, but it could have led to a system of commercially insulated, competing states that would have thrown away the blessings of continent-wide free trade. Before long, alert citizens were asking how the country could avoid such an outcome and still protect itself against the superior industry of Great Britain.

CREDITORS AND DEBTORS.   Unable to impose taxes, Congress ceased paying the interest and principal of the national debt. Thereafter, the value of government securities—Congress's promises to pay back money it had borrowed during the Revolution—dropped sharply. Speculators willing to take the chance that Congress might eventually pay its obligations bought up government IOUs at a fraction of their face value and soon held a large part of the total amount. The original holders of the securities thus got something for their money, but many felt cheated. Many state creditors felt the same way. After the war some states had taxed themselves heavily and paid their debts. Others did not, and their depreciated securities, like Congress's, soon passed into the hands of speculators.

Nor were private creditors much better off. The postwar years brought a sharp drop in general prices. Imports, as we noted, had boomed briefly after 1783 as American consumers, starved for British goods during the war, snapped up every cargo from Bristol, London, and Liverpool. To pay for this merchandise merchants and customers shipped overseas the gold and silver coin left behind by the French army or lent to Congress during the war by Dutch bankers. But there was a limit to the available cash, and the country soon reverted to its normal condition of currency dearth.

When money is scarce, it becomes more valuable relative to the things it buys. Thus prices for domestic goods soon fell sharply. This deflation hurt farmers and artisans, who produced goods for sale. It also hurt debtors, who found it hard to get money to pay their creditors. To relieve their distress, debtors demanded paper money, and in several states the legislatures passed measures to oblige them.

Most states printed only moderate amounts of the new paper currency and did not make it "legal tender" that forced creditors to accept it for debts even if they did not want to. These issues caused few problems. New York and Pennsylvania businessmen actually supported their state's paper money issues to help end the currency famine and make business easier to conduct. The situation was very different in Rhode Island. In that turbulent state the debtors were in political control and seemed determined to defraud their creditors. In 1786 the legislature, acting under debtor pressure, issued £100,000 of legal tender paper money and declared that everyone must accept it at face value whatever its purchasing power. A creditor who resisted was breaking the law, and the debt would be canceled. Soon debtors were pursuing their creditors and paying them without mercy. Creditors complained bitterly, but to no avail.

The evidence thus confirms the economic difficulties of the Confederation period. And it also suggests that they were widespread, not confined just to creditors, as Charles Beard argued. Merchants, farmers, and craftspeople, as well as creditors, had good reason to complain in these early postwar years.

The distress had important political repercussions. Citizens began to ask pointed questions. Who was to blame for the problems? Why had prices dropped? Why did the British refuse to make trade concessions to Americans? Why could Spain close the port of New Orleans without retaliation? Why were American craftspeople not protected against cheap foreign goods? Why could Rhode Island debtors arbitrarily scale down their debts? Why must national creditors sell their government securities to speculators at a fraction of their face value? The fault in every case, seemed the weak national government established by the Articles of Confederation. Before long a growing segment of the most enterprising voters had concluded that something must be done to strengthen the national frame of government if the country was to recover and fulfill its economic promise.

CONFEDERATION FINANCES.   Beard was right to identify Confederation finance as part of the background for the constitutional convention of 1787. Congress had not paid Revolutionary soldiers, security holders, or any of its other creditors—and could not deal with many of its other pressing problems—because it lacked financial resources. Under the Articles of Confederation, as we saw, the central government had no power to tax and could do no more than assign revenue quotas to the states. Raising these funds then became the responsibility of the thirteen state legislatures. Under this scheme money came in very slowly because the states, with their own expenses, were reluctant to fulfill their national obligations.

To meet its needs Congress offered large blocks of western land for sale to speculators. Under one such arrangement, 1.5 million acres of land were sold for less than eight cents an acre in hard money to a group of Boston businessmen and promoters. Congress also resorted to borrowing money from abroad as well as from Americans. But these loans were a mere stopgap, since the government could not expect bankers to continue to lend to it when it had no means to repay them. Meanwhile, though the fighting had ended, Washington's restless army remained unpaid and undischarged in its camp at Newburgh, New York.

Hoping to solve the government's revenue problems, in 1781 some members of Congress proposed an amendment to the Articles allowing Congress to levy a duty of 5 percent on all goods entering the country. The revenue from this "impost" would be used to pay the defaulted debt. Amending the Articles, however, required the unanimous consent of the states. Twelve states quickly ratified the amendment, but Rhode Island rejected the proposal. Another impost amendment, put forward in 1783, failed when New York ratified it with such crippling conditions that the other states would not accept it.

These failures had serious consequences. As we have seen, many people were forced to sell their government securities to speculators for whatever they would bring. Veterans were denied the cash bonuses Congress had promised them. Continental officers, who believed they were entitled to half-pay for life in retirement, were especially angry and were soon muttering of rebellion in the army's camp at Newburgh.

NATIONALISM.   Another important source of political change in this period was nationalism. This feeling links individual happiness to the interests and welfare of the nation as a whole; it is the emotional bond that joins citizens of a country to one another. Nationalism is a powerful force that can overwhelm individual and group interest and at times inspire sacrifice of life itself.

The active nationalists of the period were mostly young men who had served in the Continental Army or in Congress. They had fought and sacrificed for the United States. They had seen many parts of the continent, had met men like themselves from every region, and had shared with them their hopes for a new national future. Their experiences had broadened their perspectives into a "continental" view and had made them aware of the inadequacies of localism. Many former officers of Washington's army belonged to the Society of the Cincinnati, an organization formed in 1783 and dedicated to preserving the bonds forged in war and promoting the interests of the new nation. In later years the Jeffersonian Republicans would accuse its members of seeking to create an aristocracy in the United States.

The heightened continental consciousness could be seen in many areas in the immediate postwar period. Before 1776 Americans had looked to Britain and Europe for religious, cultural, and intellectual leadership. In the first years of independence they sought to end this subordination. In these years Americans established religious autonomy from Europe. American Anglicans (who took the name Episcopalians), led until now by church superiors in distant England, now acquired their own bishops and a separate church government. In 1784 the Methodists left the British-controlled Methodist Conference and organized an independent American Methodist Episcopal Church. In 1789 the pope selected the first resident American Catholic bishop, a move that recognized American independent nationhood.

Americans also declared their cultural independence from the Old World. In 1780 a group of Bostonians formed the American Academy of Arts and Sciences to encourage "every art and science" that might add to "the interest, honor, dignity, and happiness of a free, independent, and virtuous people." Five years later a reinvigorated American Philosophical Society issued its first volume of scientific transactions. A leader of the new movement for cultural independence was Noah Webster, a Connecticut-born Yale graduate. Soon after Yorktown Webster set out to create a distinctive intellectual life for "the confederated republics of America." In 1783 he published his Blue-Backed Speller, a volume, he proclaimed, that would help make America "as independent in literature as she is in politics." In the next few years he also published a grammar and a reader that used stories and examples drawn from American life as exercises for children learning their letters. Another sign of the new cultural nationalism—a dubious one perhaps—was the publication in 1787 of the first American history textbook.

To the growing body of nationalists the Confederation's political feebleness seemed humiliating. Everywhere they looked they found distressing signs of their country's plight. In June 1783 Congress had made itself look ridiculous by fleeing Philadelphia in fear of attack by unpaid and mutinous Continental troops. During the next months it wandered from town to town trying to find a decent resting place. When the new Dutch minister to the United States arrived to present his credentials, Congress was ensconced in Princeton, a small college town without proper facilities for state occasions. The embarrassed president of Congress, Elias Boudinot, wrote the representative of the nation's former ally to apologize for the inadequacy: "We feel ourselves greatly mortified that our present circumstances in a small Country village prevent us giving you a reception more agreeable to our wishes. But I hope these unavoidable deficiencies will be compensated by the sincere Joy on this occasion." In the end the ceremony went off creditably, but few who observed Boudinot's plight were proud of their country's government.

Though alert enough when threatened by physical attack, Congress seemed indifferent to everything else. In the six weeks following ratification of the 1783 peace treaty it was difficult to gather a quorum to do business. In mid-February 1784 James Tilton of Delaware wrote a fellow member that "the situation of Congress is truly alarming; the most important business pending and not states enough to take it up. . . . " Another member declared: "The Congress is abused, laughed at and cursed in every company." Is it any wonder that sincere patriots feared for their country's future?

✳ FOREIGN AFFAIRS ✳

Even more disturbing to patriotic nationalists than the domestic weakness of the Confederation was its feebleness in foreign affairs. Almost everywhere the United States was treated with contempt. France remained friendly and honored the trade privileges specified by the treaty of 1778; but Spain and Britain were antagonistic, and even minor powers felt they could defy American interests. As Jefferson, serving as American minister in Paris, wrote in 1784: "All respect for our government is annihilated on this side of the water from an idea of its want of energy."

The British, in particular, took advantage of American weakness. Besides excluding Americans from the profitable West Indies trade, they refused to evacuate a flock of forts and trading posts on American soil. They had good commercial reasons for thus violating the 1783 peace treaty: With British troops garrisoned at Michilimackinac, Detroit, Niagara, Oswego, and other posts, American fur traders were forced to surrender the trade of the Northwest to their Canadian rivals from Montreal. But the continued occupation was also a political response. The Americans had failed to live up to two provisions of the Treaty of Paris: They had not fully compensated Loyalists for their property losses, and they had not paid all prewar debts owed British merchants. Although Congress earnestly recommended that the states encourage both actions, the plea had been largely ignored. Loyalist groups and British creditors complained bitterly, but it did little good. The American government could not force its own citizens to comply with its treaty agreements.

The American minister to London, John Adams, pleaded with the British to adopt a more generous policy toward American trade and to evacuate the northwestern posts. Royal officials treated the American envoy with a "dry decency" and cold "civility," but refused to budge. Britain might have dealt more generously with the United States if Congress had been able to impose duties on British imports. As Jefferson noted, the United States "must show" the English that "we are capable of foregoing commerce with them, before they will be capable of consenting to equal commerce." But of course Congress lacked the power to exclude foreign goods, and the British knew it. As Lord Sheffield, a defender of British shipping interests, remarked, it would "not be any easy matter to bring the American states to act as a nation. They are not to be feared as such by us."

American relations with Spain during the Confederation era also revealed Congress's weakness. Besides restricting America's Mississippi commerce, Spain refused to allow United States ships to trade with its colonies in Latin America, thus cutting off a profitable relationship that had developed during the war. These blows to American interests finally goaded even the sleepy Congress to act. In 1785 it authorized John Jay, the secretary for foreign affairs, to open negotiations with Spain over these issues.

Once more the American government proved incapable of achieving results. The Spanish minister, the lady-pleasing Don Diego de Gardoqui, was willing to make concessions on trade with Spanish-American ports, since these did not threaten his nation's control over territory. He refused, however, to yield on the right of tax-free deposit at New Orleans. His position suited some influential easterners, who feared that a too-rapid growth of the West would draw off population from the older states and eventually lead to western secession from the United States. It also coincided with the interests of northeastern merchants, who stood to gain by enlarged trade opportunities with Spanish America but saw little advantage in the right of deposit. Yet it was just this right to unload their cargo at New Orleans and transfer it to oceangoing ships that was the crucial matter to westerners.

A stronger government might have forced each group to accept a compromise for the national good. As it was, the treaty finally negotiated with Spain outraged the West. In exchange for Latin American trade concessions, the United States agreed to forgo the right of deposit for twenty-five years. Unrepresented as yet in Congress, the westerners received the support of southern congressmen, who saw little gain for their section in the trade provisions and so could afford to take a nationalist position. Voting solidly against adoption, the southern representatives defeated the treaty. No one got anything. Once again, American weakness had betrayed American interests.

In the Mediterranean, too, the feeble American government was humiliated during the immediate postwar years. For centuries the Barbary states in North Africa—Morocco, Algiers, Tunis, and Tripoli—had prospered by preying on the commerce of Europe. Swift Barbary corsairs would swoop down on merchant ships and seize their cargoes; the pirates would then remove passengers and crews and hold them for ransom. Most European powers either paid tribute to the Barbary beys and bashaws in return for safe passage or provided their citizens with naval protection. Before 1776, English men-of-war had guarded American commerce against the corsairs. Now that Americans were independent, they could no longer rely on the Royal Navy, and their merchant ships soon became fair game for the raiders in the Mediterranean and off the coasts of Spain and Portugal. In 1787 the United States signed a treaty in which Morocco agreed to respect American rights. But negotiations with the other Barbary states failed because they insisted on bribes, which Congress could not pay. Unable either to pay tribute or provide naval protection for its shipping, the United States suffered continuing harassment from the North African pirates.

* THE PUBLIC DOMAIN *

In one important area of national concern—the administration of the vast public domain—the Confederation government gets at least a mixed review. When Virginia finally surrendered its claims to the Northwest in 1784, Congress found itself in possession of almost a quarter of a billion acres of some of the finest land on earth. What should be done with this princely realm? How should it be disposed of? Who should get it? Should it be considered primarily a source of revenue for the central government, or an opportunity to shape American society in some desirable way? And how should the communities carved out of this land be governed? Should they be equal politically to the original states? If the problems were immense, so were the stakes, for the course chosen would profoundly affect the nation's future.

One issue never in serious doubt was whether the "West" should be subject to the needs of white Americans. Embued with the new "romantic" sensibility which swept Europe and America toward the end of the eighteenth century, a few sensitive souls came to appreciate untamed nature. During the 1780s Philip Freneau, a Patriot poet, sang of the "wild genius of the forest" and contrasted it with the corruption of civilization. The prominent Philadelphia doctor Benjamin Rush noted about this time that "man is naturally a wild animal, and . . . taken from the woods, he is never happy." But few others in this era questioned the goals of clearing the forests and plowing the prairies of the region beyond the Appalachians and converting them into farms and towns. Even if the romantic views had been stronger and more widespread, they could not have overcome the enormous pressure for cheap land and the ethic that human progress depended on resource exploitation.

THE LAND ORDINANCE OF 1785.   The first public land issue Congress tackled was how to transfer real estate to private individuals. As yet no one seriously considered giving the land away, if for no other reason than Congress needed some source of revenue. But there remained many other unanswered questions. Should the price be high or low? Should the land be sold in large blocks to speculators, or in small parcels to farmers? One crucial issue was whether to adopt the New England system of first surveying the land and then selling it in compact blocks, or the scheme more common in the South of selling a receipt for a particular number of acres and then allowing the buyer to choose his land more or less where he pleased with the survey to follow. The New England plan had the advantages of encouraging orderly and compact settlement and of avoiding overlapping land claims. But it was likely to slow the pace of settlement by forcing people to buy bad land along with good and by requiring that each section opened be filled before others became available. The New England pattern also promised to avoid the sort of pell-mell rush to the West that was certain to disturb the Indians. On the whole, however, westerners favored the southern scheme, for all its potential for trouble, because it promised faster settlement.

The Land Ordinance of 1785 was Congress's attempt to choose a course among these conflicting alternatives. It provided that all government lands be surveyed and divided into square townships six miles on an edge. Each township in turn would be cut into thirty-six sections, each of a square mile, or 640 acres. Half the townships would be sold as complete units of over 23,000 acres each. The other half would be sold in 640-acre sections. Some land was reserved for Revolutionary veterans after the land was surveyed; all the rest would be sold at auction at a minimum price of a dollar an acre.

The Land Ordinance followed more closely the New England than the southern settlement tradition. As in New England, it mandated orderly surveying and compact tracts. Southerners, preferring relatively small tracts, got part of what they wanted in the provision for sale of single sections. On the other hand, the measure also allowed for the large block sales that speculators preferred. All in all, the scheme favored the principles endorsed by northeasterners over those desired by the rest of the country. Westerners, in particular, would not find it satisfactory. Over the next century they would agitate to alter the public land laws to favor the small farmer and the family farm over the land speculator and the large holding.

CONGRESS'S INDIAN POLICY.   Congress was no more successful in dealing with the Indian tribes than with foreign powers. In 1784 it dispatched commissioners to induce the Northwestern tribes to surrender a major portion of their lands to white settlers. At Fort Stanwix they compelled the Iroquois to give up all claims to the region for a few presents. Soon after, at Fort McIntosh, they persuaded the Chippewa, Ottawa, Delaware, and Wyandot Indians to make a similar concession. The two treaties did not accomplish their aim. Several tribes rejected them and at the same time, they opened the door to renegade whites from Kentucky, Virginia, and Pennsylvania to stake out claims on Indian lands still in dispute. By the spring of 1786 it looked as if a major Indian war was about to erupt in the Northwest.

At this point western settlers, in a pattern that would be repeated many times in later years, decided to take matters into their own hands by hiring the Indian fighter George Rogers Clark to lead an offensive against the Ohio Indians. The attack failed when the western volunteers recruited by Clark mutinied. The Indians now repudiated the two treaties and declared that white settlers would be excluded from the whole Northwest. The "line now cutting Pennsylvania," they announced, "shall bounde them on the sunrising, and the Ohio shall be the boundary between them and the Big Knives." Congress refused to accept this Indian barrier, but in its usual feeble way, could do nothing to prevent it.

THE ORDINANCE OF 1787.   Despite its weakness, the Confederation Congress could claim one major political accomplishment: the Northwest Ordinance providing government for the region north of the Ohio River and west of Pennsylvania.

In 1784, following Thomas Jefferson's suggestion, Congress proposed to divide the trans-Appalachian region into ten political communities. When the population of any of these reached 20,000, the inhabitants could adopt a constitution and apply for admission to the Union as a state equal in status to the states already comprising the Confederation. Although this measure was never put into effect, it served as the model for the Northwest Ordinance adopted three years later.

Section one of the 1787 Northwest Ordinance mandated that no fewer than three nor more than five states be formed out of the Northwest Territory. In its political provisions it was less liberal than Jefferson's plan. Section two, instead of allowing the people of a new territory self-rule from the outset, required a three-step process toward autonomy. At the outset the territory would be governed by a governor, a territorial secretary, and three judges appointed by Congress. Then, when the adult male population had reached 5,000, it could elect a legislature to share power with a council of five chosen by the governor and Congress. It could also elect a territorial delegate to Congress, though he could not vote. Finally,

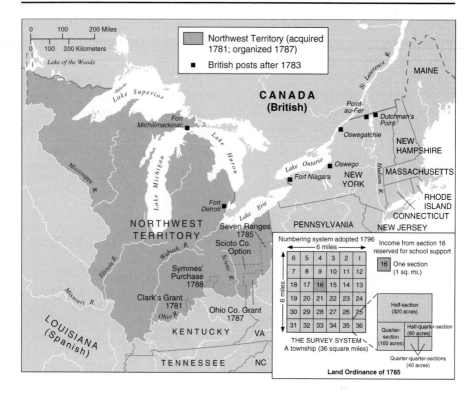

The Northwest Ordinance of 1787

when the territory's total population had reached 60,000, it could apply for admission to the Union as a self-governing state equal to all the others. Section three of the Ordinance prohibited slavery in the new communities and provided a bill of rights for their inhabitants.

The Northwest Ordinance was a momentous piece of legislation. Its exclusion of slavery ensured that the entire North would be free territory. Equally important, the ordinance determined the future of the West and the Union by establishing the principle that new states would be equal to the original thirteen. If we consider the possible alternative of holding new territories in colonial thralldom, we can see how beneficial a precedent the ordinance was. Ray Billington, a historian of the American West, has declared:

> The Ordinance of 1787 did more to perpetuate the Union than any document save the Constitution. Men could now leave the older states assured that they were

not surrendering their political privileges. [By enacting the Ordinance] Congress not only saved the Republic, but had removed one great obstacle to the westward movement.

✳ THE CONSTITUTIONAL CONVENTION ✳

The Confederation government, then, was not without accomplishments. But they were outweighed by its failures to meet the needs—political, economic, emotional—of many citizens. By 1785 it seemed clear to many vocal Americans, not just a small elite, that the nation needed a more powerful and effective central government to serve its interests and fulfill its hopes.

The road to the Constitutional Convention was not direct, however. The process of revising or replacing the Articles began in 1785 when Maryland and Virginia signed an agreement over navigation rights on the Potomac River and Chesapeake Bay. The success of this pact induced Maryland to call for a broader arrangement that would include Pennsylvania and Delaware and cover disputes over import duties, currency, and other commercial matters. Nationalists in the Virginia legislature quickly proposed that all thirteen states meet in September 1786 at Annapolis to consider common commercial problems. Only five states attended the conference, but the nationalists—led by Alexander Hamilton of New York, James Madison of Virginia, and John Dickinson of Delaware—took advantage of the situation. They convinced the delegates to petition Congress for a full-scale convention to meet at Philadelphia in May 1787 to discuss not only economic problems but fundamental political changes as well.

By this time, Congress's long decline had brought it close to paralysis. The Annapolis Convention's resolution was referred to a committee of three, which proposed to submit it to another committee of thirteen, which the legislators never got around to appointing. Congress, it seemed, intended to let the proposal die.

SHAYS'S REBELLION. Events in Massachusetts, a center of political turbulence since the 1760s, jolted the country and Congress into action. Massachusetts was one of those states that had obligated itself to pay its war debt. To meet this commitment the Bay State legislature had imposed on its citizens the heaviest taxes in New England. To farmers already suffering from low crop prices, the taxes were a disaster. Debts and bankruptcies soon mounted in the western counties, and many yeomen fell behind in their tax payments. As if this were not enough, Massachusetts law required that the pettiest commercial transactions be recorded by a court, necessitating the payment of high fees to lawyers and court officials. The large volume of legal business resulting from hard times thus added to the heavy tax load imposed on the state's rural citizens.

By the summer of 1786 discontent among farmers in the western counties had reached the flash point. In late August they convened in Worcester and condemned the taxes and heavy legal fees. Shortly afterward, an armed mob of 1,500 men, eager to end foreclosures for tax delinquency and debt default, stopped the convening of the Hampshire County court. In early September three more county courts were kept from sitting by groups of angry men.

Although the Massachusetts legislature made some effort to ease the burden of debtors, disaffected westerners began to arm and drill as if they expected to take on King George's redcoats once again. Led by Daniel Shays, a former Continental Army officer, they formed a committee to resist what they considered intolerable conditions. Meanwhile, in the eastern part of the state, people had begun to panic. In Boston Governor James Bowdoin decided to raise a military force to suppress the dissenters. Rather than impose new taxes to support this small army, Bowdoin appealed to the city's rich men, who, in their fright, promptly came up with $25,000. In January 1787 a rebel force of 1,200 met the smaller group of Bowdoin's militia at Springfield. The state troops fired a single artillery volley, and the rebels fled in panic. The uprising was over by spring.

Shays's Rebellion was actually not much of a threat to the social order, yet it frightened many people. One citizen later insisted that if the rebels had won, there would have been "an abolition of all public and private debts" followed by "an equal distribution of property." The rebellion also dismayed the country's nationalists. Washington wrote that he was "mortified beyond expression" by the disorders. For the country "to be more exposed in the eyes of the world and more contemptible" than it already was seemed "hardly possible." Congress at last took heed of the restless mood of many citizens, and on February 21 it voted to ask the states to send delegates to a constitutional convention at Philadelphia. All except maverick Rhode Island complied.

THE CHALLENGE. The convention in stately Independence Hall opened on May 14, 1787. It was an assembly of giants. Leading the rest in prestige were George Washington, Benjamin Franklin, James Madison, Robert Morris, James Wilson, John Dickinson, and Alexander Hamilton. There was also a large contingent of less famous but notably able men: George Mason, George Wythe, and Edmund Randolph, all of Virginia; John Rutledge and Charles Pinckney of South Carolina; William Paterson of New Jersey; Roger Sherman and Oliver Ellsworth of Connecticut; and Rufus King of Massachusetts. The rest of the fifty-five delegates made lesser contributions to the convention's work, though most enjoyed high standing in their states and had played important roles in national events.

Seldom has any group taken on so momentous a task. Western governments have usually been the products of historical accident and the gradual evolution of tradition and experience. The idea of a written frame of government, of a structure of fundamental law put down in precise words at one time, is an

American invention. The practice began, as we saw in Chapter 5, with the making of state constitutions after 1775. Its finest expression is the federal Constitution of 1787.

The "Founding Fathers" did, of course, draw on the traditions of the colonies and Great Britain; the English experience is embedded in every legal and governmental institution of the United States. They also relied on their understanding of the ancient world, especially Rome, and on the views of the great political and legal thinkers of modern times including Locke and Montesquieu. But in the end they were guided primarily by their own practical experience of government.

Though a number of the men at Philadelphia owned substantial amounts of unpaid Continental and state debt certificates, a more important bond among them was their nationalism, or continentalism. The period from 1781 to 1787, the delegates would have agreed, was indeed critical: America had been treated with contempt abroad while mob rule had threatened at home. There were some defenders of states' rights at Philadelphia—Robert Yates of New York, George Mason of Virginia, and Luther Martin of Maryland, for example—but most delegates believed that the Articles of Confederation had failed as an instrument of government and that the United States needed a stronger central authority.

Few of the delegates, however, wished to strengthen the government at the expense of freedom. The goal of the majority was balance, an end much harder to achieve. They wished to establish a "mixed" government, combining popular and aristocratic elements, that would protect private property, but also preserve personal liberty. They intended to construct a strong government, but one that would maintain local autonomy and local rights. In a nation of continental proportions the diversity of interests, opinions, and philosophies made the task formidable. During the deliberations small states would clash with large states, slave states with free states, commercial interests with agrarian interests, democrats with aristocrats, champions of local rights with nationalists. In the end, compromise would be unavoidable.

THE DEBATE ON REPRESENTATION.[1] Following some preliminary skirmishing over procedural rules, the convention began its real work when Edmund Randolph, acting for James Madison, submitted a proposal that has come to be known as the Virginia Plan. Randolph advocated not merely a revision of the Articles of Confederation, but a completely new government, with separate legislative, executive, and judicial departments. Congress would have two houses, and the states would be represented in each in proportion to their population. In each house the elected members would vote as individuals, not as part of a single state unit, as they did under the Articles. They would, in effect, represent themselves or their constituents, not their states. The new legislature

[1]The text of the complete Constitution may be found in the Appendix.

would be all powerful and choose the persons to fill positions in the executive and judicial branches of government.

The Virginia Plan emphasized the central government as opposed to the states. Randolph hoped to establish a "strong consolidated union, in which the idea of states would be nearly annihilated." The Articles had created a league of virtually independent states; the new plan would confer broad powers on the central government, which would "legislate in all cases to which the separate States are incompetent"—that is, in every area where it chose to assert its power. But Randolph's proposal did not spell out precisely the new government's powers.

The Virginia Plan was countered by the New Jersey Plan, submitted by William Paterson. Paterson recommended that the Articles be revised, not replaced. His new government was to be a "federal," not a truly centralized one; that is, there would be a central government, but the states would retain independent authority in some spheres. The New Jerseyite, speaking for a smaller state than Randolph, endorsed the one-house legislature of the Articles, in which each state was represented equally, regardless of its wealth or population. States would continue to vote as units in Congress, so that the states, rather than the people, would be represented in the new government. But the New Jersey Plan did improve on the Articles by granting the national government the power to tax and regulate foreign and interstate commerce. It also made federal laws and treaties superior to all state laws, another advance over the Articles.

It is easy to see that the New Jersey Plan would benefit states with small populations more than the Virginia Plan. If Paterson's proposal was adopted, they would have representation in Congress equal to that of the more populous ones. If, on the other hand, the Virginia Plan prevailed, the small states' voices would be drowned out by those of their larger neighbors. For this reason it is often said that the two plans represented a conflict between large and small states. But the disagreement was just as much between the strong centralists and their more locally oriented colleagues.

The two plans became the basis for debate, and both were modified in the discussions. On the whole, the centralizers came out ahead. The new government would have greatly enlarged powers, but they would be specified and not left to Congress to decide. It would also be a true central government. Congress would represent the citizens of the United States, not the states as entities. Members of Congress would therefore vote as individuals, and not merely to decide how the vote of their state should be cast. On the other issues of representation, a compromise was adopted. In one house, the Senate, each state would have equal representation regardless of population; in the other, the House of Representatives, population would determine the size of state delegations.

At this point the delegates had to consider the issue of what constituted "population." Were slaves property, or were they people? If they were property, they might be the basis for levying taxes, but could not be considered in calculating a state's representation in the lower house of Congress. If they were people, they should be counted for determining representation. But slaves were not free

The small room in Independence Hall, Philadelphia, where the debates on the Constitution were held in 1787.

and could not vote, so treating them as people would give the southern states a voice in Congress disproportionate to the actual number of their voters. Each voter in the South, where slaves were numerous, in effect would have more power than each voter in the North, where they were few. Northerners naturally objected to such a scheme. Southerners, noting that their wealth in slaves would force them to pay a heavy tax bill, insisted on some political compensation for the burden they would bear.

The issue was very sensitive, for it touched on the continued existence and prosperity of slavery in the South. And slavery, the South's "peculiar"—that is, special or unique—institution, was entangled in every aspect of southern life. True, ever since the Revolution had proclaimed that "all men are created equal," the supporters of slavery had been on the defensive. But slaves still tilled the South's fields, built its fences, and performed its household chores. Though slavery was fast disappearing in the North, only a handful of enlightened southerners were willing to contemplate its abolition in their own section.

The men at Philadelphia generally elected to compromise. Taxes and representation in the lower house of Congress would be based on "the whole number of free Persons," excluding Indians but including indentured servants, and "three-fifths of all other Persons." Thus, with the "three-fifths compromise," America's Founding Fathers managed the neat trick of simultaneously treating a slave as property and as three-fifths of a human being.

FREEDOM OR ORDER?   The delegates desired both the representative principle on the one hand, and order and rule by the "best men," a kind of elitism, on the other. Some leaned strongly to one side, some to the other, with most somewhere in the middle.

The give-and-take among these principles resulted in several important features of the Constitution, particularly the separation of powers. Borrowing from Montesquieu, the French political philosopher, the delegates assigned to each branch of government—executive, legislative, and judicial—distinct powers, and directed that members of each be selected in a distinct way. This separation would ensure the independence of each branch. In addition, the Founders adopted the idea that each branch must be able to "check and balance" the others. By such an arrangement the greatest freedom would be ensured, for if one branch grew too powerful and sought to dominate the others, it could be constitutionally stopped.

To this end, the chief executive was to have a veto over acts of Congress, the most democratic part of the new government. But the president was not to be all-powerful. His veto could be overridden by a two-thirds vote of Congress. The chief executive could make treaties with foreign powers, but they would have to be confirmed by a two-thirds vote of the Senate. He was to be commander in chief of the army and navy, but only Congress could declare war. Finally, he could appoint a host of high officials, but these appointments would have to be confirmed by the Senate. As a final check on the president—and his appointees—the House of Representatives could bring impeachment charges against federal officials and, if convicted by the Senate, they could be removed from office.

Standing guard against the excesses and abuses of Congress and the president was to be the third branch, the federal judiciary, capped by a Supreme Court. Although it is nowhere stated in the Constitution, legal scholars believe that the delegates at Philadelphia assumed the right of the federal courts to declare acts of Congress contrary to the Constitution and so void. To protect the judges against political pressure, they gave them lifetime tenure and declared that during their terms of office Congress could not reduce their salaries.

Checks and balances offered one way to combine strong and stable government with a popular voice. The mixture of democratic and aristocratic methods of choosing the officers of each branch was another. The president would be selected not by the direct vote of the people but by an electoral college chosen by the states as they saw fit. The number of electors from each state would be equal to the number of representatives and senators it sent to Congress. State law would determine how they would be chosen, but it was assumed that they would not be elected directly by the people. Nor was the Senate, the upper house of Congress, conceived of as a stronghold of democracy. Senators would be selected by their state legislatures. To limit popular control of Congress further, senators were to have long terms of six years; only one-third would be seeking reelection in each congressional election held every two years. Finally, the federal judiciary, including the Supreme Court, was to be appointed by the president and confirmed by the Senate, and thus far removed from popular pressure. To temper these aristocratic features, the House of Representatives would be directly controlled by the voters. Representatives would be elected for two-year terms by the same liberal rules that governed the selection of members of the lower houses of the state legislatures.

POWERS OF THE NEW GOVERNMENT. Besides establishing a new structure, the Constitution greatly enlarged the powers and scope of the national government. The new government, as we have seen, would impose its authority on the people directly, not through the states. It would also fuse the nation into a single legal whole. Under the new charter each state was required to give "full faith and credit" to all laws and court decisions of the others and to surrender to any other criminals fleeing across state lines to avoid prosecution. To protect property rights, states were forbidden to pass laws "impairing the Obligation of Contracts." The new government could also do many specific things its predecessor could not do. It could impose and collect taxes from citizens, though by the Constitution's original terms these taxes had to be proportionate to each state's population. It could regulate foreign and interstate commerce, although at the behest of the southern states which shipped large amounts of rice and tobacco abroad, it was forbidden to tax exports. The new government had sole control over the coinage of money and could establish a postal system, build post roads, and pass laws of naturalization. It was also endowed with the power to establish a system of uniform weights and measures, a uniform bankruptcy law and, to encourage invention and the arts and sciences, a patent and copyright system. Finally, the Constitution declared that the new government could "make all laws which shall be necessary and proper for carrying into Execution the foregoing Powers, and all other Powers vested by this Constitution in the Government of the United States." This provision, which is known as the "elastic clause," later became the justification for greatly expanded federal authority. In sum, a strengthened national government was to exercise broad authority over economic and political affairs, and over a single economic and legal unit.

Still, the Constitution created not a unitary but a "federal" government; it left the states with independent authority in many spheres. Crime and breaches of the peace were in the states' jurisdiction, except when a state legislature or governor specifically requested federal help to put down local violence. Social relations, including marriage, divorce, and education, were also left to the states, as were laws regarding purely local commercial relations and most business affairs.

Although slavery was considered a "domestic" institution much like the family, it could not be left solely to the states' jurisdiction. Conflict over representation had resulted in the three-fifths compromise, and the problems of slaves escaping to free states as well as the foreign slave trade also had to be considered. After much debate the Philadelphia delegates agreed that Congress could not forbid the foreign slave trade until 1808, but thereafter it might do so if a majority wished. Congress could, however, pass laws to deal with runaway slaves who crossed state lines and guarantee slaveholders the right to recover such fugitives regardless of local antislavery laws.

All through the summer and into September the delegates debated every issue. The discussion, like the weather, was often heated. To quiet ruffled tempers and encourage goodwill among the delegates, Benjamin Franklin at one point proposed that a chaplain be invited to open each morning session with a prayer. Washington, the presiding officer, also worked to maintain peace; and although he said little, his dignity and calm demeanor helped to keep the delegates' differences from getting out of hand.

Nothing could prevent disagreement, however. A number of the delegates considered the completed draft of the Constitution far too centralizing. New York's Robert Yates and John Lansing, George Mason of Virginia, Luther Martin and John Mercer of Maryland, and Elbridge Gerry of Massachusetts denounced the work of the convention for that reason. Lansing, Yates, and Mercer went so far as to quit Philadelphia in protest. On the other hand, the most extreme centralizers believed the proposed constitution did not go far enough. Alexander Hamilton wanted the states abolished outright in favor of a strong, unitary government. The views that ultimately prevailed were those of James Madison, Oliver Ellsworth, and Roger Sherman, who succeeded in mobilizing the majority around the compromise proposals.

On September 8 the convention sent the completed draft to the Committee of Style and Arrangement. This group of five polished the convention's paragraphs and rearranged them in logical order. One of its members, Gouverneur Morris of Pennsylvania, wrote a preamble that described the promotion of "the general welfare" as one of the purposes of the new framework of government. On September 17, 1787, each of the state delegations voted its approval, and the convention adjourned.

* RATIFICATION *

Now the Constitution's friends faced the problem of securing its adoption, and it seemed likely that the battle would prove difficult. The Confederation Congress had authorized the Philadelphia convention only to "revise" and "amend" the Articles of Confederation, not to propose a new form of government. Would Congress reject the convention's work? On September 29 the new Constitution was presented to Congress. That body was almost dead and had no heart for resistance. After some minor debate it recommended the plan to the separate states for consideration by convention. The more difficult task was winning state-by-state ratification.

The opposition was formidable. Certain groups of debtors, aware that state-issued paper money would be illegal under the new government, were naturally opposed to it. So were taxpayers in states that had paid their debts and feared that through new federal taxes they would pay someone else's as well, and those who considered a strengthened national government a retreat from "true republicanism." Finally, there were the temperamentally cautious people, inclined to stick to the ills they were familiar with rather than fly to others they knew not of.

At one time scholars described the battle to get the Constitution adopted as a fierce struggle. In part, this view projects back into the adoption period attitudes that gelled in the years following when political parties were beginning to form. It also reflects the fact that in a few states the adoption issue was indeed hard fought. Because it would have been difficult to achieve a successful Union without them, the debates that took place in these states were important. Still, it is clear that the "federalists"—those who favored the new federal government—won with relative ease.

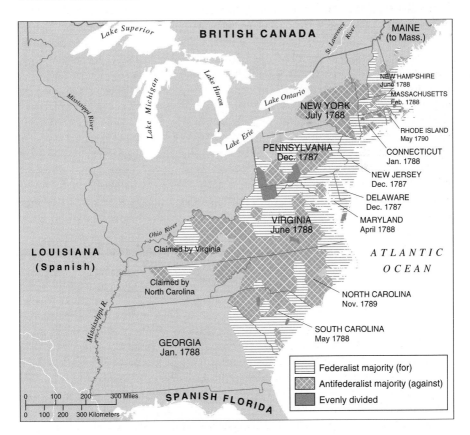

Ratification of the Constitution, 1787–1790

The delegates at Philadelphia had decided that the new government would go into operation when nine states had ratified the Constitution by special conventions. Delaware, Pennsylvania, and New Jersey were won over almost immediately, the first and third by unanimous votes in their conventions. In Pennsylvania, the delegates from Philadelphia and the port towns had to overcome opposition from the rural areas but won a two-to-one victory. Early in 1788 Georgia's convention also ratified unanimously. Connecticut soon followed with a heavy federalist majority. In Massachusetts the friends of the Constitution encountered their first serious opposition. By early estimates the state convention had a solid antifederalist majority. Among the initial opponents were the influential Sam Adams and John Hancock, for years leaders of the state's popular party. If these men could be converted, enough delegates would follow them to carry ratification. Fortunately for the Constitution, Adams was induced to change his mind by a mass meeting of Constitution supporters staged by Paul Revere. Convinced that the rally expressed the views of the state's common folk, Adams agreed to support the Constitution. Hancock, now the state's governor, was coaxed and flattered by federalists into believing he was in line for high federal office under the new Constitution.

One of the federalists' problems in Massachusetts and a number of other states was that the Constitution lacked a bill of rights to protect citizens against federal tyranny and violations of civil liberties. Some opponents of the Constitution used this primarily to delay or defeat adoption. But others, such as Hancock, were sincere in their concern. When Hancock agreed to endorse ratification, he proposed simultaneously that nine amendments be added to protect citizens against possible federal oppression. With this request tacked on to its motion, the Massachusetts convention voted 187 to 168 for adoption.

In March the federalists suffered their first actual setback when nonconformist Rhode Island overwhelmingly rejected the Constitution by a popular referendum. The state, as we saw, had been the center of debtor-imposed paper money schemes and had not even sent a delegation to Philadelphia. During the ratification battle the state's federalists did not stand a chance, so they boycotted the vote. The results were as expected: The supporters of the Constitution received only 10 percent of the votes cast.

Rhode Island's rejection did not stop the federalists' forward momentum, however. In April and May, Maryland and South Carolina joined the parade of adoptions, and by large convention majorities. Then, by a close vote on June 21, New Hampshire became the ninth state to ratify the Constitution. Under the rules that the convention had prescribed, the Constitution was now officially in force. But New York and Virginia had not acted. If these two large states voted no, it would be almost impossible to maintain a workable federal system.

Federalist forces in Virginia were strong and well organized. Among them were some of the most prestigious men in the state, including James Madison, Edmund Pendleton, George Wythe, Edmund Randolph, and John Marshall. Also working in the federalists' favor was the general assumption that the first president under the Constitution would almost certainly be the state's greatest son,

George Washington. Not yet the "father of his country," he was nevertheless a commanding figure in the new nation and seemed to embody the finest type of patriotism.

On the antifederalist side, however, there was an impressive array of talent, too, including Patrick Henry, Richard Henry Lee, James Monroe, and George Mason. Henry was the spearhead of the antifederalist attack. In an impassioned speech to the state convention he portrayed the new Constitution as dangerous to liberty. Under it the citizen would be abused, insulted, tyrannized. Henry also appealed to localism and the self-love of his listeners. "The Constitution reflects in the most degrading and mortifying manner on the virtue, integrity, and wisdom of the state legislatures," he declared. It assumed "that the chosen few who go to Congress will have more upright hearts, and more enlightened minds, than those who are members of individual legislatures." Many in his audience believed it was the finest address of his distinguished career as an orator. In the end, though, Henry's eloquence was not enough. The convention voted to ratify narrowly with the proviso that a bill of rights be added to the new frame of government.

The battle now shifted to New York. Without that state the Union would be physically split in half; with it, the Union would be complete in all essentials. For weeks the federalists had been bombarding New York newspaper readers with articles written by Hamilton, Madison, and Jay. These *Federalist Papers,* explaining, defending, and praising the new Constitution, were, of course, partisan expositions of the federalist position. But they were more than propaganda; they were also brilliant analyses by unsentimental men of the way politics was practiced in the real world. Ordinary men were not equipped to govern the country directly, they stated; they did not have the necessary knowledge or understanding. The country could be well ruled only by those who recognized that government was a "complicated science" requiring "abilities and knowledge of a variety of other subjects, to understand it." Every just and successful government must respect the wishes of ordinary people, but wisdom must temper the decisions of majorities. Majorities were frequently temporary and more often moved by passion than by mature judgment. In the future, moreover, when social inequalities had become greater than at present, majorities were certain to attack property rights. Government must be strong enough to guard against the natural but mistaken leveling tendencies of democracy.

The persuasiveness of the *Federalist Papers* and Hamilton's impassioned presentation of the federalist position at the state ratifying convention gave the adoption drive a great boost. But the pro-Constitution people had more than eloquence on their side. If New York State did not join the Union, New York City might choose to join anyway to avoid losing the lucrative commerce that flowed through it to New Jersey and southern New England. What would the state do then? In the end the logic of circumstances prevailed. On July 26, 1788, the New York convention voted 30 to 27 to adopt the Constitution.

The new Union was now secure. Early in 1789 national elections were held for the first time under the Constitution, and federalist candidates won a majority in the new Congress. In January the electoral college voted unanimously for

Washington as president and settled on John Adams as his vice president. Rhode Island and North Carolina were still outside the Union, and their citizens did not participate in the election.

Soon after the elections the new government, as promised, adopted the first ten amendments to the Constitution, now commonly called the Bill of Rights. The first nine guaranteed the rights of free speech, press, and assembly, and forbade the federal government to make any law "respecting the establishment of religion or prohibiting the free exercise thereof." They affirmed the right of the people "to bear and keep arms," protected citizens against "unreasonable searches and seizures," required jury trials in criminal and major civil cases, and forbade "excessive" bail or fines and "cruel and unusual punishments." The tenth amendment "reserved" to the states all powers not given the United States by the Constitution.

Note that these ten amendments placed limits on Congress and the federal government; they did not apply to the state governments. As most states already had similar restraints in their own constitutions, it was considered at this time unnecessary to rein them in in the same way.

With their last objections gone, and fearful of being treated as foreign nations if they did not join the Union, North Carolina and Rhode Island reversed their earlier stands and ratified the Constitution in 1789 and 1790, respectively. The United States was now a nation; it had ceased to be a league of petty states.

* CONCLUSIONS *

Between Yorktown in 1781 and Washington's inauguration in 1789 the country underwent a constitutional transformation of startling dimensions. The end of fighting did not bring the blessings of peace and freedom to the American people. Instead, it ushered in a period of declining trade, falling prices, and unemployment. It also brought national humiliation. In foreign affairs the United States was treated with contempt; even minor powers felt free to disregard American rights.

Thousands of ordinary citizens found the period deeply disappointing. Farmers, planters, craftspeople, creditors, and merchants—easterners as well as westerners, northerners as well as southerners—looked on in dismay as material conditions worsened; they longed for a way to protect their interests and improve their circumstances. Patriots, who saw their dreams of a glorious national future fading, felt despair, and demanded a more effective government to assert their country's position in the world community.

All of these groups turned to constitutional revision as their solution, and the great convention at Philadelphia was the result. Predictably, the Constitution that emerged from the deliberations reflected the feelings of the nationalists and all those who blamed weak central government for their plight. One can almost deduce the political and economic problems of the "Critical Period" from the specific grants of power to the new federal government. No doubt, that government was supported by the country's elite and the defenders of strong restraints on debtors and social levelers. But it was also endorsed by thoughtful and politically active citizens of every social persuasion. We will never be able to say for certain whether a majority of adult Americans in 1788 supported the Constitution. Yet it is likely that the federal Constitution was indeed written and adopted "by popular demand."

7

THE FIRST PARTY SYSTEM

What Issues Divided the New Nation?

1789	The French Revolution; Congress adopts the Tariff and Tonnage acts to raise the first federal revenues; Congress establishes the State, Treasury, and War departments, and prescribes the structure of the Supreme Court and the federal courts in the Federal Judiciary Act
1790–91	Hamilton presents his financial program to Congress
1790	Congress enacts Hamilton's plan for public credit in the Funding Act
1791	Congress charters the Bank of the United States
1793	War breaks out between France and Britain, Spain and Holland; France sends "Citizen" Genêt as minister to the United States; Jefferson resigns as secretary of state and is replaced by Federalist Edmund Randolph
1794	Britain authorizes the seizure of neutral ships trading between the French West Indies and Europe; The United States and Britain sign the Jay Treaty; General Anthony Wayne crushes the Indians at Fallen Timbers; rapid settlement of the Northwest Territory follows; The Whiskey Rebellion in Pennsylvania
1795	The Pinckney Treaty concluded between United States and Spain; With the Treaty of Greenville the Indians cede territory in what will later be Ohio
1796	Washington's Farewell Address; Adams elected president
1797	The French order American ships carrying British goods confiscated
1797–98	The "XYZ Affair"
1798	Congress votes to triple the size of the army and enlarge the navy; The Federalist Congress passes the Alien and Sedition Acts; Secretary of State Timothy Pickering prosecutes opposition leaders under the laws; Kentucky and Virginia declare their right to nullify acts of the national government
1800	The Convention of 1800 between France and the United States nullifies the Treaty of 1778; Jefferson elected president

Americans had every reason to expect that, under the newly adopted Constitution, the nation finally had the political machinery needed to deal with its public business. But did it?

Today every representative government operates through a political party system based on organizations of people with roughly similar views on political issues who create platforms, choose candidates for office, and formulate legislative programs. Political parties are essential attributes of modern democratic nations in which free elections select those who make and carry out the laws.

The delegates at Philadelphia in the summer of 1787 did not perceive parties in this way. They had established offices for the new federal government with defined powers and modes of selection, but they had supposed that these positions would be filled by men whose only concern would be disinterested public service, not the furthering of a particular political group or viewpoint. Public officials, moreover, would be chosen by citizens who placed the common good above their own special needs. Each issue would be decided on its own merits, not on the basis of ideology or preconceived positions. When the Philadelphia delegates considered political parties, the word they commonly used was "factions," by which they meant groupings around particular political chieftains for purely selfish reasons, such as the rewards of political office or the favor of the leader. Factions or parties, they believed, would divide citizens into hostile camps. They were not part of the legitimate machinery of government; they were dangerous cancers on it. Government by party, then, seemed a disruptive, selfish, and often corrupt way to conduct a nation's political affairs.

And yet within a decade two great national parties had emerged in the United States. Many thoughtful citizens were dismayed that the country should so quickly fall from political virtue. But this "first party system," which lasted until about 1815, became an essential part of the young republic's political life. Without it, Americans learned, it was difficult to get anything accomplished; indeed, free government itself was rendered ineffective.

What produced this momentous change of heart? Were the new parties the result of differences over ideology? Did opposing views of the Constitution create the party divisions? Were the parties deliberately planned to meet administrative or political needs? Were they the outgrowth of personality clashes among leaders driven by opposing ambitions? Let us look at the circumstances under which the parties emerged, for events often determine the shape of evolving institutions.

But first one confusing matter should be clarified. One of the two parties that appeared during the 1790s was called Federalist; the other was often referred to as Anti-Federalist, though it was also called Republican or Democratic-Republican, or sometimes Jeffersonian. These two groups must not be confused with the federalist and antifederalist partisans of the period when the Constitution was being debated. The issues that divided the two political parties of the "first party system" went beyond the disputes of 1787–1789.

* THE NEW GOVERNMENT LAUNCHED *

NATIONAL FINANCES.   Congress convened for the first time in New York early in 1789, and in the first session adopted two important tax measures: the Tariff Act of 1789, which placed duties on a wide range of imported articles, and the Tonnage Act, which taxed foreign vessels entering American ports. Congress also established three executive departments—State, Treasury, and War—and passed the Federal Judiciary Act, prescribing the structure of the Supreme Court and the federal court system.

The debate on the Tonnage Act revealed differences between Northerners, who conducted most of the nation's foreign trade, and Southerners, who exported tobacco and rice, but the disagreements were muted. It is the measure of the relative political peace of these early months that Washington could appoint Jefferson, soon to be the leading Republican, and Hamilton, soon to be the leading Federalist, as his first secretary of state and secretary of the treasury, respectively.

Yet even in this first session of the First Congress there were signs of trouble to come. One hint was the farcical dispute over how the president should be addressed. Was Washington to be called "His Elective Majesty," "His Highness the President," "His Excellency," or merely "Mr. President"? The first three titles had overtones of British monarchy; the last suggested plain American republicanism. The argument seems trivial, but it divided people into temperamental aristocrats and temperamental democrats, and foreshadowed later party differences.

Relative harmony became loud discord when, in its second session, the First Congress confronted the pressing issue of the unpaid war debts. Millions of dollars of state and national obligations were overdue. Failure to pay overseas creditors made it difficult for the American government to borrow from foreign bankers. Most of the debt, however, was owed to American citizens, including war veterans, former army suppliers, and those who had directly lent money to Congress or the states. The public creditors also included many businessmen and speculators who had bought up securities and debt certificates in the hope that they would rise in value when the government was finally able to repay them. How were all these people to be paid? And were they to be paid fully and equally?

HAMILTON'S PLAN FOR AMERICA.   The man chosen to provide practical answers to these questions was treasury secretary Alexander Hamilton of New York. Born illegitimate in the West Indies, he lacked the advantages of "good birth" and family wealth so useful in getting ahead in eighteenth-century America. But he made up for this by enormous charm, drive, and intelligence. The young man so impressed prominent men on St. Croix that they sent him to college on the mainland. Hamilton arrived in New York in 1773 in the midst of the imperial crisis and promptly joined the Patriot cause and then the Patriot army. His skill as an artillery officer soon brought him to the attention of Washington, who appointed him his aide-de-camp. After Yorktown Hamilton returned to his adopted city and set up as a lawyer.

Alexander Hamilton at about the time of his leadership of the Treasury Department.
(Portrait by John Trumbull, oil on canvas c. 1806, 30 × 24 in.
Courtesy by the National Portrait Gallery, Washington, D.C.)

Hamilton believed in strong government and had been instrumental in getting New York to adopt the Constitution. He thought the new Union was still too weak, but it was better than the old Confederation. When offered the job of secretary of the treasury, Hamilton leaped at the chance to help forge a strong national government and transform the United States into a unified and prosperous nation.

Hamilton was a political innovator with an expansive vision of America's future. The United States of 1790 was a nation of 4 million people, most of them farmers or farm workers. The first national census (1790) showed that only about 3 percent of the population lived in cities with more than 8,000 people. Hamilton recognized the importance of agriculture in America and understood that it would remain the country's economic mainstay for many years to come. But he believed that the United States must turn to manufacturing for its future prosperity. Industry would free the nation from foreign dependence. It would also transform it in positive ways. Looking at England, then fast becoming the workshop of the world, Hamilton perceived the wealth and power that might lie in store for America. As a public servant, he hoped to do more than just straighten out the country's tangled finances. In many ways the first secretary of the treasury was the first great national planner. He sought to encourage economic growth and social modernization. Although today we can see many of the environmental and human drawbacks of unrestrained industrialization, for its time Hamilton's was a progressive vision.

Hamilton incorporated these goals into three major reports submitted to Congress between January 1790 and December 1791. The *First Report on the Public Credit* proposed a plan for putting national finances on a sound basis. Now that the government had a guaranteed revenue from taxes and duties, let it pay its own creditors. It should also take over ("assume") the remaining state debts incurred during the war for independence. Hamilton knew that even with its newly acquired taxing power the government could not simply pay off these debts in one lump sum. His solution was a new issue of federal bonds that would bear an attractive interest rate. Holders of the old, defaulted debt could exchange it for the new "funded debt."

Hamilton's motives here were in part political. He hoped to strengthen the national government by winning the support of the rich and powerful, the country's chief creditors. But he also believed that a public debt would be a "blessing," rather than a "curse." The new funded debt could be used to back a new national money supply, which in turn would stimulate commerce and provide investment capital for a capital-poor nation. The new funded debt would be "an engine of business, an instrument of industry and commerce."

The secretary spelled out the way this process would operate in the *Report on a National Bank*. Congress should charter a commercial bank (called the Bank of the United States). Besides handling federal tax collections and disbursements and aiding private business transactions, a federally chartered bank would provide money for circulation and credit for investment. Investors in the Bank of the United States could use the new funded debt bonds, instead of specie, to buy bank stock. These bonds would then become the backing for an issue of "bank notes" that could then be lent to manufacturers and merchants and used as the normal cash of the country. By such means, Hamilton theorized, banks in general and the proposed federal bank in particular could become "nurseries of national wealth."

In his final important state paper, the *Report on Manufactures,* Hamilton urged Congress to support industry with subsidies, a tariff, and a system of roads, canals, and other "internal improvements." America's high labor costs and shortage of investment capital put it at a disadvantage against the better-developed European countries, but these handicaps could be overcome by government action. So long as given industries were weak, the government should nurture them. The benefits of supporting "infant industries," Hamilton claimed, would be felt not only by promoters of industry and the laboring classes but also by farmers, who would find new markets for their products in the manufacturing cities and towns that the government's protective policies would foster. Of Hamilton's three major reports, only this one on manufactures failed to result in immediate action by Congress. But it planted the seeds for later government protection of American industry.

ENACTING THE HAMILTONIAN PROGRAM.   The Funding Act of 1790 sought to enact the first portion of Hamilton's program. Part one allowed all present holders of national securities to convert them into federal bonds at face value, though at varying rates of interest. Under part two the federal government "assumed" the outstanding state debts.

The measure aroused the ire of James Madison, now a leader in the House of Representatives. Hamilton and his allies, Madison said, were not showing enough consideration for "original holders," who had helped the government during the war and had received securities in exchange. Many of these patriots had been forced to sell their securities at large discounts to speculators. Why should they not receive some part of the gain that would come when the debt was funded?

Though he dwelt on the ethical aspects of the issue, Madison was also concerned about the interests of his constituency, just as were his opponents. The southern states had already paid most of their debts. Now, under the assumption provision, burdened southern taxpayers would be asked to pay federal taxes to redeem the debts of delinquent northern states. Though it took a sectional form, the debate also reflected economic differences. To Madison and his supporters the North represented trade and commerce, the South, agriculture. The Funding Act, accordingly, seemed designed to benefit the commercial interests at the expense of the agricultural interests. After all, southerners declared, most of the speculators who would gain from the act lived in the port towns of New England, New York, and Pennsylvania.

The first part of the Funding Act passed after a bitter battle. But the assumption section seemed certain to go down to defeat until, with Jefferson's approval, Madison and Hamilton arranged a deal. In exchange for yielding on assumption, the new national capital, after moving to Philadelphia for ten years, would be located at a site on the Potomac between Maryland and Virginia. Thus sugarcoated, the Funding Act, with both sections intact, passed. In the end principle had yielded to sectional pride.

Early in 1791 Congress received Hamilton's bank bill. Madison attacked this measure, too. Once again, he was reluctant to advance commerce and industry at the expense of agriculture, but he preferred to raise constitutional objections. A strong nationalist in the 1780s, Madison now asked where in the Constitution Congress was authorized to incorporate such a bank. He rejected Hamilton's answer that certain powers of the federal government were "implied" in the Constitution.

Despite Madison's resistance, Congress established the Bank of the United States with a twenty-year federal charter. The new institution would accept deposits, make commercial loans, and perform other familiar banking services. But it would also handle the government's financial business, including its tax collections and disbursements, and issue up to $10 million in paper money, backed partly by gold but largely by the funded debt. In this way, as Hamilton intended, the federal debt would become the basis for a money circulation and a source of credit for a capital-poor land. In structure the bank would combine public and private features. Five of the twenty-five directors of the bank were to be appointed by the government, the rest by the private stockholders.

Washington was undecided about signing the bank bill. He would eventually become the Federalists' hero, but the president was not yet a strong political partisan. He understood his symbolic role as a just father who must rise above the fray, and to take an obviously partisan stand without very good reason might destroy the image. In his dilemma he turned to his cabinet—Hamilton, Jefferson, and Attorney General Edmund Randolph—for advice. Two written statements resulted, presenting the classic arguments for "loose construction" and "strict construction" of the Constitution. Hamilton defended the bank with his doctrine of implied powers. Jefferson and Randolph argued that powers not explicitly granted Congress by the Constitution were beyond its authority. Washington accepted Hamilton's views and approved the bill.

* THE BEGINNINGS OF PARTIES *

THE ECONOMIC DIVISION.   The Hamiltonian program drove a wedge through the nation, dividing Americans into opposing political camps. On one side were the emerging Federalists—speculators in government securities, merchants, manufacturers, and would-be manufacturers. Employees of the merchants and manufacturers—merchant seamen, artisans, clerks, bookkeepers, and all who worked in trade—also tended to support Hamilton's program. On the emerging Republican side were many small farmers and southern planters, especially those of middle rank.

The division along occupational lines transcended mere geography. The "commercial" classes were particularly numerous in New England and the Middle Atlantic states; southerners mostly belonged to the "cultivator" class. This situation largely accounts for the sectional split in Congress over the bank and funding. But in the South, wherever there were large pockets of people engaged in finance, trade, and industry, Federalists found numerous supporters. Similarly, in the North, where surplus crops were produced for export, the farmers were Federalists, while in more isolated farm areas cultivators expressed Republican sentiments.

THE IDEOLOGICAL DIVISION.   Economic interest, however, was not the only element that separated Federalists from Republicans. There were also differences in attitudes toward freedom, toward human nature, majority rule, and the role of government.

Republicans such as Jefferson, Madison, and John Taylor of Virginia regarded the Hamiltonian-Federalist dream as misguided and dangerous. Committed libertarians, they deplored paternalistic government. Individuals were far better judges, in general, of their own interests, they felt, than any set of government officials. Tyranny was more to be feared than chaos. Unless checked, government would grow excessively powerful and end by destroying freedom. However unfairly, they saw their opponents as disguised monarchists who were scarcely different from King George III and his ministers. Strictly limit the power of the national government, they exhorted, and assign as many functions as possible to the states.

Recent scholarship has made it clear that the Jeffersonian Republicans were believers in free markets (laissez-faire) rather than naive anticapitalists. Yet they were also "agrarians," people who cherished a society composed of small freeholders. Jefferson called the nation's farmers "the chosen people of God, if he ever had a chosen people." John Taylor proclaimed that "divine intelligence" had "selected an agricultural state as a paradise." The Jeffersonians were suspicious of the urban masses. City "artificers," wrote Jefferson, were often "the panderers of vice & the instruments by which the liberties of a country are generally overturned."

The fear of the urban "mob" was the fear of the propertyless who had no stake in society and could easily be corrupted and used by demagogues. It also reflected the Jeffersonian view that social virtue inhered in fields and flocks, not in factories, shipyards, and offices. Shadowy forms of urban wealth—stocks and bonds—were even more dubious. Drawing on views deeply embedded in Western consciousness, the agrarians attached a moral stigma to money lending and "stockjobbing." Republican prejudices logically extended to home-grown industry. In 1781 Jefferson would declaim: "While we have land to labour, then, let us

Rembrandt Peale, a famous American artist, painted this portrait of Jefferson in 1805. It was completed in time to be displayed at the president's second inauguration. (Collection of the New York Historical Society)

never wish to see our citizens occupied at a work-bench or twirling a distaff. Carpenters, masons, smiths, are wanting in husbandry; but, for the general operations of manufacture, let our work-shops remain in Europe." The preference for "husbandry" did not preclude commerce; obviously American farmers would want to trade their crop surpluses for foreign manufactures. Yet it was primarily as an adjunct to agriculture that commerce deserved favor.

Whatever their economic preferences, the Jeffersonians were optimists who believed in the ability of human intelligence to improve people's lot. They were also conservatives, in the original sense of the word: they wished to conserve what already existed. America must remain a nation of farms and forests. Their motto could have been "Keep America Green!" By contrast, for all their social and political caution, the Federalists sought to alter the economic status quo in fundamental ways.

Federalists and Republicans disagreed, too, over the value of majority rule. Federalists were elitists. They distrusted human nature and feared the rule of mere numbers. Such a regime denied power to the trained and the able, the "wellborn," and gave it to their inferiors. To Hamilton, the people were "a great beast." Harrison Gray Otis of Boston called the voters a "duped and deluded mob." John Jay of New York, first chief justice of the Supreme Court, reflected that "the mass of men are neither wise nor good, and virtue . . . can only be drawn to a point and executed by . . . a strong government ably administered."

Republicans, by contrast, proclaimed human nature to be inherently good. That human vices "are part of man's original constitution," announced one New York Jeffersonian, had been shown to be false. The evil deeds that people at times committed should be traced rather "to the errors and abuses that have at every period existed in political establishments." Jefferson himself regarded the people as eminently trustworthy. "I am," he announced, "not among those who fear the people; they, and not the rich, are our dependence for continued freedom." At moments Jefferson even sounded like a radical. In letters to friends and associates he wrote that "the tree of Liberty must be watered periodically with the blood of tyrants" and "a little revolution every twenty years is an excellent thing." In his public statements and acts he was far more reserved. We should also remember that he and his political allies tended to limit the "people" to the white tillers of the soil. Of the "mobs of great cities" they were far more suspicious. It is clear, nevertheless, that philosophically the Republicans were more democratic than their opponents.

We must not draw the distinctions between Federalist aristocracy and Republican democracy too sharply, however. Many southern Jeffersonians were slaveholders. Many deplored slavery in the abstract, but considered it indispensable. Jefferson himself did not believe in absolute human equality but in "natural aristocracy," an elite based on talent and ability, rather than birth. Nor should we assume that Hamilton and his followers were unqualified aristocrats or "monocrats," as their enemies called them. Generally they accepted representative government as unavoidable in America and never seriously intended to establish a monarchy.

Yet when all these qualifications are noted, it remains true that Federalists had less faith in majority rule than their opponents. The Republicans, in turn, had less confidence in persons of wealth and position than in "the people."

THE ROLE OF RELIGION.   Religion also separated the two emerging parties. In the 1790s the Federalists attracted Congregationalists in New England and Episcopalians in the Middle Atlantic states and the South. Leading Federalists were often outspoken defenders of traditional Christian beliefs. The Republicans won the support of a hodgepodge of Baptists, Methodists, Roman Catholics, nonbelievers, and deists. These groupings may not appear to make much sense—Roman Catholics and nonbelievers do not seem to have much in common. If we take a second look, however, we can see the pattern: Members of long-established churches, which had received financial support from state governments and so had privileged positions, voted Federalist; the others tended to prefer the Jeffersonian-Republicans.

The Republican appeal to nonbelievers is easy to understand. Jefferson himself was a deist whose religious creed rejected many orthodox Christian elements. As for the Republican appeal to Catholics and evangelical Protestants, such as Baptists and Methodists, these groups had long been victims of legal discrimination. By the 1790s they were still disqualified from holding office in some areas, and in parts of New England where Congregationalism was still the established church, they remained second-class citizens. The role of Jefferson and Madison in securing the Virginia Statute for Religious Freedom, which disestablished the Anglican church, earned the Republican leaders the gratitude of all those outside the established religious order everywhere. In Connecticut and Massachusetts the Republicans confirmed this attachment by leading the fight to end the preferred status conferred on Congregationalism. It is not surprising, then, that people who thought of themselves as religious outsiders should find Republicanism more congenial than Federalism.

Religion served to counteract economic interest as a factor in party support. A Congregational farmer in Massachusetts, for example, would seem to be represented by Republicans agrarian interests, but might well vote Federalist on the basis of religion. Of course, a rich Catholic lawyer from New York, whom we would expect to vote for the Federalists on the basis of occupation, might well support the Republicans for religious reasons. On the whole the religious factor seemed to help the Federalists more than their opponents.

* RELATIONS WITH EUROPE *

The first party system was not only a response to domestic events and attitudes. It was also derived from America's complex relations with the rest of the Atlantic world.

In 1790 Spain controlled the mouth of the Mississippi and still denied Americans the right of free deposit at New Orleans. The British continued to restrict American trade with their empire and refused to abandon the military posts they occupied in the Northwest. And even France had begun to limit American trade with its colonies, despite the commercial treaty of 1778.

REVOLUTION IN FRANCE. The outbreak of the French Revolution of 1789 would make these problems infinitely worse. The great political convulsion in France aroused strong passions in America. At first most Americans rejoiced at the overthrow of the corrupt, aristocratic, and worn-out Old Regime in the most powerful nation on the European continent. One enthusiastic Yankee orator saw the fall of the Bastille, the hated prison that symbolized French tyranny, as a "spark from the altar flame of liberty on this side of the Atlantic, which alighted in the pinnacle of despotism in France and reduced the immense fabric to ashes in the twinkling of an eye." In Boston, streets were renamed for revolutionary ideals—Royal Exchange Alley, for example, became Equality Lane. Some Americans replaced "mister" with the revolutionary "citizen" and "Mrs." with the awkward "citess." At first even men of conservative temper welcomed the change. President Washington graciously received from Lafayette the key to the Bastille as a link between the American and French struggles against tyranny.

But the fall of the Bastille was followed by the overthrow of the French monarchy, the execution of King Louis XVI, the bloody Reign of Terror, confiscation of the property of French nobles, and ever more violent attacks on the church and traditional Christianity. American public opinion quickly split. Fisher Ames, a Massachusetts Federalist, was soon denouncing revolutionary France as "an open hell, still ringing with agonies and blasphemies, still smoking with sufferings and crimes, in which we see . . . perhaps our future state." Other Federalists warned that the French "moral influenza" was to be more dreaded than a "thousand yellow fevers." Jefferson, Madison, and their allies, however, continued to admire the revolutionaries, cheering the end of "superstition" and applauding the "rule of reason." Many approved of the execution of Louis XVI and even saw virtue in the Reign of Terror.

When war broke out in 1793 between the new French Republic and England, Spain, and Holland, Americans were uncertain how to respond. France was America's formal ally, and although it had not lately taken the friendship seriously, the French Republic needed American support now that it was fighting for its life. The French saw the United States as a source of food and supplies for itself and the French colonies in the Caribbean and a possible base of operations against British and Spanish possessions in North America.

CITIZEN GENÊT. Seeking American aid, in 1793 the French government dispatched "Citizen" Edmond Genêt to the United States. Genêt immediately became a magnet for controversy. Secretary Hamilton opposed receiving him for fear that it would involve the nation in the war. Secretary Jefferson believed that if we refused, we would be repudiating our alliance with France. Neither man wished to see the United States enter the war, but Hamilton believed that it was the president's task to proclaim neutrality, and he should do so at once, while Jefferson favored a congressional announcement, but only after the United States had squeezed concessions out of both the British and the French. Washington took his treasury secretary's advice and in April 1793 issued a proclamation of neutrality asking Americans to be "impartial" toward the belligerents and forbidding actions favorable to either side. Republicans found the proclamation too even-handed. "The cause of France is the cause of man," declared one protesting Jeffersonian.

Meanwhile, hoping to make the United States a base for operations against Britain and Spain, Genêt hired George Rogers Clark, the Indian fighter and hero of the Revolution, to lead an expedition against the Spanish in Louisiana and Florida. He also issued commissions in the proposed army and authorized privateers to sail from American ports to attack British and Spanish shipping. In midsummer of 1793, Genêt demanded that Washington call Congress into special session to decide what the United States would do to aid the French Republic. If the president refused, he arrogantly declared, he would take his case to the American people over Washington's head.

Genêt's activities further polarized American opinion. The Republicans at first befriended him, and Jefferson filled the Frenchman's ears with the misdeeds of his Federalist opponents. The Federalists despised him and used his dubious activities as a stick with which to beat their opponents. The English-born Federalist journalist William Cobbett labeled the Republicans the "bastard offspring of Genêt, spawned in hell, to which they will presently return."

Before long Genêt's activities had so embarrassed the American government that even Jefferson agreed he must be sent home. France, however, was now in the hands of the radical Jacobins, who despised the moderates who had sent Genêt to America. Rather than send the amiable but foolish emissary to certain execution, Washington granted him asylum in the United States.

THE PARTISAN PRESS.   Differences over foreign policy, combined with the disagreements over the Hamiltonian program, had by now produced a combative party press that further enflamed the political rivalry. Federalist and Republican newspapers published scathing attacks on their opponents. John Fenno's *Gazette of the United States* treated Hamilton as a demigod and spewed out insults against his enemies. These "Jacobins" were working to corrupt the nation's youth and "make them imbibe, with their very milk . . . the poison of atheism and disaffection." The *General Advertiser,* edited by Franklin's grandson, Benjamin Franklin Bache, and Philip Freneau's *National Gazette* denounced the Federalists as outright monarchists and dupes of British policy. Bache even maligned Washington as the "scourge of all the misfortunes of our country," a man who had given currency "to political iniquity and to legalized corruption."

Within Washington's cabinet the relations between Jefferson and Hamilton became so bad that at the end of 1793 Jefferson resigned as secretary of state and was replaced by Edmund Randolph, a Virginia Federalist. But Jefferson's departure did not end his leadership of the Republicans. From Monticello, his hilltop home in Virginia, he continued to issue political advice, remaining in close touch with Madison, the party's chief tactician in Congress.

RELATIONS WITH ENGLAND. Just before Jefferson's departure, European affairs once more reached a crisis. This time the United States found itself pitted against the world's greatest naval power, England. The difficulty concerned neutral rights on the high seas in time of war, an issue that would not be settled for generations.

Basically the two nations disagreed over whether the United States could trade freely with France, England's enemy. The French, unable to protect their shipping against the powerful British navy, had opened their imperial trade, normally restricted to French vessels, to neutral commerce. The British, rightly, saw this as a maneuver to evade their naval advantage and invoked the Rule of 1756, which declared that trade forbidden in time of peace could not be legally pursued in time of war. In effect, a weak naval power could not protect itself by hiding behind a neutral. Britain and the United States also argued over "contraband." International law recognized the right of one nation to blockade its wartime enemy's ports and prevent neutral nations from delivering certain war goods—contraband—through the blockade. But contraband was not clearly defined, nor was the legal status of neutral trade in other goods.

Soon after Anglo-French hostilities began, Britain proclaimed a blockade of France and its colonies and deployed its navy to destroy French shipping and commerce. The French immediately lifted all restrictions on foreign imports and opened their ports to foreign ships. Neutral America seized the opportunity to supply French shipping needs. For the next two decades, as Britain and France struggled to dominate Europe, French demand stimulated American trade beyond all previous measure. Salem, Boston, Providence, New York, and Philadelphia boomed between 1790 and 1796 as the annual value of foreign trade leaped from $46 million to $140 million.

The British denounced the Americans for profiting from Britain's troubles by supplying their chief enemy with needed commodities. Even more galling, Britain was unintentionally supplying many of the seamen for the bloated American merchant fleet. Some of these were deserters from the Royal Navy, who preferred the lenient treatment and good pay of American merchant seamen to the harsh discipline, bad food, and physical dangers faced by sailors in the British navy. British merchant seamen, too, jumped ship for the higher pay and better working conditions of the American merchant marine.

To offset the loss of sailors, British men-of-war began to stop American vessels to inspect the crews for deserters, "impressing" both those deemed guilty and those who merely looked like apt recruits for the depleted Royal Navy. Americans were outraged by impressment, but their anger was tempered by fear that worsening relations with Britain would destroy entirely the lucrative trade with France. To New Englanders and residents of the middle states' ports—the chief beneficiaries of this trade—it seemed wiser to submit to British practices, however arbitrary, than to defy Britain, provoke war, and see the new trade completely shut down.

THE BRITISH AND THE INDIANS.   In one area of Anglo-American relations, however, almost all Americans agreed that British policies were deplorable. In the Northwest, British garrisons remained on American soil and British fur traders still monopolized business with the Indians. Americans were also certain that the British were encouraging the Indians south of the Great Lakes in their policy of harassing American settlers. During the winter of 1791–1792, after defeating two American military expeditions sent against them, the Indians forced the Ohio settlers to retreat to the region's two well-defended villages. President Washington now decided to settle the conflict by overwhelming force and dispatched a new army under Anthony Wayne to the Ohio region. Wayne, an abler strategist than his predecessors, trained and seasoned his troops through the winter and spring of 1793–1794. In August 1794 he confronted the Indians at Fallen Timbers and decisively defeated them.

THE JAY TREATY.   In the fall of 1793 the crisis between England and the United States came to a head when a British order in council—an executive proclamation—authorized English naval commanders to seize neutral vessels trading with the French Caribbean islands. In short order 250 American ships were boarded by British naval parties, escorted to British ports, and confiscated. The seizures infuriated Americans, and it soon seemed like 1775 all over again. Mobs roamed the streets of seaport towns, denouncing Britain and insulting and threatening Englishmen. British tempers were equally hot and it looked as if war was imminent. To avoid a military showdown, for which the United States was ill prepared, Washington sent Chief Justice John Jay to England to negotiate.

The British drove a hard bargain with the upstart Americans. They agreed to surrender the western posts and pay for American ships recently confiscated. They also yielded slightly on the long-festering issue of trade with the British Empire. The United States would be allowed to trade with British India, and small American vessels would be permitted to enter British West Indies ports. But in most other matters they refused to budge. They rejected American demands for full commercial equality with British subjects. They denied liability for the slaves they had removed from the South during the Revolution. The final agreement contained a broad definition of contraband that made many American goods liable to seizure, as well as a proviso that the United States must close its ports to French privateers. To satisfy long-standing English complaints, the United States also agreed to refer all unpaid American private debts owed English creditors to a joint commission for settlement. On western problems, too, the United States made concessions. In return for surrendering the Northwest posts, Britain would be allowed to exploit the resources of the region south of the Canadian border as in the past.

To France's friends and England's enemies the Jay Treaty seemed a sellout. Jay was denounced as an "archtraitor" and hanged in effigy by irate crowds all across the country. The agreement itself was referred to widely as "that damned treaty." For a while there was doubt that the Senate would confirm it or the president sign it. But the Senate's strong Federalist majority passed the treaty after striking out one of the more unfavorable trade provisions. Washington hesitated but approved it when he realized that the alternative might well be war with England. Even after adoption the treaty continued to rankle, and Washington was reviled for endorsing it. Jefferson claimed that he had "undone the country," and a bitterly partisan Virginian ventured the shocking toast: "A speedy death to General Washington."

Hostility to the Jay Treaty powerfully reinforced the ongoing process of party formation. In the House of Representatives—the body that would have to appropriate money to carry out several provisions of the pact—Republicans organized the first congressional party caucus ever held to consider ways to defeat the treaty. In the end their attempt failed, but the close House vote revealed the new strength of the opposition and the extent to which foreign affairs had polarized Congress along party lines.

THE WHISKEY REBELLION; THE PINCKNEY TREATY. The major disputes with Great Britain now settled, however unsatisfactorily, the Washington administration turned to differences with Spain.

In the Northwest, Britain's surrender of the military posts meant the abandonment of its Indian allies. Chastened by their defeat at Fallen Timbers, the Indians signed the Treaty of Greenville in 1795, surrendering all of Ohio except for a small strip along Lake Erie. Before many months a mass movement of white pioneer farmers into the Northwest was under way. In the Southwest, where Indian resistance to the whites was weaker, by 1796 there were already two new states—Kentucky and Tennessee—carved out of a region that had had no permanent white inhabitants twenty years earlier.

The western pioneers were a restless and unruly lot. For years frontier farmers had been angry over federal tax policy. Unable to sell their grain to distant urban customers because of high transportation costs, they had found an ingenious alternative. To make their grain portable, they made it potable, distilling it into whiskey, which could be easily carried to market in barrels. When the government imposed a tax on distilled liquors in 1791 to raise money for Hamilton's funding plan, westerners defied the authorities and threatened tax collectors with physical harm.

In 1794 the farmers of western Pennsylvania carried defiance to the point of open rebellion. The "Whiskey Rebels" closed down federal courts and robbed the mails. They attacked federal troops guarding the tax collector for the Pittsburgh district. Washington quickly ordered out the militia of Virginia, Maryland, New Jersey, and Pennsylvania. With the bellicose Hamilton as second in command, this small army marched on the rebels. The insurgents surrendered without a shot. Two were convicted of high treason and then pardoned.

The incident confirmed westerners' disgust at the trigger-happy Federalists. At the same time it showed the government that westerners were not to be trifled with. Now they were demanding that the federal government do something about Spain's refusal to allow the right of deposit at New Orleans. If the United States government did not give them what they wanted, they would take matters into their own hands and negotiate directly with Spain.

At this point Washington ordered Thomas Pinckney to Spain to arbitrate the differences between the two nations. Fortunately for the United States, Spain was ready to negotiate. In short order Pinckney and the Spanish foreign minister concluded a treaty granting the United States free navigation of the Mississippi and the right of tax-free deposit at New Orleans for three years, subject to renewal. The treaty also set the boundary between the United States and Florida at the thirty-first parallel, conceding the Yazoo Strip of southern Georgia and Mississippi to the Americans. The Jay Treaty had left many issues unresolved. The Pinckney Treaty, for the moment at least, settled the nagging problem of Mississippi navigation at virtually no cost to the United States.

WASHINGTON'S FAREWELL.   In 1796 Washington decided to retire after two terms to his plantation home at Mount Vernon on the Potomac. Before leaving, however, he delivered a formal farewell to his fellow Americans in the form of a letter published in the newspapers. The departing president's "Farewell Address" cautioned against "permanent alliances with any portion of the foreign world." But most of his message was a warning against the "spirit of party" and a tribute to the virtues of "fraternal affection" and national unity. Toward the end of his administration Washington had been drawn into the ranks of the Federalists. Still, he did not believe in the party system, and he told the American people that factionalism served to "distract the public councils and enfeeble the public administration."

With Washington gone, the Federalists were now deprived of an immense political asset. In the election of 1796 they would not have the nation's greatest popular hero at the head of their ticket. This time there would be a real contest for the presidency.

THE ELECTION OF 1796.   No one was quite sure how the presidential candidates would be selected in 1796 and how, once chosen, one would be elected to office. Washington had faced no opposition as nominee or candidate and had not campaigned. Now things were different. In a few states there were already permanent party organizations and a formal nominating procedure. In others, and at the national level, party machinery was primitive. In the end the leaders of each party informally consulted with one another and decided who to support as their party's candidates. The Republicans' choice of Jefferson was never in doubt. Among the Federalists, however, the leaders disagreed. The High, or extreme, Federalists supported Thomas Pinckney, the treaty negotiator. Moderates preferred Vice President John Adams. Because the party leaders were unable to settle on a single nominee, there were two Federalist candidates.

The contest was fought over the unpopular Jay Treaty and general foreign policy, though the Republicans tried to make the supposed monarchism of their opponents a major issue. Official electors were chosen by popular vote in only half the states; in the others the state legislatures made the choice. The Federalists won a majority in the electoral college, carrying most of the states from New Jersey north. But since they were divided between High Federalists and Adams men, the Federalist electors could not coordinate their votes. Adams received the highest number of votes and became president. Enough Federalists refused to support Pinckney, however, to give Jefferson the second highest number of votes, thereby making him vice president under the existing terms of the Constitution.

THE XYZ AFFAIR.   Adams no sooner took office than the United States found itself in an undeclared war with its recent ally, France. The French government, now in the hands of the Directory, a new ruling group, considered the Jay Treaty a virtual Anglo-American alliance and the election of Adams, the candidate of the pro-British Federalists, seemed to confirm American sympathies for England. In 1797 the French authorities ordered that impressed American sailors captured from the British be hanged and that any intercepted American ship carrying British goods be confiscated. They also refused to receive the American minister, Charles Cotesworth Pinckney.

Adams might have used these insults to break relations with France. But unlike the more inflexible High Federalists he preferred to negotiate. As commissioners to settle with the French, he appointed the previously rejected Charles C. Pinckney; John Marshall, a Virginia Federalist; and Elbridge Gerry, a Massachusetts leader with Republican leanings. At the same time, as a precaution, the administration asked Congress to provide funds to expand the army and navy.

When the American commissioners arrived in France, they were received by Charles Talleyrand, the French foreign minister. A wily and corrupt man, Talleyrand made them cool their heels and then turned them over to three of his agents. These men—mentioned in the diplomatic dispatches as X, Y, and Z—promised to speed up negotiations if the Americans paid Talleyrand and other French officials $250,000, lent France $12 million, and apologized publicly for harsh words President Adams had recently hurled their way. The commissioners refused to comply. They had not been instructed to pay a bribe, they said, and such a large loan to France would seriously damage relations with England. Besides, how could they know whether, after paying, the United States would gain a favorable treaty?

When news of the negotiations reached the United States, it produced a tremendous uproar. Americans considered the corrupt French demands an unforgivable insult to their nation. The Federalists attacked the French and their Republican friends with renewed fury and made Pinckney and Marshall, the two Federalist commissioners, into heroes. One Federalist journalist proudly boasted that when the French had asked to be bribed, Pinckney had retorted: "Millions for defense, but not one cent for tribute!" (What he actually said was far less eloquent: "No, no, not a six-pence!")

The XYZ Affair ignited a naval war between the former allies. French raiders from the Caribbean began attacking American vessels in United States coastal waters. Congress responded by voting money to triple the size of the army and build forty new ships for the navy. In May 1798 it created the Navy Department with a secretary of cabinet rank to head it. Washington was recalled to public service and placed in command of the army, with Hamilton, yearning, as always, for military glory, second in command. In July Congress nullified the French alliance of 1778, ending the pretense of special friendship for that country. For the next few years American and French ships attacked one another in the Caribbean. The Americans also helped the British and their ally, the black patriot Toussaint L'Ouverture, overthrow the French regime on the island of Hispaniola and establish Haiti as the first black nation in the New World.

The pressure on Adams to formally declare war on France was immense. But the president, aware of American unpreparedness, refused. In 1799 the French government began to show a more conciliatory attitude. Late in the year Adams sent three new emissaries to Paris to reopen negotiations. The president wanted the French to compensate Americans for their recent "spoliations" of American commerce, and insisted that France formally accept nullification of the 1778 treaty. Now led by Napoleon Bonapart, the French refused the first condition but accepted the second. On that basis the two countries signed the Convention of 1800. The United States had again avoided war.

✻ REPUBLICAN TRIUMPH ✻

The crisis with France improved Anglo-American relations and won considerable popular support for the Federalists. But it also set in motion a train of events that ultimately led to the emergence of the Republicans as the majority party.

As yet, few Americans understood the role of a "loyal opposition." Opposing the administration in power seemed disloyalty, if not treason, and they could not see the value of a second party in keeping the first honest. Partisan hostility often went beyond the bounds of decency. The Republican *General Advertiser* called the president the "old, querulous, bald, blind, crippled, toothless Adams." Vermont Congressman Matthew Lyon was almost expelled from Congress for spitting in a Federalist member's eye and wrestling with him on the floor of the House of Representatives chamber.

THE ALIEN AND SEDITION ACTS. Deep ideological differences, certainty that they were the nation's bulwark against foreign evil, and the surge of patriotism in the face of French danger all go to explain (though they do not excuse) the extreme actions that the Federalists now took. In 1798 the Federalist Congress, claiming national security as justification, passed four laws known collectively as the Alien and Sedition Acts. The Naturalization Act extended the residence requirement for naturalization as a citizen from five to fourteen years, thereby keeping the vote from recent pro-French Irish and French immigrants. The Alien Act gave the president power to expel from the country any alien considered dangerous or suspected of treasonable acts. Under the Alien Enemies Act, the president was authorized to arrest, imprison, or expel enemy aliens in the event of war. The Sedition Act made it illegal for both aliens and citizens to (1) impede the execution of federal laws; (2) bring the federal government, Congress, or the president into disrepute; (3) instigate or abet any riot, insurrection, or unlawful assembly; or (4) prevent a federal officer from performing his duties.

Under the Sedition Act Secretary of State Timothy Pickering prosecuted four leading Republican newspapers and several individuals. Ten of the indictments resulted in convictions, and a flock of foreign political activists fled the country rather than face almost certain prosecution. Despite these "successes," the Alien and Sedition Acts were a tremendous political blunder. The Federalists had their opponents on the run until the passage of these laws. Unable to support the France of the XYZ Affair and the undeclared naval war, many moderate Republicans had defected to the side of the administration. Now the government's vindictiveness and disregard of free speech propelled the waverers back to the Republican side.

To meet this challenge to civil liberties and to the power of the states relative to the national government, Jefferson and Madison induced the legislatures of Kentucky and Virginia to denounce the recent Alien and Sedition Acts on constitutional grounds. The Virginia and Kentucky Resolutions held that the Constitution was a "compact," or agreement, among the states to confer only limited powers on the national government. Whenever the national government exceeded these powers—as in the Alien and Sedition Acts—the states had the right to oppose it. The Kentucky legislature later asserted the right of states to resort to "nullification . . . of all unauthorized acts" by the national government.

Both states called on their sister commonwealths to join their protest. Few did. Where the Federalists were in control, the legislatures rejected the idea that the states were the proper judges of constitutionality. And even Republican legislatures were reluctant to approve the nullification doctrine. Nevertheless, the Virginia and Kentucky resolutions gave effective voice to widespread rank-and-file Republican outrage at the administration's disregard of civil liberties. They were also significant precedents for the later southern position on states' rights.

THE TRANSFER OF POWER.   By the time Congress ratified the Convention of 1800, Adams was out of office and Thomas Jefferson had become the third president of the United States. The 1800 presidential contest that ended in Republican victory was the precedent for peaceful and orderly surrender of power by one political party to another that America has followed ever since.[1] When the 1800 campaign opened, Adams's peace policy was popular with the moderate public and Federalists had made gains in the state elections of 1799. But the party was actually in trouble. Washington's death at the end of the year deprived it of a powerful unifying force. Soon the personal rivalry and temperamental differences

---

[1] Except in 1860 when Lincoln was elected and the lower south seceded in protest.

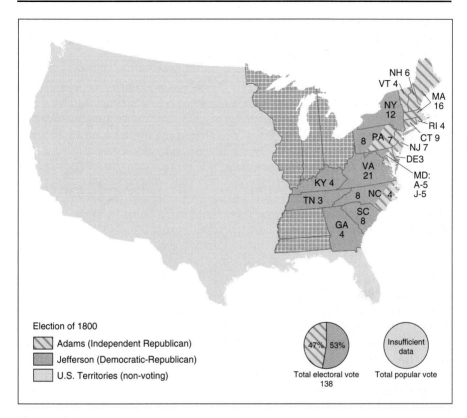

Election of 1800

Adams (Independent Republican)
Jefferson (Democratic-Republican)
U.S. Territories (non-voting)

47% 53%

Insufficient data

Total electoral vote 138

Total popular vote

Election of 1800

between Adams and Hamilton became an open scandal. Moreover, Republican efforts to woo northern business interests and town laborers had begun to produce results. Few contemporaries as yet saw these weak spots.

In May 1800 a caucus of Federalist congressmen chose Adams and Charles Cotesworth Pinckney of the XYZ Affair as their candidates. The Republicans nominated Jefferson and Aaron Burr of New York by the same congressional caucus system. Both caucuses pledged to support each candidate equally, even though this commitment created the risk that the House of Representatives, under the existing constitutional rule, would have to choose between them for president and vice president if there should be a tie in the electoral college.

And a tie in fact was what happened. During the campaign Federalists and Republicans employed such modern tactics as printed party tickets, appeals to party loyalty, and public speechmaking. When it was over, Adams and Pinckney had only 65 electoral votes, and Jefferson and Burr each had 73 votes.

Who would be president and who second in command? No one doubted that the Republicans had intended Jefferson to be their candidate for the top office; but as things stood, the House of Representatives would have to decide the question, with each state casting one vote. The Federalists would be in a position to veto whichever candidate they wished. But would they? To some Federalists it seemed that if Jefferson was bad, Burr was even worse. Hamilton admitted that Jefferson "had some pretentions to character," but Burr was a complete rogue, a man "bankrupt beyond redemption." When Jefferson's friends gave the Federalist congressman from Delaware, James Bayard, assurances that the Virginian would leave Hamilton's financial system intact, maintain the armed forces at full strength, allow most Federalist civil servants to keep their jobs, and continue to steer the nation on a neutral course in foreign affairs, Bayard threw his state's vote to the Virginian. This one-state shift decided the election. The transfer of power was now complete. Jefferson, the arch-Republican, would be the third president of the United States.

* CONCLUSIONS *

In little more than a decade, Americans had laid the foundation of a modern political party system. They had discovered that the machinery of government that the Constitution provided had to be supplemented by voluntary political institutions called parties. But they had not made a deliberate, considered decision; parties had evolved through the circumstances of the day. The need to put America's economic house in order and deal with its unsettled finances had created passionate disagreements between people with commitments to agriculture and those engaged in trade, banking, and manufacture. Differences over the French Revolution had divided the country between those who felt the exhilaration of a freer, more democratic, and more secular Europe, and those who saw revolutionary France as a dangerous enemy of religion and social order and perceived Britain as a bastion of stability.

Constitutional biases had also divided Americans. During the years of Washington's and Adams's administrations, the Federalists had, understandably, favored a broad interpretation of national powers; and they had stretched these to the limit to achieve their legislative ends. The Jeffersonians, by contrast, had fought centralized, concentrated national power and favored protection of the states' authority. Time would show that much of this difference depended on which party was "in" and which was "out." And yet we must not be too cynical about the parties' professions of constitutional principles. What started as rationalization often ended as sincere conviction.

However it came about, by 1800 the country had acquired two great national parties. Neither had a monopoly of virtue or wisdom. The Republicans had shown greater sensitivity to personal rights and freedom; ideologically, they would point the way to a more open and democratic society. But their vision of the nation's social and economic future was naive. The Federalists had seen that America's greatness could not be limited by the past. They had recognized that the United States was fated to become a land of busy workshops as well as fertile farms and pastures. Yet they had failed to understand the average person's yearning for equality and the immense value of personal liberty and free expression in a progressive society. It remained to be seen now if the party of Jefferson could avoid the excesses of its opponents and find a workable balance for the nation.

8

THE JEFFERSONIANS IN OFFICE

How Did Power Affect Republican Ideology?

1800	Jefferson elected president; Washington, D.C., becomes the national capital
1801	President Adams appoints "midnight judges" to tighten Federalist control of the courts
1802	The federal government sells its shares in the Bank of the United States; The Republican Congress repeals the Judiciary Act of 1801
1803–06	Lewis and Clark explore the West
1803	*Marbury v. Madison;* The Louisiana Purchase
1805	The Essex decision: Congress retaliates with the Nonimportation Act
1805–06	The Wilkinson-Burr conspiracy
1806–07	England and France issue decrees limiting neutral trade in Europe
1807	The Chesapeake–Leopard affair; Jefferson activates the Nonimportation Act of 1806; The Embargo Act
1808	James Madison elected president
1809	The Nonintercourse Act
1810	Macon's Bill Number Two
1811	Southern and western "War Hawks" dominate the House of Representatives; American naval ship President attacks English navy's Little Belt; Congress defeats an attempt to recharter the Bank of the United States; Battle of Tippecanoe
1812	Congress provides for a 35,000-man regular army, gives Madison the power to call up state militias, and declares war on England
1814	Napoleon defeated in Europe; British troops are transferred to America and move on Washington; The Hartford Convention; The Peace of Ghent provides settlement of minor disputes between United States and Britain, leaves major issues of war untouched

| 1815 | Andrew Jackson's victory over the British at New Orleans |
| 1817 | Rush-Bagot Agreement provides for demilitarizing United States–Canada border |

In December 1815 James Madison sent his seventh annual message to Congress. The president reported Captain Stephen Decatur's defeat of the Dey of Algiers, a victory that finally forced the Barbary pirates to cease their demands for tribute and their attacks on American ships. He also reported progress in concluding peace with the Indian tribes in the West and described the still-disturbed state of the country's finances in the wake of the recent war. But the most arresting portion of the message was its last paragraphs. In these Madison recommended a protective tariff to encourage domestic industry, a program for building roads and canals, and "a national seminary of learning" within the District of Columbia, to be financed by the federal government. This national university would serve as "a central resort for youth and genius from every part of the country, diffusing on their return [to their homes] those national feelings, those liberal sentiments, and those congenial manners which contribute cement to our Union and strength to the great political fabric of which it is the foundation."

These proposals were startling. Madison was the man who had fought Hamilton's scheme to establish a national bank and drafted the Virginia Resolution of 1798, which proclaimed the limited power of the federal government under the Constitution. His party was the party of states' rights and strict construction. Now leader of that party, he was asking Congress for some of the very things he had opposed!

What had produced this about-face? Only fourteen years had elapsed between the election of 1800, which made Thomas Jefferson president, and Madison's seventh annual message. What had taken place in this decade and a half to cause such a drastic change of direction among Republicans?

* PRESIDENT JEFFERSON *

Part of the answer is Republican adaptability. Once in office, Jefferson proved to be less dogmatic than many of his opponents had feared. In his inaugural speech Jefferson sought to quiet fears and disarm his enemies. The recent political campaign had been bitter, he noted, but now that it was over, the country must unite. His party would respect the funded debt established by the Federalists and the rights of political minorities. Though the two parties called themselves by different names, their members were "brethren of the same principle." "We are all Republicans, we are all Federalists," he declared. Nor would the victorious Republicans return the country to its feeble state before the Constitution. It was important, he said, to support "the State governments in all their rights"; but it was also necessary to preserve "the General Government in its whole constitutional vigor, as the sheet anchor of our peace at home and safety abroad."

A NEW, REPUBLICAN SPIRIT.   Despite Jefferson"s conciliatory professions, he sought to introduce "republican" principles into the conduct of the government. The new president reduced the formalities that had surrounded Washington and Adams. In place of his predecessors' regal ceremonial visits to Congress to express their wishes on new legislation or policy, Jefferson sent written messages. Instead of "levees," formal occasions at which members of the government and resplendent diplomats paid court to the president in strict order of rank, Jefferson gave state dinners at which guests took whatever seat they could find. Still more characteristic of Jefferson were his small dinners, with guests seated at a round table where no one could claim precedence over anyone else. For these informal gatherings the red-haired president often dressed in carpet slippers and a threadbare scarlet vest, his shirt not always perfectly clean. The guests discussed philosophy, the arts, literature, and science while eating food prepared by an excellent French chef, though often served by the president himself.

FEDERALIST LEGISLATION REPEALED.   Jefferson tried to break with the Federalist past in more fundamental ways as well. At first he labored to contract the role of the national government, and he was partially successful. The secretary of the treasury, Albert Gallatin of Pennsylvania, reduced the detested national debt by cutting down appropriations for the army and the navy, which the Republicans neither liked nor considered essential. At the same time the new administration was able to do away with several unpopular internal taxes imposed by the Federalists. The Republicans attacked or eliminated other Federalist policies or programs. They repealed some of the Alien and Sedition Acts, allowed others to expire, and pardoned all those the Federalists had imprisoned for sedition. Because it had a twenty-year charter, the Bank of the United States could not be dismantled until 1811, but in 1802 the federal government sold its shares of bank stock at a profit and got out of the banking business.

A STRONG ECXECUTIVE   The initial Republican attack on "big government" soon gave way to a more pragmatic approach. The third president was by temperament a vigorous leader who did what was needed to advance the national interest as he saw it. Although he had earlier condemned a powerful central government, after 1801, when he passed from opposition to power, he shifted ground. As president he decided that he could not be overburdened with constitutional scruples if he was to get things done. His critics charged him with hypocrisy, but we can see his inconsistencies as growth.

Though willing to reassure his opponents, Jefferson had no intention of allowing them to dominate the national government or tie his hands. As yet, the politicians had not raised to a lofty democratic principle the "spoils system" of replacing government personnel of the defeated party with members of the victorious one. Jefferson himself believed that the measure of fitness to hold appointive office should be merit. But not all the Federalist officeholders could be counted on to administer fairly the laws passed by a Republican Congress and approved by a Republican president. Some of them, moreover, were corrupt or incompetent. Finally, he could not disregard the fact that many Republicans could see no reason why they should not get jobs as rewards for loyal service to the president and the party. Jefferson would have preferred to allow positions to become available by retirement or death. Unfortunately, he noted, the vacancies "by death are few; by resignation none."

During Jefferson's first two years in office he replaced almost 200 Federalist officials with members of his own party. Federalist leaders, who believed that the new president had promised to leave all positions below cabinet rank alone, protested, but to no avail.

THE ATTACK ON THE JUDICIARY.   A particularly thorny problem for the incoming president was the national judiciary. United States judges were virtually all Federalists, and these men were not impartial or disinterested. Because they were appointed for life, the president could not remove them. Matters were made particularly acute, from the Republican point of view, by the Judiciary Act of 1801, passed during the final days of the Adams administration. The act relieved Supreme Court justices of the burden of having to travel from place to place to hear lower court cases; it gave that job to sixteen new circuit judges. The law improved national legal enforcement, but it also gave the Federalist party even tighter control over the federal court system. On the evening of March 3, 1801, the day before Jefferson's inauguration, Adams signed the commissions of the new circuit judges along with those of a flock of new federal marshals, attorneys, and justices of the peace. All the "midnight appointees" were Federalist party members, and it now looked as if the opposition party had locked up control of at least one branch of the government for decades to come, despite the Republican victory of 1800.

The Republicans were outraged by Adams's action. Jefferson noted that the Federalists had "retired to the judiciary . . . and from that battery all the works of Republicanism are to be beaten down and destroyed." To keep the new appointees from assuming office, Secretary of State James Madison refused to deliver their commissions. Soon after, the Republican Congress repealed the 1801 Judiciary Act and replaced it with the Judiciary Act of 1802.

At this point the commanding figure of John Marshall, chief justice of the Supreme Court, enters the picture. A Virginian of strong Federalist views, Marshall insisted that the Supreme Court had the right to check the fickle and headstrong representatives of the people by declaring acts of Congress unconstitutional. Judicial review, as this process is called, had been talked about earlier, but it had never been conclusively established. Republicans considered it "unrepublican," and claimed that the power to judge constitutionality belonged to either the executive or the legislative branch or both.

Early in 1803 Marshall saw his chance. He would assert his precious principle, but do so in a way the Republicans would find difficult to oppose. His opportunity came in the case of *Marbury v. Madison,* in which William Marbury, who
had been nominated justice of the peace for the District of Columbia by Adams
and refused his commission by Madison, sued to have the commission delivered
by the secretary of state. In 1803 Marshall, speaking for the Court, denied Marbury's claim by declaring the federal law under which he had sued to be unconstitutional. In effect, Madison and the government had won on the question of
Marbury's appointment, but their victory depended on accepting the right of the
Supreme Court to decide whether a law passed by Congress was in conflict with
the Constitution and therefore void. An important claim held by many Federalists had been established: The Supreme Court, whose members were beyond easy
reach of popular opinion, was to be the final judge of constitutionality.

Chief Justice John Marshall's ruling in Marbury v. Madison helped entrench Federalist
principles in American law. Marshall had fought at Valley Forge; his experience there,
he wrote later, had confirmed him "in the habit of considering America
as my country and Congress as my government."

Marbury v. *Madison* did not end Jefferson's attack on the existing Federalist-dominated court system. In 1803 the administration turned to impeachment to remove the most ardent Federalist partisans from the federal bench and replace them with Republicans. To launch their attack, they selected two targets: John Pickering, a federal district judge in New Hampshire, and the notorious Judge Chase of the Supreme Court. Both men were outrageously partisan Federalists; Pickering, besides being an alcoholic, was clearly insane. He was impeached by the House of Representatives and removed by the Senate with little difficulty. But Chase—however ill-tempered and unfair—convinced enough senators that he had not committed the "high crimes and misdemeanors" that were the specified constitutional grounds for removal from office. Chase's acquittal virtually ended the Republican assault on the Federalist judiciary.

* INTERNATIONAL POLITICS AND REPUBLICAN POLICY *

It was the need to deal effectively with foreign powers more than any other single factor that pushed Jefferson and his successor toward Federalist principles of strong central government.

JEFFERSON BUYS LOUISIANA.   In 1801 the United States was still entangled in the complicated issues that had grown out of the French Revolution. Britain and France were briefly at peace following the Treaty of Amiens in 1802. But then in May 1803 hostilities between the French, under Napoleon Bonaparte, and their enemies erupted once more and darkened the Atlantic world for another dozen years.

Once again America was sucked into the conflict. The first warning came in 1800 when Spain and France signed the Treaty of San Ildefonso allowing France to resume control of Louisiana. News of the deal caused great alarm in the United States. Jefferson feared France's effort to reestablish an empire in North America. It was one thing for a weak Spain to occupy New Orleans. It was far worse for a powerful and arrogant France to control the mouth of the Mississippi, and be in a position to choke off American commerce from the great river and its tributaries.

Even more than in the previous decade the United States had vital interests in the Mississippi Valley. Hundreds of thousands of Americans now lived beyond the Appalachians. Over 150 vessels regularly plied the great central river, carrying over 20,000 tons of freight annually. As Jefferson was painfully aware, whoever controlled the Mississippi wielded enormous power over the United States. If France gained control of the river and the region, he noted, "from that moment we must marry ourselves to the British fleet and nation."

When rumors of the French agreement with Spain reached the United States, Jefferson dispatched Robert R. Livingston to Paris to buy both West Florida and

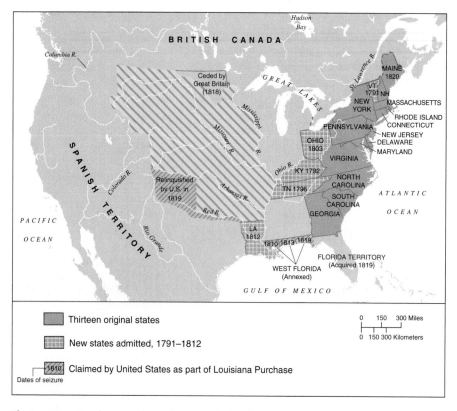

The Louisiana Purchase and New States, 1791–1812

New Orleans from Napoleon. From the outset Livingston encountered difficulties. Talleyrand, the French foreign minister, would not let him see Napoleon. The devious Frenchman was waiting to see what would happen in Santo Domingo, where a French army was struggling to put down the slave revolt led by general Toussaint L'Ouverture. Only if Toussaint were defeated could France protect Louisiana. The black liberator was eventually captured by trickery, but the Haitians refused to surrender, and a combination of black guerrillas and the yellow fever mosquito in the end defeated the French army.

News of the growing French disaster soon trickled back to Paris, making it clear to Napoleon that France must give up all thought of a new North American empire. Besides, it looked as if hostilities were about to break out again in Europe, and war, the First Consul realized, would expose Louisiana to British attack from Canada or military conquest by the Americans. The region, however, might be converted into cash, which could finance French imperial ambitions in Europe. On April 11, 1803, Napoleon told his minister of finance, Francois de

Barbé-Marbois: "I renounce Louisiana. It is not only New Orleans that I will cede, it is the whole colony without reservation. . . . "

Napoleon's new attitude completely altered the picture. Livingston, now joined by James Monroe, was confronted with a remarkable and totally unexpected proposition. Instead of only New Orleans, Barbé-Marbois asked, why not take all of the immense Louisiana territory? Another 20 million francs would pay for outstanding claims of American citizens against France dating back to the naval war of the 1790s. This offer exceeded the expectations and instructions of the American emissaries, but they grabbed it. On May 2, 1803, the American negotiators signed the treaty transferring Louisiana to the United States for $15 million.

The deal was a wonderful piece of good luck. But it left many questions unanswered and many problems unsolved. Spain had never formally surrendered the province to France and could be expected to cause trouble. There was also uncertainty about the territory's precise boundaries. When Livingston questioned Talleyrand on the colony's limits, the Frenchman had remarked cynically that the Americans had "made a noble bargain" for themselves and would no doubt "make the most of it." They would indeed; but in the meantime the unclear borders with Mexico and Canada were sure to complicate relations with Spain and Great Britain.

Most difficult of all, however, were the constitutional problems raised. Fifty thousand French and Spanish descendants of the original European settlers, and French-speaking exiles from Acadia ("Cajuns") in Canada, inhabited the colony. Under the treaty they were all to become American citizens. Did the United States have the constitutional right to incorporate these people without their consent? And what about the fact that nowhere did the Constitution confer authority on anyone to buy new territory for the nation? Federalists denounced these assumptions of powers. Each side called the other hypocritical for reversing its usual position on implied powers under the Constitution.

Jefferson himself was troubled by constitutional scruples, and for a while hesitated. But it seemed certain that the Louisiana Territory would support millions of small land-holding farmers, and that prospect was dear to the president's heart. Trying to get a bargain and preserve his principles at the same time, Jefferson proposed that Congress should simultaneously confirm the treaty and adopt a constitutional amendment expressly authorizing such territorial acquisitions. But Napoleon would not wait for the president to overcome his philosophical misgivings. Warned that the First Consul was becoming restless, Jefferson abandoned the idea of a constitutional amendment and pushed the treaty through the Senate. On December 20, 1803, in a simple ceremony at New Orleans, the French flag was lowered and the Stars and Stripes raised in its place. Louisiana, a region almost equal in extent to the original United States under the 1783 peace treaty with Britain, was now American.

THE LEWIS AND CLARK EXPEDITION. Even before Napoleon had made his startling offer, Jefferson had engaged his private secretary, Meriwether Lewis, and a former soldier, William Clark, to explore the vast region. Jefferson's motives were both political and commercial. Initially, he had sought to establish an American claim to the region through exploration. More important, the president hoped to gather the eastern Indian tribes into reservations where they could be induced to abandon their "savage" ways and settle down as "civilized" farmers. Jefferson believed this change to be advantageous to the Indians themselves. But it also promised to free vast tracts of land for white settlers. To achieve his goals Jefferson hoped to draw to regions further west the Indian traders who encouraged the Indians' nomadic ways. Lewis and Clark, accordingly, were charged with investigating the fur resources of the new region and with establishing commercial relations with the western tribes. News of the Louisiana Purchase added to these goals an intense curiosity about what exactly the United States had bought for $15 million. The expedition, the president directed, must make careful observations of the flora, animal life, minerals, soils, and geography of the regions they crossed.

Lewis and Clark's party left St. Louis in the spring of 1804. After wintering in the Dakotas, they set off for the Pacific the following April with thirty-seven men and a woman, Sacajawea, a Shoshone captive of the Dakota tribes, who was given her freedom in exchange for guiding the expedition across the Rockies. Sacajawea took them as far as the Lemhi Pass on the Continental Divide, where they were met by Shoshone tribesmen. Grateful for the return of their kinswoman, the Indians provided the expedition with horses and guides for the next stage of the journey, over the remaining ranges of the Rockies to the valley of the Clearwater River. By mid-November, after traversing the rapids of the Clearwater and the Columbia, the weary explorers arrived at the shores of the Pacific.

When the explorers returned to St. Louis in September 1806, they were received with wild enthusiasm. At the cost of only a single life and some $50,000, they had established relations with several important Indian nations; discovered usable passes through the Rockies; and provided important botanical, zoological, geological, and anthropological data about a vast stretch of western North America. Their expedition helped to open the trans-Mississippi region, and was soon followed by others that laid the groundwork for the wave of settlement that would carry millions of Americans across the continent.

THE WILKINSON-BURR CONSPIRACY. Acquisition of Louisiana had finally ended one source of western troubles: farmers' difficulty in sending their goods to market through New Orleans. But the West was still not sure that it could entrust its future to the government in Washington. Many easterners, the people of the trans-Appalachian region knew, were suspicious of growing western power and numbers. In Massachusetts, for example, extreme Federalists, members of the so-called Essex Junto, were talking of detaching New England, New York, and New Jersey from the Union and forming a new confederation of states that would insulate the commercial Northeast from the power of the allied agricultural South and West.

Western resentments and suspicions offered opportunities for ambitious and unscrupulous men to carve careers for themselves as champions of the trans-

Appalachian region. Two of the most dangerous of these adventurers were General James Wilkinson, governor of the Louisiana Territory, and Vice President Aaron Burr of New York. Though a trusted lieutenant of every American president from Washington through Madison, Wilkinson was in the pay of the Spanish government as Agent Number 13. Burr, a far more talented man, though descended from a long line of Puritan ministers, was a compulsive womanizer, a reckless pleasure seeker, and a cynic, driven by ambition and the desire to win fame and glory. He still might have attained the presidency if he had not made a fatal misstep. In 1804, angered by Hamilton's role in helping to defeat him when he ran for governor of New York, Burr challenged the former treasury secretary to a duel. The two men met on the Hudson Palisades opposite New York. Hamilton held his fire; Burr shot to kill. Mortally wounded, Hamilton was carried back to New York where he died the next day. People called Burr's action murder. From that point on, a conventional course to power was closed to Burr, and he turned to intrigue and conspiracy to achieve his ends.

Though the exact truth is still in dispute, it appears that he and Wilkinson sought British and Spanish support for a scheme to detach the West from the United States, combine it with parts of Spanish Mexico, and then set up an independent nation with themselves as rulers. To raise money Burr connived with the British minister in Washington, who seemed interested in any plan that promised to diminish American strength. Deciding that his former arrangements with Spain were more profitable, Wilkinson betrayed Burr. Posing as an American patriot anxious to defend his country's interests, he told Jefferson of Burr's scheme. Tried before Chief Justice Marshall, Burr was acquitted of treason, but rather than face various state charges against him, fled to Europe.

NEUTRAL RIGHTS ONCE MORE. Impressment, blockades, neutral rights, contraband, and Indian incitements continued to disturb America's relations with the two leading European powers after 1803. The country's foreign involvements during 1803–1812 seemed like a replay of 1793–1800 with the volume turned up.

Soon after France and England resumed their war in 1803, the British reactivated their impressment policy. Before long, British ships were hovering off East Coast ports, ready to swoop down on American ships and remove seamen from their decks for the Royal Navy. In July 1805, in the *Essex* decision, a British admiralty court declared illegal the American practice of carrying French West Indian produce to American ports and then shipping it to France. These commodities were not neutral goods, the court said, they were really French, and under the Rule of 1756 could be confiscated like other enemy goods if intercepted by the British navy.

Congress retaliated in April 1806 by passing the Nonimportation Act. Designed to force the British into a more acceptable response, this measure forbade the importation of many goods that Americans normally bought from Britain but could, if necessary, produce at home. Jefferson held the law in abeyance while British and American negotiators tried to hammer out an accommodation. These talks in fact produced an agreement but, embarrassed by how little it conceded to the United States, Jefferson refused to submit it to the Senate for confirmation.

Meanwhile, American commerce and pride continued to suffer under a barrage of measures and countermeasures by Napoleon and his chief European adversary. In May 1806 Britain announced a blockade of the European continent from the Elbe River in Germany to the port of Brest in France. Napoleon retaliated with the Berlin Decree, placing Britain under blockade and forbidding all British commerce with France. The British then threatened to confiscate all ships engaged in French coastal trade or entering those European continental ports still not off limits unless they paid British duties and secured British clearance. Napoleon replied with the Milan Decree, which declared that all vessels that obeyed his enemy's new rulings would be subject to French seizure.

The British–French war of regulations seemed designed to produce maximum irritation in America. If American merchants bowed to the British, they would offend the French, and vice versa. To make matters worse, the regulations contained large loopholes in both their provisions and their enforcement. These continued to entice Americans into the lucrative trade with Europe and the West Indies, but made it hazardous and uncertain.

THE CHESAPEAKE–LEOPARD AFFAIR. While the barrage of French–British decrees and orders in council flew through the air, the impressment issue became acute. Sir George Berkeley, British naval commander at Halifax, Nova Scotia, blamed American officials for encouraging the desertion of British seamen, and resolved to stop the practice. He was especially irked by the situation in the Chesapeake Bay region, where many deserters from the Royal Navy had taken refuge and a number had enlisted in the American navy. One of these deserters, Jenkin Ratford, now a sailor on the U.S.S. *Chesapeake,* was reported to be swaggering through Norfolk insulting British officers on leave.

On June 1, 1807, Berkeley directed his subordinates to stop the *Chesapeake,* if they should encounter it beyond American territorial waters, and search it for deserters. Soon after, H.M.S. *Leopard* overtook the American frigate as it left for the Mediterranean on a shakedown cruise. The American captain, Commodore James Barron, suspecting nothing—for the British had never attempted to impress from an American naval vessel before—allowed a British officer to come aboard. He handed Barron a demand from the British captain that the deserters be surrendered. When Barron refused, the *Leopard* fired three broadsides into the American ship, killing three Americans and wounding eighteen. Not yet fully outfitted for combat, the *Chesapeake* was able to fire back only a single token shot before it surrendered. A British search party then boarded the vessel, lined up its crew, and removed Ratford and three other deserters. Ratford was later hanged.

Never before had the British so blatantly violated American sovereignty. Indignation swept the country, and protesters organized mass meetings in dozens of cities to condemn British high-handedness. The British consul in New York had to be given police protection, and a mob attacked and almost demolished a British vessel at its pier in the harbor. Many Americans expected war; many demanded it.

THE EMBARGO. Jefferson could easily have brought a united nation into war at this point, but instead, after issuing a proclamation closing American waters to the Royal Navy, he sent an emissary to negotiate the impressment issue with the British. Unfortunately the American representative accomplished little. Not until 1811 did the British make acceptable reparation for the Chesapeake–Leopard affair. Meanwhile, the clamor in America abated and war enthusiasm cooled.

Jefferson had mixed motives for taking a moderate course in the *Chesapeake* affair. The president was conscious of American military weakness. He and his fellow Republicans were themselves responsible for this condition. Ever since the undeclared naval war with France in 1798–1800—which many Republicans believed a pro-British, Federalist venture—they had denounced standing armies and a strong navy as "dangerous to liberty" and conducive to "the spirit which leads to war." Militarism they said, went along with Federalist faith in centralized political power. Jefferson was not indifferent to American defense, but he thought a citizen militia and small, lightly armed coastal vessels using oars and sails, was sufficient. This would spare the country a large and expensive military establishment.

Jefferson also believed the United States had a better weapon against British and French high-handedness than an army and navy. Americans had wielded economic weapons effectively against Britain during the great imperial crisis before independence, and now, in December 1807, he activated the first Nonimportation Act and soon after asked Congress to place an embargo on all exports from the United States. Congress responded with the 1807 Embargo Act, which forbade American vessels to sail to foreign ports without special permission and forbade foreign vessels to carry off American goods. American ships could continue to engage in the coastal trade between domestic ports, but the owners of such vessels had to post bonds twice the value of the ships and their cargoes to guarantee that they would not sail off to foreign ports once at sea. The law did not explicitly prohibit imports in foreign ships; but if foreign ship owners could not carry American cargo on their return trips, they had little incentive to trade with the United States. The law also restricted overland trade to British colonies. In effect, Congress had sealed off the country from foreign commerce on the theory that Europe needed America more than America needed Europe.

Theory was one thing; reality was another. The law was impossible to enforce. Some state governors took advantage of its loopholes to peddle exemptions to merchants for cash or political support. Merchants, on their own, found ways to get around the law. Many risked the loss of their bond by directing their ships to Europe or the Caribbean once out of sight of land. Others conducted illegal commerce with British Canada across the Great Lakes. Defiance was greatest in New England, where Jefferson was denounced as a tyrant executing an unconstitutional law. Equally opposed were the merchants of New York and Philadelphia.

For a while, wholesale evasion made the law tolerable. But the Giles Enforcement Act of 1809 closed the loopholes, and foreign trade virtually ceased. Farmers saw the prices of their export crops plunge dramatically. But more seriously hurt were the traders of the port towns and all who depended on them. New York in 1809, one contemporary reported, "looked like a town ravaged by pestilence." The city's waterfront streets were deserted, its ships dismantled, and its countinghouses closed and boarded up. Boston and seaboard New England were hardest hit of all, with thousands of seamen, dock laborers, sail makers, and rope makers idle.

And to top it all, the law failed to achieve its ends. It hurt some British manufacturers, but it was English wage earners, Caribbean planters, and slaves who suffered the most, and none of these groups carried much political weight in Parliament. Even when the embargo finally began to pinch important British commercial interests, sheer stubbornness kept the British government from yielding to American pressure.

For a year and a half the administration sought to enforce its unpopular policy, using militia and regulars to halt the overland trade with Canada and the navy to stop violations by sea. Driven by frustration, the president, a great defender of liberty while in the opposition, proposed to declare whole communities in rebellion and subject to prosecution for treason. At one point he told a Republican congressman that in times of emergency "the universal recourse is a dictator."

Popular opposition to the infamous embargo soon reached a crescendo. In the shipping states, even Republicans pleaded that the policy be abandoned. Faced by this overwhelming pressure and the obvious failure of its policy to alter British and French behavior, the administration finally yielded. In March 1809, as one of his last official acts, Jefferson signed the Nonintercourse Act, repealing the embargo and reopening foreign trade except with Britain and France, but allowing the president to restore trade with either country, or both, if they ceased violating American rights.

MADISON TAKES THE HELM.   Soon after, Jefferson left Washington for Monticello, never again to serve in high political office. Jefferson was not proud of his presidency, but he underestimated it. He had successfully guided the United States through a major transition from the rule of one party to the rule of another; had doubled the physical size of the country; and had brought a new, more democratic tone to the nation's political culture. These were accomplishments that few presidents would match.

His successor, James Madison, was a man in the Jeffersonian mold. Cofounder of the Republican party, Jefferson's secretary of state, and one of the chief architects of the Constitution, Madison had earned the right to be his party's choice. He went on to defeat Federalist Charles Cotesworth Pinckney in the 1808 election.

Historians have generally considered Madison's presidency a failure. Although a profound student of government, an effective legislative leader, and a charming conversationalist, he lacked executive ability. In peace and war he would prove irresolute; and when he did bring himself to act, he would often blunder.

Madison's first misstep came in the second month of his presidency, when he arranged with David M. Erskine, the British minister in Washington, to suspend the Nonintercourse Act in exchange for British withdrawal of the 1807 orders in council. Erskine, however, had exceeded his instructions, and the British foreign secretary in London repudiated the agreement when he heard of it. Madison, now believed by many to be the dupe of the British, felt compelled to restore the prohibition on British–American trade.

The Nonintercourse Act having put too great an economic strain on the country, Congress in 1810 replaced it with Macon's Bill Number Two. This was a curious measure. The United States, it stated, would immediately reopen commerce with both Britain and France. If either country, however, should cease to violate American commercial rights, the president could then reimpose trade prohibitions on the other, after a three-month wait to give the slower-acting power a chance to rescind its trade restrictions. In effect, as an inducement to cease attacks on American trade, the United States promised to support against its enemy the first nation to act.

The wily Bonaparte quickly saw that he might trap America into becoming his unwitting ally against England. The Duc de Cadore, the French foreign minister, informed the American minister in Paris that the Berlin and Milan decrees had been revoked. It was a deception. In fact, on the very day Cadore told the American ambassador of the supposed French change of heart, Napoleon signed the Decree of Trianon, which ordered the confiscation and sale of all American vessels that had called at French ports after May 20, 1809. The president, however, swallowed the bait. On November 2 he announced that trade restrictions against Great Britain would be reimposed early in 1811. Without surrendering a thing, Napoleon had gotten the United States to strike a blow against France's archenemy.

FURTHER WESTERN TROUBLES.   Anglo-American tensions were further aggravated by events in the West. Though the British had finally removed their troops from the Northwest, western settlers and their spokesmen remained convinced that England, though actually innocent of the charge, was stirring up troubles with the Indians. The continued presence of British-Canadian fur traders in the Northwest, as allowed under the Jay Treaty, created further antagonisms and suspicion of British intrigue.

Actually, Americans themselves were responsible for the Indian troubles. At the behest of land speculators, frontier officials, many of them Jefferson's appointees, had for years transferred vast tracts of land from the native Americans, giving them little in return. In 1802 Governor William Henry Harrison of the Indiana Territory, using the threat of military force, had compelled the Kickapoo, Wea, and Delaware tribes to cede to the United States several million acres in what is now southern Indiana. The Treaty of Vincennes became the evil precedent for a rash of coerced agreements that compelled the northwestern and southwestern tribes to surrender millions of acres of choice lands for a few thousand dollars and a few baubles.

Disregarding Harrison's provocative actions, by 1810–1811 settlers throughout the West were certain that "British gold" was being used to encourage Indian militancy. Many of the fears and complaints centered on the activities of the Shawnee chief Tecumseh and his brother, "the Prophet," a chieftain believed to possess supernatural powers. These two remarkable men recognized that Harrison's success at land grabbing depended to a large extent on the disunity of the Indian tribes. To defeat Harrison and his kind, they proposed creating a tribal confederation that would present a united front to white officials. But beyond this, reviving the old dream of Pontiac, Tecumseh told his people that the whites must be driven "back whence they came, upon a trail of blood, they must be driven." Tecumseh at first urged his followers to exercise restraint as long as Harrison did not try to take possession of the Indian lands the whites had inveigled. Then, when Harrison indicated that he intended to proceed with the takeover, Tecumseh exhorted all-out war against the American settlers. "Burn their dwellings," he urged a meeting of Creeks, Cherokees, and Choctaws. "Destroy their stock. The red people own the country. . . . War now. War forever. War upon the living. War upon the dead; dig up their corpses from the grave; our country must give no rest to the white man's bones."

In September 1811 Harrison and a thousand troops set out to suppress the Indian rebellion. The small army reached Prophetstown and camped nearby. Just before daylight on November 7 the Indians attacked while the Americans still slept. Harrison's seasoned troops held, however, and when the American cavalry charged the Indians broke and fled.

Though the Battle of Tippecanoe would help make Harrison's reputation as an Indian fighter, it was actually a kind of defeat. The vanquished Indian rebels abandoned their capital and scattered throughout the West. Wherever they went, they carried their pan-Indian vision and their hatred of the white man. Before long the whole West, north as well as south, was in flames.

Besides the largely unfounded claims of Indian agitation, Westerners had other grievances against the British. British policies, it was said, had cut off the European market for western grain and created large unsold surpluses. Prices had dropped, causing distress to many western farmers. Though the American embargo had only made matters worse, westerners hoped it would eventually force Britain to back down, and western representatives in Congress were among the law's staunchest supporters.

Western attitudes would have been an important element in the decision to finally go to war in any case. But western views were given added weight by the skillful maneuvering of the War Hawks, some forty western and southern representatives elected to the Twelfth Congress that met in 1811. Led by Henry Clay, the group included such notable men as John C. Calhoun, William Lowndes, and Langdon Cheves of South Carolina; Felix Grundy of Tennessee; Richard M. Johnson of Kentucky; and Peter Porter of western New York. Marked off from other members of the Twelfth Congress by their aggressive nationalism and their resolve to shake the nation loose from subservience to Great Britain come what may, the War Hawks succeeded in electing Clay speaker of the House and packing the important foreign relations and naval committees with their members. Thereafter every move to condemn Britain or to appropriate money for the army and navy received their enthusiastic support.

CONGRESS VOTES FOR WAR.   No single dramatic event finally pushed the country into war. All through 1811 relations with Britain deteriorated. The British government did not take kindly to Madison's proclamation reimposing the embargo on Anglo-American trade. British cruisers were soon gathering in increasing numbers off the Atlantic coast, stopping more American vessels than ever and removing suspected British deserters in droves. Once more, impressment set off a major naval incident. In May Commodore John Rodgers, commanding the frigate *President,* stumbled on the British corvette *Little Belt* off Virginia. Rodgers chased the British vessel, overtook it, and attacked, inflicting severe damage. The *President* did not sink the smaller British ship, but most Americans felt satisfied that the disgrace of the *Chesapeake* defeat had finally been avenged.

Matters moved swiftly to a head. In April 1812 Congress gave President Madison power to call up the state militias for six months' service. On the same day British Foreign Secretary Lord Castlereagh rejected the American demand that the 1807 Orders in Council be withdrawn. But the British economy was now finally beginning to feel the bite of the embargo, and continued pressure might have forced the British to back down had a madman not shot Prime Minister Spencer Perceval, throwing the British government into turmoil. By the time it began to function again, Castlereagh was ready to suspend the Orders in Council. But news of his announcement arrived too late in America to influence events. On June 18, Congress declared war on England.

WHO WANTED WAR?   The declaration of war against Britain was not unanimous. Of 128 representatives voting, 49 voted no. In the Senate 13 out of 32 members refused to support the war declaration. Historians have tried to determine the motives for war by analyzing the vote, but the picture remains murky. Representatives of coastal New England clearly opposed war, but those from interior New England favored it. New York, too, opposed the war, but Pennsylvania, including the port of Philadelphia, voted to fight. The South, especially the Carolinas and Georgia, was almost solidly in support of the war, as was the West beyond the Appalachians.

More important perhaps than whether a congressman lived in the North, the South, or the West was whether his constituents exported farm products (in which case he tended to support the war declaration) or engaged in ocean commerce (in which case he probably voted against it). In other words, pocketbook considerations seem to have been more important than geography in determining the way individual representatives voted. Sectional factors in this view seem significant mostly because many westerners and southerners were certain that their prosperity depended on teaching the British that they must not interfere with America's export trade, whereas many New Englanders feared that war with Great Britain would lead to the complete destruction of American commerce by the powerful British navy.

Perhaps the most workable analysis, however, connects the war vote to politics and party. Generally speaking, the Federalists and John Randolph's dissenting Quid Republicans voted against the war; administration Republicans, including, of course, the War Hawks, favored it. Professor Bradford Perkins estimates that fully 90 percent "of the real, available Republican membership [of the House of Representatives] backed the bill" to declare war. Despite misgivings, the strong anti-British stand of the party ever since the 1790s, and particularly since Jefferson's embargo, committed the Republicans to taking this step.

If we look behind the war vote in Congress, we can identify something more fundamental than economic interest and party, however. The War of 1812 was the result of an upsurge of nationalism among Americans. By 1812 many citizens were determined to avenge the humiliations the United States had suffered at British hands for almost a generation. Though their country had won its formal independence in 1783, it still seemed to be under Britain's thumb. Impressment, Orders in Council, incitement of Indians, confiscation of American ships—all contributed to the anger and hurt pride that these Americans felt. Many Federalists and New Englanders might have preferred to ignore the incidents, believing it better to suffer these ills for the sake of profit and safety. Some westerners, as John Randolph charged, might have supported the war out of lust for British Canada to add to western land and wealth. But for many Americans, the prospect of continued submission to haughty Britain seemed ample reason for military resistance.

❋ THE WAR OF 1812 ❋

The war was badly bungled. Owing in part to Republican hostility to peacetime armies, American military and naval forces were feeble. Congress had provided for a 35,000-man regular army in January 1812, but at the beginning of June it consisted of only 6,700 officers and men. Worse, the troops were not stationed close to Canada, the most accessible part of British territory, but were scattered all over the country. Although he was authorized to bring 100,000 militia into federal service, the president was effectively deprived of the best-trained state troops by New England's virtual neutrality during the war. Facing the motley American army would be an uncertain number of equally nondescript Canadian militia plus 7,000 British and Canadian regulars. But behind them—once Napoleon surrendered in Europe—were thousands of tough veterans of the Duke of Wellington's Spanish campaign against the French.

The Americans were even worse off on the high seas. In June 1812 the American navy consisted of only seven seaworthy frigates and over a hundred almost worthless gunboats. By contrast, Britain had over two hundred frigates and ships of the line, most with twice the firepower of the largest American vessels. Americans would add to their navy during the war, and would send out scores of privateers against British ocean commerce, yet the American naval effort would resemble a scrappy minnow nipping at a shark's tail.

In financial matters, too, the United States was handicapped. In 1811 Congress had defeated by a close vote an attempt to recharter the Bank of the United States. The bank, as Hamilton had predicted, had helped the government manage its financial operations and had provided businessmen with much-needed credit and capital. Although hostile at first, Albert Gallatin and other Republicans eventually came to favor it. But the bank had not converted all its opponents, and it had made new enemies among some business groups. These forces had defeated renewal. Now, without a central bank to make loans to meet the government's extraordinary wartime needs, the treasury found itself in difficulties. The situation was made worse by New England's reluctance to lend to the treasury from its large reserves of available capital.

The president also faced the problem of poor communications. Contact with the interior, especially across the mountains, was slow and difficult. Roads were few throughout the nation; those crossing the Appalachians were no more than Indian trails. The Great Lakes were potentially useful, but nowhere on American territory were they connected by water to the country's major population centers. Bad communications imposed serious handicaps on military commanders, who were forced to move supplies and men along crude trails hacked out of the forest.

THE HARTFORD CONVENTION. Almost the whole area north and east of the Hudson sat out the war. Many New Englanders regarded Great Britain as the world's last hope against the tyrant Napoleon, and they condemned Madison for having made the United States France's ally. In 1814, after seeing their commerce virtually swept off the seas by the British navy, antiwar Yankees forced the calling of a convention at Hartford, Connecticut. There they intended to discuss how to deal with the war and to consider whether the discontented states should secede from the Union. Fortunately, the extremists at Hartford were outmaneuvered by the moderates, and the convention took no action beyond endorsing state nullification of federal acts and proposing constitutional amendments limiting the power of the president and Congress over foreign relations. New England disaffection stopped short of outright disloyalty, yet the hostility to the war in the Northeast would be a dead weight around Madison's neck.

THE EARLY YEARS OF THE WAR. After we acknowledge all of these difficulties, however, Madison still must bear much of the blame for the failures of the American war effort. As commander in chief, he appointed the generals, and his first choices were abysmal. Major General William Hull was sent to attack the British in Upper Canada (Ontario), but was forced to surrender to the British near Detroit. Harrison, ordered to retake Detroit, gave up much of the Northwest to the British and their Indian allies. An American invasion of the Niagara peninsula under Generals Stephen Van Rensselaer and Alexander Smyth was turned into a tragic farce when the New York militia, ordered to cross into Canada to fight the enemy, refused on the grounds that they had no obligation to fight outside their home state, and stood idly by watching the regulars across the Niagara River being slaughtered by British troops. Only the famous victories of the frigates *Constitution* and *United States* in single-ship combat with the *Guerrière* and *Macedonian* kept up American spirits in the first year of war.

Despite the disasters in the field, Madison was reelected for a second term in 1812 over De Witt Clinton of New York, the Federalist candidate. The president's 128 electoral votes represented the prowar sections, largely in the South and West; Clinton's 89 represented the antiwar regions of New England, with New York, New Jersey, and part of Maryland thrown in.

The second year of the war went only a little better than the first. In January 1815, Harrison's lieutenants were defeated in a series of battles south of the Great Lakes. Because the British seemed likely to be successful so long as they could move freely on Lake Erie, the government ordered Captain Oliver Hazard Perry to construct a small navy on the south shore of the lake. On September 1, Perry's fleet met a somewhat smaller flotilla under Captain Robert Barclay. In a fierce exchange Perry sank or captured the entire British force. "We have met the enemy and they are ours," read Perry's succinct dispatch to Harrison.

With Lake Erie under American control, Harrison moved against the British in Upper Canada. In the Battle of the Thames in early October he and his Ken-

The battle of the U.S.S. Constitution and H.M.S. Guerrière as depicted in a contemporary painting. Single encounters like this one were among the few naval victories the United States could claim in the War of 1812. They scarcely affected the outcome of the war, but they did help American morale. (Courtesy New Haven Colony Historical Society)

tucky militia encountered a small force of British regulars, Canadian militia, and some 1,500 Indians, these last led by Tecumseh. The shock of the first volley scattered the British and Canadians. The Indians held out longer, but they, too, soon turned and ran. Tecumseh was presumed dead, though his body was never found. This defeat led to the collapse of the Shawnee chief's confederation and the desertion of many tribes from the British cause.

The year 1813 also saw the outbreak of Indian troubles in the Southwest. The Creek War brought on the grim ambushes, scalpings, and indiscriminate murder of women and children often perpetrated by both sides in Indian–white wars. In August a Creek force of 1,000 killed 250 white settlers jammed for safety into Fort Mims in southern Alabama. Later that year the Tennessee militia avenged the deed by slaughtering 186 Indians near Jacksonville, Alabama.

The Indian fighting marked the rise to prominence of Andrew Jackson, a Tennessee planter-politician who commanded the government's forces as major general of the state militia. Early in 1814 Jackson marched on the Creeks in what is now Alabama. At Horseshoe Bend he attacked and massacred 800. The surviving Creeks were forced to sign a peace treaty at Fort Jackson surrendering a giant slice of territory in southern Georgia and central Alabama. For his services Jackson was made a major general in the regular army.

THE LAST CAMPAIGNS.   Meanwhile, in Europe Napoleon had finally been defeated and in April 1814 was sent into exile on the Mediterranean island of Elba. Bonaparte's surrender freed thousands of seasoned British troops for the American war, and in late summer 1814, some 11,000 of these veterans set out from Canada for New York City under George Prevost. But all hopes of cutting the United States in two along the old Champlain-Hudson route ended when American gunboats under Captain Thomas McDonough defeated an English fleet at Plattsburgh on Lake Champlain. With the Americans in control of the lake, Prevost hurriedly retreated, leaving behind a mountain of supplies and hundreds of deserters.

The second prong of the British knockout campaign, aimed at Chesapeake Bay, proved more successful. In June the British navy transported 4,000 troops directly from France to the Patuxent River. From there they advanced on the national capital and at Bladensburg, Maryland, defeated a hastily gathered force of militia, sailors, and a few regulars that tried to stop them. The British veterans then marched into Washington unopposed. Congress and the president had already fled the city, leaving behind the spirited first lady, Dolley Madison, to save Gilbert Stuart's portrait of Washington. The British burned the Capitol, the presidential mansion, and all the city's public buildings except the Patent Office.

The redcoats now turned north to Baltimore, the country's third-largest city. Here they were checked. Fort McHenry and the fortifications quickly thrown up were manned by thousands of militia, sailors, and some regulars. The British fleet bombarded the fort for two days, but it held out. To commemorate the heroic defense, Francis Scott Key wrote a poem, the "Star-Spangled Banner," and set it to the tune of an old British drinking song. It is appropriate that the only serious literary work evoked by this mismanaged war is associated with befuddlement.

As the third prong of the British campaign, in late November a British army of 7,500 under Sir Edward Pakenham landed at Lake Borgne, forty miles from New Orleans. Jackson and his troops sped south and engaged the enemy in skirmishes east of the city, slowing the British advance. On New Year's Day Jackson's skilled artillerymen severely punished the British, compelling Pakenham to wait for reinforcements.

On January 8, 1815, the British resumed their advance against Jackson's force of U.S. regulars, Kentucky and Tennessee riflemen, and New Orleans and Louisiana militiamen composed of Bayou pirates, free blacks, and young bluebloods from the city. In a dense morning fog the British regulars advanced on the Americans lined up behind a low wall. The fog lifted before the red-clad troops had gone very far and at 500 yards the American artillery opened fire with devastating effect. When the still advancing redcoats reached rifle range, Jackson ordered his men to blaze away with small arms.

The combination of rifle and artillery fire was too much for the British. In less than an hour one-third of their force was cut down, another third was milling about in confusion, and three of the highest-ranking British officers, including Pakenham, were dead. Facing reality, General John Lambert ordered retreat. On January 27 the surviving British troops sailed for home.

THE PEACE OF GHENT. The Battle of New Orleans would never have taken place if transatlantic communications had been swifter in these years. On December 24, British and American negotiators had concluded a peace at Ghent in what is now Belgium. The peace treaty, signed before Jackson's stunning victory, was an ambiguous and tentative document that brought the United States few gains. It said nothing about impressment, ignored the neutral rights and Indian issues that had bedeviled British–American relations for years, and left the Canadian–American boundary where it had been before the war. None of the goals that had prompted Americans to action were realized by the treaty.

It did not satisfy the British either. For them the war had begun as a defensive struggle, but their early military successes had led the English leaders to hope for territorial concessions from the Americans and perhaps an Indian buffer state between the United States and Canada. War weariness and fear that fighting might shortly resume in Europe led the British to abandon these goals at Ghent.

Little was accomplished by the treaty, then, except for the restoration of peace. It provided for a commission to settle the disputed boundary with Canada in the far northeast and mentioned future settlement of differences over navigation of the Great Lakes and the Newfoundland fisheries. In 1817, to implement the agreement at Ghent, Britain and the United States signed the Rush–Bagot Agreement by which both nations accepted almost total disarmament along the Canadian–American border. Applied at first solely to the Great Lakes region, it eventually converted the whole of the Canadian–American boundary into the longest unarmed frontier in the world.

Yet the fact remains that the document ending the war was less significant than the victory at New Orleans. Weeks after the Ghent negotiations had ended, the British government ordered reinforcements to Pakenham—a move that suggests that if their army had defeated Jackson, they would have refused to confirm the treaty. Great Britain had never recognized the legality of the Louisiana Purchase, and it is likely that if their troops had captured New Orleans, Britain would have carved out a sphere of influence along the lower Mississippi. Jackson's triumph ended the possibility of a new British Empire at the expense of the United States.

More important, however, the victory at New Orleans left Americans with a sense that they had defeated British tyranny a second time. It created a new national hero in the person of testy, rough-hewn Andy Jackson, and a proud new national mythology. Unspoiled, sturdy, and independent, American frontiersmen, so the myth went, had taken on Europe's best and defeated them decisively. Jackson's triumph produced a surge of patriotism that all but obliterated the disunity that had afflicted the country at the beginning of the war. However it had begun, by its glorious ending the war reaffirmed American self-respect and pride. "The war," Albert Gallatin would write a colleague, "has renewed and reinstated the national feelings and character which the Revolution had given, and which were daily lessened. The people have now more general objects of attachment. . . . They are more American; they feel and act more as a nation."

Gallatin's view is confirmed by the facts. President Madison's 1815 message to Congress expressed the new spirit that had captured the nation: Even the party of states' rights must now devote its energies to forging closer national bonds and stronger national institutions. Republicans had learned their lesson. The country had been severely handicapped by poor communications and the absence of a central bank. Perhaps Hamilton and his friends had been right after all. Why not give their ideas a try?

Ironically, although the war made the Republicans into nationalists, it destroyed the party that formerly had had a virtual copyright on the nationalist label. If the war had ended on a sour note, the Federalists might have come out of it with enhanced prestige. As it was, New Orleans made the party of Washington and Hamilton seem unpatriotic and even treasonous. After 1815 the Federalists would never again be a serious threat to the Republicans on the national level.

* CONCLUSIONS *

Between the 1800 presidential campaign and James Madison's seventh annual message to Congress, American political attitudes had taken a 180-degree turn. Jefferson's election had been a repudiation of Federalist excesses and a mandate for the party that represented local as opposed to national power. The public exaggerated Jefferson's differences from his opponents. Nevertheless, the Republican victory of 1800 represented an endorsement of a less activist national government and a repudiation of the strong centralizing bent of the Federalists.

The American people could not have foreseen that they and their leaders would do an about-face. Events would overtake everyone's theories. In the decade and a half that followed Jefferson's inauguration, the growing confrontation with

France and England required an ever more active and effective central authority. The clash also created a new sense of national priorities, especially among southerners and westerners, whose agricultural interests, as opposed to the commercial interests of New Englanders, did not conflict with a strong stand against the country's foreign enemies. The war itself made clear to many former opponents of Federalist "follies" that to function, the country must accept much that Hamilton and his allies had proposed. Finally, with the splendid climax at New Orleans, the country experienced a new sense of unity and a self-confidence that would last until immense new issues once again reactivated the divisive forces of localism.

New Orleans and the Treaty of Ghent closed one chapter of American history. For fifty years the United States had been embroiled in Europe's remote affairs. Now, with Napoleon gone, Europe settled down to a long period of relative international calm. For almost a century the United States would be spared the clash of empires that had unsettled it for so long. And with peace, Americans could go about the business of exploiting their bounteous human and natural resources and converting them into tangible wealth.

9

THE AMERICAN ECONOMIC MIRACLE

What Made it Possible?

1793	Eli Whitney invents the cotton gin
1794	The Philadelphia–Lancaster Turnpike opens
1802	West Point established
1803	The Louisiana Purchase
1807	Robert Fulton's steamboat Clermont makes a round trip between Albany and New York
1811	The federal government begins work on the National Road at Cumberland, Maryland; Fulton-Livingston interests awarded an exclusive charter from the Louisiana territorial legislature to operate steamboats on the Mississippi
1815	Entrepreneur Francis Cabot Lowell's Boston Manufacturing Company produces cotton cloth on a new power loom
1816	The Second Bank of the United States chartered
1817	New York's legislature approves funds for the Erie Canal
1818	The National Road reaches the Ohio River
1819	Financial panic and economic depression
1825	Completion of the Erie Canal: Shipping rates between Buffalo and New York fall more than 75 percent; Rensselaer Polytechnic Institute founded
1827	Mechanics Union of Trade Associates founded in Philadelphia
1828	The Baltimore and Ohio Railroad chartered
1830	Congress passes Pre-emption Act for the public domain
1837	Financial panic and economic depression
1844	Samuel F. B. Morse transmits the first intercity telegraph message
1847	Lawrence Scientific School established at Harvard

1853	The Gadsden Purchase secures an important southwestern railroad pass for the United States
1857	Financial panic and economic depression
1859	Edwin Drake drills the first successful oil well at Titusville, Pennsylvania

In 1833 Michael Chevalier, a French mining engineer, crossed the Atlantic to study the young American republic's canals and railroads. A keen student of the industrialization process then well underway in Europe, Chevalier was amazed at what the Americans had accomplished. One arresting sight was the city of Pittsburgh, where eighty years earlier the French had established Fort Duquesne amid the solitude of the unbroken forest. Now, Chevalier wrote, Pittsburgh was

> a manufacturing town which will one day become the Birmingham of America. . . .
> It is surrounded . . . with a dense black smoke which, bursting forth in volume
> from the foundries, forges, glasshouses, and the chimneys of all the factories and
> houses, falls in flakes of soot upon the dwellings and persons of the inhabitants. It
> is, therefore, the dirtiest town in the United States. . . . Nowhere in the world is
> everybody so regularly and continually busy as in Pittsburgh. I do not believe there
> is on the face of the earth a single town in which the idea of amusement so seldom
> enters the heads of the inhabitants.

The rest of the country, the French visitor found, had not changed as much from its eighteenth-century condition. The majority of Americans were still farmers, and almost all the rest were employed in petty trade and handicrafts. But, as Pittsburgh demonstrated, immense changes were taking place. By 1860, a generation after Chevalier's visit, the United States would have a dozen Pittsburghs, beehives of industry belching smoke into the air. It would also have clusters of cleaner factories humming with the sound of looms and spindles. Meanwhile, crisscrossing the fields and woods, "iron horses" would carry the products of the new mills and factories, along with great quantities of commodities created by a surging agriculture. On the eve of the Civil War the United States would be one of the world's economic giants, ahead of all but Britain, its people enjoying one of the highest per capita living standards in the world.

How did this "economic miracle" come to pass?

* FACTORS OF PRODUCTION *

Viewed in terms of individual well-being, economic growth requires not just the expansion of a nation's total output, but expansion of total output that outstrips expansion of population. Rapid growth of total goods and services may make a nation richer and increase its overall power relative to other nations. But if we are interested in the material comfort of individuals, then it is *per capita* expansion that we must consider.

Historians and economists disagree over the causes of economic growth. Some emphasize the various "factors of production"—the "inputs" of labor, natural resources, skills, capital, and technology—that must be added to the economic mix to increase "output." Other experts assume that the most dynamic element in economic expansion is the swelling demand for goods and services that comes with increases in population, changing consumption patterns, and government tax and spending policies. A third school is especially impressed by the cultural elements that encourage societies to alter both their investment and consumption patterns. In reality, to understand how the United States increased its output enough to create relative abundance for its people, we must look at each of these, for all seem to have contributed to the fortunate outcome.

RESOURCES.   From the outset the United States was richly endowed by nature. The nation in 1815 stretched over a billion acres. No other country in the world possessed so much level, well-watered, fertile agricultural land in the earth's temperate zone, where the growing season is relatively long. The nation's forests, although they initially impeded farming, were a unique resource, for virtually everything in the nineteenth century was made of wood—houses, fences, wagons, even clocks and machinery. Wood, moreover, was a major source of fuel, used by steamboats, locomotives, factory steam engines, and by most householders to cook their food and heat their homes. America was also rich in minerals. The ores of the Appalachian region from central Vermont to the Carolinas formed an "iron belt" that as early as 1800 was dotted with forges, smelters, and mines. Copper and lead deposits were found in Michigan and Missouri. Pennsylvania and Ohio had excellent coal and—though as yet unused—the country possessed vast petroleum reserves.

In water power, too, the United States was blessed. The Appalachian chain was the source of many rivers that emptied into the Atlantic. Along the fall line, where the Piedmont plateau drops abruptly to the Atlantic coast plain, scores of swift cascading streams offered a vast reserve of water power to turn mill wheels.

In 1815 relatively little of the country's land was being farmed. In the West white farmers were found only in the regions adjacent to the Ohio Valley and a few other pockets. Almost all of the Mississippi valley was forest except some tracts in present-day Indiana, Illinois, and Iowa, covered with tall prairie grass. Even in the Atlantic coast states forests and unused farm woodlots covered the landscape, especially in northern New England, New York, western Pennsylvania, and the mountain regions of the southern states.

Nor were the nation's power resources much used. Aside from some gristmills for grinding wheat and corn into flour and meal, and sawmills for slicing logs into boards, the waterpower of the fall line went largely to waste. Also neglected was the coal of eastern Pennsylvania; as long as wood was cheap, people had no incentive to exploit the unfamiliar black stone for fuel. As for petroleum, though people knew "rock oil" would burn, they did not know how to guarantee a steady supply, so it remained a curiosity sold by quacks and hucksters as medicine.

In the forty-five years following the War of 1812, the accessible and usable resources within the country's 1803 boundaries were greatly expanded. Growing

Pittsburgh in 1796 and 1857. Located at the junction of three navigable rivers, the village thrived before 1800. In 1799 businessmen set up a nail factory there, and by the 1850's Pittsburgh's population worked in coal mines, steel mills, and glass factories under an ever-present cloud of industrial soot.

population and easier access to consumers induced farmers to expand their cultivated acreage. Increasingly, similar incentives moved businessmen to build water-powered mills and exploit coal deposits. In 1859 Edwin L. Drake, backed by New Haven capitalists, found that by drilling into the ground, an abundant supply of petroleum could be assured. Drake's well at Titusville, Pennsylvania, set off a "rush" to the oil regions that resembled the earlier gold rush to California.

But besides learning to exploit its existing resources, the country added to these resources by enlarging its boundaries. Between the Louisiana Purchase in 1803 and the Gadsden Purchase fifty years later, the United States grew by 830 million acres. A large part of the new territory was arid, but it also included great tracts of fertile land in the Central Valley of California, in east Texas, and in Gulf Coast Florida; vast deposits of copper, silver, gold, lead, and zinc in the Rocky Mountain area; and unique timber resources along the coasts of California and Oregon.

LABOR. But no quantity of natural resources, without men and women to utilize them, would have contributed to the economy. The United States was a sparsely populated country in 1815. With 8.5 million people spread over 1.7 million square miles, it had under 5 inhabitants for every square mile (640 acres) of land, compared with about 80 per square mile today. In 1820 the population reached 9.6 million, including some 1.8 million blacks. Though legal importation of slaves had ceased in 1808 (when Congress implemented the constitutional provision allowing it to end the Atlantic slave trade), blacks remained about 19 percent of the country's population.

With so few people spread over so much land, the United States suffered from a chronic labor shortage. The shortage was alleviated somewhat by the youth of the population. In 1817 the median age was 17. In an era when people began to work at 13 or 14, such a young population was a distinct economic asset. Offsetting this demographic advantage, however, were the problems of disease and ill health. There were major cholera epidemics in 1832 and again in 1849–1850 that killed thousands and disrupted economic life. In low-lying, swampy areas many people suffered each summer from "fevers" or "agues," probably mosquito-borne malaria. In addition, typhus, typhoid, whooping cough, and tuberculosis killed or disabled vast numbers of working people every year. After 1815 the potential labor force was further reduced by individual efforts to limit family size. The American birthrate dropped sharply, so that by 1850 it was below that of many countries in Europe.

As in the past, the Old World helped to offset the New World's labor shortage. Between independence and 1808 the South's labor force was augmented by a large number of slave imports. Then, on January 1, 1808, the foreign slave trade became illegal. Some smuggling of captive Africans continued, but the number of slaves who arrived in the United States from abroad was drastically cut. But Europe added to America's population with each passing year. In the period 1776–1815 no more than 10,000 Europeans entered the United States annually.

In the next twenty-five years the number rose to over 30,000. Then, in the 1840s and 1850s, economic dislocations in Germany and Scandinavia and the potato blight in Ireland made life hard, in some cases intolerable, for hundreds of thousands of European peasants. During the 1840s and 1850s a staggering average of 200,000 Europeans arrived each year at American Atlantic and Gulf Coast ports. Most of these immigrants were in their most productive early adult years. Europe had nurtured them through their dependent childhood period, and they added their brawn and their skill to the American labor pool at scarcely any cost to their adopted nation. Almost all of these additions accrued to the North. European newcomers perceived the South as an alien place where slaves competed with free labor and the chances of economic success were limited. They avoided Dixie. All told, by 1860, the nation's labor force, as a result of both natural increase and transatlantic immigration, had grown to over 11 million people.

PUBLIC SCHOOLS AND ECONOMIC GROWTH. Modern economic development has depended as much on the improvement of labor force quality—the enhancement of "human capital," as economists call it—as on the sheer growth of numbers of workers. In America the upgrading of labor force skills, literacy, and discipline was the work of the system of public education.

Educational standards had been relatively high in colonial America, especially in New England, but they had declined during the half century following the Revolution. In 1835 Professor Francis Bowen of Harvard complained that New England's once celebrated school system "had degenerated into routine . . . [and] was starved by parsimony." In the West, if we can believe the students of one small rural school, the teaching level was still lower. At the end of the academic year these pupils inscribed this verse on the wall of their schoolhouse:

> Lord of love, look from above
> And pity the poor scholars.
> They hired a fool to teach this school
> And paid him fifty dollars.

But even as Bowen—and the "scholars"—wrote, labor leaders, philanthropists, businessmen, and concerned citizens were struggling to improve the country's educational system. The most effective worker for better schools after 1835 was Horace Mann, a lawyer who gave up a successful legal practice to become secretary of the Massachusetts Board of Education in 1837. Mann believed that an educated body of citizens was essential for a healthy democratic society, but as one of Mann's successors on the Massachusetts Board of Education noted: "The prosperity of the mills and shops is based quite as much upon the intellectual vigor as the physical power of the laborers." During Mann's twelve years as secretary of the board, Massachusetts doubled teachers' salaries, built and repaired scores of school buildings, opened fifty public high schools, and established a minimum school year of six months. Other states, especially in the North, soon followed the lead of the Bay State. The new school systems taught useful values as well as useful skills. Children learned punctuality, good hygiene, industriousness, sobriety, and honesty—all valuable qualities for an emerging industrial society.

Many gaps remained in the country's educational system even after the advent of the state-supported primary school. Secondary education, except in Massachusetts, remained the privilege of the rich who could afford the tuition of private "academies" for their children. One of the most serious deficiencies was in the education of girls and young women. At the elementary level young girls were treated the same as boys. Beyond the first few grades, however, female education was often inferior. American women could not attend college until Oberlin admitted its first female student in 1833. The typical secondary school or academy for young women around 1815 was a "finishing school" where the daughters of businessmen, professionals, and wealthy farmers or planters were taught French, music, drawing, dancing, and a little "polite" literature. Then, in the period of 1820–40, educational reformers, both men and women, began to conceive of a new sort of secondary schooling for women.

These reformers attacked the idea that women should be mere ornaments or drudges. In a bustling progressive society, they said, women had a vital role to play as mothers and teachers, educating the leaders of the nation in all areas of life. This "cult of domesticity" did not assert women's equality with men. But it did insist that in their own "spheres" women were an immense neglected resource and that this waste must not continue.

The new idea that women's role was important transformed female education, especially in the Northeast. Under the leadership of Emma Willard, Mary Lyon, Joseph Emerson, and Catharine Beecher, female "seminaries" were established throughout the region. Schools such as Willard's Troy Female Seminary (1821) and Lyon's Mount Holyoke Female Seminary (1836), unlike the earlier finishing schools, taught algebra, geometry, history, geography, and several of the sciences. These more "muscular" subjects were now thought appropriate for the mothers-to-be of statesmen, soldiers, and captains of industry. The most important role of these schools, however, was to provide a flood of trained women to fill the ranks of the burgeoning teaching profession.

Though the educational system still had its failings, by 1860 the United States had a highly skilled and literate labor force. It was ahead of every nation in the world except Denmark in the ratio of students to total population, and New England was even ahead of the advanced Danes. Literacy made it possible for workers to read plans and make written reports, and gave them access to new ideas and new ways of doing things. It is no accident that the ingenious Yankee tinkerer became a legendary figure or that New England became a beehive of shops, mills, and factories, producing cloth, clocks, shoes, hardware, and machinery for the rest of the nation.

TECHNOLOGY.   During the years between independence and the Civil War, the United States led the world in useful invention. In the 1780s Oliver Evans invented a new flour mill that introduced grain at the top, and automatically cleaned, ground, cooled, sifted, and barreled it as it descended. In the 1790s, Eli

By mid-century, Americans made the world's best farm machinery. Eli Whitney's gin, shown in a mid-century-version, cleaned cotton fifty times faster than a hand laborer, and incidentally increased the demand for slaves.

Whitney perfected the "gin," a machine that cleaned the sticky seeds from the cotton boll and revolutionized cotton growing in the United States. In 1787 John Fitch first hitched steam power to navigation. Twenty years later, Robert Fulton's paddle-wheeled steamboat, the *Clermont,* made the trip from New York to Albany in a record-breaking 32 hours. In the 1840s a New York University professor, Samuel F. B. Morse, developed a practical telegraph system.

Almost all those who advanced technology in these years were self-educated or had acquired their training on the job. Most of the country's first civil engineers learned their trade by working on the early turnpikes and canals. Gradually, however, more formal means to train technicians and scientists were developed. West Point (founded in 1802), Norwich University (1820), Rensselaer Polytechnic Institute (1825), and the Lawrence Scientific School at Harvard (1847) eventually provided civil engineering courses for planning the canals, designing the bridges, and surveying the railroads that would knit the country together.

GROWING MARKETS.   We can treat the expanding and ever-more-skillful population of the country as an addition to the supply side of the economic growth equation. It was also a factor on the demand side. As population increased, so did the market for everything from babies' cribs to old folks' canes. Americans were already well supplied with food, clothing, and shelter, and each addition of family income provided money for modest luxuries. Before the Civil War the finer industrial goods were commonly obtained from Britain or France, but with each passing year American industry expanded to meet the growing home market for jewelry, furniture, carriages, carpets, writing paper, clocks, fine cloth, and a thousand other sophisticated manufactured articles.

CAPITAL. The growing labor force of the United States was matched by a growing supply of physical capital. Capital, as economists use the term, is not money as such, but money invested in machines, barns, factories, railroads, mines—that is, money invested in "tools" that produce other commodities. It comes from the savings of society, what it sets aside out of its total income. When employed productively, capital becomes the basis for increasing the rate of economic growth.

During the colonial period, most capital came from abroad in the form of implements, credits, and cash brought by immigrants or lent to Americans by European promoters and merchants. After independence the United States continued to rely on foreign sources of capital. The increasing flood of immigrants did bring money to America, but loans extended by British, French, Dutch, and German bankers and businesspeople were a larger source of foreign capital. The total amount of the nation's outstanding foreign loans went from under $100 million in 1815 to $400 million by the eve of the Civil War.

Foreign trade was yet another source of capital. The United States in this period exported vast quantities of raw materials and farm products to foreign nations. Cotton from the South alone represented almost half the value of the country's total annual exports in the mid-1850s. Profits from these sales enabled the country to buy not only European consumer goods, but also machinery, iron rails, locomotives, and other capital goods. At the same time the American merchant marine, whose swift clipper ships were the nation's pride, earned income for the United States by carrying European goods to Australia, South America, and the Far East. Finally, after 1849, gold from California helped pay for capital goods imported from the advanced industrial nations of Europe. Foreign trade created fortunes for merchants, particularly in the middle states and New England, much of which was reinvested in domestic industry.

BANKS AND BANKING. The country's commercial banking system helped the growth of private capital by creating money or credit and lending it to business borrowers. The commercial banks keep only a small reserve of money against the debts they owe to their depositors and the loans they make to borrowers. On a small amount of paid-in capital or deposited savings, they can lend a large amount to investors. In effect, the commercial banks are money machines, advancing the cash or credit they create to businesspeople who want it.

This system depends on prudence to work successfully. If bankers lent to unreliable borrowers or made loans far beyond what a cautious reserve policy required, they jeopardized their firms and often the economy as a whole. Depositors, or other creditors, fearing for the safety of their savings, might demand immediate repayment. If enough of a bank's creditors simultaneously demanded their money back, the bank might be forced to "suspend payments" and close its doors. That in turn might trip off a broad "panic," with everyone demanding cash and insisting their creditors pay their debts. Serious national panics occurred in 1819, 1837, and 1857, and each ushered in a long economic downturn. For a time businesspeople would not invest and consumers would not buy. Economic activity slowed, and workers lost their jobs.

In the pre-Civil War period, banks also provided the paper money that people used in their daily buying and selling. The United States Treasury issued gold, silver, and copper coins, but this was not enough to do the people's business. Instead, in all but minor transactions, the "bank note," issued by some banking corporation, served the public as money. By law these notes were backed by a reserve of gold kept on hand to redeem each note when presented, but the requirement was often laxly enforced. The Second Bank of the United States, chartered in 1816, had little trouble keeping its circulation of paper notes "as good as gold." Many of the state-chartered banks, however, issued excessive amounts to maximize their profits. When a bank could not redeem its notes—as when it could not pay its depositors—it was forced to suspend operations. Those who held the bank's notes now found themselves with worthless paper, much as depositors in defaulted banks found themselves with worthless bank accounts.

GROWTH OF THE BANKING SYSTEM.   Despite these failings, the country's banking system proved adequate to the job of increasing the nation's pool of capital. The first modern American commercial bank was the Bank of North America, chartered by Congress in 1781 and located in Philadelphia. In 1784 the legislatures of New York and Massachusetts chartered two additional banks. Congress, acting on Hamilton's financial program, chartered the first Bank of the United States (or BUS). Like any other commercial bank, the BUS lent money, but before its demise in 1811, it took on some of the functions of a central bank. That is, it sought to control and stabilize the entire economy by providing extra funds to state bank lenders when credit was scarce and by limiting their loans when credit was excessive.

The Second Bank of the United States, chartered in 1816, was even larger than the First, with $35 million in capital compared to the $10 million of its predecessor. It, too, sought to provide a balance wheel for the economy. At times, however, it blundered badly. Under its first president, it initially followed an easy-credit policy, lending freely to businessmen and speculators. This policy helped fuel a western land boom after 1815. Then, when it tightened credit in 1819, the Bank triggered a major panic and depression.

Meanwhile, a large state banking system was growing up alongside the BUS. In 1820 there were 300 state banks; in 1860, almost 1,600. At first most state banks were established by charters granted individually by state legislatures. By the 1840s, however, banks could secure charters by applying to designated state officials and meeting general legal requirements (free banking). In some states, especially in the Northeast, these requirements were strict. In the newer parts of the country they were often slack. There the need for capital to clear land, build barns, construct railroads, and lay out towns was most acute, and interest rates— the price of money—was therefore high. Under the circumstances, it is not surprising that many western states' banking laws were lax and enforcement still laxer. This led to large issues of "wildcats," paper money backed by hope and faith rather than "specie" (gold). The practices of western banks encouraged a boom-and-bust pattern, but their free-and-easy policies undoubtedly facilitated rapid capital growth in the emerging parts of the country. All told, economic historians conclude, the banking system of this period, for all its faults, worked well for an enterprising people.

GOVERNMENT ACTIONS. Americans disagreed about the role of the government in the American economy. Jeffersonians continued to fear federal and state intrusion as a danger to political freedom. Citizens influenced by the laissez-faire ideas of Adam Smith believed that government intervention would only hamper economic progress. Private capital was in fact the predominant source of economic growth during the pre-Civil War period, but we must not dismiss the role of government in the country's pre- Civil War expansion. Through laws favorable to the easy chartering of banks and corporations, the states encouraged private capitalists to pool their savings for investment purposes. The federal tariff system, proposed by Hamilton and implemented by the Republicans in 1816, by making imports more expensive, protected American manufacturers against foreign competition and so encouraged capitalists to risk their money in factories and mills. The legal system, buffered by lawyers, contributed to the growth surge that marked these years. Never far removed from the commercial realm, lawyers came to identify ever more closely with the entrepreneurial spirit. Increasingly, judges and lawyer-dominated legislatures made the right to earn a profit superior to the individual's rights under the common law to be protected.

Governments also contributed to capital formation more directly. Many investments, such as canals, required so much money and posed so many risks that private investors hesitated to undertake them. Yet they promised to confer economic benefits on many people or whole regions. Profit on a railroad through a wilderness area, for example, might take years to appear, though it would open an undeveloped region for settlers. To encourage growth in these instances, state and local governments in the years before 1860 joined with private promoters to build roads, canals, and railroads. Sometimes the states lent money to private capitalists; in the case of the canals, they often financed projects directly. New York put up the $7 million for the Erie Canal after efforts to secure federal funds failed. Federal revenues built the National Road, begun in 1811 and completed in 1850, from Cumberland, Maryland, to Vandalia, Illinois, a distance of 700 miles. The federal government also financed the St. Mary's Falls ship canal linking Lake Huron and Lake Superior, built coastal lighthouses, dredged rivers and harbors, and, in the 1850s, contributed millions of acres of land to promoters of the Illinois Central Railroad connecting the Great Lakes with the Gulf of Mexico.

All told, the government contribution to pre-Civil War investment was enormous. One scholar has estimated that by 1860, states, counties, and municipalities had spent about $400 million toward building the country's transportation network alone. If we add to this sum the federal government's contribution and the millions spent for schools, hospitals, and other vital public facilities that helped the economy, we can see that we must qualify the myth of laissez-faire in pre-Civil War America.

* THE COURSE OF AMERICAN ECONOMIC GROWTH *

America, then, was endowed with stupendous natural resources, a skilled, acquisitive, and disciplined population, and values and institutions conducive to hard work, saving, and capital growth. How did these elements combine to produce an economic miracle?

THE BIRTH OF KING COTTON.   Most people associate nineteenth-century economic growth with factories, forges, and mines. But agricultural advance was a vital part of the process.

The outstanding advance in agriculture before the Civil War was the opening of the "cotton kingdom." Toward the end of the eighteenth century several ingenious Englishmen developed machines to spin cotton yarn and weave it into fabric. By the 1790s the mills of Lancashire in northwest England were producing cheap cotton cloth for an ever-expanding world market.

But where was the raw cotton to come from for the hungry mills? A small amount of cotton was grown on the Sea Islands off the South Carolina and Georgia coasts. Sea island cotton has smooth fibers; its seeds could easily be removed by hand. But the region where it flourished was limited. Short-staple cotton would grow throughout the South's vast upland interior, but it had burrlike green seeds that required much hand labor to remove. It was not economical to grow, even in the slave South. Contton cultivation remained confined to the narrow Carolina–Georgia coast.

Yet the South badly needed a new cash crop. Tobacco, rice, and indigo had all suffered declining markets after independence. What could be done to make short-fiber cotton a practical replacement for the declining staples?

The answer was provided by the Yankee Eli Whitney. In 1793, while visiting the Georgia plantation of Mrs. Nathanael Greene, widow of the Revolutionary War general, Whitney learned about the problem confronting southern planters. As a gesture of gratitude to his gracious hostess, he put together a simple machine that would efficiently remove the sticky seeds from the upland cotton boll. Suddenly a single laborer, using Whitney's new "gin" (from engine), could do the work of fifty hand cleaners.

The gin, and cotton culture, quickly spread throughout the lower South. Thousands of planters, white farmers, and slaves migrated into western Georgia,

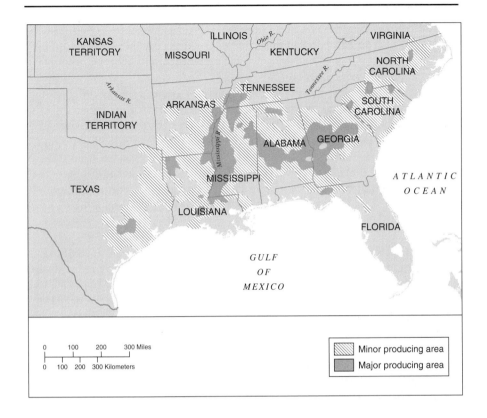

Cotton-Growing Areas

Florida, Alabama, Mississippi, Louisiana, Arkansas, and east Texas to clear fields and plant cotton. From about 2 million pounds in 1793, short-fiber cotton output shot up to 80 million pounds by 1811. In 1859 the United States produced 5 million bales of 400 pounds each and had become the world's leading supplier of raw cotton. On the eve of the Civil War cotton was "king," and its realm spanned the region from North Carolina on the Atlantic coast, 1,300 miles westward to central Texas, and from the Gulf of Mexico to Tennessee.

THE NORTH AND WEST.   If cotton was king in the South, wheat was king in the agricultural North. Grown since colonial times in almost every part of North America except New England and the deep South, it continued to be important in the Middle Atlantic states and the upper South after 1815. Thereafter, as canals and railroads made the prairies accessible, wheat growing moved westward. By 1859 Illinois, Indiana, Ohio, and Wisconsin had become the chief wheat-producing states.

The soils of the new wheat region were especially fertile and the prairies that covered large parts of several northwestern states were practically treeless; farmers did not have to clear forest cover, an occupation that consumed much of their time in the middle states. The shift of wheat growing to the Midwest accordingly increased the output per capita of American agriculture and helped to supply expanding national markets at ever-lower costs.

Labor was a problem in northern agriculture. There were generally enough hands for plowing, planting, and cultivating. But at harvest time, when the crop had to be gathered quickly, there was not enough help to go around. In the 1830s Obed Hussey and Cyrus McCormick invented horse-drawn mechanical reapers to speed the process. A man with a hand-operated "cradle" could cut from three to four acres of ripe wheat a day; with the new machine he could harvest more than four times as much. By 1860 there were some 80,000 reapers worth $246 million, at work on the fields of the North and West, more than in the rest of the world.

LAND POLICY.   Land policies too encouraged agricultural productivity. Congress in these years was under constant pressure to provide family farms for the growing population by accelerating the conversion of public lands to private use. In 1800 Congress allowed settlers to buy land in tracts of 320 acres, or half the smallest parcel previously permitted, at a minimum of $2 an acres. The same law also gave the buyer four years to pay and provided a discount of 8 percent for cash. The Land Act of 1804 lowered the minimum price to $1.64 an acre and reduced the smallest amount purchasable to 160 acres.

Federal land policies, however, were not consistent. The states and the federal government occasionally sold public land in large blocks, some of 100,000 acres or more. But these were not worked as great estates. Rather, they were bought by speculators, often on credit, and resold in small parcels to settlers. The system allowed free-wheeling businesspeople to make large profits, but even that did not prevent widespread ownership of land by people of small and middling means.

Low land prices and easy credit combined to set off periodic waves of speculation in the West. Buyers with little capital placed claims to much larger amounts of land than they could ever expect to farm themselves in hopes of selling most of it for profit later. Meanwhile, they met their payments to the government by borrowing from the banks. To prevent widespread default Congress passed periodic relief acts that delayed collection of overdue payments. Such measures did not always help, however. When speculation got out of hand in 1819, the country experienced a major depression set off by panicky speculators trying to unload their land at a time when no one wanted to buy. The Panic of 1837 also stemmed in part from western land speculation.

Not every would-be farmer waited for land to be surveyed and put up for sale. Many cleared some unsurveyed acres and farmed illegally. Such "squatters" risked losing fences, barns, houses, and the land itself when the tract they had settled and "improved" was finally offered for sale by the government. In 1830 champions of the squatters, led by Senator Thomas Hart Benton of Missouri, convinced Congress to pass the Pre-emption Act to allow those who had illegally occupied portions of the public domain on or before 1829 to buy up to 160 acres of land at the minimum price of $1.25 an acre before others were allowed to bid. In 1841 the time restrictions on the Pre-emption Act were removed.

Land policy remained relatively unchanged for more than a decade after 1841. Benton and his colleagues, joined at times by working-class leaders, continued to fight for a "homestead act" that would give land free to all bona fide settlers. But many easterners feared that free western lands would drain off eastern labor; southerners feared it would give the government an excuse to raise the tariff to offset the loss of land-sale revenues and also that it would encourage the growth of free states. The continued opposition of the South blocked a homestead law until 1862. Still, federal land policies overall accelerated the geographical expansion of the economy's agricutural sector.

FARM PRODUCTIVITY.   If agriculture had remained stagnant, rapid overall ecomic growth would not have been possible. While the reaper made farm labor more efficient and newly opened "virgin" lands yielded far more for each outlay of labor and capital than the older lands of the East, there was a serious downside to this agricultural expansion. It mined centuries-long accumulations of top-soil nutrients wastefully. But it also churned out ever-cheaper wheat, pork, beef, fruits, vegetables, and fiber in a profusion seldom attained anywhere, anytime. Without this development there would not have been an "economic miracle."

STEAMBOATS AND ROADS.   In some ways American geography favored the efficient, cheap transportation necessary for growth. The Mississippi River system combined with the Great Lakes made it possible for ships to penetrate deep into the vital interior of North America. But the lakes lacked lighthouses and port facilities and at several points were connected only by unnavigable rapids. As for the Mississippi system, flatboats and rafts could easily be floated down to New Orleans propelled by the current, but the trip upstream by poled keelboats required backbreaking labor and took far longer.

Capitalists and inventors had been working on schemes to apply steam power to river navigation for some time, but not until Robert Fulton took up the quest, backed by the powerful Livingston family, did it become economically feasible. Soon steamboats were operating on schedule up and down the Hudson. In 1811 the Fulton-Livingston interests, having already secured a legal monopoly of steamboat traffic in New York State waters, received an exclusive charter from the Louisiana territorial legislature to operate steamboats on the lower Mississippi. If unchecked, the Fulton group might have monopolized steamboat navigation on all the inland waters. However, the Supreme Court struck down these monopoly privileges in the case of *Gibbons v. Ogden* and opened up steamboat navigation to all investors. Entrepreneurs were not long in seizing the opportunity. By 1855 there were 727 steamboats on the western rivers with a combined capacity of 170,000 tons; many more plied the Great Lakes as well as the streams and coastal waters of the Gulf and the Atlantic.

It had taken four months to pole a boat upstream from New Orleans to Louisville; by 1853 steamboats made it in under four and a half days. Freight rates on the same route in this period fell from an average of $5 a hundred pounds to under 15 cents.

Impressive as the advances in inland navigation were, there still remained the problem of transportation where there were no natural waterways. Overland travelers during the colonial period had been forced to use narrow, muddy, circuitous trails. After 1800 a network of surfaced, all-weather roads for horses, carriages, and wagons began to appear, financed by tolls on users. The first major "turnpike" in the country was the Philadelphia–Lancaster Road in Pennsylvania opened in 1794. The entire country soon caught the road-building fever. In the Northeast private capital built most of the turnpikes; in the South and West state governments built the roads directly or bought stock in private turnpike companies. The federal government also joined in the rush, investing $7 million in the construction of the National Road.

CANALS.   Though turnpikes reduced the cost and time of transporting people and goods, transportation by land remained more expensive than by water. Where there were no navigable streams or lakes, the solution was canals. A few miles of artificial waterway were constructed in the Northeast just before the War of 1812. The real boom got under way in 1817, when the New York State legislature appropriated funds for constructing an enormously long canal between the Hudson River and Lake Erie, bypassing the Appalachian barrier to connect the Great Lakes with the Atlantic Ocean.

The project was an impressive achievement. The New York engineers learned on the job and improvised a score of new tools and techniques. In the end they moved millions of cubic yards of earth, constructed 83 locks, scores of stone aqueducts, and 363 miles of "ditch" 4 feet deep and 40 feet wide. The completed Erie canal, opened by a colorful ceremony in 1825, was an engineering marvel that astounded the world. Power for the canal boats was provided by horses and mules that treaded towpaths on either side of the waterway. A man or a boy led the animals; another man at the tiller kept the boat in mid-channel and signaled passengers seated on top of the cabin to duck by blowing a horn when the vessel approached a low bridge.

The canal was also an immense economic success. In 1817 the cost of shipping freight between New York City and Buffalo on Lake Erie was 19.2 cents a ton. By 1830 it was down to 3.4 cents. Freight rates to and from the upper Mississippi Valley also plummeted. By 1832 the canal was earning the state well over a million dollars yearly in tolls. The canal deflected much of the interior trade that had gone down the Mississippi and its tributaries and redirected it eastward to New York City, confirming its growing economic advantage over the nation's other business centers.

New York's experience inevitably aroused the envy of merchants in the other Atlantic ports. Baltimore, Boston, Philadelphia, and Charleston businessmen now demanded that their states follow New York's lead. At the same time, promoters,

Locks such as these on the Erie Canal near Albany made it possible for canal boats to ascend and descend from one level to another. The motive force for the boats was provided by mules walking a towpath and attached by ropes, as seen at right.
(Collection of the New York Historical Society)

speculators, farmers, and merchants in the Northwest saw that their region's prosperity depended on constructing canals to link up with the waterways built or proposed. The pressure on state governments soon got results. By the 1830s the dirt was flying all over the Northeast and Northwest as construction crews raced to create a great network of canals. In 1816 there were 100 miles of canals in the United States; by 1840 over 3,300 miles of artificial waterways criss-crossed the Middle Atlantic states, southern New England, and the Old Northwest.

Few canals built after 1825 were as successful as the Erie. Some never overcame difficult engineering problems; others never attracted sufficient business to repay investors. Still others were built too late and were overtaken by the railroads, which provided quicker and less easily interrupted service. Nevertheless, the sharp decline in freight and passenger rates was a great boon to interregional trade. Western farmers found new outlets in the East for their wheat, corn, pork, beef, and other commodities. With transportation costs lower, the price of manufactured goods in the West fell, enabling eastern manufacturers to sell more to western customers. Everyone benefited.

THE RAILROADS ARRIVE. The railroads, too, helped growth. The early steam railroads were plagued by technical problems. Engines frequently broke down or even exploded. And even on a normal trip, passengers emerged from the cars nearly suffocated by smoke or with holes burned in their clothes from flying sparks. Rails were at first flat iron straps nailed to wooden beams. When these came loose, they sometimes curled up through the floors of moving passenger cars, maiming or killing the occupants. Cattle that got in the way of trains caused derailments. Trains moving rapidly over lightly ballasted rails and around sharp curves did not always stay on the track. Some of these problems were inevitable in so new a system, but accidents were also the result of makeshift construction imposed by the shortage of capital and the desire to build quickly.

Gradually, railroad technology improved. All-iron rails, more substantial passenger cars, the "cow catcher" in front of the locomotive to push aside obstructions, more dependable boilers, and enlarged smokestacks to contain the hot sparks all made the railroads more efficient and more coomfortable. To deal with the hairpin curves characteristic of American railroads, engineers developed loose-jointed engines and cars with wheels that swiveled to guide trains around turns.

The first major American railroad was the Baltimore and Ohio, chartered in 1828. In 1833 the Charleston and Hamburg in South Carolina reached its terminus 136 miles from its starting point, making it the longest railroad in the world. By 1860 the country boasted some 30,000 miles of track, and passengers and freight could travel by rail from the Atlantic coast as far west as St. Joseph, Missouri, and from Portland, Maine, to New Orleans. The system was far from complete, and many communities remained without rail connections. Nevertheless, the accomplishment was impressive.

THE FACTORY SYSTEM.   Advances in agriculture and transportation contributed immensely to the pre-Civil War economic surge. But the most dynamic development of the antebellum economy was the rise of the factory system, initially in southern New England.

There had been large workshops here and there in the colonial period, but none of these had brought together hundreds of "operatives" and expensive power-driven machinery under one roof to produce a single uniform product. The modern factory, copied from eighteenth-century English inventors and entrepreneurs in cotton textile manufacture, arrived in the United States after independence and in a rudimentary form. The first mill using water power to spin cotton yarn was probably the Beverly Cotton Manufactory of Massachusetts incorporated in 1789. In 1790 a skilled English mechanic, Samuel Slater, linked up with Almy and Brown, a concern descended from colonial candle-makers and West Indies traders with capital to invest. In 1790–1791 the firm opened the nation's first cotton spinning mill at Pawtucket, Rhode Island. Before long, the small state was covered with spinning mills that employed whole families, including women and young children, to tend the water-powered spindles.

The Rhode Island mills only produced cotton yarn; the textile industry still needed skilled hand weavers to produce cloth. The first true textile factory to produce finished cloth arrived about twenty years later in Massachusetts. Francis Cabot Lowell, a Boston merchant hard hit by Jefferson's embargo during the

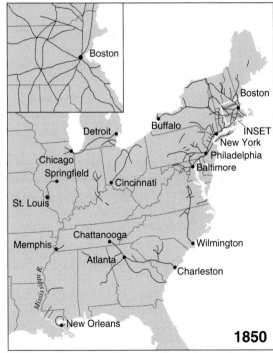

The Railroad Networks, 1850–1860

dispute with Britain over neutral rights, provided much of the entrepreneurial leadership of the Massachusetts cotton mills. Lowell visited Lancashire, center of the flourishing British textile industry, in 1810 and took careful note of the latest power looms. He carried the plans home in his head and was able to build a loom superior to the original.

Joining with other merchants, Lowell secured a corporation charter for the Boston Manufacturing Company. With their combined capital the promoters built a mill at a water power site in Waltham on the Charles River. The first cotton cloth came from the company looms in 1815 and proved superior to British imports. Between 1816 and 1826 the Boston Manufacturing Company averaged almost 19 percent profit a year.

The promoters soon found they could not produce enough cloth at the limited Waltham power site to satisfy the demand, and made plans for a complete new textile community along the swift-flowing Merrimack. The new mills at Lowell, Massachusetts, were much larger than either the Waltham factory or the earlier spinning mills in Rhode Island. Attracting enough labor for the new mills and finding housing for the workers and an attractive moral environment were major problems. The promoters solved their labor difficulties by hiring Yankee farm girls drawn to Lowell by promises of good wages and cheap, attractive dormitory housing built at company expense. The company also provided a lyceum, where the literate and pious young women who worked in the mills could hear edifying lectures, and paid for a church and a minister. By the mid-1830s Lowell was a town of 18,000 people with schools, libraries, paved streets, churches, and health facilities. The mills themselves numbered some half dozen, each separately incorporated, arranged in quadrangles surrounded by the semidetached houses of the townsfolk and the dormitories of the female workers.

Lowell became famous even across the Atlantic. Distinguished foreign visitors made pilgrimages to Lowell and were invariably impressed by what they saw. The British novelist Charles Dickens, who had encountered at home the worst evils of industrialism, noted that the girls at Lowell wore "serviceable bonnets, good warm cloaks and shawls . . . , [were] healthy in appearance, many of them remarkably so . . . , [and had] the manners and deportment of young women, not of degraded brutes."

During the "hungry forties," when the nation's economy slowed, conditions in the mills worsened. The girls' wages were cut, and when they protested, they were replaced with newly arrived Irish immigrants who were not so demanding. But for a time the Lowell system served as a showcase for the benefits of industrialization.

* INDUSTRIAL WORKERS *

UNEQUAL GAINS. In 1815, well before Lowell, the Erie Canal, and the Baltimore and Ohio Railroad, Americans were already a rich people by the standards of the day. During the next thirty-five years the wealth and income of the American people increased enormously. One scholar believes that between the mid-1830s and the Civil War alone, annual GNP (gross national product, a dollar measure of all goods and services produced) more than doubled. Growth in per capita GNP was also high, as much as 2.5 percent a year in the 1825–1837 period, for example.

Yet it is clear that all Americans did not benefit equally from the economic surge taking place. Clearly it enlarged the urban middle class by creating jobs not only for laborers and factory operatives but also for engineers, clerks, bookkeepers, factory managers, and others. Most of these "white collar" workers were native-born Americans whose familiarity with the English language and American ways gave them the pick of the new jobs.

The industrial leap also created a new class of rich manufacturers, bankers, and railroad promoters. Many were "new" men who used the industrial transformation to lift themselves out of poverty. Samuel Slater, for one, had come to America in 1789 with almost nothing; he was worth $700,000 by 1829. In fact, the economic growth of the 1815–1860 period was accompanied by growing inequality of economic condition. Studies of wealth ownership between the end of the colonial era and 1860 show a considerable increase in the proportion of houses, land, slaves, bank accounts, ships, equipment, factories, and other kinds of property, owned by the richest 10 percent of the American people, compared with everyone else.

WAGES AND WORKING CONDITIONS.   Did these growing inequalities mean that the people doing the actual hard physical labor of the nation failed to benefit from the economic growth of the period?

Leaving aside the South's slaves (see Chapter 13), taken as a whole, American wage earners made real advances during the generation preceding 1860. But individual circumstances varied. Relatively few married women worked for wages, but those who did were badly paid. When women teachers flocked to the new public schools, teachers' average wage levels fell. For traditional "women's work" the situation was similar. Female household servants in 1850 received, typically, a little over a dollar a week plus their room and board. Manufacturers of straw hats, ready-made clothes, and shoes relied on a large pool of poorly paid female workers, many employed part-time at home and paid by the "piece." These women often earned no more than 25 cents a day. The Lowell girls were relatively affluent at $2.50 to $3 a week.

But many men were paid not much better. In 1850 common laborers—ditch diggers, stevedores, carters, and the like—received 61 cents a day with board, or 87 cents without board. Skilled labor was in shorter supply and so better rewarded. Blacksmiths earned about $1.10 a day in 1852. In 1847 a skilled iron founder in Pennsylvania could make as much as $30 per week. The Boston Manufacturing Company paid machinists up to $11 a week.

To put this into perspective, the *New York Tribune* estimated in 1851 that a minimum budget of about $10 a week was needed to support a family of five in expensive New York City. This meant that an unskilled worker needed help from other family members, and they generally got it. In many families children were put to work at ten or twelve and earned enough to push total family incomes past the bare subsistence point. One scholar estimates that just after the Civil War family heads in Massachusetts earned just 57 percent of total family income; the rest came from the children.

Though the picture for labor is mixed, wage earners were better off in the United States than in Europe. An Irish railroad construction worker received wages of 75 cents a day plus board, which included meat three times a day. When he wrote home to his family in Ireland, however, he told them he ate meat three times a week. When asked why he didn't tell them the truth, the man replied, "if I told them that, they'd never believe me." In fact, the abundance of cheap food, especially items seldom part of working-class diet in Europe, invariably astonished people accustomed to foreign practice. One immigrant expressed amazement at what his New York boardinghouse offered its patrons. Breakfast included "beef steaks, fish, hash, ginger cakes, buckwheat cakes etc such a profusion as I never saw before at the breakfast tables." And at dinner there was even "a greater profusion than breakfast."

But wages and income were not the whole story. Wage earners' lives were not easy. Work hours were long. The Lowell girls spent twelve hours a day, six days a week, at their machines. Outdoor workers averaged eleven hours a day, fewer in winter, more in summer. Foreigners, seeking to explain superior American wages, believed that Americans worked harder than their own compatriots. And they probably did. Though the pace of factory labor was more leisurely than today, it was difficult for people used to the slow rhythms of the nineteenth-century farm to adjust to the remorseless pace of the factory machines.

Pre-Civil War workers and their families also experienced great insecurity. Accidents were common, and when workers were injured, they lost their jobs. Men killed in the mines or factories left behind families who had to turn to meager private charities or begrudging public support. Besides industrial disaster, there was the uncertainty of employment. A bad harvest or a particularly hard winter often left agricultural workers destitute. Severe periodic depressions produced acute hardship among laborers and factory workers. During the hard times that began in 1819, an English traveler through the East and Northwest noted that he had "seen upwards of 1,500 men in quest of work within 11 months past." Again, following the 1837 and 1857 panics, unemployment forced many wage earners to ask for city and state relief for themselves and their families. In 1857 there were food riots in several northern cities.

Still another source of distress among workers was the downgrading of skills and the loss of independence that sometimes accompanied mechanization and the factory system. The fate of the Massachusetts shoemakers is a case in point. In the opening years of the nineteenth century they had been skilled, semi-independent craftsmen. Merchants brought them cut leather and paid them a given sum for each pair of shoes they sewed and finished in their "tenfooters," the ten-by-ten sheds they worked in behind their homes. These skilled craftsmen owned their own tools and often employed their wives and grown children to help with the work. Not only were they well paid; they also enjoyed a sense of independence since they were subcontractors, not wage earners, and were the heads of their households, not only in a social and legal sense, but also in a direct economic way.

Gradually, as the market for ready-made shoes, especially for southern slaves, expanded, the shoemakers' independence and incomes declined. Merchants broke up the shoemaking process into smaller and simpler parts and "put out" the work to unmarried young women in New England country villages. Eventually power-driven machines that sewed heavy leather were introduced, enabling the merchants to establish factories where wage workers could use the expensive, capitalist-owned machines. By the eve of the Civil War the independent master craftsman working in his ten-footer had been replaced with semiskilled labor working for weekly wages in factories.

THE LABOR MOVEMENT.   Clearly many wage earners were unhappy with the new aggressive capitalism and the new factory system. In 1836 the young women at Lowell went on strike to protest a wage cut. In the end the factory owners won and the wage cut stuck. In 1860 the shoemakers of Lynn, Massachusetts, "turned out" to protest declining wages; before the strike ended, some 20,000 Massachusetts shoemakers had left their places at the machines.

All through the antebellum period workers struck for higher wages or better working conditions. Most of the strikes were unplanned uprisings in response to some unexpected blow such as a wage cut. But some grew out of long-standing grievances such as the sheer drudgery of factory life or the loss of worker independence. These grievances created a labor movement of considerable dimensions.

The small community craft societies organized in the early 1800s expanded over the next thirty years into citywide labor unions, each representing a whole trade. Later local unions joined together into national organizations. But after the Panic of 1837 employers usually defeated the strikers by threatening to hire the many unemployed. Trade unions declined and in the next two decades labor discontent generally was diverted from labor unions to political action and various reform movements.

We must not exaggerate the extent of labor discontent during these years, however. The school system, as well as the churches, worked hard to instill the "work ethic" into the labor force, and on the whole, they were successful. By and large the American workforce cooperated with economic growth. As one pre-1860 observer noted, in New England "every workman seems to be continually devising some new thing to assist him in his work, and there [is] a strong desire both with masters and workman . . . to be 'posted up' [that is, kept informed] in every improvement." Skilled English workingmen who came to American machine shops in the 1830s and 1840s were often startled to find that their American counterparts, rather than fighting the shop owners, were "fire eaters" whose "ravenous appetites for labor" made their own performance look bad. Several eminent students of American economic development are convinced that this cooperation was one of the most important elements in creating the pre-Civil War American economic miracle.

* CONCLUSIONS *

Many things contributed to the nation's impressive economic performance during the antebellum period. Nature had endowed the United States with uniquely rich resources. History had given it a vigorous, frugal, hard-working people. After 1815 Americans vastly improved on what they had inherited from nature and their own colonial past. During the succeeding decades European immigrants added their brains and brawn to the working population and its accumulated skills. Foreign investors, seeing the United States as a land of opportunity, sent their capital across the Atlantic. Government encouraged enterprise by passing general incorporation laws and tariffs, constructing schools, and investing directly in canals and roads. Skillful entrepreneurs, benefiting from low wages and low taxes, threw themselves into the task of making their communities—and themselves—rich. The country's values and ideals also contributed to material progress by creating a work ethic that made wage earners feel they had a share in the nation's economic progress.

Whatever the causes, economic growth was not an unrelieved blessing. Though most Americans benefited, the contrast between rich and poor became more pronounced. A by-product of America's spectacular economic surge, these inequalities would assume greater importance in the generations ahead.

10

JACKSONIAN DEMOCRACY

What Was It and How Did It Change Political Life?

1810	The United States claims more land as part of the Louisiana Purchase; *Fletcher* v. *Peck*
1812	James Madison reelected president
1816	Congress incorporates the Second Bank of the United States (BUS); Tariff Act for the first time protects American industry from foreign competition; James Monroe elected president
1818	Andrew Jackson's raid on Spanish Florida
1819	*Dartmouth College* v. *Woodward*; *McCulloch* v. *Maryland*; The Adams–Onís Treaty with Spain
1821	*Cohens* v. *Virginia*
1823	The Monroe Doctrine announced
1824	Henry Clay's "American System" becomes the Whig platform; John Quincy Adams is elected president by the House and Jackson's supporters suspect a "corrupt bargain"
1828	Congress passes "Tariff of Abominations"; John Calhoun writes Exposition and Protest; Andrew Jackson elected president
1830	Indian Removal Act
1832	Tariff Act lowers 1828 duties only slightly; South Carolina declares the new tariff null and void; *Worcester* v. *Georgia* upholds Cherokee land claims; Jackson vetoes the bill renewing the BUS charter; Jackson removes government deposits from the BUS
1832–34	Biddle reduces and calls in BUS loans
1833	Congress passes the Force Bill; South Carolina agrees to a compromise tariff, but nullifies the Force Bill
1835–42	Florida Seminoles forcibly resist removal west
1836	Jackson issues Specie Circular; Martin Van Buren elected president

| 1838 | Cherokees leave Georgia for Oklahoma on the "Trail of Tears" |
| 1840 | Whig William H. Harrison elected president |

March 4, 1829, was moving day in Washington. Andrew Jackson was to be inaugurated seventh president of the United States, and for weeks many of the city's oldest inhabitants had been packing their possessions and preparing to leave for new residences. To Margaret Bayard Smith, the elegant hostess who had presided over Washington society for twenty-five years, the change was a tragedy. "Never before did the city seem . . . so gloomy," she wrote. "Drawing rooms in which I have so often mixed with gay crowds, distinguished by rank, fashion, beauty, talent, . . . now empty, silent, dank, dismantled. Oh! 'tis melancholy!"

While some were leaving the still-raw capital on the Potomac, however, others were moving in. The city had filled with visitors, and the hotels overflowed. Washington endured a flood of new people every four years, of course, but this time there were more of them and they were different. Besides the usual frock-coated dignitaries and bureaucrats, rough-looking men in leather shirts and coonskin caps and equally unfamiliar types with Irish lilts to their voices strolled the capital's streets. The crowd was playful and good-humored, but also fiercely determined. Every face, according to Mrs. Smith, bore "defiance on its brow." "I never saw anything like it before," wrote the new senator from Massachusetts, Daniel Webster. "They really seem to think the country is rescued from some dreadful danger."

The determined mood of the newcomers was understandable. For fourteen years—ever since his great victory over the British at New Orleans—Andy Jackson's admirers had fought to make their hero president. The general was the most magnetic political leader since Washington; to many his personal qualities of bluntness, courtliness, and charm, combined with his stature as a military leader, would always be his chief political assets. But was hero worship the only reason for the excitement? Or was there more than personal loyalty behind the defiant brows? Was something important taking place in Washington that day? Would Old Hickory's election make a difference in the way the country was run? Would it bring new groups to power with new ideas and new programs? Obviously Webster and Mrs. Smith believed they were witnessing some sort of revolution. So did the rough-hewn men who wandered the streets of the capital in March 1829. Were they right? Was a major political change in the air? And if so, what was it? To answer these questions we must look first at the era before Jackson's election.

✻ THE ERA OF GOOD FEELINGS ✻

By 1817, when James Monroe was inaugurated as fifth president, the "first party system" had run its course. The bad judgment that had led the Federalists to oppose the War of 1812, along with the limited appeal of their aristocratic ideology, virtually destroyed them as a significant political force. Though it continued to show strength in New England, Delaware, and a few other places, the party of Washington, Hamilton, and John Adams never challenged the Republicans in a national election again.

Federalist principles lived on, however. The War of 1812, as we saw in Chapter 8, taught the Republicans the value of banks, roads, and national self-sufficiency; in 1815 President Madison had asked for a new national bank, a protective tariff, and a system of internal improvements. In Congress Henry Clay, John C. Calhoun of South Carolina, and other "new Republicans" who had learned from Hamilton, supported the president. Madison got most of what he had asked for without serious opposition. In April 1816 Congress passed a measure to incorporate a second Bank of the United States with a larger capitalization than its predecessor. A few weeks later it approved the Tariff Act of 1816, which for the first time protected American manufacturers against the lower costs and greater efficiency of European industry. Early the following year Congress enacted a major internal improvements bill. The old Federalist Gouverneur Morris watched this Republican turnaround with amazement. "The Party now in power," he mused, "seems disposed to do all that Federal men ever wished. . . . "

With the Federalist party gone, ideological tensions declined. Historians have called the decade following the War of 1812 the Era of Good Feelings. This is a useful label if we consider only presidential elections, contests without clashes of parties with distinct ideologies. It is a misnomer if it is intended to mean that political conflict had ceased. Political disagreements continued during these years, but they took the form of intraparty squabbling and personal rivalry, as in colonial times. Within the states there were frequent battles between one Jeffersonian Republican faction and another. Nationally, the differing political factions looked to Calhoun, Clay, John Quincy Adams, or Senator William H. Crawford of Georgia for leadership. But none of these men was as yet capable of evoking great enthusiasm among the voters. Moreover, the issues debated were obscure—if there were issues at all. Public indifference was widespread and the voter turnouts were small.

National elections continued, of course, but they merely confirmed the choices of Republican leaders. Every four years the Republican chieftains in Congress "caucused"—got together in closed session—and nominated the party's candidate, and in the fall their choice was duly ratified by the voters. Making matters even more cut and dried, the caucus leaders invariably chose either the incumbent or, if he had served two full terms, his secretary of state. Thus Secretary of State Madison succeeded Jefferson, Secretary of State Monroe succeeded Madison, and Secretary of State John Quincy Adams would succeed Monroe. To top off the whole cozy arrangement—and turn off the voters—four of the first six presidents were Virginians, and the other two were from Massachusetts. With so little real choice, it was no wonder that voter participation in elections declined so sharply.

THE VIRGINIA DYNASTY. The presidents from Jefferson to Monroe (1800–1825) were part of what is known as the Virginia dynasty. (John Quincy

Adams, who followed Monroe in office, belonged to this group in most respects in spite of his Massachusetts origins.) They were all cultivated gentlemen, but they were also colorless and withdrawn, and they proved surprisingly timid in domestic affairs.

John Quincy Adams, the sixth president, was a learned, intelligent man and the boldest innovator of the group, Jefferson excepted. In his first annual message to Congress he recommended federal support for a national university and a national observatory, a system of uniform weights and measures, a new Department of the Interior, reformed patent laws, and a massive program of internal improvements. But Adams, like most of the others, lacked leadership ability. However intelligent and able, he was also aloof and humorless. One associate said of him: "It is a question whether he ever laughed in his life." It is not surprising that he found the normal roughhouse of national politics distasteful. Congress, controlled by his political enemies, ignored his recommendations, and the president, too fastidious to use his influence or the power of patronage to gain its support, accomplished little.

JOHN MARSHALL'S COURT.   There would have been little innovation on the political front during the Era of Good Feelings if not for Chief Justice John Marshall. Marshall was a throwback to the earlier, confident Federalism of Hamilton. Unlike the new Republicans, he did not waiver in the cause of strengthening federal power and encouraging a climate attractive to business and enterprise. In 1810, under his leadership the Supreme Court for the first time struck down a state law as unconstitutional in *Fletcher v. Peck,* on the grounds that it violated a state contract with private parties. Nine years later, in the *Dartmouth College* case, the Marshall Court again upheld the inviolability of a private contract when it forbade the state of New Hampshire to amend the royal charter of Dartmouth College. A government charter to a private corporation, Marshall pronounced, was equivalent to a contract and so protected by the Constitution. As Justice Joseph Story, one of Marshall's colleagues, remarked, the decision would protect "private rights" against "any undue encroachment . . . which the passions of the popular doctrines of the day may stimulate any State Legislature to adopt."

At the same time, Marshall fought to expand the authority of the federal government over the states. In 1819 Maryland placed a tax on the paper money issues of the unpopular Second Bank of the United States. Marshall declared the Maryland law unconstitutional and hence void. The issue, he announced in *McCulloch v. Maryland,* was twofold: Did Congress have power to charter a federal bank in the absence of a specific provision to that effect in the Constitution; and could states tax federal property? His decision was yes on the first question and no on the second. The right of Congress to charter a bank could be readily deduced from the Constitution's "necessary and proper clause." "Let the end be legitimate," the Chief Justice declared, "and all means which are appropriate . . . , which are not prohibited, but consist with the letter and spirit of the Constitution, are constitutional." As for state taxation of federal agencies, the "power to tax" involved "the power to destroy." No state could destroy a legal creation of

Congress, and so the Maryland law was unconstitutional. In *Cohens v. Virginia* (1821), Marshall asserted that state court decisions were subject to review by the federal courts when they involved violation of federal law.

FOREIGN AFFAIRS. The Virginia dynasty presidents may have been indifferent leaders in domestic affairs, but they were vigorous and successful champions of America's international interests. In 1810 and again in 1812, while both Spain and England were preoccupied with Napoleon, the United States took possession of the western portion of Spanish West Florida on the dubious grounds it had been included in the Louisiana Purchase. Spain protested vigorously but, weakened by the international turmoil of the previous decades, could do little.

This serving of Spanish territory did not satisfy the American appetite. A remnant of the Florida panhandle still remained in Spanish hands, and still more enticing was the great southern loop of the peninsula itself. Acquiring this would not only round out the southeastern corner of the nation; it would settle the problem of escaped slaves, hostile Indians, and white renegades who periodically staged raids from Florida into Georgia and then fled back across the border into Spanish jurisdiction.

Secretary of State John Quincy Adams offered to buy Florida and at the same time settle the uncertain boundary between the Louisiana Purchase territory and the Spanish provinces in Mexico. Spain was not interested. Andrew Jackson's impetuous behavior as commander of American forces patrolling the Florida–Georgia border brought the situation to an unexpected head in 1818. Jackson was authorized to cross into Spanish territory to suppress the raiders, but told to avoid attacking Spanish posts and settlements in the colony. The general had little patience with such a namby-pamby policy. Jackson crossed the border, captured the Spanish fort of St. Marks, executed two British troublemakers—Alexander Arbuthnot and Robert Ambrister—and went on to occupy Pensacola, deposing the Spanish governor in the process.

Ordinary Americans cheered Jackson's bold acts; in Washington, London, and Madrid there was consternation. The only cool head was that of Secretary of State Adams, who saw that the general's rash behavior could be turned to America's advantage. Adams took the offensive. He dismissed Spain's loud protest, charged the Spaniards with failure to protect their own possessions, and enlarged United States claims to Spanish territory in the Far West under the Louisiana Purchase treaty.

Adams's brazen tactics worked. The Spanish minister in Washington, Luis de Onís y Gonzales, blustered and complained, but his government recognized that it could no longer hold Florida and came to terms with the United States. In February 1819, in the Adams–Onís Treaty, Spain ceded Florida to the United States and surrendered its claim to Oregon. In return, the United States assumed the payment of $5 million in debts owed by Spain to American citizens and agreed to accept the Sabine Rivers as the southwestern boundary of Louisiana, thereby excluding the Mexican province of Texas.

THE MONROE DOCTRINE.   Spain's weakness created hazards as well as opportunities for the United States. By 1820 all of Spanish America, except some Caribbean islands, had won independence. But Spain still hoped to regain control of its former possessions. These hopes were encouraged by France, Prussia, Austria, and Russia, whose monarchs in 1815 had established the Holy Alliance to resist the new forces of democracy and liberalism wherever they appeared. Among the European powers, only Great Britain opposed the alliance for fear that France might regain her lost influence in the Americas and that a revived Spanish-American empire would exclude Great Britain from the profitable trade that had developed with Latin America since its independence. To counter these dangers, the British foreign secretary, George Canning, proposed that his nation and the United States work together to prevent Spain from regaining control of her former colonies.

The American government, like the British, was dismayed at the prospect of Spanish restoration and the intervention of the great European powers in the Americas. It also feared the spread of Russian trading posts in California. But Secretary Adams was skeptical of any joint arrangement. For the United States to cooperate with Great Britain would put it in the position of "a cockboat in the wake of the British man-of-war." Far better for America to go it alone without relying on Britain's uncertain backing.

On Adams's recommendation President Monroe included a statement regarding Latin America in his December 1823 message to Congress. We now call this the Monroe Doctrine. Four principles would guide the United States in its relations with Europe and the rest of the Western Hemisphere, Monroe announced. First, no part of the American continents were "to be considered as subjects for future colonization by any European powers." Second, the new Latin American nations must remain independent republics; any attempt of the European powers "to extend their system to any portion of this hemisphere" we would consider "as dangerous to our peace and safety." Third, the United States would respect existing European colonies in America and stay out of purely European concerns. The fourth component of the Monroe Doctrine—actually announced in a separate diplomatic note to the Russian minister in Washington—asserted that the United States would oppose any transfer of existing colonies in the Americas from one European country to another.

Monroe's statement appeared to the nations of continental Europe to be "blustering," "arrogant," and "monstrous." And it was. The United States was asserting rights unrecognized by international law or treaty—rights it also could not yet defend. The pretensions of the puny American nation seemed ludicrous. "Mr. Monroe, who is not a sovereign," scoffed the French foreign minister, "has assumed in his message the tone of a powerful monarch whose armies and fleets are ready to march at the first signal. . . . Mr. Monroe is the temporary President of a Republic situated on the east coast of North America. . . . Its independence was only recognized forty years ago; by what right then would the two Americas today be under its immediate sway from Hudson's Bay to Cape Horn?"

The United States was counting on Great Britain to stand behind it in case of challenge. Nevertheless, it took courage for a nation of scarcely 10 million to defy the powers of Europe. It also took idealism. No matter how the United States might later twist the Monroe Doctrine to serve its own interests, it was originally a generous statement in defense of international freedom and republican institutions.

THE MISSOURI COMPROMISE.   One event late in Monroe's administration carried hints of serious internal political troubles ahead. In February 1819 the Enabling Act, a measure to admit Missouri to the Union, came before Congress. Carved out of the Louisiana Purchase, Missouri had been settled predominantly by southerners, and the bill accepted it into the Union as a slave state. Soon after the bill was submitted, Representative James Tallmadge of New York proposed an amendment prohibiting any further introduction of slaves into the proposed new state and providing for the emancipation of all adult children of slaves born after the date of its admission. The halls of Congress echoed with angry debate for two sessions as members attacked or defended the Tallmadge amendment. Southerners warned that if slavery were excluded from Missouri, the Union would be torn apart. Even the aging Jefferson considered the Tallmadge amendment and the attitude of the northern congressmen ominous. The Missouri debate was a "fire bell in the night," he wrote, that warned of grave danger for the Union ahead.

After months of heated wrangling, the voices of moderation prevailed. Under the Missouri Compromise of 1820 Congress admitted two states to the Union—Maine and Missouri. Maine, carved from Massachusetts, would be free; Missouri would be slave. The balance of free and slave states in the Union would thus be preserved. The compromise further provided that the southern boundary of Missouri (36° 30′ north latitude) would be the dividing point between future slave and free territory within the remaining Louisiana Purchase territory.

* JACKSON COMES TO POWER *

By this time the politicians were hard at work considering Monroe's successor. If precedent had remained a guide, there would have been little dispute; as secretary of state, John Quincy Adams would be the choice in 1824. But the voters were tired of being "King Caucus's" rubber stamp.

DEMOCRATIC REFORMS IN THE STATES.   The new attitude fueled a quiet political revolution. Between 1820 and 1840 the last vestiges of state property qualifications for voting disappeared. Several states in this period also ended "stand-up" voting, which revealed voters' preferred candidates, and replaced it with printed ballots to protect privacy and independence. Most states eliminated the remaining property qualifications for officeholding and reapportioned their legislatures to give underrepresented areas the political weight they deserved. By 1832 every state except South Carolina had also transferred the power to choose presidential electors from the legislatures to the voters. Many states also changed appointive offices into elective ones. The convention system, in which the party rank and file had a voice, soon replaced the elitist caucus as a method of nominating candidates for office. First adopted in the states, the convention soon became the norm in national politics as well.

It used to be said that these changes originated in the West and only later spread to the East. The evidence shows that it was often the other way around. In political affairs, at least, the East was the pioneer and eastern practices were carried west by emigrants. It was also at one time commonly held that Andrew Jackson and his supporters were responsible for many of the changes. In fact, most of the changes preceded rather than followed the Jackson movement.

THE ELECTION OF 1824.   There was no opposition party in 1824. Except for the small group of Anti-Masons, everyone called himself a Republican, and in the end the campaign turned out to be primarily a popularity contest. Jackson, alone among the contenders in 1824, was a genuine popular hero. Adams, however able, was associated with the old Virginia dynasty and his reserve hurt him with the voters. Clay and Calhoun were endorsed as candidates by local groups in Kentucky and South Carolina, respectively; but despite their prominent roles as national leaders during and immediately following the War of 1812, neither had national support. Calhoun soon dropped out of the race.

No candidate won a majority of the electoral college vote. Jackson was first in both the electoral and popular vote; Adams was second; and Clay trailed well behind both. The Constitution, as provided in the Twelfth Amendment, declared that in the event no candidate received an electoral vote majority, the selection of a president would rest with the House of Representatives, where each state would cast a single vote for one of the top three candidates. Jackson's supporters believed that members of the House had a moral obligation to endorse their candidate as the man who had won the most popular votes. When thirteen state delegations gave Adams a majority and the victory, they denounced the result as a denial of the people's will. When the new president appointed Clay his secretary of state, the Jackson supporters proclaimed that the two men had struck a "corrupt bargain."

Adams's administration was dogged by the "corrupt bargain" charge and by the rancor of Jackson's supporters. The country had seen nothing like this for ten years, and the effects were unfortunate. As we have noted, almost nothing in President Adams's domestic program passed Congress. Even in foreign affairs, where his great experience should have been an advantage, he accomplished little.

THE TARIFF OF ABOMINATIONS.   All through his administration Adams fought Jackson and his supporters. A major focus of their battle was the tariff.

By 1828 the last important tariff revision was already twelve years old. Now increasing numbers of wool growers, textile manufacturers, ironmasters, and even farmers, were demanding higher duties on imports to protect them from foreign competition. The "protectionists" were concentrated in the Northeast and to a lesser extent in the Old Northwest. Southerners of virtually all economic classes opposed any increase in duties because they had little industry to protect and their major crop, cotton, had no competition. Indeed, the South was happy to rely on Great Britain, the cheapest producer of manufactured goods, for its imports. In 1816, when their region's economic future was still in doubt, many southerners had endorsed the tariff. In 1828, after it had become clear that the South's fate was to be supplier of raw materials for a world market, its leading spokesmen saw the protective tariff as an instrument for increasing northern profits at the South's expense.

The issue was highly charged, and most politicians would have preferred to avoid it. But Martin Van Buren of New York's Albany Regency believed that a major tariff revision would help get his friend Jackson elected president by winning him support in the North and West. It did not work as he expected. The tariff bill, when it finally emerged from the pro-Jackson Congress, injured the manufacturers of New England by raising rates on raw materials they needed to produce their goods. At the same time, it promised that southerners would pay higher prices for many English imports. Only Middle Atlantic industrialists and the producers of hemp, raw wool, and a few other farm products got anything positive out of the bill. So objectionable was the measure that puzzled contemporaries assumed that the wily Van Buren had intended to raise the political stock of the Jackson men by giving them a universally unpopular bill they could loudly denounce. Most scholars now agree that Van Buren honestly favored the tariff of 1828. He did not intend to offend northerners; that was the doing of Congress which, in the give-and-take of tariff making, had twisted the measure out of its original shape.

The southern outcry against this "Tariff of Abominations" was universal, but it was John C. Calhoun who took it upon himself to make a constitutional case for his region's interests. Published anonymously by the South Carolina legislature, Calhoun's *Exposition and Protest* denied that Congress had the right to levy a tariff so high that it would exclude imports. The Founding Fathers had intended to impose only moderate duties on imported goods as a means to raise revenue. Calhoun went beyond those familiar low-tariff arguments to insist that if Congress persisted in taking such an unconstitutional course, any state had the right to call a convention and declare such a measure null and void. *Exposition and Protest* revealed that its author, once a confirmed nationalist, was well on his way to becoming the great southern sectional champion.

THE ELECTION OF 1828. Despite Van Buren's hopes, the 1828 presidential election revolved around personalities rather than issues. Adams, with Richard Rush of Pennsylvania as his running mate, was nominated by the "National Republican" convention at Harrisburg, the first major-party presidential convention. Jackson and Calhoun were selected by the Tennessee legislature and then placed on the ballot by their supporters in the various states. Although President Adams alone had the endorsement of the new, more democratic convention procedure, he was actually the weaker candidate. His partisans were numerous only in New England and other areas settled by New Englanders.

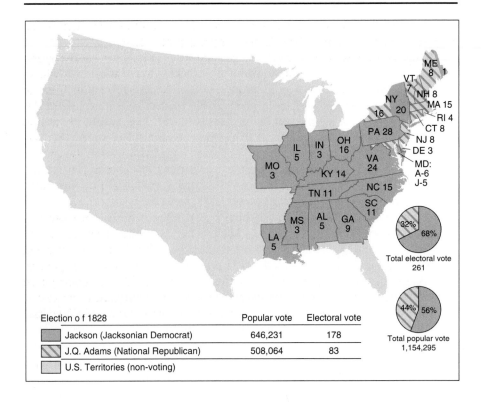

Election of 1828

Election of 1828	Popular vote	Electoral vote
Jackson (Jacksonian Democrat)	646,231	178
J.Q. Adams (National Republican)	508,064	83
U.S. Territories (non-voting)		

Total electoral vote 261

Total popular vote 1,154,295

The contest was one of the dirtiest on record. The Jackson men, brooding over their defeat in 1824, revived the "corrupt bargain" charge to discredit Adams and resorted to blatant scandalmongering. The Jackson press claimed that Adams's wife, Louisa, had been born out of wedlock and he had lived in sin with her before they were married. Equally scandalous stories were spread by the other side. Rachel Jackson, the Adams people said, had not been divorced from her first husband when she married the general. As for Jackson himself, he was a brutal man who had ordered the execution of six innocent militiamen during the campaign against the Creek Indians a decade before.

There was almost no discussion of issues. Few principles seemed to separate the candidates. One contemporary noted that no one in the New York State convention that confirmed Jackson's nomination for president knew the candidate's views on public matters. A Pennsylvanian observed that "the great mystery of the case" was that "the South should support General Jackson avowedly for the purpose of preventing tariffs and internal improvements and that we should support him for a directly opposite purpose." Adams's positions were a little easier to discern. He stood for an active and paternalistic national government, if he stood for anything, and in New England the surviving Federalists clearly found him the more congenial candidate. Yet he also received the support of many Yankee Republicans, who saw him as the spiritual descendant of Jefferson.

Only the Anti-Masons seemed to have a clear program. This curious group had appeared in New York following the mysterious disappearance of William Morgan, a former Mason who in 1826 had written a book exposing the Masonic order's rituals and other "secrets." Morgan was presumed murdered by the Masons, and the public's indignation led to the formation of a political organization dedicated to reducing the power of secret groups in national affairs. In 1828 the new party generally supported Adams, but in later years the Anti-Masons would nominate their own candidates and mount an attack on privilege in government and the economy that would be far more wide-ranging than anything undertaken by the reputedly radical Jackson party.

The 1828 contest, the Anti-Masons notwithstanding, did not contribute very much to reestablishing well-defined and competing party ideologies. Yet in several states it aroused political instincts dormant for over a decade. A two-sided contest, particularly one that included the colorful Jackson, was more gripping than either the rubber stamps of 1816 and 1820 or the multi-sided competition of 1824. In much larger numbers than four years before, voters came out to cast their ballots. Jackson won decisively, receiving 178 electoral and 646,000 popular votes to Adams's 83 electoral and 509,000 popular votes.

* KING ANDREW *

THE SPOILS SYSTEM.   Jackson's first order of business was distributing the political loaves and fishes. The new president did not eject his political opponents from office wholesale, as scholars used to believe. In his first year and a half he removed 900 of over 10,000 federal employees, only 9 percent of the total. Yet Jackson's appointment policy was something new on the political stage. The Virginia dynasty presidents had favored members of their own party in filling vacancies, but they had seldom fired opposition officeholders primarily to create new openings. Jackson and his friends took no such moderate view of the federal civil service. Loyalty to the president, they quickly made clear, would be the prime consideration in retaining office. If the number of those actually dismissed was small, it was only because so many bureaucrats were already Jackson supporters or quickly became supporters to avoid losing their jobs.

At times the Jacksonians frankly admitted the narrow political reasons for removing long-time civil servants from office. "To the victor belong the spoils of the enemy," declared the candid Senator William L. Marcy, a Jackson man, in 1832. Generally, however, they tried to pass it off as political reform. Since, in Jackson's words, "the duties of all public officers are . . . so plain and simple that men of intelligence may readily qualify for their performance," no group need be excluded from serving the nation. Scholars, accepting the Jacksonians at their own word, have often treated the spoils system as a democratization of the political process.

In fact, as practiced by Jackson, the spoils system was not particularly democratic. The privileged social position of Jackson appointees differed little from

Jackson's use of the veto, his tightening of executive control, and his personal approach to the presidency led Republicans to dub him "King Andrew." As proper for the enemies of kings, they called themselves "Whigs."

that of their predecessors. The Jacksonians chief purpose was to provide political muscle to the party system. The lure of office would be a powerful incentive to ambitious men to work for party causes, while officeholders could be assessed for party contributions out of their government salaries. The spoils system would be a useful and important component of the emerging second party system, but it should not be taken as evidence that Jackson and his party were more democratic than their predecessors.

Whatever the deficiencies of the Virginia dynasty presidents, they had maintained a high level of honesty and efficiency in the public service. The Jackson men—and their successors—undoubtedly lowered the moral and intellectual tone of American political life. The spoils system damaged civil service morale and reduced efficiency. It also encouraged corruption. In the New York customhouse, the collector Samuel Swartwout embezzled over a million dollars and escaped to England before he could be arrested.

At the same time, however, the ordinary man began to feel a sense of participation. This new mood was not at first reflected in the voting statistics, except in the 1828 presidential election. Larger election turnouts would have to wait until real two-party contests had appeared in all the states and the voters had been caught up in the rivalries of close elections. But the Jackson party did infuse a new, more open spirit into political life—a spirit essential to the success of the second party system.

JACKSON'S STYLE. Jackson was a strong president. A military man accustomed to command and unwilling to brook defiance by Congress, state legislatures, or the chief justice of the Supreme Court, he inspired either hatred or intense affection among the voters. He was not learned or even a clear and consistent thinker and acted on the prejudices he had acquired as a young man and never abandoned. A southerner and slaveholder, he had few objections to slavery and despised abolitionists. A man from the frontier state of Tennessee and a leader in the Indian wars, he had little love for Native Americans. Having been almost ruined in 1819 by the tight credit policies of the Bank of the United States, he hated banks in general and the Bank of the United States in particular. Jackson personalized almost all his political attitudes, turning political opponents into enemies who had to be destroyed lest they destroy him. Many Americans thought Old Hickory principled and spirited, but his opponents condemned his irascibility and high-handedness and called him "King Andrew." Their adoption of the name Whigs identified them as opponents of arbitrary power, much as the English Whigs had opposed royal absolutism in the late seventeenth century.

THE NULLIFICATION CRISIS. Jackson's imperiousness surfaced during the tariff controversy that marked his first term. Though he had criticized the Tariff of Abominations during the election campaign, he disappointed the South by refusing to sponsor a substantial reduction in import duties. When, in 1832, Congress passed its own measure reducing the 1828 rates only slightly, South

Carolinians, led by Vice President Calhoun, precipitated a political crisis by calling a convention and declaring the tariff void in the Palmetto State.

The South Carolina Ordinance of Nullification reflected more than southern economic discontent. By 1832, as we shall see in Chapter 12, slavery had become a major social and political issue in the nation. Just two years before, firebrand Massachusetts editor and reformer William Lloyd Garrison had begun to demand "immediate and complete emancipation" of southern slaves and had used angry language to denounce slaveholding and slaveholders. Garrison's attack frightened the South Carolina planter elite, who saw it as a serious threat to the stability and profitability of their slave-linked society. Nullification, they believed, was an appropriate weapon by which to defend the South's interests against an aggressive North that seemed likely to rally around the new antisouthern movement.

South Carolina's action was a constitutional challenge to the Union. But Jackson characteristically took it as a personal affront as well. The president called Calhoun a madman and denounced the state's move as "without parallel in the history of the world." Yet this time, at least, he sought to avoid a direct confrontation. In his December 1832 message to Congress he pointed to imminent changes in the tariff duties and told South Carolinians that their reaction was exaggerated. Soon after, he induced Congress to pass the Force Bill granting him additional powers to enforce the customs laws. Fortunately, Clay was able to patch together a compromise tariff bill that saved protection for nine years, until 1842, in exchange for dropping protection thereafter.

Finding no support in other states, the South Carolina planter elite backed down. The state legislature rescinded the Ordinance of Nullification against the 1832 Tariff Act, but at the same time, as a gesture of defiance, it nullified the Force Bill. In the relief at getting past the crisis, few complained about the state's refusal to abandon the principle of nullification.

INDIAN POLICY. Jackson's position on nullification seems to confirm his strong nationalism. But he was perfectly willing to undermine the federal government's power when it suited his purposes or accorded with one of his fundamental prejudices. A blatant instance of this was his defiance of John Marshall over Indian policy.

In 1817, as agent for the War Department, Jackson had coerced a treaty out of the Cherokees of Georgia, by which they agreed to exchange their tribal lands for an equal amount of land in the West. Those Indians who did not want to go might remain and settle down as farmers. Though the Georgia lands would have to be surrendered as tribal property, each Indian family might have 640 acres as an individual holding. To Jackson's disgust, virtually every Cherokee chose to remain in Georgia; indeed, many bought slaves and began to raise cotton on their new 640-acre plantations.

In the North, in 1818 and 1819, the government induced the Wyandot, Chippewa, and Delaware tribes to surrender enormous areas in Indiana and Illinois. But the remaining Indian tribes, both north and south of the Ohio River, threatened to impede the rush of settlers pouring into the Great Lakes Plain, the

Ohio Valley, and the Gulf Plain by the thousands. In 1825, President Monroe announced that henceforth all the tribes of the eastern portion of the nation would be removed beyond the ninety-fifth meridian to a "permanent Indian frontier." There they could live in peace, he declared, unmolested by whites and free to preserve their ancestral ways.

Under the direction of Secretary of War Calhoun, Congress soon set about removing the remaining tribes of the Northwest and South. The Indians resisted, and the new policy could only be carried out by unsavory tactics. Government agents bribed chiefs to sign treaties that committed their tribes to move, passing these off as the collective will of the Indian people. Recalcitrant tribes were "persuaded" by military threats and force. In 1825 the Osage and Kansas tribes surrendered all of Kansas and northern Oklahoma except for two reservations. Over the next fifteen years the Shawnee, Kickapoo, Sauk, Fox, Potawatomi, Ottawa, Iowa, Miami, and Peoria were similarly moved.

The Indians of the Southeast proved more stubborn. In Georgia, the Carolinas, Alabama, and Mississippi the Five Civilized Nations—the Cherokees, Creeks, Choctaws, Chickasaws, and Seminoles—owned some 33 million acres of valuable land. These Indians had become a settled agricultural people with a sophisticated political and social system and a high level of literacy. They had conformed to the white man's ways, and by all the professed principles of contemporary white Americans, they should have been left alone to enjoy their unusual blend of European and Indian cultures. But their holdings aroused the greed and envy of their white neighbors. In 1827, hoping to head off Georgia's effort to oust them, the Cherokee wrote a constitution at New Echota establishing an independent republic. The outraged Georgians called this a violation of the federal Constitution and demanded that Washington evict the Cherokees as punishment. Congress responded by offering a bribe. The tribe would receive lands in the West and each Cherokee family that agreed to leave would get $50 in cash as well as a blanket, rifle, five pounds of tobacco, and other supplies. During the summer of 1828 federal agents pressured the Cherokees to accept this offer. There were few takers.

Jackson's election, and the discovery of gold on Cherokee lands, goaded the Georgians to harsher action. A new state measure provided that beginning in 1830 the tribe would be under the jurisdiction of state rather than federal law. The Indians would now have little or no protection against unprincipled whites coveting their land. The Cherokee protested to the federal government, which responded sternly with the Removal Bill allowing the president to send any eastern tribe beyond the Mississippi if he wished, using force if needed. When the Indians asked the U.S. Supreme Court for an injunction to stop Georgia's repressive laws, the Court refused on the grounds the Cherokee were not, as they claimed, a foreign nation and so could not sue before the Supreme Court.

Now followed an orgy of greed and brutality at the Cherokees' expense. The Georgia government cancelled debts owed the Indians, stopped payment of subsidies, and seized their property. State agents sought to stir up tribal animosities to undermine the Cherokees' morale. Christian missionaries who protested this ill-treatment were clapped in jail. A renewed appeal to the U.S. Supreme Court this time produced a favorable opinion from Chief Justice Marshall in *Worcester v. Georgia* (1832). The Indians did possess the status of a "domestic dependent nation," he declared, and were therefore entitled to federal protection against the state. But Jackson refused to enforce the chief justice's opinion, supposedly retorting: "John Marshall has made his decision, now let him enforce it!"

During the months that followed federal agents found a turncoat leader who, in late 1835, agreed to abandon all the tribal lands for $5.6 million and free transportation to the West. The Cherokees denounced the agreement but realized they could no longer resist. For the next three years thousands of Indian families, grieving for their ancestral homes, set out on the "Trail of Tears" for what is now Oklahoma. The last holdouts were driven away by federal troops in the dead of winter. Many died on the way west.

Humane Americans, especially easterners, denounced Jacksonian Indian policies. The New England press labeled it "an abhorrent business." But it continued unabated. Few instances of white–Indian relations in North America exhibit the total callousness of the removal of the Civilized Tribes by Jackson and his successors.

THE ATTACK ON THE BANK.   Andrew Jackson hated banks—especially "The Bank"—even more than he hated Indians. After its inauspicious start, when it helped trip off the Panic of 1819, the Second Bank of the United States had settled down to a useful existence under its third president, Nicholas Biddle. The bank lent money to merchants, helped expedite foreign trade, handled checking accounts, issued paper money backed by gold, held the deposits of the federal government, and transferred government funds from one part of the country to the other. Most important, it served as a central bank and the economy's balance wheel. As the nation's largest commercial bank, it could force the state banks to limit their credit when it felt the economy was overheated or encourage them to lend readily when the economy was in the doldrums.

Many businesspeople supported the BUS, as did nationalist politicians. This support was not always disinterested, however. Newspaper editors and some of the most prominent men in government—including Daniel Webster, Henry Clay, and some Jacksonians—were in the bank's pay. The "God-like Daniel," who was frequently in debt, was a particularly shameless dependent of the bank, constantly asking that his "retainer" be "renewed or refreshed."

The bank also made some fierce enemies in the business community. Speculators, for one, found its conservative credit policies a hindrance. Its most important opponents, however, were agrarians primarily from the South and West, such as Senator Thomas Hart Benton of Missouri, who disliked all banks, favored "hard money," and believed that the paper notes that banks issued were unwise and immoral. Agrarians also held that banks in general, and the Bank of the United States in particular, endangered free government. With its $35 million in capital, Biddle's "monster bank" was the largest corporation in the country by far. Such size by itself gave it a potential power over the economy that was frightening. Given Biddle's sense of its regulatory responsibilities, and its influence on

Nicholas Biddle, the powerful head of the Second Bank of the United States.
Under his direction, the bank loaned business money prudently
and helped smaller banks survive temporary setbacks.

politicians, it seemed obvious to many that the bank had to be destroyed or it would destroy the country's democratic system.

The bank's twenty-year charter was due to expire in 1836. Wishing to ensure its continuity, Biddle applied for renewal in 1832. The measure passed Congress, but Jackson vetoed it. In a stinging attack, the president denounced the bank as a privileged monopoly controlled by foreign investors and warned that it would wield its great powers to punish its enemies if it became entrenched. The president undoubtedly believed that the Bank of the United States was a dangerous institution in a nation composed of many small economic units, but he also had a strong personal motive. "The Bank is trying to kill me," he told Van Buren, "but I will kill it."

The veto unleashed a storm of protest. Biddle called Jackson's veto message a "manifesto of anarchy." Webster, of course, also denounced it, as did two-thirds of the nation's press, much of the business community, and many state bankers. The veto immediately became the chief party issue during the 1832 presidential election, with Jackson's supporters treating it as an attack on monopoly and privilege and his foes condemning it as an example of King Andrew's tyrannical temperament.

WHIGS AND DEMOCRATS.   By this time the second party system was rapidly taking shape. The Jackson party, now beginning to be called the Democrats, was a heterogeneous group that differed in its programs and principles from one part of the country to another. Most Democrats tended to favor low tariffs, hard money, antimonopoly, and a government hands-off policy toward the economy. But in New York, New England, and Pennsylvania the Jackson men favored banks, protective tariffs, and government aid for internal improvements.

The Whigs were less divided in their economic principles. Their "American System" called for protective tariffs, federal aid for internal improvements, and a strong national bank. First announced by Clay in 1824, the American System projected a paternalistic national government that would nurture business, protect industrial workers from cheap foreign competition, and provide a secure market for farmers in America's growing cities.

The Whigs and the Democrats also differed somewhat in their political ideologies. The Democrats claimed to be the party of the "common man," and there was some truth to their claim. James Silk Buckingham, an aristocratic English visitor, constantly heard the Democrats attacked by their opponents as "agrarians, incendiaries, men who . . . desire to . . . seize the property of the rich and divide it among the poor." The Jackson men, wrote William Seward, a New York anti-Jackson leader, considered the parties distinctly different in their class orientation: "It's with them the poor against the rich."

Yet the differences between the parties must not be exaggerated. Each attracted voters from various classes, sections, and occupations. In the cities many "mechanics" voted for the Whigs or for various "workingmen's parties," which advocated "radical" measures such as laws limiting the workday to ten hours and abolishing the inconvenient militia service required of male voters. Farmers, too, were split, with many rural voters, especially in New England and the Yankee-settled areas of the Old Northwest, voting for the Democrats' opponents. In New York the regular Democratic party often attacked the "Locofocos," a radical equal rights wing of their own party, as "infidels," "agrarians," and the "scum of politics." Moreover, the Jackson Democrats—as much as the Whigs—were led by successful and prosperous lawyers, businessmen, and gentlemen. The high and mighty "silk-stocking" element of the Whigs may have often expressed contempt for the "rabble" that supposedly made up the political opposition, but the leading Whigs—Clay, Webster, and Seward—were popular figures who cultivated the voters and flattered them as effectively as Jackson, Van Buren, Marcy, and the other leading Democrats.

The Whigs were strongest in New England and those places where New Englanders had settled, but they had supporters in every part of the country. In the South small farmers voted Democratic; but large planters—despite their hostility to the tariff favored by Whigs—voted Whig largely because they needed cheap bank credit to market their cotton. Farmers in the West, eager for internal improvements, were also attracted to the Whigs. And in the cities the Whigs' American System attracted manufacturers and many industrial wage earners.

According to some scholars, what truly set Whigs and Democrats apart were distinctive cultural and religious styles. There is evidence that in some states, such as Michigan and New York, the Democrats were the party of laissez-faire in religion and morals as well as in economic affairs, whereas the Whigs saw nothing wrong in government officials policing the public's personal habits and behavior. Thus the Whigs often endorsed Sunday closing laws for businesses, opposed government deliveries of mail on the Christian Sabbath, and favored laws encouraging temperance. By contrast, Democrats generally believed that drinking and doing business on Sundays were private, not public, matters. These divergent attitudes also made the Whigs in the North more hostile to slavery than northern Democrats. Northern Whig voters often saw slavery as sinful and, like other sinful practices, within reach of government control; most northern Democrats believed that, however deplorable slavery was, it was none of the government's business what southerners did with their local institutions.

These outlooks in turn appealed to different cultural and religious groups. Whig policies attracted evangelical Protestants, who considered politics a valid arena for moral reform. Democratic laissez-faire appealed to Catholics, Episcopalians, and free thinkers—all groups that preferred government to pursue a hands-off policy toward personal behavior and rejected politics based on morality. Because many New Englanders belonged to evangelical denominations, areas with a New England stamp voted Whig. Many of the recent immigrants were Catholics, and they generally joined the party of Jackson.

THE ELECTION OF 1832.　But as the election of 1832 approached, these distinctions were only beginning to emerge. Jackson's opponents nominated Clay at their Baltimore convention. The Jackson supporters in turn renominated their hero, but selected Martin Van Buren as his running mate in place of Calhoun, who had defended South Carolina's nullification ordinance. Besides the two major parties, the Anti-Masons were in the field with William Wirt of Maryland as their candidate.

The chief issue in the campaign was ostensibly the Bank of the United States and the Jackson veto of the recharter bill. Actually, personalities also counted. The voters were either charmed by Clay—"Old Coon," "Harry of the West," "The Mill Boy of the Slashes"—or repelled by his easygoing ways, drinking, and card playing. Jackson was to some a great national hero and to others the imperious and impetuous King Andrew. In the end the president won a decisive victory, with Clay second and Wirt a poor third.

ECONOMIC UPS AND DOWNS.　The outstanding political event of Jackson's second term was the slow, agonizing death of the Bank of the United States.

The president interpreted his election victory as a mandate to proceed immediately against the bank, even though its charter left it four more years of life. Disregarding the advice of two successive secretaries of the treasury, he removed government deposits from the bank and placed them in twenty-three state-chartered banks Whigs promptly labeled as "pet banks."

Biddle determined to fight back no matter what the cost. "All the other Banks and all the merchants may break," he wrote a friend, "but the bank of the United States shall not break." In the next months the BUS reduced its loans and called in those already outstanding, creating a credit squeeze that caused business severe hardship. Actually, with the treasury's $10 million in deposits removed from its reserves, the bank had to contract. But to demonstrate the bank's importance to the country's prosperity, Biddle contracted faster and further than necessary.

Worse was soon to come. With the Bank of the United States no longer regulating the country's credit and money supply, a major source of financial restraint was gone. The pet banks, with millions in government money in their reserves, began to lend extravagantly. Businessmen and speculators promptly invested their borrowed money in western lands, while states initiated ambitious canal-building schemes. The nation experienced a runaway boom that drove all prices, especially those of land, to record heights.

Jackson had not struck down Biddle's "monster" only to see it replaced by a state bank system that was even more irresponsible and dangerous. Nor did he wish to see the notes of the Bank of the United States, which were backed by gold, replaced by "wildcats" of a hundred banks that were little more than vague promises to pay. To halt the unhealthy boom, in July 1836 the president issued the Specie Circular announcing that the federal government henceforth would accept only gold and silver in payment for public lands.

The Specie Circular pricked the bubble. The public abruptly lost confidence in the notes issued by the state banks and fought to convert them into specie. Hoping to hold on to their gold, the banks in turn called in their loans. Other creditors, fearful of the future, refused to lend further and clamped down on debtors. The result was a severe panic that halted business and brought down prices with a resounding crash. A decade of hard times followed.

Recent scholarship has absolved the Specie Circular of some of the blame for the panic and ensuing economic depression and has pointed to the collapse of international cotton prices as a major culprit. Jackson's supporters blamed the panic on "overbanking and overtrading." But many contemporaries condemned the president and criticized his hard-money and antibank policies. Fortunately for the Democrats, the full force of the economic collapse did not make itself felt until 1837, and so did not affect the 1836 presidential election.

* WHIGS AND DEMOCRATS AFTER JACKSON *

THE VAN BUREN ADMINISTRATION. The 1836 presidential contest was a confused affair. The Whigs, not yet a solid party, selected several regional candidates, including Webster of Massachusetts and Hugh Lawson White of

Tennessee. The better-organized Democrats, required by the two-term tradition to pass over their leader, nominated Vice President Martin Van Buren. Van Buren pledged to follow in Jackson's footsteps and won a comfortable victory in the fall.

Scarcely was the new president installed in office than the full force of the economic storm broke. Van Buren called Congress into special session to deal with the emergency, but in a classic statement of the laissez-faire position, he noted that government was "not intended to confer special favors on individuals or on any classes of them to create systems of agriculture, manufacturers, or trade, or to engage in them. . . . The less government interferes with private pursuits the better for the general prosperity."

The timid response of the new Democratic president lent support to the label "laissez-fairist" attached to the Jacksonians. But as one witty scholar has said, in many parts of the country Jackson men had "feet of Clay" and had few scruples against supporting business enterprise.

For the rest of Van Buren's ill-starred term the politicians remained preoccupied with the economy and economic legislation. To aid the treasury during the crisis, Congress ended the government's recently adopted policy of distributing to the states federal surpluses derived from excise taxes, the tariff, and land sales. In 1837 Van Buren proposed a scheme for a separate federal financial depository not dependent on banks. The proposal expressed Jacksonian suspicion of banks and paper money, and it seemed to the Whigs a crude system that would leave the country without a financial balance wheel or an effective means for regulating the state banks. Whigs and Democrats fought over the issue until 1840, when the Democrats in Congress managed to establish the Independent Treasury System. This required the treasury to collect and keep federal revenues and disburse them at need from its own vaults without relying on private banks. Moreover, government transactions with the public—salaries, taxes, bounties, and so forth—would now be confined to gold and silver. It was a primitive arrangement that handicapped business and commerce.

THE WHIGS TAKE POWER.   As the 1840 presidential election approached, Van Buren, despite his spotty record and the bad times, had few opponents among the Democrats. On the Whig side the logical choice was Henry Clay, but the Whigs were reluctant to select a man too closely identified with the political battles of the past. At their first national convention, the delegates passed over Clay and turned instead to a man without strong political commitments: William Henry Harrison.

Harrison, though now sixty-seven, had a number of distinct advantages. A southerner by birth and sure to win many votes in the South that might otherwise go to the Democrats, he was also the hero of the 1811 battle of Tippecanoe. Most important of all, Harrison had no known political principles. For a party that had lost once by running its most representative figure, the obscurity of his views was a distinct asset.

The campaign revealed how well the Whigs had adapted to the sharp political partisanship that had appeared since 1828. Their candidate, the party leaders concluded, must be kept from expressing his ideas on any controversial issue. Let Harrison "say not one single word about his principles or his creed," advised Nicholas Biddle. The Whigs' major problem, besides their candidate, was their aristocratic image. Fortunately, a careless remark by a prominent Democrat—that if Harrison were given a pension, a barrel of hard cider, and a log cabin to live in, he would never run for president—bailed them out. The Whigs immediately seized on the snobbery implied by the characterization. Picturing the wealthy Harrison as a simple man and a true democrat, they painted Van Buren as an aristocrat who lived in lordly style on his estate in Kinderhook, New York.

The "Log Cabin and Hard Cider" campaign was the first time a political party successfully marshaled the powerful forces of ballyhoo and propaganda to sell a presidential candidate to the American voters. The Whigs dressed up supporters as Indians to advertise Harrison' victory over Tecumseh. They distributed oceans of cider to thirsty voters. Whig party workers organized enormous parades with bands, giant banners, flaming torches, and flags.

The vote was huge—almost 60 percent greater than in 1836—and it was strongly Whig. Harrison and his running mate, John Tyler of Virginia, carried nineteen of the twenty-six states and received 53 percent of the popular vote, an unusually high proportion for this period. The opposition had succeeded in the difficult task of turning an incumbent president out of office and had demonstrated the vitality of the newly revived party system.

* CONCLUSIONS *

By 1840 two new political parties had come into being. After a long gap that saw government become the preserve of public-spirited gentlemen, the people once more insisted on being heard. The change was not Jackson's doing: It had begun years before, in the states. Jackson was its beneficiary, not its author.

The two new parties seemed to parallel those of Hamilton's and Jefferson's time. Whigs and Democrats superficially resembled Federalists and Jeffersonian Republicans, respectively—without the powdered hair, velvet knee breeches, and silver shoe-buckles. But on closer examination we see that the reality was different. Neither party was as closely associated with a single class as their predecessors. There was a difference in the parties' social focus: Democrats probably won the support of more small farmers than the Whigs, and because small farmers were a majority of Americans, this made them in some sense the party of the common people. But we should not make too much of this tendency. In an age that professed to be democratic, both parties had to appear to accept the voice of the "sovereign people."

The two new party organizations were not as clearly different in ideology as the old parties were, either. They disagreed over banks, tariffs, and internal improvements; but their leaders were apt to be more practical and accommodating than the Federalists and Jeffersonians. The emergence of the second party system marked the development of a pragmatic political consensus: Both parties would avoid extreme ideological positions and try to stand close to the political center. This tendency continues to some extent in the politics of our own day.

Jackson's victory did not set off a revolution in the social and political order, but it did loosen the rigid political framework of the day. By refusing to accept the gentlemanly procedures of the Virginia dynasty, the Jacksonians revitalized American political life. After 1828 the country would once more have a lively and effective two-party system, and the change would make the nation's government more responsive to public needs and public wants. It was the return of two-party government to American political life.

11

THE MEXICAN WAR AND EXPANSIONISM

Greed, Manifest Destiny or Inevitability?

1803–06	Lewis and Clark Expedition to Pacific
1812	Astor establishes fur-trading post on Pacific in Oregon
1818	A treaty between Great Britain and the United States provides for joint occupation of Oregon Territory
1819	Adams–Onís Treaty establishes the western boundaries of the Louisiana Purchase
1823	Mexico grants Stephen Austin the right to settle in Texas with 300 American families
1836	Texas declares its independence from Mexico; Texans force captured Mexican leader Santa Anna to recognize the Texas Republic
1841	President Harrison dies and John Tyler becomes president
1842	Webster–Ashburton Treaty signed by Great Britain and the United States
1844	James K. Polk elected president
1845	Congress admits Texas into the Union; Anticipating war, Polk sends General Zachary Taylor and 4,000 troops to occupy Mexican territory on north bank of Rio Grande; Polk secretly authorizes American consul Thomas Larkin to encourage the secessionist movement in California; The Slidell Mission discusses Texas's southern boundary and offers to buy New Mexico and California for $30 million
1840	Mexico declares defensive war on the United States; Congress votes for war; The Oregon dispute with Great Britain is settled by treaty
1847	Polk authorizes General Winfield Scott to attack Vera Cruz and Mexico City
1848	The Mexican-American War ends with the Treaty of Guadalupe Hidalgo; Mexican Cession adds 339 million acres to U.S.
1850	Congress admits California into the Union

On May 11, 1846, the clerk of the House of Representatives read the war message of President James K. Polk to a solemn joint session of Congress. The message was expected. Rumors had been circulating for weeks that a diplomatic break with Mexico was imminent. Just two days before, people in Washington had learned that Mexican troops had crossed the Rio Grande del Norte and attacked American army units on its eastern bank. Several Americans had been killed, others wounded.

"The cup of forbearance had been exhausted before the recent information from the frontier of the Del Norte," the president declared. "But now, after reiterated menaces, Mexico has passed the boundary of the United States, has invaded our territory and shed American blood upon American soil. She has proclaimed that hostilities have commenced, and that the two nations are now at war." "By every consideration of duty and patriotism," the president concluded, Americans must "vindicate with decision the honor, the rights, and the interests of their country."

Congress voted for war by an overwhelming majority, yet many representatives and senators were uneasy with the decision. During the next weeks and months, United States armies would go from triumph to triumph in a crescent of territory that stretched 2,000 miles from the Gulf of Mexico to the Oregon boundary; but many Americans would denounce the war. In Congress, Senator Thomas Corwin of Ohio would declare: "If I were a Mexican I would tell you 'Have you not room in your own country to bury your dead men? If you come into mine we will greet you with bloody hands, and welcome you to hospitable graves'." In the House a young Illinois Whig, Abraham Lincoln, would call the president "a bewildered, confounded, and miserably perplexed man" with a "painful" conscience. Lincoln would spend much of his single term in Congress demanding that Polk prove his allegations that the Mexicans had provoked the war by attacking Americans on their own soil.

Outside Congress there were other harsh critics. New Englander James Russell Lowell's fictional Yankee spokesman, Hosea Biglow, called the attack on Mexico "a national crime committed on behoof of slavery." An ardent enemy of slavery, Lowell was certain that the "slave power" was determined to seize Mexican territory "so's to lug new slave states in." Henry Thoreau, the writer, who admired Mexico for giving refuge to escaped slaves, believed the American invasion justified "honest men to rebel and revolutionize."

Different theories of the war's origins are implied by these charges. Lincoln and Corwin view the conflict as naked United States aggression against a weaker neighbor. Thoreau and Lowell's Hosea Biglow see the war as a southern slaveholders' plot. Modern scholars, too, have advanced competing theories of causation. Eugene Genovese perceives the cotton South as forced to expand territorially or suffer from declining profits as its soils lost their fertility and cotton ceased to produce abundant wealth. Other historians are more inclined to see Americans as inspired in 1846 by the ideological attitude of continentalism, or Manifest Destiny, which justified United States dominion over the continent—indeed, made it seem inevitable—on grounds of supposed American cultural, political, or even racial superiority. Mexican scholars agree in ascribing the war to America's sense of superiority, though they also blame it on Yankee greed. In either case, they insist, the United States was a blatant aggressor.

A final school of interpretation seeks to avoid simple praise or blame. In this view the pre-Civil War expansionist impulse was the expression of what was almost a physical law. To the west of the growing, vibrant United States, it says, lay a sparsely populated and loosely governed expanse of territory. It was almost an empty region in a political and social sense, and American expansion into it resembled the rush of air to fill a vacuum. The war, in this view, was an inevitable event arising out of the unavoidable circumstances of history and geography.

The Mexican War marked the last phase of continental expansion that carried the American people to the Pacific. The war itself added 530,000 square miles of territory to the United States, and the related settlement of the Oregon boundary dispute with Great Britain added another 258,000. The total addition was truly imperial in extent, but was it also imperialist in origin? Was it greed that led President Polk to send his war message to Congress that day in early May? Was it misplaced idealism? Or was it still some other force that brought to two neighbors to war in 1846?

∗ THE OREGON COUNTRY ∗

In 1830 the line marking the western edge of dense agricultural settlement in the United States did not extend much beyond the bottomlands of the Mississippi River. Almost all of the trans-Mississippi West remained the domain of the Indian tribes. Beyond the western boundary of the Louisiana Purchase was a vast region of mountain, desert, plateau, and rugged ocean coast still barely touched by European culture and institutions.

Political title to much of this region was uncertain. In 1819 the Adams–Onís Treaty had settled the boundary between American and Spanish possessions and surrendered Spanish claims in the Oregon country to the Americans. But title to the vase expanse of Oregon—including present-day Oregon, Washington, Idaho, British Columbia, and parts of Montana and Wyoming—remained in dispute between Great Britain and the United States. British claims rested on the voyages of Captains James Cook in the 1770s and George Vancouver in the 1790s, and on the activities of Canadian and British fur companies. American claims derived from the April 1792 discovery of the Columbia River by Captain Robert Gray, Lewis and Clark's winter camp near the Pacific in 1805–1806, and the American merchant vessels that periodically visited the northern Pacific coast.

Stretching from the northern boundary of California to the southern boundary of Russian America (Alaska) at 54°40′ north latitude, Oregon had only a few hundred American inhabitants in 1840. Yet the United States guarded its claim jealously. In 1818 Secretary of State John Quincy Adams negotiated a convention with the British providing for joint occupation of Oregon for ten years. In 1827 the Anglo-American occupation was extended for an indefinite period, subject to termination by either party on a year's notice.

THE FAR WESTERN FUR TRADE.   Ultimately, the dispute over Oregon was resolved by actual white settlement, not diplomacy. But as with so many other American frontiers, the fur traders came first, preparing the way for the settlers.

Several groups of businessmen were involved in the far northwestern fur trade. In Oregon the impresario was John Jacob Astor, a German-born entrepreneur who had come to the United States in 1783 and soon became a successful fur merchant. Astor entered the Oregon trade shortly after the United States acquired the Louisiana Territory and in 1811 established a trading post at the mouth of the Columbia, which he named Astoria. The post flourished briefly until the threat of British attack during the War of 1812 induced Astor to sell it to a Canadian firm.

After the war, the British-owned Hudson's Bay Company and the American-owned North West Company competed bitterly in the Oregon country for a while and then, in 1821, merged. Soon afterward the new company established Fort Vancouver on the north bank of the Columbia River in what is now Washington state. Head of the new settlement was Dr. John McLoughlin who sought to exclude the Americans and nail down Britain's claim to the Oregon region.

Meanwhile, in the Rocky Mountain region, other Americans, under Missourian William Ashley, were uncovering new fur-bearing regions in what is now southwestern Wyoming. Ashley saw that he needed not only a new source of furs but also a new method of collecting them. In the past, white agents had bought the furs from Indian trappers. But beginning in 1825, Ashley sent his own employees to forage the newly opened region for furs. Under Ashley's successors in the Rocky Mountain Fur Company, as many as 600 "mountain men" of American, French, Mexican, black, and mixed Indian-European backgrounds spent the year in the mountain wilds, many of them with their Indian wives and children. In the spring the trappers hunted beaver along the streams. In July they gathered at a "rendezvous," where they exchanged their "hairy bank notes" for cloth, rifles and shot, trinkets, food, liquor, and other commodities brought west by the company. Cut off from others for months at a time by the deep snows and fiercely cold winters, the mountain men turned the July meetings into wild debauches. After a week or two of heavy drinking, gambling, fighting, and general hell-raising, the trappers and their families staggered off to rest up for the coming hard year. The company agents returned east with furs worth twenty times their cost.

THE WAY WEST.   The western fur trade helped open the trans-Missouri region for white settlement. Fur company agents and officials—Kit Carson, Jim Bridger, Milton and William Sublette, and others—marked useful routes, explored unknown rivers, and discovered new mountain passes through the Great Plains, Rocky Mountain, and Great Basin regions. In 1823 one of Ashley's agents, Jedediah Smith, found South Pass, a major break in the towering mountains that blocked the overland route west. The following year Peter Ogden, of the Hudson's Bay Company, was the first white man to view the Great Salt Lake.

Not all the trans-Missouri expeditions furthered settlement. In 1806 Zebulon Pike returned from a government-authorized trip through the High Plains and

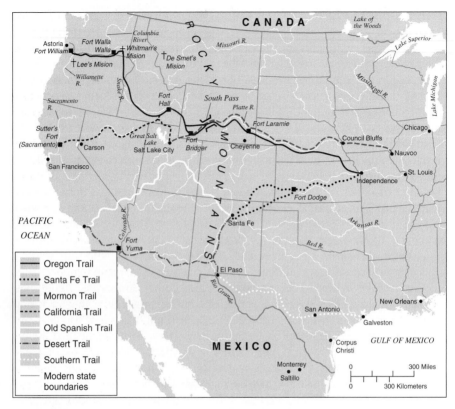

Trails to the West

judged the area too dry for cultivation. In 1820, Stephen Long, another explorer, called the region "wholly unfit for cultivation, and . . . uninhabitable by a people depending upon agriculture for their subsistence." His account of a "Great American Desert" just to the east of the mountains helped delay Plains settlement for decades and turned people's eyes to the well-watered, forested lands of Oregon farther west.

The journey of the pioneers to Oregon was a rugged overland trek across hundreds of miles of dangerous, inhospitable country. Each spring, beginning in 1841, eager Oregon-bound families assembled in Independence, Missouri, the jumpoff point for the trip west. The settlers traveled in canvas-covered farm wagons, into which they crammed supplies and as much equipment as they could carry. Oxen in teams of six drew these wagons, while women and older children—at least in good weather—walked. The men either drove or rode saddle horses to scout for game and potential danger.

Each party, moving in a broad column several wagons wide, was commanded by a captain elected by the men. Some of these were skilled guides who had made the trip before or were natural leaders. Others, however, were incompetents who had to be replaced in mid-journey.

The going at first was easy. The lush green lands of the eastern portion of the Trail were level and pleasant to cross. Three hundred miles from Independence, the pioneers reached the Platte River, in present-day Nebraska, a shallow stream "too thick to drink and too thin to plow." Following the low banks of the river for another 500 miles, the travelers encountered the Rocky Mountains. Here the real challenges began. At times the wagons bounced over terrain so rough that the trail was covered with blood from the oxen's lacerated hooves. At many spots the men were forced to put their own shoulders to the wagons and push them along by brute strength. At this point, usually, over the side would go all the heavy gear—plows, stoves, tables, sofas, even pianos—that optimistic emigrants had stowed in hopes of making their new lives more comfortable. Finally, at the Dalles in what is now central Oregon, the travelers reached the Columbia River. After caulking the wagons' seams to make them watertight, they floated down the great river to their destination, the fertile valley of the Willamette River.

In the 1830s, the travelers were mostly American Methodist missionaries bringing the Christian God and the white man's notions of morality to the Indians. During the hard times of the 1840s reports of cheap Oregon land and of insatiable markets for agricultural produce in Asia created an "Oregon fever" throughout the West. By 1845 there were over 5,000 Americans living in Oregon.

The British in Oregon watched this American influx uneasily at first. The settlers were clearly reinforcing the American claim to the Oregon country. The resident British were virtually all employees of the Hudson's Bay Company, and nowhere could they match the Americans in numbers. It soon became clear that Britain had lost the population competition south of the Columbia, where in any case the beaver had been trapped out. At this point McLoughlin generously helped the settlers in the Willamette region by providing jobs and other aid. In effect, the company surrendered what is now the state of Oregon to the Americans, though it continued for a while to oppose American entry into the region further north.

Before long, excluding Americans from that area began to seem pointless too. In 1845 the Hudson's Bay director moved the firm's chief base to Vancouver Island in what is now British Columbia. The British had conceded to the Americans control of the whole block of territory between Puget Sound and the California boundary.

* THE MEXICAN BORDERLANDS *

For a generation preceding the migration to Oregon a few Americans had been drawn to the Southwest, where Mexico, formerly a Spanish colony, loosely held a million square miles of territory. The south, the Mexican borderlands from Texas to California were generally arid, but within their limits were tracts where the land was well watered and enterprising farmers could raise lush crops. The Mexican capital city was comfortably far away, hundreds of miles to the south.

THE NATIVE PEOPLE.   About half the population of the borderlands was Indian. In Texas the Comanche, Apache, and Kiowa were nomadic peoples who for centuries had hunted buffalo on foot with bow and arrow. During the late seventeenth century they had acquired horses from Spanish Mexico, and then rifles. These new possessions made them formidable foes of both their Indian neighbors and the Spaniards who began to push up from Mexico after 1700.

Farther to the west, in what is now New Mexico and Arizona, were the Zuñis, Acomas, Hopis, and several other tribes grouped under the name Pueblo Indians. Dependent on agriculture, they lived in densely populated, settled communities (pueblos) with mud-brick (adobe) structures that resembled modern apartment houses. The Pueblo tribes were generally peaceful people; they seldom waged offensive war against their neighbors, though they were capable of fighting fiercely for their homes and rights.

Along the Pacific coast in what is now California, as many as 350,000 Indians were spread through the narrow Pacific coastal plain, in the interior valleys, and along the lower reaches of the region's rivers when whites arrived in the eighteenth century. Though the material possessions of the California tribes were meager, they had developed a complex religious and ceremonial life, and a rich oral literature of songs, stories, and myths passed on from generation to generation.

SPANISH PENETRATION.   The earliest Spanish settlers had come to the interior of the Southwest around 1600, when parties of soldiers from Mexico established Santa Fe in what is now central New Mexico. But the clergy were the chief agents of Spanish penetration. A Spanish friar of the Dominican, Franciscan, or Jesuit order would set off with a few Indian dependents for an unsettled region. When he had located a favorable spot, he returned to "civilization" and gathered a few soldiers, several families of Christianized Indians, and some fellow friars. Back on the new frontier, the "padres" recruited local Indian labor and, if all went well, in a decade or so they had established a "mission" with vineyards, cultivated fields of grain, herds of cattle, and clusters of Indian huts, all dominated by a church, elaborately decorated to beautify Christian worship and hold the attention of the Indian converts. Before long this new pocket of Spanish colonial civilization would send out other shoots to repeat the process and contribute to the steady advance of the European cultural frontier.

CALIFORNIA.   In California the missionary process began in 1769 when Franciscan friar Junípero Serra and fourteen brown-robed brothers led a party of 126 Indians and soldiers from present-day Arizona to San Diego Bay. Intended by the Spanish authorities to forestall Russian designs on California, the move combined imperial self-interest with the hope of gathering souls for the Lord. Over the next half century the friars established another twenty missions, along with two garrisoned towns (*presidios*), in what is now the state of California.

In many ways these missions were immensely successful enterprises. By 1800 they sheltered some 13,000 Indians and had taken on the attractive physical form that tourists see today: whitewashed churches with red-tiled roofs, courtyards with arched colonnades and fountains, and ingenious workshops containing the artifacts of skilled Indian artisans. It is also easy to imagine the nearby vineyards, grain fields, fruit and olive orchards, and vast grazing herds that no longer exist.

But there was another, grimmer side. Mortality in the crowded missions was high both among children and adults. The whites, as usual, brought their diseases and their almost equally lethal culture. The former killed directly; the latter killed by undermining Indian morale and family life. Demographic disaster was visited on the California Indians. All told, between 1769 and 1846 the Indian population of California dropped to about 100,000—less than one-third of what it had been when the friars first arrived.

The mission era ended in the 1830s when the Mexican government, prodded by would-be landowners, divested the missions of thousands of acres and ended the friars' paternal but stern control over the Indians. In the next few years aggressive entrepreneurs established some 700 *ranchos,* each covering thousands of acres. Devoted largely to cattle raising, each giant estate was headed by a *ranchero,* usually of Spanish descent, who supervised groups of *vaqueros* (cowboys) doing the hard common labor of herding, fence-mending, branding, and slaughtering.

Life in California in the years immediately preceding American occupation was colorful and, for the *rancheros,* almost idyllic. Little news came from the outside world to disturb the few thousand Spanish-Mexicans. Government in Mexico City was remote, and its hand rested lightly on the inhabitants. If we can believe the accounts of visitors, the life of the small Spanish elite was a round of fiestas, races, dancing, and courtship rituals.

Americans began to drift into California in small numbers in the 1830s. Some established themselves as merchants in Monterey, San Diego, and other towns. Others, arriving overland by way of the California Trail, became successful ranchers. There were immigrants directly from Europe too. The Swiss John Augustus Sutter talked the Mexican governor into granting him a vast domain near present-day Sacramento, which he named New Helvetia in honor of his homeland. Many of the newcomers converted to Catholicism and married into prosperous Mexican families.

For the former mission Indians life was little better than before. Working for the *rancheros,* they spent long days purifying tallow, tanning hides, and loading skins onto ships for markets in the United States and Europe. They were paid nothing for their labor beyond their food, clothing, and shelter. If they left the ranch, they were hunted down like runaway slaves. It is not surprising that the California Indian population continued to fall at an appalling rate.

NEW MEXICO.   Separated from the nearest settlements of northern Mexico by 600 miles of barren plains and rugged mountains, New Mexico, like California, had been settled by friars who planted missions as centers of Christian civilization and incidentally as outposts to protect New Spain against the French in Louisiana.

Unlike the indigenous peoples of California, the Indians of the New Mexico region were not easy to dominate. The Pueblo Indians were able to keep their tight-knit agricultural communities intact, and to this day preserve a distinctive and strongly defined culture. Their warlike qualities protected the nomadic Apache, Navaho, and Comanche tribes in the New Mexico–Arizona–west Texas region from the Europeans. These tribes had long preyed on the Pueblo Indians, stealing slaves and booty. They also attacked the Spaniards, who arrived about 1700, though the Europeans provoked them by enslaving captured Indians and offering bounties for their scalps. Once the Indians acquired horses from their enemies, they became formidable mounted warriors whose swift raids and quick retreats made them difficult to subdue. Indeed, not until the advent of the repeating revolver in the mid-nineteenth century would the European become the military equal of the Apache or Comanche horseman.

Despite these difficulties, the Spaniards succeeded in establishing several permanent communities in the New Mexico–Arizona region. By the 1820s New Mexico had about 40,000 settled inhabitants, many of them clustered around the provincial capital, Santa Fe. They were self-sufficient in food, but starved for manufactured goods, which distant and economically undeveloped Mexico could not supply. In the early 1820s a Missouri merchant, William Becknell, launched a lucrative trade in textiles, rifles, tools, and other goods between St. Louis and New Mexico by way of the Santa Fe Trail. By 1824 parties of as many as eighty men with a score of wagons and over a hundred pack animals were using the trail blazed by Becknell to carry goods to and from New Mexico.

TEXAS.   The American presence in Texas, then an ill-defined region between Louisiana and the northern desert of Mexico, was far weightier than in New Mexico and California. Americans in small numbers began to cross the Sabine River into Spanish-held territory early in the nineteenth century. In 1820 the newly independent Mexican Republic, hoping to develop the region, gave Moses Austin a land grant and the right to bring 300 American families as permanent settlers. In 1823, Moses's son, Stephen, established the first American colony on the banks of the Brazos River in east Texas. By 1825 the colony had 1,800 inhabitants, including 443 black slaves.

Austin's settlement was followed by others launched by various American *empresarios* under contracts with the Mexican state of Texas-Coahuila. Settlers also came as individuals and in single families, attracted by reports of the region's fertile land. Some brought slaves. Fearful of the flood of Americans, in 1830 the Mexican government prohibited further United States immigration and established military garrisons in the state. The law was not enforced, however, and by 1835 there were about 20,000 transplanted Americans living in Texas.

* THE ANNEXATION OF TEXAS *

There were inherent tensions between the Americans and Mexicans that could not easily be resolved. The Americans were mostly Protestant and resented efforts by Mexican officials to convert them to the Catholic faith. Most were south-erners determined to grow cotton with slave labor, and they disliked Mexico's laws forbidding slavery. Many transplanted Americans disdained Mexicans as cul-turally or racially inferior. Yet at first the American settlers in Texas proved re-markably loyal to their adopted country. When, in 1826, a small band of dissident Americans led by Haden Edwards revolted against the central government, the main body of settlers under Austin helped the Mexican authorities put down the insurrection.

THE TEXAS REVOLUTION. Unfortunately, neither the citizens of the United States nor the Mexican government could let the Texan-Americans alone. Many Americans regretted the surrender of Texas to Spain in the Adams–Onís Treaty of 1819. Six years later, as president, John Quincy Adams tried to undo his own work by offering Mexico $1 million for Texas. His successor, Andrew Jack-son, raised the bid to $5 million and sent Anthony Butler to Mexico City to in-duce the Mexican government to accept it. When this effort failed, Butler urged Jackson to take Texas by force.

The Mexican government, too, stirred up trouble. Almost never was there a peaceful succession of administrations in Mexico City, where two competing philosophies of government produced constant changes of policy and turmoil. "Federalists" advocated local autonomy for the individual Mexican states and weak control from Mexico City. This allowed the states to pursue policies favorable to im-migration. "Centralists," on the other hand, demanded tight, centralized govern-ment to hold the unwieldy country together. They opposed immigration and, when in power, sought to prevent liberal state colonization grants to Americans.

The shifts of factions and leaders within the Mexican government had seri-ous effects on the relations between Mexico and her newest citizens, the Texans. In 1834 Antonio Lopez de Santa Anna became the nation's leader for the second time. As a Centralist, he rescinded the autonomy his predecessors had allowed the Mexican states and established a harsh dictatorship in Mexico City.

His rise to power worsened an already uncomfortable situation for the Tex-ans. For some time the American settlers had been unhappy with their limited self-rule. Texas was part of the Mexican state of Coahuila, with its capital at Satillo, 300 miles to the west, a great inconvenience to those in the distant northern re-gion subject to its authority. Under the Federalists the Texans had hoped to achieve separate statehood for themselves, but now these hopes were dashed, and in fact there seemed a distinct possibility that the Mexican government might try to expel all Americans from Texas. When Santa Anna sent troops to garrison sev-eral points within Texas, these fears seemed vindicated. Sporadic fighting soon broke out between Texans and Mexican troops. Though there were special rea-sons for Mexican–Texan tensions, hostility to the Santa Anna government was widespread in Mexico generally, and other outlying parts of the republic rose in revolt against the dictator as well.

In 1835 Santa Anna marched north with an army to punish the Texans and confiscate their arms. Prepared to challenge him were 187 Texans commanded

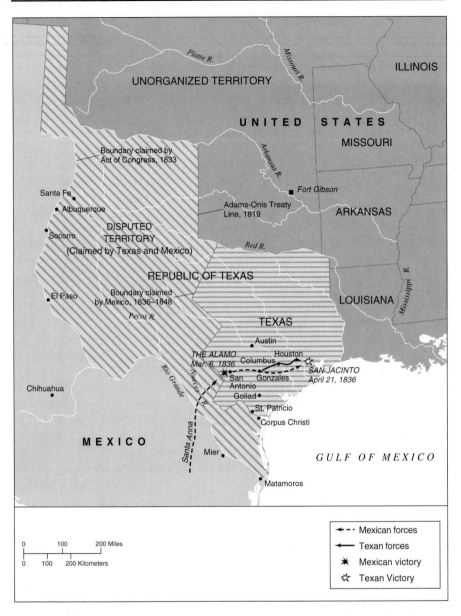

The Texas Revolution

by William B. Travis, holed up in the Alamo, an adobe-walled former mission in San Antonio. In late February 1836 Santa Anna and 4,000 troops arrived at San Antonio and surrounded the small American force. The Americans held out for two weeks, but on March 6 they were overwhelmed by the Mexicans. Every defender, including Travis and the frontier heroes Jim Bowie and Davy Crockett, died in the siege. Resentment against the Mexicans was soon being expressed by the rallying cry: "Remember the Alamo!"

Soon after, fifty-nine delegates met in the little village of Washington, adopting a declaration of Texas independence, naming former governor of Tennessee Sam Houston commander-in-chief of the Texas army, and creating a constitution that recognized slavery and granted each citizen a square league of land. In the next few weeks Houston and his men retreated before Santa Anna's army.

As Santa Anna's forces chased the Texans eastward, the Mexicans' fighting effectiveness dwindled. Meanwhile, Houston grew stronger as American volunteers crossed the border to join his small army. At San Jacinto, Houston finally turned to face the enemy. At noon on April 21, 1836, his troops attacked the Mexicans and decisively defeated them. More than six hundred Mexicans were killed in the fighting and 730, including Santa Anna himself, were captured.

San Jacinto brought Texas its independence. Houston forced the Mexican leader to sign treaties ending the war and accepting the independence of Texas. When news of Santa Anna's defeat and capture reached Mexico City, the Mexican Congress promptly repudiated the agreements on the ground that they had been coerced. Little attention was given at this point to the question of Texas's boundaries. The Mexicans would claim that it stopped at the Nueces; the Texans would insist that it reached farther west to the Rio Grande. But from the Mexican standpoint, Texas was still part of Mexico and the whole issue was irrelevant. In any event, Mexico was in no position to resume the war, and Texas settled down uneasily to a brief existence as an independent nation.

* EXPANSIONISM: ADVOCATES AND OPPONENTS *

The knotty problems of Oregon, the Mexican borderlands, and indeed virtually all of the boundaries of the United States, fell into the lap of John Tyler when, in April 1841, William Henry Harrison contracted pneumonia and died a month after his inauguration. This was the first time a president had died in office, and it was not clear whether "His Accidency" should exercise the full powers of a duly elected chief executive. The Whigs' skepticism was magnified by their knowledge that Tyler was really a Democrat who had been placed on the party ticket to win southern Democratic votes. Tyler refused to accept an inferior status and stubbornly and successfully asserted his full presidential prerogatives.

But in domestic matters Tyler's doggedness accomplished little. The Whigs had looked forward after their 1840 victory to rechartering a federal bank, raising the tariff, and carrying out other nationalist measures. Congress did pass a new federal bank bill, but Tyler, true to his Jeffersonian states' rights principles, promptly vetoed it. In short order his entire cabinet, except Secretary of State Daniel Webster, who still had important diplomatic business to complete, resigned in protest. Thereafter, Tyler and the Whig leaders in Congress remained at loggerheads. The president vetoed two Whig efforts to raise the tariff and signed the Tariff Act of 1842 only after Henry Clay's pet scheme to distribute surplus federal revenues to the states had been eliminated from the bill.

In foreign affairs, where the Constitution allows the chief executive a freer hand, Tyler was more effective. The president was a moderate expansionist. As a southerner, he craved new territory within slavery's supposed "natural limits"—the region where cotton, sugar, rice, and other warm-climate, slave-grown crops could flourish. Tyler was indifferent to expansion elsewhere.

The president's attitude affected the course of negotiations with Britain over the disputed boundary between Canada and the states of Maine, New York, Vermont, and New Hampshire. In 1838 the Maine authorities tripped off a violent clash between American and Canadian lumbermen and fur trappers when they tried to eject British subjects from parts of the Aroostook district claimed by the Canadian province of New Brunswick. Fortunately, the Maine and New Brunswick authorities agreed to a truce, but the boundary dispute continued to fester while other arguments with Britain accumulated including the unwillingness of the United States to cooperate with Britain in suppressing the illegal Atlantic slave trade and the *Caroline* affair involving an American ship that had been used by Canadian rebels to mount a revolt against Britain.

Tyler and Secretary of State Daniel Webster chose to be conciliatory toward Britain. The British, too, preferred compromise, and sent Lord Alexander Ashburton, a pro-American banker married to an American woman, to negotiate with Webster. In a few short weeks the two men hammered out the Webster-Ashburton Treaty (1842). Under its terms the United States would keep about 4.5 million acres of the 7.7 million in dispute along the Canadian-American boundary; the province of New Brunswick would get the rest. In addition, the United States government agreed to join Britain in supporting a naval squadron stationed off the African coast to capture slave ships attempting to bring Africans to the Americas. In a supplementary exchange of notes Ashburton in effect also apologized for the *Caroline* incident.

Tyler's tepid interest in northern real estate carried over to Oregon. Many Americans insisted that the United States rightfully owned all the Oregon country from the northern boundary of California at 42° north latitude to the southern boundary of Russian-America at 54° 40′. Tyler proposed to the British to divide Oregon at the forty-ninth parallel and to take even less territory if Britain forced Mexico to give the United States the port of San Francisco. The British declined the offer and the Oregon dispute remained unsettled.

VICTORY FOR TYLER.   Tyler's major foreign policy success came in Texas. No sooner had they achieved independence than the Texans sought admission to the Union. Many Americans, however, fervently opposed the annexation of Texas. Though eager to augment federal power within the existing limits of the United

States, Whigs traditionally opposed dispersion of that power over a broader area. Many northerners, moreover, feared that Texas, which would surely enter the Union as a slave state or even a number of slave states, would reinforce the "slave power" in the national government. A group of antislavery congressmen, led by former President John Quincy Adams, called the effort to annex Texas a plot by the "slavocracy" to add to southern strength in Congress. Still other citizens feared war. Annexation might well goad the Mexicans into attacking the United States.

With so many Americans hostile to slavery, skeptical of expansion, or afraid of war, Texas annexation became a political hot potato. In early 1837, just before leaving office, Jackson granted official diplomatic recognition to the Texas Republic, and during the next few years Americans established trade relations with the young nation. Annexation, however, remained stalled.

Events soon goaded the United States to action. Discouraged by American indifference, the Texans began to dicker with England and France for diplomatic recognition and for loans in exchange for free trade in cotton and generous land grants to French and British subjects. This flirtation with the European powers disturbed Americans, who recoiled at allowing the Lone Star Republic to be absorbed into the British Empire, at this point no friend of the United States. Slaveholders were particularly concerned that once Britain acquired Texas it would abolish slavery there, exposing the South's western flank to abolitionist influence. Pro-annexation sentiment was further reinforced by an influential group of capitalists who owned Texas bonds and Texas lands and believed that making Texas a state of the Union would guarantee the safety and profits of their investments.

Tyler cleverly played on the interests and fears of all these groups to secure annexation. To southerners, he emphasized the dangers of British abolitionism. To Anglophobes and patriots he suggested that British interest in Texas was part of a plot to encircle the United States. His personal friend, Senator Robert J. Walker of Mississippi, dangled the promise of Pacific ports in front of Northeastern commercial men interested in the China trade.

Despite Tyler's and Walker's efforts, the Senate defeated an annexation treaty in 1844, and Texas remained outside the Union almost to the end of Tyler's term. Annexation and Oregon became major issues in the 1844 presidential contest. The Whigs chose Henry Clay, who opposed annexation on the grounds that it would mean war with Mexico. To maintain party harmony, they avoided any mention of Oregon or Texas in their platform. The Democrats, as was their habit, became embroiled in a lengthy battle over men and policies. Martin Van Buren considered himself the party's titular leader despite his defeat in 1840, but he was opposed to annexation, and most of the party favored it. Annexationists successfully blocked his nomination, but they deadlocked the convention in the process. Maneuvering went on for days until, on the ninth ballot, James K. Polk of Tennessee, former speaker of the House of Representatives, received the prize. The Democratic platform called for the "reoccupation of Oregon and the reannexation of Texas at the earliest practicable period." The suggestion that the United States was merely exerting clear existing rights in these regions was dubious history, but it accurately expressed the expansionists' convictions.

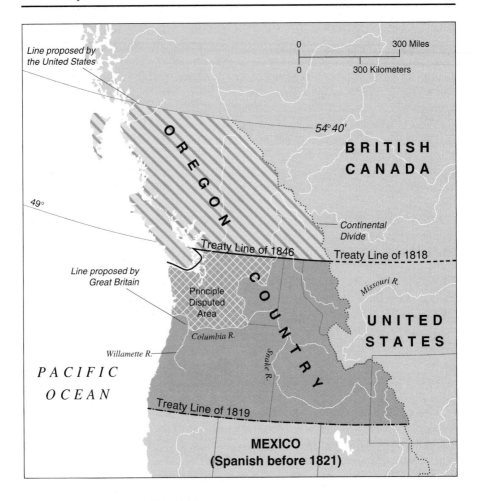

The Oregon Controversy, 1818–1846

The Democrats went on to victory, but just barely. Polk won only because James Birney, candidate of the tiny Liberty party, drew enough antislavery voters from Clay to give Polk New York by 5,000 votes and with it a paper-thin electoral majority.

Polk's election was not, then, a strong mandate for annexation. Nevertheless, many formerly undecided citizens, now concluding that annexation was inevitable, gave it their support. To Tyler this was a cue to renewed efforts. Rather than submit yet another annexation treaty, which would require the approval of two-thirds of the Senate, he asked Congress for a joint annexation resolution, which would need only a bare majority of both houses for adoption. This approach worked. By heavily Democratic majorities in both houses, Congress approved the resolution. On March 1, 1845, in the closing hours of his administration, Tyler signed the joint resolution. Texas entered the Union as a slave state in December 1845, but only after another heated debate in Congress with antislavery Whigs leading the opposition.

* MOVING TOWARD WAR *

For many months the Mexican government had been threatening retaliation if the United States absorbed Texas. Now, in the wake of the joint resolution, the Mexican minister to Washington asked for his passport and returned to Mexico City eager to report that the Americans had no stomach for war and could be easily intimidated.

The minister had not taken the correct measure of James K. Polk. A slight man of forty-nine, the new president was not impressive physically. Nor did he loom much larger intellectually. But he was a remarkably strong-willed man, resembling his hero and patron Andrew Jackson in his aggressive spirit and willfulness. Determined to make his mark, Polk mastered the details of government through sheer energy.

MANIFEST DESTINY.   Like many Americans of his day, Polk was imbued with the mystique of Manifest Destiny. A term coined by John L. O'Sullivan, a New York magazine editor, it asserted the God-given right of Americans to "overspread and to possess the whole of the continent which Providence has given us for the great experiment of liberty and federated self-government." "Make Way for the Young American Buffalo," declaimed a bombastic New Jersey defender of American destiny:

> He has not got land enough. . . . I tell you we will give him Oregon for his summer shade, and the region of Texas as his summer pasture. Like others of his race, he wants salt, too. Well, he shall have the use of two oceans—the mighty Pacific and the turbulent Atlantic shall be his.

As a sense of special American "mission," Manifest Destiny can be traced back as far as the Puritans of colonial Massachusetts Bay. Reinforced by the tremendous national energies unleashed following independence and by the aggressive economic opportunism and buoyant confidence that accompanied pre-Civil War economic growth, it reached a climax in the 1840s. It was undoubtedly a self-serving ideology. Like the French, British, German, and Japanese rationalizations of territorial ambitions at other times, it sought to justify policies based on selfish national interest. Certainly the peoples and nations who stood in the path of America's expansionist urge found it difficult to see it as divinely inspired and benevolent. And all too often, Manifest Destiny would excuse the harshest disregard of the rights of others. It also reeked of cultural and racial arrogance that implied the superiority of American civilization and "Anglo-Saxon" stock to any other in North America.

Yet American expansionism differed from its Old World equivalents. Americans have never been comfortable with colonies. The precedent of the Northwest Ordinance of 1787 was that all new territory acquired by the United States would eventually be organized into self-governing states of the Union equal to the others. This principle served as a check on American expansionism. Whether out of prejudice against other cultures and races or merely in recognition of cultural disparities, Americans have been reluctant to annex densely populated regions of peoples with different traditions, customs, and beliefs. In 1846 this attitude would help put a damper on the "All Mexico!" movement that followed the war.

Polk and his cabinet endorsed the premises of Manifest Destiny. In Oregon the president seconded his followers' cry of "Fifty-four forty or fight." He also coveted the rich province of California which he feared, incorrectly, that Britain was planning to seize. Polk's expansionism also led him to support the Texas claim to territory reaching southwestward to the Rio Grande. The Mexican government insisted that the province extended only to the Nueces River, and the precedents for this position were strong ones. Polk never questioned the Texans' claims, however, and was willing to use force to make them good.

DEBATE ON EXPANSIONISM.   Not all Americans accepted Polk's ambitious territorial goals. In New England and parts of the Northeast where antislavery sentiment was strong, the expansionists were a minority. Whig voters tended to see politics as an extension of morality: Because expansion favored slavery, it was unethical. Their party moreover had traditionally opposed expanding U.S. boundaries.

Expansionist feelings were strongest in the Mississippi Valley and among the business classes of the Northeast. In Pennsylvania and New York, commercial men and industrialists looked forward to continental markets and the access to east Asia that Pacific ports might bring. In the Mississippi Valley land hunger was the fuel for expansionism. Many people in this vast, lightly settled region already feared the disappearance of cheap land and looked to the Far West as a reserve for future generations.

Expansionism was also associated with Democratic affiliation. Democrats were less inclined to treat politics as a moral arena: They either considered the extension of slavery into new regions an irrelevant issue or, in the South, actually welcomed it. Expansionists were generally youthful. The "Young America" group among the Democrats led the movement for a totally American continent. Led by men like the thirty-two-year-old Stephen A. Douglas of Illinois and journalists such as the twenty-six-year-old Walt Whitman, Young America exhibited all the enthusiasm for great, bold deeds traditionally associated with youth. President Polk, at forty-nine the youngest man till then to hold presidential office, identified with this group.

Columbia brings a new day to North America, laying railroad tracks,
plowing fields, and stringing telegraph wire, as Indians, buffalo, and other wild animals
flee before her advance. Americans believed they were ordained by God
to farm Oregon and Texas, mine California, and build ports on the Pacific coast.
A telling symbolic depiction of the "development" ethnic that prevailed.

COMPROMISE WITH ENGLAND. Although he coveted new territory, Polk was not anxious to go to war for it. In his inaugural address he repeated the claim of the 1844 Democratic platform that the American title to Oregon was "clear and unquestionable." But in later months he blew hot and cold on Oregon, alternately threatening and appeasing Britain. Soon after his inauguration he proposed settling the Oregon dispute by extending the existing Canadian-American boundary, the forty-ninth parallel, all the way to the Pacific. When the British minister haughtily rejected this proposal, the angry Polk withdrew it. Several months later, in his first message to Congress, the president again demanded all of Oregon to the 54° 40′ line and asked Congress to give the required one-year notice to Britain ending joint occupation of the region.

The threat of a direct confrontation with the United States startled the British, and they asked the American government to renew its forty-ninth parallel offer. The touchy president refused, but allowed Secretary of State James Buchanan to tell the British that if they suggested a compromise, the American government would reconsider. In early June 1846 the British proposed extending the boundary beyond the Great Lakes along the forty-ninth parallel to the Pacific, but reserving all of Vancouver Island for themselves. Polk now submitted the plan to the Senate. The bellicose Young Americans denounced it as a betrayal of American interests, but by a vote of 41 to 14, the Senate adopted it. The Oregon question, which had dragged on since the days of John Quincy Adams a generation before, had finally been settled by good sense and compromise.

And not a moment too soon. Polk had not expected war with Mexico when he first proposed a settlement to the British; but by the time the Senate approved the Oregon treaty, Americans and Mexicans were killing one another along the entire border from Texas to California.

THE SLIDELL MISSION. Polk blundered into war. In the fall of 1845 he had dispatched John Slidell to Mexico to see if the United States could get what it wanted by negotiation. Mexico had broken diplomatic relations with the United States at the time of the Texas annexation, and Mexican patriots were still outraged at what they considered the theft of one of their country's choice provinces. Nevertheless, Polk remained hopeful of a peaceful settlement. Slidell was to say that if Mexico recognized the Rio Grande as the southwestern boundary of Texas, the United States would pay the $3.25 million that Mexico owed to American citizens as a result of disorders and defaults in that chaotic country. He was also to offer another $5 million for the province of New Mexico and $25 million more for California. He did not expect these negotiations to fail, Polk informed his envoy; but if they did, he would ask Congress "to provide proper remedies." Historians have interpreted this phrase as a threat of war, and it probably was. But Polk considered the use of force unlikely.

The Slidell mission went wrong from the beginning. The government of José Herrera was inclined to negotiate, but when news got out of Slidell's purpose hostile public opinion made it difficult for Herrera to pursue a consistent policy. Although Slidell was permitted to enter Mexico, he was held at arm's length and not allowed to present his proposals.

Soon after, the Federalist Herrera government fell. The new Centralist administration under Mariano Paredes attacked its predecessor for "seeking to avoid a necessary and glorious war" and began to negotiate with Great Britain for support against the United States if war should come. Disgusted with what he considered Mexican bad faith, Polk ordered General Zachary Taylor to move his troops to the north bank of the Rio Grande to occupy the disputed Texas border region and protect Texas against possible attack. The Mexican government soon gave Slidell his walking papers.

By the spring of 1846 Polk concluded that war was inevitable. So did the Mexicans. Confident that they would have the support of Britain, that the American war effort would be shackled by New England and abolitionist opposition, and that Mexicans, man-for-man, were better soldiers than Americans, they were not averse to conflict. On April 23 Paredes announced that Mexico had declared "defensive war" on the United States.

News soon reached Washington that the Mexicans were preparing to attack Taylor's army. Early in May, Polk discussed a war declaration with his cabinet, but before Secretary of State Buchanan could prepare a statement of grievances against Mexico, news reached the capital that Mexican troops had crossed the Rio Grande and attacked a unit of Taylor's troops in the disputed region. Two days later Polk's war message was read to Congress. War was declared by a vote of 40 to 2 in the Senate and 174 to 14 in the House.

* WAR WITH MEXICO *

The war lasted almost two years, cost 13,000 American lives, and $100 million. It was a remarkable triumph for American arms. This time the combination of a small regular army and a mass of volunteers worked well. Young men flocked to the recruiting offices. Many enlistees came from the Mississippi Valley and especially the newer slave states, where the spirit of Manifest Destiny was at its most fervent. Leading these spirited troops was a cadre of well-trained officers from the military academy at West Point. Besides skilled military leadership, the country also enjoyed excellent morale. Many Whigs remained skeptical of the war, and antislavery citizens strongly opposed it. But it was a short and relatively popular war. Most Americans eagerly followed the armies in the field and cheered each victory.

TAKING THE BORDERLANDS. Never before had American soldiers fought over so vast an area. In June the small Army of the West under Stephen Watts Kearny set out from the Missouri River for Santa Fe, the capital of New Mexico and the major commercial town of the Southwest. On August 18, 1846, Kearny's men took the city without a fight. A month later Kearny departed for California, reaching San Pascual near San Diego with 100 half-naked, half-starved and exhausted men in December.

By this time major battles had been fought in northern Mexico where the main American force under Old Rough-and-Ready—Zachary Taylor—confronted a Mexican army of poorly trained soldiers under General Mariano Arista. At Palo Alto, on May 8, 1846, American artillery blew great holes in the Mexican ranks. When Arista launched his mounted lancers against the American infantry, they were repulsed with heavy losses. Once more the Mexicans attacked, this time with infantry. The Americans replied with devastating fire from their eighteen-pounder cannon. The fighting stopped at darkness, and the next morning Taylor awoke to discover the Mexicans had disengaged. At Resaca de la Palma, the next day (May 9, 1846), the two armies clashed once again. This time the Mexican defeat was decisive and Arista and his army retreated across the Rio Grande. On May 17 the American troops occupied Matamoros, the major Mexican port at the mouth of the great river.

The Mexican War, 1846–1848

Taylor's two battles made him an instant hero at home. Congress awarded him two gold medals, and war enthusiasm soared. A recruiting poster of these early months caught the mood of the nation: "Here's to Old Zach! Glorious Times! Roast Beef, Ice Cream, and Three Months' Advance!" Volunteers poured into the recruiting offices. A call by the Tennessee authorities for 2,800 men brought a response of 30,000. By August Taylor's army on the border had swelled to 20,000 troops.

On August 19 Old Rough-and-Ready began to move on Monterrey, capital of Nuevo León. Once more the American artillery proved devastating. After several days of fighting in and around the city, the Mexicans agreed to withdraw after extracting an armistice that allowed them to keep their sidearms and remain unmolested for eight weeks. On September 25, 1846, Taylor raised the Stars and Stripes over Monterrey. He had lost 800 killed and wounded.

This fierce-looking man is Zachary Taylor, "Old Rough-and-Ready," the American commander in northern Mexico. Though a soldier, unskilled in politics, he proved to be a competent president during the two years he served in office before his death.

Although another American victory, Monterrey damaged Taylor's reputation. Critics charged that he should not have allowed the Mexicans such generous terms. President Polk's skepticism was reinforced by his fear that the Whig general would be a political rival in 1848. In January 1847 he ordered Taylor to remain at Monterrey while four-fifths of his troops were transferred to General Winfield Scott for an invasion of the Mexican heartland by way of Vera Cruz, the port on the Gulf of Mexico east of Mexico City.

CONQUEST OF CALIFORNIA. Meanwhile, in California, important events were unfolding even before formal hostilities. In 1845 Polk had secretly authorized Thomas O. Larkin, the American consul in the California capital, to help stir up a secessionist movement among the numerous American residents. In June, however, before Larkin's plans could mature, a group of Americans proclaimed the "Republic of California" and adopted a national flag emblazoned with a star, a stripe, and a crudely drawn grizzly bear. By coincidence, at this point Captain John C. Frémont arrived in California with a contingent of American troops supposedly sent for exploring purposes. The hotheaded young officer took over leadership of the Bear Flag Revolt, and he and his men soon clashed with a force led by the Mexican governor, and routed it. On July 1 Frémont occupied the Mexican fort at San Francisco while governor Jose Castro fled south to Los Angeles.

Now officially at war with Mexico, the United States prepared to conquer the province. In early July a naval squadron under Commodore John D. Sloat arrived in Monterey and raised the U.S. flag over the Mexican custom house. The next day Sloat read a proclamation stating that "henceforth California will be a portion of the United States." In ill health, Sloat was soon replaced by Robert Stockton, who joined with Frémont to impose American authority on the province.

The task proved more difficult than expected. Mexican troops drove the Americans out of Los Angeles, Santa Barbara, and San Diego. Virtually the whole of southern California was in Mexican hands when Stephen Kearny arrived outside of San Diego with his small force from the east. Kearny attacked the Mexican troops defending the town and was beaten off. Kearny was rescued by Stockton and together the two leaders, with larger forces, retook the towns previously lost, occupying Los Angeles on January 10. As Stockton and Kearny moved north, the California Battalion under Frémont moved south from Sacramento. On January 13 the remaining Mexican forces in California signed the Capitulation of Cahuenga. The beautiful province was now American territory by right of conquest.

VICTORY IN MEXICO. The United States now controlled all the Mexican borderlands from the Gulf of Mexico to the Pacific Ocean. But the war was far from over. Santa Anna was once more back in the picture, having inveigled the *Norteamericanos* into allowing him safe conduct through the naval blockade by promising to make peace on their terms. Once home he reneged and took command of the Army of Liberation. By February the erratic strong man was leading an army of 20,000 troops against Taylor still holed up in Monterrey with an army one quarter the size. The two forces met at Buena Vista, and once again American artillery proved decisive. After three days of fighting, the badly bloodied, hungry Mexican army retreated southward to meet a new American threat, this time coming from the east.

Winfield Scott ("Old Fuss and Feathers"), commanding 12,000 men, arrived off Vera Cruz in early March, hoping to take the steamy tropical city quickly to avoid the summer yellow-fever scourge. Scott surrounded Vera Cruz and pounded it with big guns manned by naval crews. On March 29 the city surrendered and Scott quickly turned it into his base of operation for the advance on the Mexican capital high up on the country's cool central plateau.

In early April American troops began their march to the "Halls of Montezuma." At Cerro Gordo, fifty miles inland, Scott's 9,000 men routed the larger Mexican army in hand-to-hand fighting with bayonets and muskets used as clubs at a cost of 63 killed and 337 wounded. In the fierce heat of the lowlands many of the Americans had thrown away their blankets and warm clothing, and as they now climbed into the cold of the highlands they suffered severely. They were also harassed by Mexican guerrillas who picked off stragglers, couriers, and isolated detachments. In mid-May Scott occupied Puebla, eighty miles from the capital, and remained there until reinforcements, under Franklin Pierce, arrived from the United States in August. Fighting soon resumed, with the Americans defeating Santa Anna once more at both Contreras and Churubusco.

Santa Anna now withdrew to Mexico City and requested an armistice while he and the U.S. peace commissioner attached to Scott's army, Nicholas Trist, parlayed. Meanwhile, the Americans camped outside the capital waiting for Mexican surrender. Negotiations soon broke down, and the fighting resumed. The final American assault on the capital took place in early September with a series of battles culminating in the American assault on the fortified hill of Chapultepec, bravely defended by a thousand Mexican troops including the young cadets of the Mexican military academy. The Americans scaled the rocky hill with ropes and ladders and on the evening and early morning of September 13–14 fought their way into the capital. The formal capture of Mexico City was marked by the raising of the American flag by the U.S. marine battalion.

But Santa Anna refused to capitulate. As the Americans were entering the capital, he and a force of 8,000 men attacked the small American garrison left behind at Puebla. When this operation failed Santa Anna fled the country, leaving the unavoidable surrender and peace negotiations to the ad interim president, Pedro Anaya.

THE PEACE. As wars go, the Mexican conflict was brief; the fighting lasted less than a year and a half. The peace negotiations, however, dragged on for months. With Santa Anna gone neither President Anaya nor any other Mexican leader could at first muster the will and authority to accept defeat and the inevitable loss of territory. In the United States, indecision about American territorial goals further delayed settlement. At the outset of fighting the territorial ambitions of Americans had been relatively modest: California and New Mexico. But with each new dazzling victory the national appetite grew until the cry "All Mexico!" became a powerful slogan and movement.

For a while the "All Mexico!" surge seemed unstoppable. It was attractive to the country's commercial interests, which saw an opportunity to build a canal across the Isthmus of Tehuantepec, a narrow part of the North American continent. By absorbing all of the defeated nation, American enterprise, progress, glory, and greatness might all be furthered simultaneously. Manifest Destiny would be fulfilled!

But the "All Mexico!" advocates did not reckon with the Mexicans themselves. In New Mexico and California, and in the Mexican heartland, the occupying American troops were soon facing attacks by Mexican irregulars. At Taos, New Mexico, Mexican and Indian guerrillas killed the American governor, Charles Bent, and had to be subdued by soldiers hastily brought in from Santa

Fe. If the United States insisted on all of Mexico, it could expect more of this resistance. Who knew how long the fighting might last?

The issue was ultimately decided by the reluctance of most Americans to take on the responsibility of governing a large non-English-speaking population with different institutions and traditions. Meanwhile, peace negotiations proceeded slowly. In October 1847 Polk recalled Trist, but the headstrong, ambitious Virginian, on the advice of General Scott, continued to negotiate with Mexican officials. Fortunately for Trist, Santa Anna's successors finally concluded that they could not avoid concessions. On February 2, 1848, they signed an agreement with Trist at Guadalupe Hidalgo.

The Treaty of Guadalupe Hidalgo gave the United States the provinces of California and New Mexico and confirmed the Rio Grande as the southwestern boundary of Texas. The Mexican Cession included the present states of California, Nevada, and Utah, and parts of Arizona, New Mexico, Wyoming, and Colorado. In return, the United States agreed to pay Mexico $15 million and to assume the $3.5 million of American citizens' claims against the Mexican government.

These terms differed only marginally from those Slidell had proposed before the war, and some Americans opposed them. After a costly and total military victory, why take only as much as you had asked for in the first place? President Polk himself disliked the treaty because it had originated with Trist, whom he had relieved of his commission. But most Americans were inclined to accept it. "Admit all [the treaty's] faults," wrote one newspaper editor, "and say if an aimless and endless foreign war is not far worse. . . . We are glad to get out of the scrape even upon these terms." This accommodating spirit prevailed when the treaty came before the Senate, and it was ratified by 38 votes to 14.

* CONCLUSIONS *

And so the war ended on a relatively moderate and conciliatory note. The Mexican government could consider the $15 million an acknowledgment of American guilt; Americans could see themselves as forbearing and generous.

But what were the causes? The war was part of a process of territorial expansion over which Americans—and even more clearly their government—had relatively little control. Greed (or acquisitiveness, if one prefers) was part of the American character and could not easily have been checked by laws or moral exhortation, even if the United States government had wanted to. No agency could have kept American citizens from moving into the loosely held Mexican borderlands. Whatever Washington had done, it is likely that New Mexico and California would have taken the same course as Texas. American migration would have been followed by secession, demands for annexation, and eventual incorporation into the United States. No doubt war would have been part of the process.

The Mexican War, then, was in some ways almost inevitable. Had Mexico been a strong and stable country, Mexican–American relations would undoubtedly have taken a different turn. We cannot blame the victim for his misfortunes, but it is hard not to conclude that Mexico's history, which found it after independence a poor, disorganized nation, racked periodically by violence, with a powerful, dynamic, and materialistic neighbor to the North, was a crucial factor in its fate. A wise Mexican has observed: "Poor Mexico, so far from God, so near the United States!"

The joke, however, was on the Americans. At the war's start the writer Ralph Waldo Emerson predicted that the United States would conquer Mexico, but that the victory would "poison us." As we shall see in Chapter 14, it almost did.

12

AMERICANS BEFORE THE CIVIL WAR

What Were They Really Like?

1790	The geographic center of American population is east of Baltimore
1793	Congress adopts first fugitive slave law
1794	Black preacher Richard Allen establishes the congregation that becomes the first African Methodist Episcopal Church
1821	Emma Willard founds the Troy Female Seminary (the Emma Willard School) in New York
1825	Robert Owen founds New Harmony (Indiana)
1831	First issue of William Lloyd Garrison's The Liberator; Nat Turner's Rebellion in Virginia: 57 whites and about 100 slaves die
1833	American Antislavery Society organizes; Oberlin becomes the first college to admit women as full degree candidates
1837	Abolitionist editor Elijah Lovejoy, defending his printing press against a mob, is murdered in Illinois; Mary Lyon founds a women's academy, now Mount Holyoke College, in Massachusetts
1838	Sarah Grimké publishes Letters on the Equality of the Sexes
1840s	"Potato famine" sends hundreds of thousands of Irish to the United States
1844	Protestants riot against Irish Catholics in Philadelphia
1848	John Humphrey Noyes founds Oneida Community (New York); Lucretia Mott and Elizabeth Cady Stanton organize the first Women's Rights Convention at Seneca Falls, New York
1849	Elizabeth Blackwell receives a medical degree from Geneva College

1850	Hawthorne's *The Scarlet Letter* published
1851	Maine passes the first state prohibition law; Melville's *Moby Dick* published
1855	First edition of Walt Whitman's *Leaves of Grass*
1865	The first all-women's college, Vassar, is established

In the decades before the Civil War, America and Americans fascinated people of other nations. Hundreds of educated Europeans visited the new country to see for themselves what manner of society was emerging on the North American continent. Most European travelers were impressed by the relative equality they encountered here. Harriet Martineau, an English writer and intellectual, observed after her 1834 visit that few in America were "very wealthy; few are poor; and every man has a fair chance of being rich." Frances Trollope, who spent the years 1827–1830 in Cincinnati, noted that in America maids and other domestics refused to consider themselves inferior to their employers, referring to themselves as "help" rather than "servants."

Not every visitor agreed that Americans were democratic. Some detected a deep streak of snobbery in the United States. Isidor Löwenstern, a Viennese scholar who traveled through the country in 1837, observed that "distinctions of rank have their defenders in America as zealous as in the Old World. . . ." Women, he wrote, were especially snobbish. The ladies of Philadelphia, for example, took "infinite pains and all their cleverness to differentiate themselves, and as much as possible to avoid contact with inferior classes."

Foreign observers also argued over the much-touted American individualism. The Swedish novelist Fredrika Bremer considered it a prominent American characteristic that "every human being must be strictly true to his own individuality—must stand alone with God, and from this innermost point of view must act alone according to his own conscientious convictions." On the other hand, Martineau complained that Americans suffered from a "fear of singularity"; and the French visitor Alexis de Tocqueville believed that public pressure to conform constituted a "tyranny of the majority" in America almost as stifling as European despotism.

Still another disagreement among the foreign observers of pre-Civil War America was whether Americans were practical, hardheaded, and materialistic or romantic, sentimental, and idealistic. Trollope, no slouch herself at seeking wealth, wrote that she never met an American who was not trying to increase his fortune. "Every bee in the hive is actively employed in search of that honey . . . vulgarly called money; neither art, science, learning, nor pleasure can seduce them from its pursuit." Yet Bremer noted that Americans respected books and learning, and she was surprised by how much social and charitable work they performed. Nor did all observers believe that Americans worshiped money above all other things. Of all the cities of the world, wrote the Hungarian politician Ferencz Pulszky after his 1852 visit, Boston was "the only one where knowledge and scholarship" had "the lead of society." There a "distinguished author, an eminent professor, an eloquent preacher, are socially equals of the monied aristocracy."

What a confusing set of contrasts! Visitors saw equality; they saw snobbery. Americans were individualists; they were conformists. A practical, materialistic people, they also seemed to be scholars, poets, and philanthropists. How can we reconcile these conflicting views of antebellum Americans? Let us examine American culture, institutions, social structure, and values between 1815 and 1860. In this chapter we shall focus primarily on the pre-Civil War North and the West, saving the South for separate attention in Chapter 13.

*   THE MOVING FRONTIER   *

Generations of scholars have seen the West, where the older society and culture of the East touched the still unsettled frontier, as the key to American character and institutions. In the forty-five years following 1815 the West, the fastest growing part of the nation, became home to 15 million Americans. By 1860, eleven years after the great Gold Rush, even distant California had almost 380,000 people. The country had over 31 million inhabitants when the first shots of the Civil War were fired, and half of them lived in states and territories where settled white communities had not existed at the time of Washington's inauguration seventy years before.

Americans generally moved west along lines of latitude. Thus the heavy migration from New England first crossed the Berkshire Hills to central New York, then swept through the Mohawk Valley into northern Ohio, northern Illinois, and southern Michigan. One branch of the Yankee exodus reached out to distant Oregon. New Yorkers and Pennsylvanians tended to settle the middle portions of the trans-Appalachian region. Most southerners moved to the lower parts of the Old Northwest, close to the Ohio River, and to the newer slave states of Kentucky, Tennessee, and the Gulf region. Southern blacks as well as whites moved westward. Most blacks accompanied their masters to the cotton fields of the interior; others, however, were transported by slave dealers in gangs and sold to cotton planters in the new region. Meanwhile, the Indians were continually pushed westward, ahead of the powerful flood of white and black settlers.

THE MIGRANTS' MOTIVES.   Reasons for moving west of course varied from person to person, group to group, and region to region. Some western pioneers were the "loners" of traditional romantic accounts who could not stay put once they had seen the smoke of a neighbor's hearth on the horizon. But people "lit out for the territories" for other reasons. Some were refugees—fleeing the law, their creditors, their spouses, or their own pasts generally. Married women and children went west without much choice because their husbands or fathers did. On the other hand, many single women regarded the West as a land of opportunity. Western farmers needed wives, and unmarried women could easily find in the West the husbands and the security and social status that only marriage and a family of one's own could confer.

Economic considerations, however, probably outweighed personal and social motives. New England's first emigrants streamed to the cheap lands of the Genesee country of western New York in the 1790s following the rapid rise in land prices at home. In the 1820s there was another New England exodus as tenants and agricultural laborers, dislodged by conversion of arable land to sheep pasture, moved west. In the next few decades, unable to undersell the cheap commodities of the fertile Mississippi Valley, many Yankee farmers from Massachusetts or Connecticut simply gave up and joined the westward exodus.

The people of the Middle Atlantic region, where soils were good, had less reason to move than their Yankee neighbors. But by the 1840s and 1850s, many New Yorkers, children of transplanted New Englanders or the transplants themselves, began a second migration to Wisconsin and Iowa, responding once again to the lure of cheap, fertile land.

The older South also felt the economic attraction of the West. Declining soil fertility pushed people out of the Chesapeake region and the older cotton areas of South Carolina and Georgia, while the more fertile cotton lands across the mountains exerted a simultaneous pull. The rich lands of the free prairie states also saw an influx. Many Southerners, mostly slaveless farmers, preferred southern Ohio, Indiana, and Illinois to the new western Cotton Kingdom.

THE FRONTIER TYPE.   Many scholars believe the western environment transformed eastern migrants. The West, according to Frederick Jackson Turner, the late nineteenth-century historian of the frontier, was "productive of individualism. . . . It produced antipathy to control, and particularly any direct control." The West was also egalitarian. Among the pioneers, "one man is as good as another. . . . An optimistic and buoyant faith in the worth of the plain people, a devout faith in man prevailed in the West." It also encouraged idealism. "From the beginning of that long westward march of the American people America has never been the home of mere contented materialism. It has continually sought new ways and dreamed of a new perfected social type."

The truth is more complex than this western myth. Western individualism was not unqualified. Community cooperation and social control existed on the frontier. Westerners joined in social activities and mutual-aid efforts such as barn raising, fence building, cooperative harvesting, quilting bees, and assisting in childbirth. In politics westerners, like other Americans, rejected unqualified laissez-faire and seldom hesitated to pass laws to control the economic and social practices of their neighbors when regulation suited their purposes.

Turner also exaggerated the extent to which the movement westward involved individuals and isolated families. New Englanders often settled in compact communities modeled on the traditional "towns" of Massachusetts and Connecticut. At times entire eastern communities pulled up stakes as an entity and headed west. The migration of the persecuted Latter-day Saints (Mormons) from upstate New York ultimately to the intermontain region near the Great Salt

Lake is a particularly striking instance of group migration. The new Mormon "Zion," moreover, scarcely conformed to the stereotype of a community dominated by rugged individualists. In Utah, the Mormons established a closely regulated society in which decisions were made by elders and by Brigham Young, the charismatic Mormon leader.

Still, westerners were probably more individualistic than easterners. Spread more thinly over the land, without the steady support of close neighbors, they faced an untamed physical environment and had to be self-reliant or perish. But individualism had another, less attractive side: lawlessness. Westerners were much given to brawling and violent behavior. During the 1840s Iowans' use of the bowie knife made them world-famous for bloodthirstiness. Cutting, eye gouging, and nose biting were common ways of settling disagreements in the antebellum West. Although the use of vigilantes was an effort to impose law on lawless communities, it also expressed westerners' penchant for taking the law into their own hands.

In general, western compliance with social norms was rather poor by eastern or European standards. "I have rarely seen so many people drunk," wrote a traveler in the West in the 1830s. Tobacco chewing, spitting, and swearing were almost universal. Charles Dickens concluded after his American visit in the 1840s that westerners could scarcely speak without "many oaths . . . as necessary . . . words."

Turner's assertions about western egalitarianism and lack of concern for materialism must also be qualified. It is true that outside the Southwest, where slavery left its deep impression, the rural West achieved a rough equality of material condition. As we saw in Chapter 9, abundant land and a democratic, if imperfect, system of land distribution created a large body of farm owners of middle rank by 1860. Even more significant, however, is the fact that western attitudes were egalitarian. One westerner did not regard another as superior merely because he possessed a better education or a more impressive pedigree.

But communities in the Southwest were also full of "cotton snobs" and newly minted gentlemen. In the fast-growing western cities class distinctions developed very quickly. And no matter how indifferent they were to ancestry, westerners were generally impressed by money. Pioneer farmers had come west to achieve modest independence at least; to get rich if they could.

Turner's agreeable, positive picture, then, is an overstatement. Real westerners were cruder, more materialistic, and less egalitarian and individualistic in their behavior than he claimed. But their values were indeed individualistic and egalitarian, and values affect actions.

* NEW PRESSURES IN THE NORTHEAST *

What about the rest of the country? Did the West's qualities mark Americans elsewhere as well? Turner claimed that they did. The West, he said, was the ultimate source of the democratic values of the nation as a whole. Attitudes and institutions developed on the frontier were carried back east, helping to make the entire country an open, democratic society.

Such an interpretation, however, leaves many things out of account. In the pre-Civil War years the Northeast was engulfed in a rush of economic changes that turned farm people into factory wage earners and brought to America's shores thousands of newcomers from Europe. These changes had vital effects unrelated to the frontier experience of the West.

PROBLEMS OF URBANIZATION.   One social force that Turner ignored was urbanization. In 1800 only five towns—New York, Philadelphia, Boston, Charleston, and Baltimore—had over 10,000 inhabitants. These small cities were primarily centers of foreign trade, and even inland urban communities were mostly distribution centers for buyers and sellers.

As the economy changed and grew, the new factories and mills attracted a wave of people to the older towns and created new ones in the Northeast. Cities also sprouted or expanded in the West. Wherever located, cities brought people together in schools, concert halls, theaters, clubs, churches, libraries, political parties, and other associations, creating a sense of community and shared interests and values. But cities were also troubled places with many disruptive social problems. One was the lack of transportation. At first cities were so small that people could get around on foot. By the eve of the Civil War, however, Baltimore, Boston, Chicago, Cincinnati, St. Louis, and New Orleans all had over 100,000 people; Philadelphia had over 500,000; and New York-Brooklyn, over a million. Such metropolises required public transportation systems. Omnibuses— elongated wheeled carriages pulled by horses—arrived in the 1830s. But not until the appearance two decades later of the horse-drawn streetcar running on rails did the major towns acquire reasonably good transit systems.

Housing was another major urban problem, and it was never adequately solved. As middle-class people abandoned the city centers to move to newer neighborhoods, their dwellings were cut up into small apartments. Sometimes landlords built shacks in the gardens and backyards of older middle-class houses for the newcomers. By the 1850s most large cities had acquired the latest urban development: the slum.

Poor housing was matched by poor water supply, poor waste disposal, and poor health services. Early in the nineteenth century, Philadelphia, Cincinnati, and Pittsburgh built aqueducts to bring pure country water into their cities, but it was mid-century before New York, Boston, and other towns abandoned use of polluted wells and streams. Waste disposal in most American cities was primitive. Slop water from baths (infrequently taken), sinks, and "necessary houses" was often merely dumped into the streets. Where sewers existed, they were often connected to the same stream that supplied the community's drinking water. Scavenging pigs took care of much of the cities' garbage disposal. Although the pigs performed a civic duty, their droppings, along with those of horses by the thousands, were a major source of urban pollution. On a sweltering August day in 1852, one New Yorker noted, "the streets smell like a solution of bad eggs in ammonia."

It is not surprising that health was poor in antebellum cities. Typhoid fever and typhus were common. The devastating cholera epidemics of 1832 and

1849–1850 came from the infected water supplies. Smallpox, yellow fever, and malaria were other common urban afflictions. Not all these diseases were actually water-borne, but doctors thought they were, and the alarm they caused moved public-spirited citizens to improve water supplies and establish boards of health.

CRIME AND VIOLENCE.   The traditional social restraints of America often broke down in the antebellum cities. Cities became catch basins for the antisocial with weak ties to families and other groups. Those who failed or found only marginal places in the urban economy, moreover, often succumbed to temptations or turned to antisocial occupations. Inevitably cities were full of burglars, footpads, pickpockets, and ruffians who preyed on law-abiding citizens. Cities were often nurseries of vice as well. One 1858 estimate claimed that there was one prostitute for every fifty men in American cities.

Even small communities were not exempt from the general violence and disorder of antebellum American life. No Fourth of July or election day passed without broken heads and blood in the streets of America's villages and hamlets. The metropolises were worse, of course. City slums, like New York's notorious Five Points, fostered gangs that conducted full-scale wars with one another and with the police. Crammed with the poor and outcast, districts of urban immigrants were especially violence-prone, a fact that led many native Americans to conclude that the foreign-born were a danger to society. Riots were frequent in antebellum

Troops in Philadelphia attempt to stop a riot between Catholics and bitterly anti-Catholic "nativists" in 1844. Fierce nationalists, the nativists objected to the Catholic's tie to a foreign authority: "the bloody hand of the Pope."

cities. In 1837, Boston volunteer firemen and Irish mourners clashed violently at a funeral procession on Broad Street and state militia had to be called out to quell the mayhem. Still worse was the Astor Place Riot in New York in 1849 when twenty-two people lost their lives and the new, luxurious Astor Place Opera House was severely damaged by a working-class mob.

At first, American cities had few means to deal with disorder. Until the 1840s the law was enforced by elected constables by day and a part-time "watch" at night. The increasing violence and rioting that marked these years of tensions between the native- and foreign-born and the urban erosion of rural-derived social controls made this antique system inadequate. In 1838, Boston established a professional daytime police force to supplement the night watch. In the following decade New York gave up the night watch entirely and established a twenty-four-hour-a-day police force. Before long most other large eastern cities had taken the same road to a modern city police system.

SURGING IMMIGRATION. Increasing tensions between native-born Americans and recent immigrants clearly challenged the principle of equality. Immigration from Europe, as we saw, had been light during the half century following the Revolution. Then in the 1830s the number of new arrivals grew to almost 600,000; in the 1840s, to 1.7 million; and in the 1850s, to 2.3 million. Most of the newcomers came from Britain, Germany, and the southern part of Ireland.

The two largest groups, the Irish and the Germans, did not fare equally well in America. For centuries the Catholic Irish peasants had been denied economic and political rights and had lived as impoverished tenants on lands owned by rich Protestant landlords. In the late eighteenth and early nineteenth centuries the introduction of the potato permitted peasant families to raise more food on their small plots of ground, and Ireland's population soared. When the potato crop failed during the mid-1840s, hundreds of thousands of Irish fled to escape starvation. With their paltry possessions, most crossed the Atlantic to America.

Too poor to buy land or pay the fare to the West once they arrived, Irish families usually stayed in the eastern cities, where they took the lowest paying jobs— as construction workers, day laborers, factory hands, porters, handymen, and teamsters. Many Irish women and girls worked part-time as laundresses or garment workers or became maids, cooks, and charwomen in the homes of middle-class native-born Americans.

The Germans were more fortunate. Though they were seeking better lives in America, many had owned their own land at home, and they brought with them to their new country the money they received from its sale. They were also, on the whole, more skilled than the Irish. Some were even members of the middle class—lawyers, doctors, musicians, soldiers, college professors, and business-people—who were fleeing the antiliberal persecutions that followed the failure of the German Revolution of 1848. (The educated German immigrants of this period are often referred to as "Forty-eighters.")

Many of the German arrivals could leave the crowded labor markets of the large port cities for the cheap lands of Illinois and Wisconsin. Those who stayed in the East were often able to do better for themselves than the Irish. Every American city had German mechanics, printers, and craftsmen. Many Forty-eighters made their mark in business, medicine, academic life, and even politics. Carl Schurz, Gustav Koerner, and other German political refugees quickly rose to prominent positions in American public life.

DISCRIMINATION. Most immigrants found America a mixed blessing. True, there were jobs, and for some, land. No one starved. Immigrant children could go to free schools. The more fortunate and enterprising could pull themselves up from unskilled laborers to the level of small businesspeople, often providing services for their compatriots or selling them the imported old-country goods they craved.

Still, the social environment of their adopted land was not ideal. Americans talked about equality and took pride in the openness of their borders, but they disliked the immigrants and often treated them harshly. During the fifty-year period of slack immigration following the Revolution, native-born white Americans had become unused to large blocks of aliens in their midst, and felt overwhelmed by the deluge of newcomers after 1830. Many viewed the immigrants as lawbreakers, tipplers, and clannish people who refused to adopt the customs of their new country. Confusing causes with consequences, native-born Americans also held the immigrants responsible for their squalid housing, their raggedness, their bad health, and the unsanitary conditions in which they lived.

Native-born Americans also deplored the immigrants' religion. Virtually all the Irish, and many of the Germans, were Catholic. Protestant Americans had a long tradition of anti-Catholicism derived from the religious conflicts of the sixteenth century English Reformation. Before 1830 the American Catholic community had been small, unobtrusive, and assimilated. With the deluge of the 1830–1860 period, however, there suddenly appeared in every town and city Catholic churches, schools, convents, hospitals, and seminaries. A central Catholic hierarchy soon took shape. For the first time Americans encountered the unfamiliar sight of priests and nuns in black garments on their streets. They also experienced the newcomers' relaxed "Continental Sunday," which turned the sober Protestant Sabbath into an exuberant day of visiting, picnicking, playing, and imbibing.

Latent anti-Catholicism soon became active anti-Catholicism. Protestant laymen and ministers accused the highly centralized Catholic Church of antidemocratic tendencies. Catholics, moreover, were undermining the public school system, Protestants said, by establishing parochial schools and demanding that the state support them. A few bigoted extremists even revived the time-worn accusations of rampant vice and immorality among Catholic priests and nuns.

Encouraged by such propaganda, between 1830 and 1860 the nation's cities witnessed violent confrontations between immigrant Catholics and militant native Protestants. More common, however, was the day-to-day discrimination that immigrants encountered. Landlords often would not rent to foreigners, especially the Irish. During the 1850s newspaper help-wanted ads frequently carried the warning "Irish Need Not Apply." Many immigrants achieved a tolerable economic life only because the chronic American labor shortage often gave employers little alternative to offering them jobs.

In the 1850s, when immigration was at its height, antiforeign, anti-Catholic feelings spawned a political movement based on bigotry. During the 1840s various antiforeign "nativist" societies sought to exclude foreigners from America or to reduce their influence in American life. About 1850, one of these, the secret Order of the Star-Spangled Banner, began to be called Know-Nothings from the guarded response of its members when asked to describe the organization. In the next few years the Know-Nothings abandoned their secrecy and became a force in American political life. The new party fell as quickly as it rose, splitting into factions and losing members when it was unable to deal with the overriding issue of slavery in the territories (see Chapter 14). By 1858 it was all but dead, but it left behind a harsh legacy of political nativism that has never completely disappeared from America.

FREE BLACKS. Even more than religion and nationality, race tested America's egalitarian ideals. Two hundred thousand free blacks lived in the northern and western states in 1850. The free black community of the North included many talented men and women. Some of the most stylish restaurants, barbershops, and catering establishments in northern cities were run by blacks. The larger cities also sheltered able black ministers and journalists. But these people were exceptional. The great majority of northern free blacks were unskilled laborers at the bottom of the social pyramid. Both north and south, white Americans generally treated blacks with disdain. The one notable exception were northern abolitionists, especially the followers of William Lloyd Garrison, many of whom truly embraced an ethic of human equality.

Bigotry harshly affected the life of almost every free black. They were denied admission to white schools, refused jobs they were qualified to perform, living without even elementary civil rights in most northern states. In many northern communities, Jim Crow laws (the name derived from the popular "blackface" minstrel show) mandated separate public facilities for blacks and whites. The Northwest states, pandering to white wage earners' fears of job competition, excluded blacks from taking up residence within their borders, where state "black laws" also disqualified them from serving on juries, testifying against whites in court, or joining the militia.

Their exclusion from many spheres of life inspired some free blacks to creative solutions. When in 1794 the St. George Methodist Church of Philadelphia tried to segregate blacks, the popular black preacher, Richard Allen, established the African Methodist Episcopal Church, which eventually had thousands of communicants all through the North and South. Free black Christians of other denominations likewise established separate churches rather than accept inferior status within white ones. Blacks also founded separate Masonic, Odd Fellows, and other fraternal lodges when they were not admitted to full equality in existing white associations.

As the years passed, conditions got worse rather than better for free black Americans. Before the 1830s there had been a place, if a lowly one, for blacks in the northern economy. With the influx of immigrants, their lot deteriorated. Employers would hire newly arrived Germans and Irish before free blacks. The immigrants themselves, especially the Irish, were hostile to blacks, seeing them as competitors in the labor market. Tensions between blacks and Irish sometimes erupted into savage riots in which scores of people were injured.

WOMEN. American equality was also marred by discrimination based on gender. Antebellum America, like every other Western society, was male-dominated. It was difficult for any woman, except perhaps a strong-willed and self-sufficient widow, to live independently of a man, whether father, husband, or brother. Under the law the earnings and property of married women belonged to their husbands. Their husbands could beat them without the law's intervention except in aggravated cases. Their children were not their own in a strict legal sense, and in a divorce they usually lost all claim to their offspring. Nor were matters better in public realms. Women could not hold office or vote. Virtually all the professions were closed to them except schoolteaching, and as we have seen, women schoolteachers were paid lower salaries than men. Indeed, most women's work outside the home tended to be unskilled and poorly paid.

Few married women worked for wages in this era. Working women usually were either young, unmarried girls waiting for future husbands and families, or older spinsters or widows who had no choice but to support themselves. Consequently, the life of a typical American woman was conditioned largely by her role and function in her family household. Here matters were improving somewhat, at least for the middle class, in these pre-Civil War years. For the wives of businessmen, professionals, and highly skilled workers, there were servants, usually young immigrant women, to help with the heavy chores of the typical household in the pre-electric, pre-running water, pre-telephone era. In addition, falling birthrates lessened the burden of raising children. Although birth-control methods were crude, by the eve of the Civil War, the numbers of children born each year per family had dropped about 40 percent from the 1800 levels.

Other improvements came as new working conditions took men out of the household. Increasingly, among middle-class city people, fathers went to work in the morning, leaving wives and children at home. This emerging pattern encouraged acceptance of a distinct women's "sphere"—the family circle—where their role was supreme. Reinforced by the idea that in a free republic women educated the sons who eventually led the nation, the concept of a distinct women's sphere raised the status of women within the family. Women were still their husband's inferiors, but in the nursery and the kitchen they were supreme.

Despite some advances in status, women continued to suffer from male condescension. Male-dominated society claimed to honor women but often treated them as emotional and physical invalids. Women were thought to be frail creatures, nervous and sickly, and not competent to bear the full burdens of adulthood. Society surrounded them with a wall of stifling conventions and expectations, epitomized in the "cult of true womanhood." A "true" woman was sweet and gentle, modest and nurturing, pious and reverent, and irreproachably chaste. Even within the bonds of marriage, women were expected to be "pure" and deny their "animal" urges.

There were perhaps some advantages to these misconceptions and myths. Some women, especially those of the middle class, were spared heavy physical chores and the pressures of making a living. But no matter how intended or used, the practice of treating women like children diminished their lives and deprived society of their talents.

✳ THE ARTS IN ANTEBELLUM AMERICA ✳

Though foreign travelers often condemned Americans for their crude materialism and indifference to the "finer things," there was another side to the nation's values. Americans were also an artistic, imaginative, and creative people who made important contributions to the arts in the antebellum era.

AN AMERICAN LITERATURE. "Who reads an American book?" sneered the English critic Sydney Smith in 1820. By the time he uttered his famous insult, many educated Europeans were doing that very thing.

In 1800 Americans were apologetic about their lack of literary distinction. During the earliest years of the Republic the air resounded with voices clamoring for a national literature that would use American themes and avoid slavish imitation of Europe. Energy and enthusiasm were not enough to produce such a literature, however; genius was required. Abruptly, in the opening years of the new century, two New Yorkers—Washington Irving and James Fenimore Cooper—provided it.

Irving leaped to international fame in 1819 with publication of a set of assorted short pieces, *The Sketch Book of Geoffrey Crayon, Gent.* These were written in England primarily on English themes. But included in *The Sketch Book* were two brilliant stories, "The Legend of Sleepy Hollow" and "Rip Van Winkle," that had as their setting the picturesque Hudson Valley with its stolid Dutch burghers and the misty green Catskill Mountains steeped in myths and legends. Though in reality based on German sources, this seemed to be authentic American material that answered the call for a native literature.

More authentically "American" than Irving's short stories were the novels of James Fenimore Cooper. The first of these, *The Pioneers* (1823), set in the rapidly changing upstate New York of Cooper's childhood, recounted the struggles to impose "civilization" and the forces of "progress" on the pristine wilderness. Its cast of characters includes the untutored but wilderness-wise Natty Bumppo (Leatherstocking), his noble Indian friend, Uncas, and the symbol of change, Judge Marmaduke Temple. Bumppo is the hero of four other Leatherstocking

Tales, including *The Last of the Mohicans* (1826). In these he personifies the "natural" man pitting his skills and sinews against the dangers of wild nature and wild men as well as the corrosive effects of civilization.

THE NEW ENGLAND RENAISSANCE. Irving and Cooper made New York the nation's first literary capital. By the following decade there were major writers elsewhere as well. In the South William Gilmore Simms's novels dealt with the South during the Revoution and paralleled the work of Cooper. The poets Paul Hamilton Hayne and Henry Timrod, were southern nationalists who sought to carve out a specific southern poetic genre. The one southern writer of undisputed stature was Edgar Allen Poe, born in Boston but raised in Virginia.

Poe began his writing career as a poet, imitating Byron, Shelley, and the other great English romantics. But his short stories—including "The Gold Bug," "The Fall of the House of Usher," "The Murders in the Rue Morgue," and "The Pit and the Pendulum"—have fascinated and moved generations of readers in Europe and America. To us, the somber Poe often seems less "American" than less introspective writers such as Irving and Cooper. Yet in his fondness for hoaxes, mysteries, and violence, he was very much in the national mood.

Far more consistent with American pride were the literary giants who burst forth in New England, especially in and around Boston. In the generation before the Civil War the Massachusetts capital was the ideal seedbed for a literary flowering. With only 100,000 people in 1840, Boston was a city where face-to-face contact among those of like mind and taste was easily achieved. The city, moreover, had a tradition of learning based on the proximity of Harvard College and the heritage of a scholarly and intellectual New England clergy.

Boston's literary renaissance owed much to transcendentalism—an approach to God, humanity, and nature compounded of diverse elements of European romanticism, German philosophy, and oriental mysticism. Although they borrowed from foreign sources, the transcentalists were distinctly American in their views and values: Humans were perfectible, God was forgiving, each person must follow his or her own inspiration, and all men and women had within them part of the divine spark. High-minded and humane, the transcendentalists rejected mere material gain.

The transcendental mood was best expressed in the essays of Ralph Waldo Emerson. Emerson's calm optimism, reasonable and humane views, social generosity, pure motives, and high-mindedness seemed noble and reassuring. He respected American practicality and praised self-reliance, but at the same time he deplored excessive concern with material progress.

In Concord, outside Boston, Emerson was surrounded by a group of talented and idealistic men and women, including Bronson Alcott, Henry David Thoreau, George Ripley, William Ellery Channing, Margaret Fuller, Elizabeth Peabody, and, for a time, Nathaniel Hawthorne. At Emerson's Tuesday evenings these bright people discussed their host's ideas and those of congenial European writers and thinkers. Their thoughts reached the cultured public through a small magazine, *The Dial,* first published in 1840. In the early 1840s Ripley and a few others of the Emerson circle established Brook Farm, a cooperative experimental community at West Roxbury, Massachusetts, a venture that tested their utopian belief in human perfectibility and innate goodness.

If Emerson was the theorist of transcendentalism, Thoreau was the actor. Thoreau was far more sensitive than his contemporaries to the primacy of nature. "In Wildness is the preservation of the World," he told an audience in Concord. In 1845 he put his own precepts to the test by going to live in the woods at Walden Pond. There he discovered the essentials of existence and concluded that human beings needed very little of a material sort to be happy. Thoreau was also a courageous individualist, defying the authorities during the Mexican War by refusing to pay his taxes to support what he felt was an unjust attack on America's weaker neighbor.

Nathaniel Hawthorne, the most creative of the Boston group, was, unlike his Concord acquaintances, a sardonic, skeptical man with a strong sense of the human capacity for evil. These qualities and perceptions he incorporated into many memorable short tales, and into the longer works *The Scarlet Letter* (1850) and *The House of the Seven Gables* (1851). Hawthorne's disagreements with some members of Emerson's group prompted him to satirize the impracticality of their social experiments in *The Blithedale Romance* (1852), a novel about Brook Farm.

MELVILLE AND WHITMAN.   Emerson's transcendentalism was even less acceptable to another great American writer: New Yorker Herman Melville. Melville's first novels related his adventures among the natives of the South Seas. In 1850 he began *Moby Dick,* in outward form a sea adventure, but actually a far more profound book. In his study of Captain Ahab and Ahab's single-minded determination to destroy the white whale, Melville created a powerful allegory of human obsession. *Moby Dick,* with its dark and complex themes, was not as enthusiastically received by antebellum American readers as Melville's earlier work, but today it is thought to be one of America's greatest novels.

Like Melville, Walt Whitman was not fully appreciated until this century. A writer of distinctly American character, Whitman carried individualism to the point of egotism. His "Song of Myself" begins with the famous lines:

> I celebrate myself and sing myself,
> And what I assume you shall assume,
> For every atom belonging to me as good belongs to you.

In this mood he reveals the boastfulness that we associate with the American frontier, although he himself spent much of his life in Brooklyn and Camden, New Jersey. Whitman was also a sensualist; whatever Americans of this generation did in private, few if any ever publicly proclaimed their lustiness, their admiration of personal beauty, and their delight in physical love as he did.

THE PEOPLE'S LITERATURE.   The Boston and New York writers appealed primarily to the educated middle class. The best were skeptical of American materialism and several exhibited a streak of pessimism that ran against America's postcolonial tendency to envision a bright future. They were the first group of American intellectuals at odds with the dominant values of their society. The literature of the masses, however, was unapologetically upbeat and frankly endorsed get-ahead materialism and conformity. During the antebellum period, presses poured out a flood of inexpensive novels that reinforced positive American folk attitudes.

Much of the audience for literature of any sort in these years was female; American men were too busy with practical matters to read books. Convinced that only women writers could tap this audience successfully, publishers sought out women skilled with words. A genteel occupation that could be practiced at home, writing presented one of the few opportunities besides teaching for middle-class women to earn their living in a respectable way, and they quickly took advantage of it.

Much of the output was potboiler literature. Mary Agnes Fleming, Catharine Maria Sedgwick, Susan Warner, Sarah Payson Willis, and other women churned out countless novels praising domesticity, chastity, true love, and assorted household virtues. These were often cloyingly sentimental. To sustain interest the authors included such melodramatic stock types as the "other woman," the weak husband, and the martyred wife. In the end justice triumphed, and no one but the villain— or villainess—got hurt. Meanwhile, on the way to the denouement, the reader was exposed only to the sweetest, noblest, and most conventional sentiments.

The literature of antebellum America thus expressed many of the contradictions of the nation. Most of the better writers were skeptical of commercial values. They celebrated the individualism of the nonconformist who resisted the dominant teachings of the day or defied nature. In Melville, Poe, and Hawthorne we also detect despair and pessimism, attitudes scarcely approved by Americans or ascribed to them by most foreign observers. Popular literature, on the other hand, sang the praises of family, country, and traditional virtue and refused to carp at darker American characteristics.

PAINTING AND ARCHITECTURE.   The other arts are equally suggestive of the nation's inner contradictions. Many American painters considered their fellow citizens unappreciative materialists with philistine attitudes toward art. John Vanderlyn, a painter of elegant nudes, insisted that "no one but an artistic quack would paint in America." Washington Allston, like Vanderlyn trained in Europe, returned to the United States to experience the frustration that eventually led to his emotional breakdown and the collapse of his promising career. Later critics of the United States would cite Allston as a victim of the blighting effect of American materialism and lack of true appreciation for "culture" and the fine arts.

On the whole, however, the dissenters were outnumbered by the celebrators of America. Thomas Cole, Asher B. Durand, and the lesser artists of the Hudson River school chose as their subjects the American countryside, especially the scenery of the Northeast. Still closer to the popular taste were painters such as William Sidney Mount and George Caleb Bingham, whose scenes of rural life and homey anecdotes in paint resembled the sentimental popular novels but excelled them in quality. George Catlin and John Audubon were less mannered and less sentimental about the American environment. Catlin's superb pictures of American Indians have enough accuracy and detail to delight an anthropologist. Audubon, of course, was a great naturalist as well as an excellent draftsman, and his watercolor and crayon sketches of American birds are scientific documents as well as objects of great beauty.

Americans between 1815 and 1860 were both practical house builders and romantic artists in stone, brick, and wood. The practical side was to be found in the innovative "balloon frame" house that abandoned the heavy joined timbers of earlier house construction, and substituted a light skeleton of uprights and cross pieces attached by nails encased in siding of boards or shingles. The resulting structure was well suited to a fast-growing society that needed enormous amounts of new housing, had abundant timber, and was willing to sacrifice individuality and permanence for speed and cheapness.

Of course, there were people in both town and country who wanted more than a box with a roof in which to live. In this era they commissioned workers in the Greek-revival style to build gracious mansions with white pillars and public buildings indebted to the ancient Greeks and Romans. The Capitol and White House in Washington are both examples of the style. A competing genre was the nostalgic romanticism of the Gothic style. Gothic was better suited to churches and homes than to public buildings, though James Renwick's Smithsonian Institution is a distinguished exception. For churches Gothic was a natural style, and the traditions of the great European cathedrals and English parish churches were continued beautifully in such structures as Richard Upjohn's Trinity Church and Renwick's Grace Church in New York. It was in private homes, however, that the Gothic style flourished best. It lent itself not only to mansions; in some ways it was even more suitable for wooden cottages.

* THE PERFECT SOCIETY *

The social scene of the pre-Civil War North, like the cultural flowering, contained elements that contradicted the charges of American materialism and conformity. Northern society exhibited a degree of dissent, a willingness to confront established social institutions, and a zeal for replacing them with new ones, that could be found almost nowhere else in the world. This was a time, according to Emerson, when "madmen, madwomen, men with beards, Dunkers, Muggletonians, Comeouters, Groaners, Agrarians, Seventh Day Baptists, Unitarians and Philosophers—all came successively to the top, and seized their moment, if not their hour, wherein to chide, or pray, or preach, or protest."

RELIGIOUS ROOTS OF REFORM. The reform movements of the years preceding 1860 drew some of their energy and substance from the new religious spirit that swept the nation. At the beginning of the nineteenth century American Protestantism was languishing. Piety had declined drastically both on the frontier and in the East. In New England and in those parts of upstate New York and the Great Lakes states where Yankees had immigrated, ministers worried that "the Sabbath would be lost, and every appearance of religion vanish."

Then, during the years preceding 1860, traveling bands of Methodist, Baptist, and Presbyterian evangelists induced thousands of Americans to consider their sins, contemplate a new life, affirm or reaffirm their faith, and join the church. During the second "Great Awakening" outdoor revivals drew hordes of rural citizens to marathon preaching sessions where eloquent evangelists such as Charles Grandison Finney, Francis Asbury, and Peter Cartwright exhorted sinners to abandon their evil ways and find salvation in God's everlasting love. In the wake of each visting evangelist, new members poured into the Methodist, Presbyterian, and Baptist churches. Many of the "saved" joined new denominations. Western New York, called the "burnt-over" district for the wave after wave of revivalism that swept across it, became a religious hothouse that fostered a score of new sects, among them the Latter-day Saints (Mormons), Adventists, and Shakers.

Leaders of more sedate groups such as the Episcopalians and Congregationalists often attacked the new preachers as ranters, and orthodox Calvinists deplored their rejection of predestination. But orthodox Calvinism was also at war during these years with Unitarianism, an offshoot of Congregationalism that had divested itself of Calvinist pessimism along with the orthodox Christian belief in the Trinity. Heirs of Enlightenment rationality, Unitarians rejected what they considered the supernatural and irrational elements in traditional Christian belief.

Unitarianism and evangelicalism attracted different sorts of individuals. The first appealed to educated merchants and professional people, especially in the Boston area; the second made greater headway among farmers and lower-middle-class artisans and tradespeople. For all their social differences, however, Unitarians and evangelicals agreed that men and women could effect their own salvation and perfect both themselves and their society. The converted, proclaimed the evangelist Finney, "should aim at being holy and not rest till they are as perfect as God." Sin was selfishness; virtue, selflessness and benevolence toward others. Sin, said the new breed of religious leaders, was voluntary; humanity could reject it; and collective sin—social evils—could be rooted out by human will, education, and cooperative public action.

This "Perfectionist" doctrine quickly penetrated organizations already involved in efforts to improve society. By 1820 these groups were in close contact with one another in an informal "benevolent empire" that devoted its attention to world peace, temperance, foreign missions, antislavery, and other good causes. The benevolent societies usually had limited, practical goals. But perfectionism gave a previously locking passion, and at times a fanaticism, to the wave of humanitarian reform that swept the North and the West.

THE DESIRE FOR SOCIAL CONTROL. Many reformers were also inspired by a belief that society was experiencing a severe breakdown and fears that social chaos would result if steps were not taken to check the collapse. Reformers of this sort often blamed crime, insanity, and alcoholism on family failure in an industrializing, urbanizing environment. To men and women who held such views, "asylums," where victims of family collapse could find havens from the harsh new world and learn to cope with their difficulties, seemed the solution.

Penitentiaries were one form of asylum. Existing jails and prisons were unsanitary places with wretched food, where first offenders were mixed with hardened criminals. They did nothing to rehabilitate lawbreakers. The reformed system of penitentiaries endorsed by Louis Dwight, Elam Lynds, and others separated first offenders from repeaters, provided better sanitation, and allowed prisoners some privacy. But as a would-be substitute for family discipline, it also imposed solitary confinement, hard physical labor, and regimentation. In the Auburn system of New York, established in 1816, prisoners were marched to and from work in tight lockstep and flogged for violating prison rules. In the end the penitentiary system failed in its primary aim of rehabilitating criminals. Yet the changes were considered models of enlightenment in their day, and dozens of European observers came to view the American penal system and learn from it.

Another sort of asylum was envisioned by Dorothea Dix. In an earlier era "lunatics" had been kept at home in the care of their families. Increasingly, however, mobility and the growing reluctance of families to carry the burden of unproductive relatives forced the community to care for the mentally disturbed. Unfortunately, there were few mental hospitals, and the insane were often treated like animals. Mental patients in Massachusetts, Dix reported, were kept in "cages, closets, cellars, stalls, pens!" They were "chained, naked, beaten with rods, and lashed into obedience." Dix demanded that her state establish hospitals to provide the insane with humane treatment. With the aid of Samuel Gridley Howe, Horace Mann, and Dr. Luther Bell, by 1860 she had induced almost every state to provide improved facilities for mental defectives and the insane.

Not every social ill the reformers attacked lent itself to the asylum solution. Antebellum America had a serious alcohol problem. Captain Basil Hall, an English visitor of the 1820s, noted the "universal practice of sipping a little at a time, but frequently . . . during the whole day." Americans themselves worried about their countrymen's drinking habits. Ministers asserted that drunkenness and "lewdness" went hand in hand. The guardians of public morals believed that alcoholism was especially prevalent among the working class and immigrants; but in fact, all classes had their share of drunkards who squandered their wages, beat their wives, neglected their children, and committed vicious crimes while under the influence of "demon rum."

The temperance reform movement developed two wings. The moderates wished to educate society on the evils of alcohol in order to reduce excessive drinking. The "total abstainers" condemned all drinking as a sin and demanded state prohibition laws to outlaw the production, transport, and consumption of alcoholic beverages. In the 1840s, the prohibitionists, under the leadership of Neal Dow, gained control. Dow's first success came in 1851 when Maine, his native state, passed the first statewide prohibition law. In the next few years a dozen states, mostly in the North and West, adopted "Maine Laws."

GROWING FEMALE ASSERTIVENESS. At one time scholars ascribed the large number of women within the reform movements to the "natural tenderness" or the intrinsic nurturing quality of women. Today we are more likely to seek an explanation in the social setting of the day, especially in the experience of middle-class women.

The cult of domesticity had given mothers higher prestige and sanctioned better education for women than previously. Yet society still believed that women's proper sphere was the home and family. To the young women pouring out of the new seminaries, or otherwise affected by the new partial liberation, the countless remaining restraints on women's public role seemed increasingly galling.

At first women activists found it very difficult to assert their own rights. Striving for the betterment of others seemed more acceptable, for these efforts were related to women's traditional helping role. Many reform-minded middle-class women turned to the problems of working girls forced into prostitution in order to eke out a living in the cities. Hundreds of middle-class women during these years also joined missionary societies to bring the message of Christ to the benighted frontier and to the "heathen" Chinese, Hawaiians, Burmese, and Africans across the oceans. Women also participated in record numbers in the ranks of the American Peace Society, which opposed recourse to war as a means of settling disputes among nations.

The antislavery movement also attracted women reformers, and their experience in the momentous attack on black bondage was a catalyst in overcoming their reluctance to aid themselves. Within the antislavery movement few objected to women helping to raise money through such activities as bazaars or cake sales, for example. But at least a few bolder women wanted to take more active roles as speakers and organizers. The first woman to put such urges into practice was Angelina Grimké, a young woman who left the South in 1829 with her more retiring sister, Sarah, when they could no longer stand the scourge of slavery. In 1837, after becoming Quakers, the sisters began to give antislavery talks to small groups of women who came to hear about the "peculiar institution" from those who knew it firsthand. Before long Angelina was addressing large gatherings of both men and women in New York and New England.

For women to speak before mixed audiences was a shocking break with tradition. Many moderate antislavery leaders decried Grimké's speeches and deplored the growing participation of women in the movement. But not the abolitionist radicals. Frederick Douglass, a black antislavery leader who felt discrimination based on biology with special poignancy, praised Grimké and endorsed female activism. So did the firebrand William Lloyd Garrison. "As our object is *universal* emancipation," wrote Garrison, "to redeem women as well as men from a servile to an equal condition—we shall go for the rights of women to their utmost extent."

Despite, or perhaps because of, her opponents, Angelina Grimké evolved into one of the earliest feminists. In 1838 she published *Letters on the Equality of the Sexes,* in which she denounced the traditional education and indoctrination of women designed to keep them in an inferior status. Women should be treated as full human beings. "Whatsoever it is morally right for a man to do," she announced, "it is morally right for a woman to do."

Other women, too, were propelled by the antislavery movement into grappling with their own social and political inferiority. When the 1840 World's Antislavery Convention in London excluded nine American female delegates from its sessions, two of these, Lucretia Mott and Elizabeth Cady Stanton, resolved to launch a new movement dedicated to improving the status of American women. In the summer of 1848 Mott and Stanton brought together 250 people in a women's rights convention at Seneca Falls, New York. Seneca Falls marked the true beginning of the women's rights movement in the United States. The delegates issued a Declaration of Sentiments modeled after the Declaration of Independence, replacing King George III with "man" as the oppressor. It demanded a series of changes to reduce women's legal inferiority and denounced male efforts to diminish women's "confidence in [their] own power" and lessen their "self-respect." The most radical demand, one that clearly violated the notion that women's "proper sphere" was domestic life, was for the "elective franchise"—votes for women!

Seneca Falls did not create a national women's rights organization. Instead, it energized a flock of local and state groups, often informal and temporary, and produced several rounds of state and national conventions where the Seneca Falls Declaration was refined and augmented. The informal networks of women's rights advocates during the 1850s continued to fight for state laws to eliminate gross legal discrimination against women and scored some further successes. They also succeeded in securing new recruits for feminism. They made no impression on resistance to female voting, however. Even women reformers doubted the wisdom of the drive for female suffrage. It seemed so extreme as to stigmatize the entire movement.

Besides group efforts to defeat male domination of society, many middle-class women strove individually to improve their position. The inaccessibility of higher education to women was breached when first Oberlin, in 1833, and then other colleges, admitted women as full degree candidates. In 1865 the first all-women's college, Vassar, was established.

With degrees in hand, women could now take on the professions. In 1850 Antoinette Brown took a theology degree at Oberlin and became the first ordained woman minister. The female breakthrough in medicine came with the Blackwell sisters, who earned their degrees at Geneva College, the only school that would admit them for medical training. Other women began to take law courses and set up practices as attorneys. In almost every case women professionals encountered resistance and ridicule in these years. But by the Civil War women had at least broken the crust of male domination of the public sphere, and it was apparent that more advances would follow.

ANTISLAVERY SENTIMENTS. Antislavery not only energized women reformers; it was a momentous and controversial reform movement in its own right.

In the decades following the Revolution the Quakers continued to oppose slavery, although they avoided harsh attacks on slaveholders. For a time after 1783 there were antislavery societies even in the South itself.

One expression of antislavery sentiment in this early period was the colonization movement dedicated to returning free blacks to Africa. Some members of the American Colonization Society (founded in 1817), especially southerners, saw their movement primarily as a means of getting rid of a dangerous group that threatened the survival of slavery. Others believed that returning blacks to Africa could serve as a first step in eventually freeing all the slaves. Whatever their motives, promoters of colonization did not take into account the costs of transporting millions of people to Africa, or the feelings of black Americans themselves that America was their native land. Under the auspices of the Colonization Society, a few thousand free blacks, former slaves, and Africans taken from illegal slave ships were sent to Liberia, a new black republic founded on the West African coast. But as a serious solution to the slavery problem, colonization remained not only mistaken, but unworkable.

During the late 1820s the antislavery movement took on a new dimension when it linked up with religious Perfectionism and was converted into a crusade for immediate and total abolition. The instigator of the change was William Lloyd Garrison, a pious young printer from Newburyport, Massachusetts, who developed a white-hot determination to drive slavery from the land. Garrison's "immediatism" rejected the quiet tone and step-by-step approach of the Quakers as dealing too gently with sin. Now was the time to demand abolition—if necessary in a way that did not spare people's feelings.

On January 1, 1831, the first issue of Garrison's *Liberator* appeared. It rang with the fervor for liberty and the righteous determination to end the evil of slavery that would make its editor the hope of the oppressed and the despair of moderates. In words that still inspire, Garrison wrote:

> I *will be* as harsh as truth, and as uncompromising as justice. On this subject, I do not wish to think, to speak, or write with moderation. . . . I am in earnest—I will not equivocate—I will not excuse—and I will not retreat a single inch—and I will be heard.

Despite its militant tone the *Liberator* at first attracted little attention. Then in August 1831 Nat Turner, a slave preacher, instigated a slave uprising in the Virginia tidewater that led to 57 white and 100 slave deaths. A wave of horror rolled across the South. Though Garrison had had nothing to do with the revolt, southerners were certain that he had inspired Turner. They demanded that he and his fellow abolitionists be stopped by every means possible. Garrison was not deterred. As the years passed, he became even more uncompromising and intransigent. A thorough Perfectionist, he became convinced that the criminal code, war, and government itself were all efforts to coerce human beings and were equally evil. By condoning slavery, the federal Constitution seemed particularly wicked, and in 1843 Garrison began to place at the head of his editorial column the words:

> Resolved, that the compact which exists between the North and South is a "Covenant with Death, and an Agreement with Hell,"—involving both parties in atrocious criminality,—and should be immediately annulled.

Not all abolitionists were as militant as Garrison. Lead by the dynamic Theodore Weld, western abolitionists refused to adopt the extreme positions and language of the Garrisonians. They were also not as certain as Garrison that women's rights and other reforms were the proper concern of abolitionists. In 1840 the Weld group, joined by eastern moderates under the Tappan brothers of New York, split from the Garrisonians to form the American and Foreign Antislavery Society with headquarters in New York, leaving the Garrisonians in possession of the American Antislavery Society with headquarters in Boston.

Conservative white Americans, even in the North, saw the abolitionists as dangerous to social and political order. Mobs attacked Garrison in Boston, and murdered antislavery leader Elijah Lovejoy in Alton, Illinois, when he refused to shut down his antislavery printing press. When not subject to physical violence, abolitionists were denounced as fanatics, dangerous agitators, and heretics. They were frequently denied basic constitutional rights. When Prudence Crandall attempted to admit a black girl to her Connecticut school in 1833, local whites broke her windows and poisoned her well. Eventually she was driven from the state. Antiabolitionist feeling penetrated to the highest levels of public life. President Andrew Jackson attacked the antislavery advocates as extremists bent on instigating slave insurrections; his postmaster general denied abolitionists the use of the mails to distribute their newspapers, books, and pamphlets. In 1836, the House of Representatives adopted the "gag rule" placing all antislavery petitions of abolitionists "on the table," where they were simply ignored.

The physical, verbal, and legal assaults did not keep men and women from joining the antislavery movement. In fact, by converting abolitionism into an issue of free speech, the attacks may have created sympathy for it and attracted recruits. Hundreds of men and women—many of New England ancestry, with occasional southerners such as the Grimké sisters and Alabama planter James G. Birney—flocked to the antislavery organizations. A majority of prominent abolitionists were white, but many free blacks also joined the movement. Unfortunately, blacks within the antislavery societies were often snubbed by white abolitionists who, though they defended human equality in the abstract, could not overcome their actual prejudice against black people. Despite such prejudice, Frederick Douglass, the brilliant black editor of the antislavery *North Star*; Henry Highland Garnet, an eloquent black preacher; and Sojourner Truth, an illiterate former slave who spoke with effective simplicity for the cause of freedom, all became prominent members of abolitionist societies.

UTOPIAN SOCIALISM.　　Each of these reform movements was an attempt to cure some perceived ill of American society while leaving the main structure untouched. Some Americans, however, rejected the very foundations of their society and chose to withdraw from it almost entirely or to demand drastic change from the bottom up.

These militants considered America too competitive and individualistic, too given over to the pursuit of wealth, and too severely marred by inequality and exploitation. Yearning for a society closer to human scale where men and women could deal with one another face to face, eager to erase the distinctions between rich and poor, hopeful of replacing competition with cooperation, and determined to eliminate human drudgery, they went off to the woods or the frontier to found communities based on some idealistic economic, social, or religious philosophy.

Several of the new utopian communities were inspired by the writings of Charles Fourier, a French thinker who opposed capitalism as inhumane and competitive. Fourier proposed in its place a system of small cooperative communities—"phalanxes"— scattered about the countryside where men and women could work at farming and industry while living in a communal structure. No one would own the community's capital; all would share both the labor and the profit. Government of each phalanx would consist of a Council of Seven, five of whom would be women.

A communitarian experiment that owed as much to religious as to political principles was Oneida, led by John Humphrey Noyes, a Yale-educated minister who settled with his followers in western New York in 1847. At Oneida, Noyes preached against what he called "the Sin system, the Marriage system, the Work system, and the Death system," combining religious evangelism and socialist economics. All work at Oneida was reduced to what seemed essential and unavoidable. Women, particularly, were freed from drudgery by simplified methods of housekeeping.

Noyes's most radical experiment was "complex marriage." He and his followers believed that monogamy (a single spouse) was selfish and interfered with a true sense of community. Instead, every man at Oneida was considered the husband of every woman and vice versa. Outsiders called this "free love" and reviled it as an utter breakdown of morality. But the Oneidans responded that no one in the community was forced to accept sexual relations he or she did not desire. Though Oneida members practiced birth control, some children were born into the community; they were treated in an unusually permissive way, being allowed, for example, to sleep until awakened by the natural rhythms of their bodies.

The Oneida community avoided the bickering that destroyed so many other communitarian experiments by a scheme of self-criticism whereby members could air their grievances before the whole group and work them out. Oneida also developed a firm economic foundation. Recognizing that a community such as his was better suited to industry than agriculture, Noyes trained members in embroidery and silk making and mobilized their ingenuity in developing manufactures. The community basked in prosperity for many decades, becoming, ironically, the basis for a major commercial cutlery firm that is still in business today.

There were many other experimental communities in this era. It is estimated more than 100 such establishments with 100,000 members were formed in the United States between 1820 and 1860. As Emerson wrote an English friend in 1840: "We are all a little wild here with numberless projects of social reform. Not a reading man but has a draft of a new community in his waistcoat pocket."

Most communities founded on some sort of political or philosophical plan were short-lived. New Harmony, a socialist experiment on the banks of the Wabash sponsored by the British philanthropist Robert Owen, lasted two years and then disbanded when internal bickering destroyed all chance of harmony. Icaria, designed as an experiment in communal ownership and use of capital, attracted a small group of French people to the new state of Texas in 1847. A year later it was defunct. The longest-lived of the Fourierist communities—at Red Bank, New Jersey—lasted only a dozen years.

Communities with a religious base were generally more successful than ones founded on a political ideal. Among the most enduring "utopian" communities were those established by the English Quaker Mother Ann Lee, who came to America in 1774 and organized her first small "Shaker" settlement soon after. By the late 1840s there were about 6,000 Shakers living in a score or more communities scattered across the northern states. In their trim, spare, simple villages the Shakers followed a life that combined economic cooperation with a pursuit of spiritual perfection that precluded sexual relations. Shakers prospered collectively by selling seeds, medicinal herbs, bonnets, cloaks, and cabinetwork, and lasted as a group well into the twentieth century.

The commercial success of the religious communities illustrates the paradoxes of antebellum America. Secular faiths were unable to deal with the craving for brotherhood and cooperation. During the pre-Civil War era no political or economic philosophy could overcome the acquisitiveness and individualism of the larger society. A religious perspective was more effective. But to survive, the religious communities found it necessary to become successful economic enterprises.

✳ CONCLUSIONS ✳

What were pre-Civil War Americans in the North and West truly like, then? Americans were competitive and individualistic; they were crude, bad-mannered, violent, and bigoted. They were also humane, romantic, creative, and socially speculative. It seems fitting to call them, as one historian has, a "people of paradox."

These inconsistencies can be traced to the special circumstances of the northern part of the nation in these years. The whole region north of Dixie was in a state of extraordinary flux. Still agricultural and rural, it was rapidly becoming commercial, industrial, and urban. Still largely composed of native-born Protestants whose forebears had arrived in the colonial era, it was experiencing a deluge of newcomers from Europe, many of them Catholic. Besides the tensions these changes created, there were antagonisms between East and West. Easterners often disliked western manners and practices, yet they themselves were moving west in vast numbers and learning to adjust to western economic competition. These transplanted easterners were undoubtedly influenced by the western practices they deplored.

One important fact should be kept in mind as we consider the country's evolution: Virtually all the changes we have described in this chapter followed lines of latitude. In shifts of people, institutions, values, and problems, Northeast mixed with Northwest. This is not to say that the two sections did not retain many distinctive features, but by 1860 Northeast and Northwest were far more alike than either was to the South. This development of distinctive North–South sectional identities would soon have momentous consequences for the nation.

13

THE OLD SOUTH

What Is Myth and What Was Real?

1807	Congress prohibits the slave trade with Africa, but illegal importation of black slaves continues
1822	Denmark Vesey and thirty-five slaves are hanged for planning a slave rebellion in South Carolina
1831	Nat Turner leads an unsuccessful slave rebellion in Virginia; Tariff of Abominations precipitates nullification crisis in South Carolina
1832	In response to Turner's rebellion the Virginia legislature debates the abolition of slavery
1836	Under pressure from southern congressmen, the House of Representatives adopts a "gag rule" prohibiting discussion of all abolitionist petitions
1849	John Calhoun writes Disquisition on Government: He states his theory of the "concurrent majority" in the Senate the following year
1852	Harriet Beecher Stowe's *Uncle Tom's Cabin* is published
1857	Hinton R. Helper's The *Impending Crisis of the South* is published
1858	James Hammond in a famous speech declares there has to be a "mud sill" upon which to erect a civilized cultured life
1860	Abraham Lincoln elected president; Slaves in the South number about 4 million, sixteen times the number of free blacks; South Carolina secedes from the Union

Magnolias and moonlight; white mansions with tall colonnades; beautiful hoop-skirted ladies and handsome, dignified white-suited gentlemen; thoroughbred horses; rich laughter and song drifting up from the slave quarters; waltzes and entrancing talk in the big plantation house—this was the Old South, a society that achieved for a brief moment a brilliance and happy harmony based on mutual respect of classes and races, an ideal of excellence, and good prices for cotton.

Or was it? There is another picture that is almost the complete opposite. In this view the Old South—the slave states in the half century before 1860—was an abhorrent region where a privileged white minority lorded it over millions of black slaves and "poor white trash." The typical elite planter was a newly rich "cotton snob," who abused his black chattels and showed contempt for the non-slaveholding class he himself had so recently left behind. The poor whites, in turn, were shiftless, slovenly, violent, and ignorant people who lived by a little desultory farming and trading whiskey with the slaves for stolen plantation goods. Beneath the poor whites were the exploited slaves. Oppressed by a regime of terror and physical violence, they fought back by contrived laziness, deceit, flight, or violence.

What was the Old South really like? Are both descriptions essentially fables? Is one fable truer than the other? Or is there some truth in both?

* AN UNEXPECTED DIVERSITY *

One myth about the Old South is that it was utterly distinct in its climate and geography. Climate did make a difference. The lower South was indeed warmer than the rest of the nation, and this enabled it to grow short-fiber cotton successfully in its lower reaches. It was too warm for wheat; its chief grain crop was corn. It had poor pasturage and so the corn-eating hog, rather than the grass-eating cow, was the basis of its animal husbandry. But there was little to separate the climate of Maryland from that of Pennsylvania—and yet the first state was part of the Old South, the second of the North. Nor was the South's topography unique. The Appalachian plateau, the Atlantic coastal plain, and the Mississippi Valley were geographical features shared by the nation's two sections. In short, it was not primarily the natural environment that defined the Old South.

SOUTHERN AGRICULTURE.   Another myth is that the Old South was a single agricultural unit. When we think of Dixie in this period, we imagine a gigantic cotton field. Yet cotton was only one of the region's many crops, and not even the most valuable. Corn, which grew everywhere, fattened the section's farm animals and, in the form of "pone," "hominy," and "roasting ears," fed most of its people. The southern corn crop was valued at $209 million in 1855; the cotton crop at only $136 million.

Other staple crops brought in cash. Kentucky hemp, Louisiana sugar, Carolina rice, and Virginia, North Carolina, and Kentucky tobacco were important in their regions. Although none even came close to cotton as a source of income, they contributed to the region's remarkable diversity.

INDUSTRY.   Another myth about the Old South is that it was economically backward. Until recently, historians believed that cotton growing was actually an unproductive enterprise. It exhausted the soil, so that only by constant expansion into virgin land could the planter ensure himself a decent profit. Cotton also supposedly deflected capital from more productive enterprise. Southerners poured their money into new land and slaves rather than into machines and factories. And even if they had been willing to invest in industry, the older view went, the slave system would have prevented it. Slaves lacked the necessary skills, incentives, and education for industrial work. Moreover, to set up successful industrial enterprises where the labor force itself was property was too great a burden for would-be investors. Finally, a slave society inevitably encouraged aristocratic values and contempt for hard physical work—attitudes at odds with successful industrialization. Given all these qualities of a slave society, it was not surprising, said critics, that the South remained bound to agriculture and achieved a slower rate of economic growth than the rest of the nation.

Few scholars today accept these ideas without serious qualifications. It is true that the Old South developed its manufacturing potential more slowly than the Northeast. But the reasons have little to do with slavery. Most slaves, it is true, were unskilled laborers, yet some served as "drivers" or even overseers supervising large work gangs. Moreover, many slaves were skilled craftspeople. On the cotton plantations there were coopers, masons, carpenters, brick makers, gardeners, and the like. On the sugar plantations of Louisiana black experts supervised most of the delicate operations of sugar refining. Slave women were often skilled seamstresses, weavers, cooks, and midwives. Some even practiced medicine, on white as well as black patients. Clearly slaves could have supplied the workforce for an industrial economy.

Nor did prospective factory owners in the South have to buy their employees. Many planters hired their slaves out at prevailing wage rates. Hired slaves worked as municipal workers in southern cities; they worked by the day for southern householders. They also worked in southern factories and industries. Hired slaves were miners in Virginia, Kentucky, and Missouri. Deck hands on the river steamers of the Old South were generally black bondsmen, as were the construction workers on railroads and canals. Cotton mills in South Carolina, Alabama, and Florida used slave "operatives," and in Virginia slaves worked in tobacco factories and at the Tredegar iron mills of Richmond, which would produce most of the Confederacy's artillery.

Clearly, then, the slave-labor system did not exclude industry and business from the Old South. Neither did southern values. Dixie planters were generally practical men who studied agriculture as a business, encouraged experimentation in crops and animal breeding, and organized their labor force efficiently. In fact, according to some historians, the "gang" system of labor they developed on the cotton and sugar plantations was one of the most efficient work patterns for agriculture ever devised. While the hours were moderate, the intensity of the effort was high and the output of the slaves impressive. All told, one scholar writes, the pre-Civil War southern plantation was "a modern business organization, and possibly even a leading business organization of its time."

A final demonstration of plantation slavery's efficiency was the actual overall economic performance of the antebellum South. The Old South was a remarkably productive community. Its industrial development was ahead of all but a very few European countries in cloth output and railroad mileage. In 1860 there were almost 200 textile mills scattered through the region, plus hundreds of tobacco factories, flour and lumber mills, and other manufacturing establishments that, primarily, processed the section's agricultural products.

Most interesting are the comparative figures of sectional income. In 1860 the average per person income for the entire United States was $128 (in 1860 dollars). For the North as a whole it was $141. For the South, if we include both slave and free people, it was only $103, less than either. But if we only include the free population, the South's per capita income rises to $150, a figure higher than both the North and the national average. And it was also growing at a faster rate than the country as a whole. Between 1840 and 1860 the economy of the entire United States grew at the average yearly rate of 1.4 percent for each man, woman, and child. The Old South's growth rate was 1.7 percent.

Taken together, then, it is clear that the gap between the Old South and the North in the matter of industrialization did not arise from slavery or aristocratic disdain for "trade." Rather, it resulted from a rational estimate of profits on investment that induced planters to put their capital into agriculture rather than manufacturing.

SOCIAL DIVERSITY. The Old South's social system has also been misperceived. In the past, few scholars questioned the existence of a well-defined three-tiered society of rich planters, poor whites, and black slaves. But in reality each layer was far more complex than this view suggests.

The top layer was very thin indeed. In 1860 only 2,200 southerners owned 100 or more slaves, and these 2,200 made up less than 1 percent of the 383,000 slaveholding families in that year. The lordly domain, and the lordly planter aristocrat, was a rarity in the Old South.

The typical slaveholder was a member of the middle class. Seventy-one percent of slaveholders in 1860—almost 200,000—had fewer than 10 slaves. These farmers ate plain food and lived in houses that were little more than enlarged wood-frame structures or even modified log cabins. Although aspiring to wealth and gentility, they were often rough in their speech and in their ways.

Even more numerous were the white yeoman farmers who worked their acres themselves, helped by their grown sons and some occasional hired labor. As described by Professor Frank Owsley and his students, they were independent, democratic, and lived comfortably but simply.

The white yeomanry was particularly numerous in hilly upland regions and the "pine belts," away from the rich bottomland of the Mississippi, Tombigbee, Pearl, and other rivers where the great plantations flourished. The bottomland was both malarial and expensive and the yeomen gave it a wide berth. Yet even in the delta regions of Mississippi and Alabama, small farmers could be found.

The yeoman class was not without political power. Voting qualifications were almost as broad in the Old South as elsewhere in the country, and southern politicians had to heed the yeomen's wishes. Moreover, in some areas the yeoman-small planter class was able to manipulate election districts so that counties where the white population was proportionately greatest—and where the small farmers pre-dominated—could dominate the state legislatures.

But in revising the traditional view, we must not go too far. Wealth in the South was more concentrated than in the North. Few northern farms equaled the thousands of acres of some cotton plantations. Moreover, with a "prime" male field hand selling for about a thousand dollars in, say, 1850, any owner of a half dozen slaves was a wealthy person. If we include only nonslaveholders, southern yeomen were poorer than their northern counterparts.

Nor can we deny that there was a class of very poor rural southern whites. Where infertile soils and steep terrain made farming difficult, small groups of white families made a precarious living by growing corn, raising hogs, and hunting. These rural poor were often despised. Fanny Kemble, a visiting English actress, called them "the most degraded race of human beings claiming an Anglo-Saxon origin that can be found on the face of the earth." Kemble hated slavery and sought to demonstrate that it degraded whites as well as blacks. But it is clear that whether explained by slavery, isolation, nutritional diseases like pellagra, or natural selection, there was indeed a group of destitute whites who inhabited the rural nooks and crannies of pre-Civil War southern society.

We must also qualify Owsley's view of the Old South's yeoman democracy. Although the South's white farmers had to be heeded politically, they did not wield most of the region's political power. In the Carolinas, Georgia, Maryland, and Virginia voting was rigged in favor of the plantation areas. In the newer states slaveholders often enjoyed special advantages such as relatively low property taxes. And even where the yeomen made their numbers felt, the planter aristoc-racy often occupied positions of influence far beyond their formal power. Tal-ented sons of the yeomanry with political ambitions had to acquire land and slaves to succeed in public life.

The South's white, nonslaveholding yeomen often resented both slavery and planter leadership. Their spokesman was Hinton R. Helper of North Carolina, whose book, *The Impending Crisis of the South* (1857), is a blistering attack on the planter class. The planters, he claimed, had retarded the South's growth and op-pressed its yeomen. As a group, they were "so depraved that there . . . [was] scarcely a spark of honor or magnanimity to be found among them." Helper, like many whites of his class, also despised blacks, but he was willing to use fire to fight fire. To destroy the power of the planters, he proposed to rally the non-slaveholders against them—with the help, if need be, of the slaves.

✷ LIFE UNDER SLAVERY ✷

The black South too has long been covered by a thick crust of myths. The older legend depicts "happy darkies" singing in the fields. Lovable but childlike creatures, they did not feel the oppression of slavery the way white people would. Indeed, on a day-to-day basis, slavery was a rather benign institution, and mas-ters and slaves found it possible to develop mutual respect and to live comfort-ably with inequality. There is a newer picture that is the diametric opposite.

Slavery, it says, was a system of organized terror that either broke the spirit of black people or drove them to blind fury against their oppressors. Slaves were often whipped or maimed and were consigned to an incessant round of brutal, degrading labor. Worst of all, masters broke up the slaves' families and violated black women.

The truth is more complex than either description allows. Slave life was very diverse. Like most southern whites, most blacks were employed in agriculture. Only a small portion of the southern population in 1860 was urban, and only about 17 percent of the total city population of the slave states was black. Yet black urbanites provided the black community with much-needed leaders and were an important element in the general cultural life of cities such as New Orleans and Charleston.

This sketch by the English-born architect Benjamin Latrobe shows Virginia slaves working under the eye of an overseer. We are repelled by the arrogant and indolent pose of the overseer, a response that the artist, who hated slavery, was probably trying to encourage.

Most southern blacks were slaves; but on the eve of the Civil War about 250,000 (the same number as in the North) were free. Free blacks lived predominantly in the upper South. Many were urban. In 1860 Baltimore's free black population outnumbered its slaves ten to one; Washington, D.C., had over 9,000 free blacks and fewer than 1,800 slaves.

Wherever free blacks lived in the South, their lot, as in the North, was not enviable. A few were successful in business, the skilled trades, the professions, or agriculture. Some free blacks even owned slaves of their own, and a tiny number were planters with considerable property, including slaves. Most, however, were unskilled laborers who huddled in the slums of the large southern towns, worked at menial tasks, suffered the contempt of whites, and were denied fundamental civil rights.

The South's slaves numbered about 4 million in 1860, sixteen times the number of free blacks. The great majority worked the soil. Whereas whites were mostly associated with small farm units, almost three-fourths of the South's slaves were found on relatively large plantations.

Working on a large plantation had some advantages for slaves. Where there were many slaves, there were many different jobs. On the large plantations slave women found employment as seamstresses, cooks, nurses, or maids in the master's house; slave men worked as butlers, coachmen, and valets. Black house servants were not free, but they were the envy of other slaves. Their jobs kept them out of the fields and brought them into contact with the more interesting world of the "big house." It also enabled them to control their working conditions to some degree. Abusing a good cook or laundress might ruin dinner or make it impossible to get a clean shirt, after all. Even slaves who were not house servants enjoyed some advantages on large plantations. Besides working in the field, they might serve as drivers, skilled mechanics, or craftsmen. Because skilled workers were often hired out in towns and were sometimes allowed to negotiate their own terms of hire, these slaves were unusually free—for slaves.

Even the field hands on the large plantations were often better off than those on smaller establishments. It is true that the labor was intense. Worked in gangs under close supervision, the slaves were expected to be productive, and they were. The output per worker on large plantations was consistently higher than on small ones. Planters usually perceived that generosity was a more effective means to encourage hard work than force, and acted accordingly. But where an absentee master employed a white overseer to manage his plantation, slaves were sometimes treated more severely. Still, the overall estimate that the workload was seldom excessive on large plantations remains valid.

The physical comfort of slaves on large plantations was better than on small ones. Every slaveholder was interested in making money and understood that profits depended in part on maintaining a healthy, contented, well-nourished labor force. But only large plantations could provide medical services, weather-tight cabins, and the varied diet needed to maximize the efficiency of slave workers.

The one out of four slaves living on farms or small plantations no doubt had closer contact with the white owner and his family. They often ate at the same table with the master and sometimes even slept in the same cabin. But slaves who lived in such close quarters with their owners were constantly subject to white scrutiny, always made aware of their inferior social status, and had less opportunity to meet other blacks. In addition, small farmers were more likely to run into financial problems and be forced to sell their slaves. Blacks then faced the grim prospect that their families would be broken up.

SLAVE CULTURE.   We now know that slavery did not prevent the development of a distinctive black American culture. This culture achieved a remarkable flowering in music and oral literature particularly. Slaves sang about God and salvation, about their work, about love and passion, and about their daily lives. They composed humorous songs, bitter songs, and even rebellious songs that explicitly called for freedom. Talented black storytellers drew on the West African tradition of oral history, fable, and legend, combined it with Bible stories, and filled their tales with the animals and people of the southern environment. The stories, like the songs, often expressed the slaves' true feelings about their condition. One of the best-known group of tales featured Brer Rabbit, who manages to outwit stronger animals with his resourcefulness and trickery.

The slaves' religion helped them create a group identity. West Africans accepted a supreme God, though they did not think of him as a jealous, exclusive deity. This belief enabled transplanted slaves to accept the Christian faith of their European masters. Blacks found the enthusiastic Protestantism of the Baptists and Methodists especially congenial, though they never fully accepted the Protestant emphasis on guilt.

Observers of the Old South never failed to comment on the deep religious commitments of black men and women and often noted that their piety put their "betters" to shame. Southern whites generally welcomed these religious feelings, and many planters employed white ministers to preach to their slaves, who seized the chance to attend religious services on the plantation. In the towns they often went to white churches, though they had to sit in separate places in the back or in the gallery. But blacks preferred religious autonomy. Throughout the antebellum period black preachers, most of them self-taught, ministered to the needs of their people, sometimes in secret. During slave days, as in more recent years, black clergymen served as the social and political leaders of their people.

Masters hoped that slaves learned from Christianity the message of submission, obedience, and sobriety. Black Christianity actually had very different consequences. Like black music and literature, it helped preserve a sense of black independence. Blacks found in their version of Christianity a message of hope and freedom. The popularity of spirituals like "Go Down Moses" suggests how closely the slaves identified with the Children of Israel, enslaved in Egypt, and how eagerly they awaited liberation from bondage. Perceptive whites understood the subversive quality of black Christianity, and during times of slave unrest slaveowners often forbade religious meetings on the plantation.

Slavery, however lenient in some places and at certain times, remained grounded on coercion. Slaves were punished by having privileges withdrawn or extra work piled on. They were also subject to physical punishment. Slaves were flogged for stealing, for disobeying orders, for running away, for fighting and drinking. Young men were more likely to be lashed than other slaves, but no group was exempt from physical punishment. At times slaves were whipped without apparent cause. Mary Boykin Chesnut, wife of a South Carolina planter-politician, admitted that "men and women are punished when their masters and mistresses are brutes, not when they do wrong." Even slaves who were not themselves physically chastised were deeply affected by it; to witness grown men or women being flogged was an intimidating experience that drove home the lesson that the white owner was indisputable master.

SLAVERY AND THE FAMILY. One of the most affecting parts of Harriet Beecher Stowe's antislavery novel, *Uncle Tom's Cabin* (1852), is the description of how Arthur Shelby, a kindly Kentucky master, is forced to sell the little slave boy Harry to a coarse and brutal slavetrader in order to pay his debts. Harry's mother, Eliza, flees with him before the sale and mother and child escape to free territory across the ice-choked Ohio River. *American Slavery as It Is,* an important abolitionist tract, denounced slavery's disregard of black family life, its encouragement of moral laxity, and the opportunity it afforded for the sexual exploitation of black women.

Everything recorded in the antislavery tracts took place. Slave families were indeed broken up by sale; the experience of Eliza and Harry was not unique. The threat of separation was always a powerful weapon of social discipline. And slavery was at war with black family life in other ways. Nowhere in the Old South did the law recognize the sanctity of slave marriages; to have done so would have limited the power of slaveholders to dispose of slaves as they wished.

On the other hand, the picture is not totally bleak. Masters often found it advantageous to encourage strong marriage ties among their slaves because they reduced rivalries and made for a more efficient workforce. Generally speaking, slaves themselves preferred the married to the single state. But whether the initiative came from the master or from the slaves themselves, the result was a surprisingly large number of strong, loving, and permanent slave unions and stable slave families.

One of the most lurid charges leveled by abolitionists against the slave system is that it allowed white men to exploit black women sexually. There is truth to this accusation. Some slaveowners and white overseers had virtual harems. Less sensational, but more telling, the 1860 census records that 10 percent of the slave population had partly white ancestry. We must assume, given the disparity in power between white men and slave women, that the relationships that produced racially mixed offspring were frequently imposed on black women. Yet as Professor Eugene Genovese remarks: "Many white men who began by taking a black girl in an act of sexual exploitation ended by loving her and the children she bore. They were not supposed to, but they did. . . . "

Miscegenation—mating across racial lines—was rare on the well-run plantation, though less unusual in cities and towns. Wherever it took place, it was considered scandalous. Even a beloved black partner could never expect to be recognized and respected by the white community. Harmful to slave discipline and deeply resented by both slave men and women, it was also condemned by white society, which held that all sexual relations outside marriage were deplorable. Slave families, whose solidarity was formidable considering the trying conditions, were disrupted by the practice. White women, particularly, considered it a threat to their families, which explains why southern white women were often hostile to slavery. But miscegenation did take place, and it must be considered another count in the indictment of slavery.

THE "BOTTOM LINE" OF SLAVERY.   Slaves, then, were scarcely the "happy darkies" of myth. The most obvious evil of slavery was its denial of individual freedom. Ultimately, the slaves' lives were not their own. Slaves were not free to move. They could not withhold their labor or maximize the benefits from it. They could not express their personalities fully. The peculiar institution directly repudiated those sacred rights of life, liberty, and the pursuit of happiness that all Americans professed to cherish. Slaves knew of white America's professions, and the disparity between principles and performance undoubtedly made the pain of bondage all the greater.

And there was much else. Slavery provided no effective remedy for cruelty. There were laws against sadistic torture and mutilation of slaves; but the laws could not be easily enforced because the slave was a legal nullity who could not testify against whites in court. Masters might prefer to preserve slave families, but because nothing required them to do so, and they seldom kept families intact if it conflicted with their pressing financial interests. Slavery also denied black people the full use of their abilities. Opportunities to become drivers or to acquire some skill were no substitute for the ability to reach the highest reaches of business or the professions. In addition, it was illegal to teach slaves to read and write. Some masters ignored the law and themselves instructed their slaves to read or permitted literate blacks to teach their fellow bondsmen. Yet in 1860 more than nine out of ten slaves could not read, a condition that severely limited their access to many areas of knowledge and experience. When talented slaves like Josiah Henson, Solomon Northrup, and Frederick Douglass were free to tell their stories, they utterly condemned the system that denied them their humanity. Slavery, wrote Frederick Douglass in his Autobiography, "could and did develop all its malign and shocking characteristics." It was "indecent without shame, cruel without shuddering, and murderous without apprehension or fear of exposure, or punishment."

Finally, slavery reinforced racism. It was a mark of inferiority that affected all black men and women and did not disappear even when black people secured their freedom. Slavery accordingly amplified the original racial antipathies of white Americans and made black skin a stigma strong enough to survive even the destruction of the peculiar institution itself.

* THE SOUTHERN MIND *

Perhaps the most beguiling myth about the Old South is that it was a genial, cultivated society. The picture is not entirely false. Among the planters there were kindly and charming ladies and gentlemen who read the classics, appreciated music, and kept in touch with the best thought of England and Europe. The region also had many literate, upright yeomen whose natural dignity, independence, and generous hospitality would have warmed the heart of Jefferson. Nor were all southern whites hostile to change. The South, for example, joined the crusade against demon rum and against mistreatment of convicted felons. It was even a little ahead of the North in showing concern for the insane. During the 1820–1850 period, moreover, many southern states adopted the principle of universal white male suffrage. Yet by 1860 the white South had also become a land of fear and suspicion where dissent seemed treason and those who denied the region's superiority over all other societies were cruelly ostracized or brutally driven out. In such an atmosphere culture languished or became the servant of self-defense, and all chance of reform ended.

A classic Old South plantation house. This one is in Louisiana.

SLAVE REVOLTS.   The South's fears were directly related to slavery. Although most southerners refused to acknowledge that slavery was a cruel and exploitative system, many recognized that the slaves resented their bondage and would end it if they could. Slaves revealed their hatred of the system by the day-to-day resistance of ignoring directions, engaging in work slowdowns, abusing equipment, and running away. Occasionally a male slave would attack his master or overseer.

The most feared of all forms of slave resistance was the slave revolt, eruptions of collective racial violence that sent shock waves through white society. Several of these occurred in the Old South era. In 1800 a slave named Gabriel Prosser was foiled in his attempt to organize an army to capture the city of Richmond. A decade later, 500 slaves began a march on New Orleans and had to be dispersed by troops. In 1822 Denmark Vesey, a free black from Charleston, organized a slave insurrection that was betrayed by a slave. Vesey and thirty-four other blacks were hanged. Most frightening of all, however, was the Nat Turner uprising in the Virginia Tidewater in 1831. In late August, Turner, a slave foreman and preacher, aided by several other slaves, killed his owner and his owner's family. Then, with seventy fellow bondsmen gathered along the way, he marched through the countryside, killing and burning. Before the rebellion was put down by state and federal troops, over fifty whites had lost their lives. Most of Turner's band were either captured or killed in skirmishes with the soldiers during the first forty-eight hours, and thirteen slaves and three free blacks were later hanged. It took an additional two months to capture the resourceful Turner, who was then tried and executed.

Though slave revolts were far less common in the American South than in other New World slave societies, they revealed the true feelings of blacks in a particularly dramatic way and planted a chill in the hearts of white southerners. There were times when southerners seemed positively obsessed with the fear of a "servile insurrection" that might result in the mass destruction of white lives and property. This nervousness fed on itself; for each instance of actual slave unrest in the antebellum South, there were a hundred rumors of slave plots.

QUIETING THE OPPOSITION.   Occasionally, fears led to honest soul-searching among southerners. Soon after the suppression of Nat Turner's insurrection, when slavery had not yet become sacred and untouchable, the Virginia legislature conducted a frank debate on the possible abolition of slavery in the state. Some representatives, primarily from the state's western, nonslaveholding districts, attacked the peculiar institution as "offensive to the moral feelings of a large portion of the community," "ruinous to the whites," degrading to labor, and a danger to the social order of the South. In the end, unfortunately, the debate led nowhere; slavery in Virginia, as elsewhere, was by now so intertwined with the culture and economy of the community that to a majority of whites abolition seemed a cure worse than the disease.

This 1832 debate was the last serious public discussion of abolition in the South. Thereafter the response to slave unrest was unqualified repression. Laws requiring slaves to carry passes when they were away from their masters were more carefully enforced. The patrol system—posses of white men traveling about checking on slaves found off the plantation—was tightened. After 1832, in scores of southern communities, innocent slaves were jailed or even executed in panicky reaction to anticipated slave uprisings.

These fears cast a pall over the political and intellectual life of the South. Many southerners became convinced that the restlessness of the slaves was the work of outside agitators: free blacks, black merchant seamen, and above all, northern abolitionists. To deal with the problem southern legislatures passed laws that made manumission (the freeing of slaves by their owners) increasingly difficult, and restricted the rights and movements of free blacks. Several states even sought to expel free blacks from their limits. In Maryland and Missouri the state legislatures appropriated sums for the purpose of returning ("colonizing") free blacks to Africa. South Carolina tried to prevent slaves from being "contaminated" by black merchant seamen working for northern and foreign firms by forbidding black sailors to set foot on the state's soil.

The fiercest southern response was reserved for the abolitionists. Of all the outside groups that endangered the peace and safety of the South, they seemed the worst. Governor John Floyd of Virginia accused these "unrestrained fanatics" of fomenting the Nat Turner revolt. Other southerners called them "a pestilent sect," "ignorant and infatuated barbarians." Even though they were federal employees, postmasters throughout the South refused to deliver abolitionist newspapers and books. When antislavery activists denounced this as censorship of the mails, Postmaster General Amos Kendall, a Kentuckian by adoption, refused to intervene. "We owe an obligation to the laws," he conceded, but "we owe a higher one to the communities in which we live."

De facto censorship of the mails was the mildest of the South's efforts to preserve its system by cutting off the free exchange of ideas. After the Virginia debate of 1832 the subject of abolition was considered closed. Almost everywhere in the slave states toleration for social and intellectual dissent weakened. White southerners who refused to go along with the majority view, such as James G. Birney of Alabama, the Grimké sisters of South Carolina, and Cassius M. Clay of Kentucky, were denounced, threatened, and eventually driven from the South. Southern leaders sought to suppress abolitionist agitation elsewhere as well. In 1836, as we have seen, the southern delegation in Congress, annoyed at the barrage of petitions asking for abolition of slavery in the District of Columbia, induced the House of Representatives to adopt a rule automatically laying such petitions "on the table" without action. This "gag rule" remained in force for eight years despite attacks by antislavery advocates and civil liberties champions, who assailed it as a denial of free speech and a violation of the constitutional right of petition.

ARGUMENTS IN FAVOR OF SLAVERY. The South also mounted a counterattack against its critics that produced some interesting—and generally deplorable—results. In the eighteenth century, southerners seldom defended slavery in the abstract. Indeed, they often conceded that, ideally speaking, slavery was a violation of human rights. Its ultimate justification was necessity: The South could not survive without black laborers, and as it was unthinkable that blacks could be anything but social and economic subordinates, they must remain slaves. However unavoidable, slavery seemed clearly wrong to many thoughtful southerners during these years.

After about 1800, however, southern leaders and publicists ceased to question the institution of slavery and began to defend it. Slavery, they said, was sanctioned by the Bible and the Christian faith. In the Old Testament God made Ham, the second son of Noah, into a servant of his two brothers. Ham's descendants, the dark races, must therefore serve the light-skinned progeny of Shem and Japheth. The New Testament enjoined "servants" to be obedient and dutiful to their masters. It is difficult to tell how seriously white southerners took the biblical defense of slavery. It was possible to extract other meanings from the Bible, as both black and white abolitionists had reason to know. For those already disposed to defend the peculiar institution on more practical grounds, it was nevertheless comforting to have the Scriptures' reinforcement.

The most sophisticated proslavery argument, however, was sociological. In the writings of Virginian George Fitzhugh, slavery was converted from a necessary evil to a "positive good." Fitzhugh considered the North's vaunted freedom a failure. It had not brought comfort and security to the white masses: It had brought them slums, social dislocation, and "wage slavery." By rejecting egalitarianism and individualism and accepting the idea of social hierarchy, the South had avoided the cruelty of a competitive society. Slaves, unlike free white laborers, were not tossed on the human rubbish heap after they had ceased being useful to their employers. The South, moreover, was free of such intellectual and moral taints as Mormonism, Perfectionism, Fourierism, trade unionism, and other disgusting and deplorable consequences of freedom. "In the whole South," Fitzhugh proclaimed, "there is not one Socialist, not one man rich or poor, proposing to subvert and reconstruct society."

Fitzhugh's attack on northern society and its turbulent democracy quickly became a commonplace of southern opinion. It was repeated by Calhoun on the floor of the Senate. It filled the pages of newspapers, books, and pamphlets, and was heard from pulpits throughout Dixie. Senator James Hammond of South Carolina gave it classic form in his famous speech of 1858, in which he declared that there had to be a "mud sill" upon which to erect a civilized, cultured life. This mud sill was a class "to do the menial duties, to perform the drudgery of life . . . a class requiring but a low order of intellect and but little skill." Far better, said Hammond, that these people be black, as in the South, than white, as in the North.

ROMANCE AND CULTURE. The need to justify the South's way of life profoundly affected southern culture and social values. Influenced by the novels of Sir Walter Scott, literate southerners came to equate their society with the rigidly ordered and conservative social systems of medieval Europe. Southerners of the best sort, they asserted, were true gentlemen whose forebears were the cavaliers who fled England after the defeat of Charles I by the Puritan Cromwell. They were, claimed one Alabaman, "directly descended from the Norman Barons of William the Conqueror, a race distinguished . . . for its warlike and fearless character, a race at all times . . . renowned for its gallantry, chivalry, honor, gentleness and intellect. . . . " Northerners, by contrast, were descended from Cromwell's Puritan Roundheads, people without breeding or gentility who, to top it all, exhibited the "severe traits of religious fanaticism."

This romantic fantasy permeated upper-class southern life. In the Old South's cultural imagination, plantations became feudal manors, planters became chivalrous knights, slaves became respectful serfs. Southerners came to idealize the warrior virtues. They esteemed horsemanship and adopted fox hunting as a plantation sport. They held medieval tournaments where young gallants jousted for prizes while lovely belles showered them with roses from the sidelines. In time only a military career could compete with planting as a proper calling for a gentleman.

Upper-class southern women were an essential part of the cult of chivalry. Southern "ladies" were placed on pedestals and treated with elaborate gallantry and outward deference. But the southern white woman's life was often quite different. Most were not plantation mistresses, but the wives and daughters of common farmers. There was little pampering or chivalry in the lives of these women. And even the mistress of a great plantation often worked hard. Managing a large household and many house slaves was a complex and demanding job full of emotional turmoil. The house slaves were often "part of the family" and the tension between women's familial feelings for their servants and their need to exploit them for their own comfort was evident in the diaries of southern ladies. Meanwhile, the myth of female helplessness and need for protection limited the freedom and autonomy of southern white women even more than "women's sphere" restricted their contemporary northern sisters.

It is not surprising that the forces that encouraged the flowering of this elaborate social mythology tended to stifle artistic growth in the antebellum period. William Gilmore Simms and Edgar Allan Poe aside, few southern writers rose above mediocrity. After Thomas Jefferson's death in 1826 there were few creative southern architects. All the important American painters of the antebellum years either were northerners or lived in the North or Europe. Although many popular songs—like Stephen Foster's "Swanee River," "My Old Kentucky Home," "Old Black Joe," and "De Camptown Races"—had southern themes, the composers, including Foster himself, were mostly northerners. Even the minstrel show, which fused theater, comedy, and music into a unique form of entertainment, was basically a northern white commercialization of southern black folk culture and owed little to the white South.

Southern defensiveness also affected intellectual life. On the whole, the colleges and universities of the Old South were not great centers of learning, though for a while, in the 1830s, the best university in the country was Jefferson's University of Virginia, and South Carolina College had the most distinguished social science faculty. Many young southerners at the time went to Harvard, Yale, or Princeton. By the 1850s the growing fear of dissent had brought hundreds of southern students back home. The increasing restrictions on free inquiry meanwhile drove such interesting social thinkers as Francis Lieber of South Carolina College and Henry Harrisse of the University of North Carolina to move north. Harrisse, before his departure, trenchantly attacked the intellectual intolerance he saw all around him.

> You may eliminate all the suspicious men from your institutions of learning, you may establish any number of new colleges which will relieve you of sending your sons to free institutions. But as long as people study, and read, and think among you, the absurdity of your system will be discovered and there will always be found some courageous intelligence to protest against your hateful tyranny.

By contrast with the fertile, innovative contemporary North, the South, then, was a cultural backwater. It was a region turned inward and intent on building up a false self-image and a false self-confidence.

SOUTHERN POLITICAL IDEOLOGY. Yet defensiveness has its uses. Southerners were able to detect the flaws in the individualistic, tumultuous society of the North and raise questions about democratic political assumptions. This conservative critique was a defense mechanism, but it called attention to the inconsistencies and hypocrisies of free society.

Southerners seriously questioned majoritarian democracy. Although most southern states had established universal white male suffrage, some of the most articulate southerners continued to doubt the wisdom of voter majorities. Pure and simple majority rule was obviously a disadvantage to the South. If mere numbers were considered in making national political decisions, the South would be consigned to certain defeat. Well before 1860 it had fallen behind the North in population and hence in congressional representation. Sectional parity had been maintained in the United States Senate, if not in the House, by admitting into the Union one slave state for each free one. But almost certainly more free than slave states would eventually be carved out of the western territories; and when this took place, the South would lose its fragile political equality with the North in Congress.

Southerners worried about their section's decline and sought to discover its causes. A number, including J. D. B. De Bow, William Gregg, and Edmund Ruffin, concluded (contrary to fact) that the cause was slow economic growth owing to the South's vassalage to the North. During the late 1830s, when southern political victory had removed the tariff from center stage, the attack shifted to the North's commercial dominance. According to the apostles of sectional commercial independence, virtually every aspect of the South's economy except the raising of crops was controlled by northern business interests. Much of the South's shipping was done in northern vessels. Almost all imports came through New York, and until the 1850s even the cotton crop generally went to New York before being shipped to Europe. Northern capitalists and their agents also controlled most of the South's banking. Northern cotton "factors" (agents) residing in the South dominated agriculture, extending credit to planters and farmers, sending crops to market, and buying supplies their customers wanted.

The picture of northern dominance painted by the critics was exaggerated. Not all the South's business was handled by outsiders; the section produced a substantial crop of home-grown merchants, bankers, and manufacturers who often combined town business with plantation ownership. Yet most southerners assumed northern dominance, chafed under it, and periodically determined to end it. Gregg, a successful textile magnate, constantly urged his fellow southerners to invest their capital in manufactures to make their section independent of the North and Europe. The publicist and editor De Bow used his *Review* to call for southern economic independence. "Action, Action, Action!!!" the *Review* demanded. "Not in the rhetoric of Congress, but in the busy hum of mechanism, and the thrifty operators of the hammers and anvil." Ruffin condemned southern farming practices and advocated improved agricultural methods to stem the flow of yeomen from the South and to help equalize free- and slave-state populations.

Beginning in 1837, southern merchants and publicists convened in various cities to consider ways to liberate their section from its supposed economic bondage to the North. Delegates discussed at great length how to end "the abject state of colonial vassalage" to the North by such devices as direct shipping of cotton to Europe from southern ports. The conventions achieved few concrete results, but they were effective forums for the display of antinorthern feelings. Toward the end of the 1850s, when sectional antagonisms exploded, the conventions went on record against northern books, magazines, and teachers and passed resolutions demanding the reopening of the transatlantic slave trade, which had been closed since 1808.

The growing imbalance of population and potential power between the two sections of the country was an unpleasant fact of life that southerners had to face. How could the South remain a part of the Union and, as the weaker partner, defend its unique and controversial interests?

This problem obsessed John C. Calhoun in his later years. During the tariff crisis of 1831–1832 Calhoun had resurrected the theory of nullification first raised in the 1790s as part of the Kentucky Resolution. But nullification seemed more and more inadequate. Between the 1830s and his death in 1850, the South Carolinian sought a new formula to protect his section's minority interests. In a succession of treatises, speeches, and letters, Calhoun's solution evolved into a critique of the democratic concepts of the age. People were not all equal, he concluded. The Declaration of Independence expressed a noble theory, but an invalid one. The best societies, like those of classical Greece and Rome, recognized the inherent inequality of human beings and exploited the inferior groups to construct great civilizations. If people were unequal, it stood to reason that some should lead and others follow; otherwise the inferior many would impose their will on the superior few and the result would be a tyranny of the ignorant. In the United States, a despotism of numbers would result in sectional oppression: The North with its greater population would trample on the rights of the South.

How could those rights be protected? A "concurrent majority" was Calhoun's solution. Before any law that vitally concerned the interests of either section went into effect, let it be ratified by both sections of the country. This arrangement could be guaranteed by a dual presidency, with one president selected by the

North and the other by the South. Both would have to approve any important measure passed by Congress before it became law. In this way the South could exercise a veto over a domineering North and check the normal tendency of a majority to ride roughshod over the rights of a minority.

John C. Calhoun died before the inner logic of his theories was expressed in deeds. He had not wished to see the Union destroyed; he hoped to preserve it by finding an accommodation with which the South could live. It is fitting, however, that when the people of Charleston received news of South Carolina's secession from the Union in 1860, they unfurled a banner bearing Calhoun's image.

✳ CONCLUSIONS ✳

The Old South was not a moonlight and magnolias society; it was too diverse for that. The happy harmony of that fabled state was marred by regional, class, and economic divisions. The South was not all multi-acred delta estates. It consisted of small farms in the back country and the mountain regions and poor whites living from hand to mouth by grazing, hunting, and foraging. Though upper-class southerners sought to create a fantasy land of medieval chivalry, they were at best marginally successful. The Old South was ruled by a planter elite, but only with the consent of a substantial yeomanry and through the mechanism of universal white male suffrage. And even the life of the planter was not what the South's spokesmen and writers sought to make it. Under the veneer of an aristocratic indifference to money was the firm reality of hard striving and profit maximizing that made the chivalrous pose possible.

The Old South, despite its economic success, was not a serene and confident society. Even if it was not solely the land of "the whip and the lash" as depicted by its opponents, it lived on the coerced labor of millions of black men, women, and children. Most of these slaves were able to accommodate to the system. They managed to snatch some satisfactions from the life of bondage and maintain a degree of personal and cultural autonomy. Yet there was some basis for the fear of white southerners that they lived on the edge of a social volcano that could erupt at any time. The fear begat a degree of defensiveness that imposed conformity and intolerance of change and dissent.

To the very end of the slave era southerners would continue to share with other Americans memories, political values, and cultural attributes. Yet with each passing year the South diverged more and more from the liberal mainstream of the United States and the values of the Atlantic world. Before long many southerners would consider themselves people with distinct interests and a separate destiny. The consequences would be tragic.

14

THE COMING OF THE CIVIL WAR

What Caused the Division?

1780	Pennsylvania becomes the first state to prohibit slavery
1787	The Northwest Ordinance prohibits slavery north of the Ohio River and west of Pennsylvania
1812	Louisiana is admitted into the Union as a slave state
1820	The Missouri Compromise
1832–34	The South Carolina nullification crisis
1839	Antislavery leaders found the Liberty party
1846	Congressional debate on the Wilmot Proviso worsens sectional controversy
1848	The California Gold Rush; Formation of the Free-Soil party; Zachary Taylor elected president
1850	The Compromise of 1850, including passage of the Fugitive Slave Act
1852	Harriet Beecher Stowe's *Uncle Tom's Cabin*, published; Franklin Pierce elected president
1854	The Kansas–Nebraska Act; The Republican party is formed by antislavery Whigs and Democrats
1856	John Brown murders five proslavery settlers in Kansas; James Buchanan elected president
1857	Dred Scott decision; Buchanan accepts Kansas; fraudulent constitution
1858	The Lincoln–Douglas debates focus national attention on the Illinois election for United States Senator
1859	John Brown's raid on Harpers Ferry
1860	The Democratic party breaks up at its national convention; Abraham Lincoln is nominated by the Republican national convention, and elected president
1860–61	South Carolina, Georgia, Louisiana, Mississippi, Florida, Alabama, and Texas secede from the Union

| 1861 | Delegates of six seceded states adopt a constitution and elect Jefferson Davis president; Lincoln says the federal government will hold its property in the South; Confederates fire on Union-held Fort Sumter; Arkansas, North Carolina, Virginia, and Tennessee secede |

The Civil War was the greatest crisis that ever befell the United States, the only one that threatened its very survival. No sooner had the fighting broken out than thoughtful citizens on both sides urgently asked: Why? Why had a union so promising, so prosperous, so self-confident, so triumphant, come to this terrible state? Students of American history still ponder the question today.

* A HOUSE DIVIDING *

On the eve of the American Revolution an outspoken Massachusetts citizen would not have felt seriously out of place in the social or intellectual environment of South Carolina. Similarly, southerners visiting the North could speak their minds without shocking or offending their hosts. North and South in, say, 1770 were not so far apart in their economic or labor systems. Agriculture was the chief occupation of all Americans from New Hampshire to Georgia by a wide margin. Slavery existed in every colony. There were more slaves in the South, but a considerable part of the workforce north of the Mason-Dixon Line were half-free indentured servants. By 1800 even the religious differences that had separated Puritan New England from the Anglican South had receded as both regions felt the effects of evangelical revivalism and the breakdown of established churches.

Then, in the generation and a half following the War of 1812, differences between North and South multiplied. As we saw in Chapters 9 and 12, the North began to industrialize and evolve into an open, culturally diverse society. The South, meanwhile, confirmed its stake in plantation agriculture and embraced the social conformity and defensiveness described in Chapter 13. These structural differences were essential elements in sectional estrangement, but they are abstract and tell us little about the texture and daily reality of North–South conflict.

IDEOLOGICAL DIFFERENCES. We must not exaggerate the sectional contrasts. Both North and South were complex societies with a variety of dissenters from the prevailing orthodoxies. Only a minority of northerners were abolitionists, transcendentalists, or Perfectionists; many considered such people meddlers or fanatics. And the North was full of "doughfaces"—"northern men with southern principles"—who supported the South's positions in the emerging sectional debates. Even the conformist South was not homogeneous. Southerners such as J. B. D. De Bow and William Gregg urged their section to emulate the North's success in commerce and manufacturing, while among the small farmers in the upland regions and the backcountry were those who despised both slavery and the slaveholding class.

Yet there gradually emerged two distinct sectional outlooks, which each year grew further apart and more militant and antagonistic. Southern political and intellectual leaders increasingly glorified a society based on slavery, condemned dissent, rejected commercial values, endorsed inequality, and resisted social change. It became ever more difficult as the years passed for dissenters to defy the overwhelming weight of sectional opinion.

The North also adopted distinctive guiding beliefs in these years, though more slowly and never so universally as the South. The heart of the emerging northern ethos was freedom, though this term meant different things to different people. To northern reformers it meant freedom to engage in social experiment. To northern intellectuals it meant freedom to speculate and criticize. To northern manufacturers it meant freedom from government control, though not exemption from government aid. To northern farmers it meant freedom to take up cheap land in the West. To northern wage earners it meant freedom to move wherever opportunity offered and to advance in life. Northern opinion leaders and officials never attempted to impose these sentiments on the people. Nevertheless, the whole thrust of northern society created an increasing agreement on the importance of "free" values and attitudes, especially in contrast to the South and what it represented.

ECONOMIC CONFLICT. The widening gap between the northern and southern value systems has been seen as a reflection of competing economies: northern commerce and industry versus southern agriculture. There is no question that the differing economic interests of the antebellum North and South pushed them into political conflict along a wide front. We saw in Chapter 10 how, during Jackson's presidency, the northern-sponsored tariff provoked the South into angry reaction that threatened the Union. In 1846 southern political leaders were able to secure the Walker Tariff lowering duties on imported goods and the tariff of 1857 reducing rates still further. By the eve of the Civil War the tariff had become a hot political issue in Pennsylvania and New England; this time it was northern groups that felt aggrieved.

Nor was the tariff the only economic issue dividing the sections. Northern commercial interests favored federal subsidies to the American merchant marine to enable it to compete with foreign carriers; southerners saw little benefit to themselves in such measures and opposed paying the taxes required. Northern merchants and manufacturers favored federal appropriations for dredging rivers and harbors to improve navigation; southerners, believing that they would benefit from such measures less than northerners, fought the appropriations.

But the two most important economic issues disturbing the sectional waters during the generation preceding 1860 were a Pacific railroad and a homestead act. By the 1850s most Americans, North and South, endorsed building a railroad to connect the settled and developed portions of the United States with the newly acquired Mexican Cession and the Pacific Coast. The location, however, triggered sharp sectional controversy. Southerners wanted to link New Orleans with San

Diego or Memphis with San Francisco. Northerners demanded a route farther north to connect the Great Lakes with either San Francisco or Puget Sound.

Building a railroad across hundreds of miles of empty country required a large federal subsidy but the sectional bickering produced an impasse. In 1853, Mississippian Jefferson Davis, secretary of war in the pro-southern administration of Franklin Pierce, arranged to buy a 30,000-square-mile slice of northern Mexico. The move in part derived from southern yearning for more real estate. But the Gadsden Purchase also contained within its limits one of the better passes through the Rocky Mountains and was intended to improve the chances of a southern route for a Pacific railroad. The scheme did not work as intended. After the United States acquired the property, northern congressmen vetoed the route. Southerners, in turn, were able to frustrate the choice of a central or northern connection.

The two sections also battled over a homestead bill. Many ordinary southerners were interested in acquiring free farms in the West, and some southern political leaders responded by favoring a homestead act. A more substantial portion of southern opinion feared that free land would draw farmers from the South to regions where slavery could not take root and so benefit the free states. In the 1854 debate over a homestead bill, one southern congressman insisted bluntly that the proposed legislation was "tinctured with Abolitionism." Eventually, in 1860, a coalition of northeastern and northwestern congressmen passed a homestead measure over the opposition of a virtually united South. President James Buchanan, a "northern man with southern principles," vetoed it.

THE ROLE OF SLAVERY.　These clashes over economic policies are not sufficient, however, to explain why the sections eventually came to blows. Not all the battling over tariffs, railroad subsidies, and internal improvements pitted the sections against one another. Often the divisions were within each section, not between them. Furthermore, sectional conflict over economic policy had raged before 1840 and would continue after 1865; yet only after 1848 did divisive forces actually threaten the Union. In the nullification crisis of 1832, the Tariff of Abominations failed to arouse strong disunionist sentiment outside of South Carolina. A generation later eleven states left the Union when confronted with a similar threat to the South's "rights." Clearly, in the decade following the Mexican War, the bonds among the slave states grew stronger while those attaching them to the Union as a whole weakened. It was only in the decade following the Mexican War that grievances were converted to outrage and outrage to secession. What events and forces reinforced southern cohesion and loosened the South's ties to the rest of the nation?

✻ THE DILEMMA OF TERRITORIAL EXPANSION ✻

The country's territorial expansion was a critical element in the snowballing North–South struggle. If the nation had not confronted the question of slavery extension after 1846, the sections might have remained at peace. But it was not to be. In the past, as the country added new territory it became necessary to redraw the boundary between slavery and freedom first established by state emancipation acts and by the

Northwest Ordinance of 1787 (slavery excluded from the Northwest), and the Southwest Ordinance of 1790 (slavery allowed in the Southwest). Slavery already existed in parts of the Louisiana Purchase when the United States bought it in 1803. Then, in 1819-1820, as we saw, another part of the Louisiana Purchase, Missouri Territory, was admitted to the Union as a slave state, while the remainder of the purchase was divided by Congress along the line of 36°30' north latitude into slave and free regions.

THE WILMOT PROVISO. As of 1820 the whole of the existing United States had been assigned to one labor system or the other either by Congress or by individual states themselves. For the next fifteen years the territorial limits of slavery ceased to trouble Americans very much. Then, in 1835, Texas revived the issue. Many opponents of annexation, feared that admitting Texas to the Union would tip the balance in favor of slavery. Southerners, on the other hand, considered admission of Texas "as indispensable to their security." Despite much northern opposition, Texas was admitted to the Union in 1845.

The events of 1846–1848 reopened the slavery extension issue with a vengeance. Besides Oregon, the United States acquired by conquest the vast Mexican Cession in the far Southwest. While many southern leaders considered the region uncongenial to slavery, they railed against the idea that slavery should be arbitrarily excluded by law from a region that had been won by the exertions of an army two-thirds of whose volunteers came from slave states. When, in August 1846, only three months into the Mexican War, Democratic Congressman David Wilmot of Pennsylvania submitted a resolution requiring that a "fundamental condition" of acquiring "any territory from the Republic of Mexico" be that "neither slavery nor involuntary servitude shall ever exist in any part of said territory," he triggered a political explosion.

Wilmot belonged to a group of northern Democrats hostile to the Polk administration for its sacrifice of northern interests by supporting tariff reduction, surrendering half of the Oregon region to the British, and vetoing rivers and harbors improvement legislation. The South, they feared, totally controlled the Democratic party, treating its northern members as outcasts. Some of this same group felt that Martin Van Buren, the former president, had deserved the party presidential nomination in 1844, and resented the desertion of their hero by southern Democrats in favor of Polk.

The Wilmot Proviso produced a fever of sectional excitement. The aging Calhoun countered the proviso with resolutions denying that Congress had the power to exclude slavery from the territories. Southerners were soon denouncing the North. The "madmen of the North and the Northwest have . . . cast the die," proclaimed the *Richmond Enquirer,* "and numbered the days of the glorious Union." On the other side, every northern legislature but one endorsed the proviso. By solid northern votes, both Whig and Democrat, the House passed the proviso, but it was kept from coming to a vote in the Senate. In February 1847 the House once more approved it, but then, under administration pressure, a contingent of northern Democrats reconsidered, and the bill was defeated.

The issue of slavery or freedom in the Mexican Cession territory remained very much alive, with public opinion divided into several distinct positions. Many northerners continued to favor total exclusion of slavery from the newly acquired

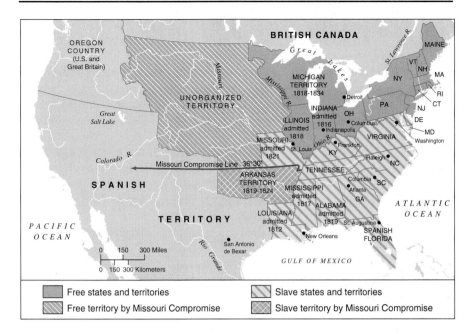

The Missouri Compromise, 1820

region. Northern and southern moderates endorsed extending the Missouri Compromise 36°30' line to the Pacific Coast to separate slavery from freedom. Calhoun and his supporters demanded that slaveholders have equal access to all the territories. The southern elder statesman considered it a matter of life or death for the South. "If we flinch we are gone," he wrote a friend.

A new compromise position soon emerged that middle-of-the-road politicians rushed to support. "Popular sovereignty" proposed "leaving to the people of the territory to be acquired, the business of settling the matter [of slavery] for themselves." The scheme appealed to many Americans as an expression of grassroots democracy: Let the people of the local community, rather than Congress, decide. But the details were not so clear. When would the people decide? When the territory entered as a state? During the territorial stage by vote of the territorial legislature? And did popular sovereignty supersede Congressional enactment regarding slavery in the territories entirely? All this was puzzling. But its very ambiguity was the great virtue of the formula: It could please many people simultaneously and give the appearance of agreement when there really was none.

FREE SOIL. Slavery extension inevitably colored the 1848 presidential campaign. Within both the Whig and Democratic parties there was a range of views from pro-Wilmot Proviso, through popular sovereignty, to the Calhounite position. The Whigs nominated as their candidate "Old Rough and Ready," Zachary Taylor, the hero of Buena Vista, and eschewed a party platform entirely. The antislavery "conscience Whig" faction denounced the choice of Taylor, a slaveholder, as an alliance between the "lords of the lash" (the southern planters) and the "lords of the loom" (the New England textile manufacturers).

The Democrats' differences over slavery extension were amplified by the split in the large New York delegation between the Barnburners, who opposed southern dominance in the party, and the Hunkers, who favored conciliating the South. The Barnburners were also loyal followers of Van Buren; the Hunkers his enemy. When the presidential nominating convention refused to exclude their Hunker opponents, the Barnburners left in a huff and nominated Van Buren in a separate convention. Meanwhile, led by southern and western moderates, the regular Democratic convention chose Lewis/Cass of Michigan on a vague slavery plank that satisfied virtually no one. When the convention voted down the proposal by Alabaman William Lowndes Yancey endorsing southern rights in the territories, Yancey too walked out.

A third political group soon began to coalesce out of the discontented pro-Wilmot Proviso elements of both parties, joined with the minuscule Liberty party. Formed in 1839 by abolitionists, the Liberty party had nominated Senator John P. Hale of New Hampshire on a platform that demanded prohibition of slavery wherever federal power over the institution extended. Its leaders soon arranged a coalition with the Van Burenites that promised to combine Van Buren's vote-getting power with a strong platform against slavery extension. Meeting at Buffalo in August 1848, the rebels nominated Van Buren for president with Charles Francis Adams, son of the sixth president, as his running mate. The new Free-Soil party adopted a platform calling for "free soil, free speech, free labor, and free men."

The new party covered a range of positions. A minority were outright abolitionists who hoped to see slavery ended throughout the United States. A larger group was more interested in preserving the territories for free labor than destroying slavery in the South. Their position was summarized by Senator Preston King of New York: "If slavery is not excluded by law" from the national territories, he declared, "the presence of the slave will exclude the laboring white man." Yet many delegates at Buffalo saw the free-soil position as the first step toward ending slavery and left Buffalo convinced that the new party's showing in the fall would mark the start of slavery's downfall.

Unfortunately, the slaves' deliverance would have to wait until a later day. Taylor achieved an electoral as well as a popular majority, doing particularly well in the South. Van Buren won only a meager 300,000 votes, 14 percent of the northern popular vote. But the Free-Soil campaign was a portent. The new organization elected ten members to Congress, who would be outspoken antislavery advocates in the bitter debates just ahead. It also broke new political ground. Most northern voters were not yet ready for a single-issue, purely sectional, party, but the outlines of such an organization were now coming into view.

GOLD IN CALIFORNIA.   Though a southerner and a slaveholder, as president, Zachary Taylor proved to be a bulwark of the Union.

The immediate problem was California. In January 1848 a laborer working for John Augustus Sutter, a Swiss businessman long settled in the Mexican province, found gold while constructing a water mill channel near Sacramento. Sutter tried to keep the discovery a secret, but the news soon leaked out. In December, after California was safely American, President Polk confirmed the lucky strike in his annual message to Congress, setting off a stampede to the gold fields. By the early months of 1849 over sixty ships packed with gold seekers were on their way to the Pacific Coast by way of Cape Horn or Panama. In the spring thousands of others set out overland on the California Trail established by settlers earlier in the decade.

The forty-niners were usually disappointed. Hundreds sickened and died aboard ship or along the trail. By the fall, the route across the plains was lined with the skeletons of horses and cattle and the graves of gold seekers. Among those who reached the diggings, few struck it rich. Some gave up and straggled home. Others settled down in the new country to farm, labor, keep store, or practice professions. By mid-1849 thousands of people from every state, section, race, and nationality had made California their home,

President Taylor understood that California would soon need some better form of government than the existing military regime. He also saw that allowing a lengthy territorial phase to precede statehood was potentially disruptive, for it would permit the free-soil forces in Congress to raise the Wilmot Proviso issue once again. To avoid another bitter debate over slavery in the territories, the president urged the Californians, and also the residents of New Mexico, to apply directly for admission to the Union as states. The Californians quickly complied under a constitution that excluded slavery. New Mexico, more sparsely settled and in turmoil over its Texas boundary, failed to heed his call.

Taylor's scheme offended the proslavery forces. California's admission as a free state would give the North a majority in the Senate. The change would be largely symbolic, but it seemed a dangerous precedent. "Our only safety," announced Southern firebrand James Hammond, "is in equality of POWER." Responding to the perceived danger, southern extremists called for a convention to meet in Nashville in June 1850 to discuss southern rights and consider the possibility of secession from the Union.

DIVISIVE ISSUES IN CONGRESS.   California was not the only sectional friction point in 1850. Opponents of slavery for years had demanded that the capital of the nation not be disgraced by the presence of slave pens and auction blocks. For their part, southerners fumed over "personal liberty laws," attempts by northern states to nullify the federal fugitive slave law of 1793 by forbidding state officials to help federal authorities capture southern runaway slaves. Many of these escapees were actually aided by northern abolitionists through the "underground railroad," a network of houses, barns, and cellars stretching from slave territory to Canada, where slaves could hide while escaping to freedom. In truth, probably no more than a thousand slaves a year ever escaped to freedom, but many southerners believed that their countrymen in the North were scheming to destroy slavery by attrition.

Texas, too, figured in the reemerging sectional conflict. It claimed part of eastern New Mexico, and militant southern rights advocates supported the new slave state's claim, while Free-Soilers opposed it. Moreover, the Lone Star State had joined the union with millions of dollars of unpaid public debts. Texas's creditors included some leading politicians and businessmen, many open to any deal that would protect their interests.

Finally, there was the status of New Mexico. That vast region was not really ready for statehood, but it too needed some sort of government. Should Congress decide the slave question while the region was still in a territorial stage? Or should some version of the popular-sovereignty formula be applied?

THE COMPROMISE OF 1850.   Fortunately for the Union, two Senate leaders—Henry Clay of Kentucky and Stephen Douglas of Illinois—quickly took matters in hand and forged a sectional armistice.

In his seventies, Clay did not intend to see his beloved Union torn apart. Across the Senate aisle, on the Democratic side, was another devoted unionist, Stephen A. Douglas of Illinois. Thirty-seven years old, Douglas was at the prime of his career. Historians have often judged this stubby, dynamic man an opportunist, but events would show that the ambitious "Little Giant" sincerely loved the Union and, when necessary, would put its welfare before his own. In their effort to prevent a disruptive sectional showdown, Clay and Douglas would have the help of Daniel Webster, the Whig elder statesman from Massachusetts.

Most members of the Thirtieth Congress desired a peaceful settlement, but several took positions that made a confrontation unavoidable. On the extreme southern side, looming above the rest, was the ailing John Calhoun, a fierce partisan for his beloved South. On the militant northern side were Senators Salmon Chase of Ohio and Charles Sumner of Massachusetts, both newcomers and ardent Free-Soilers, and the former Whig governor of New York, the diminutive, affable, cigar-smoking William Henry Seward. The veteran Seward was a militant antislavery man who seemed more devoted to freedom than the Union.

In the end, the Union cause proved stronger than southern rights, antislavery, or free soil. In January 1850 Clay presented a set of proposals to the U.S. Senate designed to settle all outstanding sectional issues simultaneously. His package included eight resolutions. Six were paired, half to satisfy the North, half to please the South. California was to be admitted to the Union as a free state; the rest of the Mexican Cession would be organized as territories "without . . . any restriction or condition on the subject of slavery." Texas was to surrender its boundary claims in New Mexico, and the federal government would assume its public debt. The slave trade in the District of Columbia would be ended; slavery itself in the District would be made inviolate. Two final resolutions favored the South: Congress would never interfere with the interstate slave trade; it would enact a more effective fugitive slave law. Under the urging of friends, Clay agreed to combine his proposals into a single "omnibus" bill.

It soon became clear that the Clay bill would not win easy support. The venerable Calhoun was too feeble to address the Senate himself, but he denounced

Stephen Douglas, the "Little Giant," sought to prevent southern secession by endorsing the principle of popular sovereignty. Although "the great persuader" managed a compromise in 1850, southern and northern Democrats were unwilling to allow the question of slavery to be resolved by popular votes in each new state. (Courtesy of National Portrait Gallery, Smithsonian Institution, Washington, D.C.)

the Clay proposals through a Virginia colleague while he, wrapped in flannels to keep his ravaged frame warm, looked on from the Senate floor. Northern aggressiveness was dividing the Union, Calhoun charged, and the only way to save it was to guarantee the South's right to veto unfriendly northern action. William Seward spoke for the militant northern side. Clay's compromise was "radically wrong and essentially vicious" for it failed to check slavery extension. The Constitution sanctioned excluding slavery from the territories, but beyond the Constitution there was a "higher law," the law of God, and under it all men were free and equal. The voice of the middle, the compromisers and peace-makers, was heard on March 7 when Daniel Webster, in one of his finest speeches, defended the Clay measures. Geography itself excluded slavery from the Mexican Cession; why antagonize the South by excluding it by law? "I would not take pains to reaf-

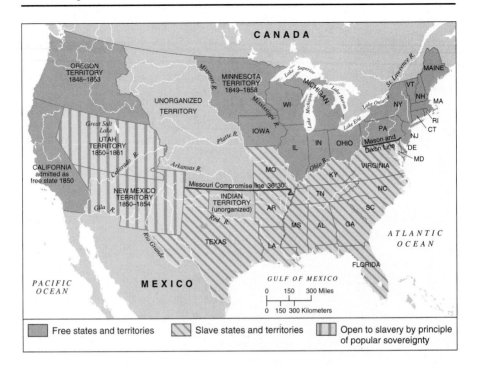

Free states and territories   **Slave states and territories**   **Open to slavery by principle of popular sovereignty**

The Compromise of 1850

firm an act of nature, nor reenact the will of God." The temporizing address earned Webster angry denunciation in his own strongly antislavery state.

Webster's support was not enough. In late July, after almost six months of debate, the omnibus bill went down to defeat. By this time President Taylor had died of a stomach complaint. A southerner, he had nevertheless worked behind the scenes for his own plan to admit both California and New Mexico as free states without a trade-off for the South. His death placed Millard Fillmore of New York in the White House. Though a northerner, Fillmore favored the compromise. Another gain for the compromise forces was the failure of the Nashville convention to take disunionist actions. Instead, the delegates had adjourned to see what Congress would finally do.

Stephen Douglas took over management of the sectional issues after the defeat of Clay's omnibus bill. A skilled parliamentarian, he split the measure into five separate bills: California would enter the Union as a free state; the Texas border would be adjusted in favor of New Mexico; New Mexico would be organized as two territories—New Mexico and Utah—and when admitted as states they could decide either for slavery or freedom; the slave trade would be abolished in the District of Columbia; there would be a new, stricter, fugitive slave law. With the help of Fillmore, Douglas convinced a group of northern Democrats and upper-South Whigs to support all the measures. When combined with southern or northern partisans who would support those particular measures that favored their section, these moderate center votes were enough to pass the whole package. What Clay could not achieve with a single measure had now been accomplished with five.

The Compromise of 1850 heartened unionists all over the country. Profoundly relieved at having escaped disunion, Congress celebrated the end of the unruly session with an enthusiasm that left many members with hangovers the next day. Jubilant crowds surged through the streets of Washington toasting Clay, Douglas, and Webster. In the country at large moderates gained confidence; many citizens agreed with Cass that the slavery question was finally "settled in the public mind." Soon after, the Nashville convention finally adjourned without taking a disunionist position.

FUGITIVE SLAVES AND NORTHERN SYMPATHIES. It seemed that the Union had been saved. But as the months passed, it became clear that the Compromise of 1850 would not put an end to sectional discord. Indeed, the Fugitive Slave Act component seemed only to inflame sectional antagonisms.

The new fugitive slave law deprived suspected runaway slaves of virtually every right normally granted in American jurisprudence to those accused of violating the law. By merely submitting an affidavit to a federal commissioner, a person could claim ownership of an avowed black runaway. The commissioner might, on investigation, reject the affidavit, but if he did, he received a fee of only $5; if he ordered the suspect's return, he pocketed $10. During the investigation, the accused could not testify on his or her behalf. Still worse, the law required that any free citizen could be forced to join in the pursuit of any fugitive on pain of stiff fines and jail sentences. In effect, the law made every American a potential slave-catcher.

Anger at the law's disregard of civil liberties was amplified by its enforcement. The sight of black men and women, many long-time residents of the North, being dragged off to jail in chains and taken south to bondage by federal authorities converted hundreds of indifferent northerners to antislavery overnight. In Syracuse, Boston, Oberlin (Ohio), New York City, and even Baltimore, people hid escapees, attacked slave-catching officials, rescued fugitives from jail and whisked them away to Canada.

Public outrage prompted nine northern states to enact new personal liberty laws providing state attorneys to defend fugitives, appropriating funds to pay their defense costs, and denying the use of public buildings to detain accused escapees. At the South's behest, the federal government challenged the state personal liberty laws, and in *Ableman* v. *Booth* (1859) the Supreme Court declared the laws unconstitutional. Obviously, in the heat of sectional rivalry, both sections were sacrificing venerable constitutional scruples.

One northerner appalled by the Fugitive Slave Act was Harriet Beecher Stowe. As a little girl she had wept when her father, the Reverend Lyman Beecher, prayed for "poor, oppressed, bleeding Africa," and as a young woman she had been shocked at the sight of escaped slaves being plucked off the streets of Cincinnati by slave-catchers. In 1851 she wrote a series of slave-life sketches for the *National Era,* an abolitionist journal. She soon expanded these into a novel that appeared in 1852 as *Uncle Tom's Cabin*. The book was a huge success. In the sentimental style of the day, it recounted the story of a lively and vivid cast of characters, black and white, enmeshed in the tragic web of slavery and victimized by its inherent cruelty. By the end of its first year the book had sold 300,000 copies, and eight presses were running day and night to keep up with the demand.

Southerners denounced *Uncle Tom's Cabin* as inaccurate and biased. Stowe, they said, was an ignorant and dangerous woman. But in Europe and the North the book was acclaimed a masterpiece. It aroused such strong sympathy for slaves and such utter detestation of slavery that it could not help but heighten sectional antagonism. Legend has it that when President Lincoln met Harriet Beecher Stowe during the Civil War, he remarked: "So this is the little lady who wrote the book that made this big war!"

✷ WORSENING TENSIONS ✷

If, in 1850, it seemed that Clay, Webster, and Douglas had finally checked the mounting sectional antagonism, appearances were deceiving. Within three years the two older men would be dead. Douglas would remain, but events would show that he lacked the political skill that had enabled his seniors to hold the nation together.

Meanwhile, there was a new occupant of the White House. In 1852 the Democrats nominated Franklin Pierce, Mexican War general, U.S. senator from New Hampshire, and a doughface Democrat who had long supported the South. The Whigs, badly divided on the slavery issue, chose as their candidate their own Mexican War hero, Winfield Scott. With the Barnburners now back in the Democratic fold, Pierce won a resounding victory in both sections. The Whigs carried only two southern states. They had been reduced to a northern party almost entirely.

SOUTHERN DREAMS OF EMPIRE. For four years, fugitive slaves notwithstanding, the nation avoided further sectional crisis. The Compromise of 1850 had put to rest the slavery expansion question in the Mexican Cession, the only part of the country where the legality of slavery had been uncertain. The entire country appeared once again to be staked out for all time as either slave or free. The slavery expansion issue in existing U.S. territory seemed solved.

But there remained the destabilizing possibility of further geographical expansion. Southerners had never abandoned the yearning for new territorial acquisitions, especially to the south. The United States had already wrenched immense chunks out of Mexico; why not more from that chaotic country? Also tempting were the Central American republics and the rich island of Cuba, the latter still feebly held by Spain. Through most of the 1850s southern political leaders continued to lust for more territory to extend the nation's imperial reach and, mayhap, provide more slave states to balance off the growing North. Expansion also seemed necessary for the South's economic health. As Mississippi Senator Jefferson Davis expressed it, "Slave labor is wasteful labor, and it therefore requires a still more extended territory than would the same pursuits if they could be prosecuted by the more economic labor of white men."

This sectional version of Manifest Destiny sometimes took private forms. In the 1850s American "filibusterers" launched military raids into Mexico, often for private gain, but also for the purpose of carving out new slave states to the south. The most famous of these adventurers was William Walker, a "grey-eyed man of destiny" who, in 1856, invaded Nicaragua with a small army and overthrew its government. Walker was soon ousted by a coalition of Central American states, but tried twice more, and eventually was executed by a Nicaraguan firing squad.

In these years, strongly influenced by southern attitudes and values, the American government itself went hunting after loose real estate to the south. Mexico was an obvious target, and the Gadsden Purchase was originally a more ambitious scheme to acquire Mexican land, drastically scaled down by skeptical northern senators. But successive American administrations coveted Cuba even more. The "Pearl of the Antilles" already possessed a flourishing slave-plantation economy based on sugar and would be a congenial addition to the South. It was owned by Spain, but Spain was weak and perhaps could be induced to surrender its distant island colony. The Pierce administration made acquiring Cuba its major foreign policy goal and in 1854 dispatched Pierre Soulé, a flamboyant Louisianan, to Madrid as minister to try to buy the island. Soulé was to offer the Spanish government $130 million for Cuba. If the offer was rejected, Secretary of State William Marcy instructed, Soulé should direct his "efforts to the next desirable object, which is to detach that island from Spanish dominion."

When Spain refused to sell, Soulé met at Ostend, Belgium with the other major American diplomats in Europe, John Mason and James Buchanan, to consider what to do. The three men composed a memo to Marcy that bristled with arrogant self-assertiveness. Cuba was "as necessary to the North American republic as any of its present . . . family of states," they wrote. If Spain refused to sell the island to the United States, then "by every law, human and Divine, we shall be justified in wresting it from Spain." When it became public, the Ostend Manifesto created an uproar. Antislavery groups attacked it as a "manifesto of Brigands." Many northerners considered it an outrageous assertion of American power. Embarrassed by the incident, Pierce recalled Soulé and abandoned the attempt to acquire Cuba.

THE KANSAS–NEBRASKA ACT. The most damaging blow to sectional harmony during the 1850s, ironically, was the work of Stephen Douglas, a devoted unionist. The Little Giant had done much to cool sectional anger in 1850, but he undid most of his good work in January 1854 when he introduced a bill to establish a territorial government in the Nebraska country, a part of the Louisiana Purchase.

Douglas was moved by several considerations. An ardent expansionist, he hoped to accelerate western settlement by fostering community building on the frontier. Related to this goal was his interest in a transcontinental railroad that would link Chicago to the Pacific Coast and bring prosperity to his home city and, incidentally, increase the value of his Chicago real estate holdings.

The 1820 Missouri Compromise had excluded slavery from the Nebraska country. Douglas's new bill, as originally submitted, declared, as had the Utah and New Mexico territorial acts of 1850, that at the point of admission to statehood the people of the region could accept or reject slavery notwithstanding the Missouri Compromise. This was not enough for southern senators David Atchison of Missouri, James Mason and Robert M. T. Hunter of Virginia, and Andrew Butler of South Carolina, who perceived that if slaves were excluded from a region during the territorial period, the new communities would probably enter as free states. Douglas sought to placate the group by agreeing to allow the people of the territory to deal with slavery before the point of statehood. This "popular sovereignty" would open the possibility of at least one new slave state in the Louisiana Purchase territory, a region seemingly closed by law to slavery for all time.

But the powerful southern bloc insisted on even more: that the new measure include a specific repeal of the Missouri Compromise. Knowing that his bill could not pass without southern support, Douglas complied. The revised bill explicitly repealed that part of the Missouri Compromise that forbade slavery in the Louisiana Purchase north of 36°30'. It also divided the region into two territories: Kansas to the south, Nebraska to the north. In effect, Douglas had opened a door once closed to slavery in a large slab of the unsettled west.

For four raucous months Congress debated the Kansas–Nebraska bill. Douglas defended the repeal provision by the specious claim that the 1850 Utah and New Mexico territorial bills had implicitly repealed the 36°30' provision. Moreover, he said, echoing Daniel Webster in 1850, there was little likelihood that geography and climate would allow slavery to take root in the Nebraska country. Southerners supported the bill as an overdue recognition of their rights to the common territory of all the American people paid for by common sacrifice and taxes.

The Kansas–Nebraska bill outraged many Northerners. In the words of the Appeal of the Independent Democrats, a manifesto authored by two Ohio Free-Soilers, Senator Salmon Chase and Congressman Joshua Giddings, the Kansas–Nebraska bill was "a gross violation of a sacred pledge," a "criminal betrayal" and "part and parcel of an atrocious plot" to make the Nebraska country "a dreary region of despotism inhabited by slaves and masters." At one point feelings ran so high that northern and southern partisans came close to blows in Congress.

Douglas, with president Pierce's support, pushed the bill through Congress. But it was an ominous victory. The bill split the northern Democrats in two; it was passed by a solid South plus those northern Democrats who stayed with the Pierce administration. A large bloc of anti-administration northerners deplored it. The law, a clear victory for the South, reopened wounds thought closed, if not fully healed.

NATIONAL PARTIES BREAK UP.   The Kansas–Nebraska Act put unbearable strains on an already weakened party system. From Maine to California Democratic newspapers screamed with outrage at the actions of Douglas and Pierce. The Kansas–Nebraska bill, announced one, was "a triumph of Slavery [and] Aristocracy over Liberty and Republicanism." Democratic party loyalists defended

Douglas and the administration, but many northern Democrats worried that their constituents would repudiate them at the polls. Whig divisions went even deeper. The Whigs had lost most of their southern support and were in trouble in the free states as well. Now, Kansas–Nebraska further divided the party's two wings. The pro-Nebraska stand of the southern Whigs in Congress had profoundly disillusioned such men as Horace Greeley, editor of the influential *New York Tribune,* and he proclaimed the North's "indignant resistance" to the measure.

The times seemed ripe for a new nativist party that could shift attention to alien and Catholic "plots" and away from slavery and during 1854–1855 the Know Nothings seemed likely to become a formidable player on the political stage. With a platform calling for extending the time required for naturalization from five to fourteen years, permitting only citizens to vote, and restricting officeholding to native-born Americans, the Know-Nothings expressed the rampant xenophobia and anti-Catholic feelings of the decade. But they also expressed the disenchantment with the existing party system.

Many contemporaries expected the Know-Nothings to replace the Whigs as the other major party. And indeed Whigs, north and south, joined the new organization in large numbers, further draining Whig strength. But many American voters despised their nativist attitudes. As the Illinois "Conscience Whig" Abraham Lincoln, noted, "Our progress in degeneracy appears to me to be pretty rapid. As a nation, we begin by declaring that 'all men are created equal.' We now practically read 'all men are created equal, except negroes.' When the Know-Nothings get control, it will read 'All men are created equal except negroes, and foreigners, and Catholics'."

Happily for those stranded northern Whigs who like Lincoln could not stomach bigotry, an alternative soon appeared. In 1854–1855 anti-Nebraska political organizations sprang up all through the North in the wake of Douglas's ill-advised bill. At a meeting at Ripon, Wisconsin, in February 1854, one of these groups adopted the name Republican. Several months later another anti-Nebraska group met at Jackson, Michigan, and gave the Republicans their new platform: no slavery in the territories, repeal of the Kansas–Nebraska and Fugitive Slave Acts, and abolition of slavery itself in the District of Columbia. The new party grew rapidly in strength, recruiting many northern Whigs and a portion of northern Democrats. After 1856, many erstwhile northern Know-Nothings, seeing their party losing strength, also joined the Republicans convinced that it was more reliably Protestant and native American than its Democratic rival.

"BLEEDING KANSAS". The Republican surge was accelerated by the outbreak of a vicious guerrilla war in Kansas. From the outset leaders of the two sections recognized that settlers would soon pour into Kansas and their origins would determine whether Kansas became a slave or a free state. Both sides threw down the gauntlet. "We will engage in competition for the virgin soil of Kansas," Seward told his Senate colleagues, "and God give the victory to the side which is stronger in numbers as it is in right." Senator Atchison, from Missouri, the slave state adjacent to Kansas, responded in kind: "We are playing for a mighty stake;

if we win we carry slavery to the Pacific Ocean, if we lose we lose Missouri, Arkansas, and Texas and all the territories; the game must be played boldly."

In fact, a majority of Kansas-bound settlers were relatively indifferent to the sectional confrontation. Most free-staters were from the Midwest and were more interested in free farms than free soil. The contingent of Yankees financed by Eli Thayer's New England Emigrant Aid Society was exceptional in its antislavery zeal. The other side too consisted largely of men and women seeking better lives rather than a particular social system. Most of the slave-state people came from Missouri; a few brought their slaves with them. Their opponents called them "border ruffians," but most were ordinary southern farmers.

Yet within weeks of passage of the Kansas–Nebraska Act, friends and foes of slavery in the territory were at each other's throats: Ambushes, arson, and murder quickly became the order of the day in "Bleeding Kansas." The struggle over Kansas was not over slavery alone. The government's failure to properly extinguish Indian claims or make essential land surveys created confusion and conflict. There were also disputes over water rights, town-site locations, and other issues connected with establishing new communities. But obviously differences in social philosophy made things worse. Men who disagreed over such issues were more prone to fight when they also held irreconcilable views on slavery. In any case, Americans elsewhere viewed the struggle as a bitter confrontation of the nation's two social systems and responded accordingly.

The early maneuvers favored the South. In late 1854 and early 1855, territorial governor Andrew Reeder called elections for territorial representative to Congress and the territorial legislature. The results were rigged. Though free-state residents by this time probably outnumbered their opponents, several thousand Missourians crossed the river to vote illegally, giving the slave-state forces majorities. Reeder recognized the fraud, but he refused to authorize new elections. In short order, the proslavery legislature passed a harsh slave code and disqualified from office citizens who did not support slavery. In response, the free-state forces fortified the town of Lawrence and organized their own free-state party. Soon after, at a convention held in Topeka, they drew up a constitution prohibiting slavery in Kansas and convened a free-state legislature in opposition to the one recognized by Reeder. In time, Governor Reeder declared his sympathy for the free-state group. President Pierce, responding to southern pressure, replaced him with William Shannon, a more reliable proslavery man.

The struggle soon took a more dangerous turn. In the spring of 1856 a small army of proslavery men descended on Lawrence, destroyed the free-state printing press, tore down the hotel, burned several private homes, and ransacked the town. Southern newspapers depicted the raiders as gallant knights battling for a holy cause. Northern Free-Soilers denounced the "border ruffians." In New Haven, Connecticut, the popular Brooklyn minister, Henry Ward Beecher, urged an antislavery congregation to send more settlers to Kansas equipped with Sharps rifles. Thereafter many Kansas-bound northerners carried the deadly repeater rifles, now dubbed "Beecher's Bibles."

Among those who turned to violence in Kansas was one John Brown of Osawatomie, a stern, latter-day Old Testament patriarch who had failed in virtually everything he attempted and identified his own suffering with that of the slaves. He soon came to see himself as an instrument of an avenging God to smite the slaveholders in Kansas. Angered by the attack on Lawrence, in May 1856, the Browns and a small band of followers took revenge by hacking to death in cold blood five slave-state settlers at Pottawatomie Creek.

The Pottawatomie massacre set off a virtual war in Kansas. Spring planting was neglected while bands of southern "border ruffians" and northern "bushwhackers" roamed the territory pillaging, burning, and killing. Scores died and millions of dollars of property was destroyed in the disorders. The events in Kansas raised sectional tensions in the rest of the country. As atrocity succeeded atrocity, even moderate citizens found it difficult to check mounting resentments of people from the other section.

THE BROOKS–SUMNER INCIDENT.   One of the more militant antislavery leaders in Congress was the junior senator from Massachusetts, Charles Sumner. No one was a more courageous and consistent defender of blacks. At the same time, few men in public life were as dogmatic, as certain of the unfailing rectitude of their positions, or as unwilling to give their opponents credit for honesty or good intentions as he. Sumner had watched the struggle over Kansas with growing dismay and on May 19, 1856, he rose in the Senate to deliver a blistering two-day denunciation of the South in a speech he called "The Crime against Kansas."

Elaborately prepared, sonorous, full of learned allusions, the address descended to crude personal attacks on Douglas, the president, Senator Atchison, and others. But Sumner reserved his sharpest barbs for Andrew Butler, the venerable senator from South Carolina, calling him a Don Quixote, a foolish blunderer, and a liar, and cruelly alluding to his physical infirmities. Two days later, Butler's young kinsman, South Carolina Congressman Preston Brooks, entered the Senate chamber as Sumner was sitting at his desk writing letters and struck him over the head repeatedly with a cane until the Senator was bloody and unconscious.

The South considered Brooks's attack the just chastisement of a blackguard. Several southern communities presented Brooks with replacements for his shattered walking stick. The assault and the South's response shocked most northerners. The Massachusetts legislature denounced it as "a gross breach of Parliamentary privilege—a ruthless attack upon the liberty of speech—an outrage of the decencies of civilized life, and an indignity to the Commonwealth of Massachusetts." Northerners who prized free speech noted that, having suppressed dissent everywhere on their home ground, southerners were now trying to squelch it in the sacred halls of Congress itself. A small incident in itself, the Brooks-Sumner affair confirmed many northerners' skepticism of southern "chivalry" and convinced them that it was time to curb "the arrogant and aggressive" demands of the "slave power."

* REPUBLICANS AND THE WORSENING CRISIS *

Bleeding Kansas, the Brooks–Sumner affair, and *Uncle Tom's Cabin* all garnered recruits for the emerging Republican party. The new organization was a purely sectional party. It had virtually no support in the lower South and little in the border slave states. Its heartland was the "upper North" where the population was predominantly Yankee (New England)-derived. In the "lower North"—southern New York, Pennsylvania, New Jersey, and the southern parts of the Old Northwest—Republicanism competed with strong remaining attachments to the Democrats.

Only a small minority of Republicans were out-and-out abolitionists. All believed that the federal government could and should prevent slavery from expanding. Many agreed with Lincoln that slavery, if contained, would retreat and eventually die. Others were indifferent to the eventual fate of the "peculiar institution"; it was sufficient that the western territories be kept open to free labor. Those businessmen who supported the Republicans at this stage were putting ideology ahead of economic advantage, as most merchants, bankers, and manufacturers saw the new party as a divisive influence that would upset the country's economy along with its politics.

The Republicans ran their first presidential candidate in 1856 when they nominated the California hero John C. Frémont. That year their platform demanded a free Kansas and congressional prohibition of "those twin relics of barbarism—Polygamy,* and Slavery." As an afterthought, it also endorsed government aid for a Pacific railroad and for internal improvements. The Democrats chose former Pennsylvania Senator James Buchanan of Ostend Manifesto fame, largely because he had been serving as U.S. minister to London and was one of the few prominent Democratic politicians free of "bleeding Kansas" taint. A third candidate, ex-President Fillmore, ran on the flagging Know-Nothing ticket and received the support of surviving Whigs.

The Republicans depicted Frémont as the champion of the "laboring classes" against the slaveholders. The Democrats appealed to white fears of black equality and of political disunity if Frémont and the "black Republicans" won. In the end, Buchanan carried the entire lower North, plus California, and fourteen of the fifteen slave states (Maryland supported Fillmore). Frémont won the rest of the North, a showing that alarmed southerners and filled them with foreboding.

BUCHANAN'S POLICIES. Buchanan was a well-meaning but indecisive leader whose talents lay in the maneuvering of American politics as usual. Republicans sized him up as just another doughface Democrat, subservient to the South, and his choice of many southerners and proslavery northerners as advisers confirmed their judgment.

---

*Polygamy, as practiced by some Mormons in Utah, offended many traditional Christians and had become a political issue.

Even before his inauguration, Buchanan set out to undermine the Free-Soil position by intruding into the pending case of a Missouri slave, Dred Scott, then before the Supreme Court. Through the auspices of antislavery activists, Scott was suing for his freedom on the grounds that his former owner had taken him to free territory, including a portion that had been closed to slavery by the Missouri Compromise. The case was that long-awaited opportunity to have the federal courts settle once and for all the divisive question of whether the people of a territory or Congress—as opposed to the people of a fully sovereign state—could exclude slavery from part of the United States.

Southerners anticipated that the decision would go their way. The chief justice, Roger Taney, was a proslavery Marylander, and four of the associate justices were also southerners. But the southern leaders wanted at least one free-state judge to support their side to give it credibility. President-elect Buchanan now induced his fellow Pennsylvanian, justice Robert Grier, to side with the proslavery majority. Knowing the certain Dred Scott outcome, on March 4, in his inaugural address, Buchanan noted that whatever the court's decision, "in common with all good citizens" he would "cheerfully submit" to it.

The actual decision two days later was a bombshell. Taney's opinion covered a number of issues that did not seem necessary to decide. First, said the chief justice, Scott was still a slave. His freedom was denied. Second, as a black person and a slave Scott was not a citizen and therefore had "no rights which the white man was bound to respect." Third, his stay in Wisconsin territory did not make him free since Congress did not have the power to exclude slavery from a territory and the law that had supposedly permitted it, the Missouri Compromise, was unconstitutional. Because Congress could not exclude slavery from a territory, neither could a territorial legislature, which was merely a creation of Congress. Most scholars today agree with the dissenting opinion of Justice Benjamin Curtis of Massachusetts, noting that some blacks had been legal citizens of the United States in past periods and that in no way did a congressional prohibition of slavery in the territories violate the Constitution. But the Supreme Court had spoken: Only the people of a state could keep slavery out of any part of the United States; the hands of Congress and a territorial legislature were tied. And some antislavery partisans feared that the Dred Scott decision even called into question whether a *state* could exclude slave property within its borders.

The Dred Scott ruling was politically destabilizing. It annulled the core Republican principle that it was the right and, indeed, the duty of Congress to ban slavery from the territories. It also appeared to void the Douglas popular-sovereignty position that the local populace had the right to exclude slavery from an organized territory.

Buchanan soon gave the Republicans and the Douglas wing of his own party further grounds for dismay when he approved the Kansas state constitution adopted by a proslavery convention at Lecompton in late 1857. By the convention's terms, this document was to be submitted to the Kansas voters with a choice of two clauses regarding slavery. One recognized the full rights of slaveholders and, in effect, made Kansas a slave state. The other stated that "slavery shall no longer exist" in Kansas, but "the right of property in slaves now in this Territory shall in no manner be interfered with." The voters could choose one or the other; in effect, there was no way of excluding slavery from Kansas totally.

Republicans denounced the Lecompton proposal as "the Great Swindle." Douglas charged it was a perversion of true popular sovereignty. Even Robert Walker, Buchanan's choice as Kansas's territorial governor, called it "a vile fraud, a bare counterfeit." In Kansas most free-state partisans boycotted the referendum and, not surprisingly, the more extreme proslavery version passed overwhelmingly.

When the Lecompton constitution came before Congress for approval as part of the Kansas statehood bill, the Buchanan administration rallied behind it as did virtually the entire House and Senate delegations from the South. In his message transmitting the bill to Congress, Buchanan noted that Kansas "is at this moment as much a slave state as Georgia or South Carolina." Douglas and most northern Democrats fought the bill as a travesty of popular sovereignty and a measure that would sink them and their party generally in the upcoming elections. At one point a free-wheeling fistfight broke out on the floor of the House with "fifty middle-aged and elderly gentlemen pitching into each other like so many . . . savages."

By wielding his patronage power aggressively, President Buchanan managed to eke out a victory for Lecompton in the House, but in the Senate Douglas Democrats joined the Republicans to defeat the bill by a narrow vote. A compromise bill, including a generous federal land grant to the state and a provision allowing acceptance or rejection of the entire constitution, was soon resubmitted to the Kansas voters. In August 1858 they rejected it by a vote of 11,300 to 1,788. Kansas would not enter the Union until 1861, after secession of the southern states.

THE EMERGENCE OF LINCOLN. The troubles of the Buchanan presidency were compounded by the Panic of 1857 and the economic slump that followed. Although the downturn was probably to be expected after ten years of buoyant economic growth and speculation, the North blamed it on southerners in Congress for lowering their tariff protection. Southerners, on the other hand, largely unaffected by a falling stock market and urban unemployment, saw the panic as a vindication of the slave economy. Enjoying high world prices for cotton, they gloated at the misfortunes of northern commerce and industry.

Midway through Buchanan's term, the politicians were already looking ahead to 1860. Douglas was the obvious presidential front-runner for the Democrats. But the Little Giant had hurt his chances with southerners by his stand on the Lecompton constitution and his view that, under Dred Scott, slaveholders might have the right to take their slaves into the territories, but it would be a "barren and worthless right" unless the people of the territory provided a slave code and the other supportive laws the peculiar institution needed to survive. In effect, by refusing to act on slavery at all, the people of a territory could exclude it.

Abe Lincoln was a very young man when this portrait was painted.
He became better looking!

The formula dismayed states' rights defenders. Before long, southern Democrats were demanding a federal slave code to get around the Douglas position.

Among the Republicans there was no lack of political talent or ambition as 1860 approached. But more and more people were beginning to hear the name of Abraham Lincoln of Illinois.

We who recognize Lincoln's greatness may find it difficult to see him as he was in the 1850s. The lanky, homely prairie lawyer was pithy, shrewd, and folksy, and combined keen realism with an idealistic strain. But as yet he gave little sign that he was capable of leading a great nation through trying times.

Only gradually did he become politically "available." Following his single term in the House of Representatives (1847–1849), Lincoln had returned to Springfield, Illinois, and private law practice. For the next few years he devoted his professional life to defending slanderers, petty thieves, and the Illinois Central Railroad in the courts. All the while, however, he kept up his connections with the Illinois Whigs and shared their doubts and anxieties when their party began to disintegrate. He did not formally become a Republican until his law partner, without authorization, signed his name to a call for a local Republican convention. In 1856 Lincoln campaigned for Frémont.

In 1858 Illinois Republicans gave Lincoln the party's official nomination for U.S. Senate. The move was unusual. Senators were then chosen by the state legislators and there was no reason to campaign among the voters and no need for a formal nomination. This time, however—in hopes of defeating the formidable Douglas—the state Republican leaders decided to make the year's election for state officials hinge on the victory or defeat of their senatorial choice. The voters would be casting their ballots, actually, for individual state legislators, with the senatorial candidates, in effect, standing in for each party.

The campaign format too was unusual. At first the two candidates went their separate ways, speaking to individual audiences. Lincoln's acceptance speech, the famous "House-Divided" address, made slavery a moral issue by contrast with Douglas's purely political focus. The country, he announced, could not remain permanently half slave and half free. "A house divided against itself cannot stand." Under the Democrats it would become all slave; under the Republicans all free, for the Republicans intended to "arrest the further spread of [slavery], and place it where the public mind shall rest in the belief that it is in the course of ultimate extinction."

Before long the candidates agreed to conduct a direct debate. Beginning in late August 1858 in the northern Illinois city of Ottawa, they would meet on the same platform in seven towns, ending in Alton in mid-October. In each they would fire questions at one another while the public watched and listened. The contest attracted national attention because it had national implications. To be a serious contender in the 1860 presidential race, Douglas had to defeat his opponent. People from all over the country followed the debates in the newspapers, and their interest gave Lincoln invaluable national exposure.

Although the face-to-face format was unusual, the open-air political rally had long been a midwestern diversion, and thousands came to watch and listen to the speakers. The banners, the marching cadets, the glee clubs, and the general holiday atmosphere encouraged the candidates to banter and name-calling, but generally the level of discourse and discussion was high.

The debates zeroed in on race and slavery in the territories. Douglas at times appealed to crude white racism and fear of a mass invasion of Illinois by blacks if slavery were abolished. If, in the House-Divided speech, Lincoln sounded a bit like an abolitionist, at other points, especially in the southern part of the state where many of the voters were of southern descent, he pandered to the anti-black prejudices of his audience. When Douglas accused the "Black Republican party" of favoring racial equality and full civil rights for blacks, Lincoln said he did not believe that black people were the equal of whites, and as long as there were differences he expected the white race to have the superior position. Nevertheless, Lincoln's moral revulsion against slavery came through clearly. At Alton, in the last debate, he announced that "the sentiment that contemplates the institution of slavery . . . as a wrong is the sentiment of the Republican party." Slavery was "a moral, social, and political wrong."

The Dred Scott decision inevitably engaged the debaters. At Freeport, Lincoln tried to embarrass his opponent by asking him to reconcile his popular sovereignty doctrine with Chief Justice Taney's decision in Dred Scott denying the right of the people of a territory to exclude slavery. Douglas repeated the formula he had already advanced: All a territorial legislature needed to do was refuse to enact a slave code and slavery was effectively kept out. Though not new, this Freeport Doctrine publicized Douglas's differences with his southern colleagues and increased the tension between him and the party's southern wing.

On election day the voters of Illinois gave the Republican candidates for the legislature more total popular votes than they gave the Democrats. But the Democrats won more counties than their opponents, and the legislature reelected the Little Giant to the Senate. Having survived the challenge, Douglas was now clearly the front-runner for the Democratic presidential nomination in 1860. Lincoln, though he had lost, was now a national figure. In February 1860 he traveled to New York to speak before the city's wealthy and influential Republicans. His Cooper Union address impressed his distinguished audience. Old Abe would now be a presidential contender, too, on the Republican side.

HARPERS FERRY.   But first the country would have to undergo another ordeal of violence over slavery, and once again John Brown would be the instigator. Though many people knew of his role in the Pottawatomie massacre, Brown was never indicted and remained free to concoct other schemes to scourge the slaveholders. Between 1856 and 1859 he worked out a mad plan to foment a slave revolt that would bring down the institution of slavery. Starting with a nucleus of armed escapees in the inaccessible Virginia Blue Ridge, he and his band would advance south along the Appalachians attracting runaways and spreading slave insurrection all through the eastern slave country. Brown solicited money for his scheme from New England abolitionists and antislavery philanthropists. Not all approved. Frederick Douglass, for one, believed that invading Virginia with two dozen men was harebrained and told Brown as much.

Warnings did no good. In the fall of 1859 Brown, his sons, and a small band of black and white supporters bought guns and drew up plans for an assault on the federal armory at Harpers Ferry in what is now West Virginia. The armory would provide the weapons and light the spark for his insurrection. On the night of October 16 the rebels seized the armory and all its rifles and ammunition. But the slaves did not rise at the news. Instead, Brown and his small band remained holed up in the armory building not knowing what to do next. On the eighteenth a detachment of U.S. marines led by Colonel Robert E. Lee stormed the building and captured the surviving members of the implausible revolt.

Brown's raid raised sectional antagonisms to fever pitch. To southerners it was proof that the North would stop at nothing to undermine slavery, including igniting a dreaded servile insurrection. Hundreds of southern students at northern colleges packed their bags and returned home in protest. Georgians attacked the crew of a northern ship at Savannah and a New Yorker, newly installed as president of an Alabama college, was forced to flee for his life.

Brown was tried for treason, convicted, and sentenced to hang. During the trial and in the weeks between sentencing and execution, he conducted himself with great dignity. Many northerners had initially condemned the attack, and even Lincoln and *New York Tribune* editor Horace Greeley believed Brown tragically misguided. But Brown's bearing and eloquent words after his capture made him a hero to many in the North. Henry David Thoreau compared him to Jesus, and novelist Louisa May Alcott named Brown "Saint John the Just." When he was hanged on December 2, he became, in the eyes of antislavery advocates, a martyr to the cause of human freedom. In two short years Union soldiers, advancing against the slave South, would be singing the words: "John Brown's body lies a-moldering in the grave but his truth is marching on."

THE PARTY CONVENTIONS OF 1860.   Harpers Ferry kept the country in an uproar well into 1860, and by that time the nation was in the throes of the most fateful presidential election of its history.

The Democratic convention convened in April 1860 at Charleston, South Carolina, in the heart of "Secessia." Led by the fiery William Yancey of Alabama, the southern leaders threatened to walk out unless the convention endorsed a federal territorial slave code plank. The Douglas majority, certain that a such a plank would ensure Democratic defeat in November, refused to yield. When the Douglasites won the platform fight, Yancey and forty-nine other southern rights' delegates marched out of the convention hall. Meeting elsewhere in town, the minority adopted their cherished plank and waited to see what their adversaries would do. The majority continued to meet, but were unable to give Douglas the nomination by the required two-thirds of the delegates still present despite fifty-seven ballots. Frustrated, they adjourned, promising to convene at Baltimore six weeks later to try again.

Unity still could not be achieved. The southern rights' bolters, some now back, as well as some newly chosen southern delegates, once again walked out. This time they held their own convention and nominated Vice President John C. Breckinridge of Kentucky on a federal slave code platform. Meanwhile, the remaining Baltimore delegates chose Douglas on a popular sovereignty platform.

On May 9 the remaining Whigs organized the Constitutional Union party with a fuzzy platform that endorsed the Union and "the enforcement of the laws." They chose as their candidates John Bell of Tennessee and Edward Everett of Massachusetts.

The Republicans met in Chicago confident of victory. As the delegates crowded into the dynamic young metropolis on the lake, the Republican front-runner seemed to be Senator William Seward of New York. But Seward was the author of "the higher law" doctrine, and in 1858 had made another provocative speech declaring that the two sections of the country were doomed to an "irrepressible conflict." Many Republicans considered him too radical to carry the lower North. Salmon Chase, the antislavery senator from Ohio, did not appear much better. At the other end of the Republican scale was Edward Bates of Mis-

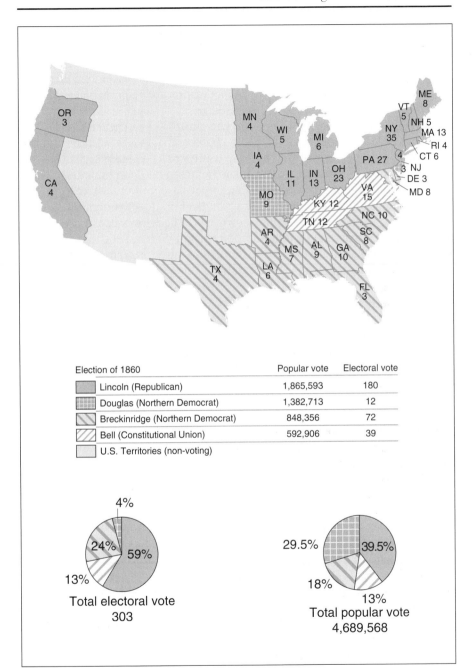

The Presidential Election of 1860.

souri. But Bates was too moderate, and colorless besides. Simon Cameron of Pennsylvania, another possible nominee, was weighed down with a reputation for both party inconsistency and shady financial dealing.

The Lincoln forces made much of their rivals' weaknesses and pictured their candidate as the perfect balance between moderation and radicalism. He was also from the Midwest, they emphasized, a region the Republicans had to carry to win in November. Skilled maneuverers, the Lincoln managers packed the galleries with enthusiastic, leather-lunged Lincoln supporters. Old Abe won the nomination on the third ballot. His running mate was Hannibal Hamlin of Maine.

The party platform, like the candidate, represented the more moderate Republican position. It demanded the exclusion of slavery from the territories, but endorsed the right of each state to "order and control its own domestic institutions." It also condemned the John Brown raid. The Republicans proved more sensitive to the economic interests of the North and West in 1860 than four years before. The party platform endorsed a homestead law, a protective tariff, a northern-route Pacific railroad, and federal aid for internal improvements.

THE UNION DISSOLVES. None of the candidates favored disunion. Douglas, of course, was a passionate unionist, and the platform of John Bell's party was little more than an assertion of national unity. The Republicans, for their part, soft-pedaled the slavery extension issue, especially in the lower North, to avoid frightening off moderate and timid voters. Even John Breckinridge decried secession, though, as Douglas correctly noted, every secessionist voter was also a Breckinridge supporter.

The Republican campaign was marked by enthusiastic marches, banners, parades, and rallies. The young party emphasized the "free labor" theme, with Lincoln, the humble "rail-splitter," depicted as the perfect exemplar of its message. Lincoln's opponents sought various fusion arrangements to deny the Republicans victory by carrying the entire South plus a few crucial northern states. These efforts failed except in a few localities, and it was soon clear that the nation faced the probability of a Republican president representing an exclusively northern constituency.

Weeks before the results were in, the *Charleston Mercury* predicted that if Lincoln won, "thousands of slaveholders will despair of the institution." Other southern journals and politicians warned that the Republican administration would appoint abolitionist federal officials in the South who would work to undermine slavery. If slavery collapsed, white farmers and wage earners would be forced to compete with the cheap labor of freed blacks. The prospect of a Black Republican victory seemed intolerable. One Atlanta editor announced: "Let the consequences be what they may, whether the Potomac is crimsoned in human gore, and Pennsylvania Avenue is paved ten fathoms deep with mangled bodies . . . the South will never submit to such humiliation and degradation as the inauguration of Abraham Lincoln."

The election results did not endorse extremism of either sort. Lincoln won a clear electoral college majority over his combined opponents, carrying every free state except New Jersey, where he split the electoral vote with Douglas. Yet he won only 39 percent of the popular vote, virtually all from the free states. Douglas was second in popular votes with 29 percent, but in every state but Missouri he was second to someone else, and so could only claim 12 electoral votes. Together, the Little Giant and Bell, both strong unionists, won more popular votes in the slave states than Breckinridge. Even if we judge Breckinridge's support to be mainly secessionist, the 1860 election was scarcely a mandate for disunion.

News of the result found the South Carolina legislature in session and it quickly approved a secession convention. On December 20, 1860, by a unanimous vote, this convention declared that the "union now subsisting between South Carolina and other States . . . is hereby dissolved." In the next few weeks six more states—Alabama, Mississippi, Florida, Georgia, Louisiana, and Texas—joined the rush to leave the Union. Few outright opponents of secession were to be found at the secession conventions of the lower South, though in each there was a contingent of "cooperationists," people who favored waiting until the South as a whole decided to leave the Union. The largest fraction of all consisted of "immediate secessionists," who demanded secession without delay and without qualifications. All through the lower South the immediate secessionist group represented the counties that were richer, more closely tied to slavery and cotton, and traditionally more Democratic than Whig.

SECESSION WINTER.   People who lived through the months between the election and Lincoln's inauguration in March remembered it vividly as a time of acute public anxiety. Southerners hovered between hope and despair, not knowing how the federal government would respond to secession and fearful that the confusion of the time would encourage slave revolt. Meanwhile, officials of the seceded states seized federal customs houses, post offices, mints, arsenals, and forts, and army officers, members of Congress, and other federal officials of southern birth declared their allegiances to their native states.

In early February delegates from six of the seceded states met in Montgomery, Alabama, and organized a new federation to replace the old. Choosing Jefferson Davis of Mississippi and Alexander Stephens of Georgia as provisional president and vice president, respectively, they adopted a frame of government for the Confederate States of America that in most ways resembled the old federal Constitution. The Confederate constitution, however, declared slavery everywhere protected by law, forbade protective tariffs, gave the president the right to veto specific portions of bills passed by congress, and confined him to a single six-year term of office.

Northerners, too, felt confused and apprehensive in those secession winter months. In Washington rumors circulated that southern sympathizers intended to seize the capital. In New York City, where merchants and bankers had close business ties with the South, and where most of the white working class were Democrats, there was disturbing talk from the Democratic mayor, Fernando Wood, about taking the city out of the Union. Many northern moderates supported compromise to close the sectional breech before it became irreparable.

President Buchanan did not approve of secession, but neither did he believe that the federal government had the right to take coercive steps to save the Union.

As Seward would express it, his position seemed to be that "no state has a right to secede unless it wishes to." Buchanan hoped above all that violence would not erupt during his remaining weeks in office; thereafter secession would be his successor's problem. Surrounded at first by southern advisers, the president was unable to check the progressive disintegration of the Union.

Republicans themselves were divided and indecisive. A few strong antislavery partisans, like Horace Greeley, advised letting "the erring sisters depart in peace," thereby freeing the Union of the taint of slavery. Some Republican moderates favored compromise on the territorial issue, perhaps by extending the Missouri Compromise line to the California border. Other Republicans, confusing "conditional Unionism" in the South with true Unionism, advised going slow until the forces of unity reasserted themselves in Dixie.

The core of the party, however, refused to compromise with secession. It was wrong and dangerous. If the lower South could leave the Union, why not the other slave states, and then perhaps the West? Once allowed, could anything stop total dissolution of the Union? And for what purpose? The South had lost a political contest played by the rules; could it now cry foul? Secession was not rebellion against tyranny, as in 1776, but an attack on the most benign, most democratic government the world had ever known. And how could the separation be effected without serious harm? The new Confederacy would control the mouth of the Mississippi. Could that vital spot be allowed to fall into unfriendly hands? And who would get the territories? No, the only option was to resist secession.

The eyes of the country during these tense months inevitably turned to the president-elect. Many sincere unionists urged Lincoln to make some major conciliatory gesture on the slavery extension issue. Lincoln was willing to support a constitutional amendment forbidding the federal government to meddle in slavery in the states and even agreed to enforce the Fugitive Slave Act if it was made fairer. But he would not surrender exclusion of slavery from the territories. If he did, the issue would only have to be fought all over again in the future. As he told a fellow Republican: "The tug has to come, and better now than any time hereafter."

Meanwhile, desperate efforts were under way in Congress and the states to patch together another sectional compromise. The most promising proposal was the scheme of Kentucky Senator John J. Crittenden to extend the Missouri Compromise line through the remaining federal territory. But it, along with several others, required that the Republicans abandon their core issue. The Crittenden plan also opened the door for slavery to be extended to territories "hereafter acquired." Republicans in Congress rejected the Crittenden compromise as well as the others.

MAJOR ANDERSON'S ORDEAL. With each passing day the crisis deepened. Increasingly, the attention of the country focused on the two southern military posts still in federal hands—Fort Sumter in Charleston harbor, and Fort Pickens at Pensacola, Florida. Their status, like so many issues of the preceding decade, had become charged with tremendous emotional and symbolic importance. Even Buchanan was unwilling to give up the forts, though he had done little to prevent other southern seizures of federal property. In January he despatched the merchant steamer *Star of the West* with munitions and troops to reinforce the beleaguered Union army commander at Sumter, Major Robert Anderson. The South Carolina militia forced the steamer to turn back, leaving Anderson's garrison as desperate as ever.

By inauguration day, March 4, 1861, the issue of the forts had still not been settled. Lincoln's inauguration address adopted a conciliatory tone. The Union was "perpetual"; secession was the "essence of anarchy." The government would "hold, occupy, and possess" federal property and "collect the duties and imposts." On the other hand, the new president declared, he would not insist on delivering the federal mails if such service were "repelled," nor would he appoint "obnoxious strangers" to federal offices in the South. Ultimately, the "momentous issue of civil war" was in the hands of the South. The federal government would not assail the South, but at the same time he, as president, was sworn to "preserve, protect, and defend" the government. Lincoln ended with an appeal to "the mystic chords of memory" that joined the North and South in a common history and heritage.

Once in charge, Lincoln was compelled to grapple with the question of the forts. Pickens could be reinforced by sea without difficulty. The issue of Sumter, under the direct guns of Confederate forces on shore, continued to fester. William Seward, now secretary of state, advised that it be evacuated and let Confederate commissioners in Washington believe that it would be done. But Lincoln was under great pressure from Republicans around the country to save Sumter. And if he was going to do it, it would have to be quickly. Major Anderson reported in early March that his supplies were running low and he could not hold out much longer.

On March 20 the president ordered an expedition to reinforce Anderson. Seward still objected, and composed a memorandum advising abandonment of Sumter. Hoping to take charge of the nation's affairs from a man he considered weak and vacillating, he went beyond this suggestion, however, and made the preposterous proposal that the United States provoke a diplomatic crisis with Britain and France that would induce still patriotic southerners to rush to the Union's defense. Lincoln quickly and firmly put Seward in his place. He alone, he told his puffed-up subordinate, must execute the nation's policies.

Lincoln proceeded with the Sumter relief expedition but took care to notify southern officials of his intentions. As a further precaution against provoking the South, he divided the expedition into two parts. One would only be for resupplying Major Anderson. The federal government would hold troop reinforcements in reserve to be used only if the supply ships were fired on. If the southern authorities did that, the onus of war would be on the South's head. The upper South, he hoped, would not see the expedition as an attack.

To Jefferson Davis and his colleagues the continued presence of U.S. property in the middle of Charleston harbor was a reproach to the very idea of Confederate independence and sovereignty. On April 9 Davis ordered the Confederate general in command at Charleston, Pierre Gustave Beauregard, to demand Anderson's surrender before the relief expedition arrived. If he refused, the Confederate batteries should open fire. Anderson rejected the ultimatum, but told the Confederates frankly that his supplies were low and he would have to surrender soon in any case. Beauregard decided that this reply was unsatisfactory.

At 4:30 a.m., on April 12, 1861, the first cannon shot arced over Charleston harbor to land on Fort Sumter. For thirty-four hours the bombardment continued, breaching the fort's walls and starting fires. True to his pledge to hold his post, Major Anderson returned the barrage. On the afternoon of April 13, his ammunition exhausted, he lowered the Stars and Stripes and surrendered.

* CONCLUSIONS *

And so the war came. For the next four years the nation would suffer the agonies of fratricidal strife and skirt the edge of dissolution. What had brought the United States to this disastrous result?

Slavery comes closest to explaining the origins of the Civil War. But it was not moral outrage over the peculiar institution primarily that set northern armies on the march to crush the Confederacy. At the outset, only a small minority of northerners saw the war as a crusade against a fundamental social evil.

The actual role of slavery was more subtle and indirect. Southerners had developed a deep stake in the peculiar institution and feared both social and economic cataclysm if it failed. And that failure seemed the goal of the "Black Republican" party and the northern majority that brought it to power in 1860. Southerners were also infuriated by the evident intent of their northern fellow citizens to deny them their "rights" in the common territory of the nation. Northerners, for their part, had come to fear and despise an aggressive and demanding "slave power" that sought to trample the rights of free men.

Slavery defined the South and set it off against the North. Deeply woven into the fabric of southern life, it helped to create a southern sense of distinctiveness. This sense took the form of a combined sectional aggressiveness and defensiveness, and these, in turn, made the clash of economic interests more bitter than it need have been. Slavery also converted the Mexican Cession—a national boon— into a source of constantly escalating friction that could not be contained by the existing party system or the other institutions that transcended section.

Yet we must also allow for the role of individuals and of accident. Sectional conflict might have been contained if this generation of Americans had possessed the statesmanship necessary for compromise. Douglas, who could have filled the role played by Webster and Clay in the past, badly miscalculated in 1854 and helped wreck the Union. The other leaders of the decade, many of them talented men, were far too closely tied to sectional interests to bridge the chasm opening between the sections.

Whatever the route taken, the nation's greatest ordeal now began.

15

THE CIVIL WAR

How Did the War Change the Nation?

1861	Confederates fire on Fort Sumter; President Lincoln calls up 75,000 state militia; Lincoln suspends *habeas corpus* for the first time and endorses severe penalties for treason; The First Battle of Bull Run; Congress grants Lincoln power to take over railroads and telegraphs, imposes internal revenue taxes on manufactures, and passes an income tax law; The Second Confiscation Act
1862	The Union treasury begins to issue $450 million of "greenbacks"; Ironclads Monitor and Merrimac battle; Albert S. Johnston stops Grant's advance in the West at the battle of Shiloh Church, Tennessee; Union forces capture New Orleans; The Confederate States of America institute a draft; The Homestead Act; George McClellan's peninsular campaign is checked by Robert E. Lee; The Morrill Land Grant College Act; The first black Union regiments are authorized; Congress passes the first of two Pacific Railway Acts; The Second Battle of Bull Run; McClellan stops Lee's advance at Antietam Creek, Maryland; Lincoln issues the Emancipation Proclamation
1863	The Emancipation Proclamation goes into effect; Congress adopts a draft for the Union army; Joseph Hooker is defeated by Lee and "Stonewall" Jackson at Chancellorsville, Virginia; Democratic Congressman Clement Vallandigham is arrested and eventually banished to the South; Fifty pro-Union counties in Virginia are admitted into the Union as West Virginia; Battle of Gettysburg, Pennsylvania, the turning point of the war; Grant captures Vicksburg, Mississippi, and ensures Union control of the Mississippi River; The New York draft riots
1863, 1864	National Banking Acts establish uniform banking and currency practices

| 1864 | Sherman captures Atlanta, Georgia, and marches to the sea; Second Pacific Railway Act passed by Congress; Lincoln reelected |
| 1865 | Lee asks Grant for terms of surrender and they conclude a peace at Appomattox Court House; Lincoln is assassinated by John Wilkes Booth, and Andrew Johnson becomes president |

Looking back at the events of 1861–1865, most ex-Unionists and ex-Confederates were certain that they had witnessed a profound transformation of the nation. Vast armies had fought and many thousands had died. The two warring governments had spent billions of dollars on arms, supplies, and services. The war had destroyed slavery and decisively shifted power to the North. It seemed to mark a great divide between a sleepier agrarian nation and a bustling America of great factories and teeming cities.

Yet some scholars have had doubts about the extent of Civil War change. The war, they say, may have formally destroyed slavery, but the nation's black people had to wait until almost our own day for anything resembling real freedom. The war, moreover, did not promote the economic growth of the United States nor was it the great watershed between an agrarian and an urban-industrial world. In fact, many historians believe, the Civil War retarded economic development and slowed the shift from agriculture to industry, from country to city.

How *did* the war affect the nation? As we discuss the awesome "brothers' war," we must, if we are to answer the question, consider not just the battles and campaigns but also the social, political, and economic changes that accompanied the strife and carnage.

* NORTH Versus SOUTH *

The Civil War was a confrontation of two armies, two economies, two ideologies, and two governments. With the advantages of hindsight, we might assume that in each of these areas the Union had the advantage. But few Americans living in 1861 perceived it this way, and the fact that the war lasted so long and cost the Union so dearly confirms contemporary perceptions.

THE BALANCE OF FORCES. An objective, neutral observer making up a Confederate–Union balance sheet in April 1861 might well have bet on the South. With 9 million people, the seceded states had less than half the population of the North, and 3 million of its inhabitants were blacks, whom the Confederacy was unwilling to arm. The South also seemed outclassed economically. In 1860 the whole of what became the Confederate States of America had only 18,000 manufacturing establishments, employing 110,000 workers. The North had over 100,000 factories and shops, with 1.3 million employees. In transportation facilities the North was also far ahead of the South, with more than 70 percent of the nation's railroad track and twice as many horses and mules as the Confederacy.

The southern economy had the advantage of an abundance of food to feed its citizens, its draft animals, and its armies. Cotton also seemed to be a strength. Cotton was useful for cloth and uniforms, but more importantly, it promised to invigorate Confederate diplomacy. Without cotton, southerners thought, Europe's great textile industry, particularly Britain's, would shut down. To restore a dependable supply of American cotton and save itself from industrial ruin, England would have to intervene on the South's behalf. To guarantee that Britain felt the pinch, early in the war southern states embargoed cotton, and patriotic Confederate citizens pressured growers to limit the amount of cotton they planted. Some cotton was even burned. The campaign cut the South's 1862 cotton output to a third of its prewar volume.

The Confederacy also appeared to have important strategic advantages. For the South to win, it only had to survive. For the North to win, it had to conquer. The Confederacy would enjoy "interior" lines of communication; retreat from its borders would only shorten the distance between the South's core and its armies in the field, making it easier to supply and deploy troops. The North faced the opposite situation. As its attacking armies advanced farther and farther into enemy territory, they would experience the problems of constantly lengthening lines of communication. In the end, if only the North's difficulties and costs could be made painful enough, southern independence seemed assured.

The key was whether the North's will to fight could survive the strain. Many believed that here, too, the Confederacy had the edge. The South was fighting for its rights, its freedom. As Jefferson Davis proclaimed in his farewell speech to the United States Senate, Mississippi had left the Union only "from the high and solemn motive of defending and protecting the rights we inherited, and which it is our duty to transmit unshorn to our children." By contrast, only the North's desire to dominate, to achieve selfish economic and political ends, could explain its refusal to grant the South its due. A better cause promised better morale and better morale promised victory.

The South seemed also to possess superior military talent. Secession deprived the United States Army of a third of its officers, and the best third at that. Men such as Joseph E. Johnston, Edmund Kirby-Smith, and above all Robert E. Lee took commissions in the Confederate armed forces only after great personal anguish. Their choice made, however, they supported the southern cause with dedication and skill; especially in the early months, before the Union discovered its own talented military leaders, they contributed immeasurably to Confederate successes.

At the level of the common soldier, too, the Confederacy appeared to have the advantage. Southerners were an outdoor people, who knew how to use rifles, and were better adapted to physical hardship. Confederate sympathizers had little doubt that young southern farm boys would make better soldiers than the hollow-chested Yankee clerks from the counting-houses and shops of the northern cities.

LEADERSHIP. Yet despite appearances, we can now see that almost all the real advantages lay with the North. Abraham Lincoln was the Union's greatest single asset. Leading the Union for four of the most dangerous years it ever faced, he

During the weeks following Fort Sumter, the martial spirit affected everyone:
Notice the enthusiasm as New York's Seventh Regiment leaves for the front.
So many northerners tried to enlist that the United States turned down thousands.

managed to make the essentially right political decisions. The mobilization of Union resources to fight a great—and in many quarters unpopular—war required prodigious political juggling. Northern state governors, even Republicans, at times clashed with the federal authorities, especially over military recruiting. Within his own party Lincoln had to deal with both radicals and conservatives. At times he felt compelled to limit civil liberties to preserve order and to prevent "agitators" from discouraging enlistment. He also faced the problem of the border states, which remained in the Union only precariously and had to be dealt with deftly to avoid pushing them into the Confederate camp. Finally, there was slavery: Emancipation was the North's moral trump card, but should it be played? And if so, when?

The president often had better military instincts than his generals. His chief claim to military leadership, however, was his choice of men. He was not always right, but he was capable of learning. Eventually he recognized the military genius of Ulysses S. Grant and William T. Sherman and gave them a free hand in managing the Union armies. The combination of their talents was an important step toward victory.

Lincoln's selection of civilian subordinates was also, on the whole, wise and successful. William Seward, once he recognized that he was not the prime minister, served the administration admirably as secretary of state. Though secretary of the treasury Salmon Chase had no significant experience in finance, he guided the government through some of the most difficult financial shoals it would ever encounter. Lincoln's choice of Simon Cameron, the powerful Republican leader of Pennsylvania, as secretary of war was a mistake. Cameron was both corrupt and incompetent. Fortunately, Lincoln quickly discovered his error, sent Cameron to Russia as American minister, and chose Ohio Democrat Edwin Stanton for the post. Often caustic and intolerant, Stanton was a prodigious worker and a passionate and skilled defender of the Union cause.

Lincoln's chief success, however, was as a symbol of the Union's will to survive and an articulator of goals beyond mere survival. His major state papers and speeches rank among the most inspiring evocations of the democratic spirit. Taking what could easily be interpreted as a war of conquest, Lincoln transformed it into a struggle for the finest aspirations of the American people. The war was a "people's contest," a "struggle . . . to elevate the condition of men—to lift artificial weights from all shoulders—to clear the paths of laudable pursuit for all—to afford all an unfettered start and a fair chance in the race of life." The Union's survival, Lincoln told his fellow citizens, was humanity's "last, best hope." If it should be defeated, democracy would fail, and the forces of darkness and tyranny triumph. If, however, the Union prevailed, government "of the people, by the people, for the people" would "not perish from the earth."

And what of the Confederacy's leader, Jefferson Davis? A West Point graduate, Franklin Pierce's secretary of war, and former United States senator from Mississippi, Davis seemed eminently suited to guide the besieged Confederacy. He was honest, courageous, and intelligent; and his sharply etched, lean features and dignified bearing gave him the look of a national leader. Davis, however, had to have his hand in everything, both civilian and military, and often he botched the job. According to Stephen R. Mallory, Davis's secretary of the navy, the Confederate president "neither labored with method or celerity himself, nor permitted others to do so for him." He was also argumentative and, unlike his northern counterpart, insensitive to public opinion.

✳ THE WAR BEGINS ✳

The first responsibility of each president was to raise an army. Immediately after the attack on Fort Sumter, Lincoln had called for 75,000 state militia to join the small regular army for three months' service. The war, he expected, would be brief, and the troops would be home for late spring planting. Except in the border states, the public response was quick and enthusiastic. Young men regarded the war as a glorious lark, and they flocked to recruiting offices. State quotas were quickly oversubscribed; and militia regiments, many composed of untrained youths without rifles or proper uniforms, rushed off for Washington to meet their country's call.

Lincoln's move to put down the rebellion tripped off a furious reaction in the still uncommitted slave states. Between April 17 and May 20 four more—Virginia, Arkansas, Tennessee, and North Carolina—seceded and joined the Confederacy, bringing with them more of the South's manpower and much of its agricultural and industrial capacity. Meanwhile, war fever also seized the South and thousands of young southerners rushed to join the army to defend southern rights. The Confederacy had the opportunity to make a formidable force out of this raw material, but it let the chance slip. Like Lincoln, the Confederate Congress believed the war would end by winter, and it accepted many short-term volunteers who soon had to be replaced.

BULL RUN.   The fighting would be bloody, bitter, and seemingly interminable. Many of the early clashes took place in the strategically important border regions— Kentucky, Missouri, eastern Tennessee, and western Virginia—where the two sections touched one another and where the people were deeply divided in their allegiances. The battle of Bull Run in July 1861, twenty miles from Washington, was the first major military confrontation. There, 30,000 men under Union General Irvin McDowell met a smaller force commanded by Confederate General Pierre Beauregard. The Confederates were outgunned and outnumbered, but better led and better coordinated. For a time the Union forces held the upper hand, but when the Confederates, screaming their shrill "rebel yell," counterattacked, the federals panicked, abandoning their rifles and artillery, and fleeing pell-mell to the safety of Washington. Accompanying them in their headlong retreat was an array of civilians, including several congressmen and many ladies, who had come out from the Union capital on a warm summer's day to watch the expected rebel rout.

The defeat at Bull Run (called the battle of Manassas by Confederates) seemed to confirm Confederate claims that southerners were superior fighters. On the other hand it provided a healthy antidote to northern over-optimism. Republican governors from all over the North telegraphed the War Department offering new state regiments to protect the capital and prepare for resuming the march south. These men, moreover, would be enlisted for three years. Patriotism, the glamor of a uniform, and the love of adventure were still potent stimulants to enlistment; another 75,000 volunteers streamed into training camps near Washington prepared to put down the "rebellion."

LINCOLN'S EARLY COMMANDERS.   The man who took charge of this force was George B. McClellan, a small, wiry man with a bristling black moustache and a Napoleonic complex. As a young officer, "Little Mac" had served in the Mexican War; but he had spent most of his military career in the Corps of Engineers, and when the war broke out in early 1861 he was a civilian railroad director. His training and experience as an organizer and administrator helped him pull the army together. McClellan drilled his troops rigorously, welding the new arrivals and the ragged, dispirited mob that had fled to Washington from Bull Run into a confident, spit-and-polish army. He was soon being hailed as a savior.

McClellan, however, lacked the needed daring and drive of a good field commander. As a Democrat, moreover, he was suspicious of the president and his party. He took months to equip and train his men before resuming the attack. Finally in March 1862, after insistent goading by Lincoln, McClellan's magnificent army of 130,000 set out for Richmond from Hampton Roads, where they had arrived by sea. At Williamsburg, in early May, McClellan first encountered the enemy. The engagement was inconclusive. For the next two months McClellan fought a series of battles—the Peninsular Campaign—against two of the South's ablest military leaders, Robert E. Lee and Thomas J. ("Stonewall") Jackson. He managed to avert defeat; but his army returned to Washington in June bruised and badly battered. Nothing had been achieved.

In the West, Union forces under the Virginian George H. Thomas and the shaggy, hard-drinking Ulysses S. Grant were having better luck. In late January Thomas defeated the Confederates at the Battle of Mill Springs in Kentucky. Several weeks later Grant captured Fort Donelson on the Cumberland River, taking 14,000 Confederate prisoners. Soon Nashville fell to Union forces. Grant believed that he was now in a position to crush the Confederate army in the West decisively, but he underestimated the recuperative powers of his foe. On April 6, 1862, Albert Sidney Johnston attacked the exposed Union position near Shiloh Church, Tennessee, and pushed back the federal troops commanded by William Tecumseh Sherman. A confused two-day battle brought heavy casualties to both sides, including the death of the Confederate commander. Ultimately, the Confederate attack was repulsed, but Grant's men, exhausted and hungry, could not muster the energy to pursue the beaten Confederates.

McClellan's lack of offensive zeal disturbed Lincoln. In addition, the general was thoroughly detested by the emerging circle of "Radicals" in the Republican party, who advocated abolition of slavery and a more aggressive policy to defeat the South. In July 1862 the president replaced McClellan as field commander in the East with General John Pope.

For the next year the tide of war swept back and forth, with Lincoln unable to find a field commander to match Lee. When Pope was beaten by Lee and Jackson in the Second Battle of Bull Run (August 29–30, 1862), Lincoln turned once again to McClellan, who once again disappointed him. McClellan stopped Lee's advance into Maryland at Antietam (September 17, 1862) but lost the opportunity of decisively defeating the far smaller Confederate force. In November Lincoln decided to replace McClellan with Ambrose E. Burnside. The choice was unwise. In December 1862 at Fredericksburg, Virginia, the new Union commander sent massed infantry against entrenched Confederate troops, whose rifles and artillery slaughtered the charging blue-clad federals. Lincoln replaced Burnside with Joseph Hooker, who quickly demonstrated that he was no better. At Chancellorsville, Virginia (May 2–4, 1863), Lee and Jackson severely mauled Hooker's Army of the Potomac. The only consolation for the Union forces was that Jackson was accidentally killed by his own men.

UNION STRATEGY.   The Union was not only slow in finding a competent military leader; it also had difficulty evolving a clear, overall military strategy. To many northerners "On to Richmond!" seemed at first plan enough. Others considered it simple-minded, though in fact, to the end the Union concentrated excessively on taking the Confederate capital. In 1861 the aged commander in chief, Winfield Scott, proposed that the North, like the great Anaconda snake, should seize its victim in its coils and squeeze it to death. Union forces would contain the South along its borders, blockade the Confederate coast, and cut the South in half along the Mississippi River. Seeing that its cause was hopeless, the South would surrender. The Anaconda Plan was greeted with derision by the northern press and never adopted as such.

Yet several features of the Anaconda were in fact incorporated into Union strategy. In April 1862 Union forces under general Benjamin F. Butler took New Orleans, the South's largest city and control point for access to the Mississippi. Bit by bit the Union forces advanced up and down the banks of the river. In the summer of 1863 the final Confederate positions fell when Grant, aided by Admiral David Porter's river gunboats, took Vicksburg and Port Hudson. The Confederacy was now cut in two by a Union controlled north–south corridor.

THE NAVAL WAR.   The squeeze tactics were especially effective at sea, where each month the northern naval blockade grew tighter. In early 1862 the *Merrimac,* a Confederate ironclad converted from a scuttled United States naval vessel, threatened to break the Union blockade of Hampton Roads, Virginia. The federal navy rushed its own brand new ironclad, the *Monitor,* to the scene. The two vessels battled to a draw, and the southern ship retired, never again to challenge Union naval supremacy.

Its naval advantage was to stand the North in good stead. In the western theater federal gunboats on the Mississippi and its tributaries supported Union military operations with their cannon and kept river supply lines open. Along the Atlantic and Gulf coasts the seagoing Union fleet made possible successful amphibious attacks against southern ports such as New Orleans, Mobile, Savannah, and Port Royal. Most useful, however, was the coastal blockade. Each month the sea noose around the South drew tighter. In 1861 the federal navy captured one Confederate vessel in ten that tried to escape to the open sea; by 1865 its record had improved to one in two, and growing Confederate shortages of many products hitherto imported from Europe attested to the mounting effectiveness of the blockade.

The Confederates had their moments of glory at sea. Many Confederate blockade-runners evaded Union cruisers and dashed to Bermuda or some other British-American port and returned with weapons, medicines, foodstuffs, and luxuries. On the high seas the *Alabama* and other Confederate raiders destroyed Union shipping worth millions of dollars. Despite these successes, the Confederates were never able to challenge the Union navy on the waters, and each month saw the northern advantage grow as its shipyards turned out scores of new vessels to augment Union naval strength. In June 1864 the United States Navy's *Kearsarge* finally caught up with Captain Raphael Semmes of the *Alabama* off Cherbourg, France, and put an end to his spectacular commerce raiding career.

THE DIPLOMATIC WAR.   Europe's need for cotton had promised the Confederacy a chance to win diplomatic recognition and possibly military help from Britain and France. The South also hoped that Britain would seize the chance to cut the United States down to size by helping to divide it in half. The South counted on support from Europe's upper classes, who admired the southern planter elite more than the crude, money-mad Yankees. The French, for the most part, followed Britain's anti-Union lead. But, after establishing a puppet regime in Mexico that challenged the Monroe Doctrine, they had their own reasons for favoring a Yankee defeat and an enfeebled, distracted United States.

In the end King Cotton diplomacy proved to be a disappointment. Britain was overstocked with cotton in 1861 and for a time felt no pinch. Thereafter, the British imported cotton from Egypt and India to replace some of the lost southern supply. The North also had one high card that its enemy lacked: the prospect of emancipation. Though they were not averse to southern independence, the British middle and working classes could not morally support the slave system. If the North could convince the British people of its antislavery intentions, the London government would find it difficult to throw its weight against the Union.

For three years the Union and the Confederacy fought desperately to curry favor with the British. The South won the early diplomatic rounds when, in November 1861, the U.S.S *San Jacinto* stopped the British merchant vessel the *Trent,* removed the Confederate commissioners to France (John Slidell) and England (James M. Mason), and brought them as prisoners to Boston. Furious at this violation of their high seas rights, the British demanded their release, as well as reparations and an apology. Lincoln and secretary of state Seward sat on the situation for a time and then, concluding that war with Great Britain was not expedient, quietly returned the commissioners with an apology. But the *Trent* affair gave the Confederates a diplomatic edge. Early in 1862 the British government permitted the Confederates to use British shipyards to build and outfit the *Alabama* and other sea raiders, and soon after allowed the Confederate navy to contract with the Laird shipbuilding firm in Scotland for several powerful, ironclad "rams." For a while, too, English investors were receptive to lending money to the Confederacy.

The tide turned, however, when British friends of the United States, Richard Cobden and John Bright, appealed to antislavery opinion and succeeded in creating a strong pro-Union current. The efforts of these sympathetic Britons, the tireless maneuvering of Lincoln's minister to England, Charles Francis Adams, and, above all, Union victories on the battlefield, combined to shift British opinion away from the Confederacy. In October 1863 the British government seized the Laird rams before the Confederates could take delivery, ending their threat to the Union blockade. Though the North's worst diplomatic fears were allayed by the end of 1862, the possibility of a falling-out between Britain and the Union gave hope to the South almost to the end of the war.

✻ WAR AND SOCIETY ✻

The military, naval, and diplomatic drives of North and South were sustained by stupendous efforts of their respective home fronts. The raising of troops, the marshaling of financial and economic resources, and the containment of internal dissent were all vital parts of the great struggle on both sides to achieve victory.

CONSCRIPTION. Throughout the war both combatants relied primarily on volunteers to fill their military ranks. For the first year the system worked well. Typically, in the North, a prominent local citizen who craved adventure, influence, or a military reputation opened a recruiting office and issued a call for

Major Battles of the Civil War, 1861–1865

volunteers. When enough men had signed up they formed a company; ten companies equaled a regiment. The men of the company chose their own junior officers, who in turn chose the senior regimental officers. Usually the senior officers included the sponsors of the regiment.

The pure volunteer system did not last. A few months of bitter fighting and growing casualty lists dampened youthful enthusiasm and patriotism; fewer and fewer volunteers turned up at the recruiting offices. Yet the war consumed manpower at a frightful rate. More than 2.1 million men fought for the Union and about 800,000 for the Confederacy. Over half of all northern men of military age eventually wore the Union blue; over four-fifths of the South's young white males donned Confederate gray. Relatively few combatants escaped wounds or death. Some 360,000 Union men lost their lives; about 260,000 Confederates did not survive. Union wounded totaled another 275,000; Confederate wounded, at least 100,000.

By the middle of 1862 both governments were forced to resort to conscription. The South's April 1862 draft law made all able-bodied white males between 18 and 35 liable for military service, but exempted civil servants, militia officers, clergymen, and teachers. A supplemental measure that fall, intended to prevent slave disorders and encourage agricultural output, exempted a white male on each plantation with twenty slaves or more. Finally, the southern draft allowed any draftee to hire a substitute to go in his place.

The wounded near Fredericksburg. The emptiness and despair on these soldiers' faces contrast with the confidence and optimism of the early volunteers. With inadequate food, shelter, and sanitation, the ideals of glory and victory gave way to the realities of pain and death.

In the Union, the March 1863 Enrollment Act made every healthy male aged 20 to 45 subject to a federal draft with the exception of those who were the sole support of widows, motherless children, or indigent parents. The law also allowed a potential draftee to pay someone else to take his place or to pay a $300 commutation fee exempting him from service. Because the law was intended primarily to stimulate flagging enlistment, each congressional district could fill an assigned quota with volunteers. Only if state and local officials could not raise the necessary numbers within fifty days would the draft be invoked to make up the difference.

Conscription in both sections produced anger, resentment, and a multitude of abuses. In the North local officials offered large bounties to avoid the drafting of local citizens. "Bounty jumpers" made a business of accepting hundreds of dollars from several districts, one after the other, and then failing to report for duty. In both sections, critics charged that the draft benefited the rich. The "twenty-slave clause" in the Confederate draft supposedly favored the planter class over the small farmers. The provision for buying substitutes in both draft systems, though intended primarily to soften the harsh law, also seemed tilted toward those with ready cash. Under the North's Enrollment Act, moreover, rich districts were able to outbid poorer ones for able-bodied substitutes and so spare more of their citizens from military duty. These provisions led to charges in both North and South that it was "a rich man's war and a poor man's fight."

Recent research into the social makeup of Union and Confederate armies, however, casts doubt on the charge of class bias in Civil War military recruitment. Allowing for the youth of most soldiers, the occupations and class affiliations of the boys in blue and the boys in gray resembled those of their societies as a whole. In both sections the sons of the rich and the sons of the poor apparently risked their lives in proportionate numbers. Both armies had many foreign-born soldiers. In the Union the foreign-born troops reached 26 percent of the total.

Still, the draft acts aroused deep resentments and led to resistance in both sections. In the South young men escaped to the remotest mountains and often joined with deserters from the Confederate army to defy the authorities. Union draft resistance took an especially violent form in New York City where the working class, Democratic in its politics and often resentful of blacks, blamed the draft on the despised Republican administration. Soon after federal officials began to draw the first names of New York draftees in July 1863, mobs of whites attacked symbols of the Union cause, looting the homes of prominent Republicans, destroying the offices of the *New York Tribune,* burning down the city's Colored Orphan Asylum, and lynching a half-dozen innocent black people. The federal government rushed troops from the Gettysburg battlefield to end the anarchy, and General George Meade's veterans fired volleys into the mob. When, after four days, the ghastly riots finally ended, more than a hundred people were dead.

Conscription did not raise many soldiers directly. In the North only 46,000 men were actually drafted into service. But many thousands more volunteered rather than accept the stigma of forced recruitment. All told, a recent student of the draft system concludes, it worked moderately well to get the job done.

Whatever its failings, conscription was a novel exercise of central government power. The three previous American wars had been fought by volunteers. Now, under the goad of necessity, both Union and Confederate governments had asserted a right never claimed before—to compel men to risk their lives for the nation. But this innovation was only one of many pointing to enhanced power for the national government and to the physical and social consolidation of the country.

THE BEGINNINGS OF MODERN NATIONAL FINANCE.   Paying for the war was a major challenge for both governments. At one point the Union treasury was disbursing $2 million a day for munitions, supplies, military pay, and other war-related expenses.

The Confederacy initially tried to meet most of its costs with money borrowed from foreign and domestic sources. This approach yielded little, for few capitalists at home or abroad would lend money to the South except at outrageous interest rates. A "produce" loan of cotton and other crops was equally disappointing. As early as 1861, following the precedent of the Revolution, the Confederate treasury turned to paper money, unbacked by gold, mere IOUs.

Though the Confederate printing presses spewed out over $1.5 billion in paper money during the war, even that sum proved inadequate. Before many months the value of Confederate currency had fallen so low that the government was forced to adopt other means for paying its bills. In early 1863 the Confederate Congress authorized the impressment of slaves for the building of fortifications and for other government work. It also empowered the government to detail soldiers for work in vital war factories. In April 1863 it assumed the authority to take from farmers a tenth of all the major crops they produced.

In the North the need to supply the military forces led to a parallel, though less drastic, inflation of national power, and because it was the Union government that survived, that growth was momentous for the nation's future. With access to the markets of Europe, the gold of the West, and most of the country's banking capital, Union Secretary of the Treasury Salmon Chase was better able than his Confederate counterpart to tax and borrow. By 1865 Congress had imposed internal revenue taxes on hundreds of manufactured items, created a Bureau of Internal Revenue to administer the tax laws, and established America's first income tax. Using the excuse that heavily taxed American manufactures must be protected against cheaper foreign wares, the Republican Congress also raised tariff rates to levels never before reached, drastically reversing the prewar trend under the Democrats.

Internal taxes and import duties were not enough, however, and the Union, too, resorted to borrowing. Under Chase's prompting, Congress authorized the sale of several hundred million dollars of bonds, paying 6 percent interest in gold. The treasury's chief agent, Philadelphia banker Jay Cooke, advertised this issue in every northern newspaper and sent his agents to peddle the securities from door to door. Eventually he sold $362 million in bonds. By the war's end these bond sales and other loans had pushed the Union debt to the immense figure of $2.5 billion.

The treasury's financial needs produced a major revolution in the country's banking system. The state banks that had supplied the country's currency and credit since the demise of the Second Bank of the United States in 1836 proved inadequate to meet the country's political emergency. Matters were brought to a crisis in December 1861, when public hoarding of gold and excessive treasury borrowing forced the banks to cease redeeming their notes in specie. Without a gold reserve imposing a limit on their paper money issues, the banks were free to turn on the printing presses. The country now faced the prospect of a deluge of worthless paper bank notes to meet its currency needs.

To avoid this chaotic situation and at the same time tap the banks for funds, Chase proposed a national currency backed by government bonds and issued by a new system of federally chartered banks. Under the National Banking Acts of 1863 and 1864, businesspeople who bought a specified amount of federal bonds could organize new banks under federal charter and issue bank notes backed by the government securities. Now, instead of a multitude of privately issued bank notes unsecured by gold, the country would have a uniform paper money system under strict federal control. And after the war these notes would be doubly safe, for then, it was assumed, gold would once more return to normal circulation and the government and the banks would be able to redeem their obligations in "specie" on demand. The measure also sought to put the state banks out of business or force them to convert to national banks by taxing their note issues.

The national banking system did help the treasury finance the war. By June 1863 there were 450 national banks in existence, with millions of dollars' worth of federal bonds in their reserves, representing large revenues to the federal government. More important, however, for the first time in a generation Washington was back in the business of regulating the country's banking affairs.

Still, this was not enough to pay the Union's bills, and there seemed no alternative to treasury-issued paper money, as in the South. The Union's "greenbacks" would be "legal tender" with its value further shored up by a promise to redeem them in gold after the war. Limited in amount to $450 million, they did not appreciate drastically. By late 1864 northern prices were about two and a half times those of 1860. In the South prices had risen fiftyfold.

GOVERNMENT BECOMES BIG BUSINESS.   The demands of war enormously swelled the size of the Union government. Disbursements and tax collections brought an army of clerks to the Treasury Building across from the White House, while in the field hundreds of treasury agents fanned out to regulate the illegal cotton trade between northern buyers eager for scarce fiber and southerners avid for the means to pay for scarce imported goods. The War Department's scale of operation became even greater than the treasury's. Under Quartermaster General Montgomery Meigs, it performed prodigious labors in supplying the army. During the year ending June 30, 1865, alone, the Quartermaster Department purchased 3.4 million trousers, 3.7 million pairs of drawers, and 3.2 million flannel shirts, laying out for these and countless other articles over $431 million. In 1861 the federal civil service had employed 40,000 people; by 1865 there were 195,000, a fivefold increase.

Government orders invigorated the North's economy. The giant War Department procurement effort lowered costs in private armories. It also stimulated production in a wide array of businesses directly connected to the war effort. By 1864 production of coal, iron, copper, and leather was greater than before the war. Frequently the scale of government orders encouraged standardization and mechanization of production, establishing a model for postwar development. The canning industry was stimulated by government orders: When Gail Borden's condensed milk factory opened in early 1861, its entire output was "immediately commandeered" for the army. All told, the index of manufacturing for the North alone by 1864 was 13 percent higher than for the whole nation in 1860.

ORGANIZING AGRICULTURE. In the South invading armies, the breakdown of transportation, and the erosion of the slave labor system led to agricultural decline. In the North agriculture burgeoned under wartime need. The departure of thousands of young men from the farms precisely when the demand for farm products reached an all-time peak accelerated the acceptance of horse-drawn harvesters and mowers. During the entire decade of the 1850s American farmers had bought 100,000 of these machines; in 1864 manufacturers were turning out that many each year.

The expansion of northern farm output during the war was only obliquely a consequence of government action. But the government had an important direct impact on the social side of American agriculture. For years various northern and western farming groups had demanded favors of the federal government. Now, with the South out of the Union and the Republicans in control, the barriers came down. In 1861 Congress authorized a department of agriculture within the Patent Office to be headed by a commissioner. In 1862 it enacted the Morrill Land Grant College Act, setting aside several million acres of federal land for support of agricultural and industrial higher education. The 1862 Homestead Act provided that any citizen or any alien who declared his intention of becoming a citizen and who was also head of a family and over 21 might claim 160 acres of land on specified surveyed portions of the public domain. After residing on this land, adding improvements, and paying a small registration fee, he would become its owner, with no further strings except the usual local taxes. The law would be less than perfect in the way it was administered, yet it represented a triumph of the ideal of a free family farm and a fulfillment of Republican promises to western farm groups.

THE WAR AND ECONOMIC GROWTH. The war undoubtedly stimulated the northern economy in many ways. At one time scholars believed that it accelerated overall American economic growth and marked the basic shift of the American economy from an agricultural to an industrial base. It is now clear, as we saw in Chapter 9, that the structural transformation from rural-agricultural to urban-industrial was already well under way by 1860; it did not require the trigger of the Civil War. But the issue of the war's stimulating effect on the economy is less clear. Figures that lump together data for both sections show a slowing down of the American economy during the 1860s, the war period. Total commodity output in the United States was growing at the average rate of 4.6 percent a year in 1840–1859; during the period 1870–1899 it would increase annually by an average of 4.4 percent. In 1860–1869, however, it was only 2.0 percent, less than half these rates.

Given the economic surge in so many wartime northern industries, this is puzzling. But these figures add South to North, and during the war the South's economy suffered devastating blows from northern invasion and from the failure to repair and replace factories, railroads, barns, livestock, and other items that make up a nation's capital stock. Any gains in northern output, then, must be set against large declines in the South. But there are other good reasons. With a million or so young men in the army, the Union lost a vast amount of productive labor, and total output inevitably suffered. Labor and capital were already fully employed in 1861, and government outlays for war were mostly at the expense of the private sector with little addition to the net output of the economy.

There is a related question to consider here. Did the *political* effects of the war have significant economic consequences? With the South out of the Union, it proved possible to at least agree on the building of a Pacific railroad, to pass a protective tariff, and to restructure the nation's banking system. Clearly, the Union government under the Republicans was more friendly and helpful to economic "progress" than its southern and Democratic-dominated predecessor. And this shift of power and ideology would persist for years beyond 1865, with inevitable effects on the country's future economic development. It is difficult to avoid the conclusion that although the war may not have been caused by sectional economic rivalry, its consequences may well have favored the predominant interests of the business-industrial classes over the agrarian classes.

DISSENT. Despite the war-kindled patriotism, dissent flourished in both the Union and the Confederacy. In each it would create serious difficulties for the government. Ironically, repression would be stronger in the North, which prided itself on its intellectual freedom, than in the South, with its tradition of intolerance.

Dissent in the North ranged from mild disagreement with Republican policies to violent opposition that bordered on treason. The so-called War Democrats often differed with Lincoln and the Republicans over the best way to achieve victory, but they followed the lead of Stephen Douglas in offering their wholehearted support to the Union. The Little Giant died in June 1861, depriving the War Democrats of their outstanding leader; but to the end of the struggle, they were among the Union's staunchest supporters.

More critical of the administration's positions were the Peace Democrats. As the months passed, a segment of the opposition party became convinced that the Union must accept a negotiated peace that would restore the prewar sectional balance. At the depths of Union fortunes a substantial fringe of Peace Democrats even talked of letting the Confederacy go, in effect conceding victory to the South.

Called Copperheads by their enemies, the Peace Democrats were especially numerous among Catholic immigrants in the urban centers and among the southerners who had settled in the free states of the Midwest before 1860. Ideologically, especially in the Midwest, they were often opponents of the centralizing tendencies of the Republicans and of the new powers of the federal government. Men such as Clement Vallandigham, Samuel S. Cox, George Pendleton, and Daniel Voorhees regarded the Lincoln administration as the agent of "revived Whiggery." They, along with most other Democrats, also denounced the administration's efforts to make slavery's abolition a part of the Union cause and to abridge freedom of speech and of press. They were dissenters as well against the cultural values that the Republicans represented. The Lincoln party, they held, was the embodiment of moralistic New England puritanism. Congressman Cox blamed the war on the New England "tendency to make government a moral reform association."

The Copperheads were not the only opponents of the Lincoln administration's policies. Anti-Union feelings in the slave states that remained in the Union—Delaware, Maryland, Kentucky, and Missouri—was often intense. In several border states during the war pro-Union neighbor fought pro-Confederate neighbor with a viciousness that sometimes went beyond anything found on the battlefields. In Missouri guerrilla war made the state resemble "Bleeding Kansas" during the 1850s as roving bands of irregulars attacked innocent and not-so-innocent citizens of the opposite persuasion. In suppressing the disorders in the border region, Union commanders frequently alienated the prosouthern populace and stirred up even greater dissatisfaction.

Inevitably, Lincoln had to consider how much dissent was permissible in a nation threatened with dissolution. The president was strongly committed to free speech. But his first responsibility, he felt, was to preserve the Union.

To head off his opponents and those he considered dangerous to the Union cause, Lincoln employed a combination of guile, persuasion, and coercion. Within his own party he had to contend with the Radicals, Republicans who fervently opposed slavery and believed that the president was not moving fast enough or firmly enough against the South. They particularly deplored his unwillingness to use the war as an opportunity to destroy slavery and his reluctance to employ blacks in the armed forces. Republican conservatives pulled the other way, saying that the war to restore the Union must not be "abolitionized." To attack slavery would only drive the border states out and confirm southern determination to resist. Lincoln dealt with the opposing wings of his party, as he explained at one point, by carrying "a pumpkin in each end of the bag." In his cabinet this meant balancing Seward against Chase and seeing to it that neither prevailed. In Congress this meant listening to all Republican voices, keeping his options open, and moving only when it helped the Union cause.

Dealing with dissenters outside the party was more difficult. The remaining Democrats in Congress were often a thorn in the president's side. Several historians believe that a functioning two-party system during the war was a significant northern advantage over the South. It kept opposition to the administration within the bounds of party conflict, they say, and prevented it from becoming destructive and irresponsible. On the other hand, in the South, without a working party system, attacks on the Davis administration quickly turned into damaging personal assaults on the president, which seriously undermined his authority. Whatever the case, to Lincoln, Democratic opposition at times seemed indistinguishable from disloyalty, and it was hard for him to resist wielding his authority as commander in chief to suppress his critics.

CIVIL LIBERTIES DURING CRISIS.   Lincoln's first response to the dangers of disloyalty came in mid-1861 when, to contain anti-Union sentiment in several districts of the country, he suspended the writ of *habeas corpus,* a fundamental constitutional protection against unlawful imprisonment. In September 1862 he expanded the area in which the suspension applied and authorized the arrest by military commanders of all "Rebels and Insurgents, their aiders and abettors within the United States, and all persons discouraging volunteer enlistments, resisting militia drafts, or guilty of any disloyal practice." All told, the Union government arrested about 15,000 civilians during the war for disloyal activities, espionage, sabotage, or some other action detrimental to the Union cause. A number of times it also interfered with freedom of the press by excluding "disloyal" newspapers from the mail and on a few occasions shut down papers accused of hurting the Union cause. None of this was admirable behavior for a democratic government. Yet, all told, given the serious danger to the nation's survival, the government and the military avoided excess in suppressing dissent.

The most famous, or infamous, breach of civil liberties by the Lincoln administration was the arrest of Clement Vallandigham. In May 1863 the former congressman, campaigning for the Democratic nomination for governor of Ohio, deliberately provoked the government by denouncing the war as a failure, demanding repudiation of the Emancipation Proclamation, and calling for a negotiated peace with the Confederacy. General Burnside, then military commander in Ohio, promptly arrested Vallandigham and a military commission sentenced him to prison for the duration of the war.

The affair embarrassed Lincoln. The incident made the administration seem despotic while at the same time converting the ex-congressman into a free-speech martyr. On the other hand, the president did not see how he could ignore those people who threatened Union survival. "Must I shoot a simple minded soldier boy who deserts," he wrote a group of Democrats who protested the Vallandigham arrest, "while I must not touch the hair of a wily agitator who induces him to desert?" Lincoln solved the problem by banishing the Ohio Democrat to the Confederacy. Vallandigham soon escaped to Canada and resumed his campaign for governor long distance. But he was no longer an embarrassment to the administration.

THE EMANCIPATION PROCLAMATION.   The Lincoln administration's willingness to invade civil liberties is a further instance of war-inflated government power. Fortunately, repression did not become a permanent feature of American political life. And in race relations, the use of government war powers worked a profound, permanent, and beneficent change.

Lincoln and the Radicals differed on the question of slavery. As part of a Union-first policy, the president initially tried to steer clear of the issue. As long as the border slave states might join the Confederacy, Lincoln sought to focus the public mind on reuniting the nation rather than on ending the "peculiar institution." When General John C. Frémont, the former Republican presidential candidate, proclaimed in late 1861 that all slaves held by rebels within his Missouri command were free, Lincoln overruled him. The president also refused to use a feature of the Second Confiscation Act of 1861 that allowed the emancipation of captured slaves employed by the Confederacy against the Union. When Horace Greeley publicly criticized him for his inaction against slavery, Lincoln replied that his "paramount object" in the struggle was "to save the Union, . . . not either to save or destroy slavery."

But Lincoln and the Radicals were not free agents: Both were at the mercy of circumstances. To begin with, blacks were not passive observers of emancipation. In the North black abolitionists joined their white colleagues in asserting that the war was a struggle over slavery and that to win it the Union must destroy the hateful institution. Slavery, Frederick Douglass proclaimed, was "a tower of strength" to the Confederacy. "The very stomach of this rebellion is the negro in the condition of a slave. Arrest that hoe in the hands of the negro and you smite the rebellion in the very seat of its life."

Even more compelling than the words of free northern blacks were the deeds of southern slaves. Despite the absence from the farms and plantations of thousands of young white men, generally, slaves continued to work at their accustomed tasks: They did indeed serve as "the very stomach" of the rebellion. They failed to rebel because resistance in the heavily armed and militarized wartime South would have been suicidal. But they did not acquiesce. When Union armies drew near, the odds changed dramatically, and blacks showed their real feelings. Black refugees in the thousands fled to the Union lines. At first federal officials did not know what to do with these homeless and destitute people, since slavery was still legal and they were still the property of white owners. Faced with this situation, General Benjamin F. Butler shrewdly called them "contraband of war" and paid them to work as free laborers on military fortifications. Other military commanders, following Butler's lead, employed thousands of "contrabands" at military jobs. Other refugees were set to work growing cotton for northern mills or took jobs with private employers for money wages. Long before the end of the war a substantial part of the South's slaves had, in effect, liberated themselves from bondage.

More than informal self-liberation, however, was required to demolish the pernicious institution as a legal system beyond all possibility of resurrection. Lincoln originally hoped that compensated emancipation and colonization in either Africa or Central America would finish slavery. At one point he pushed a measure through Congress appropriating a half million dollars to settle freed slaves on an island off Haiti. But blacks were hostile to colonization, and in the border states slaveholders proved unwilling to consider freeing their slaves even if paid. Lincoln now had to consider simply ending slavery—an institution representing $4 billion worth of private property—by direct action under presidential war powers. However much he despised slavery, it was a momentous step to take, and he was reluctant to act.

The hope that the destruction of slavery would shorten the war finally tipped the balance in favor of abolition by federal proclamation. Three considerations worked powerfully on the president. One was Frederick Douglass's point: the reliance of the Confederacy on slave labor. If the slaves knew that the federal government intended to set them free, they would cease to be a source of strength for the Confederacy. Another consideration was the potential value of black soldiers. If the North could tap this human reservoir, it could offset the immense losses on the battlefields and the declining zeal of white volunteers. A final factor was the moral advantage of turning the war for the Union into a war for human freedom. If the Union cause were identified with the destruction of slavery, it would be difficult for any European power to aid the Confederacy.

By July 1862 Lincoln had concluded that a proclamation of emancipation was "absolutely essential for the salvation of the Union." He postponed making his intentions known, however, fearing that if the news came at a time of military difficulties, it would be taken as an act of desperation. On September 22, following Lee's defeat at Antietam, he issued a preliminary emancipation proclamation declaring that on January 1, 1863, in every part of the South then still in rebellion, all slaves would be "thenceforward and forever free." As scheduled, on New Year's Day, 1863, the final Emancipation Proclamation took effect. Technically, it affected only those places where federal law could not be enforced—the Confederacy. It said nothing about slavery in the border states, and had the Union lost the war, it would have become a symbol of futility. But the Union won, and the proclamation in the end effectively sounded the death knell for slavery all over the United States.

It also affected the Union's standing abroad. Henry Adams, serving as his father's secretary at the American legation in London, wrote home after news of the proclamation reached Britain: "The Emancipation Proclamation has done more for us here than all our former victories and all our diplomacy."

BEHIND THE LINES.   The war caused dramatic changes in civilians' lives. In the South it produced great hardship for virtually every citizen. As prices rose, as transport broke down, as the blockade took effect, southern living standards deteriorated. In Richmond a clerk in the Confederate War Department complained bitterly in 1863 that the inhabitants of the city were "almost in a state of starvation" though there was abundant food in the Confederacy as a whole. In Mobile, food riots, led by women carrying banners reading "Bread or Blood" and "Bread and Peace," broke out in 1863. All through the South tea and coffee, both imported items, became scarce; and southern consumers turned to parched wheat, corn, peanuts, and even acorns as substitutes. When commodities were available, they often sold at prices far beyond the means of the average consumer.

The North too experienced an inflationary surge. Prices rose faster than money wages, reducing the average worker's real income by about 20 percent and causing some labor unrest behind northern lines. But the effects were less extreme and never seriously threatened social order.

Northern women were significant beneficiaries of the war. Before 1861 employment opportunities for women had been limited. With thousands of able-bodied men now in the Union armies, traditional sex barriers weakened. Many women joined the vastly expanded War and Treasury departments as secretaries, copyists, and clerks. In the private sector the number of women factory operatives, schoolteachers, and clerical workers also increased. Unfortunately, unskilled women workers were among those most seriously hurt by rising prices.

One of the most important breakthroughs for women was the creation of a female nursing profession. Though Florence Nightingale, an Englishwoman, had already proved the competence of women as military nurses during the 1850s Crimean War in Europe, male authorities resisted their use in Union military hospitals. They did not count on the determination and patriotism of strong-willed women such as Clara Barton and Dorothea Dix, who insisted on sharing the work and sacrifices of the war effort. In the end some 10,000 white women served as nurses in the North receiving $12 a month. About 4,000 black women worked for the Union as practical nurses, cooks, laundresses, and orderlies at $10 a month. Dix was appointed superintendent of women nurses for the Union army. Though women on both sides organized societies to aid the war effort, only in the North were these carried beyond the local level.

Many of the gains in paid employment for women were temporary. After 1865, as government departments contracted and men returned to civilian life, women were forced back into their parlors or kitchens. But the Civil War did much to establish nursing as a profession for women and to develop formal training and certification in that field. Clara Barton, who founded the American Red Cross twenty years after the Civil War, noted that by the time the war ended, "woman was at least fifty years in advance of the normal position which continued peace . . . would have assigned her."

* THE LAST YEARS OF BATTLE *

Lee's defeat of Hooker at Chancellorsville in May 1863 lifted the spirits of the entire Confederacy. Yet the South's situation, taken as a whole, did not seem encouraging. In the West, Grant was advancing on Vicksburg and would soon place that strategically important Mississippi city under siege. Along the Atlantic coast the Union was preparing to attack Charleston. All through the Confederacy, prices were soaring; the blockade's noose was growing tighter. Something must be done to prevent the South's collapse.

With some misgivings, the Richmond government adopted Lee's plan to invade the North. This move could relieve the pressure in the West, skim much-needed supplies from the prosperous northern countryside, encourage the peace forces in the North, and perhaps even lead to the capture of Washington or Philadelphia. On June 15 General Robert Ewell's corps, under Lee's overall command, forded the Potomac heading north. The remainder of the Army of Northern Virginia soon joined it and together the combined Confederate force swept across the Mason-Dixon Line into Pennsylvania. As the Confederates advanced they levied tribute on local storekeepers, farmers, and bankers, and destroyed railroad property and Republican Congressman Thaddeus Stevens's iron works. Lee's advance alarmed the entire Union. Having lost faith in Hooker, Lincoln placed George G. Meade in command of the Army of the Potomac to face the threat.

GETTYSBURG. The choice was a good one: Meade was able, though neither colorful nor aggressive. Moving north parallel and to the east of Lee, Meade and the Confederates converged at Gettysburg, a small town fifty miles from the Pennsylvania state capital at Harrisburg. Meade's men dug in on ridges both to the south and to the north of town and prepared to repulse the Confederate attack. The 88,000 federals not only outnumbered Lee's 75,000 but also had superior artillery.

The battle was a seesaw affair lasting three full days (July 1–3, 1863). Lee's forces came close to sweeping the federals off their position several times. The fighting was exceptionally bloody, some of it hand to hand. Union artillery was devastating and so were union rifles. The replacement of the smooth-bore musket by the far more accurate rifle as the standard infantry weapon gave the defense a tremendous advantage. Masses of infantry charging an entrenched enemy were ripped to pieces by the minié balls (lead bullets that expanded to fit the rifled barrel) of the defenders. It was the misfortune of the Confederates that Lee believed in the concept of the offensive-defensive—fighting what was basically a defensive war by aggressive attack on the enemy. In the new era of the rifle this approach produced ferocious casualties, and so it was at Gettysburg. Each brave charge of the gray-clad Confederates was sent hurtling back after fearful carnage.

On the last day of battle the Confederates launched forty-seven regiments, 15,000 men, under General George Pickett against the Union center on ominously named Cemetery Hill. The men in gray advanced across the open field against murderous artillery fire and swept to the top of the Union emplacement. Then, their momentum exhausted, they reeled back, leaving behind several thousand dead and wounded.

Pickett's charge was the last spurt of Confederate strength. Lee expected Meade to counterattack, but the federals were almost as exhausted as the Confederates and sat tight. Seizing this opportunity to disengage safely, Lee ordered a general retreat. Soon he and his ragged army were safely back in Virginia.

Lee's defeat at Gettysburg coincided with Grant's capture of Vicksburg following a long campaign and costly siege. Then, in the fall of 1863, Grant and General George H. Thomas won the battles of Lookout Mountain and Missionary Ridge and finally pushed the Confederates out of ravaged Tennessee. Called to command all the Union forces, Grant came east in March 1864 to take over the Virginia front. In the next months he aimed sledgehammer blows at Lee and his lieutenants in the densely forested country between Washington and Richmond. The gains in ground were negligible, and the losses on both sides were appalling. Yet Grant realized that the attrition was easier for the Union to bear than for the enemy. Southern manpower was by now all but exhausted; the North, though weary, still had human reserves.

"JOHNNY REB" AND "BILLY YANK."   Although Gettysburg had been the war's turning point, many dismal months of fighting remained. The chief sufferers toward the end, as in the beginning, were the common soldiers of the Union and the Confederacy. Of the two, "Billy Yank" had the easier time, especially after the North's factories began to operate at high gear. The resources of the Union assured him enough food and clothing to keep the inner and outer man reasonably content. But his life was no picnic. Being a Union soldier involved long periods of hard foot-slogging over rough roads in every sort of weather, days of boredom in bivouac, followed, finally, by terrifying exposure to flying lead and iron. If wounded, his chances for survival were poor. The medical profession did not use anesthesia and lacked any knowledge of the sources of infection. Many of the injured died of shock, gangrene, or loss of blood. Many who survived battle were swept away by diseases picked up in unsanitary camps or as a result of exposure and exhaustion.

"Johnny Reb" experienced all these afflictions and several more besides. The southern soldier often lacked adequate shoes, clothing, and food. Despite Confederate ingenuity in manufacture and supply, much of his equipment, including his rifle and ammunition, was captured from the Yankees. There was seldom enough to go around.

The men of both armies had their good moments. Within units, many lifelong friendships were forged in the heat of battle. But however warmly veterans later recalled their fighting days, soldiering was not an occupation that many men cared to stay at indefinitely, and in both armies the desertion rates were stupendous. In all, 200,000 Union men and 104,000 Confederates deserted, almost 10 percent of all Yankees and 13 percent of all "Rebs."

BLACK SOLDIERS.   One source of northern strength denied the South was the manpower of black Americans. Defenders of equality strongly favored the use of black troops. As Frederick Douglass declared: "Once let the black man get upon his person the brass letters, U.S.; let him get an eagle on his button, and a musket on his shoulder, and bullets in his pocket, and there is no power on earth which can deny that he has earned the right to citizenship." But many white Northerners were immovable bigots who feared the very consequences that Douglass welcomed. In February 1863 forty-three Democratic congressmen signed a statement condemning Republican plans to enlist black soldiers as a plot to establish "the equality of the black and white races."

As it became more and more difficult to fill the depleted ranks of the Union Army, however, the opposition faded. Why not share the burden of dying for the Union with one of the chief beneficiaries of the war, many whites began to ask. By early 1863, with Lincoln's enthusiastic support, the War Department authorized the creation of black regiments composed of northern free blacks and, in larger numbers, of ex-slaves freed by the Emancipation Proclamation. At first the Confederate government declared that any captured member of a black regiment, whether white officer or black private, would be severely punished. But when Lincoln threatened to retaliate against captured Confederates, the Richmond government backtracked.

Black troops fought bravely in many bloody engagements. Placed almost invariably under white officers and treated initially as second-class soldiers in matters of pay, bounties for service, and other benefits, black troops nevertheless established a record for courage and enterprise equal to any group in the Union army. In March 1863 Lincoln called black troops "very important, if not indispensable" to the Union war effort. By the end of the fighting the Union armed forces had enrolled 179,000 black soldiers and another 20,000 black sailors.

The valor of foreign-born and black fighting men had favorable effects on ethnic and racial attitudes in the North. Antiforeign sentiment declined. Racial bigotry continued, but the legal and social positions of northern blacks improved. Midwestern legislatures repealed state laws discriminating against free blacks or denying them the right to reside within state borders. Several cities ended the common practice of segregating blacks on streetcars and in schools. America scarcely became a racial paradise, but the shining record of black troops fighting for the Union made many white citizens reconsider their prejudices.

THE ELECTION OF 1864. The lessening of ethnic conflict in the North was not matched by a decline in political strife. Nobody proposed passing over the presidential election of 1864 in the interest of national harmony. At Baltimore the Republicans renominated Lincoln and chose Andrew Johnson, the Tennessee Unionist Democrat, as his running mate. Johnson's selection was intended to reach out to non-Republicans, and to reinforce this strategy the delegates re-named their party the National Union Party. The Democrats turned to General McClellan as their presidential candidate. McClellan was a war Democrat, but his running mate, George Pendleton of Ohio, supported a negotiated peace with the South, as did the Democratic platform. During the campaign the Republicans charged their opponents with disloyalty, and they were not completely wrong. The Richmond government yearned for Democratic victory, and southern agents secretly poured money into the campaigns of midwestern Democrats. For a time the Democrats believed they could ride to victory on the wave of discouraging northern defeats during the late spring—the Wilderness, Spotsylvania, Peters-burg, and the Crater. Lincoln himself was pessimistic and thought it "exceedingly probable that this Administration will not be reelected."

But then the military tide turned. In early May a Union army of 100,000 men led by William T. Sherman cut south from Tennessee and advanced on Atlanta, Georgia, a major rail junction and manufacturing center. Through much of July and all of August Sherman halted before the city while he and his Confederate foe, John B. Hood, maneuvered for advantage. Then on September 2, Union troops marched into the abandoned city. Sherman telegraphed the president: "Atlanta is ours, and fairly won." On August 23, meanwhile, the Union navy under admiral David G. Farragut captured Mobile, shutting down a major port for Confederate blockade runners. In the Shenandoah Valley of Virginia, the Union cavalry commander, Philip Sheridan, won a smashing victory against Jubal Early's troops in late September. These victories were reflected in the polls. On November 8 the Lincoln-Johnson ticket swept the electoral college by 212 to 21 and won a popular majority of 400,000 votes.

LAST BATTLES, THE LAST CASUALTY. The months following the election saw the rapid collapse of southern hopes. On November 15 Sherman and his veteran army left Atlanta heading east for Savannah on the Atlantic coast. Before departing the city, the general ordered everything of military worth burned. The flames got out of control, and a third of Atlanta went up in smoke.

Sherman's "march to the sea" was considered foolhardy by many military experts. Cutting himself off from his supply bases and advancing through the heart of enemy country could spell disaster. Sherman rejected the doubters: He would survive by living off the country while cutting a swath of destruction through the heart of Dixie. The general had a theory of warfare that, alas, would see much application in our own day. Winning wars, he believed, was not merely a matter of winning battles and killing enemy soldiers. It was also instilling fear into the enemy people and destroying their morale. Fortunately, in 1864–1865, this did not yet mean brutal extermination of civilians. But it did mean massive destruction of property. Sherman's men demolished everything in a fifty-mile belt on either side of their march. One of their favorite targets was southern railroads. Yankee foragers ("bummers") also destroyed fences, crops, and farm houses. Another Yankee target was slavery. Union troops marching to Savannah liberated every black in sight. Before long Sherman's troops were being trailed by a column of thousands of liberated slaves, the able-bodied and lame, the young and old, men and women.

On December 22 Sherman reached Savannah and turned north, heading for a rendezvous with Grant and the Army of the Potomac. Through South Carolina he continued to apply his "total war" tactics. One result was the destruction by fire of Columbia, the capital of the state. In the West, meanwhile, General George Thomas had smashed Hood's army at Nashville. Grant, too, was finally able to achieve the breakthrough he had long sought south of Washington. During the early weeks of 1865 Grant pressed hard against Lee in Virginia. In early April, with the help of Sheridan's cavalry, he took the important center of Petersburg, which had eluded him for many months. Lee and his army slipped away, but by now southern morale had virtually collapsed. President Davis proposed to recruit black troops to shore up the faltering Confederate cause, promising these men freedom for themselves and their families in exchange for risking their lives. It is doubtful if many black men would have fought for the Confederacy under these terms, but the issue was moot. On April 2 Confederate officials began to flee Richmond to avoid capture by Grant's army. The following day, with the city burning, the federals arrived in the Confederate capital. The first blue-clad troops to enter were the men of the all-black Fifth Massachusetts Cavalry.

On April 7 Robert E. Lee—his army hungry, demoralized, and encircled—asked Grant for terms. On Sunday, two days later, the two commanders met at the crossroads hamlet of Appomattox Courthouse and agreed on surrender terms. Grant was generous. The Confederate officers and men were to be released on their promise not to take up arms again. The Confederates would surrender all weapons and war material, but the men might keep their personal equipment, including their horses and mules. These, Grant said, they would need to help them "work their little farms." The brief ceremony over, 26,000 Confederates laid down their arms.

Lincoln came to the Confederate capital in early April to view the prize of four years' outlay of Union blood and treasure. In the next few days his mind ran much to the problems of political reconstruction, and after his return to Washington he made a major address on the subject. On April 14, 1865, the happy though tired chief executive went with his wife, Mary, and some friends to the theater to see the British comedy *Our American Cousin*. During the third act a dark-haired man entered the presidential box, fired a single shot at Lincoln, and leaped to the stage. Amid the confusion and the shrieks, he shouted something that sounded like "Sic Semper Tyrannis" ("Thus always to tyrants"), the Virginia state motto, and escaped. Early the next morning Abraham Lincoln died.

The assassin was John Wilkes Booth, an actor and Confederate sympathizer who, with a few other disgruntled southerners, had concocted a plot to destroy the man they held responsible for Confederate defeat. The plotters also intended to assassinate Seward, Vice President Johnson, and other high Union officials. Booth was cornered in Virginia on April 26 and either shot himself or was shot by a zealous Union soldier. He died before disclosing the full conspiracy; false rumors of complicity by Secretary Stanton or the Confederate leaders soon gained wide circulation.

* CONCLUSIONS *

The war was over; but was an era also over? Had the war transformed American life?

The war did not change the United States from an agricultural to an industrial society. That process was already underway before 1860 and would not be completed until well after 1865. Meanwhile, the events of 1861–1865 did fuse the country into a more coherent social and economic whole. It made possible a transcontinental railroad and created a national banking system and a new national currency. It trained thousands of men to manage large-scale operations and mass movements of people and goods—talents that when applied to private enterprise would help to create modern "big business" and further integrate the country. Though it took years beyond 1865 for the full effects to work themselves out, the war also helped to universalize the commercial values of the Northeast. The South would be slow to embrace the new ethos, but for good or ill the rest of the country would find Yankee enterprise and "get-ahead" more acceptable after 1865 than before. Even the intellectuals who had been emphatically critical before 1860 found liberal capitalist society more palatable after the experience of 1861–1865.

The war also ended for all time the threat of secession. States' rights would continue to be an issue in American political life, but never again would one part of the nation threaten to leave the Union.

Finally, the war destroyed slavery. It did not end problems of racial adjustment; they are still with us today. But it did sweep away a benighted, oppressive institution that rigidly prescribed the relations of the races and replaced it with alternatives that, however imperfect, permitted reform and improvement.

16

RECONSTRUCTION

What Went Wrong?

1877	Compromise of 1877: Hayes is chosen as president, and all remaining federal troops are withdrawn from the South
By 1880	The share-crop system of agriculture is well established in the South

Almost no one has had anything good to say about Reconstruction, the process by which the South was restored to the Union. Contemporaries judged it a monumental failure. To most southern whites it seemed a time when Dixie was subjected to a cruel northern occupation and civilization itself was buried under an avalanche of barbarism. For the freedmen—as the former slaves were called—the period started with bright promise but ended in bitter disappointment, with most blacks still on the bottom rung of society. Contemporary Northerners, too, generally deplored Reconstruction. They had hoped it would remake the South on the national model. But it had not, and most were relieved when the last federal troops withdrew in 1877 and the white South once more governed itself.

Nor have later Americans generally thought well of Reconstruction. A half century ago most historians accused the Republicans who controlled Reconstruction after the Civil War of being blinded by vindictiveness and botching the job. Scholars of the next generation rejected this view, but believed the chance to modernize and liberalize southern society had been missed because the North had neither the will nor the conviction to take the bold steps needed. Recently some younger historians have declared that by failing to guarantee the political rights of the freedmen and provide them with land, the North sold out the black people, leaving them little better off than before the Civil War.

Obviously, then, from many points of view, Reconstruction has seemed a failure. What went wrong? And were the results as bad as most critics have believed?

* THE LEGACY OF WAR *

A month after Appomattox, Whitelaw Reid, a correspondent for the Republican *Cincinnati Gazette,* went south to see what the war had done to Dixie. Reid was struck by the devastation he encountered. Hanover Junction, near Richmond, Reid reported, "presented little but standing chimneys and the debris of destroyed buildings. Along the [rail]road a pile of smoky brick and mortar seemed a regularly recognized sign of what had once been a depot." Not a train platform or water tank had been left, he wrote, and efforts to get the road in running order were often the only improvements visible for miles. Interior South Carolina, hard hit by General Sherman's army, "looked for many miles like a broad black streak of ruin and desolation." In the Shenandoah Valley of Virginia be-

THE FALL OF RICHMOND V⁴ ON THE NIGHT OF APRIL 2ⁿᵈ 1865.

Richmond, Virginia, the Confederate capital, being abandoned by the Jefferson Davis government in the last days of the war.

tween Winchester and Harrisonburg, scarcely a horse, pig, chicken, or cow remained alive. Southern cities, too, were devastated. Columbia, capital of South Carolina, was a blackened wasteland with not a store standing in the business district. Atlanta, Richmond, Selma, and other southern towns were also devastated. All told, over $1 billion of the South's physical capital had been reduced to ashes or twisted wreckage.

Human losses were appalling. Of the South's white male population of 2.5 million in 1860, a quarter of a million (10 percent) had died of battle wounds or disease. Most of these were young men who represented the region's most vigorous and creative human resource. Of those who survived, some were maimed and many were worn out emotionally.

The South's economic institutions were also wrecked. Its banking structure, based on now-worthless Confederate bonds, had collapsed. Personal savings had been wiped out when Confederate currency lost all its value. Even more crushing, the region's labor system was in ruins. Slavery as an economic institution was dead, but no one knew what to replace it with. Many blacks remained on the farms and plantations and continued to plant, cultivate, and harvest. But many others—whether to test their new-found freedom, hunt for long-lost relatives, or just to take their first holiday—wandered the roads or fled to the towns, abandoning the land on which the South's economy was based.

The war had left behind damaging resentments. After struggling for independence against the "tyrannical government in Washington" and "northern dominance" for four years, white southerners could not help feeling apprehensive, angry, and disappointed. Now, even more than in 1860, a weak South would be oppressed by the North, its arrogance reinforced by victory. Northerners, for their part, would not easily forget the sacrifices and losses they had suffered in putting down what they considered the illegal and unwarranted rebellion; nor would they easily forgive the "atrocities" committed by the Confederacy. At Andersonville, Georgia, for example, during July 1864, 31,000 Union prisoners had been confined in a sixteen-acre stockade, protected from the weather only by tents and fed on scanty rations. As many as 3,000 prisoners had died in a month, a rate of 100 a day. To the northern public the Confederate prison officials, and especially the camp commandant, Captain Henry Wirz, seemed beasts who must be punished.

The American people, then, faced a gigantic task of physical, political, and psychological restoration. By the usual measure, the period of restoration, or Reconstruction, lasted for some twelve years, until 1877. It was a time of upheaval and controversy, as well as new beginnings. In its own day the problems associated with Reconstruction dominated the political and intellectual life of the country, and they have fascinated and repelled Americans ever since.

* ISSUES AND ATTITUDES *

During the years of Reconstruction all Americans agreed that racial and political readjustments were necessary. But what changes and how to make them deeply divided contemporaries, North and South, black and white, Republican and Democrat.

People's views tended to cluster around five major positions: Radical Republican, northern conservative, southern conservative, southern Unionist, and southern freedman. Let us allow each to speak for itself. The monologues that follow are fabricated, but they express the essential position each group took on Reconstruction.

RADICAL REPUBLICANS. *"The South must be made to recognize its errors, and southerners must acknowledge that now that they have been defeated, they can no longer decide their own fate. It is now in the hands of the victorious North. Southerners can avoid our wrath and show they deserve to be readmitted as citizens of the United States in a number of ways. At the very least, they must reject their former leaders and choose new ones who have not been connected with the Confederacy. They must take oaths of loyalty to the United States. They must reject all attempts to repay the Confederate debt incurred in an unjust cause. Most important of all, they must accept the fact that the former slaves are now free and must be treated as the political equals of whites.*

"Many former slaves worked and fought for the Union, and we must now help them through the difficult transition to full freedom. As to how this end can best be accomplished, not all of us agree. A few hold that it will be necessary for the freedmen to get land so they can support themselves independently. But we all believe that at the very

minimum they must be given the right to vote and, during the early stages of the change, must be protected against privation and exploitation. No doubt they will be grateful for the efforts of their Republican friends in defeating the slave power, destroying slavery, and defending them against those who do not accept the new situation. This gratitude will incline them to vote Republican. But that is all to the good. The Republican party is the great hope of the nation. It is the party of freedom and economic progress. It is not afraid to use government to encourage that progress. In a word, it is the party that has, since its founding, proved that it is the best embodiment of both the nation's moral and practical sense."

NORTHERN CONSERVATIVES. *"We, the northern conservatives, are generally of the old Democratic persuasion. Most of us opposed secession and supported the war. But we agree that now that the war is over and secession defeated, we must forget the past. Let southerners—white southerners, that is—determine their own fate. It is in the best American tradition to let local communities decide their own future without undue interference from the national government. Let us confirm this great principle of local self-determination, and let us allow the South back into the Union on its own terms.*

"We must not try to force black suffrage or social equality down the throats of the former Confederates. Almost all white Americans believe that Negroes are ill-equipped to exercise the rights of citizens. The Radicals insist on giving them the vote only because they want to secure continued control of the national government and to guarantee the predominance of the values and goals of the Northeast, the nation's commercial-industrial region, against the very different interests and goals of the country's agricultural West and South. It is clearly hypocritical of the supposed champions of the freedmen to be so timid in supporting Negro suffrage in the northern states, where such a stand is politically unpopular and where there are too few Negroes to add to their voting strength. We must reject such hypocrisy and restore peace and tranquillity to the nation as quickly and completely as possible."

SOUTHERN CONSERVATIVES. *"The war we fought and lost was for a noble cause, and it brought out the best in our southern people. We must never forget the sacrifice and heroism of the gallant men in gray. Perhaps secession was a mistake, but that fact will never diminish the grandeur of our struggle.*

"But let us now get back to the business of daily living. We of the South must be allowed to resume our traditional political relations with the rest of the states. We must be free to determine our own fate with a minimum of conditions. Above all, we must be permitted to steer our own course on race relations. The 'carpetbaggers' who come down from the North looking for easy money, and the southern renegade 'scalawags' willing to betray their own people for the sake of power, are self-serving and contemptible. They do not understand or accept southern traditions.

"True, we must recognize that Negroes are no longer slaves and we must make certain concessions to their private rights, but in the public realm these must be limited by their capacities. Above all, Negroes must not be allowed to exercise political power. They

are not the equal of whites. They can be duped and deceived by their professed 'friends' into supporting the Republican party, but actually their interests will be best served by those who have always been the leaders of southern society and who remain the Negroes' natural protectors."

SOUTHERN UNIONISTS.   "At long last we are free to speak our minds! For four long years we have been persecuted and intimidated by the secessionists. Now that they have been defeated, we deserve recognition and favor. Unfortunately the rebels are still in the majority. They say they have accepted the new circumstances of the South, but many of them have not, and we are in a vulnerable position. At the very least we must be protected by our northern friends against hostile unreconciled rebels. Moreover, we should be rewarded for our loyalty to the Union with an important place in the new order.

"We do not all agree about the role of the ex-slaves in the South's future, but many of us recognize that they are entitled to equal political rights now that they are free. Given the vote, they will inevitably—and rightly—look to us for leadership. Ex-rebels may call us scalawags and worse; that is to be expected. But we can help transform the South from a sleepy backward region dominated by the former planter class into a bustling, thriving region of farms, factories, and cities."

SOUTHERN FREEDMEN.   "We are now free men and women and must be accorded all the privileges of free people as expressed in the Declaration of Independence. We contributed to Union victory in war and have earned the right to be treated as equals. We are also the largest group in the South truly loyal to the Union. Southern whites, with some exceptions, cannot be trusted. They are unreconciled to defeat, and if the North fails to protect us and guarantee our rights as free men and women, these ex-Confederates will once more seize power and nullify the Union victory. The federal government, then, must continue for an indefinite period to take an active role in the process of southern Reconstruction.

"We do not expect white southerners to treat us as social equals; but we must have equality before the law and full civil rights, including, of course, the right to vote. We must also have economic independence, which means not only the right to sell our labor in the open market but also the right to our own land. Thousands of the South's best acres, abandoned by disloyal owners during the war, are controlled either by the Freedmen's Bureau or by the army. Giving us this land would enable us to secure our independence and prevent our being kept in permanently subordinate positions. We also deserve access to education. Literacy is an important tool for achieving economic independence. If the cost of a public school system means that southern state taxes must rise, so be it."

Several of these positions overlapped. But it would clearly be difficult to reconcile those people who wanted to return to prewar conditions as quickly as possible and those who hoped to make social transformation a requirement for readmitting the South to the Union. In the next dozen years there would be fierce battles between the contending parties, some almost as passionate as the war itself.

* PRESIDENTIAL RECONSTRUCTION *

Even before Lee's surrender in 1865 the Lincoln administration confronted the problem of how to govern the conquered territory and subdued people. In 1862 the president appointed military governors for those parts of four Confederate states under federal control. But while military administrators might suffice for a while, they ran counter to the American tradition of civilian rule and could only be considered a temporary resolution of the problem.

LINCOLN'S TEN-PERCENT PLAN. Lincoln sought to keep in his own hands the process of restoring southern self-rule and normalizing the South's relations with the rest of the country. He believed this would be more efficient, but he also inevitably preferred guiding the final stage of reuniting the Union himself. The president favored a lenient process, one that would not create too many hurdles to the South's readmission to the Union, impose severe punishment on white southerners, or require unrealistic changes of heart. He agreed, however, that any scheme had to guarantee the South's acceptance of slavery's demise.

Lincoln waited almost a year from the time of the Emancipation Proclamation to announce his plan for reconstruction. Issued on December 8, 1863, his Proclamation of Amnesty and Reconstruction, usually called the Ten-Percent Plan, offered full pardon and full restoration of all rights to white southerners who pledged future loyalty to the Union and accepted the abolition of slavery. Excluded from the pardon and restoration were high-ranking Confederate political and military leaders. When loyal southerners in any rebel state equalled at least ten percent of the number of voters in the 1860 elections, this group could convene and establish a new state government to supersede the old. The new constitution adopted must abolish slavery but it could also temporarily accept laws for the freed slaves "consistent . . . with their present condition as a laboring, landless, and homeless class." The state governments that met these conditions would be entitled to admission to the Union and to representation in Congress.

The Ten-Percent Plan did not please several important groups. Blacks and their allies condemned it for ignoring black suffrage and saying nothing about civil rights for the freedmen. Radical Republicans deplored the easy requirements for amnesty. They preferred to impose an "ironclad oath" on southerners, requiring them to declare that they had never willingly helped the Confederacy. Under the president's scheme, they felt, far too many Confederate collaborators would be restored to full rights.

The differences between the president and Congress came to a head in early 1864 when Louisiana applied for readmission under terms close to Lincoln's blueprint. The state's March 1864 constitutional convention produced a new frame of government establishing a minimum wage and nine-hour day on all public works, adopting a progressive income tax, and creating a system of free public education. The delegates, however, also rejected black suffrage despite the president's suggestion that the vote be given to "some of the colored people . . . as for instance, the very intelligent, and especially those who have fought gallantly in our ranks."

The exclusion of all blacks from suffrage angered the Radicals in Congress. In July 1864 they adopted the Wade-Davis Manifesto, which proposed postponing the reconstruction process until a majority of a given state's white males had pledged to support the United States Constitution. At that point, elections would be held for a state constitutional convention with only those who had taken the Ironclad Oath permitted to vote. In addition, though it stopped short of requiring black suffrage, Wade-Davis proposed that the freed slaves be guaranteed equality before the law. Lincoln feared that the measure would force him to repudiate the Louisiana government and so pocket-vetoed it. But, he said in mock innocence, he had no objection if other southern states chose Wade-Davis rather than his own plan. Despite the disagreement with Congress, by the time of Appomattox Unionist governments recognized by Lincoln were operating in Louisiana, Arkansas, and Tennessee.

JOHNSON TAKES CHARGE. Lincoln's assassination profoundly altered the course of political reconstruction. Had he lived, his popularity, prestige, and flexibility might have induced Congress to accept major portions of his plan. Yet Congress resented the war-swollen powers of the president and would certainly have insisted on playing a major role in restoring the Union. It seems unlikely that either side would have gotten its own way entirely. Lincoln's successor had to confront this inevitable struggle with Congress without the martyred president's skills and popularity.

Like Lincoln, Johnson was an ambitious self-made man from southern yeoman stock. He was not a Republican and had been put on the Union national ticket in 1864 to attract War Democrats. He did not share the nationalist principles of the Republicans. Rather, he was a defender of local power, even states' rights. Nor did he share the antislavery views of many Republicans. He despised his state's privileged planter class and considered secession a plot to perpetuate the elite's power, but at the same time, he had little respect for blacks. A fierce democrat when it came to the rich and powerful, he drew the equality line at the white race.

Johnson lacked Lincoln's winning personal qualities. Lincoln was confident in his own abilities. Johnson suffered from severe self-doubts, a weakness that made him susceptible to flattery. Lincoln was gregarious. Johnson was a loner with few friends or close advisers. Lincoln was flexible, a natural compromiser. Johnson was a rigid man who could be cajoled out of a position, but when defied directly, refused to budge. This stubbornness, in turn, often drove potential allies into the waiting arms of Radical Republicans. The president's characteristics became apparent only gradually, however. At first the Radical Republicans, tired of dealing with the wily Lincoln, had rejoiced at Johnson's succession. As military governor of Tennessee during the war he had declared that "treason . . . must be made infamous and traitors . . . punished," and they concluded that he would be harder on the South than his predecessor.

An idealized portrait of Andrew Johnson. His photographs show a coarser-featured man, an image more in keeping with his actual origins and early life.

During his first eight months in office Congress was not in session and the president had a relatively free hand in formulating Reconstruction policy. Johnson formally announced his Reconstruction plan in two proclamations issued on May 29, 1865. The first offered pardon and amnesty to participants in the rebellion who pledged loyalty to the Union and support for the end of slavery. All who took the oath would have returned to them all property confiscated by the Union government during the war, except for slaves. Exempted from this blanket pardoning process were fourteen classes of Southerners who were required to apply individually for pardons from the president. These included most high Confederate officials and owners of taxable property worth more than $20,000. This last proviso reflected Johnson's southern yeoman prejudice against the old planter class as the source of disunion and secession.

The second proclamation designated William Holden as provisional governor of North Carolina and directed him to call a convention to amend the state's existing constitution so as to create a "republican form of government." Voters would be restricted to those who had taken the oath of allegiance; they would not include ex-slaves or any blacks. Johnson soon extended the same process to six other southern states while also recognizing the new governments of Louisiana, Arkansas, and Tennessee, three states Lincoln had already accepted back into the Union. Johnson made it clear that he expected the conventions to accept the abolition of slavery and pledge not to repay any public debts incurred in the Confederate cause. He also asked them to consider giving voting rights to a few educated and property-holding blacks in order to "disarm" those clamoring for full civil rights for ex-slaves. Otherwise they could decide for themselves what sort of government and laws they would adopt.

In the next few months Johnson chose provisional governors from among each unreconstructed state's "loyalists" to manage the process he had prescribed. He often turned to members of the old Whig elite. These men typically had been skeptical of secession but had gone with their states when the decision to leave the Union was made. Few favored any changes in the undemocratic and unprogressive systems of the prewar era; none supported civil equality for blacks. The governors wielded broad patronage power and, during their months in office, used it to win the support of the Old South's planter and merchant class regardless of their Unionism or willingness to accept a new social and political order.

Meanwhile, each of the unreconstructed states held elections for a convention and adopted new state constitutions. Each acknowledged the end of slavery and all, except stubborn South Carolina, pledged to repudiate its Confederate debts. No state conceded blacks the vote, however, though several revised their formulas for representation to favor the white small farmer counties over the plantation regions. Soon afterward, they held statewide elections for permanent governors and other officials and chose state legislators and congressional delegates.

During the summer and fall conservative white southerners had reason to feel reassured that, despite Johnson's tough talk about disunionists and his disdain for the planters, the president did not intend to disturb their region's social and political systems. In August he overruled Freedmen's Bureau Commissioner Oliver Howard's Circular 13 setting aside forty-acre tracts of land for the freedmen to farm and ordered the return of land confiscated during the war from disloyal southerners. He also yielded to southern demands for removing black troops, whose presence whites considered a "painful humiliation" and a force for undermining plantation labor discipline. At the same time the president scattered pardons wholesale to those who applied to him directly. By 1866 he had given out almost 7,000 of these. Whatever his initial response to the old planter elite, the president had become the protector of the South's old order.

THE JOHNSON GOVERNMENTS.   During the months the "Johnson governments" operated without restraint from Washington their deeds strengthened the Radicals and destroyed any possibility that Congress would accept the president's Reconstruction policy.

Several actions especially offended northern Unionists. In the elections for new state and federal officials southern voters selected few real Unionists. Chosen to represent the former Confederate states in the upcoming Congress were four Confederate generals, five Confederate colonels, six Confederate Cabinet officers, fifty-eight former Confederate Congressmen, and Alexander H. Stephens, vice president of the Confederate States of America. Many of the newly-elected state officials were also tainted with secession. It was natural for white southerners to turn to former secessionists for their leaders. But this blatant display of Confederate sympathies outraged many Northerners.

The new state legislatures compounded the offense. Despite the president's recommendations, several refused to ratify the Thirteenth Amendment, passed by Congress in January 1865, that placed the abolition of slavery on a sound constitutional basis. Mississippi and South Carolina also refused to repudiate their wartime state debts. None of the Johnson governments allowed even a handful of blacks to vote. But worst of all, each of them enacted a set of laws to govern race relations (the Black Codes) that jarred Union sensibilities.

These codes did extend to the freedmen several rights of normal citizens. They legalized marriages between blacks, including earlier slave-era relationships; permitted ex-slaves to buy, own, sell, and otherwise transfer property; and gave the freedmen the right to appear, plead, and testify in court in cases involving fellow blacks. But the codes also sought to give the ex-slaves permanent second-class legal, economic, and political status. Under the Black Codes, black southerners could not offer their labor freely on the market. Mississippi required black workers to produce each January a written document showing they had a contract to work for the coming year. Laborers who left their jobs before a contract expired forfeited any wages already earned and could be arrested. "Vagrants"—defined as the idle, disorderly, and those who "misspend what they earn"—could face fines or forced plantation labor. The South Carolina code demanded a stiff annual tax for blacks working as anything other than farmers or servants. In Florida, blacks who broke labor contracts could be whipped, sold into indenture for up to one year, or placed in the pillory. In several states blacks were forbidden to bear arms, were subject to more severe punishment for given offenses than whites, and could not live or buy property in specified locations. Most states prohibited interracial marriage. Most rankling of all were apprenticeship laws, which allowed the courts to "bind out" black minors to employers for a period of time without their own consent or that of their parents.

Blacks eloquently protested the codes. One black man wrote the Freedmen's Bureau: "I think very hard of the former owners for Trying to keep my Blood when I kno that Slavery is dead." A black Union veteran exclaimed: "If you call this Freedom, what do you call Slavery!"

One of the real advances afforded by the emancipation was the legal recognition of black marriages. After 1865 black men and women seized the opportunity to solemnize relationships begun under slavery or to contract new ones. Officiating at this wedding is a chaplain from the Freedmen's Bureau.

Inevitably many Northerners considered the president's version of Reconstruction deplorable. Wendell Phillips prophetically noted that without the right to vote, blacks in the South would be consigned to "a century of serfdom." But nothing so offended Northern opinion as the Black Codes. The *Chicago Tribune* declared that the people of the North would turn one of the worst offending states, Mississippi, into a "frog pond" before they would allow its Black Code "to disgrace one foot of soil in which the bones of our soldiers sleep and over which the flag of freedom waves." Another critic called the codes "an outrage against civilization." Meanwhile, northern congressmen were receiving almost daily reports from white southern Unionists that the former secessionists were crowing about how they once again had the upper hand and would make life difficult for their opponents. Simultaneously, northern travelers in Dixie recounted unpleasant experiences with unreconstructed "rebels." Hotels and restaurants often refused them service and individual southerners insulted them.

The outrage over the Johnson governments' policies and the Black Codes should not deceive us about the extent of racial liberalism in the nation at large. Northern Democrats were often blatant racists who had no scruples against appealing to the voters' prejudices and resisted every attempt to confer the franchise on blacks. Republicans, generally, were less bigoted and, in any case, believed that the freedmen's votes were needed to keep former rebels from regaining power in the South. But even many Republicans were reluctant to accord black Americans the full rights of citizenship, at least where they themselves lived. In the fall of 1865 three northern states—Connecticut, Wisconsin, and Minnesota—placed constitutional amendments on their ballots to allow the handful of black males within their borders to vote. A substantial minority of Republican voters opposed the changes, and together with the Democrats, helped defeat the black franchise in all three. In effect then, a majority of all white voters opposed letting blacks vote and this reality inevitably tempered the radical ardor of Republican politicians in districts where elections were closely contested.

✴ CONGRESS TAKES OVER ✴

By the time the Thirty-Ninth Congress assembled on December 4, 1865, the Republican majority was determined to take over the process of southern reconstruction to assure that rebels would not get their way. Its first act was to reject the Congressional delegations sent by the Johnson governments to Washington. Prompted by the Radicals, the Clerk of the House, Edward McPherson, skipped the names of the newly elected southern congressmen as he called the roll. Immediately after, the two houses established a Joint Committee on

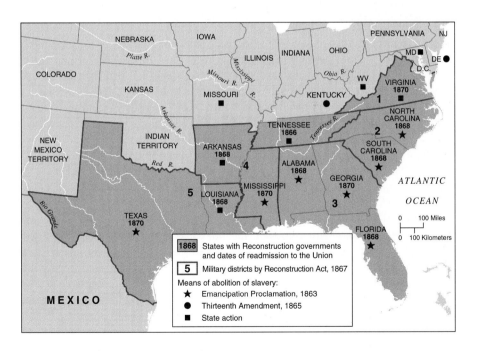

Reconstruction of the South, 1865–1877

Reconstruction to look into conditions in the South and consider whether any former Confederate states were entitled to representation. Consisting of fifteen Senators and Representatives, three of them Democrats, their views stretched across the political spectrum, although the "too ultra" Charles Sumner was deliberately excluded.

Despite his policies, Johnson had still not completely alienated the Republican moderates and they listened to his conciliatory annual message with respect. For a time the Republican congressional centrists took charge. This changed abruptly when moderate Lyman Trumbull of Illinois introduced a bill to extend the life of the Freedmen's Bureau and broaden its authority.

Established in March 1865, just before the war ended, the bureau aided refugees, both white and black, found employment for freedmen, and supplied transportation home for those displaced by the war. It had established hospitals and schools and drawn up guidelines for bringing ex-slaves into the free labor market. In enlarging the bureau's scope, the Trumbull bill gave Congress the additional power to protect freedmen against discrimination, including the right to punish state officials denying blacks their civil rights, and authorized it to build and run schools for the ex-slaves. It was generally considered a moderate measure.

The Civil Rights bill of 1865, on the other hand, was far-reaching in scope. It declared all persons born in the United States, including blacks (but not Indians), citizens, and specified their rights regardless of race. These included the right to make contracts, bring lawsuits, and enjoy the "full and equal benefit of all laws and proceedings for the security of person and property." To ensure that no state denied citizens these rights, it authorized federal district attorneys and marshalls, as well as the Freedmen's Bureau, to sue in the federal courts. In many ways the law foreshadowed the civil rights measures of the mid-twentieth century.

Johnson refused to sign either bill. The Freedmen's Bureau, he said in his veto message, was a vast patronage boondoggle that would create a horde of bureaucrats to oppress ordinary citizens. Moreover, it violated the Constitution; never before had the federal government been called on to provide economic relief to individuals. The president soon after attacked the Civil Rights bill as another unwarranted extension of federal power. The bill was a "stride toward centralization and the concentration of all legislative powers in the national Government."

In the end Congress was unable to muster the two-thirds needed to pass the Freedmen's Bureau bill, though it managed to override the Civil Rights veto. The fight over the Freedmen's Bureau destroyed the hope of moderates that Johnson could be trusted with Reconstruction. It was the opening round of a struggle that lasted until the end of Johnson's term, with each new battle driving more and more moderates into the Radical camp.

THE FOURTEENTH AMENDMENT.   While Congress and the President fought for supremacy, the Joint Committee on Reconstruction set to work on its own comprehensive plan to restore Dixie to the Union. Even with the Thirteenth

Amendment finally approved by the states and the Civil Rights bill enacted into law, Radicals worried that the rights of black Americans were vulnerable. Certainly, if it proved necessary to rely on the federal courts, they would have little security. Although it was not until April 1866 that the Supreme Court, in the case of *Ex Parte Milligan,* voided the Lincoln administration's wartime imposition of martial law on civilians in Indiana, the justices already seemed hostile to the Republican philosophy of federal supremacy. What would prevent them from striking down the Civil Rights Act or any other measure that Congress passed to protect the freedmen? With this in mind, the first initiative of the Joint Committee was another amendment to the Constitution to put the principles of the Civil Rights bill beyond the reach of the president, the states, and unfriendly federal judges.

As finally hammered out and submitted to the states for adoption, the Fourteenth Amendment contained four clauses, the first two of which were of major significance.

The original Bill of Rights had only limited the federal government's power over citizens. Now the Constitution would place restraints on the states as well. The first clause defined citizenship to include all those born or naturalized in the United States. It then declared that no state could make or enforce any law that abridged the rights of American citizens, or deprived any person of "life, liberty, or property without due process of law." Nor could any state "deny to any person within its jurisdiction the equal protection of the laws." In effect, individuals could not be executed, imprisoned, or fined by the states except through the normal processes of law with all their constitutionally-protected procedures and safeguards, nor could the states treat any individual or class of individuals as inferior to others. Clause one vastly expanded federal power over the states and served in the end many purposes besides ensuring racial justice in the South.

Clause two, concerning suffrage, was not what the most radical of the Republican leaders wanted. Congress might have bluntly declared unconstitutional all political discrimination on racial grounds. Instead it deferred to continuing northern racial prejudice by a series of evasions. Rather than giving the vote outright to all adult male citizens, it merely declared that whenever a state denied any age-qualified male citizen the right to vote, that state's representation in Congress would be reduced proportionately. The South, with its large black population, would now have a strong incentive to grant full voting rights to black males. (Otherwise it would send far fewer representatives to Congress than its total population warranted.) Northern states, however, with few black residents, could continue to deny them suffrage without serious penalty. Not until after the adoption of the Fifteenth Amendment (1870) were "race, color, or previous condition of servitude" completely eliminated as legal grounds for denying adult men the vote.*

---

*The proposed amendment's two minor clauses (1) denied public office to those who had taken oaths of allegiance as state or federal officials and then served in the rebellion; and (2) repudiated any state debt incurred in aid of the Confederate cause.

* CONGRESSIONAL RECONSTRUCTION *

To assure adoption of the new constitutional amendment, Congress made its passage by the southern state legislatures a condition of readmission to the Union. But this incentive did not work. By the end of 1866 Texas, South Carolina, Georgia, Florida, North Carolina, Arkansas, and Alabama had all rejected it. In fact, the ratification process dragged even in the North, and not until well into 1867 did the amendment receive the necessary approval by three-fourths of the states.

By now the president's abrasive personality and backward-looking views had alienated almost all the Republicans in Congress. But there still remained a nub of conservative Republicans. In April 1866 these leaders joined with moderate Democrats to form the National Union Executive Committee. In August they held a National Union Convention in Philadelphia to form a third party based on sectional reconciliation and immediate return of the southern states to the Union. The highlight of the convention was the affecting ceremony of Massachusetts and South Carolina delegates, representing the two sectional poles, marching into the convention hall in pairs, arm and arm.

Though the president gave the National Union movement his blessing, it came to little. For one thing, the conservative forces could not overcome the impression of southern intransigence created by news from the South. In May an angry white mob invaded the black section of Memphis, killing forty-six people. In late July another white mob assaulted delegates to a black suffrage convention in New Orleans. Before federal troops could arrive, the attackers had murdered thirty-seven blacks and three of their white supporters. Here was proof, if any were needed, that the South would never accept the consequences of defeat without northern coercion.

Despite poor prospects, the president campaigned aggressively for the National Union movement in the 1866 off-year elections. Against the advice of friends, he set out on a "swing around the circle," giving speeches attacking the Radicals as the country's real traitors, defending the South as loyal, justifying his generous pardoning policy, and even offering his life to save the Union and the Constitution. Wherever he went, his critics heckled him unmercifully and goaded him into rash, undignified replies. He probably did his cause more harm than good. Radical Republicans won a decisive victory almost everywhere. The new Congress would retain its three-to-one Republican majority.

But even before the Fortieth Congress convened, the second session of the Thirty-ninth, its Republican leaders encouraged by the 1866 election mandate, passed the First Reconstruction Act (also called the Reconstruction Act of 1867). By December 1866 Johnson had lost all Republican support and the Radicals felt the time was ripe to replace all the Johnson state governments by a system that would finally express the will of the Union's most progressive forces.

The First Reconstruction Act swept aside the existing state regimes in the former Confederacy and divided the South into five military districts, each under a general who was empowered to use troops if necessary to protect life and property. The military commanders would supervise the choice of delegates to state conventions that would write new constitutions and establish new state governments. All adult males would be eligible for voting for the conventions regardless of race, except those excluded for participating in the rebellion. The new constitutions had to provide for a similar broad electorate for legislature, governor, and other public officials, and required that their work be accepted by a majority of the same, color-blind, pool of voters. When the new constitutions had been so ratified, when Congress had approved them, and when the new state legislatures had ratified the Fourteenth Amendment, the states would then be admitted to the Union and their delegations to Congress seated.

JOHNSON IMPEACHED.   Radicals feared Johnson would use his appointment authority and general executive powers to frustrate their plans. And before long he did, removing several of the military commanders as too radical and issuing orders to others intended to negate Congress's intentions.

To hedge him in, Congress passed a series of additional measures in 1867. To prevent the president taking advantage of an interval between congressional sessions, in January it approved a bill that called the new Congress into special session immediately after the old one had expired. In March it passed, over Johnson's veto, the Tenure of Office Act requiring Senate consent for the dismissal of all federal officeholders appointed with Senate approval. A third measure required that all presidential orders to the army be issued through the general of the army. This happened to be Grant, a man who had come to support the Radical Republican position on Reconstruction. At the same time, to goad dilatory southern voters to take steps under the First Reconstruction Act, Congress passed the Second Reconstruction Act. A Third Reconstruction Act in July tightened control by the five military commanders over the provisional governments in the South and sought to broaden the rules excluding ex-Confederates from the Reconstruction process.

For some Radicals these measures seemed insufficient, and in January 1868 they attempted to remove Johnson from office through impeachment. As yet most moderates did not believe there were grounds for such a drastic proceedure, however, and the indictment was quashed in committee. But then Johnson handed his opponents their opportunity. In August, during a congressional recess, the president suspended from office Secretary of War Edwin Stanton, a man inherited from Lincoln who supported the Radicals, and appointed Grant as interim Secretary. In January 1868 the Senate refused to accept Stanton's dismissal, and Grant, against the wishes of Johnson, stepped down. Defiant, the president once more removed Stanton and replaced him with Lorenzo Thomas. But Stanton, with the urging of congressional Radicals, barricaded himself in his office and refused to leave or to allow Thomas to enter. However ludicrous, the Stanton affair seemed to provide grounds for impeachment that had not existed before. The president, exclaimed one moderate, had "thrown down the gauntlet and says to us plainly as words can speak it: 'Try this issue now betwixt me and you: either you go to the wall or I do'." On February 24, 1868, the House formally voted to impeach the president by a strict party vote of 126 to 47.

The impeachment trial, conducted before the Senate sitting as a court, was the show trial of the century. The major charge against the president was his "unlawful" removal of Stanton. Attorney General Henry Stanbery, the president's counsel, argued that Stanton had been appointed by Lincoln, not Johnson, and so was not covered by the Tenure of Office Act. The law, moreover, was unconstitutional, and it was the right of the president to challenge it to bring it before the courts.

During the six weeks of the trial intense excitement reigned in Washington and the country. Radicals insisted that acquittal would be a victory for rebels and traitors. Democrats, and Johnson's few remaining moderate supporters within Republican ranks, claimed that conviction would mean that Congress had successfully usurped the power of the executive branch. The president's defenders also noted that the man next in line for the presidency was the president *pro tempore* of the Senate, the truculent Radical, Benjamin Wade.

On May 16, 1868, Johnson was acquitted by one vote. Most historians believe that he should not have been impeached in the first place. There can be no question that he was stubborn and at times boorish, and that he used his execu-

In August 1866 President Johnson announced that "peace, order, tranquility, and civil authority now exist . . . in the United States." Dissatisfied with Johnson's idea of peace and order, the House voted his impeachment less than two years later. Here a packed gallery follows the trial of the century.

tive power to impede Congress. Nor is there much dispute among scholars today that his racial policies were misguided. In a parliamentary system such as Britain's he would have been removed by a legislative vote of "no confidence." But the Founders had deliberately created an independently elected executive with the right to disagree with Congress. It seems unlikely that they intended impeachment to serve as a way to remove an official from office except for breaking the law or for gross incapacity. The Radicals in effect, then, were seeking implicitly to change the Constitution in a vital aspect.

✻ RECONSTRUCTION IN THE SOUTH ✻

THE ELECTION OF 1868.   Johnson still had almost a year to go before his term ended, but achieved little in the months remaining. During this period he spent much of his time maneuvering for the Democratic presidential nomination. The Democrats did not want him. In the West many preferred George Pendleton of Ohio, a Democratic Senator who favored the "Ohio Idea," a scheme to relieve taxpayers' burdens and stimulate the economy by paying the large federal debt in paper money ("greenbacks"). Eastern Democrats claimed the Ohio Idea would call into question all debts, public and private, shake the financial markets, and set loose the forces of social anarchy. It took twenty-two ballots before Governor Horatio Seymour of New York, a "hard money" man, nosed out Pendleton. The "soft money" group was able to get the Ohio Idea incorporated into the party platform but, as soon as nominated, Seymour repudiated it.

The Republicans turned, not to their most militant wing, but to the center. The acquittal of Johnson had weakened the Radicals and they could not stop the nomination of Ulysses Grant, the great war hero. General Grant had not opposed the Radicals' policies after 1865 but he was a pragmatist, rather than a zealot, and reassured the moderates. The Republican platform denounced the Ohio Idea as "repudiation" and a "national crime," and defended the civil rights of the freedmen in the South.

The election was remarkably close. In the South, armed and violent whites succeeded in intimidating many blacks from going to the polls. In eleven Georgia counties with black majorities no votes at all were recorded for Grant. But the Republicans did manage to carry all but two states in Dixie thanks to black voters and won most of the North. With 53 percent of the popular vote, Grant won the election.

By the time the new president was inaugurated in early 1869, the governments organized under the congressional reconstruction acts—composed of white and black Republicans and decidedly Radical in temper—had been admitted to the Union, and the Fourteenth Amendment had been incorporated into the Constitution. In a narrow legal sense, Reconstruction was now complete. But in fact, the situation in the newly restored states remained uncertain and tense.

ECONOMIC RECOVERY.   In the South itself, important changes had taken place since April 1865. Damaged southern railroads were quickly rebuilt after Appomattox and the system extended to new regions. Much of the needed capital was supplied by investors in the North and in Britain, who anticipated a favorable business climate in the South. The southern state governments, both the Johnson regimes and the ones established under Congress's aegis, also contributed, going heavily into debt to lend money to railroad enterprises. Industry too recovered. Between the 1860s and 1880, southern manufactures increased in value almost 55 percent. In agriculture cotton became even more important after 1865 than before the war. By 1878 the South's cotton output had almost reached its prewar peak. By the 1890s the region was producing twice as many bales as in 1859.

TENANTRY AND SHARECROPPING.   It was primarily in its social aspects, however, that Reconstruction transformed the southern economy. Before 1861, defenders of slavery had denied that blacks could function in a free labor market. During the war the Treasury Department put this theory to the test in the South Carolina Sea Islands near Port Royal and demonstrated that when ex-slaves were given land, they made successful farmers. The Port Royal venture collapsed when the Treasury Department failed to transfer land title to the freedmen as it had promised, selling the abandoned Sea Island property to the highest bidder instead.

Efforts to create a class of black farm owners in the South resumed after the war. Thaddeus Stevens and other Radicals in Congress introduced legislation to transfer confiscated rebel estates to newly enfranchised blacks. Only landowning, they believed, could protect blacks against exploitation and keep them from being virtually reenslaved. The former slaves themselves yearned to become landowners. "We all know that the colored people want land," a South Carolina carpetbagger declared. "Night and day they think and dream of it. It is their all and all." Whitelaw Reid quoted an elderly black man he had met on his trip to the South: "What's de use of bein' free if you don't own land enough to be buried? Might juss as well stay slave all yo days."

Yearnings often became expectations. Many blacks came to believe that the government intended to give them "forty acres and a mule," and they were bitterly disappointed when it proved untrue. In the end, a large black yeomen class failed to appear. Ultimately the Radicals were not so very radical, and their respect for private property rights—even those of ex-rebels—took precedence over their concern for the freedmen. Most were certain that the ballot offered sufficient protection to the freedmen; a social revolution was not needed.

Black southerners might have accumulated some money and purchased land. Southern land prices were low in the 1870s, and a few hundred dollars could have bought a black family a small farm. In 1865, Congress chartered the Freedmen's Bank to support such black self-help efforts. But the bank was poorly managed and could not withstand the financial panic of 1873. When it closed its doors the following year, it took with it over $3 million of hard-won savings from thousands of black depositors. There was still another impediment to freedmen buying land: White southerners believed that if blacks owned land they would not work for white landlords and employers. It is easy to see why they made it difficult for black farmers to buy land even when they could pay cash. Yet despite all the difficulties, by 1880 about a fifth of all black farmers owned their land.

Though only a minority of southern blacks ever became independent farm owners, most continued working the land. For a while after Appomattox they worked for cash wages under contracts supervised by the Freedmen's Bureau. But it was difficult for landlords to find cash in the months following the war. The freedmen, for their part, resented the harshness with which some bureau agents enforced labor contracts against them. Still more unsatisfactory from the freedmen's point of view was the return to gang work and the planters' close supervision of every aspect of their labor and their lives. The system reminded them too much of slavery and seemed a mockery of freedom.

Out of this mutual dissatisfaction with wage-paid farm labor emerged a tenant system that by 1880 had become characteristic of much of the cotton-growing South. Tenantry included whites as well as blacks. Thousands of Confederate privates returned home to become, not successful planters, but tenants on lands owned by former slaveholders.

Tenantry took many forms. Tenants might pay rent either in cash or in part of the crop. Though the system was not as desirable as ownership, a cash tenant was at least free from constant supervision and sometimes could save enough to buy land for himself. The greater number of tenant farmers, however, especially among the freedmen, were either sharecroppers or share renters. The former contributed only their labor, and in return for use of the land and a house, usually divided the crop equally with the landlord. A share renter could provide his own seed, mule, and plow as well, and usually got three fourths of what he produced.

Linked to tenantry was the crop-lien system, a credit arrangement by which a storekeeper (who sometimes was the landlord as well) would extend credit to the tenant for supplies during the crop-growing season. When the harvest came and the cotton was sold, the tenant would then repay the debt. Buying on credit was expensive, since it included an interest charge. It also gave dishonest storekeepers a chance to cheat. Tenants who could not meet their debts could not change the merchant they dealt with; they became virtual "debt-peons," tied to him almost like serfs.

The new labor regime that emerged in the South during Reconstruction was an obvious advance over slavery. Some blacks managed to become landowners despite all the difficulties. Most were released from the degradation of close personal supervision by whites. Economically they were better off as sharecroppers than as slaves. Roger Ransom and Richard Sutch conclude that whereas slaves received in food, clothing, housing, and medical attention about 23 percent of what whites received, the freedmen after 1865 obtained a full half of average white income. In addition to these economic advances, blacks were now able to make decisions about their economic lives that they never could before. Almost

Tenant farmers, 75.3%
(includes sharecroppers
and cash tenants)

Farm owners, 24.5%

Farm managers, 0.2%
↓

Black Status

Tenant farmers, 36.1%

Farm owners, 63.0%

Farm managers, 0.9%
↓

White Status

The status of farm operators in former slave states, 1900

all decided that black women would no longer work in the fields; like white women, they would stay home and become proper housewives and mothers. Many black children too left the labor market to attend school.

Yet the freedmen's fate represented a missed opportunity for the nation. Many of these gains were a one-time advance, made just after the war. Thereafter, while the country as a whole became richer, black living standards in the South remained stagnant. Indeed, the sharecrop–crop-lien system proved to be an economic trap for the entire lower South. Because they did not own the land, sharecroppers had no incentive to improve it. Landlords, too, had little incentive, for they could only hope to recover a limited portion of the greater output that might come from additional capital investment. Tenantry also tied the South to a one-crop system and prevented diversification. As one sharecropper complained in the 1880s: "We ought to plant less [cotton and tobacco] and more grain and grasses, but how are we to do it; the man who furnishes us with rations at 50 percent interest won't let us; he wants money crops planted." Failure to diversify also produced serious soil exhaustion that could only be offset by expensive additions of fertilizers. Worse still, cotton prices steadily declined for a generation after 1865, pulling down the entire cotton-tied southern rural economy.

For whatever reasons, the South as a section experienced a relative economic decline. With each year Dixie fell further behind the rest of the nation in almost every measure of material abundance and social well-being: literacy, infant mortality, longevity, health, and per-capita income. By 1890, the section had become America's problem area.

SOCIAL AND CULTURAL CHANGE.   Despite the imperfect economic adjustment, the end of slavery brought considerable social and cultural gains for black Americans. Black men and women enjoyed a new freedom of movement, which some exercised by going to the cities or departing for more prosperous parts of the country. At the end of Reconstruction several thousand blacks left the lower South and moved north or west. A particularly large movement of "exodusters" to Kansas after 1878 alarmed southern white leaders, who feared that the South might lose its labor force.

The end of slavery freed blacks to express themselves in ways never before possible. Slavery had not destroyed black culture, but it had made it difficult for blacks to demonstrate the full range of their talents and to exercise their organizational abilities. Emancipation released energies previously held in check. Blacks withdrew from white churches in large numbers and formed their own. These churches gave talented former slaves an opportunity to demonstrate leadership beyond anything previously possible. Unlike politics, which was largely closed to talented black men after 1877, the Protestant ministry continued to provide leadership opportunities.

The end of slavery also expanded educational opportunities for blacks. Before the war slaves had been legally denied education. After 1865 northern

educators and philanthropists seized on Dixie as missionary territory to be converted to "civilization." In the months after Appomattox hundreds of Yankee
teachers, hoping to uplift a benighted region, went South to establish schools
and bring the blessings of literacy. The Freedmen's Bureau also labored to end il-
literacy and sought to train blacks in trades. The most permanent impact was
achieved by southern self-help. Before long every southern state, under Radical
guidance, had made some provision for educating black children. The southern
educational system long remained poor and segregated (except for a time in the
cosmopolitan city of New Orleans); yet the schools managed to make a dent in
ignorance. By 1880 a quarter of all blacks could read and write; twenty years
later the figure had risen to half. College training for blacks, nonexistent in the
South before 1860, became available as well. Southern state governments
founded separate black colleges and universities. Meanwhile, the Freedmen's Bureau and white philanthropists helped charter such black private colleges as Atlanta University in Georgia, Fisk University in Tennessee, and Howard University
in Washington, D.C.

Despite the gains, segregation by race became a central fact of life in the
South. In 1875 Congress passed a strongly worded Civil Rights Act guaranteeing
to all persons, regardless of color, "the full and equal enjoyment of all the ac-
commodations . . . of inns, public conveyances . . . , theaters, and other places of
public amusement"; but separation and social inequality persisted; in fact, the
separation of the races became more complete than before the war. In most communities, trains, buses, and theaters had white and black sections. In private life
the racial spheres were still more exclusive, and blacks almost never entered the
homes of white people except as servants. Even southern Radicals seldom treated
blacks as social equals.

THE SOUTHERN RADICAL GOVERNMENTS.   In many ways, the most
serious deficiency of Reconstruction was its failure to create a democratic political culture. Blacks fully participated in the creation and running of the state
governments established by the five military commanders under the terms of
the Reconstruction Acts. They voted in the elections for state constitutional
conventions, served in those conventions, voted in the state elections for state
and federal office that followed, and served in these offices. Participation did
not mean domination, however. Even where the Republicans were in control,
and even in South Carolina and Mississippi, where the black population outnumbered the white, they held only a minority of political offices. The rest
were filled by native-born southern whites and northern-born white immigrants to Dixie.

One of the persistent myths of Reconstruction is that black political officials
during the years of Republican rule in the South were unusually corrupt and incompetent. But that was not the case. Among the fifteen black southerners
elected to Congress were a number of exceptionally able, honest, and well-
educated men. Maine congressman James G. Blaine, who served with many of
the black legislators, said of them: "The colored men who took their seats in

*The first colored senator and representatives in the 41st and 42nd Congress of the United States.
As a group they acquitted themselves competently.*

both Senate and House . . . were as a rule studious, earnest, ambitious men, whose public conduct . . . should be honorable to any race." On the level of state government, black officeholders ranged from excellent to poor. All in all, as legislators and officials, their successes did not fall noticeably behind those of their white colleagues.

Native-born white Republican leaders in the South have also been unduly disparaged. "Scalawags" were denounced by their opponents as "the vilest renegades of the South," as men "who have dishonored the dignity of white blood, and are traitors alike to principle and race." In fact, many were former Unionists and members of the South's prewar Whig business class who were attracted to the Republican party because of its pro-business, pro-growth policies. And they were not the tiny minority of the white population that we would expect if they were merely renegades. In 1872, for example, 20 percent of the South's white voters cast their ballots for Republican candidates.

Nor were the northern whites who participated in the southern Republican state governments the "itinerant adventurers" and "vagrant interlopers" that southern conservatives charged. Called "carpetbaggers," after the cheap carpet-cloth suitcases carried in those years by travelers, many were former Union soldiers who had served in Dixie and come to like it as a place to live. Others were sincere idealists committed to establishing a new social order. Obviously many white southern Republicans—scalawags and carpetbaggers alike—hoped to take personal advantage of new circumstances, but there is no reason to consider them any more venal, corrupt, or self-serving than politicians in general.

On the whole the Radical-dominated southern state governments were remarkably effective and reasonably honest. Of course, measured by the standards of the tight-fisted prewar South, they seemed big spenders. And they did run up large debts. But the new governments took on functions not required of their predecessors. They sought to help railroads and other businesses. They established the South's first state-supported school systems and sharply increased public spending for poor relief, prisons, and state hospitals. Though still far behind the North in providing social services, under Radical rule the South began to catch up with the rest of nineteenth century America.

The new Radical governments were also more democratic and egalitarian than were the prewar southern state regimes. The constitutions adopted under congressional Reconstruction made many previously appointive offices elective and gave small farmers better representation in the legislatures than before the war. They also extended the vote to white males who did not meet the old property qualifications. The new state governments reduced the number of crimes punishable by death and granted married women more secure control over their property, reforms most northern states had adopted before 1860. They swept away the unequal treatment of black workers that had been incorporated into the Black Codes. Some of the Radical regimes even pursued policies that foreshadowed the modern social welfare state. South Carolina financed medical care for its poor citizens. Alabama paid legal fees for poor defendants. Not for another century would the South—or the nation as a whole—see anything like this again.

REDEMPTION.   Regardless of their accomplishments, many white southerners despised the Radical regimes and accused them of corruption. Some were in fact corrupt, but generally no more than was normal in state affairs during those years. Southern conservatives also disliked the reforms they initiated, because they were new, because they seemed to be Yankee-inspired, and because they were expensive. Landlords, in particular, denounced the new programs for raising taxes on real estate, which before the war had been lightly taxed. But above all, conservatives found it difficult to accept the Republican-dominated state governments because they were part of the new racial regime. After 250 years of slavery, the white South found it hard to consider a black person the political equal of a white one.

After 1867 the southern states became arenas for ferocious struggles between the political forces of the new era and those of the old. For a while the Radical governments succeeded in holding onto political office, especially in states where they were most firmly entrenched—Alabama, Missis-

When the Freedmen's Bureau set up schools for blacks, former slaves of all ages flocked to them. Wrote Booker T. Washington, "It was a whole race trying to go to school." The Show Hill School, here, abandoned classical education in favor of industrial training, which was deemed more appropriate to black needs.

sippi, Texas, Florida, Louisiana, and South Carolina. But in the end they could not match the experience, self-confidence, and ruthlessness of the defenders of bygone times, who hoped to "redeem" the South from "Black Republicanism."

A major weapon of the "redeemers" was the Ku Klux Klan. Formed in 1866 in Tennessee by young Confederate veterans primarily as a social club, the Klan quickly evolved into an antiblack, anti-Radical organization. To intimidate black voters, hooded, mounted Klansmen swooped down at night on isolated cabins, making fearsome noises and firing guns. They also torched black homes, attacked and beat black militiamen, ambushed both white and black Radical leaders, and lynched blacks accused of crimes. During the 1868 presidential campaign Klansmen assassinated an Arkansas congressman, three members of the South Carolina legislature, and several Republican members of state constitutional conventions. Some conservative apologists dismissed the Klan as an organization composed of white riffraff, but in fact, as one Radical newspaper noted, it included "men of property . . . respectable citizens."

At its height in the late 1860s, the Klan's outrages went virtually unchecked. Law enforcement officials felt impotent to deal with the violence. Witnesses of Klan misdeeds were often scared off from testifying against it. In several southern states the Klan created a reign of terror and lawlessness that threatened to undo the entire Reconstruction process. Then in 1870 and 1871

Secret societies like the Knights of the White Camelia, the Pale Faces, and the Knights of the Ku Klux Klan organized to frustrate Reconstruction. Describing itself as an "institution of Chivalry, Humanity, Mercy, and Patriotism," the Klan violently intimidated blacks.

Congress passed three Force Bills, which declared "armed combinations" and Klan terrorist tactics illegal. The bills gave the president the right to prosecute in federal courts all those who sought to prevent qualified persons from voting. For the first time the federal government had defined certain crimes against individuals as violation of federal law. President Grant invoked the measures in nine South Carolina counties, and soon hundreds of Klansmen were indicted for illegal activities.

The Klan quickly declined, but not the determination of southern conservatives to cow the black population and take control of the South away from Radicals and their supporters. The redeemers abandoned hooded robes, flaming crosses, and night rides, but not other forms of intimidation. In their successful effort in 1875 to redeem Mississippi, conservatives used the powerful weapon of ostracism to force white Republicans to change their party. One who succumbed to their tactics, Colonel James Lusk, told a black fellow Republican: "No white man can live in the South in the future and act with any other than the Democratic party unless he is willing and prepared to live a life of social isolation and remain in political oblivion."

Tougher tactics were often effective against black voters. Blacks who voted Republican were denied jobs or fired from those they had. More stubborn black Republicans were threatened with violence. During the 1875 Mississippi election thousands of white Democrats armed themselves with rifles and shotguns, and then, to make the message clear, entered the names of black Republicans in "dead books." In Vicksburg, Yazoo City, and other Mississippi towns blacks were shot and killed in preelection fights.

The Democrats captured the Mississippi legislature and elected the only state official running for statewide office. The Republican governor, Adelburt Ames, faced with impeachment by the new legislature, agreed to resign. Mississippi had been "redeemed." Similar processes took place in other southern states, so that by 1876 only Louisiana, Florida, and South Carolina remained under Republican administrations—and these regimes stayed in power only because they were protected by federal troops.

THE END OF RECONSTRUCTION.   Clearly the redeemers were effective tacticians and organizers. But their success also depended on the weakening commitment of Northerners to Radical rule in the South.

The decline of Northern resolve had several sources. Many honest Republicans came to see the defense of the black man as an excuse for continued domination by the corrupt wing of their party. Whenever a new scandal was uncovered in the Grant administration—and there would be many—it would be buried under an appeal for Republican unity against the ex-rebels. The process came to be called "waving the bloody shirt." By the middle of the 1870s many Republicans had concluded that abandoning blacks and their friends in the South was better than continuing to uphold the corrupt element in their own party.

Fatigue and racism also played their parts. How long, many Northerners asked, could the country invest energy and money to sustain a system that the "best elements" of southern society opposed? The ex-slaves would never make good citizens, and there was no point in continuing the hopeless battle. Such arguments were reinforced by a growing conviction among northern commercial and industrial groups that stability in the South would be better for business than the political agitation that constantly disturbed the nation.

The end came in 1876. In the presidential election of that year the Democrats nominated Samuel J. Tilden of New York, an honest but colorless corporation lawyer. The Republican candidate was Rutherford B. Hayes, the aloof but upright governor of Ohio. The Democratic platform promised to withdraw federal troops from the South and endorsed traditional Democratic low-tariff, small-government positions. The Republicans declared that they would never abandon the black man and would continue to support positive government, a protective tariff, and "sound money."

The election was so close that the results were challenged. The Democrats claimed they had carried New York, New Jersey, Connecticut, Indiana, and the entire South. The Republicans insisted that the votes of Florida, Louisiana, and South Carolina—the still "unredeemed" states—rightfully belonged to them. They also challenged one Democratic vote in Oregon, where electors had split between the two candidates. As in 1824, the election was thrown into the House of Representatives. For the next four months the country's political life was in an uproar as the politicians tried to settle the election issue before Inauguration Day in March 1877.

Both sides brought every weapon to bear on the dispute—propaganda, legal maneuvering, congressional commissions, and threats of violence. Some historians believe that one hidden issue during the disputed election period was railroads. Southerners, they say, believed that only the Republicans would approve a land grant to the Texas and Pacific Railroad, designed to connect New Orleans and other important southern cities with the Pacific Coast. This reasoning led influential southern leaders, many former Whigs with little love for the Democrats, to seek a bargain with the Republicans. What seems more likely than this "Compromise of 1877" was something less devious: that Southerners merely traded electoral votes for removing federal troops from the South. But whoever

Southern black voters after 1865 were alternately courted and coerced by white politicians. The Democrats found force more necessary than did the Republicans to win black votes. In this Radical Republican cartoon two Democrats (the one at right looking remarkably like Jefferson Davis) make no pretense of winning "hearts and minds."

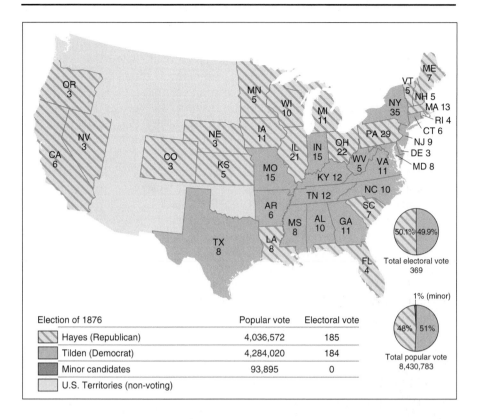

Election of 1876	Popular vote	Electoral vote
Hayes (Republican)	4,036,572	185
Tilden (Democrat)	4,284,020	184
Minor candidates	93,895	0
U.S. Territories (non-voting)		

Presidential Election of 1876

is right, soon after Hayes's inauguration as nineteenth president of the United States, the last federal soldiers were withdrawn from Dixie. The redeemers quickly moved in. Reconstruction was over.

* CONCLUSIONS *

Reconstruction was not an unrelieved disaster. During these momentous years southerners repaired the physical devastation of the war and reestablished their states' constitutional relations with the Union. Meanwhile, black southerners were able to create for themselves important new islands of freedom—freedom to move, freedom to create social and cultural institutions of their own, freedom for black women to leave the fields. They also improved their material well-being. As sharecroppers, blacks kept a larger share of the wealth they produced than as slaves. Also on the credit side were the Radical-sponsored Fourteenth and Fifteenth amendments. Once embedded in the Constitution, they would become the bases for a "second Reconstruction" in our own day.

Yet there is much that is dismaying about Reconstruction. Americans of this era failed to meet the great challenges that faced them. Instead of a prosperous black yeomanry, the South would be left with a mass of impoverished semi-peons who for generations would be a reproach to America's proud claims of prosperity and equality. Instead of political democracy, Reconstruction would bequeath a legacy of sectional fraud, intimidation, and shameless racial exclusion. Rather than accelerating southern economic growth, Reconstruction would chain the South to a declining staple crop agriculture and leave it ever further behind the rest of the nation.

Who was to blame for this failure? One answer is that Americans were trapped by the past. Deep-seated prejudices and memories of slavery blinded most white southerners (and many Northerners) to the need for racial justice. Traditional individualism and the commitment to self-help obscured the fact that the special circumstances of black dependence resulting from slavery called for imaginative government aid. And there were the accidents of events and personalities. Would Lincoln have seen realities more clearly? Certainly the accession of Andrew Johnson, a stubborn man of limited vision and conventional racial views, did nothing to solve the unique problems of the day. Refusing to recognize the North's need to exact some penance from the defeated South, he needlessly antagonized even moderates and drove them into the Radical camp. The result was a legacy of sectional hatred that poisoned American political life for generations.

Meanwhile, the nation was turning away from the "everlasting southern problem" to what many citizens believed were more important matters. The South and Reconstruction became increasingly remote as the country as a whole experienced a surge of economic expansion that dwarfed anything of the past.

APPENDIX

In Congress, July 4, 1776

The Declaration of Independence

The Unanimous Declaration of the Thirteen United States of America

When in the Course of human events, it becomes necessary for one people to dissolve the political bands which have connected them with another, and to assume among the powers of the earth, the separate and equal station to which the Laws of Nature and of Nature's God entitle them, a decent respect to the opinions of mankind requires that they should declare the causes which impel them to the separation.

We hold these truths to be self-evident, that all men are created equal, that they are endowed by their Creator with certain unalienable Rights, that among these are Life, Liberty, and the pursuit of Happiness.

That to secure these rights, Governments are instituted among Men, deriving their just powers from the consent of the governed.

That whenever any Form of Government becomes destructive of these ends, it is the Right of the People to alter or to abolish it, and to institute new Government, laying its foundation on such principles and organizing its powers in such form, as to them shall seem most likely to effect their Safety and Happiness. Prudence, indeed, will dictate that Governments long established should not be changed for light and transient causes; and accordingly all experience hath shewn, that mankind are more disposed to suffer, while evils are sufferable, than to right themselves by abolishing the forms to which they are accustomed. But when a long train of abuses and usurpations, pursuing invariably the same Object evinces a design to reduce them under absolute Despotism, it is their right, it is their duty, to throw off such Government, and to provide new Guards for their future security.

Such has been the patient sufferance of these Colonies; and such is now the necessity which constrains them to alter their former Systems of Government. The history of the present King of Great Britain is a history of repeated injuries and usurpations, all having in direct object the establishment of an absolute Tyranny over these States. To prove this, let Facts be submitted to a candid world.

He has refused his Asset to Laws, the most wholesome and necessary for the public good.

He has forbidden his Governors to pass Laws of immediate and pressing importance, unless suspended in their operation till his Assent should be obtained; and when so suspended, he has utterly neglected to attend the them.

He has refused to pass other Laws for the accommodation of large districts of people, unless those people would relinquish the right of Representation in the Legislature, a right inestimable to them and formidable to tyrants only.

He has called together legislative bodies at places unusual, uncomfortable, and distant from the depository of their public Records, for the sole purpose of fatiguing them into compliance with his measures.

He has dissolved Representative Houses repeatedly, for opposing with manly firmness his invasions on the rights of the people.

He has refused for a long time, after such dissolutions, to cause others to be elected; whereby the Legislative powers, incapable of Annihilation, have returned to the People at large for their exercise; the State remaining in the mean time exposed to all the dangers of invasion from without, and convulsions within.

He has endeavoured to prevent the population of these States; for that purpose obstructing the Laws for Naturalization of Foreigners; refusing to pass others to encourage their migrations hither, and raising the conditions of new Appropriations of Lands.

He has obstructed the Administration of Justice, by refusing his Assent to Laws for establishing Judiciary powers.

He has made judges dependent on his Will alone, for the tenure of their offices, and the amount and payment of their salaries.

He has erected a multitude of New Offices, and sent hither swarms of Officers to harass our people, and eat out their substance.

He has kept among us, in times of peace, Standing Armies without the Consent of our legislatures.

He has affected to render the Military independent of and superior to the Civil power.

He has combined with others to subject us to a jurisdiction foreign to our constitution, and unacknowledged by our laws; giving his Assent to their Acts of pretended Legislation:

For quartering large bodies of armed troops among us:

For protecting them, by a mock Trial, from punishment for any Murders which they should commit on the Inhabitants of these States:

For cutting off our Trade with all parts of the world:

For imposing Taxes on us without our Consent:

For depriving us in many cases, of the benefits of Trial by Jury:

For transporting us beyond Seas to be tried for pretended offences:

For abolishing the free System of English Laws in a neighbouring Province, establishing therein an Arbitrary government, and enlarging its Boundaries so as to render it at once an example and fit instrument for introducing the same absolute rule into these Colonies:

For taking away our Charters, abolishing our most valuable Laws, and altering fundamentally the Forms of our Governments:

For suspending our own Legislatures, and declaring themselves invested with power to legislate for us in all cases whatsoever.

He has abdicated Government here, by declaring us out of his Protection and waging War against us.

He has plundered our seas, ravaged our Coasts, burnt our towns, and destroyed the Lives of our people.

He is at this time transporting large Armies of foreign Mercenaries to compleat the works of death, desolation and tyranny, already begun with circumstances of Cruelty & perfidy scarcely paralleled in the most barbarous ages, and totally unworthy the Head of a civilized nation.

He has constrained our fellow Citizens taken Captive on the high Seas to bear Arms against their Country, to become the executioners of their friends and Brethren, or to fall themselves by their Hands.

He has excited domestic insurrections amongst us, and has endeavoured to bring on the inhabitants of our frontiers, the merciless Indian Savages, whose known rule of warfare, is an undistinguished destruction of all ages, sexes and conditions.

In every stage of these Oppressions We have Petitioned for Redress in the most humble terms: Our repeated Petitions have been answered only by repeated injury. A Prince, whose character is thus marked by every act which may define a Tyrant, is unfit to be the ruler of a free people.

Nor have We been wanting in attentions to our British brethren. We have warned them from time to time of attempts by their legislature to extend an unwarrantable jurisdiction over us. We have reminded them of the circumstances of our emigration and settlement here. We have appealed to their native justice and magnanimity, and we have conjured them by the ties of our common kindred to disavow these usurpations, which, would inevitably interrupt our connections and correspondence. They too have been deaf to the voice of justice and of consanguinity. We must, therefore, acquiesce in the necessity, which denounces our Separation, and hold them, as we hold the rest of mankind, Enemies in War, in Peace Friends.

We, therefore, the Representatives of the United States of America, in General Congress, Assembled, appealing to the Supreme Judge of the world for the rectitude of our intentions, do, in the Name, and by Authority of the good People of these Colonies, solemnly publish and declare,

That these United Colonies are, and of Right ought to be Free and Independent States; that they are Absolved from all Allegiance to the British Crown, and that all political connection between them and the State of Great Britain, is and ought to be totally dissolved; and that as Free and Independent States, they have full Power to levy War, conclude Peace, contract Alliances, establish Commerce, and to do all other Acts and Things which Independent States may of right do.

And for the support of this Declaration, with a firm reliance on the protection of divine Providence, we mutually pledge to each other our Lives, our Fortunes and our sacred Honor.

JOHN HANCOCK

NEW HAMPSHIRE
Josiah Bartlett
William Whipple
Matthew Thorton

MASSACHUSETTS BAY
Samuel Adams
John Adams
Robert Treat Paine
Elbridge Gerry

RHODE ISLAND
Stephen Hopkins
William Ellery

CONNECTICUT
Roger Sherman
Samuel Huntington
William Williams
Oliver Wolcott

NEW YORK
William Floyd
Philip Livingston
Francis Lewis
Lewis Morris

NEW JERSEY
Richard Stockton
John Witherspoon
Francis Hopkinson
John Hart
Abraham Clark

PENNSYLVANIA
Robert Morris
Benjamin Rush
Benjamin Franklin
John Morton
George Clymer
James Smith
George Taylor
James Wilson
George Ross

DELAWARE
Caesar Rodney
George Read
Thomas M'Kean

MARYLAND
Samuel Chase
William Paca
Thomas Stone
Charles Carroll, of Carrollton

VIRGINIA
George Wythe
Richard Henry Lee
Thomas Jefferson
Benjamin Harrison
Thomas Nelson, Jr.
Francis Lightfoot Lee
Carter Braxton

NORTH CAROLINA
William Hooper
Joseph Hewes
John Penn

SOUTH CAROLINA
Edward Rutledge
Thomas Heyward, Jr.
Thomas Lynch, Jr.
Arthur Middleton

GEORGIA
Button Gwinnett
Lyman Hall
George Walton

Resolved.   *That copies of the Ceclaration be sent to the several assemblies, conventions, and committees or councils of safety, and to the several commanding officers of the continental troops; that it be proclaimed in each of the United States, at the head of the army.*

The Constitution of the United States of America

PREAMBLE

We the People of the United States, in Order to form a more perfect Union, establish Justice, insure domestic Tranquility, provide for the common defence, promote the general Welfare, and secure the Blessings of Liberty to ourselves and our Posterity, do ordain and establish this Constitution for the United States of America.

ARTICLE I

Section 1. All legislative Powers herein granted shall be vested in a Congress of the United States, which shall consist of a Senate and House of Representatives.

Section 2. The House of Representatives shall be composed of Members chosen every second Year by the People of the several States, and the Electors in each State shall have the Qualifications requisite for Electors of the most numerous Branch of the State Legislature.

No Person shall be a Representative who shall not have attained to the Age of twenty-five Years, and been seven years a Citizen of the United States, and who shall not, when elected, be an Inhabitant of that State in which he shall be chosen.

Representatives and direct Taxes shall be apportioned among the several States which may be included within this Union, according to their respective Numbers. [which shall be determined by adding to the whole Number of free Persons, including those bound to Service for a Term of Years, and excluding Indians not taxed, three fifths of all other Persons.][1] The actual Enumeration shall be made within three Years after the first Meeting of the Congress of the United States, and within every subsequent Term of ten Years, in such Manner as they shall by Law direct. The Number of Representatives shall not exceed one for every thirty Thousand, but each State shall have at Least one Representative; and until such enumeration shall be made, the State of New Hampshire shall be entitled to chuse three; Massachusetts eight; Rhode Island and Providence Plantations one; Connecticut five; New York six; New Jersey four; Pennsylvania eight; Delaware one; Maryland six; Virginia ten; North Carolina five; South Carolina five; and Georgia three.

When vacancies happen in the Representation from any State, the Executive Authority thereof shall issue Writs of Election to fill such Vacancies.

The House of Representatives shall chuse their Speaker and other Officers; and shall have the sole Power of Impeachment.

Section 3. The Senate of the United States, shall be composed of two Senators from each state, [chosen by the Legislature thereof,][2] for six Years; and each Senator shall have one Vote.

Immediately after they shall be assembled in Consequence of the first Election, they shall be divided as equally as may be into three Classes. The Seats of the Senators of the first Class shall be vacated at the Expiration of the second year, of the second Class at the Expiration of the fourth Year, and of the third Class at the Expiration of the sixth Year, so that one third may be chosen every second Year; [and if Vacancies happen by Resignation, or otherwise, during the Recess of the Legislature of any State, the Executive thereof may make temporary Appointments until the next Meeting of the Legislature, which shall then fill such Vacancies.][3]

---

[1]Bracketed material superseded by Section 2 of the Fourteenth Amendment.

[2]Bracketed material superseded by Clause I of the Seventeenth Amendment.
[3]Bracketed material modified by Clause 2 of the Seventeenth Amendment.

No Person shall be a Senator who shall not have attained to the Age of thirty Years, and been nine Years a Citizen of the United States, and who shall not, when elected, be an Inhabitant of that State for which he shall be chosen.

The Vice President of the United States shall be President of the Senate, but shall have no Vote, unless they be equally divided.

The Senate shall chuse their other Officers, and also a President pro tempore, in the Absence of the Vice President, or when he shall exercise the Office of President of the United States.

The Senate shall have the sole Power to try all Impeachments. When sitting for that Purpose, they shall be on Oath or Affirmation. When the President of the United States is tried, the Chief Justice shall preside: And no Person shall be convicted without the Concurrence of two thirds of the Members present.

Judgment in Cases of Impeachment shall not extend further than to removal from Office, and disqualification to hold and enjoy any Office of honor, Trust or Profit under the United States: but the Party convicted shall nevertheless be liable and subject to Indictment, Trial, Judgment and Punishment, according to Law.

Section 4. The Times, Places and Manner of holding Elections for Senators and Representatives, shall be prescribed in each State by the legislature thereof; but the Congress may at any time by Law make or alter such Regulations, except as to the Places of chusing Senators.

[The Congress shall assemble at least once in every Year, and such Meeting shall be on the first Monday in December, unless they shall by Law appoint a different Day.][4]

Section 5. Each House shall be the Judge of the Elections, Returns and Qualifications of its own Members, and a Majority of each shall constitute a Quorum to do Business; but a smaller Number may ad-

journ from day to day, and may be authorized to compel the Attendance of absent Members, in such Manner, and under such Penalties as each House may provide.

Each House may determine the Rules of its Proceedings, punish its Members for disorderly Behaviour, and, with the Concurrence of two thirds, expel a Member.

Each House shall keep a Journal of its Proceedings, and from time to time publish the same, excepting such Parts as may in their Judgment require Secrecy; and the Yeas and Nays of the Members of either House on any questions shall, at the Desire of one fifth of those Present, be entered on the Journal.

Neither House, during the Session of Congress, shall, without the Consent of the other, adjourn for more than three days, nor to any other Place than that in which the two Houses shall be sitting.

Section 6. The Senators and Representatives shall receive a Compensation for their Services, to be ascertained by Law, and paid out of the Treasury of the United States. They shall in all Cases, except Treason, Felony and Breach of the Peace, be privileged from Arrest during their Attendance at the Session of their respective Houses, and in going to and returning from the same; and for any Speech or Debate in either House, they shall not be questioned in any other Place.

No Senator or Representative shall, during the Time for which he was elected, be appointed to any civil Office under the Authority of the United States, which shall have been created, or the Emoluments whereof shall have been encreased during such time; and no Person holding any Office under the United States, shall be a Member of either House during his Continuance in Office.

Section 7. All Bills for raising Revenue shall Originate in the House of Representatives; but the Senate may propose or concur with Amendments as on other Bills.

Every Bill which shall have passed the House of Representatives and the Senate, shall, before it becomes a Law, be presented to the President of the United States; If he

---

[4]Bracketed material superseded by Section 2 of the Twentieth Amendment.

approve he shall sign it, but if not he shall return it, with his Objections to that House in which it shall have originated, who shall enter the Objections at large on their Journal, and proceed to reconsider it. If after such Reconsideration two thirds of that House shall agree to pass the Bill, it shall be sent, together with the Objections, to the other House, by which it shall likewise be reconsidered, and if approved by two thirds of that House, it shall become a Law. But in all such Cases the Votes of both Houses shall be determined by Yeas and Nays, and the Names of the Persons voting for and against the Bill shall be entered on the Journal of each House respectively. If any Bill shall not be returned by the President within Ten Days (Sundays excepted) after it shall have been presented to him, the Same shall be a Law, in like Manner as if he had signed it, unless the Congress by their Adjournment prevents its Return, in which Case it shall not be a Law.

Every Order, Resolution, or Vote to which the Concurrence of the Senate and House of Representatives may be necessary (except on a question of Adjournment) shall be presented to the President of the United States; and before the Same shall take effect, shall be approved by him, or being disapproved by him, shall be repassed by two thirds of the Senate and House of Representatives, according to the Rules and Limitations prescribed in the Case of Bill.

Section 8. The Congress shall have Power To lay and collect Taxes, Duties, Imposts, and Excises, to pay the Debts and provide for the common Defence and general Welfare of the United States; but all Duties, Imposts and Excises shall be uniform throughout the United States;

To borrow Money on the credit of the United States;

To regulate Commerce with foreign Nations, and among the several States, and with the Indian Tribes;

To establish an uniform Rule of Naturalization, and uniform Laws on the subject of Bankruptcies throughout the United States;

To coin Money, regulate the Value thereof, and of foreign Coin, and fix the Standard of Weights and Measures;

To provide for the Punishment of counterfeiting the Securities and current Coin of the United States;

To establish Post Offices and post Roads;

To promote the Progress of Science and useful Arts, by securing for limited Times to Authors and Inventors the exclusive Right to their respective Writings and Discoveries;

To constitute Tribunals inferior to the supreme Court;

To define and punish Piracies and Felonies committed on the high Seas, and Offences against the Law of Nations;

To declare War, grant Letters of Marque and Reprisal, and make Rules concerning Captures on Land and Water;

To raise and support Armies; but no Appropriation of Money to that Use shall be for a longer Term than two years;

To provide and maintain a Navy;

To make Rules for the Government and Regulation of the land and naval Forces;

To provide for calling forth the Militia to execute the laws of the Union, suppress Insurrections and repel Invasions;

To provide for organizing, arming, and disciplining, the Militia, and for governing such Part of them as may be employed in the Service of the United States, reserving to the States respectively, the Appointment of the Officers, and the Authority of training the Militia according to the discipline prescribed by Congress;

To exercise exclusive Legislation in all Cases whatsoever, over such District (not exceeding ten Miles square) as may, by Cession of particular States, and the Acceptance of Congress, become the Seat of the Government of the United States, and to exercise like Authority over all Places purchased by the Consent of the Legislature of the State in which the Same shall be, for the Erection of Forts, Magazines, Arsenals, dock-Yards, and other needful Buildings;—And

To make all Laws which shall be necessary and proper for carrying into Execution the foregoing Powers, and all other Powers vested by this Constitution in the Government of the United States, or in any Department or Officer thereof.

Section 9. The Migration or Importation of such Persons as any of the States now existing shall think proper to admit, shall not be prohibited by the Congress prior to the year one thousand eight hundred and eight, but a Tax or duty may be imposed on such Importation, not exceeding ten dollars for each Person.

The Privilege of the Writ of Habeas Corpus shall not be suspended, unless when in Cases of Rebellion or Invasion the public Safety may require it.

No Bill of Attainder or ex post facto Law shall be passed.

No Capitation, or other direct, Tax shall be laid, unless in Proportion to the Census or Enumeration herein before directed to be taken.[5]

No Tax or Duty shall be laid on Articles exported from any State.

No Preferences shall be given by any Regulation of Commerce or Revenue to the Ports of one State over those of another; nor shall Vessels bound to, or from, one State, be obliged to enter, clear, or pay Duties in another.

No Money shall be drawn from the Treasury, but in Consequence of Appropriations made by Law; and a regular Statement and Account of the Receipts and Expenditures of all public Money shall be published from time to time.

No Title of Nobility shall be grated by the United States: And no person holding any office of Profit or Trust under them, shall, without the Consent of the Congress, accept of any present, Emolument, Office, or Title, of any kind whatever, from any King, Prince, or foreign State.

Section 10. No State shall enter into any Treaty, Alliance, or Confederation; grant Letters of Marque and Reprisal; coin Money; emit Bills of Credit; make any Thing but gold and silver Coin a Tender in Payment of Debts; pass any Bill of Attainder, ex post facto Law, or Law impairing the Obligation of Contracts, or grant any Title of Nobility.

No State shall, without the Consent of the Congress, lay any Imposts or Duties on Imports or Exports, except what may be absolutely necessary for executing its inspection Laws: and the net Produce of all Duties and Imposts, laid by any State on Imports or Exports, shall be for the Use of the Treasury of the United States; and all such Laws shall be subject to the Revision and Control of the Congress.

No State shall, without the Consent of Congress, lay any Duty of Tonnage, keep Troops, or Ships of War in time of Peace, enter into any Agreement or Compact with another State, or with a foreign Power, or engage in War, unless actually invaded, or in such imminent Danger as will not admit of delay.

ARTICLE II

Section 1. The executive Power shall be vested in a President of the United States of America. He shall hold his Office during the Term of four Years, and, together with the Vice President, chosen for the same Term, be elected, as follows.

Each State shall appoint, in such Manner as the Legislature thereof may direct, a Number of Electors, equal to the whole Number of Senators and Representative to which the State may be entitled in the Congress; but no Senator or Representative, or Person holding an Office of Trust or Profit under the United States, shall be appointed an Elector.

[The Electors shall meet in their respective States, and vote by Ballot for two Persons, of whom one at least shall not be an Inhabitant of the same State with themselves. And they shall make a List of all the Persons voted for, and of the Number of Votes for each; which List they shall sign and certify, and transmit sealed to the Seat of the Government of the United States, directed to the President of the Senate. The President of the Senate shall, in the Presence

---

[5]Modified by the Sixteenth Amendment.

of the Senate and House of Representatives, open all the Certificates, and the Votes shall then be counted. The Person having the greatest Number of Votes shall be the President, if such Number be a Majority of the whole Number of Electors appointed; and if there be more than one who have such Majority, and have an equal Number of Votes, then the House of Representatives shall immediately chuse by Ballot one of them for President; and if no Person have a Majority, then from the five highest on the List the said House shall in like Manner chuse the President. But in chusing the President, the Votes shall be taken by States, the Representation from each State having one Vote; A quorum for this Purpose shall consist of a Member or Members from two thirds of the States, and a Majority of all the States shall be necessary to a Choice. In every Case, after the Choice of the President, the Person having the greatest Number of Votes of the Electors shall be the Vice President. But if there should remain two or more who have equal Votes, the Senate shall chuse from them by Ballot the Vice President.]⁶

The Congress may determine the Time of chusing the Electors, and the Day on which they shall give their Votes; which Day shall be the same throughout the United States.

No Person except a natural born Citizen, or a Citizen of the United States, at the time of the Adoption of this Constitution, shall be eligible to the Office of President; neither shall any Person be eligible to that Office who shall not have attained to the Age of thirty-five Years, and been fourteen Years a Resident within the United States.

[In Case of Removal of the President from Office, or of this Death, Resignation, or Inability to discharge the Powers and Duties of the said Office, the Same shall devolve on the Vice President, and the Congress may by law provide for the Case of Removal, Death, Resignation or Inability, both of the President and Vice President,

declaring what Officer shall then act as President, and such Officer shall act accordingly, until the Disability be removed, or a President shall be elected.⁷

The President shall, at stated Times, receive for his Services, a Compensation, which shall neither be encreased nor diminished during the Period for which he shall have been elected, and he shall not receive within that Period any other Emolument from the United States, or any of them.

Before he enter on the Execution of his Office; he shall take the following Oath or Affirmation—"I do solemnly swear (or affirm) that I will faithfully execute the Office of the President of the United States, and will to the best of my Ability, preserve, protect and defend the Constitution of the United States."

Section 2. The President shall be Commander in Chief of the Army and Navy of the United States, and of the Militia of the several States, when called into the actual Service of the United States; he may require the Opinion, in writing, of the principal Office in each of the executive Departments upon any Subject relating to the Duties of their respective Offices, and he shall have Power to grant Reprieves and Pardons for Offences against the United States, except in Cases of Impeachment.

He shall have Power, by and with the Advice and Consent of the Senate, to make Treaties, provided two thirds of the Senators present concur, and he shall nominate, and by and with the Advice and Consent of the Senate, shall appoint Ambassadors, other public Ministers and Consuls Judges of the supreme Court, and all other Officers of the United States, whose Appointments are not herein otherwise provided for, and which shall be established by Law; but the Congress may by Law vest the Appointment of such inferior Officers, as they think proper, in the Presidents alone, in the Courts of Law, or in the Heads of Departments.

---

⁶Bracketed material superseded by the Twelfth Amendment.

⁷Bracketed material modified by the Twenty-fifth Amendment.

The President shall have Power to fill up all Vacancies that may happen during the Recess of the Senate, by granting Commissions which shall expire at the End of their next Session.

Section 3. He shall from time to time give to the Congress Information of the State of the Union, and recommend to their Consideration such Measures as he shall judge necessary and expedient; he may, on extraordinary Occasions, convene both Houses, or either of them, and in Case of Disagreement between them, with Respect to the Time of Adjournment, he may adjourn them to such Time as he shall think proper; he shall receive Ambassadors and other public Ministers; he shall take Care that the Laws be faithfully executed, and shall Commission all the Officers of the United States.

Section 4. The President, Vice President and all civil Officers of the United States, shall be removed from Office on Impeachment for, and Conviction of, Treason, Bribery, or other high Crimes and Misdemeanors.

ARTICLE III

Section 1. The judicial Power of the United States, shall be vested in one supreme Court, and in such inferior Courts as the Congress may from time to time ordain and establish. The Judges, both of the supreme and inferior Courts, shall hold their Offices during good Behaviour, and shall, at stated Times, receive for their Services, a Compensation, which shall not be diminished during their Continuance in Office.

Section 2. The judicial Power shall extend to all Cases, in Law and Equity, arising under this Constitution, the Laws of the United States, and Treaties made, or which shall be made, under their Authority;—to all Cases affecting Ambassadors, other public Ministers and Consuls;—to all Cases of admiralty and maritime Jurisdiction;—To Controversies to which the United States shall be a Party;—to Controversies between two or more States;—between a State and Citizens of another State;—between Citizens of different States;—between Citizens of the same State claiming Lands under Grants of different States, and between a State, or the Citizens thereof, and foreign States, Citizens or Subjects.[8]

In all Cases affecting Ambassadors, other public Ministers and Consuls, and those in which a State shall be Party, the supreme Court shall have original Jurisdiction. In all the other Cases before mentioned the supreme Court shall have appellate Jurisdiction, both as to Law and Fact, with such Exceptions, and under such Regulations as the Congress shall make.

The Trial of all Crimes, except in Cases of Impeachment, shall be by Jury; and such Trial shall be held in the State where the said Crimes shall have been committed; but when not committed within any State, the Trial shall be at such Place or Places as the Congress may by Law have directed.

Section 3. Treason against the United States, shall consist only in levying War against them, or in adhering to their Enemies, giving them Aid and Comfort. No Person shall be convicted of Treason unless on the Testimony of two Witnesses to the same overt Act, or on Confession in open Court.

The Congress shall have Power to declare the Punishment of Treason, but no Attainder of Treason shall work Corruption of Blood, or Forfeiture except during the Life of the person attained.

ARTICLE IV

Section 1. Full Faith and Credit shall be given in each State to the public Acts, Records, and judicial Proceedings of every other State. And the Congress may be general Laws prescribe the Manner in which such Acts, Records and Proceedings shall be proved, and the Effect thereof.

Section 2. The Citizens of each State shall be entitled to all Privileges and Immunities of Citizens in the several States.

A Person charged in any State with Treason, Felony, or other Crime, who shall

---

[8]This paragraph modified in part by the Eleventh Amendment.

flee from Justice, and be found in another State, shall on Demand of the executive Authority of the State of which he fled, be delivered up, to be removed to the State having Jurisdiction of the Crime.

[No Person held to Service or Labour in one State, under the Laws thereof, escaping into another, shall, in Consequence of any Law or Regulation therein, be discharged from such Service or Labour, but shall be delivered up on Claim of the Party to whom such Service or Labour may be due.][9]

Section 3. New States may be admitted by the Congress into this Union; but no new State shall be formed or erected within the Jurisdiction of any other State; nor any State be formed by the Junction of two or more States, or Parts of States, without the Consent of the Legislatures of the States concerned as well as of the Congress.

The Congress shall have Power to dispose of and make all needful Rules and Regulations respecting the Territory or other property belonging to the United States; and nothing in this Constitution shall be so construed as to Prejudice any Claims of the United States, or of any particular State.

Section 4. The United States shall guarantee to every State in this Union a Republican Form of Government, and shall protect each of them against Invasion; and on Application of the Legislature, or of the Executive (when the Legislative cannot be convened) against domestic Violence.

ARTICLE V

The Congress, whenever two thirds of both Houses shall deem it necessary, shall proposed Amendments to this Constitution, or, on the Application of the legislatures of two thirds of the several States, shall call a Convention for proposing Amendments, which, in either Case, shall be valid to all Intents and Purposes, as Part of this Constitution, when ratified by the Legislatures of three fourths of the several States, or by Conventions in three fourths thereof, as the one or the other Mode of Ratification may be proposed by the Congress; Provided that no Amendment which may be made prior to the Year One thousand eight hundred and eight shall in any Manner affect the first and fourth Clauses in the Ninth Section of the first Article; and that no State, without its Consent, shall be deprived of its equal Suffrage in the Senate.

ARTICLE VI

All Debts contracted and Engagements entered into, before the Adoption of this Constitution, shall be as valid against the United States under this Constitution, as under the Confederation.

This Constitution, and the Laws of the United States which shall be made in Pursuance thereof; and all Treaties made, or which shall be made, under the Authority of the United States, shall be the supreme Law of the Land; and the Judges in every State shall be bound thereby, any Thing in the Constitution or Laws of any State to the Contrary notwithstanding.

The Senators and Representatives before mentioned, and the members of the several State Legislatures, and all executive and judicial Officers, both of the United States and of the several States, shall be bound by Oath or Affirmation, to support this Constitution; but no religious Test shall ever be required as a Qualification to any Office or public Trust under the United States.

ARTICLE VII

The Ratification of the Conventions of nine States, shall be sufficient for the Establishment of this Constitution between the States so ratifying the Same.

DONE in Convention by the Unanimous Consent of the States present the Seventeenth Day of September in the Year of our Lord one thousand seven hundred and eighty seven and of the Independence of the United States of America the Twelfth. IN WITNESS whereof We have hereunto subscribed our Names.

---

[9]Bracketed material superseded by the Thirteenth Amendment.

GEORGE WASHINGTON—*President and deputy from Virginia*

NEW HAMPSHIRE
John Langdon
Nicholas Gilman

MASSACHUSETTS
Nathaniel Gorham
Rufus King

CONNECTICUT
William Samuel
Johnson
Roger Sherman

MARYLAND
James McHenry
Daniel of St. Thomas
Jenifer
Daniel Carroll

NEW YORK
Alexander Hamilton

VIRGINIA
John Blair
James Madison, Jr.

NEW JERSEY
William Livingston
David Brearley
William Paterson
Jonathan Dayton

NORTH CAROLINA
William Blount
Richard Dobbs
Spaight
Hugh Williamson

PENNSYLVANIA
Benjamin Franklin
Thomas Mifflin
Robert Morris
George Clymer
Thomas FitzSimons
Jared Ingersoll
James Wilson
Gouverneur Morris

SOUTH CAROLINA
John Rutledge
Charles Cotesworth
Pickney
Charles Pinckney
Pierce Butler

GEORGIA
William Few
Abraham Baldwin

DELAWARE
George Read
Gunning Bedford, Jr.
John Dickinson
Richard Bassett
Jacob Broom

Attest: William
Jackson, *Secretary*

THE AMENDMENTS

ARTICLES in addition to, and Amendment of the Constitution of the United States of America, proposed by Congress, and ratified by the Legislatures of the several States, pursuant to the fifth Article of the original Constitution.

ARTICLE I

[*Articles I through X, now known as the Bill of Rights, were proposed on September 25, 1789, and declared in force on December 15, 1791.*]

Congress shall make no law respecting an establishment of religion, or prohibiting the free exercise thereof; or abridging the freedom of speech, or of the press; or the right of the people peaceably to assemble, and to petition the Government for a redress of grievances.

ARTICLE II

A well regulated Militia, being necessary to the security of a free State, the right of the people to keep and bear Arms, shall not be infringed.

ARTICLE III

No Soldier shall, in time of peace be quartered in any house, without the consent of the Owner, nor in time of war, but in manner to be prescribed by law.

ARTICLE IV

The right of the people to be secure in their persons, houses, papers, and effects, against unreasonable searches and seizures, shall not be violated, and no Warrants shall issue, but upon probable cause, supported by Oath or affirmation, and particularly describing the place to be searched, and the persons or things to be seized.

ARTICLE V

No person shall be held to answer for a capital, or otherwise infamous crime, unless on a presentment or indictment of a Grand Jury, except in cases arising in the land or naval forces, or in the Militia, when in actual service in time of War or public danger; nor shall any person be subject for the same offence to be twice put in jeopardy of life or limb; nor shall be compelled in any criminal case to be a witness against himself, nor be deprived of life, liberty, or property, without due process of law; nor shall private property be taken for public use, without just compensation.

ARTICLE VI

In all criminal prosecutions, the accused shall enjoy the right to a speedy and public trial, by an impartial jury of the State and district wherein the crime shall have been committed, which district shall have been previously ascertained by law, and to be informed of the nature and cause of the accusation; to be confronted with the witnesses against him; to have compulsory process for obtaining witnesses in his favor, and to have the Assistance of Counsel for his defence.

ARTICLE VII

In Suits at common law, where the value in controversy shall exceed twenty dollars, the right of trial by jury shall be preserved, and no fact tried by a jury shall be otherwise reexamined in any Court of the United States, than according to the rules of the common law.

ARTICLE VIII

Excessive bail shall not be required, nor excessive fines imposed, nor cruel and unusual punishments inflicted.

ARTICLE IX

The enumeration in the Constitution, of certain rights, shall not be construed to deny or disparage others retained by the people.

ARTICLE X

The powers not delegated to the United States by the Constitution, nor prohibited by it to the States, are reserved to the States respectively, or to the people.

ARTICLE XI

[*Proposed March 4, 1794; declared ratified January 8, 1798*]

The Judicial power of the United States shall not be construed to extend to any suit in law or equity, commenced or prosecuted against one of the United States by Citizens of another State, or by Citizens or Subjects of any Foreign State.

ARTICLE XII

[*Proposed December 9, 1803; declared ratified September 25, 1804*]

The Electors shall meet in their respective states and vote by ballot for President and Vice-President, one of whom, at least, shall not be an inhabitant of the same state with themselves; they shall name in their ballots the person voted for as President, and in distinct ballots the person voted for as Vice-President, and they shall make distinct lists of all persons voted for as President, and of all persons voted for as Vice-President, and of the number of votes for each, which lists they shall sign and certify, and transmit sealed to the seat of the government of the United States, directed to the President of the Senate;—The President of the Senate shall, in the presence of the Senate and House of Representatives, open all the certificates and the votes shall then be counted;—The person having the greatest number of votes for President, shall be the President, if such number be a majority of the whole number of Electors appointed; and if no person have such majority, then from the persons having the highest numbers not exceeding three on the list of those voted for as President, the House of Representatives shall choose immediately, by ballot, the President. But in choosing the President, the votes shall be taken by states, the representation from each state having one vote; a quorum for this purpose shall consist of a member or members from two-thirds of the states, and a majority of all the states shall be necessary to a choice. [And if the House of Representatives shall not choose a President whenever the right of choice shall devolve upon them, before the fourth day of March next following, then the Vice-President shall act as President, as in the case of the death or other constitutional disability of the President.][10]—The person hav-

---

[10]Bracketed material superseded by Section 3 of the Twentieth Amendment.

ing the greatest number of votes as Vice-President, shall be the Vice-President, if such number be a majority of the whole number of Electors appointed and if no person have a majority; then from the two highest numbers on the list, the Senate shall choose the Vice-President; a quorum for the purpose shall consist of two-thirds of the whole number of Senators, and a majority of the whole number shall be necessary to a choice. But no person constitutionally ineligible to the office of President shall be eligible to that of Vice-President of the United States.

ARTICLE XIII

[*Proposed January 31, 1865; declared ratified December 18, 1865*]

Section 1. Neither slavery nor involuntary servitude, except as a punishment for crime whereof the party shall have been duly convicted, shall exist within the United States, or any place subject to their jurisdiction.

Section 2. Congress shall have power to enforce this article by appropriate legislation.

ARTICLE XIV

[*Proposed June 13, 1866; declared ratified July 28, 1868*]

Section 1. All persons born or naturalized ion the United States, and subject to the jurisdiction thereof, are citizens of the United States and of the State wherein they reside. No State shall make or enforce any law which shall abridge the privileges or immunities of citizens of the United States; nor shall any State deprive any person of life, liberty, or property, without due process of law; nor deny to any person within its jurisdiction the equal protection of the laws.

Section 2. Representatives shall be apportioned among the several States according to their respective numbers, counting the whole number of persons in each State, excluding Indians not taxed. But when the right to vote at any election for the choice of electors for President and Vice President of the United States, Representatives in Congress, the Execu-

tive and Judicial officers of a State or the members of the Legislature thereof, is denied to any of the male inhabitants of such State, being twenty-one years of age, and citizens of the United States, or in any way abridged, except for participation in rebellion, or other crime, the basis of representation therein shall be reduced in the proportion which the number of such male citizens shall bear to the whole number of male citizens twenty-one years of age in such State.

Section 3. No person shall be a Senator or Representative in Congress, or elector of President and Vice President, or hold any office, civil or military, under the United States, or under any State, who, having previously taken an oath as a member of Congress, or as an officer of the United States, or as a member of any State legislature, or as an executive or judicial officer of any state, to support the Constitution of the United States, shall have engaged in insurrection or rebellion against the same, or given aid or comfort to the enemies thereof. But Congress may by a vote of two-thirds of each House, remove such disability.

Section 4. The validity of the public debt of the United States, authorized by law, including debts incurred for payments of pensions and bounties for services in suppressing insurrection or rebellion, shall not be questioned. But neither the United States nor any State shall assume or pay any debt or obligation incurred in aid of insurrection or rebellion against the United States, or any claim for the loss or emancipation of any slave; but all such debts, obligations and claims shall be held illegal and void.

Section 5. The Congress shall have power to enforce, by appropriate legislations, the provisions of this article.

ARTICLE XV

[*Proposed February 26, 1869; declared ratified March 30, 1870*]

Section 1. The right of citizens of the United States to vote shall not be denied or abridged by the United States or by any State on account of race, color, or previous condition of servitude.

Section 2. The Congress shall have power to enforce this article by appropriate legislation.

ARTICLE XVI

[*Proposed July 12, 1909; declared ratified February 25, 1913*]

The Congress shall have power to lay and collect taxes on incomes, from whatever source derived, without apportionment among the several States, and without regard to any census or enumeration.

ARTICLE XVII

[*Proposed May 13, 1912; declared ratified May 31, 1913*]

The Senate of the United States shall be composed of two Senators from each State, elected by the people thereof, for six years; and each Senator shall have one vote. The electors in each State shall have the qualifications requisite for electors of the most numerous branch of the State legislatures.

When vacancies happen in the representation of any State in the Senate, the executive authority of such State shall issue writs of election to fill such vacancies: *Provided,* That the legislature of any State may empower the executive thereof to make temporary appointments until the people fill the vacancies by election as the legislature may direct.

This amendment shall not be so construed as to affect the election or term of any Senator chosen before it becomes valid as part of the Constitution.

ARTICLE XVIII

[*Proposed December 18, 1917; declared ratified January 29, 1919; repealed by the Twenty-first Amendment December 5, 1933*]

Section 1. After one year from the ratification of this article the manufacture, sale, or transportation of intoxicating liquors within, the importation thereof into, or the exportation thereof from the United States and all territory subject to the jurisdiction thereof for beverage purposes is hereby prohibited.

Section 2. The Congress and the several States shall have concurrent power to enforce this article by appropriate legislation.

Section 3. This article shall be inoperative unless it shall have been ratified as an amendment to the Constitution by the legislatures of the several States, as provided in the Constitution, within seven years from the date of the submission hereof to the States by the Congress.

ARTICLE XIX

[*Proposed June 4, 1919; declared ratified August 26, 1920*]

The right of citizens of the United States to vote shall not be denied or abridged by the United States or by any State on account of sex.

Congress shall have power to enforce this article by appropriate legislation.

ARTICLE XX

[*Proposed March 2, 1932; declared ratified February 6, 1933*]

Section 1. The terms of the President and Vice President shall end at noon on the 20th day of January, and the terms of Senators and Representatives at noon on the 3d day of January, of the years in which such terms would have ended if this article had not been ratified; and the terms of their successors shall then begin.

Section 2. The Congress shall assemble at least once in every year, and such meeting shall begin at noon on the 3d day of January, unless they shall by law appoint a different day.

Section 3. If, at the time fixed for the beginning of the term of the President, the President elect shall have died, the Vice President elect shall become President. If a President shall not have been chosen before the time fixed for the beginning of his term, or if the President elect shall have failed to qualify, then the Vice President elect shall act as President until a President shall have qualified; and the Congress may by law provide for the case wherein neither a President elect nor a Vice President elect shall have qualified, declaring who shall then act as President, or the manner in which one who is to act shall be elected, and such person shall act accordingly until a President or Vice President shall have qualified.

Section 4. The Congress may by law provide for the case of the death of any of the persons from whom the House of Representatives may choose a President whenever the right of choice shall have devolved upon them, and for the case of the death of any of the persons from whom the Senate may choose a Vice President whenever the right of choice shall have devolved upon them.

Section 5. Sections 1 and 2 shall take effect on the 15th day of October following the ratification of this article.

Section 6. This article shall be inoperative unless it shall have been ratified as an amendment to the Constitution by the legislatures of three-fourths of the several States within seven years from the date of its submission.

Article XXI

[Proposed February 20, 1933; declared ratified December 5, 1933]

Section 1. The eighteenth article of amendment to the Constitution of the United States is hereby repealed.

Section 2. The transportation or importation into any State, Territory, or possession of the United States for delivery or use therein of intoxicating liquors, in violation of the laws thereof, is hereby prohibited.

Section 3. This article shall be inoperative unless it shall have been ratified as an amendment to the Constitution by conventions in the several States, as provided in the Constitution, within seven years from the date of the submission hereof to the States by the Congress.

Article XXII

[Proposed March 24, 1947; declared ratified March 1, 1951]

Section 1. No person shall be elected to the office of the President more than twice, and no person who has held the office of President, or acted as President, for more than two years of a term to which some other person was elected President shall be elected to the office of the President more than once. But this Article shall not apply to any person holding the office of President when this Article was proposed by the Congress, and shall not prevent any person who may be holding the office of President, or acting as President, during the term within which this Article becomes operative from holding the office of President or acting as President during the remainder of such term.

Section 2. This article shall be inoperative unless it shall have been ratified as an amendment to the Constitution by the legislatures of three-fourths of the several States within seven years from the date of its submission to the States by the Congress.

Article XXIII

[Proposed June 16, 1960; declared ratified April 3, 1961]

Section 1. The District constituting the seat of Government of the United States shall appoint in such manner as the Congress may direct:

A number of electors of President and Vice President equal to the whole number of Senators and Representatives in Congress to which the District would be entitled if it were a State, but in no event more than the least populous state; they shall be in addition to those appointed by the States, but they shall be considered, for the purposes of the election of President and Vice President, to be electors appointed by a State; and they shall meet in the District and perform such duties as provided by the twelfth article of amendment.

Section 2. The Congress shall have power to enforce this article by appropriate legislation.

Article XXIV

[Proposed August 27, 1962; declared ratified February 4, 1964]

Section 1. The right of citizens of the United States to vote in any primary or other election for President or Vice President, for electors for President or Vice President, or for Senator or Representative in Congress, shall not be denied or abridged by the United States or any State by reason of failure to pay any poll tax or other tax.

Section 2. The Congress shall have power to enforce this article by appropriate legislation.

Article XXV

[*Proposed July 6, 1965; declared ratified February 23, 1967*]

Section 1. In case of removal of the President from office or of his death or resignation, the Vice President shall become President.

Section 2. Whenever there is a vacancy in the office of the Vice President, the President shall nominate a Vice President who shall take office upon confirmation by a majority vote of both Houses of Congress.

Section 3. Whenever the President transmits to the President pro tempore of the Senate and the Speaker of the House of Representatives his written declaration that he is unable to discharge the powers and duties of his office, and until he transmits to them a written declaration to the contrary, such powers and duties shall be discharged by the Vice President as Acting President.

Section 4. Whenever the Vice President and a majority of either the principal officers of the executive departments or of such other body as Congress may by law provide, transmit to the President pro tempore of the Senate and the Speaker of the House of Representatives their written declaration that the President is unable to discharge the powers and duties of his office, the Vice President shall immediately assume the powers and duties of the office as Acting President.

Thereafter, when the President transmits to the President pro tempore of the Senate and the Speaker of the House of Representatives his written declaration that no inability exists, he shall resume the powers and duties of his office unless the Vice President and a majority of either the principal officers of the executive department or of such other body as Congress may by law provide, transmit within four days to the President pro tempore of the Senate and the Speaker of the House of Representatives their written declaration that the President is unable to discharge the powers and duties of his office. Thereupon Congress shall decide the issue, assembling within forty-eight hours for that purpose if not in session. If the Congress, within twenty-one days after receipt of the latter written declaration, or, if Congress is not in session, within twenty-one days after Congress is required to assemble, determines by two-thirds vote of both Houses that the President is unable to discharge the power and duties of his office, the Vice President shall continue to discharge the same as Acting President; otherwise, the President shall resume the powers and duties of his office.

Article XXVI

[*Proposed March 23, 1971; declared ratified July 5, 1971*]

Section 1. The right of citizens of the United States, who are eighteen years of age or older, to vote shall not be denied or abridged by the United States or by any State on account of age.

Section 2. The Congress shall have power to enforce this article by appropriate legislation.

Presidential Elections

Year	Candidates Receiving More than One Percent of the Vote (Parties)	Popular Vote	Electoral Vote
1789	GEORGE WASHINGTON (No party designations)		69
	John Adams		34
	Other Candidates		35
1792	GEORGE WASHINGTON (No party designations)		132
	John Adams		77
	George Clinton		50
	Other Candidates		5
1796	JOHN ADAMS (Federalist)		71
	Thomas Jefferson (Democratic-Republican)		68
	Thomas Pinckney (Federalist)		59
	Aaron Burr (Democratic-Republian)		30
	Other Candidates		48
1800	THOMAS JEFFERSON (Democratic-Republican)		73
	Aaon Burr (Democratic-Republican)		73
	John Adams (Federalist)		65
	Charles C. Pinckney (Federalist)		64
	John Jay (Federalist)		1
1800	THOMAS JEFFERSON (Democratic-Republican)		162
	Aaon Burr (Democratic-Republican)		14
1808	JAMES MADISON (Democratic-Republian		122
	Charles C. Pinckney (Federalist)		47
	George Clinton (Democratic-Republican)		6
1812	JAMES MADISON (Democratic-Republican)		128
	De Witt Clinton (Federalist)		89
1816	JAMES MONROE (Democratic-Republican)		183
	Rufus King (Federalist)		34
1820	JAMES MONROE (Democratic-Republican)		231
	John Quincy Adams (Independent-Republican)		1
1824	JOHN QUINCY ADAMS (Democratic-Republican)	108,740	84
	Andrew Jackson (Democratic-Republican)	153,544	99
	William H. Crawford (Democratic-Republican)	46,618	41
	Henry Clay (Democratic-Republican)	47,136	37
1828	ANDREW JACKSON (Democratic)	647,286	178
	John Quincy Adams (National Republican)	508,064	83
1832	ANDREW JACKSON (Democratic)	687,502	219
	Henry Clay (National Republican)	530,189	49
	William Wirt (Anti-Masonic) John Floyd (National Republican)	33,108	7

Year	Candidates Receiving More than One Percent of the Vote (Parties)	Popular Vote	Electoral Vote
1836	MARTIN VAN BUREN (Democratic)	765,483	170
	William H. Harrison (Whig)		73
	Hugh L. White (Whig)	739,795	26
	Daniel Webster (Whig)		14
	W. P. Mangum (Anti-Jackson)		11
1840	WILLIAM H. HARRISON (Whig)	1,274,624	234
	Martin Van Buren (Democratic)	1,127,781	60
1844	JAMES K. POLK (Democratic)	1,338,464	170
	Henry Clay (Whig)	1,300,097	105
	James G. Birney (Liberty)	62,300	0
1848	ZACHARY TAYLOR (Whig)	1,360,967	163
	Lewis Cass (Democratic)	1,222,342	127
	Martin Van Buren (Free Soil)	291,263	0
1852	FRANKLIN PIERCE (Democratic)	1,601,117	254
	Winfield Scott (Whig)	1,385,453	42
	John P. Hale (Free Soil)	155,825	0
1856	JAMES BUCHANAN (Democratic)	1,832,955	174
	John C. Fremont (Republican)	1,339,932	114
	Millard Fillmore (American)	871,731	8
1860	ABRAHAM LINCOLN (Republican)	1,865,593	180
	Stephen A. Doublas (Democratic)	1,382,713	12
	John C. Breckinridge (Democratic)	848,356	72
	John Bell (Constitutional Union)	592,906	39
1864	ABRAHAM LINCOLN (Republican)	2,206,938	212
	George B. McClellan (Democratic)	1,803,787	21
1868	ULYSSES S. GRANT (Republican)	3,013,421	214
	Horatio Seymour (Democratic)	2,706,829	80
1872	ULYSSES S. GRANT (Republican)	3,596,747	286
	Horace Greeley (Democratic)	2,843,446	—*
	Other Candidates		63
1876	RUTHERFORD B. HAYES (Republican)	4,036,572	185
	Samuel J. Tilden (Democratic)	4,284,020	184
1880	JAMES A. GARFIELD (Republican)	4,453,295	214
	Winfield S. Hancock (Democratic)	4,414,082	155
	James B. Weaver (Greenback-Labor)	308,579	0
1884	GROVER CLEVELAND (Democratic)	4,879,507	219
	James G. Blaine (Republican)	4,850,293	182
	Benjamin F. Butler (Greenback-Labor)	175,370	0
	John P. St. John (Prohibition)	150,869	0

*Greeley died shortly after the election: the electors supporting him then divided their votes among other candidates.

Year	Candidates Receiving More than One Percent of the Vote (Parties)	Popular Vote	Electoral Vote
1888	BENJAMIN HARRISON (Republican)	5,447,129	233
	Grover Cleveland (Democratic)	5,537,857	168
	Clinton B. Fisk (Prohibition)	249,506	0
	Anson J. Streeter (Union Labor)	146,935	0
1892	GROVER CLEVELAND (Democratic)	5,555,426	277
	Benjamin Harrison (Republican)	5,182,690	145
	James B. Weaver (People's)	1,029,846	22
	John Bidwell (Prohibition)	264,133	0
1896	WILLIAM McKINLEY (Republican)	7,102,216	271
	William J. Bryan (Democratic)	6,492,559	176
1900	WILLIAM McKINLEY (Republican)	7,218,491	292
	William J. Bryan (Democratic; Populist)	6,356,734	155
	John C. Wooley (Prohibition)	208,914	0
1904	THEODORE ROOSEVELT (Republican)	7,628,461	336
	Alton B. Parker (Democratic)	5,084,223	140
	Eugene V. Debs (Socialist)	402,283	0
	Silas C. Swallow (Prohibition)	258,536	0
1908	WILLIAM H. TAFT (Republican)	7,675,320	321
	William J. Bryan (Democratic)	6,412,294	162
	Eugene V. Debs (Socialist)	420,793	0
	Eugene W. Chafin (Prohibition)	253,840	0
1912	WOODROW WILSON (Democratic)	6,296,547	435
	Theodore Roosevelt (Progressive)	4,118,571	88
	William H. Taft (Republican)	3,186,720	8
	Eugene V. Debs (Socialist)	900,672	0
	Eugene W. Chafin (Prohibition)	206,275	0
1916	WOODROW WILSON (Democratic)	9,127,695	277
	Charles E. Hughes (Republican)	8,533,507	254
	A. L. Benson (Socialist)	585,113	0
	J. Frank Hanly (Prohibition)	220,506	0
1920	WARREN G. HARDING (Republican)	16,143,407	404
	James M. Cox (Democratic)	9,130,328	127
	Eugene V. Debs (Socialist)	919,799	0
	P. P. Christensen (Farmer-Labor)	265,411	0
1924	CALVIN COOLDIGE (Republican)	15,718,211	382
	John W. Davis (Democratic)	8,385,283	136
	Robert M. La Follette (Progressive)	4,831,289	13
1928	HERBERT C. HOOVER (Republican)	21,391,993	444
	Alfred E. Smith (Democratic)	15,016,169	87
1932	FRANKLIN D. ROOSEVELT (Democratic)	22,809,638	472
	Herbert C. Hoover (Republican)	15,758,904	59
	Norman Thomas (Socialist)	881,954	0

Year	Candidates Receiving More than One Percent of the Vote (Parties)	Popular Vote	Electoral Vote
1936	FRANKLIN D. ROOSEVELT (Democratic)	27,752,869	523
	Alfred M. Landon (Republican)	16,674,665	8
	William Lemke (Union)	882,479	0
1940	FRANKLIN D. ROOSEVELT (Democratic)	27,307,819	449
	Wendell L. Willkie (Republican)	22,321,018	82
1944	FRANKLIN D. ROOSEVELT (Democratic)	25,606,585	432
	Thomas E. Dewey (Republican)	22,014,745	99
1948	HARRY S. TRUMAN (Democratic)	24,179,345	303
	Thomas E. Dewey (Republican)	21,991,291	189
	J. Strom Thurmond (States' Rights)	1,176,125	39
	Henry Wallace (Progressive)	1,157,326	0
1952	DWIGHT D. EISENHOWER (Republican)	33,936,234	442
	Adlai E. Stevenson (Democratic)	27,314,992	89
1956	DWIGHT D. EISENHOWER (Republican)	35,590,472	457
	Adlai E. Stevenson (Democratic)	26,022,752	73
1960	JOHN F. KENNEDY (Democratic)	34,226,731	303
	Richard M. Nixon (Republican)	34,108,157	219
1964	LYNDON B. JOHNSON (Democratic)	43,129,566	486
	Barry M. Goldwater (Republican)	27,127,188	52
1968	RICHARD M. NIXON (Republican)	31,785,480	301
	Hubert H. Humphrey (Democratic)	31,275,166	191
	George C. Wallace (American Independent)	9,906,473	46
1972	RICHARD M. NIXON (Republican)	45,631,189	521
	George S. McGovern (Democratic)	28,422,015	17
	John Schmitz (American Independent)	1,080,670	0
1976	JAMES E. CARTER, JR. (Democratic)	40,274,975	297
	Gerald R. Ford (Republican)	38,530,614	241
1980	RONALD W. REAGAN (Republican)	42,968,326	489
	James E. Carter, Jr. (Democratic)	34,731,139	49
	John B. Anderson (Independent)	5,552,349	0
1984	RONALD W. REAGAN (Republican)	53,428,357	525
	Walter F. Mondale (Democratic)	36,930,923	13
1988	GEORGE H. BUSH (Republican)	48,881,221	426
	Michael Dukakis (Democratic)	41,805,422	112
1992	WILLIAM J. B. CLINTON (Democratic)	44,908,254	370
	George H. Bush (Republican)	39,102,343	168
	H. Ross Perot (Independent)	19,741,065	—

Chief Justices of the Supreme Court

Term	Chief Justice
1789–1795	John Jay
1795	John Rutledge
1795–1799	Oliver Ellsworth
1801–1835	John Marshall
1836–1864	Roger B. Taney
1864–1873	Salmon P. Chase
1874–1888	Morrison R. Waite
1888–1910	Melville W. Fuller
1910–1921	Edward D. White
1921–1930	William H. Taft
1930–1941	Charles E. Hughes
1941–1946	Harlan F. Stone
1946–1953	Fred M. Vinson
1953–1969	Earl Warren
1969–1986	Warren E. Burger
1986–	William Rehnquist

Presidents, Vice Presidents, and Cabinet Members

President and Vice President	Secretary of State	Secretary of Treasury	Secretary of War	Secretary of Navy	Postmaster General	Attorney General	Secretary of Interior
1. George Washington (1789) John Adams (1789)	Thomas Jefferson (1789) Edmund Randolph (1794) Thomas Pickering (1795)	Alexander Hamilton (1789) Oliver Wolcott (1795)	Henry Knox (1789) Timothy Pickering (1795) James McHenry (1796)		Samuel Osgood (1789 Timothy Pickering (1791) Joseph Habersham (1795)	Edmund Randolph (1789) William Bradford (1794) Charles Lee (1795)	
2. John Adams (1797) Thomas Jefferson (1797)	Timothy Pickering (1797) John Marshall (1800)	Oliver Wolcott (1797) Samuel Dexter (1800)	James McHenry (1797) John Marshall (1800) Samuel Dexter (1800) Roger Griswald (1801)	Benjamin Stoddert (1798)	Joseph Habersham (1797)	Charles Lee (1797) Theophilus Parsons (1801)	
3. Thomas Jefferson (1801) Aaron Burr (1801) George Clinton (1805)	James Madison *1801	Samuel Dexter (1801) Albert Gallatin (1801)	Henry Dearborn (1801)	Benjamin Stoddert (1801) Robert Smith (1801) J. Crowninshield (1805)	Joseph Habersham (1801) Gideon Granger (1801)	Levi Lincoln (1801) Robert Smith (1805) John Breckinridge (1805) Cesar Rodney (1807)	
4. James Madison (1809) George Clinton (1809) Elbridge Gerry (1813)	Robert Smith (1809) James Monroe (1811)	Albert Gallatin (1809) George Campbell (1814) Alexander Dallas (1814) William Crawford (1816)	William Eustis (1809) John Armstrong (1813) James Monroe (1814) William Crawford (1815)	Paul Hamilton (1809) William Jones (1813) Benjamin Crowninshield (1814)	Gideon Granger (1809) Return Meigs (1814)	Caesar Rodney (1809) William Pinckney (1811) Richard Rush (1814)	
5. James Monroe (1817) Daniel D. Thompkins (1817)	John Quincy Adams (1817)	William Crawford (1817)	Isaac Shelby (1817) George Graham (1817) John C. Calhoun (1817)	Benjamin Crowninshield (1817) Smith Thompson (1818) Samuel Southard (1823)	Return Meigs (1817) John McLean (1823)	Richard Rush (1817) William Wirt (1817)	
6. John Quincy Adams (1825) John C. Calhoun (1825)	Henry Clay (1825)	Richard Rush (1825)	James Barbour (1825) Peter B. Porter (1828)	Samuel Southard (1825)	John McLean (1825)	William Wirt (1825)	

Presidents, Vice Presidents, and Cabinet Members (continued)

President and Vice President	Secretary of State	Secretary of Treasury	Secretary of War	Secretary of Navy	Postmaster General	Attorney General	Secretary of Interior
7. Andrew Jackson (1829) John C. Calhoun (1829) Martin Van Buren (1833)	Martin Van Buren (1829) Edward Livingston (1831) Louis McLane (1833) John Forsyth (1834)	Samuel Ingham (1829) Louis McLane (1831) William Duane (1833) Roger B. Taoney (1833) Levi Woodbury (1834)	John H. Eaton (1829) Lewis Cass (1831) Benjamin Butler (1837)	John Branch (1829) Levi Woodbury (1831) Mahlon Dickerson (1834)	William Barry (1829) Amos Kendall (1835)	John M. Berrien (1829) Rober B. Taney (1831) Benjamin Butler (1833)	
8. Martin Van Buren (1837) Richard M. Johnson (1837)	Louis McLane (1833)	Levi Woodbury (1837)	Joel L. Poinsett (1837)	Mahlon Dickerson (1837) James K. Paulding (1838)	Amos Kendall (1837) John M. Niles (1840)	Benjamin Butler (1837) Felix Grundy (1838) Henry D. Gilpin (1840)	
9. William H. Harrison (1841) John Tyler (1841)	Daniel Webster (1841)	Thomas Ewing (1841)	John Bell (1841)	George E. Badger (1841)	Francis Granger (1841)	John J. Crittenden (1841)	
10. John Tyler (1841)	Daniel Webster (1841) Hugh S. Legaré (1843) Abel P. Upshur (1843) John C. Calhoun (1844)	Tomas Ewing (1841) Walter Forward (1841) John C. Spencer (1843) George M. Bibb (1844)	John Bell (1841) John McLean (1841) John C. Spencer (1841) James M. Porter (1843) William Wilkins (1844)	George E. Badger (1841) Abel P. Upshur (1841) David Henshaw (1843) Thomas Gilmer (1844) John Y. Mason (1844)	Francis Granger (1841) Charles A. Wickliffe (1841)	John J. Crittenden (1841) Hugh S. Legaré (1841) John Nelson (1843)	
11. James K. Polk (1845) George M. Dallas (1845)	James Buchanan (1845)	Robert J. Walker (1845)	William L. Marcy (1845)	George Bancroft (1845) John Y. Mason (1846)	Cave Johnson (1845)	John Y. Mason (1845) Nathan Clifford (1846) Isaac Toucey (1848)	
12. Zchary Taylor (1849) Millard Fillmore (1849)	John M. Clayton (1849)	William M. Meredith (1849)	George W. Crawford (1849)	William B. Preston (1849)	Jacob Collamer (1849)	Reverdy Johnson (1849)	Thomas Ewing (1849)

President / VP							
13. Millard Fillmore (1850)	Daniel Webster (1850) Edward Everett (1852)	Thomas Corwin (1850)	Charles M. Conrad (1850)	William A. Graham (1850) John P. Kennedy (1852)	Nathan K. Hall (1850) Sam D. Hubbard (1852)	John J. Crittenden (1850)	Thomnas McKennan A. H. H. Stuart (1850)
14. Franklin Pierce (1853) William R. King (1853)	William L. Marcy (1853)	James Guthrie (1853)	Jefferson Davis (1853)	James C. Dobbin (1853)	James Campbell (1853)	Caleb Cushing (1853)	Robert McClelland (1853)
15. James Buchanan (1857) John C. Breckinridge (1857)	Lewis Cass (1857) Jeremiah S. Black (1860)	Howell Cobb (1857) Philip F. Thomas (1860) John A. Dix (1861)	John B. Floyd (1857) Joseph Holt (1861)	Isaac Toucey (1857)	Aaron V. Brown (1857) Joseph Holt (1859)	Jeremiah S. Black (1857) Edwin M. Stanton (1860)	Jacob Thompson (1857)
16. Abraham Lincoln (1861) Hannibal Hamlin (1861) Andrew Johnson (1865)	William H. Seward (1861)	Salmon P. Chase (1861) William P. Fessenden (1864) Hugh McCulloch (1865)	Simon Cameron (1861) Edwin Stanton (1862)	Gideon Welles (1861)	Horatio King (1861) Montgomery Blair (1861) William Dennison (1864)	Edward Bates (1861) Titian J. Coffey (18653) James Speed (1864)	Caleb B. Smith (1861) John P. Usher (1863)
17. Andrew Johnson (1865)	William H. Seward (1865)	Hugh McCulloch (1865)	Edwin M. Stanton (1865) Ulysses S. Grant (1867) Lorenzo Thomas (1868) John M. Schofield (1868)	Gideon Welles (1865)	William Dennison (1865) Alexander Randall (1866)	James Speed (1865) Henry Stanbery (1866) William M. Evarts (1868)	John P Usher (1965) James Harlan (1865) O. H. Browning (1866)
18. Ulysses S. Grant (1869) Schuyler Colfax (1869) Henry Wilson (1873)	Elihu B. Washburne (1869) Hamilton Fish (1869)	George S. Boutwell (1869) William A. Richardson (1873) Benjamin H. Bristow (1874) Lot M. Morrill (1876)	John A. Rawlins (1869) William T. Sherman (1869) William W. Belknap (1869) Alphonso Taft (1876) James Cameron (1876)	Adolph E. Bone (1869) George M. Robeson (1969)	John A. J. Creswell (1869) James W. Marshall (1874) Marshall Jewell (1874) James N. Tyner (1876)	Ebenzer R. Hoar (1869) Amos T. Akerman (1870) G. H. Williams (1871) Edwards Pierrepont (1875) Alphonso Taft (1876)	Jacob D. Cox (1869) Columbus Delano (1870) Zachariah Chandler (1875)

Presidents, Vice Presidents, and Cabinet Members (continued)

President and Vice President	Secretary of State	Secretary of Treasury	Secretary of War	Secretary of Navy	Postmaster General	Attorney General	Secretary of Interior
19. Rutherford B. Hayes (1877) William A. Wheeler (1877)	William M. Evarts (1877)	John Sherman (1877)	George W. McCrary (1877) Alexander Ramsey (1879)	R. W. Thompson (1877) Nathan Golf, Jr. (1881)	David M. Key (1877) Horace Maynard (1880)	Charles Devens (1877)	Carl Schurz (1877)
20. James A. Garfield (1881) Chester A. Arthur (1881)	James G. Blaine (1881)	William Windom (1881)	Robert T. Lincoln (1881)	William H. Hunt (1881)	Thomas I. James (1881)	Wayne MacVeagh (1881)	S. I. Kirkwood (1881)
21. Chester A. Arthur (1881)	E. T. Frelinghuysen (1881)	Charles J. Folger (1881) Walter Q. Gresham (1884) Hugh McCulloch (1884)	Robert T. Lincoln (1881)	William E. Chandler (1881)	Timothy O. Howe (1881) Walter Q. Gresham (1883) Frank Hatton (1884)	B. H. Brewster (1881)	Henry M. Teller (1881)
22. Grover Cleveland (1885) T. A. Hendricks (1885)	Thomas F. Bayard (1885)	Daniel Manning (1885) Charles S. Fairchild (1887)	William C. Endicott (1885)	William C. Whitney (1885)	William F. Vilas (1885) Don M. Dickinson (1888)	A. H. Garland (1885)	L. Q. C. Lamar (1885) William F. Vilas (1888)
23. Benjamin Harrison (1880) Levi P. Morgan (1889)	James G. Blaine (1889) John W. Foster (1892)	William Windom (1889) Charles Foster (1891)	Redfield Procter (1889) Stephen B. Elkins (1891)	Benjamin F. Tracy (1889)	John Wanamaker (1889)	W. H. H. Miller (1889)	Jon W. Noble (1889)
24. Grover Cleveland (1893) Adlai E. Stevenson (1893)	Walter Q. Gresham (1893) Richard Olney (1895)	John G. Carlisle (1893)	Daniel S. Lamont (1893)	Hilary A. Herbert (1983)	Wilson S. Bissel (1893) William L. Wilson (1895)	Richard Olney (1893) Judson Harmon (1895)	Hoke Smith (1893) David R. Francis (1896)

President	Secretary of State	Treasury	War	Navy	Attorney General	Postmaster General	Interior
25. William McKinley (1897) Garret A. Hobart (1897) Theodore Roosevelt (1901)	John Sherman (1897) William R. Day (1897) John Hay (1898)	Lyman J. Gage (1897)	Russell A. Alger (1897) Elihu Root (1899)	John D. Long (1897)	Joseph McKenna (1897) John W. Griggs (1897) Philander C. Knox (1901)	James A. Gary (1897) Charles E. Smith (1898)	Cornelius N. Bliss (1897) E. A. Hitchcock (1899)
26. Theodore Roosevelt (1901) Charles Fairbanks (1905)	John Hay (1901) Elihu Root (1905) Robert Bacon (1909)	Lyman J. Gage (1901) Leslie M. Shaw (1902) George B. Cortelyou (1907)	Elihu Root (1901) William H. Taft (1904) Luke E. Wright (1908)	John D. Long (1901) William H. Moody (1902) Paul Morton (1904) Charles J. Bonaparte (1905) V. H. Metcalf (1906) T. H. Newberry (1908)	Philander C. Knox (1901) William H. Moody (1904) Charles J. Bonapart (1907)	Charlese E. Smith (1901) Henry Payne (1902) Robert J. Wynne (1904) George B. Cortelyou (1905) George von L. Meyer (1907)	E. A. Hitchcock (1901) James R. Garfield (1907)
27. William H. Taft (1909) James S. Sherman (1909)	Philander C. Knox (1909)	Franklin McVeagh (1909)	Jacob M. Dickinson (1909) Henry Stimson (1911)	George von L. Meyer (1909)	G. W. Wickersham (1909)	Frank H. Hitchcock (1909)	R. A. Ballinger (1909) Walter L. Fisher (1911)
28. Woodrow Wilson (1913) Thomas R. Marshall (1913)	William I. Bryan (1913) Robert Lansing (1915) Bainbridge Colby (1920)	William G. McAdoo (1913) Carter Glass (1918) David F. Houston (1920)	Lindley M. Garrison (1913) Newton D. Baker (1916)	Joephus Daniels (1913)	J. C. McReynolds (1913) T. W. Gregory (1914) A. Mitchell Palmer (1919)	Albert S. Burleson (1913)	Franklin K. Lane (1913) John B. Payne (1920)
29. Warren G. Harding (1921) Calvin Coolidge (1921)	Charles E. Hughes (1921)	Andrew W. Mellon (1921)	John W. Weeks (1921)	Edwin Denby (1921)	H. M. Daugherty (1921)	Will H. Hays (1921) Hubert Work (1922) Harry S. New (1923)	Albert B. Fall (1921) Hubert Work (1923)
30. Calvin Coolidge (1923) Charles G. Dawes (1925)	Charles E. Hughes (1923) Frank B. Kellogg (1925)	Andrew W. Mellon (1923)	John W. Weeks (1923) Dwight F. Davis (1925)	Edwin Denby (1923) Curtis D. Wilbur (1924)	H. M. Daugherty (1923) Harlan F. Stone (1924) John G. Sargent (1925)	Harry S. New (1923)	Hubert Work (1923) Roy O. West (1928)

Presidents, Vice Presidents, and Cabinet Members (continued)

President and Vice President	Secretary of State	Secretary of Treasury	Secretary of War	Secretary of Navy	Postmaster General	Attorney General	Secretary of Interior
31. Herbert C. Hoover (1929) Charles Curtis (1929)	Henry L. Stimson (1929)	Andrew W. Mellon (1929) Ogden L. Mills (1932)	James W. Good (1929) Patrick J. Hurley (1929)	Charles F. Adams (1929)	Walter F. Browh (1929)	W. D. Mitchell (1929)	Ray L. Wilbur (1929)
32. Franklin D. Roosevelt (1933) John Nance Garner (1933) Henry A. Wallace (1941) Harry S. Truman (1945)	Cordell Hull (1933) E. R. Stettinius, Jr. (1944)	William H. Woodin (1933) Henry Morgenthau, Jr. (1934)	George H. Dern (1933) Harry H. Woodring (1936) Henry L. Stimson (1940)	Claude A. Swanson (1933) Charles Edison (1940) Frank Knox (1940) James V. Forrestal (1944)	James A. Farley (1933) Frank C. Walker (1940)	H. S. Cummings (1933) Frank Murphy (1939) Robert Jackson (1940) Francis Biddle (1941)	Harold L. Ickes (1933)
33. Harry S. Truman (1945) Alben W. Barkley (1949)	James F. Byrnes (1945) George C. Marshall (1947) Dean G. Acheson (1949)	Fred M. Vinson (1945) John W. Snyder (1946)	Robert P. Patterson (1945) Kenneth C. Royal (1947) *Secretary of Defense* James V. Forrestal (1947) Louis A. Johnson (1949) George G. Marshall (1950) Robert A. Lovett (1951)	James V. Forrestal (1945)	R. E. Hannegan (1945) Jesse M. Donaldson (1947)	Tom C. Clark (1945) J. H. McGrath (1949) James P. McGranery (1952)	Harold L. Ickes (1945) Julis A. Krog (1946) Oscar L. Chapman (1949)
34. Dwight D. Eisenhower (1953) Richard M. Nixon (1953)	John Foster Dulles (1953) Christian A. Herter (1959)	George M. Humphrey (1953) Robert B. Anderson (1957)	Charles E. Wilson (1953) Neil H. McElroy (1957) Thomas S. Gates (1959)		A. E. Summerfield (1953)	H. Brownell Jr. (1953) William P. Rogers (1957)	Douglas McKay (1953) Fred Seaton (1950)
35. John F. Kennedy (1961) Lyndon B. Johnson (1961)	Dean Rusk (1961)	C. Douglas Dillon (1961)	Robert S. McNamara (1961)		J. Edward Day (1961) John A> Gronouski (1963)	Robert F. Kennedy (1961)	Stewart L. Udall (1961)

President	Secretary of State	Secretary of Treasury	Secretary of Defense	Attorney General	Postmaster General	Secretary of Interior
36. Lyndon B. Johnson (1963) Hubert H. Humphrey (1965)	Dean Rusk (1963)	C. Douglas Dillon (1963) Henry H. Fowler (1965) Joseph W. Barr (1968)	Robert S. McNamara (1963) Clark M. Clifford (1968)	Robert F. Kennedy (1963) N. deB. Katzenbach (1965) Ramsey Clark (1967)	John A. Gronouski (1963) Lawrence F. O'Brien (1965) W. Marvin Watson (1968)	Stewart L. Udall (1963)
37. Richard M. Nixon (1969) Spiro T. Agnew (1969) Gerald R. Ford (1973)	William P. Rogers (1969) Henry A. Kissinger (1973)	David M. Kennedy (1969) John B. Connally (1970) George P. Schultz (1972) William E. Simon (1974)	Melvin R. Laird (1969) Elliot L. Richardson (1973) James R. Schlesinger (1973)	John M. Mitchell (1969) Richard G. Kleindienst (1972) Elliot L. Richardson (1973) William B. Saxbe (1974)	Winton M. Blount (1969)	Walter J. Hickel (1969) Rogers C. B. Morton (1971)
38. Gerald R. Ford (1974) Nelson A. Rockefeller (1974)	Henry A. Kissinger (1974)	William E. Simon (1974)	James R. Schlesinger (1974) Donald H. Runsfield (1975)	William B. Saxbe (1974) Edward H. Levi (1975)		Rogers C. B. Morton (1974) Stanley K. Hathaway (1975) Thomas D. Kleppe (1975)
39. James E. Carter, Jr. (1977) Walter F. Mondale (1977)	Cyrus R. Vance (1977) Edmund S. Muskie (1980)	W. Michael Blumental (1977) G. William Miller (1979)	Harold Brown (1977)	Griffin B. Bell (1977) Benjamin R. Civiletti (1979)		Cecil D. Andrus (1977)
40. Ronald W. Reagan (1981) George H. Bush (1981)	Alexander M. Haig, Jr. (1981) George P. Schultz (1982)	Donald T. Regan (1981)	Caspar W. Weinberger (1981)	William French Smith (1981)		James G. Watt (1981) William Clark (1983)
41. Ronald W. Reagan (1985) George H. Bush (1985)	George P. Schultz (1985)	James A. Baker III (1985)	Caspar W. Weinberger (1985)	Edwin Meese III (1985)		Donald P. Hodel (9185)
42. George H. Bush (1988) James D. Quayle Ii	James A. Baker III (1988)	Nicholas Brady (1988)	Richard B. Cheney (1988)	Richard L. Thornburgh (1988)		Manuel Lujan, Jr. (1988)
43. William J. B. Clinton (1993) Albert Gore, Jr. (1993)	Warren Christopher (1993)	Lloyd Bentsen (1993)	Les Aspin (1993)	Janet Reno (1993)		Bruce Babbit (1993)

Writing About History
Dr. Robert Weiss

What is "history"? We employ the word constantly to refer to everything from the "history" of the world to an individual's "history." But how often do we stop to think about what the word means? The following essay addresses this question, and provides some fundamental principles for reading, researching, and writing historical reports and essays.

∗ WHAT IS HISTORY? ∗

History can best be defined as a record and interpretation of past events. This statement is not very complicated, yet it is not as simple as it may appear. Let us examine it more carefully.

The "record" part is straightforward. Since the purpose of history is to inform us about what happened in the past, it must include substantial data, or "facts" (a troublesome word that some social scientists avoid). Names, dates, places, and events are the essence of history. But historical writing is not a compendium of facts. It consists of facts placed in a sequence to tell a connected story. A work of history is not merely a story, however. It also must analyze what happened and *why*—that is, it must interpret the past for the reader in a useful and informative manner. It is not sufficient, for example, to state that the American Revolution began in 1775–76, and then give an account of the relevant individuals and events, such as George Washington, Thomas Jefferson, Lexington and Concord, and the Declaration of Independence. The historian must proceed to the next step: Why did the Revolution occur in 1776? Here again, historians must resort to concrete data, including the Proclamation of 1763, the Boston Massacre, the Boston Tea Party, and the Intolerable Acts. Rather than simply composing a catalog of events, however, the historian must weave the material into a well-integrated narrative that analyzes the *process* whereby the American colonies severed their political ties to make certain value judgments concerning the role and significance of these events. Which were more important, and which were less important? What was the relationship of each event to the others, and what does each tell us about the behavior of the American colonists?

To address questions like these, historians must place their material within an appropriate historical context. An account of a past event is not very instructive unless it is analyzed as a component of a larger sequence of events within a specific social, political, and economic setting. The Boston Tea Party, for example, would be analyzed in relation to such factors as British financial expenses incurred during the French and Indian War, colonial views regarding commerce and taxation, Britain's relationship with its empire, and the role of merchants in American colonial society. Only by examining such factors can we hope to understand why both sides behaved as they did.

Historical interpretation takes place on many levels. Some historians focus on the "larger forces" in history, such as the industrial revolution of the nineteenth century and the communications revolution of the twentieth century. Obviously these developments exerted a profound effect on the way we live. The emphasis on context, however, also acknowledges the human element in history. Human beings are the actors in the historical drama, and an effective historical work attempts to explain why people behaved as they did. A history of the American Revolution, for example, would be incomplete if documented the events leading up to American independence, but offered no insights as to *why* formerly loyal subjects of the British crown took up arms against their mother country. To understand human behavior, the historian, like the psychologist or psychiatrist, must examine the effects of "larger forces" and specific events on people as well as the ways in which the people themselves perceived these forces and events. To appreciate the American desire for independence in 1776, one must view the events of the 1700s through eighteenth-century, not twentieth-century eyes.

A note of caution should be introduced here. To understand the behavior of various groups is not necessarily to endorse it. By using the proper resources, the historian can understand such phenomena as the Reign of Terror during the French Revolution, the development of slavery in the American South, and the ascendancy of Hitler in Germany. But this claim does not imply that the historian approves of guillotines, slavery, or Nazism. Rather, it asserts the historian's responsibility to analyze all facets of history, even those that he or she finds personally reprehensible.

The preceding paragraphs indicate the "subjective" nature of the interpretive process. When historians make the transition from recording data to interpreting that data, they are imposing an order and a meaning on a set of circumstances that they usually did not experience firsthand. Moreover, historians' interpretations often differ from those of various parties who *did* experience the events. While historians' interpretations should always be based on evidence, there comes a point at which they must transcend that evidence and rely on their own insights, values, and experiences in forming conclusions. Historians collect facts, and when they feel they have mastered them, they draw conclusions as to their significance and their relationship to one another. This process is not unique to the history profession, but is characteristic of all the natural and social sciences. Like all scientists, historians must pursue the maximum feasible "objectivity" in forming their conclusions while acknowledging the impossibility of total objectivity. Historians must be aware of their personal biases and values so they can monitor the effects of these biases on their interpretations of the past. At the same time, writers of history should never allow the fear of "subjectivity" to stifle the creative process.

* READING HISTORY *

An understanding of the fundamentals of historical writing will make the student of history a more discerning and selective reader. Although no two historical works are identical, most contain the same basic elements and can be approached in a similar manner by the reader. When reading a historical monograph, concentrate on the two basic issues discussed in the preceding section: facts and interpretation.

Interpretation. The first question the reader should ask is: What is the author's argument? What is his theme, his interpretation, his thesis? A theme is not the same as a topic. An author may select the Civil War as a *topic*, but he then must propose a particular theme or argument regarding some aspect of the war. (The most common, not surprisingly, is *why* the war occurred.)

Discovering the author's thesis is usually easy enough because most writers state their arguments clearly in the preface to their book. Students often make the critical error of skimming over the preface—if they read it at all—and then moving on to the "meat" of the book. Since the preface indicates the manner in which the author has used his data to develop his arguments, students who ignore it often find themselves overwhelmed with details without understanding *what* the author is attempting to say. This error should be avoided always.

The more history you read, the more you will appreciate the diversity of opinions and approaches among historians. While each author offers a unique perspective, historical works fall into general categories, or "schools," depending on their thesis and when they were published. The study of the manner in which different historians approach their subjects is referred to as *historiography.* Every historical subject has a historiography, sometimes limited, sometimes extensive. As in the other sciences, new schools of thought supplant existing ones, offering new insights and challenging accepted theories. Below are excerpts from two monographs dealing with the American Revolution. As you read them, note the contrast in the underlying arguments.

1. "Despite its precedent-setting character, however, the American revolt is noteworthy because it made no serious interruption in the smooth flow of American development. Both in intention and in fact, the American Revolution conserved the past rather than repudiated it. And in preserving the colonial experience, the men of the first quarter century of the Republic's history set the scenery and wrote the script for the drama of American politics for years to come."*

2. "The stream of revolution, once started, could not be confined within narrow banks, but spread abroad upon the land. Many economic desires, many social aspirations were set free by the political struggle, many aspects of colonial society profoundly altered by the forces thus set loose. The relations of social classes to each other, the institution of slavery, the system of landholding, the course of business, the forms and spirit of the intellectual and religious life, all felt the transforming hand of revolution, all emerged from under it in shapes advanced many degrees nearer to those we know."†

What you have just read is nothing less than two conflicting theories of the fundamental nature of the American Revolution. Professor Jameson portrays the Revolution as a catalyst for major social, economic, and political change, while Professor Degler

---

*Carl N. Degler, *Out of Our Past,* rev. ed. (New York: Harper and Row, Harper Colophon Books, 1970), p. 73.

†J. Franklin Jameson, *The American Revolution Considered As a Social Movement* (Boston: Beacon Press, 1956), p. 9.

views it primarily as a war for independence that conserved, rather than transformed, colonial institutions. The existence of such divergent opinions makes it imperative that the reader be aware of the argument of every book and read a variety of books and articles to get different perspectives on a subject.

All historical works contain biases of some sort, but a historical bias is not in itself bad or negative. As long as history books are composed by human beings, they will reflect the perspectives of their authors. This need not diminish the quality of historical writing if historians remain faithful to the facts. Some historians, however, have such strong biases that they distort the evidence to make it fit their preconceived notions. This type of history writing (which is the exception rather than the rule) is of limited value, but when properly treated can contribute to the accumulation of knowledge by providing new insights and challenging the values—and creative abilities—of other historians.

Evidence. Once you are aware of the author's central argument, you can concentrate on his use of evidence—the "facts"—that buttress that argument. There are several types of questions that you should keep in mind as you progress through a book. What types of evidence does the author use? Is his evidence convincing? Which sources does he rely on, and what additional sources might he have consulted? One strategy you might adopt is to imagine that *you* are writing the monograph. Where would you go for information? What would you look at? Then ask yourself: Did the author consult these sources? Obviously no writer can examine *everything.* A good historical work, however, offers convincing data extracted from a comprehensive collection of materials.

As you begin to ask these questions, you will develop the skill of critical learning. Used in this sense the word *critical* does not mean reading to discern what is wrong with the narrative. Rather, it refers to analytic reading, assessing the strengths and weaknesses of the monograph, and determining whether the argument ultimately works. All historical works should be approached with a critical—but open—mind.

One important point to remember is that you need not accept or reject every aspect of a historical monograph. In fact, you most likely will accord a "mixed review" to most of the books you read. You may accept the author's argument but find his evidence inadequate, or you may be impressed by his data but draw different conclusions from it. You may find some chapters tightly argued but others unconvincing. Even if you like a particular book, almost inevitably you will have some comments, criticisms, or suggestions.

* RESEARCHING HISTORY *

Most history courses, especially advanced ones, require some type of research project. Research skills are vital to history, and can be developed by observing certain rules.

The first rule is to know exactly what you are researching. Every history project begins with a question or problem. Thus the first step is to select a manageable question. Remember, a question is different from a topic. You may choose the American Revolution as a topic, for example, but you then must choose some aspect of the Revolution that interests you. Obviously a project such as "Discuss the American Revolution in all its aspects" is not realistic. You may be interested in the causes of the Revolution. This is a legitimate question, but still a broad one, more appropriate for a book than a paper. You would do better to select a more specific question, such as "Was the American Revolution really a revolution?" This question poses a specific problem, which will require you to collect data and then formulate a definite argument.

Once you have chosen the question, you begin the search for information. There are several possible sources you may wish to explore. First, you might want to consult your professor, who should be familiar with the relevant literature. This approach could be productive; on the other hand, the professor may want you to develop research skills on your own. In that case, a good encyclopedia, such as the *Encyclopaedia Britannica,* will provide a brief but useful overview of a topic and will cite the works from which the information was collected. Even more valuable is an American history work textbook. The bibliography section for the appropriate chapters—and, if included, a list of recommended readings—will direct you toward the appropriate literature.

The library card catalog constitutes another vital source of information. It contains there types of cards, which may be file separately or together, but are always in alphabetical order: author, title, and subject cards. Author cards are filed according to the author's last name; title cards, according to the book's title (excluding "the"); and subject cards by major topical groupings. Obviously subject cards are the most appropriate when you are looking for sources and ideas. If you are uncertain as to *how* your particular topic is filed, choose a heading that sounds appropriate. To come back to our sample topic, possibilities include: "American Revolution"; "Revolution—United States"; "United States—History—Revolution." If you should pick the wrong heading, the catalog will usually have one card under that heading referring you to the proper subject category. If you already have compiled a lit of names and/or authors, you can save much time by gong directly to the author and title cards.

The following is the card for a famous work in American history. Note the diversity of information that the card contains. (See below).

This information not only helps you to locate a book, but can indicate whether the book is relevant to your topic. Often, however, you cannot determine a book's usefulness until you have examined its table of contents and perhaps skimmed through a chapter or two.

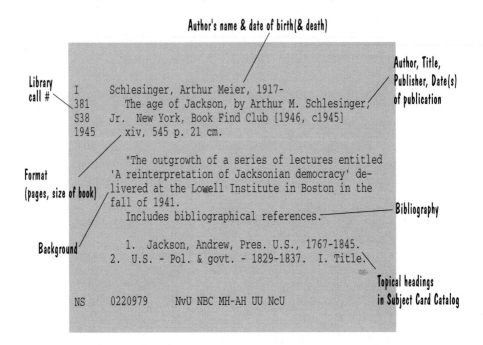

Author's name & date of birth(& death)

Library call #

Author, Title,
Publisher, Date(s)
of publication

```
I        Schlesinger, Arthur Meier, 1917-
381         The age of Jackson, by Arthur M. Schlesinger,
S38      Jr.  New York, Book Find Club [1946, c1945]
1945        xiv, 545 p. 21 cm.
```

Format
(pages, size of book)

```
            "The outgrowth of a series of lectures entitled
         'A reinterpretation of Jacksonian democracy' de-
         livered at the Lowell Institute in Boston in the
         fall of 1941.
            Includes bibliographical references.
```

Bibliography

Background

```
            1.  Jackson, Andrew, Pres. U.S., 1767-1845.
         2.  U.S. - Pol. & govt. - 1829-1837.  I. Title.
```

Topical headings
in Subject Card Catalog

```
   NS     0220979     NvU NBC MH-AH UU NcU
```

As you search for materials, you should be aware that historical sources are divided into two general categories: primary and secondary. Primary sources are those produced by the historical characters themselves or their contemporaries: correspondence, diaries and journals, autobiographies, government publications, newspapers, and similar documents. Secondary sources include books, magazine articles, and Ph.D. dissertations written by later scholars or writers. In most cases, primary sources are more impressive, since they provide a firsthand account of the events in question. Unfortunately they are often more difficult to locate. In the case of the American Revolution, for example, much primary information does exist, including correspondence, newspapers, and governmental materials. While some of these materials, such as the letters of Washington and Jefferson, are available in printed form in many university libraries, other materials exist only in the original manuscripts and are confined to special libraries, state historical societies, and similar institutions.

Fortunately primary materials are not required for all assignment. Consult your professor and use your own judgment to determine what types of sources are most appropriate for your project.

Once you have selected your sources, the task of note-taking begins. Thorough notes are the key to successful research. When you locate a source on the library shelves, the first step is to fill out a note card listing the author, title, publisher, and publication date. You might also note the library call number, in case you need to consult the book again. Once you have recorded this information, the next step is to read the appropriate sections of the book or article, and to jot down any information that may be helpful to you on additional cards. The general rule is one idea per card. Following this procedure allows you to arrange and rearrange your notes in the course of your writing. As you are taking notes, rephrase the data in your own words. Or, if you use the author's language, be sure to put quotation marks around it to indicate it is a direct quote. Always include on your card the author, title, and the page(s) on which you found the information. This will be useful when you wish to cite the material in a footnote. Remember, if you are using a book, you need not read the entire book, but only those sections relevant to your topic. Magazine articles should be read in their entirety.

* WRITING HISTORY *

Once you have collected your data, you face the often difficult task of putting your ideas on paper. Composing a history essay allows for few legitimate shortcuts. By adhering to a particular set of procedures, however, you can minimize difficulties while enhancing the quality of your writing.

The first step in writing a paper is to create an outline. Although students often avoid this stage in their haste to "get started" on their project, the outline performs a critical role in the creative process. Not only does it contribute to a more logical and coherent development of ideas, but it also helps you see and eliminate many structural problems before you become engrossed in the actual writing. As a general rule, the earlier you can spot any problem, the easier it is to resolve. The outline may be as general or specific as you wish. It serves not as an ironclad script for you to follow, but as a general framework to provide direction for the narrative. It can be modified later to accommodate ideas that occur to you as you proceed.

After you complete the outline, you should begin your paper with a clear statement of your argument. For example, if you are addressing the question of whether the American Revolution really was a revolution, you should begin by taking a clear position on the question. It is important to note that the position need *not* be a simple "yes" or "no"; it may be more complicated than that. History is seldom black and white; most often it consists of many gray areas. Whatever position you take, it should be made explicit. If you fail to do this, the effectiveness of your writing will be diminished, since your readers may not be aware of the point of your essay. A common mistake students make is to treat a paper like a mystery story, giving readers the "clues" first and supplying the "solution" at the end. This style is not conducive to good history. State your argument in the beginning so that your readers will be able to follow—and assess—your narrative.

From your introduction you should move smoothly into your narrative. It is here that you develop your argument, using your evidence in a convincing manner. The narrative should exhibit a logical sequence of ideas, not a random collection of data. While evidence is crucial, the key to successful writing is in the elaboration of evidence. Contrary to a popular slogan, the facts do not speak for themselves. Rather, the author must explain the relevance of his facts to his central argument. Few people, for example, would dispute the statement that George Washington crossed the Delaware River to surprise the Hessians at Trenton. The author, however, must explain why this event was significant to his topic. Otherwise it becomes a mere fact of passing interest, without any greater meaning.

History involves the process of change over time, and an effective narrative must illustrate his process. To do so, the narrative must connect diverse facts so that they form a cohesive story. Each sentence should follow logically from the preceding one, and lead into the next one; each paragraph should do the same. To accomplish this, you must pay particular attention to *transition;* that is, moving from one topic to a related topic. Too often students shift from one topic to another without explaining the connection between the two. A historical essay that shifts immediately from Washington's crossing of the Delaware to Jefferson's authorship of the Declaration of Independence creates confusion as to the course of the narrative. A successful transition can be effected by inserting a sentence such "While some individuals fought for independence on the battlefield, others pursued it in the halls of the Continental Congress."

This sentence establishes a concrete relationship between the two events.

In addition to elaborating your evidence, you must cite the sources of this evidence. Any information that is not "common knowledge" should be demarcated by a footnote. If you are uncertain as to proper footnote use and form, consult a stylistic manual such as Kate Turabian's *A Manual for Writers*. Although some footnotes can be complicated, the basic forms for books and articles are illustrated below.

For books:

Robert E. Brown, *Middle-Class Democracy and the Revolution in Massachusetts, 1691–1780* (Ithaca: N.Y.: Cornell University Press, 1955), p. 27.

Notice that the footnote includes the author, title, publisher, date, and page on which the information was found. As mentioned earlier, it is essential that you record this information when taking notes.

Articles are footnoted as follows:

Jesse Lemisch, "Jack Tar in the Streets: Merchant Seamen in the Politics of the American Revolution," *William and Mary Quarterly*, 3rd Series 25 (July, 1968): 347–381.

This footnote includes the author, title, the journal in which the article appears, and the date and edition of publication. The pages indicated are those from which the information was taken. Note that the title of the book or journal is underlined, while the title of the article is placed within quotation marks.

For an article by one author appearing in a work edited by another:

Gordon S. Wood, "Rhetoric and Reality in the American Revolution," in *Essays on the American Revolution*, ed. David L. Jacobsen (New York: Holt, Rinehart and Winston, 1970), pp. 50–52.

This form combines various elements of the previous two styles (all forms are based on Turabian's *Manual*.)

In addition to knowing *how* to footnote, you must learn *when* to footnote. All specific data that are not common knowledge, as well as all direct quotes, should be cited. Never use historians' words or ideas without giving them credit in a footnote. To do so constitutes plagiarism, which is a serious offense within the academic world. For stylistic purposes, most readers prefer one comprehensive footnote at the end of a paragraph to a footnote at the end of each individual sentence. (A single footnote may cite several sources.) In the case of a direct quote, however, a footnote must appear at the end of a sentence. If you use a series of quotations, one multiple footnote may suffice. The word *footnote* implies that the citations should appear on the bottom of the page on which the cited material appears. While this is the most convenient arrangement for the reader, it complicates the typing of the paper substantially. Therefore, most professors will accept a separate footnote section at the end of the narrative.

One final word regarding footnotes. While you must cite a source every time you take data from it, you need only give the full citation the *first* time you cite the source. After that, an abbreviated footnote is acceptable. For example:

Brown, *Middle-Class Democracy*, p. 11.

Adopting this form can save you considerable time in the typing of your paper.

Although all individuals must develop their own style of presenting evidence, a few basic rules should be observed. Keep your language clear and succinct. Avoid wordiness and redundancies. Expressions such as "a determined, headstrong, ambitious, unyielding, persevering individual" are repetitious and stylistically unacceptable. Make sure you have command of your vocabulary; do not employ "impressive" words if you are unsure of their precise meaning. Avoid excessive quoting. Quotes are a highly effective means of illustrating ideas and attitudes, but when used excessively, they *become* the narrative, rather than highlighting the narrative. Let your characters speak for themselves, but remember that the final argument must be yours.

Learn to employ active rather than passive verbs in your writing. "Congress passed a law" reads better than "A law was passed," and is also more informative since it reveals *who* passed the law. Since history is a record of the past, it should be written in the past tense.

Incorrect: "Hitler invad*es* Russia in June of 1941"

Correct: "Hitler invad*ed* Russia in June of 1941."

Since you are, in a sense, telling a story, humorous anecdotes and interesting asides, when used properly, can make your narrative more readable. If your writing includes extensive quantitative (numerical) data, you might want to incorporate the information into charts or appendices to avoid interrupting the flow of your narrative.

When you have completed the actual narrative, you should summarize your argument *briefly* in your conclusion. Just as your introductory paragraph prepares your readers for your argument, your conclusion affirms the major ideas that you want to communicate to your readers.

After the narrative comes the bibliography, which is a list of all the sources you have used in the course of your work. Several differences distinguish a bibliography from footnotes. While the sequence of footnotes is determined by your narrative, the bibliography is arranged in alphabetical order. Most bibliographies are divided into primary and secondary sources, and subdivided into general categories, such as books, articles, newspapers, and government documents. Moreover, the bibliographic form differs slightly from that of footnotes. Examples of proper bibliographic form follow:

Brown, Robert E. *Middle-Class Democracy and the Revolution in Massachusetts, 1691–1780.* Ithaca, N.Y.: Cornell University Press, 1955.

Lemisch, Jesse. "Jack Tar in the Streets: Merchant Seamen in the Politics of the Revolutionary America." *William and Mary Quarterly.* 3rd Series 25 (July, 1968): 371–407.

Wood, Gordon S. "Rhetoric and Reality in the American Revolution." In *Essays in the American Revolution,* pp. 43–65. Edited by David L. Jacobsen. New York: Holt, Rinehart and Winston, 1970.

Although the form differs from that of footnotes, most of the information is the same. Note that in the case of articles, however, the bibliography gives the page numbers for the entire article, while the footnote gives only those pages from which information has been extracted. Note also the way the authors' last names stand out in a biography enabling the reader to see at a glance which sources you have used. (The bibliographic form used here comes from Turabian's manual. If you have any questions regarding the bibliography, consult Turabian or some other manual.)

The final stage in writing a paper is proofreading. Ideally, you should compose a first draft, proofread it carefully, and then rewrite the paper where necessary. If you write only one draft, make your corrections as neatly as possible. Unless otherwise instructed, papers should be typed, double-spaced.

Finally, pay strict attention to deadlines. Allot adequate time for each project, including time for typing and proofreading. If you encounter any difficulties, inform your professor immediately. Do not wait until the due date to reveal that you cannot submit your paper on time.

BIBLIOGRAPHIES

CHAPTER 1 *The New World Encounters the Old*

Alvin M. Josephy. *The Indian Heritage of America* (1968). An overall survey of the Indian peoples of both American continents, region by region and era by era.

Brian M. Fagan. *The Great Journey: The Peopling of Ancient America* (1987). How Asian peoples first settled the Americas across "Baringia," the land bridge that once connected the Old World to the New.

Francis Jennings. *The Invasion of America: Indians, Colonialism, and the Cant of Conquest* (1975). Jennings seeks to redress the traditional story that makes the Indians into "savages" and the Europeans into the civilized party to the Old World-New World encounter after 1492.

Alfred W. Crosby. *The Columbian Exchange: Biological and Cultural Consequences of 1492* (1972). Crosby sees the contacts between Europeans and the native peoples of America as a two-way street—both for good and ill.

J. H. Parry. *The Age of Reconnaissance: Discovery, Exploration, and Settlement. 1450–1650* (1963). An excellent review of the roots and course of late medieval-early modern European overseas expansion.

Samuel Eliot Morison. *The European Discovery of America: The Northern Voyages, 400–1600 (1971);* and *The Southern Voyages, 1492–1616 (1974).* Both of these volumes are superb blends of lucid text, maps, and photographs by a sailor-historian who was a master of his craft.

Samuel Eliot Morison. *Christopher Columbus, Mariner* (1955). This is the condensed paperback edition of one of the great biographies in American historical literature, *Admiral of the Ocean Sea.*

Charles Gibson. *Spain in America* (1966). An informative and tightly written analysis and interpretation of Spanish-American history from the earliest explorations to the nineteenth century.

C. R. Boxer. *The Portuguese Seaborne Empire, 1415–1825* (1969).This is by far the best modern account of that epic expansion.

Carlo M. Cipolla. *Before the Industrial Revolution: European Economy and Society, 1000–1700* (1980). A first-rate survey of the economy of early modern Europe.

J. H. Parry. *The Spanish Seaborne Empire* (1966). The best work on the subject, complementing Parry's broader *Age of Reconnaissance.*

G. V. Scammell. *The World Encompassed: The First European Maritime Empires, 800–1650* (1981). The best, and most recent, treatment of European expansion in the Middle Ages and early modern period.

CHAPTER 2 *The Old World Comes to America*

Thomas J. Wertenbaker. *The First Americans, 1607–1690 (1927).* Still an excellent and well-written survey of the early settlement patterns of British America.

James Morton Smith, editor. *Seventeenth Century America: Essays in Colonial History* (1959). Includes several important essays on early colonization as well as good chapters on early Indian–white relations in North America.

Carl Bridenbaugh. *Vexed and Troubled Englishmen, 1590–1642* (1974). A social history of ordinary English people during the early years of American colonization.

Edmund Morgan. *The Puritan Dilemma: The Story of John Winthrop* (1958). A fine biography of the early Puritan leader of Massachusetts who did so much to make that colony a success.

Alden T. Vaughan. *American Genesis: Captain John Smith and the Founding of Virginia* (1975). The early history of the Jamestown colony approached through the biography of the colorful soldier John Smith.

Edmund S. Morgan. *American Slavery, American Freedom: The Ordeal of Colonial Virginia* (1975). An excellent account of the early years of the Virginia colony, which also deals interestingly with the issues of race and labor relations between whites and Indians and between whites and black slaves in the first permanent British North American colony.

Abbot Emerson Smith. *Colonists in Bondage: White Servitude and Convict Labor in America, 1607–1776* (1947). Tells how indentured servants and convicts were induced, seduced, kidnapped, and "spirited" to America.

Daniel Mannix and Malcolm Cowley. *Black Cargoes: A History of the Atlantic Slave Trade* (1962). An eye-opener for readers who have accepted the conventional wisdom about early black Africa and the international slave trade.

John Barth. *The Sot-Weed Factor* (1964). A long historical novel which spoofs the heroic accounts of early American settlement.

David Galenson. *White Servitude in Colonial America: An Economic Analysis* (1981). Traces the shift in the colonial workforce from indentured servitude to slavery and relates it to changing costs of both skilled and unskilled labor.

Barnard Bailyn. *Voyagers to the West: A Passage in the Peopling of America on the Eve of the Revolution* (1986). Deals with immigration from Britain on the eve of the Revolution.

Philip D. Curtin. *The Atlantic Slave Trade: A Census* (1969). A detailed demographic examination of the Africa–America slave trade.

CHAPTER 3   *Colonial Society*

Daniel Boorstin. *The Americans: The Colonial Experience* (1958). A bold attempt to demonstrate how the American environment altered transplanted Old World institutions and culture.

John Demos. *A Little Commonwealth: Family Life in Plymouth Colony* (1970). A fascinating study of family life in Plymouth Colony, drawn from both the written records and the archeological evidence of surviving artifacts, houses, and utensils.

Philip Greven. *Four Generations: Population, Land, and Family in Colonial Andover, Massachusetts* (1970); and The *Protestant Temperament* (1977). The first is a demographic study of a seventeenth-century New England town that shows the remarkable longevity and prosperity of the early settlers. The second deals with child-rearing practices in America from 1600 to 1830.

Kenneth Lockridge. *A New England Town, The First Hundred Years: Dedham, Massachusetts, 1636–1736* (1970). A brilliant study of one New England town during its first century. A model study.

Carl Bridenbaugh. *Myths and Realities: Societies of the Colonial South* (1952). A brief and readable treatment of the often neglected southern colonial heritage.

James R. Lemon. *The Best Poor Man's Country: A Geographical Study of Early Southwestern Pennsylvania* (1972). An interesting study of the interplay of the institutions and physical environment of early Pennsylvania.

Peter Wood. *Black Majority* (1975). One of the best treatments we have of colonial slavery. Wood believes that transplanted Africans contributed significantly to the culture and institutions of early southern society.

Louis B. Wright, editor. *The Cultural Life of the American Colonies, 1607–1763* (1957). Summarizes developments in colonial religion, literature, education, science, architecture, theater, and music.

Henry F. May. *The Enlightenment in America* (1976). Sees the American Enlightenment as a complex three-part development, with the phase described in this chapter (the defense of balance and order) as the most characteristically American.

Charles Sydnor. *Gentlemen Freeholders: Political Practices in Washington's Virginia* (1952). Emphasizes the "popular" features of colonial Virginia's political life by contrast with the aristocratic ones given prominence by earlier authors.

Robert E. Brown and B. Katherine Brown. *Virginia 1705–1786: Democracy or Aristocracy?* (1964). The authors see colonial Virginia as a remarkably democratic society in a political sense.

Robert E. Brown. *Middle-Class Democracy and the Revolution in Massachusetts, 1691–1780* (1955). Massachusetts described as a middle-class democratic society by the eve of the Revolution.

Jack P. Green. *The Quest for Power: The Lower Houses of Assembly in the Southern Royal Colonies, 1689–1763* (1963). Deals with the struggle of the southern provincial assemblies to become independent legislatures rather than rubber stamps of royal governors or Parliament.

Nathaniel Hawthorne. *The Scarlet Letter* (1850). An incomparable introduction to the gloomy, brooding, morbid side of Puritan New England.

Michael Zuckerman. *Peaceable Kingdoms: New England Towns in the Eighteenth Century* (1970). Emphasizes the consensus aspect of New England towns.

Christine Leigh Heyrman. *Commerce and Culture: The Maritime Communities of Colonial Massachusetts, 1690–1750* (1984). A fine description of colonial life in Marblehead and Gloucester, two major New England ports.

David Freeman Hawke. *Everyday Life in Early America* (1988). An interesting depiction of daily life in colonial America.

Darrett B. Rutman and Anita H. Rutman. *A Place in Time: Middlesex County, Virginia, 1650–1750* (1984). The Rutmans demonstrate that the colonial Chesapeake region was not the structureless, individualistic place that scholars had formerly believed.

Gloria Main. *Tobacco Colony: Life in Early Maryland, 1650–1720* (1982). Deals with the social abstractions of colonial Maryland—demographic processes and the impact of market forces on development—and also with the concrete details of daily life.

David Hackett Fischer. *Albion's Seed: Four British Folkways in America* (1989). Advances the view that four distinctive cultural patterns were transmitted from Britain to colonial America and that they persisted relatively intact and unblended, through the colonial period and beyond.

Jon Butler. *Awash in a Sea of Faith: The Christianization of the American People* (1990). Butler says that the "Great Awakening" phenomenon has been greatly exaggerated.

CHAPTER 4 *Moving Toward Independence*

John H. McCusker and Russell Menard. *The Economy of British America, 1607–1789: Needs and Opportunities* (1985). A recent survey of the colonial economy that pulls together much of the newest research and suggests new directions and new areas of investigation for future scholars.

Alice H. Jones. *Wealth of a Nation to Be: The American Colonies on the Eve of the Revolution* (1980). The definitive study of just how wealthy Americans were in the late eighteenth century and how their wealth was distributed among the various members of society.

Arthur M. Schlesinger. *The Colonial Merchants and the American Revolution, 1763–1776* (1917). A good older work that examines the contribution of colonial traders to the origins of the Revolution.

James Henretta. *The Evolution of American Society, 1700–1815: An Interdisciplinary Analysis* (1973). An interesting attempt by a social historian to integrate the social, economic, and political history of early America.

Jackson T. Main. *The Social Structure of Revolutionary America* (1965). Main depicts the colonists as prosperous and socially mobile. Colonial America, he says, was indeed "the best poor man's country in the world."

Edmund S. Morgan and Helen M. Morgan. *The Stamp Act Crisis: Prologue to Revolution* (1953). The best short treatment of this crucial step along the road to independence.

Bernard Bailyn. *The Ideological Origins of the American Revolution* (1967). Shows how the libertarian ideas forged in the seventeenth- and early eighteenth-century English struggle with the crown helped mold the actions of American Patriots after 1763.

Robert A. Gross. *The Minutemen and Their World* (1976). This study of the town of Concord, Massachusetts, before 1776 captures the hopes, frustrations, and fears of a small American community caught in the vortex of great imperial changes.

Pauline Maier. *From Resistance to Revolution: Colonial Radicals and the Development of American Opposition to Great Britain, 1765–1776* (1972). Views the "radical" leaders of the American independence movement as orderly and prudent men who opposed mob violence.

Bernard Bailyn. *The Ordeal of Thomas Hutchinson* (1974). A fine study of the mind and views of a leading American Tory.

Merrill Jensen. *The Founding of a Nation: A History of the American Revolution, 1763–1776* (1968). A long and well-written study of the whole sweep of events, from the French and Indian War onward, that culminated in the Declaration of Independence.

John C. Miller. *Sam Adams: Pioneer in Propaganda* (1936). A classic older study of a major Revolutionary radical.

Dumas Malone. *Jefferson the Virginian* (1948). The best treatment of Jefferson during the years he was intimately involved in the colonial struggle with Great Britain.

Carl Van Doren. *Benjamin Franklin* (1941). A classic of American biography by a brilliant stylist.

Douglas Southall Freeman. *Washington: An Abridgment* (1968). This is the one-volume condensation of Freeman's monumental seven-volume life of Washington.

CHAPTER 5 *The Revolution*

Howard H. Peckham. *The War for Independence: A Military History* (1958). A brief narrative of the military aspects of the Revolution.

Samuel Eliot Morison. *John Paul Jones: A Sailor's Biography* (1959). This portrait of the Revolutionary War sea captain also describes the growing pains of the tiny American navy.

Henry S. Commager and Richard B. Morris, editors. *The Spirit of '76: The Story of the American Revolution as Told by Participants* (1958). A vast miscellany of letters, diaries, journals, diplomatic correspondence, parliamentary debates, and more.

Alfred F. Young, editor. *The American Revolution* (1976). A volume of essays emphasizing class conflict in several states during the Revolution.

James Franklin Jameson. *The American Revolution Considered as a Social Movement* (1925). The classic statement of the social dimensions of the American Revolution.

Richard B. Morris. *The American Revolution Reconsidered* (1967). An attempt to update Jameson.

Mary Beth Norton. *Liberty's Daughters: The Revolutionary Experience of American Women, 1750–1800* (1980). An important and interesting book that supports the view that the Revolution helped to improve the lot and increase the freedom of women.

Arthur Zilversmit. *The First Emancipation: The Abolition of Slavery in the North* (1967). The best study of the process by which the northern states excluded slavery from their borders.

Jack Sosin. *The Revolutionary Frontier, 1763–1783* (1967). Tells the important story of the West in both the origins and the course of the Revolution.

Gordon Wood. *The Creation of the American Republic, 1776–1787* (1968). An important reinterpretation of the Revolutionary period as well as the Confederation era that emphasizes the rise of a republican ideology.

Kenneth Roberts. *Arundel* (1930) and *Rabble in Arms* (1933). Benedict Arnold is a principal character in these two entertaining historical novels and he is sympathetically portrayed.

John R. Alden. *A History of the American Revolution* (1969). This is probably the best single-volume history of the Revolution.

Richard Morris. *The Peacemakers: The Great Powers and American Independence* (1965). Deals with the diplomacy of the Revolution.

Arthur Bowler. *Logistics and the Failure of British Arms in America, 1775–1783* (1975). A specialized study of the military aspects of the Revolution that points the finger at supply problems as the reason for British defeat.

Gordon S. Wood. *The Radicalism of the American Revolution* (1992). A sophisticated restatement of the thesis that a real revolution took place in 1775–1783.

CHAPTER 6 *The Origins of the Constitution*

Merrill Jensen. *The New Nation: A History of the United States During the Confederation, 1781–1787* (1948). Seeks to refute the notion that the Confederation era was a critical period.

Marion Starkey. *A Little Rebellion* (1955). An entertaining account of Shays's Rebellion.

Jackson Turner Main. *The Anti-Federalists: Critics of the Constitution, 1781–1788* (1961). Main sees the opponents of a stronger central government in the 1780s as largely isolated farmers who were not tied to the sale of commercial crops and so had little interest in foreign trade.

Irving Brant. *James Madison: The Nationalist, 1780–1787* (1948). Describes government under the Articles of Confederation and Madison's dismay at the weaknesses of his country during the 1780s and his efforts that culminated in the federal Constitution.

Charles A. Beard. *An Economic Interpretation of the Constitution of the United States* (1913). Beard's thesis is that the fathers of the Constitution constructed a frame of government that was designed to serve the economic needs of their class.

Robert E. Brown. *Charles Beard and the Constitution* (1956). A reexamination of Beard's thesis that finds it seriously wanting.

Forrest McDonald. *We the People: The Economic Origins of the Constitution* (1958); and *E Pluribus Unum: The Formation of the American Republic, 1776–1790* (1965). The first of these two books challenges Beard's description of the economic factors and groups behind a stronger central government in the 1780s. The second is an interesting if sometimes highly personal discussion of the drive toward the Constitution and the formation of a new national government.

Benjamin F. Wright, editor. *The Federalist* (1961). *The Federalist Papers,* written by Madison, Hamilton, and John Jay, are essential to understanding the thinking of the Constitution's supporters.

Robert A. Rutland. *The Ordeal of the Constitution: The Anti-Federalists and the Ratification Struggle of 1787–88* (1966). Sympathetic to the antifederalists who opposed ratification of the Constitution, Rutland explains the strategy of the two opposing groups and the reasons for antifederalist defeat.

Irving Brant. *The Bill of Rights: Its Origin and Meaning* (1965). This full treatment (515 pages) of the first ten amendments to the Constitution deals with the Bill of Rights' roots in both English and American experience, its creation early in the new republic, and its application over the many years that have ensued.

CHAPTER 7   *The First Party System*

John C. Miller. *The Federalist Era, 1789–1801* (1960). One of the best short political histories of the administrations of Washington and Adams.

Lance Banning. *The Jeffersonian Persuasion: Evolution of a Party Ideology* (1978). Banning sees the Jeffersonian Republicans as men whose view of the political world was largely a product of "real Whig" ideology—which also influenced those who led the Revolution.

Richard Hofstadter. *The Idea of a Party System, 1780–1840* (1969). Deals with the emergence of parties in the United States as a part of our intellectual history.

Joseph E. Charles. *The Origins of the American Party System* (1956). The first modern interpretation of the first party system by a promising scholar who died young.

John C. Miller. *Alexander Hamilton: Portrait in Paradox* (1959). Miller considers Hamilton's preoccupation with the creation and maintenance of a strong Union the key to all his ideas and policies.

Paul A. Varg. *Foreign Policies of the Founding Fathers* (1963). Analyzes the economic and ideological factors in early foreign policy, the conflict between moralism and realism in policy-making, and the contribution of foreign-policy disagreements to the early formation of national political parties.

Harry Ammon. *The Gênet Mission* (1973). A brief, pro-Jefferson account of Edmond Genét's mission to enlist American support for republican France against England.

Leland Baldwin. *The Whiskey Rebels: The Story of a Frontier Uprising* (1939). The Whiskey Rebellion and its background treated with special attention to the feelings of those involved.

Manning J. Dauer. *The Adams Federalists* (1953); and Stephen G. Kurtz. *The Presidency of John Adams: The Collapse of Federalism, 1795–1800* (1957). These are two essential monographs on the Federalist party after the departure of Washington from the political scene.

Paul Goodman. *The Democratic Republicans of Massachusetts: Politics in a Young Republic* (1964). A superior state study of the Jeffersonians in a commonwealth where it was an uphill fight for the followers of the Sage of Monticello.

James T. Flexner. *George Washington and the New Nation, 1783–1793* (1969); and *George Washington: Anguish and Farewell, 1793–1799* (1972). These two volumes cover Washington's presidency and last years as completely as the student could wish.

Reginald Horsman. *The Frontier in the Formative Years, 1783–1815* (1970). Tells the important story of the West during the early years of the republic.

James M. Smith. *Freedom's Fetters: The Alien and Sedition Laws and American Civil Liberties* (1956). Written during the era of Joe McCarthy, it sees the 1790s as a rehearsal for the later age of repression.

Joyce Appleby. *Capitalism and a New Social Order: The Republican Vision of the 1790s* (1984). Appleby seeks to depict the Jeffersonians as forward-looking democratic innovators rather than nostalgic agrarians.

Stanley Elkins and Eric McKitrick, *The Age of Federalism: The Early American Republic, 1788–1800* (1993). A long, but readable and insightful review of the years of Federalist ascendancy.

CHAPTER 8   *The Jeffersonians In Office*

Merrill Peterson. *Thomas Jefferson and the New Nation: A Biography* (1970). Peterson relates Jefferson's private life and his thought to his public role, and is lucid on the political issues of the day.

Fawn Brodie. *Thomas Jefferson: An Intimate History* (1973). Criticized by many scholars for suggesting an intimate relationship between Jefferson and his female slave, Sally Hemmings, this work is a superior psychobiography of our third president.

Forrest McDonald. *The Presidency of Thomas Jefferson* (1976). This brief, well-written volume has a strong point of view that not every scholar can accept.

Bernard De Voto, editor. *Journals of Lewis and Clark* (1953). The chronicle of the twenty-eight-month-long search for an overland route to the Pacific.

Leonard Levy. *Thomas Jefferson and Civil Liberties: The Darker Side* (1963). A revisionist study that depicts the third president as a man who often violated his own precepts in matters of civil liberties.

Henry Adams. *History of the United States During the Administrations of Jefferson and Madison* (1881–1891). This nine-volume work is a classic of American historical literature.

Reginald Horsman. *The War of 1812* (1969). The best one-volume history of the war.

Bernard Sheehan. *Seeds of Extinction: Jeffersonian Philanthropy and the American Indian* (1973). Describes how the Indian reformers of Jefferson's day, hoping to lead the tribes from "savagery" to "civilization," only managed to drive them brutally into the interior, thereby making way for white speculators and settlers.

Bernard Mayo. *Henry Clay: Spokesman of the New West* (1937). The story of Clay's life to 1812, when he was the thirty-five-year-old Speaker of the House of Representatives and leader of the War Hawks.

Bradford Perkins. *Prologue to War: England and the United States, 1805–1812* (1961). Perkins ascribes the drift of Britain and America toward war to the condescending attitude of the English and to American insistence on neutral trade in a world beset by war.

Julius Pratt. *Expansionists of 1812* (1925). Emphasizes how American interest in acquiring Canada, Florida, and possibly Mexico influenced the decision for war in 1812.

Gore Vidal. *Burr* (1973). A historical novel about Aaron Burr in the form of a memoir. Vidal is very much biased toward Burr.

CHAPTER 9   *The American Economic Miracle*

George R. Taylor. *The Transportation Revolution, 1815–1860* (1951). Still the best single-volume treatment of the American economy during the period covered by this chapter.

Stuart Bruchey. *The Roots of American Economic Growth, 1607–1861: An Essay in Social Causation* (1965). More up-to-date in its reliance on modern economists' growth theory than the Taylor book, though Bruchey also stresses the importance of national values and political, scientific, and technological developments.

Alan Dawley. *Class and Community: The Industrial Revolution in Lynn* (1976). Describes the shoemakers of Lynn, Massachusetts, as strongly opposed to the emerging industrial values and practices of the age and determined to preserve a preindustrial working-class ethic even if that meant resisting "progress."

H. J. Habakkuk. *American and British Technology in the Nineteenth Century* (1962). Compares English and American technology during the early industrial revolution.

Ronald Shaw. *Erie Water West: A History of the Erie Canal, 1792–1854* (1966). The social and political history of the great canal.

Mark Twain. *Life on the Mississippi* (1883). A beautifully written narrative of Twain's experiences as apprentice to a Mississippi River steamboat pilot before the Civil War.

Norman Ware. *The Industrial Worker, 1840–1860: The Reaction of American Industrial Society to the Advance of the Industrial Revolution* (1924). An older work that examines the roots of the American labor movement and sees it as a reaction to the loss of skill and autonomy ushered in by the factory system.

Hannah Josephson. *Golden Threads: New England Mill Girls and Magnates* (1949). A well-written social and economic history of the early New England textile industry.

Anthony Wallace. *Rockdale: The Growth of an American Village in the Early Industrial Revolution* (1978). A fascinating study of an early textile community near Philadelphia, written by an anthropologist.

Paul E. Johnson. *A Shopkeeper's Millennium: Society and Revivals in Rochester, New York, 1815–1837* (1979). Describes the religious roots of the pre-Civil War work ethic.

Merritt Roe Smith. *Harpers Ferry Armory and the New Technology: The Challenge of Change* (1977). Smith shows how the cultural milieu of a community affected its industrial performance.

Sean Wilentz. *Chants Democratic: New York City and the Rise of the American Working Class, 1788–1850* (1984). An interesting account of what the author considers a class-conscious labor movement in pre-Civil War New York.

CHAPTER 10 *Jacksonian Democracy*

George Dangerfield. *The Era of Good Feelings* (1952). An elegantly written narrative history of the years between the War of 1812 and the rise of Jackson as a major political figure.

Robert Remini. *Andrew Jackson* (1966). Concentrates on Andrew Jackson's role in strengthening the presidency, his deft handling of the Calhounites, the nullification crisis, and his battle with the BUS.

Thomas Govan. *Nicholas Biddle, Nationalist and Public Banker* (1959). The public life of the BUS president during the years when the "Monster Bank" was locked in combat with "King" Andrew. Govan is pro-Bank and anti-Jackson.

John William Ward. *Andrew Jackson: Symbol for an Age* (1955). Deals with Jackson's popular image as a folk hero.

Arthur M. Schlesinger, Jr. *The Age of Jackson* (1945). The classic defense of Jacksonian democracy by a master of historical prose.

Marvin Meyers. *The Jacksonian Persuasion: Politics and Belief* (1957). Meyers concludes that the Jacksonians were moralistic rather than materialistic, a conservative set of men who pined for an America already past.

Richard P. McCormick. *The Second American Party System: Party Formation in the Jacksonian Era* (1966). McCormick describes how the second party system actually came together during the 1820s and 1830s.

Lee Benson. *The Concept of Jacksonian Democracy: New York as a Test Case* (1961). Benson claims that religion, culture, and ethnicity were more important determinants of party affiliation in New York during the second party system than class or occupation.

Ronald Formisano. *The Birth of Mass Political Parties: Michigan, 1827–1861* (1971). A study of the second party system in a state where the ethnocultural interpretation of party choice works exceptionally well.

William W. Freehling. *Prelude to Civil War: The Nullification Controversy in South Carolina, 1816–1836* (1966). Treats nullification primarily as a frightened reaction of the South Carolina planter class to abolitionism.

Richard N. Current. *John C. Calhoun* (1963). A short, well-written biography of the 1812 "War Hawk" who eventually became secretary of war, vice president, and ardent defender of southern minority "rights."

Grant Foreman. *Indian Removal: The Emigration of the Five Civilized Tribes of Indians* (1932). The sympathetic story of the forced migration of the Choctaws, Creeks, Chickasaws, Cherokees, and Seminoles from their homes in the Southeast to Oklahoma.

Marvin E. Gettleman. *The Dorr Rebellion: A Study in American Radicalism, 1833–1849* (1973). A sympathetic attempt to find native American radical roots, but not uncritical of the Dorr rebels.

Edward Pessen. *Jacksonian America: Society, Personality, and Politics* (1978). A highly critical view of Jackson and the Jacksonians. Pessen denies most of the egalitarian virtues usually ascribed to both.

Charles Sellers. *The Market Revolution: Jacksonian America, 1815–1846* (1991). Restores Jackson as the champion of the masses in the effort to hold back the forces of all-conquering capitalism.

CHAPTER 11   *The Mexican War and Expansionism*

Bernard De Voto.   *Across the Wide Missouri* (1947). De Voto delightfully chronicles the Rocky Mountain fur trade that flourished in the 1820s and 1830s.

Francis Parkman.   *The Oregon Trail* (1849). This is a fascinating contemporary depiction of the trans-Mississippi West by a literary artist. A classic.

John David Unruh.   *The Plains Across: The Overland Emigrants and the Trans-Mississippi West, 1840–1860* (1978). The best overall treatment of emigration by way of the various overland "trails" from the settled areas of the East to the West Coast before the Civil War.

Henry Nash Smith.   *Virgin Land: The American West as Symbol and Myth* (1950). Examines how the nineteenth-century West influenced the life and helped to shape the character of American society as a whole.

George R. Stewart.   *Ordeal by Hunger: The Story of the Donner Party* (1936). The harrowing story of eighty-nine California-bound people who were stranded in the High Sierra during the winter of 1846–1847.

Ray Allen Billington.   *The Far Western Frontier, 1830–1860* (1956). A colorful survey of the Far West in the generation before the Civil War.

Frederick Merk.   *Manifest Destiny and Mission in American History* (1963). The best discussion of this important topic by one of the deans of western history.

David M. Pletcher.   *The Diplomacy of Annexation: Texas, Oregon, and the Mexican War* (1973). Treats the background of the Mexican War and the economic and political interests of the United States, Mexico, Britain, and France during the 1830s and 1840s.

Norman A. Graebner.   *Empire on the Pacific: A Study in American Continental Expansion* (1955). Graebner concludes that it was not Manifest Destiny or the "pioneering spirit," but rather the desire of eastern commercial interests for ports on the Pacific that explains American expansion to the Pacific Coast.

Eugene Genovese.   *The Political Economy of Slavery: Studies in the Economy and Society of the Slave South* (1965). Depicts expansionism as the effort of a southern planter elite to save slavery from a trap of soil exhaustion and declining profitability.

Otis Singletary.   *The Mexican War* (1960). A good, brief treatment of the war against Mexico.

Julie Roy Jeffrey.   *Frontier Women: The Trans-Mississippi West, 1840–1880* (1979). A fresh, entertaining discussion of women along the way to, and in, the Far West, from Oregon onward.

Oakah Jones, Jr.   *Santa Anna* (1968). Depicts the Mexican leader as an honest patriot rather than the rank opportunist of other portraits.

CHAPTER 12   *Americans Before the Civil War*

Roger Brown.   *Modernization: The Transformation of American Life, 1600–1865* (1976). An attempt to place social change in America within the framework of "modernization" where custom and personal, face-to-face relations among people are replaced by impersonal, contractual relations.

Keith Melder.   *The Beginnings of Sisterhood* (1977). A fine, brief treatment of the social background and early course of the women's rights movement.

Nancy Cott. *The Bonds of Womanhood: "Women's Sphere" in New England, 1780–1835* (1977). Sees women's lives being transformed by the growing separation of family and work during the early years of the Republic.

Linda Gordon. *Woman's Body, Woman's Right: A Social History of Birth Control in America* (1976). A book with a strong thesis: "Birth control represented the single most important factor in the material basis of woman's emancipation in the course of the last century."

Russel B. Nye. *Society and Culture in America, 1830–1860* (1974). A superior intellectual and cultural history.

Oscar Handlin, editor. *This Was America* (1949). Contains excerpts from many of the accounts by foreign travelers that scholars have used to paint antebellum America's portrait.

John Kasson. *Rudeness and Civility: Manners in Nineteenth-Century Urban America* (1990). An interesting discussion of the role of the arbiters of manners, especially the authors of etiquette books, on standards of behavior in nineteenth-century American cities.

Ray Allen Billington. *America's Frontier Heritage* (1966). Billington examines Turner's frontier thesis and revises it in light of relatively recent scholarship.

Oscar Handlin. *Boston's Immigrants, 1790–1880* (1968). Catches the essence of the urban immigrant experience primarily before the Civil War in microcosm.

Ray Billington. *The Protestant Crusade, 1800–1860: A Study of the Origins of American Nativism* (1938). This case study of mass reaction describes the development of anti-Catholic and antiforeign feeling that reached its peak in the 1850s.

Leon F. Litwack. *North of Slavery: The Negro in the Free States, 1790–1860* (1961). Litwack's thesis is that by 1860 most blacks in the states where slavery was forbidden were segregated from whites, economically oppressed, and without civil rights.

David Rothman. *The Discovery of the Asylum: Social Order and Disorder in the New Republic* (1971). Rothman sees the origin of much of the antebellum reform impulse in the attempt by society to make up for the deficiencies of the American family.

Richard Wade. *The Urban Frontier: The Rise of Western Cities, 1790–1830* (1959). Wade makes the point that the antebellum West consisted of fast-growing urban centers as well as farms.

Milton Brown, Sam Hunter, John Jacobus, Naomi Rosenblum, and David Sokol. *American Art: Painting, Sculpture, Architecture, Decorative Arts, Photography* (1979). This large, beautiful, and expensive volume covers all the visual arts from the beginning of colonial settlement through the 1960s.

Leonard Arrington. *Great Basin Kingdom: An Economic History of the Latter-Day Saints, 1830–1900* (1958). An economic history of the Mormons from their beginnings in upstate New York to the twentieth century.

Jack Larkin. *The Reshaping of Everyday Life, 1790–1840* (1988). How Americans of all classes, all occupations, and both races and genders lived day-to-day before the Civil War.

CHAPTER 13 *The Old South*

William R. Taylor. *Cavalier and Yankee: The Old South and American National Character* (1961). Examines the myth of the southern cavalier—a symbol of the agrarian South and the opposite, supposedly, of the money-minded, unchivalrous Yankee.

Frederick Law Olmsted.   *The Cotton Kingdom: A Traveler's Observations on Cotton and Slavery in the American Slave States* (1861). Edited and introduced by Arthur M. Schlesinger, Sr. (1953). In this colorful report, the planner of New York's Central Park demonstrates, to his own satisfaction at least, that dependence on slave-grown cotton fostered "lazy poverty" and was a barrier to the South's broad economic progress.

Grady McWhiney.   *Cracker Culture: Celtic Ways in the Old South* (1988). Seeks to explain the yeoman culture of the white Old South by tying it to the origins of much of its population in the Celtic fringe of the British Isles rather than the English-speaking parts.

Benjamin A. Botkin, editor.   *Lay My Burden Down: A Folk History of Slavery* (1945). This one-volume oral history was compiled from the Slave Narrative Collection made by the U.S. government during the 1930s.

John W. Blassingame.   *The Slave Community: Plantation Life in the Ante-Bellum South* (1972). Demonstrates the extent to which slaves were able to create islands of freedom in which to conduct their personal lives.

Robert W. Fogel and Stanley L. Engerman.   *Time on the Cross: The Economics of Negro Slavery* (1974). An econometric study of Old South slavery that suggests that it was profitable. It has drawn a lot of criticism both for its methods and for its conclusions.

Herbert Gutman.   *The Black Family in Slavery and Freedom, 1750–1925* (1976). An important study of the evolving black family from the colonial era until well after emancipation. Gutman supports the view that black slave families were strong units.

Eugene Genovese.   *Roll Jordan Roll: The World the Slaves Made* (1974). According to Genovese, American slaves did more than merely survive; they formed a "black nation" in the South based on religion and strong family ties.

Clement Eaton.   *Freedom of Thought in the Old South* (1940). This older work presents a critical view of antebellum southern intolerance of intellectual dissent.

Ulrich B. Phillips.   *Life and Labor in the Old South* (1929). Now seventy years old, this is the nearest thing we have to a scholarly version of the moonlight and magnolias view of the Old South.

Robert Fogel.   *Without Consent or Contract: The Rise and Fall of American Slavery* (1989). This is Fogel's "second thoughts" about the institution of slavery. It seeks to alter the slavery-was-not-so-bad impression of his earlier work.

Frank Owsley.   *Plain Folk of the Old South* (1949). The best summation of the school of southern history, which emphasizes the small farmers rather than the slaves and large planters.

Ann F. Scott.   *The Southern Lady from Pedestal to Politics, 1830–1930* (1970). Makes the point that in the Old South white middle-class women were indeed pampered and patronized.

William Styron.   *Confessions of Nat Turner* (1967). Nat Turner, the black preacher who instigated the 1831 Virginia slave uprising, tells his own story in this widely acclaimed, though flawed, historical novel.

CHAPTER 14   *The Coming of the Civil War*

Michael Holt.   *The Political Crisis of the 1850s* (1978). Holt believes that the breakup of the Union can be ascribed to the need of the two parties to define themselves in different and opposed ways.

Holman Hamilton.   *Prologue to Conflict: The Crisis and Compromise of 1850* (1964). Hamilton provides a dramatic and incisive analysis of the strategy of the factions that drew up the Compromise of 1850.

David Potter. *The Impending Crisis, 1848–1861* (1976). A masterful analysis of the political turmoil that ended with the secession of the South.

Robert E. May. *The Southern Dream of a Caribbean Empire, 1854–1861* (1973). May concludes that sectional conflict increased when the Republican-controlled Congress refused to support southern expansion into Central America and the Caribbean.

Eugene Berwanger. *The Frontier Against Slavery: Western Anti-Negro Prejudice and the Slavery Extension Controversy* (1967). The author weighs the effects of this bigotry on the laws and politics of the old Northwest, as well as Iowa, Kansas, Nebraska, Oregon, and California.

James A. Rawley. *Race and Politics: "Bleeding Kansas" and the Coming of the Civil War* (1969). In this analysis of the free-soilers' motives, Rawley emphasizes their race prejudice.

Eric Foner. *Free Soil, Free Labor, Free Men: The Ideology of the Republican Party Before the Civil War* (1970). According to Foner, Republican leaders viewed the North–South conflict as one between two very different societies.

Stephen B. Oates. *To Purge This Land with Blood: A Biography of John Brown* (1970). Oates depicts Brown as a nineteenth-century Calvinist in a time made violent and fanatic by the slavery controversy.

David H. Donald. *Charles Sumner and the Coming of the Civil War* (1960). An excellent, perceptive biography of a major figure in the rise of political antislavery. It is critical of Sumner as intolerant, ambitious, and at times self-deceived.

Harriet Beecher Stowe. *Uncle Tom's Cabin* (1852). Stowe's major theme is not the day-to-day brutality of slavery, but its more indirect consequences in the break-up of black families and the corruption of slaveholders themselves.

J. Mills Thornton III. *Politics and Power in a Slave Society: Alabama, 1800–1860* (1978). Thornton believes that Alabama's secession in 1860 ultimately derived from its white citizens' fear that the North's actions endangered equality and freedom for the South's white people.

William L. Barney. *The Secessionist Impulse: Alabama and Mississippi in 1860* (1974). Barney ties the secession of two key slave states to fear of abolitionist plots, racial anxieties, the work of firebrands, and uneasiness over severe food shortages during the months of crisis.

Kenneth Stampp. *And the War Came* (1950). A close analysis, by an outstanding Civil War scholar, of the final secession crisis and Lincoln's part in it.

Don E. Fehrenbacher. *The Dred Scott Case: Its Significance in American Law and Politics* (1978). The best treatment of the Dred Scott decision.

Kenneth Stampp. *America in 1857: A Nation on the Brink* (1990). A dean of Civil War History examines the state of the American Union in a single year, "probably the year when the North and South reached the political point of no return."

William E. Gienapp. *The Origins of the Republican Party, 1852–1856* (1987). The best recent study of this important subject.

CHAPTER 15   *The Civil War*

David H. Donald (ed.). *Why the North Won the Civil War* (1960). Five historians discuss the social and institutional structure of the Confederacy, the war-making potentials of North and South, northern political parties, military affairs, and Civil War diplomacy.

David H. Donald. *Lincoln* (1995). The best one-volume biography of our sixteenth president.

Richard N. Current. *The Lincoln Nobody Knows* (1958). What was Lincoln really like as a person? Current discusses Lincoln's domestic life, religious view, and political goals.

Clement Eaton. *Jefferson Davis* (1977). The best recent biography of the Confederate president. Written by a southern scholar, it is objective and fair.

Bruce Catton. *Mr. Lincoln's Army* (1951); *Glory Road* (1952); and *A Stillness at Appomattox* (1956). Catton captures the sights, sounds, and smells of battle, besides telling us what went on in the minds of the military commanders. The view is from the Yankee side of the line.

T. Harry Williams. *Lincoln and His Generals* (1952). Williams deals with Lincoln "as a director of war and his place in the high command and his influence in developing a modern command system for this nation."

Adrian Cook. *The Armies of the Streets* (1974). Spiraling inflation, racial and class resentments, and opposition to the new Union draft brought four days of looting, burning, and lynching of blacks to New York in July 1863.

George M. Frederickson. *The Inner Civil War* (1965). The war, says Frederickson, induced reformers to reject their anti-institutional, individualistic attitudes as "feeble sentimentalities" and to favor an uncritical nationalism.

Frank L. Klement. *The Copperheads in the Middle West* (1960). Sees the Copperheads as the forerunners of Gilded Age agrarian dissenters.

Margaret K. Leech. *Reveille in Washington, 1860–1865* (1941). A panorama of life, society, and politics in wartime Washington.

Bell I. Wiley. *The Life of Johnny Reb: The Common Soldier of the Confederacy* (1943); and *The Life of Billy Yank: The Common Soldier of the Union* (1952). Drawn from ordinary enlisted men's letters, diaries, and other records, these are vivid, down-to-earth accounts of the amusements and inconveniences of camp life and the brutal experience of battle as it appeared to the ordinary soldier.

Benjamin Quarles. *The Negro and the Civil War* (1953). Deals with black Americans in both North and South, and with black soldiers as well as black civilians.

Emory M. Thomas. *The Confederate Nation, 1861–1865* (1979). This study of the Confederacy claims that if the South had won its independence, it would have been as thoroughly transformed by the wartime experience as the North.

Martin Duberman. *Charles Francis Adams, 1807–1886* (1960). An exemplary biography of a moderate antislavery leader who became United States minister to England during the Civil War and Lincoln's most important diplomatic representative abroad during the years of Union crisis.

MacKinlay Kantor. *Andersonville* (1955). This historical novel is about the infamous Confederate prison near Americus, Georgia, where almost 13,000 Union soldiers died in the last months of the war.

James McPherson. *Battle Cry of Freedom* (1988). Each generation feels the need to retell the epic of the Civil War. This is the best of the recent crop.

Ralph Andreano, editor. *The Economic Impact of the American Civil War* (1959). A collection of articles on the subject of the Civil War as an accelerator of economic growth.

CHAPTER 16   *Reconstruction*

Eric L. McKitrick. *Andrew Johnson and Reconstruction* (1960). Andrew Johnson, says the author, failed to see that the North needed evidence of southern contrition before it could forgive and allow a return to normal relations between the two regions.

Clement Eaton. *The Waning of the Old South Civilization, 1860–1880* (1968). Eaton concludes that the New South retained much of the old, especially its devotion to states' rights, white supremacy, and the cult of southern womanhood.

Albion W. Tourgée. *A Fool's Errand: A Novel of the South During Reconstruction* (1879). Edited by George M. Frederickson (1966). An autobiographical novel by a "carpetbagger" lawyer from Ohio who settled in North Carolina after the Civil War and became a Radical superior court judge.

Allen W. Trelease. *White Terror: The Ku Klux Klan Conspiracy and Southern Reconstruction* (1971). The definitive study of the first Klan after the Civil War and a potent indictment of all its doings.

Joel Williamson. *After Slavery: The Negro in South Carolina During Reconstruction, 1861–1877* (1965). Williamson concludes in this detailed study of race relations in one key Reconstruction state that racial segregation was not wholly a product of "redemption."

Willie Lee Rose. *Rehearsal for Reconstruction: The Port Royal Experiment* (1964). Though the ex-slaves ultimately lost the rich cotton lands to their former owners, the temporary success of the Port Royal experiment tells us what might have been if the northern commitment to black freedom and racial justice had been stronger.

Roger Ransom and Richard Sutch. *One Kind of Freedom: The Economic Consequences of Emancipation* (1977). An important book by two "cliometricians" about how emancipation affected the economic well-being of the freedmen and the South as a whole.

LaWanda Cox and John Cox. *Politics, Principles, and Prejudice, 1865–1866: Dilemma of Reconstruction America* (1963). A study of presidential Reconstruction that gives the Radicals much credit for idealism and suggests how much personal political advantage actually entered into Andrew Johnson's decisions.

Leon Litwack. *Been in the Storm So Long: The Aftermath of Slavery* (1980). Professor Litwack tells us what black men and women felt about the new world of freedom after 1863.

Herbert Gutman. *The Black Family in Slavery and Freedom, 1750–1925* (1976). Excellent social history, not only of the slavery period but also of the post-slavery experience of black families.

Kenneth Stampp. *The Era of Reconstruction, 1865–1877* (1965). An excellent overall view of the "new" Reconstruction history by a man who helped pioneer it.

C. Vann Woodward. *Reunion and Reaction: The Compromise of 1877 and the End of Reconstruction* (1951). Concludes that the agreement to end the presidential election dispute of 1876–1877 was a behind-the-scenes agreement to exchange continued Republican supremacy for major economic favors to southern business groups.

Jonathan Wiener. *Social Origins of the New South, 1860–1885* (1978). A Marxist-oriented study of post-bellum southern society that emphasizes the continued domination of the planter class and the near-slavery of the freedmen.

Eric Foner. *Reconstruction, America's Unfinished Revolution, 1863–1877* (1988). A long history of Reconstruction that reflects the revisionist research of the past generation as well as the political and cultural perceptions of today. (The reader could substitute Foner's briefer version, *A Short History of Reconstruction* (1990)).

CHAPTER 17 *The Triumph of Industrialism*

Edward C. Kirkland. *Dream and Thought in the Business Community, 1860–1900* (1956). This intellectual history of Gilded Age businessmen is based on their private correspondence, congressional testimony, and published writings.

Matthew Josephson. *Edison* (1959). According to Josephson, Edison's Menlo Park laboratory was his greatest invention: It was the first industrial research laboratory, applying scientific theory and technical knowledge to practical problems.

Harold C. Livesay. *Andrew Carnegie and the Rise of Big Business* (1975). This brief book—not a full biography—makes Carnegie's role in the post-Civil War economic surge clear.

Frederick Lewis Allen. *The Great Pierpont Morgan* (1949). A breezy, entertaining biography of Morgan that succeeds in defining his place in American economic life.

Irvin G. Wyllie. *The Self-Made Man in America: The Myth of Rags to Riches* (1954). Wyllie follows the myth of the self-made individual from colonial times to 1929.

Theodore Dreiser. *The Financier* (1912). The hero of this novel is modeled after the Gilded Age streetcar magnate Charles Yerkes.

Herbert Gutman. *Work, Culture, and Society in Industrializing America* (1976). A collection of essays by a leading social historian emphasizing the experience of working-class life in the half century following 1865.

Stephen Thernstrom. *Progress and Poverty: Social Mobility in a Nineteenth-Century City* (1964); and *The Other Bostonians: Poverty and Progress in the American Metropolis* (1973). Both books deal with social mobility for working people and the middle class in nineteenth-century America. The results were mixed: In Newburyport movement up the social and occupational ladder for wage earners was modest and difficult; in Boston it was remarkably easy, especially for native-born Americans, Northern Europeans, Protestant immigrants, and Jews.

Stanley Buder. *Pullman: An Experiment in Industrial Order and Community Planning, 1880–1930* (1967). As much urban as labor history, this book tells the story of the town of Pullman and views it as an example of unsuccessful paternalism.

David Montgomery. *Beyond Equality: Labor and the Radical Republicans, 1862–1872* (1967). An interesting attempt to connect the Gilded Age labor movement to the egalitarian ideas of the 1860s Radical Republicans.

Daniel Walkowitz. *Worker City, Company Town: Iron and Cotton Worker Protest in Troy and Cahoes, New York, 1855–1884* (1978). A study of two New York industrial towns with different ethnic mixes and with different property distribution patterns.

David Brody. *Steelworkers in America: The Nonunion Era* (1960). Brody shows not only what produced discontent among American steelworkers before 1919, but also what encouraged labor's stability and acquiescence.

Harold C. Livesay. *Samuel Gompers and Organized Labor in America* (1978). Goes beyond biography and tells us much of the evolving labor movement, particularly the AFL, during the years 1890 to 1920.

Daniel T. Rogers. *The Work Ethic in Industrial America, 1850–1920* (1975). Examines the intellectual defense of hard work and steady application that accompanied industrialization in the United States.

Daniel Bell. *Marxian Socialism in the United States* (1962). Bell, a former Marxist, is critical of socialism in this short history.

Nick Salvatore. *Eugene V. Debs: Citizen and Socialist* (1982). Written by a scholar sympathetic to, but not uncritical of, the Socialist leader.

Charles Francis Adams, Jr., and Henry Adams. *Chapters of Erie* (1866). The classic account of the chicanery of Jay Gould and his confederates. The work of patrician descendants of Presidents John Adams and John Quincy Adams.

Maury Klein. *The Life and Legend of Jay Gould* (1986). Professor Klein attempts the difficult here: rehabilitating the reputation of Jay Gould.

Ron Chernow. *Titan: The Life of John D. Rockefeller, Sr.* (1998). A new, first rate biography of the man who parlayed business acumen and rigid, puritan morals into the country's largest fortune.

CHAPTER 18 *Age of the City*

Maury Klein and Harvey A. Kantor. *Prisoners of Progress* (1976). The authors briskly describe American industrialization and the growth of cities between 1850 and 1920.

Sam B. Warner. *Streetcar Suburbs: The Process of Growth in Boston, 1870–1900* (1962). Warner describes the developing economic and social segregation of city and suburbs as the middle and upper classes left Boston, spurred on by the "rural ideal."

Thomas Kessner. *The Golden Door: Italian and Jewish Immigrant Mobility in New York City, 1880–1915* (1977). A case study of urban social mobility for two important New Immigrant groups.

Philip Taylor. *The Distant Magnet: European Immigration to the U.S.A.* (1971). This volume by an English scholar deals with European immigration to the United States for the whole period from 1830 to 1930.

Stanford Lyman. *Chinese Americans* (1974). Tells of the constant tension in Chinese-Americans between desires for community and ethnic integrity and acceptance in the wider world of Caucasian America.

Matt S. Meier and Feliciano Rivera. *The Chicanos: A History of Mexican Americans* (1972). A brief survey of the whole sweep of Mexican-American history.

John Higham. *Strangers in the Land: Patterns of American Nativism, 1860–1925* (1955). Higham demonstrates how the post-Civil War European immigrant often became a scapegoat when Americans suffered a loss of confidence as a result of depression, war, or some other crisis.

Abraham Cahan. *The Rise of David Levinsky* (1917). Written by a Jewish immigrant journalist and editor who settled in New York's Lower East Side, it vividly describes sweatshops, problems between the established German Jews and the newer arrivals from eastern Europe, and conflicts between generations in immigrant families.

Seymour Mandelbaum. *Boss Tweed's New York* (1965). Tweed was not a good man, but he was a useful one—as Professor Mandelbaum shows in this study of Thomas Nast's favorite villain.

Zane Miller. *Boss Cox's Cincinnati* (1968). Cox, too, was useful, but more enlightened and honest than Tweed.

Humbert Nelli. *The Italians in Chicago, 1880–1930* (1970). A model study of an urban ethnic group of the New Immigration following 1880.

Melvin Holli. *Reform in Detroit: Hazen Pingree and Urban Politics* (1969). Pingree was the "potato-patch mayor" of Detroit who fought the transit magnates and brought reform with a heart to his city.

Theodore Dreiser. *Sister Carrie* (1900). Recounts the experiences of a young rural woman who comes to Chicago to make her fortune and succeeds primarily by choosing, and using, the right lovers.

Gunther Barth. *City People: The Rise of Modern City Culture in Nineteenth-Century America* (1980). A fine treatment of the culture of Gilded Age American cities.

CHAPTER 19   *The Trans-Missouri West*

Walter P. Webb.   *The Great Plains* (1931). The classic study of the Great Plains. Webb shows the important ways in which geography and climate modified transplanted institutions.

Fred A. Shannon.   *The Farmer's Last Frontier: Agriculture, 1860–1897* (1945). This older work is still the indispensable study of agriculture in the generation following the Civil War.

Allan G. Bogue.   *Money at Interest: The Farm Mortgage on the Middle Border* (1955); and *From Prairie to Corn Belt* (1963). Bogue denies that eastern moneylenders made excessive profits from western farmers. He also claims that corn belt farmers did very well for themselves in the late nineteenth century.

Everett Dick.   *The Sod-House Frontier, 1854–1890* (1954). The subtitle of this book is: "A Social History of the Northern Plains from the Creation of Kansas & Nebraska to the Admission of the Dakotas."

Rodman W. Paul.   *Mining Frontiers of the Far West, 1848–1880* (1963). Combines excellent scholarship with a sense of the romantic aspect of the great western mining bonanzas.

R. K. Andrist.   *The Long Death: The Last Days of the Plains Indians* (1964). A skillful overview of the tragic destruction of the Plains tribes by the encroachment of "civilization."

Robert W. Mardock.   *Reformers and the American Indian* (1970). Surveys the Indian reformers through to the Dawes Act of 1887 and sees them as sincere but limited and culture-bound.

Ernest Staples Osgood.   *The Day of the Cattlemen* (1929). A brief classic study of the range cattle industry of the northern Plains.

Robert Utley.   *The Lance and the Shield: The Life and Times of Sitting Bull* (1993). An impressive new scholarly treatment of Sitting Bull and his tribe and also, along the way, a reexamination of Indian–white relations after the Civil War.

Robert Dykstra.   *The Cattle Towns* (1968). A study of the cattle towns between 1876 and 1885 that emphasizes the nature of town life in the cattle communities and talks as much of drygoods merchants as of cowboys and dance-hall girls.

Gene M. Gressley.   *Bankers and Cattlemen* (1966). The subtitle of this book is "The Stocks-and-Bonds, Havana-Cigar, Mahogany-and-Leather Side of the Cowboy Era."

Hamlin Garland.   *Main-Travelled Roads* (1891). Garland, who settled with his parents on the Iowa prairie, learned early that "farming is not entirely made up of berrying, tossing the new-mown hay, and singing 'The Old Oaken Bucket' on the porch by moonlight."

Frank Norris.   *The Octopus* (1901). In this description of California wheat growers in the Central Valley, the Southern Pacific Railroad is depicted as "a giant parasite fattening upon the lifeblood of an entire commonwealth."

Robert Utley.   *The Last Days of the Sioux Nation* (1963). The best, most complete treatment we have of the Ghost Dance uprising and the Wounded Knee massacre.

CHAPTER 20   *The Gilded Age*

H. Wayne Morgan, (editor).   *The Gilded Age: A Reappraisal* (1970). Twelve contributors write on civil service reform, labor, the robber barons, science, the currency question, the party system, Populism, foreign policy, popular culture, and the arts.

Richard Jensen. *The Winning of the Midwest: Social and Political Conflict, 1888–1896* (1971). Using statistical data, Jensen demonstrates how political affiliations during the Gilded Age were often determined by social and religious values rather than by pocketbook issues.

John G. Sprout. *"The Best Men": Liberal Reformers in the Gilded Age* (1968). A fine study of Gilded Age reform focusing on the Liberal Republican movement of 1872 and the later Mugwumps.

Irwin Unger. *The Greenback Era: A Social and Political History of American Finance, 1865–1879* (1964). Deals with post-Civil War finance as an example of who controlled political power in the Gilded Age. The author of *These United States* tends to be partial to this work.

Morton Keller. *Affairs of State: Public Life in Late-Nineteenth-Century America* (1977). Shows how the social and economic transformation of the nation between 1865 and 1900 was reflected in its political life.

Matthew Josephson. *The Politicos, 1865–1896* (1938). The classic older treatment of Gilded Age politics. According to Josephson, the political leadership of the period was thoroughly unprincipled.

Allan Nevins. *Grover Cleveland: A Study in Courage* (1932). One of the best political biographies for the era remains this older work by a master of narrative history, Allan Nevins.

Ari Hoogenboom, *Rutherford B. Hayes* (1996). Another fine biography of a Gilded Age political leader.

Mark Twain and Charles Dudley Warner. *The Gilded Age* (1873). This satire on the "all-pervading speculativeness" in business life and corruption in politics gave the Gilded Age its name.

Mary R. Dearing. *Veterans in Politics: The Story of the G. A. R.* (1952). A study of the Civil War Union veterans' organization, the Grand Army of the Republic, as a political pressure group and a bulwark of the Republican party after 1865.

John D. Hicks. *The Populist Revolt: A History of the Farmers' Alliance and the People's Party* (1931). This is the standard older treatment of late-nineteenth-century agrarian insurgency. Hicks sees the Populists as the forerunners of twentieth-century American liberalism.

O. Gene Clanton. *Populism: The Humane Preference in America, 1890–1990* (1991). A strong defense of Populism as a humane alternative to mainstream politics of the 1890s.

Lawrence Goodwyn. *Democratic Promise: The Populist Movement in America* (1976). An impassioned defense of the Populists against their detractors.

Louis W. Koenig. *Bryan: A Political Biography of William Jennings Bryan* (1971). The best one-volume biography of Bryan. Fair without being enthusiastic.

Paul Kleppner. *The Cross of Culture: A Social Analysis of Midwestern Politics 1850–1900* (1970). Kleppner's book is the pioneer study of Gilded Age cultural politics.

Morton White. *Social Thought in America: The Revolt Against Formalism* (1957). Written by a Harvard philosopher who has made American thought his province, it is by far the best study of the changes in social thought as molded by Darwinism in these years.

Richard Hofstadter. *Social Darwinism in American Thought* (1944). This work deals not only with the conservatives who used Darwin to defend the social and economic status quo, but also with those who used evolutionary ideas to defend reform.

Lawrence Vesey. *The Emergence of the American University* (1965). The best one-volume study of the new currents in graduate and professional training that arose during this period.

Lawrence A. Cremin. *The Transformation of the School: Progressivism in American Education, 1876–1957* (1961). Examines the roots, the course, and the eventual transformation of the "progressive movement" in education that John Dewey helped to launch.

Arthur M. Schlesinger. *The Rise of the City, 1878–1898* (1933). This older book is still one of the few good treatments of popular culture as a whole during the Gilded Age.

Oliver W. Larkin. *Art and Life in America* (1949). This work covers far more than the period of this chapter, and so can be consulted selectively by the student of the Gilded Age.

John Burchard and Albert Bush-Brown. *The Architecture of America: A Social and Cultural History* (1966). What applies to Larkin's book also applies to this work.

Lewis Mumford. *The Brown Decades: A Study of the Arts in America, 1865–1895* (1931). This still readable and useful book was a ground-breaking attack on Victorian architecture and a defense of the "modern" trend.

W. A. Swanberg. *Citizen Hearst* (1961). A colorful, critical biography of William Randolph Hearst, one of the creators of yellow journalism, by an outstanding popular biographer.

Sidney Hook. *John Dewey* (1939). An intellectual biography of Dewey by one of his most articulate disciples.

Burton Bledstein. *The Culture of Professionalism: The Middle Class and the Development of Higher Education in America* (1976). Bledstein makes a linkage between the ambition of the mid-nineteenth-century American middle class, the development of the professions, and the rise of the university.

Justin Kaplan. *Mr. Clemens and Mark Twain* (1966). As the title suggests, Kaplan sees Mark Twain as a deeply divided personality, a man who wanted both wealth and success and yet despised all they represented.

Gunther Schuller. *Early Jazz* (1968). The best discussion of jazz from its origins to the early 1930s—by a fine modern composer.

CHAPTER 21 *The American Empire*

Walter LaFeber. *The New Empire: An Interpretation of American Expansion, 1860–1898* (1963). A study of late-nineteenth-century American expansionism by a scholar who believes that "economic forces [were] the most important causes" of the expansionist impulse.

Ernest R. May. *American Imperialism* (1968). May ascribes American expansionism at the end of the nineteenth century to the appearance of a foreign policy elite inspired by the example of Britain, France, and Germany.

Walter Millis. *The Martial Spirit: A Study of Our War with Spain* (1931). Sees the war's origins in the gradual development of a warlike spirit that derived from a mixture of boredom, greed, politics, and the yearning for glory.

Julius W. Pratt. *Expansionists of 1898: The Acquisition of Hawaii and the Spanish Islands* (1936). Pratt criticizes the view, common in his day, that the Spanish-American War was the work of business groups anxious to acquire markets.

Graham A. Cosmas. *An Army for Empire: The United States Army in the Spanish-American War* (1971). This study of the army and the War Department during the war with Spain seeks to refute the usual picture of bungling and general incompetence.

Kenton J. Clymer. *John Hay: The Gentleman as Diplomat* (1975). A study of Secretary of State John Hay's thought about such matters as race, expansion, England, and China.

Howard K. Beale. *Theodore Roosevelt and the Rise of America to World Power* (1956). An effective, if not always fair, attack on TR for his jingoism and imperialistic arrogance.

Joseph Wisan.   *The Cuban Crisis as Reflected in the New York Press* (1934). Wisan probably ex-aggerates the significance of the Hearst–Pultizer circulation battle in New York as a cause of the Spanish-American War, but this study does tell us much about American values and prejudices, and how prowar groups played on them.

Frank A. Freidel.   *Splendid Little War* (1958). The words and pictures of news correspondents, artists, and photographers tell the story of the war in Cuba.

Robert Beisner.   *Twelve Against Empire: The Anti-Imperialists, 1898–1900* (1968). Beisner stud-ies twelve prominent Americans who opposed the Spanish-American War. All upper-class Republicans or former Mugwumps, they believed that acquiring unwilling colonies ran counter to American principles and would threaten democracy at home.

Leon Wolff.   *Little Brown Brother* (1961). War in the Philippines lasted from 1898 to 1902, but after 1898 the United States, as explained in this work, fought not Spain but Filipino guerrillas.

Thomas J. McCormick.   *China Market: America's Quest for Informal Empire, 1893–1901* (1967). Informed by Vietnam era views, this book claims America's China policies were intended to solve the problems of domestic economic overproduction through an Open Door agreement to assure American domination of the China market.

David C. McCulloch.   *The Path Between the Seas: The Creation of the Panama Canal, 1870–1914* (1977). A lively account of the building of the great isthmian canal, from the early French effort to the final success under the auspices of the United States.

CHAPTER 22   *Progressivism*

Richard Hofstadter.   *Age of Reform: From Bryan to F.D.R.* (1955). Urban and middle-class in origin, according to Hofstadter, the progressive movement failed to achieve real reform because its members distrusted organized labor and immigrants and were obsessed with threats to their own status from both the left and the right.

Lincoln Steffens.   *Autobiography* (1931). The famous muckraker eventually became disillu-sioned with the liberal values that motivated progressivism, concluding that capitalism itself was responsible for political corruption and social oppression.

James Harvey Young.   *The Toadstool Millionaires: A Social History of Patent Medicines in Amer-ica Before Federal Regulation* (1962). This funny and tragic tale of the gullible, hypocon-driacal public and the patent-medicine manufacturers will tell you something about modern advertising.

Allen F. Davis.   *Spearheads for Reform: The Social Settlements and the Progressive Movement, 1890–1914* (1967). Shows the frustration of settlement workers' efforts for social justice in the wards. Davis evaluates their success in citywide and national politics, especially their influence on education, housing, unions, and female and child labor.

David Thelen.   *The New Citizenship: Origins of Progressivism in Wisconsin, 1885–1900* (1972). This well-written monograph on progressivism in Wisconsin emphasizes the role con-sumer anger and frustration played in launching the new reform movement.

August Meier.   *Negro Thought in America, 1880–1915* (1963). Analyzes what Booker T. Wash-ington, W. E. B. Du Bois, and other black leaders' thought about contemporary politics, economics, migration, colonization, racial solidarity, and industrial and elite education.

James Weldon Johnson.   *Autobiography of an Ex-Coloured Man* (1912). This is a fictional com-posite autobiography of blacks before World War I by a real black composer and lyri-cist, lawyer, a founder of the NAACP, and chronicler of Harlem.

Henry F. Pringle.   *Theodore Roosevelt* (1931). Pringle's long and graceful biography follows the many TRs: sickly boy, university dude, reformer in New York City, Dakota rancher, Washington office seeker, Rough Rider in Cuba, president, Bull Mooser, and anti-Wilsonite.

Upton Sinclair.   *The Jungle* (1906). Sinclair, a socialist, intended this novel to arouse the nation's indignation about the meatpackers' working conditions. Instead, his nauseatingly detailed descriptions of the meat prepared for public consumption turned the nation's stomach.

Roy Lubove.   *The Progressives and the Slums* (1962). Focusing on New York City, Lubove has written a fine study of how the progressives dealt with one of the key social problems of the day—the slums.

William Harbaugh.   *The Life and Times of Theodore Roosevelt* (1975). Harbaugh's, biography of TR is more up-to-date and more in tune with recent scholarship than Pringle's.

Samuel P. Hays.   *Conservation and the Gospel of Efficiency: The Progressive Conservation Movement, 1890–1920* (1959). This was a ground-breaking book when it appeared and is still important for the serious student of progressivism. Emphasizes the progressives' obsession with efficiency.

John D. Buenker.   *Urban Liberalism and Progressive Reform* (1973). Buenker believes that we must not ignore the interest in, and support of, progressivism by urban working people and their political spokespersons in Congress and the state legislatures.

George Mowry.   *The California Progressives* (1951). This study of progressivism in a banner progressive state helped introduce the thesis that the progressives were middle-class citizens suffering from acute social anxiety as a result of threats to their status.

Arthur Link.   *Woodrow Wilson and the Progressive Era* (1954). Still the best study of the Wilsonian phase of progressivism. Link admires his subject, but he can also see his flaws.

Aileen Kraditor.   *The Ideas of the Woman Suffrage Movement, 1890–1920* (1965). A study of the thought of the women's suffrage movement leaders during the final drive that brought success.

William O'Neill.   *Everyone Was Brave: A History of Feminism in America* (1971). A lively, intelligent discussion of feminism with an especially good section on feminist politics in the Progressive Era.

CHAPTER 23   *World War I*

N. Gordon Levin.   *Woodrow Wilson and World Politics: America's Response to War and Revolution* (1968). Levin maintains that the "effort to construct a stable world order of liberal—capitalist internationalism"—safe from "imperialism of the Right" and "revolution of the Left"—was basic to Wilson's foreign policy and all subsequent American policy-making.

Robert E. Quirk.   *An Affair of Honor: Woodrow Wilson and the Occupation of Veracruz* (1962). Quirk's treatment of the Tampico incident and the shelling and occupation of Veracruz by American marines is brief and well written.

Walter Millis.   *Road to War: America, 1914–1917* (1935). Writing when most citizens believed that America's entry into World War I was a mistake, Millis blames Allied propaganda, American businessmen, and anti-German prejudice for dragging the nation into an unnecessary conflict.

Arthur S. Link.   *Woodrow Wilson and the Progressive Era, 1910_1917* (1954). Half of this book is devoted to Wilson's foreign policy and the advent of war with the Central Powers. Link sees the president as motivated by idealism and a sincere desire to stop brutal aggression.

Frederick Luebke. *Bonds of Loyalty: German-Americans and World War I* (1974). Luebke describes the unfair treatment of German-Americans during 1917–1918.

Ralph Stone. *The Irreconcilibles: The Fight Against the League of Nations* (1970). This is the best study of Lodge and his anti-League colleagues.

Randolph S. Bourne. *War and the Intellectuals: Collected Essays, 1915–1919*. Edited and introduced by Carl Resek (1964). Bourne, a brilliant political commentator, ridicules the tendency of many of his fellow intellectuals to justify American intervention in progressive and moral terms. Why did the United States fight? Because, Bourne says, "War is the health of the State."

John Dos Passos. *Three Soldiers* (1921). Three young men of very different temperaments and backgrounds meet in an army training camp and go to war. Dos Passos traces their spiritual destruction in this novel.

Erich Maria Remarque. *All Quiet on the Western Front* (1929) The author of this novel was a German private serving in the trenches of the Western Front. He recounts the death of spirit and passion in living men under the extreme conditions of trench warfare.

Florette Henri. *Black Migration: Movement North, 1900–1920* (1975). A sympathetic survey of the migration of 1.25 million blacks from the South, the "hard-luck place," to northern cities, where wages were higher and jobs more plentiful.

Ernest May. *The World War and American Isolation, 1914–1917* (1959). A balanced study of American entrance into World War I that uses the German as well as the Allied archives.

Robert Ferrell. *Woodrow Wilson and World War I, 1917–1921* (1985). Ferrell celebrates Wilson's soaring idealism but also criticizes his stubbornness and racial bigotry.

CHAPTER 24   *The Twenties*

Frederick Lewis Allen. *Only Yesterday: An Informal History of the 1920s* (1931). This 1932 best-seller vividly sketches the politics, morals, fashions, heroes, business, and arts of the "bally-hoo" twenties.

Irving Bernstein. *The Lean Years* (1960). Bernstein describes the very different responses of organized and unorganized 1920s workers to change, the role played by employer associations, and the courts' use of injunctions to break strikes.

Ray Ginger. *Six Days or Forever? Tennessee v. John Thomas Scopes* (1958). Ginger's sharp, witty portraits of Darrow and Bryan are entertaining, and quotations from the court proceedings make this book valuable for research as well as good general reading.

William E. Leuchtenburg. *The Perils of Prosperity, 1914–1932* (1958). Leuchtenburg treats the cultural conflicts of the 1920s, industrial development, labor, morals, and the nature and limits of the decade's prosperity. He emphasizes the confrontation of the city and the small town.

Robert S. Lynd and Helen M. Lynd. *Middletown: A Study in Modern American Culture* (1929). In this classic sociological study of Muncie, Indiana, during the 1920s, the Lynds examine the effects of mass production, the car, electricity, and advertising on attitudes toward work, leisure, education, the family, and the community.

Robert K. Murray. *Red Scare: A Study in National Hysteria, 1919–1920* (1955). A fine study of the post-World War I Palmer raids. Murray is highly critical of the attorney general's brutal disregard of civil liberties.

William Manchester. *Disturber of the Peace: The Life of H. L. Mencken* (1951). Superpatriots, public officials, intellectuals, reformers, and "homo boobiens"—none were safe from Mencken's gibes.

Roderick Nash. *The Nervous Generation: American Thought, 1917–1930* (1970). Nash writes of the uncertainty and contradiction in American thinking about war, democracy, the nation, aesthetics, nature, humanity, and ethics during the 1920s.

Andrew Sinclair. *Prohibition: Era of Excess* (1962). Sinclair explores the social and psychological forces behind the enactment and repeal of Prohibition.

Edmund Moore. *A Catholic Runs for President, 1928* (1956). A good treatment of the Smith-Hoover battle.

Joan Hoff Wilson. *Herbert Hoover, Forgotten Progressive* (1975). Portrays Hoover as a progressive, rather than the reactionary New Dealers believed him to be.

Norman Furniss. *The Fundamentalist Controversy, 1918–1931* (1954). Discusses the Scopes trial and much else regarding the conservative Protestant surge of the twenties.

Paula Fass. *The Damned and the Beautiful: American Youth in the 1920s* (1977). The title is misleading; this is really a book about college youth in the twenties. But on that subject it is the last word.

Geoffrey Perrett. *America in the Twenties: A History* (1982) A brilliant account of a period that has often inspired brilliant writing.

Ann Douglas. *A Terrible Honesty: Mongrel Manhattan in the 1920s* (1995). The book's thesis is that during the 1920s the nation's metropolis profited from a rare blend of blacks and whites, Jews and Christians, men and women who joined together to create a tolerant, sophisticated, culture that quickly conquered the western world.

CHAPTER 25 *The New Deal*

John Kenneth Galbraith. *The Great Crash, 1929* (1955). This account of the great Wall Street panic of 1929 explains its causes and effects without resorting to technical jargon.

Peter Temin. *Did Monetary Forces Cause the Great Depression?* (1976). Tackles the question: Was it money mismanagement that produced the Depression? Author says no, and accepts instead the Keynesian view that weak investment was the culprit.

William E. Leuchtenburg. *Franklin D. Roosevelt and the New Deal, 1932–1940* (1963). In this excellent short history of Roosevelt and the New Deal, Leuchtenburg maintains that Roosevelt assumed "that a just society could be secured by imposing a welfare state on a capitalist foundation."

Richard H. Pells. *Radical Visions and American Dreams: Culture and Social Thought in the Depression Years* (1973). In a well-written analysis of articles, books, novels, plays, and films of the 1930s, Pells seeks to demonstrate an underlying conservatism in the thought of the intellectual elite.

Studs Terkel. *Hard Times: An Oral History of the Great Depression* (1970). Terkel interviews miners, farmers, migrant farm workers, corporation presidents, a "Share Our Wealth" organizer, hobos, and teachers. Depression poverty created feelings of confusion, shame, and guilt in many of these people.

Robert S. Lynd and Helen M. Lynd. *Middletown in Transition: A Study in Cultural Conflict* (1937). Returning to Muncie, Indiana in the 1930s, the Lynds found that its citizens believed the Depression to be a temporary problem that did not require radical changes.

James Agee and Walker Evans.   *Let Us Now Praise Famous Men* (1941). Evans's photography complements Agee's sensitive, compassionate record of the daily lives of three white tenant cotton farmers in Alabama during the hard years of the 1930s.

Theodore Rosengarten.   *All God's Dangers: The Life of Nate Shaw* (1974). An aged black Alabama cotton farmer tells of his years as a sharecropper in a world dominated by white landlords, bankers, fertilizer agents, gin operators, sheriffs, and judges.

Robert E. Sherwood.   *Roosevelt and Hopkins: An Intimate History* (1948). Only about a third of this dual biography concerns the New Deal years, but that third is one of the best brief histories of political leadership during the Depression.

James M. Burns.   *Roosevelt: The Lion and the Fox* (1956). The best discussion of Roosevelt as a domestic leader. Burns describes FDR's early life and his preparation for ultimate greatness.

Paul Conkin.   *The New Deal* (1967). Conkin sees the New Deal as a lost opportunity to equalize wealth and power in the United States.

John Steinbeck.   *The Grapes of Wrath* (1939). Recounts the story of midwestern farmers fleeing the Depression by heading west to California, and their reception there.

Michael Bernstein.   *The Great Depression: Delayed Recovery and Economic Change in America, 1929–1939* (1989). The most recent discussion of the causes of the Great Depression. Rather technical at times.

Frank Freidel.   *Franklin D. Roosevelt: A Rendezvous with Destiny* (1990). A one-volume distillation of decades-long research and writing on Roosevelt by the dean of Roosevelt scholars.

Lizabeth Cohen.   *Making a New Deal: Industrial Workers in Chicago, 1919–1939* (1990). A first-rate study of ethnic life and ethnic politics in Chicago during the New Deal era and the decade immediately preceding.

CHAPTER 26   *World War II*

William Langer and S. Everett Gleason.   *Challenge to Isolation, 1937–40* (1952); and *Undeclared War, 1940–41* (1953). These weighty studies are defenses of Roosevelt's foreign policy and support the view that war between Germany and the United States was inevitable.

James M. Burns.   *Roosevelt: The Soldier of Freedom* (1970). Also sees foreign policy before and during the war through Roosevelt's eyes.

Robert Dallek.   *Franklin D. Roosevelt and American Foreign Policy, 1932–1945* (1979). A monumental study (540 pages) covering all of Roosevelt's foreign policy.

Charles A. Beard.   *President Roosevelt and the Coming of the War, 1941* (1948). Written by the dean of American progressive historians just before his death, this book indicts Roosevelt for bringing on an unnecessary war in 1941 to revive the flagging fortunes of his party and the New Deal.

Samuel Eliot Morison.   *The Two-Ocean War: A Short History of the United States Navy in the Second World War* (1963). Morison had the good fortune to witness much actual sea action in both the Atlantic and Pacific, so this well-written account is based on some firsthand knowledge.

Barbara Tuchman.   *Stilwell and the American Experience in China, 1911–1945* (1971). General "Vinegar Joe" Stilwell brilliantly commanded American forces in China until 1944, when Chiang Kai-shek had him recalled for advocating increased aid to Chinese Communist forces.

Dwight D. Eisenhower. *Crusade in Europe* (1948). An account in Eisenhower's own words of the American war effort in Europe that led to the final defeat of the Germans.

John Morton Blum. *V Was for Victory: Politics and American Culture During World War II* (1976). Shows the greed, bigotry, dishonesty, and stupidity as well as the selflessness, goodwill, patriotism, and intelligence of Americans "back home" during the war.

Richard Lingeman. *Don't You Know There's a War On? The American Home Front, 1941–45* (1970). Lingeman's book is lighter fare than Blum's and better at catching the flavor of American civilian life during the war.

Audrie Gardner and Anne Loftis. *The Great Betrayal: The Evacuation of the Japanese-Americans During World War II* (1969). A critical account of an event that weakened the moral position of the United States in a war against the enemies of freedom.

James P. Baxter. *Scientists Against Time* (1946). This popular history of the Office of Scientific Research and Development tells how industrial and university scientists worked with the military to develop improved radar, antisubmarine devices, rockets, blood substitutes, and medicines.

John Hersey. *Hiroshima* (1946). A gripping account of how the first atomic bombing affected six survivors: a clerk, two doctors, a poor widow with three children, a German missionary priest, and the pastor of a Japanese Methodist church.

John Toland. *The Rising Sun: The Decline and Fall of the Japanese Empire, 1936–1945* (1970). An American journalist-scholar tells the story of Japan's tragic try for world greatness. Rather sympathetic to Japan.

Robert Leckie. *Delivered from Evil: The Saga of World War II* (1987). A vivid, well-written journalistic history of the war on all fighting fronts.

CHAPTER 27 *Postwar America*

Dean Acheson. *Present at the Creation* (1969). Acheson's own account of his State Department experiences from 1941 to 1953, it is, not surprisingly, a strong defense of the Truman Doctrine, the Marshall Plan, NATO, and the Korean intervention.

Athan Theoharis. *Seeds of Repression: Harry Truman and the Origins of McCarthyism* (1971). Theoharis blames the liberals, rather than the political right, for McCarthyism.

Thomas C. Reeves. *The Life and Times of Joe McCarthy: A Biography* (1982). A masterly and unfailingly interesting biography by a careful scholar.

William F. Buckley, Jr., and L. B. Bozell. *McCarthy and His Enemies* (1954). A favorable view of Joe McCarthy by two conservatives associated with the *National Review.*

Alan Weinstein. *Perjury: The Hiss-Chambers Case* (1978). A definitive study that concludes that Hiss was guilty as charged.

Walter LaFeber. *America, Russia, and the Cold War* (1975); and David Horowitz, editor, *Containment and Revolution* (1967). "Revisionist" studies of the Cold War that strongly endorse the view that American policy was the predominant, and avoidable, cause of the confrontation with the Soviet Union.

Daniel Yergin. *Shattered Peace: The Origins of the Cold War and the National Security State* (1977). The United States after 1945, says Yergin, vacillated between the position that it could accommodate to the Soviet Union and that it was impossibile to compromise with an aggressive, expansionist power.

Alonzo Hamby. *Beyond the New Deal: Harry S Truman and American Liberalism* (1973). This solid volume is a defense of Truman and Truman liberalism.

Charles C. Alexander. *Holding the Line: The Eisenhower Era, 1952–1959* (1975). The title suggests the author's view of the Eisenhower administration.

Douglas T. Miller and Marion Nowak. *The Fifties: The Way We Really Were* (1977). The authors see the fifties as a time of real but neglected problems.

David Riesman, Reuel Denney, and Nathan Glazer. *The Lonely Crowd: A Study of the Changing American Character* (1950). The influential study that made Americans worry about the loss of "inner direction." An important cultural document.

Scott Donaldson. *The Suburban Myth* (1969). Suburbs, Donaldson believes, were the most realistic solution of the mid-twentieth-century housing problem—the negative attitudes of American intellectuals notwithstanding.

Richard O. Davies. *The Age of Asphalt: The Automobile, the Freeway, and the Condition of Metropolitan America* (1975). Davis describes the reason for the 1956 Highway Act and discusses the neglected alternatives that might have eased our energy and urban crises.

Richard Kluger. *Simple Justice: The History of Brown v. Board of Education and Black America's Struggle for Equality* (1975). The best single volume on the civil rights movement in the 1950s. Focuses on the famous 1954 school desegregation decision of the Supreme Court.

Bruce Cook. *The Beat Generation* (1971). Cook's thesis is that the Beat movement of the 1950s anticipated much of the cultural and political radicalism of the 1960s.

Jack Kerouac. *On the Road* (1957). A Beat novel of characters frantically moving across the American landscape of the 1950s.

Ralph Ellison. *Invisible Man* (1952). A beautifully written, convincing, and often amusing novel of the coming of age of a young black man who is caught up in—and then dumped by—the Communist party.

Max Hastings. *The Korean War* (1987). This lively review of the Korean "police action" depicts the conflict as a dress rehearsal for Vietnam, with many of the same frustrations and confusions as the later war.

J. Ronald Oakley. *God's Country: America in the Fifties* (1986). Oakley shows that all was not necessarily well in the Garden of Eden, what with racism, the Cold War, and Joe McCarthy.

CHAPTER 28 *The Dissenting Sixties*

William O'Neill. *Coming Apart: An Informal History of America in the 1960s* (1971). A witty, highly readable, and opinionated overview of the mores, politics, culture, and thought of the 1960s.

Irwin Unger and Debi Unger. *1968: Turning Point* (1988). A panorama of the 1960s from the perspective of its culminating year. Strongly recommended.

Allen Matusow. *The Unraveling of America: A History of Liberalism in the 1960s* (1984). A critical examination of 1960s political liberalism as seen from the moderate left.

Arthur M. Schlesinger, Jr. *A Thousand Days: John F. Kennedy in the White House* (1965). A highly sympathetic portrait of the Kennedy presidency by a professorial participant in it.

Herbert Parmet. *Jack: The Struggles of John F. Kennedy* (1980); and *JFK: The Presidency of John F. Kennedy* (1983). A more balanced assessment of Kennedy and his administration than Schlesinger's.

Lyndon B. Johnson. *The Vantage Point: Perspectives of the Presidency, 1963–69* (1971). Johnson defends his administration's policies—not only the Great Society programs, but also the intervention in Vietnam.

Michael Harrington. *The Other America: Poverty in the United States* (1962). In this influential book, Harrington rediscovered poverty in America after the experts had said it no longer existed.

Irving Bernstein. *Guns Or Butter: The Presidency of Lyndon Johnson* (1996). A compendious survey of the Johnson presidency with particularly good sections on the Great Society.

Irwin Unger. *The Best of Intentions: The Triumph and Failure of the Great Society Under Kennedy, Johnson, and Nixon* (1996). Reviews the origins of the Great Society programs of the Sixties and gives them mixed reviews.

Doris Kearns. *Lyndon Johnson and the American Dream* (1976). A fascinating combination of psychological study, biography, and memoir, written by a scholar who enjoyed Johnson's trust and confidence from 1967 to his death in 1973.

Eric Goldman. *The Tragedy of Lyndon Johnson* (1969). Written by the White House "intellectual in residence," this critical book catches the tragic downfall of Lyndon Johnson.

Norman Podhoretz. *Why We Were in Vietnam* (1982). The author, a leading neoconservative intellectual, makes the best case possible for American involvement in Vietnam.

George Herring. *America's Longest War: The United States and Vietnam, 1950–1975* (1986). Herring was a dove who believed that America's containment policy, as displayed in Vietnam, was "fundamentally flawed in its assumptions."

Frances Fitzgerald. *Fire in the Lake: The Vietnamese and the Americans in Vietnam* (1972). Discusses the Vietnamese people and their history to provide the setting for the Vietnam War.

David Halberstam. *The Best and the Brightest* (1972). A sharply critical account of the foreign policy "establishment" under Kennedy and Johnson and how its members entangled the United States in the Vietnam War.

Nancy Zaroulis and Gerald Sullivan. *Who Spoke Up? American Protest Against the War In Vietnam, 1963–1975* (1984). A blow-by-blow account of the anti-Vietnam War movement. Encyclopedic.

Betty Friedan. *The Feminine Mystique* (1963). Friedan devastatingly attacks the 1950s cult of female domesticity and leaves it a shambles among most intellectuals and a large proportion of college-educated women. Helped launch the Sixties New Feminism.

Alice Echols. *Daring to Be Bad: Radical Feminism in America, 1967–1975* (1989). The author considers radical feminism "the most vital and imaginative force within the women's liberation movement."

David Garrow. *Bearing the Cross: Martin Luther King, Jr., and the Southern Christian Leadership Conference* (1986). Not so eloquent as Stephen Oats's *Let the Trumpet Sound* (1982), but better balanced on King.

Taylor Branch. *Parting the Waters: America in the King Years, 1954–63* (1988). An effective invocation of the early, more successful years of the civil rights movement.

Morris Dickstein. *Gates of Eden: American Culture in the Sixties* (1977). Written by a professor of literature who is young enough to have been at the center of things himself during the 1968 student uprising at Columbia University.

Theodore Roszak. *The Making of a Counter Culture: Reflections on the Technocratic Society and Its Youthful Opposition* (1969). Both a description of the 1960s counterculture phenomenon and an influential force in its emergence.

Charles Perry. *The Haight-Ashbury: A History* (1984). A depiction of "hippie heaven" during its brief glory period.

W. J. Rorabaugh. *Berkeley at War: The 1960s* (1989). The best treatment of the free speech movement as well as the later struggles in Berkeley between the young radicals and the university and political authorities.

James Miller. *Democracy Is in the Streets: From Port Huron to the Siege of Chicago* (1987). A sympathetic treatment of the student New Left during its heyday.

Todd Gitlin. *The Sixties* (1987). A positive, and nostalgic, treatment of the Sixties' insurgencies by a founder of SDS who became a journalism professor.

CHAPTER 29   *The Uncertain Seventies*

Richard Nixon. *Six Crises* (1962). Tells Nixon's own version of major early crises in his life, including the Hiss case, the Checkers Speech, Eisenhower's heart attack, his near-catastrophic visit to Caracas, the "kitchen debate" with Khrushchev, and the 1960 presidential contest with Kennedy.

Gary Wills. *Nixon Agonistes: The Crisis of the Self-Made Man* (1970). One of the best analyses of Richard Nixon and his place in American political history.

Theodore White. *Breach of Faith: The Fall of Richard Nixon* (1975). An excellent summary of Watergate by a master of political journalism who once admired Nixon.

Richard Nixon. *Memoirs* (1978). Not ultimately convincing, perhaps, but it does make it clear that Nixon was a fallible human being, not some inhuman monster. Written after Watergate.

Joan Hoff Wilson. *Nixon Reconsidered* (1994). Seeks to rehabilitate Nixon as a kind of liberal who expanded the Great Society programs of his predecessor.

Henry Kissinger. *The White House Years* (1979). A fascinating inside report on the making of American foreign policy during Nixon's first four years, by his national security adviser at the time.

John Osborne. *White House Watch: The Ford Years* (1977). A moderate appreciation of the Ford administration by a liberal journalist.

Robert Shogan. *Promises to Keep: Carter's First Hundred Days* (1977). A journalist's favorable report on the Carter administration's first three months in office.

Haynes Johnson. *In the Absence of Power: Governing America* (1980). An indictment of the Carter administration for its feebleness and lack of competence.

Studs Terkel. *Working People Talk About What They Do All Day and How They Feel About What They Do* (1974). Here 130 people from a wide range of American types talk about the frustrations and gratifications of earning a living in the 1970s while maintaining their sense of individual worth.

Barry Commoner. *The Politics of Energy* (1979). An indictment of American energy policy by a man who believes that most of the nation's energy difficulties have been caused by big-business groups greedy for profits.

Robert B. Stobaugh and Daniel Yergin, editors. *Energy Future: Report of the Energy Project at the Harvard Business School* (1978). The authors of these essays consider the 1970s energy crisis real and urge strict conservation as the way to deal with it.

William Quandt. *Decade of Decision: American Policy Toward the Arab-Israeli Conflict* (1977). The single best volume on this important subject.

Christopher Lasch. *The Culture of Narcissism: American Life in an Age of Diminishing Expectations* (1979). A pessimistic and somewhat carping book about what has gone wrong with American culture in the 1970s.

Ralph E. Smith, editor. *The Subtle Revolution: Women at Work* (1979). A survey of the enormous changes that have taken place in women's roles in the American economy since 1945, with special emphasis in the 1970s.

Kirkpatrick Sale. *Power Shift: The Rise of the Southern Rim and Its Challenge to the Eastern Establishment* (1975). A good analysis of the political rise of the Sun Belt and its significance for national affairs.

CHAPTER 30   *The "Reagan Revolution"*

Ronnie Dugger. *On Reagan: The Man and His Presidency* (1983). A highly critical view of Reagan and his administration by the publisher of the *Texas Observer,* a liberal magazine.

Elizabeth Drew. *Campaign Journal: The Political Events of 1983–1984* (1985). This volume is not as readable as Theodore White's *The Making of the President* series, but it is probably better reportage.

Charles Murray. *Losing Ground: American Social Policy, 1950–1980* (1984). Though this work deals with the years before Reagan's presidency, it conveys many of the conservative attitudes toward social policy that characterized the Reagan administration.

Sidney Blumenthal. *The Rise of the Counter-Establishment: From Conservative Ideology to Political Power* (1986). A critical, liberal-oriented analysis of the conservative surge of the 1970s and 1980.

Thomas Ferguson and Joel Rogers. *Right Turn: The Decline of the Democrats and the Future of American Politics* (1986). The authors conclude that Reaganism triumphed, not because public opinion shifted right, but because a new elite, composed of rich businesspeople, manipulated the electoral process successfully to achieve their conservative ends.

Robert S. McElvaine. *The End of the Conservative Era: Liberalism After Reagan* (1987). Placing his faith in a theory of conservative–liberal cycles, McElvaine believes the impetus behind the Reagan Revolution had waned by the mid-1980s.

Randy Shilts. *And the Band Played On: Politics, People, and the AIDS Epidemic* (1987). A San Francisco reporter chronicles the AIDS plague, both as an unfolding human tragedy and as a story of folly and error.

Garry Wills. *Reagan's America* (1988). An impressionistic, skeptical view of Ronald Reagan's life and career by a liberal scholar of the American presidency.

Jack W. Germond and Jules Witcover. *Wake Us When It's Over: Presidential Politics of 1984* (1985). This description of the 1984 election emphasizes the work of professional media and campaign advisers who packaged the candidates and brainwashed, misled, and deceived the voting public in the process.

David Stockman. *The Triumph of Politics: The Inside Story of the Reagan Revolution* (1986). The Reagan budget director's account of how he sold the president and his advisers an economic policy that he himself was unsure of and how, in his estimate, it failed.

Martin Anderson.   *Revolution* (1988). A "supply-side," true-believer's view of the Reagan Revolution.

Donald Regan.   *For the Record: From Wall Street to Washington* (1988). Bitter at being made the scapegoat for the Iran-Contra fiasco, Reagan chief-of-staff Don Regan reveals the confusion in the White House, Nancy Reagan's influence on the president, and various astrologers' influence on her.

Peggy Noonan.   *What I Saw at the Revolution* (1990). A witty and wry account of what it was like to be a speechwriter for Ronald Reagan.

Nancy Reagan.   *My Turn: The Memoirs of Nancy Reagan* (1989). The former First Lady gets her licks in in this volume—after taking it on the chin herself.

Clyde Prestowitz.   *Trading Places: How We Allowed Japan to Take the Lead* (1988). Japan-bashing at its most convincing by a former U.S. trade official who had to negotiate with the Japanese.

Laurence Tribe.   *Abortion: The Clash of Absolutes* (1990). A sophisticated history and analysis of the abortion war by a strong pro-choice constitutional lawyer at Harvard Law School.

Kevin Phillips.   *The Politics of Rich and Poor: Wealth and the American Electorate in the Reagan Aftermath* (1990). Phillips, a conservative political analyst, is disillusioned by Reaganomics and foresees a new populist uprising based on class resentment just down the road.

Paul Freiberger and Michael Swaine.   *Fire in the Valley: The Making of the Personal Computer* (1984). The best single-volume history of a subject so new that the ancient past is 1975.

CHAPTER 31   *A Different America?*

Arthur M. Schlesinger, Jr.   *The Disuniting of America* (1992). A noted liberal expresses fear that recent tribalism will undermine a shared history and set of values among Americans.

Ronald Takaki.   *A Different Mirror: A History of Multicultural America* (1992). Himself a Japanese-American, Takaki celebrates the diversity of America and emphasizes the plight of ethnics and people of non-European ancestry in a society dominated mostly by people of North European background.

Robert Hughes.   *The Culture of Complaint: The Fraying of America* (1992). A prominent Australian-born art critic who finds both the purveyors of political correctness and many of their shriller conservative critics rather foolish people.

Katherine Roiphe.   *The Morning After: Fear, Sex and Feminism* (1993). A young Ivy League graduate who condemns what she considers the excesses of feminist responses on campus to male behavior toward women.

Catherine MacKinnon.   *Only Words* (1993). A leading feminist attorney attacks pornography as demeaning to women and calls for strict laws against it.

Dinesh D'Souza.   *Illiberal Education: The Politics of Race and Sex on Campus* (1991). A sharp indictment of "politically correct" attitudes and teachings on American campuses by a young conservative, Asian by birth, who rejects the philosophy behind affirmative action and other forms of ethnic preference.

Joe Klein.   *Primary Colors* (1996). An amusing novel about a presidential campaign, featuring a thinly disguised Bill Clinton, by "Anonymous," a thinly disguised political reporter, Joe Klein.

David Maraniss.   *First in His Class: A Biography of Bill Clinton* (1995). A critical review of Clinton's early life. Shows the talents and the failings.

* PHOTO CREDITS *

3 American Museum of Natural History.   **12** Colored engraving, 1592, by Theodor de Bry. The Granger Collection. **18** "The Syphilitic" woodcut, 1496 by Albrecht Durer. The Granger Collection.

26 Line engraving, 1591. The Granger Collection.   **38** American Antiquarian Society.

47 Engraved from the original as published by Church. The Granger Collection.   **66** Library of Congress.

75 1698. Library of Congress.   **79** The Saint Louis Art Museum.

104 Watercolor by Baron von Clossen. Library of Congress.   **122** Lithograph, American, 19th century. The Granger Collection.

129 The Historic New Orleans Collection.   **143** Independent National Historical Park Collection.

155 Oil on canvas c. 1806, by John Trumbull, 30 x 24 in. National Portrait Gallery, Smithsonian Institution, Washington, D.C., gift of Henry Cabot Lodge.   **159** Oil on canvas, 1805, by Rembrandt Peale. The New-York Historical Society Museum.

178 Library of Congress.   **192** By Michel Felice Corne "Battle between the U.S.S. Constitution and H.M.S. Guerriere" 1812 oil on canvas, 32.75 x 47.75 inches, New Haven Colony Historical Society.

200 Pittsburgh 1796 and 1857. Carnegie Library of Pittsburgh.   **204** Corbis-Bettmann.   **213** Engraving by John Hill c 1830–32. The New-York Historical Society, New York City.

232 AP/Wide World Photos.   **237** Watercolor on paper by J. B. Longacre. National Portrait Gallery, Washington, D. C.

261 Oil on canvas, 1872 "American Progress" by John Gast. The Granger Collection.   **265** Steel engraving by Alonzo Chappel, 1863. The Granger Collection.

276 New York Public Library.

299 "An Overseer Doing His Duty" Watercolor by Benjamin Latrobe. The Granger Collection.   **304** Superstock, Inc.

321 Unknown "Stephen A. Douglas" c. 1859. Albumen silver print 8.6 x 8.5 cm. National Portrait Gallery, Smithsonian Institution, Washington, D.C.   **333** Library of Congress.

346 Wood engraving after Thomas Nast from a contemporary American newspaper. The Granger Collection.   **353** Library of Congress.

371 Currier & Ives, Nath. & James, "Fall of Richmond, Virginia" 1857–1907. Private collection/Bridgeman Art Library, London/Superstock.   **377** Oil on canvas by Arthur Stumpf. National Portrait Gallery, Smithsonian Institution.   **380** Library of Congress.   **386** Corbis-Bettmann.   **393** Library of Congress.   **395** Corbis–Bettmann   **396** Rutherford B. Hayes Presidential Center.   **398** Corbis-Bettmann.

406 Drawn from a copyrighted photograph by Pach, New York. New York Public Library.   **416** State Historical Society of Wisconsin, International Harvester Collection, WHi(X3)30648.

435 William H. Rau, photographer. Library of Congress.   **446** Electricity Building World's Columbian Exposition, Chicago, watercolor by Frederick Childe Hassam, The Granger Collection.   **447** Oil painting by Leo McKay, "Steeplechase Park, Coney Island." Museum of the City of New York. 54.167.

462 Library of Congress.   **465** From the Collections of the Henry Ford Museum and Greenfield Village. NDPC.030655/37.102   **490** Cartoon—The Sacrilegious Candidate. Library of Congress.

521 Library of Congress.   **525** Chicago Historical Society.

544 Undated photo. Corbis-Bettmann.   **552** Theodore Roosevelt and William Howard Taft cartoon on cover of Puck, August 1, 1906. "The Crown Prince" Culver Pictures, Inc.

Index